Other books by A.P. Thirlwall

Inflation, Saving and Growth in Developing Economies
Regional Growth and Unemployment in the United Kingdom (*with R. Dixon*)
Financing Economic Development
Balance-of-Payments Theory and the United Kingdom Experience (Fourth Edition *with H. Gibson*)
Nicholas Kaldor
UK Industrialisation and Deindustrialisation (Third Edition *with S. Bazen*)
The Performance and Prospects of the Pacific Island Economies in the World Economy
Economic Growth and the Balance-of-Payments Constraint (*with J. McCombie*)
The Economics of Growth and Development: Selected Essays, vol. 1
Macroeconomic Issues from a Keynesian Perspective: Selected Essays, vol. 2
The Euro and 'Regional' Divergence in Europe
The Nature of Economic Growth: An Alternative Framework for Understanding the Performance of Nations
Trade, the Balance of Payments and Exchange Rate Policy in Developing Countries
Essays on Balance of Payments Constrained Growth: Theory and Evidence (*with J. McCombie*)
Trade Liberalisation and the Poverty of Nations (*with P. Pacheco-López*)
Economic Growth in an Open Developing Economy: The Role of Structure and Demand
Essays on Keynesian and Kaldorian Economics

Edited works

Keynes and International Monetary Relations
Keynes and Laissez-Faire
Keynes and the Bloomsbury Group (*with D. Crabtree*)
Keynes as a Policy Adviser
Keynes and Economic Development
Keynes and the Role of the State (*with D. Crabtree*)
European Factor Mobility: Trends and Consequences (*with I. Gordon*)
The Essential Kaldor (*with F. Targetti*)
Further Essays in Economic Theory and Policy, vol. 9, Collected Economic Papers of N. Kaldor (*with F. Targetti*)
Causes of Growth and Stagnation in the World Economy (the Mattioli Lectures of N. Kaldor *with F. Targetti*)
Economic Dynamics, Trade and Growth: Essays on Harrodian Themes (*with G. Rampa and L. Stella*)

Other books by Penélope Pacheco-López

Trade Liberalisation and the Poverty of Nations (*with A.P. Thirlwall*)
Strategic Directions on Industrial Policy in Mongolia

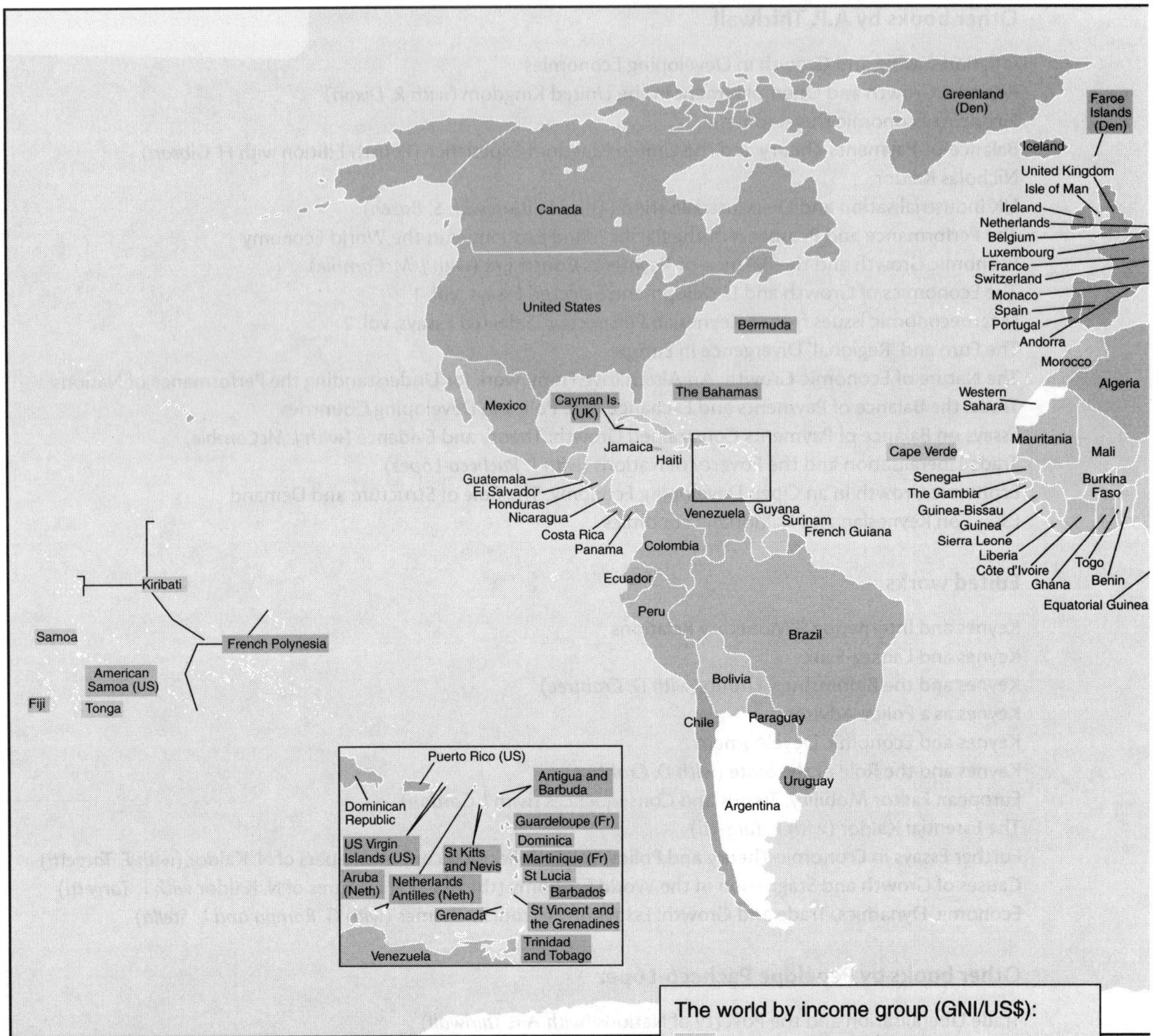

Source: International Bank for Reconstruction and Development, the World Bank

The world by income group (GNI/US$):

Low Income < $1025

Lower-middle Income $1026–$4035

Upper-middle Income $4036–$12,475

High Income > $12,476

No data

Income group classified according to the 2015 GNI per capita, calculated using the World Bank Atlas method.

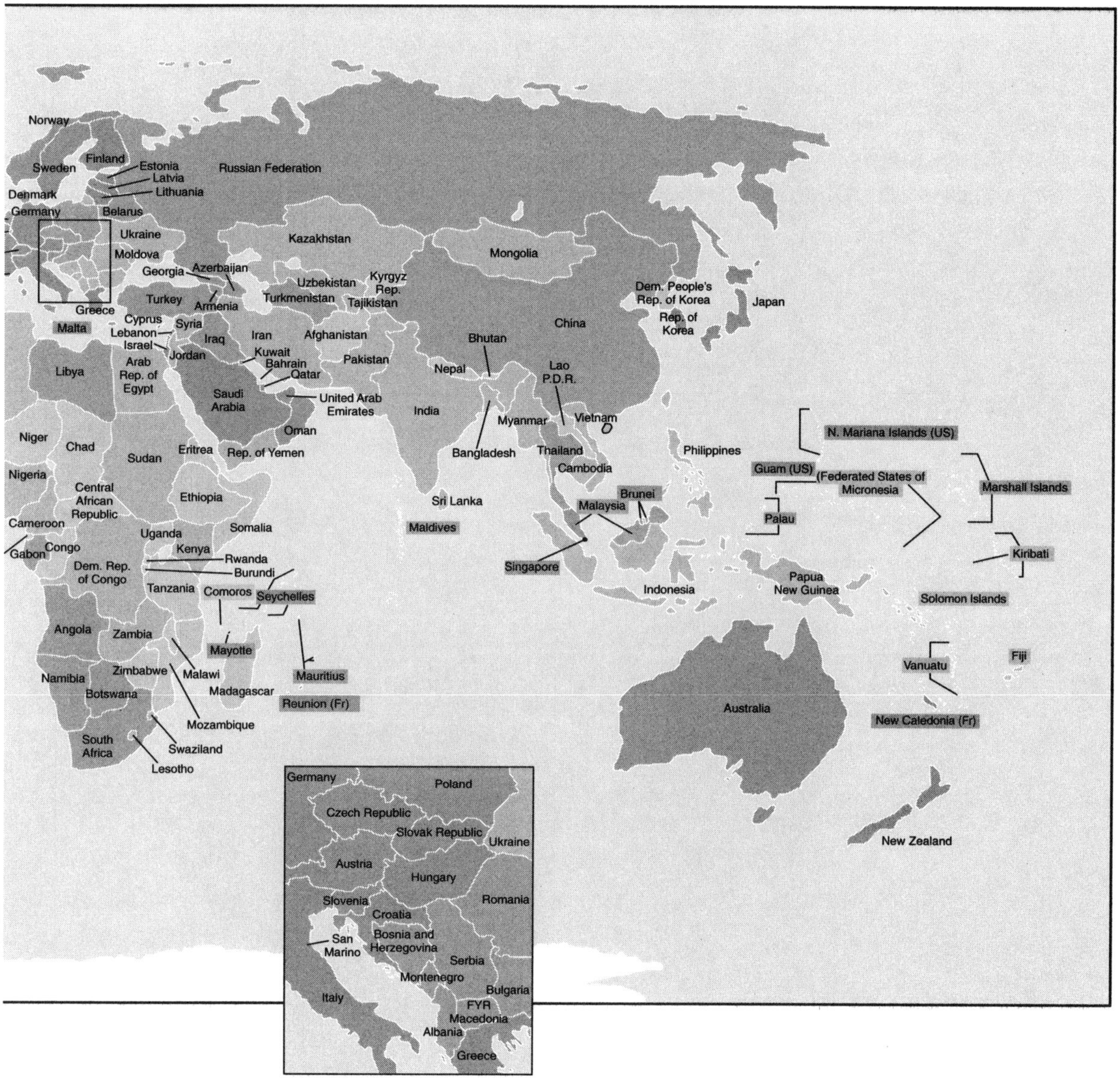

Norway
Sweden
Finland
Estonia
Latvia
Lithuania
Denmark
Germany
Belarus
Russian Federation
Ukraine
Moldova
Kazakhstan
Mongolia
Georgia
Azerbaijan
Uzbekistan
Kyrgyz Rep.
Turkey
Armenia
Turkmenistan
Tajikistan
Dem. People's Rep. of Korea
Japan
Greece
Cyprus
Syria
Rep. of Korea
China
Malta
Lebanon
Israel
Iraq
Iran
Afghanistan
Kuwait
Bahrain
Qatar
Jordan
Bhutan
Libya
Arab Rep. of Egypt
Pakistan
Nepal
Lao P.D.R.
Saudi Arabia
United Arab Emirates
India
Myanmar
Vietnam
Oman
N. Mariana Islands (US)
Niger
Chad
Sudan
Eritrea
Rep. of Yemen
Bangladesh
Thailand
Philippines
Cambodia
Guam (US)
Federated States of Micronesia
Marshall Islands
Nigeria
Central African Republic
Ethiopia
Sri Lanka
Brunei
Malaysia
Palau
Cameroon
Somalia
Maldives
Uganda
Congo
Kenya
Gabon
Rwanda
Burundi
Dem. Rep. of Congo
Singapore
Kiribati
Tanzania
Comoros
Seychelles
Indonesia
Papua New Guinea
Solomon Islands
Angola
Zambia
Mayotte
Fiji
Vanuatu
Malawi
Mauritius
Namibia
Zimbabwe
Madagascar
Botswana
Reunion (Fr)
Australia
Mozambique
New Caledonia (Fr)
South Africa
Swaziland
Lesotho
New Zealand
Germany
Poland
Czech Republic
Slovak Republic
Ukraine
Austria
Hungary
Slovenia
Romania
Croatia
San Marino
Bosnia and Herzegovina
Serbia
Montenegro
Bulgaria
Italy
FYR Macedonia
Albania
Greece

ECONOMICS OF DEVELOPMENT

THEORY AND EVIDENCE

TENTH EDITION

A.P. Thirlwall

Professor of Applied Economics, University of Kent, UK

Penélope Pacheco-López

Consultant to Development Agencies

BLOOMSBURY ACADEMIC

LONDON • NEW YORK • OXFORD • NEW DELHI • SYDNEY

BLOOMSBURY INDIA
Bloomsbury Publishing India Pvt. Ltd
Second Floor, LSC Building No. 4, DDA Complex, Pocket C – 6 & 7,
Vasant Kunj, New Delhi 110070

BLOOMSBURY, BLOOMSBURY ACADEMIC and the Diana logo
are trademarks of Bloomsbury Publishing Plc

Palgrave in the UK is an imprint of Macmillan Publishers Limited, registered in England,
company number 785998, of 4 Crinan Street, London, N1 9XW.
Palgrave® and Macmillan® are registered trademarks in the United States,
the United Kingdom, Europe and other countries.

First edition 1972, Second edition 1978, Third edition 1983, Fourth edition 1989
Fifth edition 1994, Sixth edition 1999, Seventh edition 2003,
Eighth edition 2006, Ninth edition 2011, Tenth edition 2017
This edition published 2022

This edition published with permission from Bloomsbury Publishing Plc
50 Bedford Square, London, WC1B3DP, UK

A catalogue record for this book is available from the British Library.

A catalog record for this book is available from the Library of Congress.

ISBN: 978-93-54354-13-7

10 9 8 7 6 5 4 3 2 1

Printed and bound in India Gopsons Papers Pvt. Ltd.

To find out more about our authors and books visit
www.bloomsbury.com and sign up for our newsletters.

To Oliver
from
Mum and Dad

A PERSONAL MESSAGE FROM THE AUTHORS

(Courtesy of Spencer Scott of the University of Kent photographic unit)

The economic and social development of poor countries and reducing divisions in the world economy between rich and poor are two of the greatest challenges facing mankind. Vast differences in income and wealth between countries and peoples are not only morally indefensible but also pose a grave threat to peace and stability in the world.

John Maynard Keynes, the great English economist, once described what drew him to economics; he said, it was 'its intellectual rigour combined with its potentiality for good'. He treated the subject of economics as a moral science, the purpose of which is to understand economic behaviour and thereby be able design policies to make the world a more civilized place in which to live. It is this 'potentiality for good' that attracts so many of today's top economists to development economics.

We have written this textbook on the economics of development so that students can apply their knowledge of economics to the plight of poor developing countries in the hope that they will better understand the divided world in which we live and think about issues of development in whatever capacity they may subsequently work.

We have been teaching and practising development economics for many years and have encountered thousands of students in different parts of the world and from different countries, many of whom have gone on to work in the development field – as employees in international institutions and nongovernmental organizations concerned with economic and social development, or as teachers and researchers in poor countries. If new generations of students studying development economics are inspired to do the same, this volume will have achieved its purpose.

We hope you will enjoy the book, and that when you reach the end, you will feel that the study of the economics of development has enriched your experience as an economist and as a citizen of the world.

Wherever you live, we wish you good luck in your studies.

Anthony Thirlwall and Penélope Pacheco-López

BRIEF CONTENTS

CONTENTS

Part II Factors in the development process

Part III The perpetuation of underdevelopment

LIST OF FIGURES

LIST OF TABLES

LIST OF CASE EXAMPLES

PREFACE

The first edition of this book was published in 1972 and was entitled *Growth and Development: with Special Reference to Developing Economies*. After eight editions, in 2011, the title of the ninth edition was changed to *Economics of Development: Theory and Evidence* to reflect more accurately the contents of the book, which elaborates the theory of economic development, combined with empirical evidence on the functioning of developing countries in the world economy with respect to the important mainsprings of growth and development, such as capital formation, technical progress, institutions, national and international finance, trade, and particularly export performance.

This new edition of the book, now jointly with Dr Penélope Pacheco-López, who has worked in many international economic organizations, gives the opportunity to substantially revise the content of the book, to update statistics, and rewrite chapters to include new theoretical ideas and institutional material in order to improve the exposition to aid students and teachers alike.

But the purpose of the book remains the same: to introduce students to the exciting and challenging subject of development economics, which draws on several branches of economics in order to elucidate and understand the development difficulties facing the economies of the world's poor developing countries. This does not mean that the book provides a recipe or blueprint for development: far from it. There can be no general recipes of this nature, and even if there were, they would have to include more than economic ingredients.

The book combines description and analysis, with an emphasis on the elaboration of simple and useful theoretical economic models for an understanding of the issues that comprise the subject matter of development economics. We make no apology for the use of conventional economic theory. We concur with Theodore Schultz (1980), Nobel Prize-winning economist, who has said of development economics:

> This branch of economics has suffered from several intellectual mistakes. The major mistake has been the presumption that standard economic theory is inadequate for understanding low income countries and that a separate economic theory is needed. Models developed for this purpose were widely acclaimed until it became evident that they were at best intellectual curiosities. The reaction of some economists was to turn to cultural and social explanations for the alleged poor economic performance of low income countries. Quite understandably, cultural and behavioral scholars are uneasy about this use of their studies. Fortunately, the intellectual tide has begun to turn. Increasing numbers of economists have come to realize that standard economic theory is just as applicable to the scarcity problems that confront low income countries as to the corresponding problems of high income countries.

This is not to say, of course, that *all* standard theory is useful and relevant for an understanding of the development process; in particular, the relevance of static equilibrium theory may be questioned. Nor is it possible to ignore non-economic factors in the growth and development process. The fact is, however, that the desire for material improvement in developing countries is very strong, and, in the final analysis, growth and development must be considered an economic process, in the important practical sense that it is unlikely to proceed very far in the absence of an increase in the quantity and quality of the resources available for production. The book lays particular emphasis on the economic obstacles to development and the economic means by which developing countries may raise their rate of growth of output and living standards in order to reduce poverty.

For those new to the book, or for those using the ninth edition, we outline the main contents of each chapter and the changes introduced into this tenth edition.

Part I Development and underdevelopment comprises four major chapters that provide a basis for understanding the nature of poverty and underdevelopment in low-income countries, and the theories of economic growth and development that have been put forward over time. This part constitutes important background for the rest of the book.

Chapter 1 addresses the subject of development economics, the meaning of development and the challenge of development economics. The globalization and interdependence of the world economy is emphasized, and there is discussion of the call for a new international order, including the new Sustainable Development Goals, agreed in 2015.

Chapter 2 portrays the magnitude of the development gap between rich and poor countries in the world economy and discusses the measurement of poverty, including the Human Development Index (HDI) of the UN Development Programme (UNDP) and the Multidimensional Poverty Index (MPI) of the Oxford Poverty and Human Development Initiative. There is also a new section on randomized control trials (RCTs) for understanding the best way to reduce poverty. There is a discussion of the World Bank's approach to tackling poverty based on the ideas of empowering the poor and extending their capabilities, as discussed in its *World Development Report 2000/2001*. New research is also reviewed on whether the global and international distribution of income is widening or narrowing.

Chapter 3 outlines the characteristics of underdevelopment and gives quantitative evidence of various dimensions of the development gap with respect to employment and unemployment, hunger and the distribution of income within countries. The major characteristics of underdevelopment identified include the dominance of low-productivity agriculture and lack of industrialization, low levels of capital accumulation, rapid population growth, an export trade dominated by primary products, the 'curse of natural resources' and weak governance and institutions. These topics are discussed more fully in later chapters. The process of structural change is also addressed, as is the notion of industrialization as the engine of growth.

Chapter 4 introduces students to various economic growth theories. There are sections on classical growth theory (Adam Smith, Malthus, Ricardo and Marx), the Harrod–Domar growth model, neoclassical growth theory, and the 'new' endogenous growth theory that now dominates the literature on the applied economics of growth, with its stress on the importance of physical and human capital formation and research and development effort as the prime determinants of growth. Many empirical studies are surveyed, with regard to the production function approach to understanding the growth process and the macrodeterminants of growth approach using 'new' growth theory. There is also discussion of the work of Hausmann, Rodrik and others on growth accelerations, and the concept of 'growth diagnostics' and binding constraints on growth. If you find the technical details too difficult, you should proceed straight to Chapter 5, but you will be missing a lot.

Part II Factors in the development process contains five chapters: the role of agriculture and surplus labour in developing countries; the role of capital accumulation and technical progress for growth; a new chapter on human capital – education, gender, nutrition and health; the importance of institutions conducive to development; and the role of the state in economic development.

Chapter 5 deals with the different contributions that agriculture makes to the development process, one of which is a source of cheap labour for industry. Particular attention is paid to the influential Lewis model of economic development with unlimited supplies of labour. There is explicit treatment, following on from Lewis, of the interaction and complementarity between agriculture and industry, with a number of interesting insights into the importance of demand expansion from agriculture as a stimulus to industrial growth and of achieving an equilibrium terms of trade between the two sectors. There is also a discussion of barriers to raising agricultural productivity, highlighted by the World Bank's *World Development Report 2008: Agriculture for Development*. There is an Appendix on how markets function in the rural agricultural sector, and how the land, labour and credit markets interlock, based on uncertainty of agricultural output and the risk aversion of agents.

Chapter 6 explores the role of capital accumulation and technical progress in the development process. The choice of appropriate techniques of production is also explored, and the potential conflicts involved in moving towards the use of more labour-intensive techniques – between employment and output and between employment and saving. The role played by multinational corporations in dictating technological choice is also examined.

Chapter 7 is a new chapter on the role of education, women, nutrition and health in the development process. An educated, skilled and healthy workforce of men and women is vital in the production process to absorb new technology and for working efficiency.

Chapter 8 discusses the role of institutions in the development process. The importance of property rights and the rule of law is particularly emphasized, and the various institutions for regulating markets and providing social insurance. The important work of Rodrik on democracy is reviewed, and also the pioneering work of Acemoglu, Johnson and Robinson on the relationship between institutional development in colonized countries in the past and institutions today, and the debate on the importance of institutions versus geography in explaining differences in economic development.

Chapter 9 explores the role of the state in economic development and its role in resource allocation compared to reliance on the market mechanism. Market imperfections, market failure and corruption are highlighted, as are the limited capabilities of the state, drawing on the extensive analysis contained in the World Bank's *World Development Report 1997*. Some of the broader issues of development strategy are also considered, including the case for planning. There is a revised section on failed states, conflict and violence.

Part III The perpetuation of underdevelopment comprises three chapters that focus on factors that can perpetuate underdevelopment, including poverty itself (causing a vicious circle), rapid population growth and the impact of development on the environment.

Chapter 10 explores dualism and Myrdal's concept of the process of circular and cumulative causation, and describes the mechanisms by which economic divisions between regions and between countries tend to be perpetuated and widened. It includes the early centre–periphery models of Prebisch and Kaldor, together with discussion of the new economic geography pioneered by Krugman. The views of Marxist writers, including Emmanuel's model of unequal exchange, are also presented.

Chapter 11 discusses population and development and attempts to evaluate the debate on whether population expansion is a growth-inducing or growth-retarding force. The costs and benefits of population growth are examined, together with the different ways an optimum population may be defined. The facts on population growth are clearly outlined, with a discussion of the determinants of fertility.

Chapter 12, written by our colleague Professor Iain Fraser, discusses how environmental issues may be incorporated into social cost–benefit analysis, and the new and important concept of sustainable development, which is the subject of the World Bank's *World Development Reports 1992, 2002* and *2010*. There are sections on the Stern Review on climate change, the impact of climate change on the poor, and the outcome of the climate change conference in Paris in December, 2015.

Part IV Financing economic development covers domestic and foreign resources.

Chapter 13 deals with the financing of development from domestic resources. There is discussion of the theory of financial liberalization, together with critiques and empirical evidence of the relation between real interest rates, saving, investment and growth. There is new material on the financial system in developing countries and the relationship between financial development and economic development. Fiscal policy and taxation are also discussed, together with the topic of forced saving through inflation. New research is reported on the relation between inflation and growth, and the impact of inflation targeting.

Chapter 14 discusses the finance of development from external resources. All the statistics relating to foreign resource inflows have been updated, including the importance of remittances from abroad. The whole aid debate is reviewed, and the impact of aid on development. There are sections on the macroeconomic impact of aid and the critics of aid. Structural adjustment lending by the World Bank and the role of foreign direct investment in the development process are examined. The debt-servicing problems created by foreign borrowing are thoroughly surveyed, and there is extensive discussion of international debt and the concept of optimal borrowing.

Part V Trade, the balance of payments and development contains two chapters.

Chapter 15 discusses trade theory, trade policy and economic development. The static and dynamic gains from trade are thoroughly explored (including the theory of customs unions and free trade areas), as are the ways in which the present pattern of trade works to the relative disadvantage of poor countries. The tendency of the terms of trade to deteriorate and for balance of payments difficulties to arise are stressed. There are sections on the theory and practice of trade liberalization, and the impact that trade liberalization has had on export growth, import growth, the balance of payments, economic growth, domestic income inequality and international inequality. What trade policies poor countries should pursue are also examined, and the arguments given for various forms of protection.

Chapter 16 explores the important concept of balance of payments constrained growth and the various policy responses to this constraint at the national and international level. The latter involves a consideration of the extensive facilities afforded by the International Monetary Fund (IMF) for balance of payments support. Some of the criticisms levelled at the IMF are also considered. There is an analysis of the different types of exchange rate systems that developing countries can adopt, and lessons to be drawn from the financial crisis in East Asia in 1997. The chapter ends with a discussion of Special Drawing Rights as a potential form of international assistance to developing countries.

This new edition continues to provide the addresses of websites, chapter by chapter, to guide students to relevant information and data on the internet. When the next edition of this book becomes due in 2022, the facts pertaining to developing countries will again be out of date, and no doubt there will have been new institutional changes and innovations in thinking about development strategy. To keep abreast with what is going on, students are encouraged to consult publications such as the World Bank's *World Development Report*, the IMF's *Finance & Development* (a quarterly magazine published in several different languages), *The Human Development Report* (published by the UN Development Programme) and *The Least Developed Countries Report* and *Trade and Development Report* (published by the UN Conference on Trade and Development), as well as journals such as *World Development*, *Journal of Development Studies*, *Journal of Development Economics*, *Journal of International Development*, *Economic Development and Cultural Change*, *Oxford Development Studies* and the *World Bank Economic Review*.

Please visit the book's website, www.palgravehighered.com/Thirlwall-Econ-Of-Dev-10e, which contains PowerPoint slides for lecturers, as well as web links to additional resources and videos.

Also, visit the authors' websites: www.kent.ac.uk/economics/staff/profiles/tony-thirlwall.html and www.kent.ac.uk/economics/staff/profiles/penelope-pacheco-lopez.html.

Reference

Schultz, T.W. (1980) 'The Economics of Being Poor', *Journal of Political Economy*, 88: 639–51.

UNIVERSAL DECLARATION OF HUMAN RIGHTS

On 10 December 1948, the General Assembly of the United Nations adopted and proclaimed the Universal Declaration of Human Rights. Since then, it has been translated into more than 350 languages worldwide and more than 100 African languages. There are 30 Articles, but we would like to highlight this one in particular:

> **Everyone has the right to a standard of living adequate for the health and well-being of himself and of his family, including food, clothing, housing and medical care and the necessary social services and the right to security in the event of unemployment, sickness, disability, widowhood, old age or other lack of livelihood in circumstances beyond his control. (Article 25)**

ACKNOWLEDGEMENTS

There are a number of individuals who work at and with Palgrave without whose help this tenth edition of *Economics of Development* would not have been possible. Kirsty Reade, economics publisher, and Aléta Bezuidenhout, associate editor for economics, have been a constant source of help and advice throughout the writing and production process. Georgia Walters, senior production editor, prepared the manuscript for copy-editing and supervised the final production. Maggie Lythgoe did a superb job in copy-editing the manuscript and preparing it for typesetting, correcting our English grammar on the way. Jon Peacock undertook the Herculean task of obtaining permissions from publishers and international organizations to use third-party material. To all those above, our sincere thanks. Finally, we give photographic and other acknowledgements.

Photographic acknowledgements

1. Gunnar Myrdal, UN photo
2. Muhammad Yunus, Getty Images
3. Robert Solow, photo by Donna Coveney/MIT, reproduced by kind permission of Professor Solow
4. Amartya Sen, reproduced by kind permission of Stephanie Mitchell/Harvard University
5. Dani Rodrik, reproduced by kind permission of Pinar Dogan and Professor Rodrik
6. Hans Singer, Gary Edwards/Institute of Development Studies
7. Raúl Prebisch, reproduced by kind permission of Dr Eliana Diaz Prebisch
8. Nicholas Kaldor, reproduced by kind permission of the Estate of Professor Kaldor
9. Walt Rostow, Time & Life Pictures/Getty Images
10. Adam Smith, Time & Life Pictures/Getty Images
11. Thomas Malthus, Getty Images
12. Karl Marx, Getty Images
13. Arthur Lewis, Getty Images
14. David Ricardo, Getty Images
15. Roy Harrod, Getty Images
16. Joseph Stiglitz, AFP/Getty Images
17. Paul Krugman, Getty Images
18. Albert Hirschman, reproduction by kind permission of Katia Hirschman Salomon
19. Angus Deaton, reproduction by kind permission of Professor Deaton and Princeton University
20. Elinor Ostrom, Chris Meyer/Trustees of Indiana University

Other acknowledgements

Unless stated otherwise below, all third-party material has been used under a Creative Commons Attribution 3.0 IGO license (https://creativecommons.org/licenses/by/3.0/igo/legalcode), a Creative Commons Attribution-NoDerivs 4.0 licence (https://creativecommons.org/licenses/by-sa/4.0/legalcode), or an Open Government Licence v3.0 (http://www.nationalarchives.gov.uk/doc/open-government-licence/version/3/).

Table A5.1 Land concentration and farm size in Asia and Latin America is from Otsuka K, Chuma H and Hayami Y. "Land and Labor Contracts in Agrarian Economies: Theories and Facts". *Journal of Economic Literature* Vol. 30, No. 4 (Dec., 1992), pp. 1965-2018, with permission from the American Economic Association.

Case Example 11.1 Reducing fertility in Bangladesh, with permission from the Centre for Global Development, Washington DC.

Case Example 15.2 Impact of trade liberalization in Africa, with permission from Christian Aid. Please refer to www.christianaid.org.uk for more up to date information regarding the issues concerned.

Case example 6.2 Bridging the technology divide; Case example 7.2 Women and work; Figure 13.2 Financial access gap between high- and low-income countries, 2009; Case example 13.1 Vietnam's bank on wheels; Case example 14.6 Poverty reduction strategy in IMF-supported programmes; Table 16.3 Countries classified by exchange rate regime, 2014; Table 16.4 IMF's non-concessional lending facilities; and **Table 16.5 IMF concessional lending facilities to low income countries,** all with permission from the International Monetary Fund.

Case example 13.4 A meta-analysis of financial liberalization and economic growth, with permission from Robert Lensink.

Table 13.3 Tax effort indices estimated over 1985–95, with permission from Marcelo Piancastelli.

Table 14.2 Total flow of financial resources from DAC countries to developing countries and multilateral organizations, by type of flow; Table 14.3 ODA and total net flow of financial resources from DAC countries; Table 14.4 Total net flow of financial resources from the UK to developing countries and multilateral agencies, 2014; Table 14.7 Concessional and non-concessional flows by multilateral organisations; Table 14.8 Distribution of World Bank lending, 2014; Table 14.10 DAC members' ODA terms, 2007 (all http://www.oecd.org/dac/stats/statisticsonresourceflowstodevelopingcountries.htm); and **Table 14.9 Grant element in loans at different discount rates**, all with permission from the Organisation for Economic Co-operation and Development.

Case example 10.1 Regional disparities in per capita income in India, with permission from Taylor & Francis Ltd.

Table 1.2: Sustainable Development Goals, from *Global Sustainable Development Report*, UN Department of Economic and Social Affairs © 2015 United Nations; **Table 3.3 Population growth**

from Population Division *2015 World Population Prospects* by UN Department of Economic and Social Affairs, available at https://esa.un.org/unpd/wpp/ 2015, © 2015 United Nations; **Figure 7.2 People affected by HIV/AIDS (all ages), 1990–2014** UNAIDS © 2015 United Nations **Case example 7.5 Two success stories against AIDS: Senegal and Rwanda** UNAIDS © 2015 United Nations; **Table 7.14 Regional HIV/AIDS data, 2014** UNAIDS © 2015 United Nations; **Figure 11.1 Average annual rate of population change** from *Population Division 2015 World Population Prospects*, UN Department of Economic and Social Affairs © 2015 United Nations; **Table 12.1: Key environmental indicators data** from *UNEP Yearbook*. United Nations Environment Programme © 2012 United Nations; **Table 12.2: Energy use and CO2 emissions, 2006** from *Trade and Development Report 2009* by UNCTAD © 2009 United Nations; **Case example 15.1 Trade liberalization in eight countries** © 2015 United Nations; and **Table 15.3 Changes in the real terms of trade for commodities** © 2003 United Nations, all with permission from the United Nations.

Table 7.1 Education for All 2000–15: goals and their assessment; and **Table 7.3 Public spending on education, by region and income level**, with permission from the United Nations Educational, Scientific and Cultural Organization (UNESCO).

Case example 7.4 Childhood stunting; **Table 7.13 The post-2015 global TB strategy**; and **Table 7.16 Leading causes of DALYs, 2012**, with permission from the World Health Organization.

I

DEVELOPMENT AND UNDERDEVELOPMENT

1

THE STUDY OF ECONOMIC DEVELOPMENT

- Introduction
- Development economics as a subject
- Academic interest in development
- The new empirical development economics
- A new international economic order
- Sustainable Development Goals
- Globalization and interdependence of the world economy
- The meaning of development and the challenge of development economics
- The perpetuation of underdevelopment
- Summary
- Discussion questions
- Websites

Introduction

We ask the reader (especially the young student) to consider, behind a veil of ignorance (Rawls, 1972), what sort of world they would prefer to have been born into. A world in which nearly a billion people live on less than $1.90 a day (the official World Bank poverty line), with only a 5% chance of living a luxurious lifestyle or in a fairer world that provides a decent living standard for everyone wherever they are born – whether in Norway, the richest country, or Burundi, the poorest? Whatever answer you give, you will have shown an interest in **development economics**, which seeks to understand and explain why some countries are poor and others rich, and how to reduce poverty in poor countries to give everyone on the planet a minimum standard of life and freedom from hunger and fear of the future.

Development economics, as it is understood and taught today, is a relatively new subdiscipline of economics dating from the early years after the Second World War; but, in fact, the economic progress of nations has always been at the heart of economic enquiry, at least since the time of the great classical economists of the late eighteenth century and the first half of the nineteenth century – Adam Smith, Thomas Malthus, David Ricardo, John Stuart Mill and Karl Marx. These writers were all concerned with understanding the growth and development process of countries and the factors determining the distribution of income between classes of people. Modern development economics has, in many ways, revived the old interests of the classical economists concerning the importance of saving, investment, capital accumulation, trade, and the mobilization of surplus labour for structural change out of agriculture into manufacturing industry and service activities.

In this chapter we start by considering development economics as a subject – and academic interest in development issues – and why there has been a revival of development economics in the past 70 years, with many of the world's best economists researching and writing on development matters. One of the major contributory factors has been the poorer countries of the world calling for a fairer deal from the functioning of the world economy, which they view as being biased against them. This demand for a **new international economic order** has been endorsed by all the major multilateral agencies established after the Second World War to oversee international relations and a smoother functioning of the world economy after the economic chaos of the prewar era: the United Nations (UN) and its several affiliates, the World Bank for Reconstruction and Development and the International Monetary Fund (IMF). We shall discuss what a new international economic order might consist of, and the components of the new **Sustainable Development Goals** laid down in 2015, to be achieved by 2030, which replaced the Millennium Development Goals 2000–15.

Another major factor responsible for the growing interest and concern with developing countries, and the process of economic development itself, has been the increased **globalization** of the world economy, which has led to a greater **interdependence** between countries of the world. We shall consider what globalization means, and what forms interdependence takes.

We then turn to the meaning of development and the challenge of development economics, focusing particularly on the ideas of Denis Goulet and Amartya Sen, who argue powerfully and persuasively that economic development must mean much more than just a rise in the average level of per capita income of a country. A concept of development is required that embraces all the economic and social objectives and values that countries strive for – not simply material progress but, in particular, the self-esteem of peoples and nations, and freedom.

We end the chapter by considering the perpetuation of underdevelopment and poverty; that is, the forces in the world economy that historically have produced and continue today to create divisions between rich and poor countries, and even to widen them. Differences in the structure of production between countries, unequal trade, the dependency of poor countries on rich countries, and the operation of international institutions can all interact to produce 'vicious circles' of poverty and relative stagnation for countries that get left behind in the development 'race'.

Development economics as a subject

The study of **development economics** as a separate subject in economics is a relatively new phenomenon. For the student today, it will be difficult to appreciate that as recently as 60 years ago a course in development economics was a rare feature of an undergraduate programme in economics, and that textbooks on economic development were few and far between. Today, no respectable department of economics is without at least one course in economic development; there are scores of texts and thousands of case studies and articles on the subject.

The political and public concern with poverty and the poorer nations of the world is of equally recent origin. As far as poverty is concerned, Ravallion (2013), a former research director at the World Bank, has charted the evolution of attitudes to poverty over the past three centuries and concludes that the current worldwide consensus on raising people out of poverty is surprisingly recent. Up to the nineteenth century, the plight of the poor was largely blamed on themselves and, besides, poverty was socially useful because it provided plentiful cheap labour for industrial development. In the nineteenth century, some protection was provided for the poor in some Western countries, but little concerted action to reduce poverty itself. It was not until the second half of the twentieth century that a coherent theoretical framework emerged to show how high levels of poverty stifled effort, investment and growth, through lack of education, poor health and nutrition (see Chapter 7).

As far as poorer nations are concerned, the majority of the national and international bodies that exist today to promote development, such as national development banks, the World Bank and its affiliates, and agencies of the UN, were established after the Second World War in the 1940s and 1950s. Before the war, when most of today's poor countries were still colonies, there was much less focus on the economic and social problems of the developing (dependent) economies than there is today. Perhaps the facts were not so well known, or perhaps the attention of most people was focused on depression and unemployment in developed countries. Whatever the reason, the situation today is very different. The development of low-income and middle-income countries, meaning above all the eradication of acute poverty, is now regarded as one of the greatest social and economic challenges facing mankind, together with environmental pollution and climate change. As the Pearson Report (1969) remarked a generation ago, 'the widening gap between the developed and the developing countries has become the central problem of our times'.

What accounts for this change in attitude and upsurge of interest in the economics of development and the economies of poor countries? A number of factors can be pinpointed, which interrelate with one another:

1. In the wake of the great depression of the 1930s, and in the aftermath of war, there was renewed interest among professional economists in the growth and development process and the theory and practice of planning.
2. The poor countries themselves have become increasingly aware of their own backwardness, which has led to a natural desire for more rapid economic progress.
3. The absolute numbers of poor people are considerably greater now than in the past, and greater awareness has struck a humanitarian chord in the world at large.

4. There has been a growing recognition by all concerned of the interdependence between countries in the world economy. The old Cold War between the capitalist West and the communist East led the major developed countries to show a growing economic and political interest in poor and ideologically uncommitted nations. The political and military ramifications and dangers of a world divided into rich and poor countries are even more serious now than they were in the past. The recognition of interdependence has also been heightened in recent years by the process of globalization, making all countries more vulnerable to shocks and financial crises, which spread through trade and capital movements.

Academic interest in development

As mentioned earlier, academic interest in the mechanics of growth and development is a *renewed* interest rather than an entirely new preoccupation of economists. The progress and material well-being of people and nations have traditionally been at the centre of economic writing and enquiry. It constituted one of the major areas of interest of the classical economists. Adam Smith, David Ricardo, Thomas Malthus, John Stuart Mill and Karl Marx all dealt at some length (albeit with divergent opinions on many issues) with the causes and consequences of economic advance (see Chapter 4). It is entirely natural that thinkers of the day should comment on the contemporary scene. There is perhaps an analogy here between the preoccupation of the classical economists at the time of Britain's Industrial Revolution in the eighteenth and nineteenth centuries and the concern of many economists today with the economics of development and world poverty. The list of modern-day economists who have turned their fertile minds to the study of economic development reads like a *Who's Who* of economics. Distinguished economists (past and present) who immediately come to mind are Abhijit Banerjee, Kaushik Basu, Pranab Bardhan, Jagdish Bhagwati, Hollis Chenery, Paul Collier, Partha Dasgupta, Angus Deaton, Esther Duflo, Albert Hirschman, Harry Johnson, Nicholas Kaldor, Michal Kalecki, Paul Krugman, Simon Kuznets, Harvey Leibenstein, Arthur Lewis, James Mirrlees, Gunnar Myrdal, Raúl Prebisch, Dani Rodrik, Joan Robinson, Paul Rosenstein-Rodan, Walt Rostow, Jeffrey Sachs, Theodore Schultz, Amartya Sen, Hans Singer, Nicholas Stern, Joseph Stiglitz and Jan Tinbergen (our apologies to those we left out).

The question is often posed of what lessons, if any, the present developing countries can draw from the first-hand observations of the classical writers or, more directly, from the development experience of the present advanced nations. One obvious lesson is that while development can be regarded as a natural process, it is also a lengthy one, at least if left to itself. It is easy to forget that it took Europe the best part of three centuries to progress from a subsistence state to economic maturity. Much of development economics is concerned with the timescale of development, and how to speed up the process of development in a way that is consistent with freedom and democracy. Later in the present millennium, when primary poverty in most countries will, one hopes, have been eradicated, courses in development economics will undoubtedly take a different form. The emphasis will be on intercountry comparisons rather than on the process of development as such and on the growth pains accompanying the transition from a primarily agrarian to an industrial or service economy.

As far as classical economic theory is concerned, the gloomy prognostication of Ricardo, Malthus and Mill that progress will ultimately end in stagnation would seem to be unfounded. It has certainly been confounded by experience. Population growth and diminishing returns in agriculture have not been uniformly depressive to the extent that Ricardo and Malthus supposed. Rising productivity and per capita incomes have accompanied the growth of population and the extension of agriculture. Classical development economics greatly underestimated the beneficial role of technical progress and international trade in the development process. It is these two factors above all others that seem to have confounded the pessimism of much of classical theory. With access to superior technology, there is hope, and some evidence, that material progress in today's developing countries will be much more rapid than in countries at a similar stage of development 200 years ago. The pool of technology on which to draw, and the scope for its assimilation, is enormous. Used with discretion, it must be considered as the main means of increasing welfare.

The role of trade, however, is more problematic. Much will depend on how rapidly the developing countries can alter their industrial structure, and on movements in the terms of trade. Currently, the developing countries are probably in an inferior position compared with the present advanced countries at a comparable stage of their economic history. There are potential dynamic gains from trade, but the static efficiency gains based on primary production are weak, and the terms of trade in most commodities are worse. The gains from trade accrue mainly to the rich industrialized countries, notwithstanding the rapid increase that periodically takes place in some commodity prices, as witnessed in recent years. The fact that the gains from trade are unequally distributed does not, of course, destroy the potential link between trade and growth, or constitute an argument against trade. Rather, it represents a challenge for altering the structure of trade and the terms on which it takes place.

Then there is the question of planning. Classical economists were generally opposed to interference with the market mechanism, believing that the free play of market forces would maximize the social good. But fashions change in economics, and after the Second World War there was a much greater acceptance of interference with the market mechanism, so that planning in developing countries was seen by many as one of the main means by which economic development could be accelerated. In many countries, the experience of planning has not been favourable, however, and planning has come into disrepute, not least because of the economic disarray of the rigidly planned economies of the old Soviet Union and Eastern Europe. It should never be forgotten, however, that no country in the world ever made such a swift economic advance in such a short space of time as the Soviet Union did after 1918, through a planned allocation of resources that favoured investment at the expense of consumption. The fact that planning may be operated too rigidly, or for too long and go wrong, should not be allowed to obscure the fact that it also has merits, and that unfettered free enterprise can also lead to economic failure and social deprivation. There can be market failure as well as government failure. What is required in most developing countries is a judicious mix of public and private enterprise, with the use of markets combined with different types of government involvement, for the maximization of social welfare. The state has a role to play in economic development (see Chapter 9).

Planning requires a certain amount of model-building, and this too has been inspired by economists. The most common type of model, which forms the basis of much of the model-building that developing countries practise, is to calculate the investment requirements necessary to achieve a target rate of growth of per capita income – commonly referred to as the Harrod–Domar model (see Chapter 4). Neither the models of Harrod (1939) or Domar (1947) were designed for the purpose to which they are now put in developing countries, but their growth equations have proved to be an indispensable component of macroeconomic planning. In Chapter 9, we shall consider the strengths and weaknesses of using this type of aggregate model in development planning, and the arguments for and against planning in general.

As a result of the apparent failure of development planning and the slow progress made by many developing countries in the 1970s, the status of the discipline of development economics began to be called into question in the 1980s and several obituaries of the subject were written (see, e.g., Hirschman, 1981; Little, 1982; Lal, 1983). We will concentrate here on the worries expressed by Hirschman, the practitioner who first rang the alarm bells most vigorously. Hirschman argues that development economics was originally born out of a rejection of monoeconomics (that is, the universality of neoclassical economics) on the one hand and neo-Marxism on the other, which asserted that economic relations between developed and less developed countries could only lead to the development of underdevelopment. The two themes at the forefront of the rejection of monoeconomics were the existence of a massive amount of surplus labour in agriculture in developing countries, and backwardness or late industrialization – the latter requiring active state intervention. In terms of policy, the major strategic themes emphasized and pursued by developing countries were the mobilization of underemployed manpower, rapid capital accumulation and industrialization, for all of which planning was thought to be necessary.

Hirschman's first explanation of the alleged demise of development economics is the resurgence of neoclassical orthodoxy and rejection of the view that there is a separate economics applicable to poor countries, as distinct from developed ones. The defence of monoeconomics has been buttressed by the observed success of some ostensibly free-market developing countries, such as South Korea, Hong Kong, Taiwan and Singapore (the so-called 'East Asian miracle' countries), and the failure of planning in others.

Early development economics not only asserted the need for a separate economics applicable to developing countries, but also believed that the integration of developing countries into the world economy would bring material benefits to rich and poor alike. Hirschman's second explanation of the alleged demise of development economics is that the subject has not only been attacked by the neoclassical school, but also by neo-Marxists who reject the claim of mutual benefit. Thus, development economics has been squeezed, as if in a vice, from both ends of the politico-economic spectrum.

What can be said in response? It is not difficult to defend the traditional preoccupations of development theory and development policy. Amartya Sen (1983) and Syed Naqvi (1996) show that the focus on **mobilizing surplus labour, capital accumulation** and **industrialization** has not been misplaced. It can be seen from the international evidence that many high-growth countries (and this is particularly true of Southeast Asian countries, including China) have drawn extensively on surplus labour from the rural sector, that investment and growth are highly correlated across countries, and that the best growth performers are those countries where the share of industrial output in gross domestic product (GDP) is rising most rapidly. Those defending the rejection of monoeconomics have not retreated into their shells, and very few economists would disagree that there is mutual benefit to be had from country interaction. It is not conceivable that the majority of developing countries would be absolutely better off if they were isolated and autarchic, although this is not to say that some 'delinking' and strategic protection may not be desirable and that the gains from globalization and interdependence could not be more equitably distributed across countries.

But is there a separate 'development economics'? Most observers would still argue that poor countries differ from the rich in such a way that different concepts, models and theories are required to understand their functioning in many respects. While it might be argued that the basic microeconomic assumptions about how people behave are similar for all countries, developing countries still differ *structurally* from rich ones and therefore require different models. The differences between the two sets of countries are large, particularly in relation to resource allocation and matters relating to long-term growth. It is not accidental that social cost–benefit analysis has been largely developed and refined within the context of developing countries, or that developing countries have been the breeding ground for theories of tendencies towards disequilibrium in economic and social systems – models of virtuous and vicious circles and centre–periphery models of growth and development. But as Arthur Lewis (1984), one of the fathers of development economics, once said in his presidential lecture to the American Economic Association, the central task of development economics is to provide a general framework for an understanding of the pace and rhythm of growth and development. As Lewis (1984) put it:

> the economists' dream would be to have a single theory of growth that took an economy from the lowest level … past the dividing line … up to the level of Western Europe and beyond … or to have at least one good theory for the developing economy … to the dividing line.

That is what development economics is all about. **Development economics is the only branch of economics that attempts to understand and explain the nature of the development process** (Naqvi, 1996).

But even if the need for a separate development economics could not be established, would this jeopardize the status of the subject? It might be argued that in the interests of scientific respectability, there is a strong case for thinking of economics as a unified body of theory and doctrine, and not a subject of compartments. What leads to compartmentalization is the wide diversity of subject areas, which then gives rise to the descriptive labels of monetary economics, labour economics, regional economics and so on, but all these subdisciplines employ a large measure of economic theory that is common to economics as a whole.

What distinguishes the subdiscipline is first and foremost the area of application and only secondarily the distinctive theory. A favourite definition of economics is that 'economics is what economists do'. By analogy, 'development economics is what development economists do'. The development literature indicates that they do a number of things that other economists do not do, and in the process they both invent new models, and adapt and modify existing theory in the light of circumstances. Any contribution that a subdiscipline makes by way of theoretical development enriches economics as a whole, and may well have application elsewhere. New models, concepts and ideas invented by development economists include the following:

- The concept of the low-level equilibrium trap
- The theory of the 'big push'
- Dynamic externalities
- Models of dualism
- The theory of circular and cumulative causation
- The concept of dependency
- Growth pole analysis
- Models of population and growth
- Models of rural–urban migration
- Refinements to social cost–benefit analysis
- The notion of immiserizing growth
- Models of structural inflation
- The concept of dual-gap analysis
- The theory of missing markets
- The study of rent-seeking, and so on.

None of these innovations has been borrowed from other branches of economics, but other branches of economics have borrowed liberally from the expanding toolkit forged by development economists. International economics is no longer taught within the straitjacket of equilibrium economics. Labour economics has taken on board the concepts of dualism and dual labour markets, while structural inflation and dual-gap analysis are part of the language of macroeconomics. As Bardhan (1993) concludes:

> While the problems of the world's poor remain as overwhelming as ever, studying them has generated enough analytical ideas and thrown up enough challenges to the dominant paradigm to make all of us in the profession somewhat wiser, and at least somewhat more conscious of the possibilities and limitations of our existing methods of analysis.

Finally, how should one respond to the charge that development economics has not produced the results expected of it? As Hirschman (1981) put it, the developing countries were 'expected to perform like wind-up toys and "lumber through" the various stages of development single-mindedly ... these countries were perceived to have only *interests* and no passions'. If the expectations have not materialized, this probably has more to do with the expectations being unrealistic than with deficiencies in the theory and practice of development economics. This, in turn, may have something to do with economists in general losing their historical sense and perspective. The process of development is a long and protracted one. It took over 200 years for the present developed countries to progress from Rostow's traditional stage of economic development to economic maturity and high mass consumption. Arthur Lewis (1984) bemoaned the loss of historical perspective, which he attributed to the poor training of economists:

> If our subject is lowering its sights, this may be because the demise of economic history in economics departments has brought us a generation of economists with no historical background. This is in marked contrast with the development economists of the 1950s, practically all of whom had some historical training, and guided by Gerschenkron and Rostow, looked to history for enlightenment on the processes of development.

Students beware: learn your history!

Where do we stand today? At present, there is a resurgence of academic interest in the growth and development process, inspired by the 'new' endogenous growth theory and the increased availability of large datasets that facilitate interesting and rigorous econometric work on the major determinants of intercountry growth performance. Paul Krugman (1992) described the 1950s and 1960s as the years of 'high development theory', when many important models of development were formulated but were lost sight of because they were not formulated rigorously enough. Now the ideas are being brought back into play by more skilled theoreticians. The central core of ideas that emerged in the 1950s and 1960s, which were largely swept away during the neoclassical counter-revolution, but which Krugman believes still remain valid, were **external economies, increasing returns, complementarity between sectors** and **linkages**. It is these ideas that have been recaptured by the 'new' endogenous growth theory (and which remained alive outside the mainstream in the works of economists such as Nicholas Kaldor and Kenneth Arrow – see Chapter 4).

'New' growth theory provides an answer to the question of why per capita income differences in the world economy seem to be as persistent as ever when conventional neoclassical growth theory predicts convergence. The answer is that there are many externalities that prevent the marginal product of capital from falling as countries grow richer, so that the level of investment matters for growth, and growth is endogenous in this sense – not simply determined by an exogenously given rate of technical progress, common to all countries. Indeed, technical progress is also largely endogenous, determined by research and development and education. This theory tells us what sustains growth, but it does not address the question of what it is that gets growth started. To answer this, we need to go to the roots of economic development, which initially lie in the performance of the rural economy and agriculture (see Chapter 5).

The new empirical development economics

In recent years, theorizing in development economics has left centre-stage and given way to a much greater amount of empirical work made possible by the availability of large datasets at both the macro- and micro-level, and the development of user-friendly software for data handling. Whether this shift is desirable is debatable, and has been debated by the distinguished development economists Abhijit Banerjee, Pranab Bardhan, Kaushik Basu, Ravi Kanbur and Dilip Mookherjee in the prestigious Indian periodical, *Economic and Political Weekly* (Kanbur, 2005). One inherent danger of empirics is always 'measurement without theory', but today most empirical work in development economics is not of this type. It is mainly to test theoretical hypotheses about decision-making and economic behaviour at the micro-level, and about relationships between variables at the macro-level. In the former case, randomized control trials (RCTs) have become popular (see Banerjee and Duflo, 2011). In the latter case, the problem is one of deducing causation from correlations when most variables in the economic system are endogenous, that is, dependent on each other. One big advantage of RCTs is that they overcome the econometric problems associated with regression and correlation analysis relating to causation, endogeneity and identification. Some economists argue (e.g. Mookherjee, in Kanbur, 2005) that there is now too much empirics and not enough theory – that the balance has swung too far. The debate, however, is a sterile one because for understanding social science in general, and in the attack on poverty in particular, both theory and empirics are required. One without the other leaves economic policy-making in limbo. The way forward suggested by Mookherjee is a four-stage approach:

- Stage 1: empirical description of the relevant phenomenon.
- Stage 2: formulation of a relevant theory that might explain the phenomenon.
- Stage 3: testing and estimation of theory, maybe leading to a modification or replacement of previous theories.
- Stage 4: use of 'best' theory for purposes of prediction and policy evaluation.

This is the most sensible strategy for development economists to follow. As Kanbur (2005) concludes: 'good sense will surely prevail and we will have both more theory and more good empirical work – a goldilocks solution for development economics'.

A new international economic order

Another major factor accounting for the upsurge of interest in the growth and development process has been the poor nations' own increased awareness of their inferior economic and political status in the world, and their desire for material improvement and greater political recognition through economic strength. This was precipitated by decolonization in the 1950s and 1960s and increased contact with developed nations, and has been strengthened from within by rising expectations as development has proceeded. Development is required to provide people with the basic necessities of life, for their own sake, and to provide a degree of self-esteem and freedom for people, which is precluded by poverty. Wealth and material possessions may not necessarily provide greater happiness but they widen individuals' choices, which is an important aspect of freedom and welfare. The developing countries have also called for a fairer deal from the functioning of the world economy, which they view, with some justification, as biased in favour of countries that are already rich.

The official call for a **new international economic order** was first made during the Sixth Special Session of the United Nations General Assembly in 1974. The UN pledged itself:

> to work urgently for the establishment of a new international economic order based on equity, sovereign equality, common interest and cooperation among all states, irrespective of their economic and social systems, which shall correct inequalities and redress existing injustices, make it possible to eliminate the widening gap between the developed and the developing countries and ensure steadily accelerating economic and social development and peace and justice for present and future generations.

The programme of action called for such things as:

- Improved terms of trade for the exports of poor countries.
- Greater access to the markets of developed countries for manufactured goods.
- Greater financial assistance and the alleviation of past debt.
- Reform of the International Monetary Fund and a greater say in decision-making on international bodies concerned with trade and development issues.
- An international food programme.
- Greater technical cooperation.

The call for a new international economic order has been reiterated several times by various UN agencies. In 1975, the United Nations Industrial Development Organization (UNIDO) produced the **Lima Declaration**, which set a target for developing countries to secure a 25% share of world manufacturing production by the year 2000 compared with the share then of 10%. The target was just met, thanks to rapid industrial growth in East Asia and the Pacific, and the share now stands at just over 30%. On the monetary front, in 1980, the **Arusha Declaration** demanded a UN Conference on International Money and Finance to create a new international monetary order 'capable of achieving monetary stability, restoring acceptable levels of employment and sustainable growth' and 'supportive of a process of global development'. This goal has not been achieved. Since the breakdown of the Bretton Woods system in 1971/72, no formal international monetary order has been created.

In 1995, a UN World Development Summit was held in Copenhagen, focusing on social development and employment issues. The **Copenhagen Declaration** made several commitments:

- Full employment, equality between men and women, and universal access to education and healthcare should be basic priorities.
- Overall development aid should be increased for spending in areas of social policy.
- Developed countries should allocate 20% of their aid to basic social projects and, in return, developing countries should spend at least 20% of their budgets on social needs.
- The IMF and the World Bank should pay more attention to social factors when designing programmes.

Progress in these areas has been slow.

The United Nations Conference on Trade and Development (UNCTAD), based in Geneva, regularly calls for new policy initiatives in the four major areas of debt relief, international aid, commodity policy, and trade promotion for developing countries.

Then, prior to the new millennium in 2000, the countries of the world, through the UN and other bodies, agreed on a set of **Millennium Development Goals**, which set 8 goals and 18 development targets to be achieved by the year 2015 compared to the position in 1990 (see Table 1.1).

Table 1.1 Millennium Development Goals and Targets

Goals and targets
Goal 1: Eradicate extreme poverty and hunger
Target 1: Halve, between 1990 and 2015, the proportion of people whose income is less than $1 a day. *Target 2*: Halve, between 1990 and 2015, the proportion of people who suffer from hunger.
Goal 2: Achieve universal primary education
Target 3: Ensure that, by 2015, children everywhere, boys and girls alike, will be able to complete a full course of primary schooling.
Goal 3: Promote gender equality and empower women
Target 4: Eliminate gender disparity in primary and secondary education, preferably by 2005 and in all levels of education no later than 2015.
Goal 4: Reduce child mortality
Target 5: Reduce by two-thirds, between 1990 and 2015, the under-five mortality rate.
Goal 5: Improve maternal health
Target 6: Reduce by three-quarters, between 1990 and 2015, the maternal mortality ratio.
Goal 6: Combat HIV/AIDS, malaria and other diseases
Target 7: Have halted by 2015 and begun to reverse the spread of HIV/AIDS. *Target 8*: Have halted by 2015 and begun to reverse the incidence of malaria and other major diseases.
Goal 7: Ensure environmental sustainability
Target 9: Integrate the principles of sustainable development into country policies and programmes and reverse the loss of environmental resources. *Target 10*: Halve, by 2015, the proportion of people without sustainable access to safe drinking water. *Target 11*: By 2020, to have achieved a significant improvement in the lives of at least 100 million slum dwellers.
Goal 8: Develop a global partnership for development
Target 12: Develop further an open, rule-based, predictable, non-discriminatory trading and financial system (includes a commitment to good governance, development, and poverty reduction – both nationally and internationally). *Target 13*: Address the special needs of the least developed countries (includes tariff and quota-free access for exports, enhanced programme of debt relief for HIPC (the Heavily Indebted Poor Country Initiative) and cancellation of official bilateral debt, and more generous official development assistance for countries committed to poverty reduction). *Target 14*: Address the special needs of landlocked countries and small island developing states (through the Programme of Action for the Sustainable Development of Small Island Developing States and 22nd General Assembly provisions). *Target 15*: Deal comprehensively with the debt problems of developing countries through national and international measures in order to make debt sustainable in the long term. *Target 16*: In co-operation with developing countries, develop and implement strategies for decent and productive work for youth. *Target 17*: In co-operation with pharmaceutical companies, provide access to affordable essential drugs in developing countries. *Target 18*: In co-operation with the private sector, make available the benefits of new technologies, especially information and communications technologies.

Source: UNDP, 2002.

The most important commitment was to half the proportion of people living in absolute poverty, using $1 a day as the poverty line. This meant a reduction from a poverty rate of 41.6% in 1990 to 20.8% in 2015. This target was met globally, largely as a result of the dramatic fall in the numbers in poverty in China. Taking Africa and Asia as a whole, the target was not met.

Other goals met were halving the proportion of people without access to safe water, and reducing the incidence of malaria and tuberculosis. Important targets not met were: reducing by three-quarters the incidence of infant and maternal mortality; universal primary education; gender equality, and the HIV reversal target.

Sustainable Development Goals

In 2015, a new set of **Sustainable Development Goals (SDGs)** was set out at a special conference of the UN. There are 169 proposed targets grouped into 17 goals, which are listed in Table 1.2. The SDGs are more ambitious than the Millennium Development Goals, extending to such things as urbanization, infrastructure and climate change. Each of the goals addresses one or more aspects of poverty, and all are mutually reinforcing. For example, higher school enrolment, especially for girls, reduces poverty and mortality. Better basic healthcare will increase school enrolment and reduce poverty. Many poor people depend on the environment for their living, so a better environment will help poor people. However, the multiplicity of goals and targets have been criticized for being

Table 1.2 Sustainable Development Goals

Goal 1	End poverty in all its forms everywhere
Goal 2	End hunger, achieve food security and improved nutrition and promote sustainable agriculture
Goal 3	Ensure healthy lives and promote well-being for all at all ages
Goal 4	Ensure inclusive and equitable quality education and promote lifelong learning opportunities for all
Goal 5	Achieve gender equality and empower all women and girls
Goal 6	Ensure availability and sustainable management of water and sanitation for all
Goal 7	Ensure access to affordable, reliable, sustainable and modern energy for all
Goal 8	Promote sustained, inclusive and sustainable economic growth, full and productive employment and decent work for all
Goal 9	Build resilient infrastructure, promote inclusive and sustainable industrialization and foster innovation
Goal 10	Reduce inequality within and among countries
Goal 11	Make cities and human settlements inclusive, safe, resilient and sustainable
Goal 12	Ensure sustainable consumption and production patterns
Goal 13	Take urgent action to combat climate change and its impacts
Goal 14	Conserve and sustainably use the oceans, seas and marine resources for sustainable development
Goal 15	Protect, restore and promote sustainable use of terrestrial ecosystems, sustainably manage forests, combat desertification, and halt and reverse land degradation and halt biodiversity loss
Goal 16	Promote peaceful and inclusive societies for sustainable development, provide access to justice for all and build effective, accountable and inclusive institutions at all levels
Goal 17	Strengthen the means of implementation and revitalize the global partnership for sustainable development

Source: United Nations, 2015.

too diffuse and lacking focus. It may be self-defeating to have so many 'priorities' if any of them are to be achieved. Clearly, the most important goals are the first four: ending poverty everywhere; ending hunger; ensuring healthy lives, and equal access to education for everyone.

Globalization and interdependence of the world economy

A third major factor responsible for the growing concern with poor nations is the increased **globalization** of the world economy, leading to a greater **interdependence** between countries of the world. There have been three major eras of globalization in the past 150 years. The first was from 1870 up to the First World War (1914), which witnessed large-scale capital flows and labour migration from Europe to the American continent and the colonies. The second started after the Second World War (1945) with the freeing of trade. The third phase started in the 1980s, based on technological advances in communications and transport. Fischer (2003) has given a useful, succinct definition of globalization:

> the ongoing process of greater economic interdependence among countries reflected in the increasing amount of cross-border trade in goods and services, the increasing volume of international financial flows and increasing flows of labour.

As far as the interdependence between developed and developing countries is concerned, developing countries depend on developed countries for resource flows and technology, while developed countries depend heavily on developing countries for raw materials, food and oil, and as markets for industrial goods. The term 'globalization' refers to all those forces operating in the world economy that increase interdependence, while making countries more and more dependent on forces outside their control, as time, space and borders diminish in importance. Foremost among these forces are:

- The widening and freeing of trade. Over 30% of the world's output of goods and services is now traded.
- The growth of global capital markets and the greater flow of short-term speculative capital: over $3 trillion are exchanged on the world's currency markets every day.
- More foreign direct investment (FDI) by giant multinational corporations with greater power and assets than many national governments.
- The growth of global value chains with firms sourcing inputs from the cheapest international markets.
- The greater movement of people than ever before, breaking down cultural barriers, but also leading to the spread of disease (e.g. AIDS) and international crime in drugs, people-trafficking, prostitution and arms.
- The spread of information technology (IT), which can exacerbate contagion in financial markets.
- New institutions, such as the World Trade Organization (WTO), with authority over national governments, and new multilateral agreements on trade, services, intellectual property, which reduce national autonomy.

All these aspects of globalization and interdependence make countries more vulnerable to shocks such as:

- World recessions and downturns in world trade, as occurred in the early 1980s and precipitated the debt crisis.

- Financial crises, such as the Asian crisis of 1997, and the banking crisis in the US and UK in 2007/8, which became contagious and spread like a disease, affecting not only the countries of origin but other parts of the world too.
- Commodity price rises (including the price of oil), which in 2008 more than doubled for several basic foods, such as maize and rice, leading to food riots in several poor countries.

In recent years, there have been major protests at meetings of the WTO and the World Economic Forum in Davos (Switzerland) by groups concerned with the damage done by globalization, particularly to the poorer countries in the world economy, which tend to be most exposed to, and suffer most from, the forces of competition and global capital movements. Competitive markets may be the best guarantee of efficiency, but not necessarily of equity. As the *Human Development Report* of the United Nations Development Programme (UNDP, 1999) put it:

> The challenge of globalisation in the new century is not to stop the expansion of global markets. The challenge is to find the rules and institutions for stronger governance – local, national, regional and global – to preserve the advantages of global markets and competition, but also to provide enough space for human, community and environmental resources to ensure that globalisation works for people – not just for profits.

So far, more progress has been made in promoting the institutions of globalization than in protecting people against the consequences of globalization. The UNDP calls for globalization tempered by:

- **Ethics** – less violation of human rights
- **Equity** – less disparity within and between nations
- **Inclusion** – less marginalization of people and countries
- **Human security** – less instability of countries and less vulnerability of people
- **Sustainability** – less environmental destruction
- **Development** – less poverty and deprivation.

When the actions of any one country, or group of countries, result in consequences for others (good or bad), the effects become a type of **public good** or **externality**. The task of the international community in these circumstances is to maximize the spread of public 'goods' that confer positive externalities (e.g. technology, information, healthcare) and to minimize the spread of public 'bads' (e.g. disease, pollution, financial contagion). It is in the self-interest of the international community to assist developing countries in particular, not only because they are poor but also to enable them to make their contribution to the provision of essential global public 'goods' (and to minimize the production of public 'bads', e.g. AIDS in Africa).

Globalization and, particularly, interdependence mean that the malfunctioning of one set of economies impairs the functioning of others. This was never more evident than in the world economy in the 1980s, when the rising price of energy and the debt crisis led to mounting economic chaos. The 1980 Brandt Report, entitled *North–South: A Programme for Survival*, and its sequel *Common Crisis: North–South Co-operation for World Recovery* (Brandt Commission, 1983), stressed the mutual benefit to all countries of a sustained programme of development in poorer countries, and documented the prevailing adverse trends in the world economy, which pointed to a sombre future if not tackled cooperatively:

- Growing poverty and hunger in developing countries.
- Rising unemployment with inflation.

- International monetary disorder.
- Chronic balance of payments deficits and mounting debts in most developing countries.
- Protectionism, and tensions between countries competing for energy, food and raw materials.

Nothing much has changed since the 1980s. Poverty and hunger are still rife in the world. Tens of millions of people in poor countries lack productive employment. Civil wars in North Africa are leading to the mass migration of refugees and dispossessed people to Europe. There is international monetary disorder. There are chronic global imbalances of payments between countries, and international debt continues to grow. And there are growing tensions between countries for energy, food and raw materials. Development economics addresses itself to many of the issues contributing to disarray in the world economy.

There is not only a moral case for greater efforts to raise living standards in poor countries, but a purely practical case that it is in the interests of the developed countries themselves. The ability of poor countries to sustain their growth and development means a greater demand for the goods and services of developed countries, which generates output and employment directly and also helps to maintain the balance of payments stability of these countries, which is so crucial if there is to be a reciprocal demand for the goods of developing countries. Any constraint on demand in the system arising from, say, poor agricultural performance in poor countries, or a balance of payments constraint on demand in developed countries, will impair the functioning of the whole world economy and reduce the rate of progress below potential. Herein lies the importance of the transfer of resources to poor countries to maintain their momentum of development (global Keynesianism), and of international monetary reform to smooth the burden of balance of payments adjustment and to shift more of the burden of adjustment from the deficit to the surplus countries.

The Brandt Report (1980) called for:

- A long-term programme to meet the basic needs of poor countries, involving additional resource transfers of $4 billion a year ($15 billion at 2016 prices).
- A major effort to improve agricultural productivity to end mass hunger and malnutrition.
- Commodity schemes to stabilize the terms of trade for primary commodities.
- Easier access to world markets for the exports of developing countries.
- Programmes for energy conservation.
- The development of more appropriate technologies for poor countries.
- An international progressive income tax, and levies on trade and arms production, to be used by a new World Development Fund (to fund development programmes rather than projects).
- A link between the creation of new international money and aid to developing countries.
- Policies to recycle balance of payments surpluses (as accumulated by the Arab oil exporting countries since 1973 and China since the 1990s, for example) to deficit countries to remove balance of payments constraints on demand and remove the risk of a slide into international protectionism.

To this list, we could add new forms of global governance to cope with the consequences of globalization, which also represent the interests of those countries that suffer most from the effects of globalization: the poor and marginalized. This list of priorities is as relevant today as it ever was.

We shall discuss many of these issues in the course of this book. Such a programme of action would be of mutual benefit to all parties, rich and poor. It would create investment confidence, which is the crucial ingredient maintaining the dynamics of any economic system; it would also stimulate trade and investment, and help the prospects of sustained growth in the world economy.

It would be wrong to give the impression, however, that developed countries' concern with world poverty is motivated exclusively by the selfish realization that their own survival depends on economic and political harmony, which cannot thrive in a world perpetually divided into rich and poor. There has also been an affirmation by many developed countries of a **moral obligation** towards poorer nations. Not all aid and development assistance is politically inspired. Particularly over the past four decades, developed countries have shown a genuine humanitarian concern over the plight of poor developing countries. The goal of a greater degree of income equality between the citizens of a nation seems to be gaining support, albeit slowly, as an objective among nations. Moreover, the propagation of this ideal is not confined to the supranational institutions that have been especially established to further it. Recent years have witnessed the spontaneous creation of several national pressure groups in different parts of the world, whose platform is the abolition of world poverty. In the UK, bodies such as Drop the Debt and Make Poverty History have a strong voice. Aid from voluntary agencies to developing countries now amounts to over $10 billion annually. But whatever the motive for concern, the reality of world poverty and underdevelopment cannot be ignored. Furthermore, acute poverty in developing countries is likely to persist for many years to come. The economist has a special responsibility to contribute to an understanding of the economic difficulties that poor countries face and to point to possible solutions. This textbook is devoted to that end.

We start by considering the meaning of development and the perpetuation of underdevelopment. Then in Chapters 2 and 3, we consider the measurement of poverty, the magnitude of the development gap in the world economy, and the major characteristics of underdevelopment, particularly the economic structure of developing countries geared to the production and export of primary products and low value-added manufactured goods.

The meaning of development and the challenge of development economics

Development implies change, and this is one sense in which the term 'development' is used; that is, to describe the process of economic and social transformation within countries. This process often follows a well-ordered sequence and exhibits common characteristics across countries, which we shall discuss later in the chapter. But if development becomes an objective of policy, the important question arises: development for what? Not so long ago, the concept of development was conceived of almost exclusively in terms of growth targets, with very little regard to the beneficiaries of growth or the composition of output. Societies are not indifferent, however, to the distributional consequences of economic policy, to the type of output that is produced, or to the economic environment in which it is produced. A concept of development is required that embraces the major economic and social objectives and values that societies strive for. This is not easy. One attempt is by Goulet (1971, 2006), who distinguishes three basic components or core values in this wider meaning of development, which he calls **life-sustenance**, **self-esteem** and **freedom**:

- **Life-sustenance** is concerned with the provision of basic needs, which we shall discuss in Chapter 3. The basic needs approach to development was initiated by the World Bank in the 1970s. No country may be regarded as fully developed if it cannot provide all its people with such basic needs as housing, clothing, food and minimal education. A major objective of development must be to raise people out of acute poverty and, at the same time, to provide basic needs.
- **Self-esteem** is concerned with the feeling of self-respect and independence. No country can be regarded as fully developed if it is exploited by others and does not have the power and

influence to conduct relations on equal terms. Developing countries seek development for self-esteem; to eradicate the feeling of dominance and dependence that is associated with inferior economic status.

- **Freedom** refers to freedom from the three evils of 'want, ignorance and squalor', so that people are more able to determine their own destiny. No person is free if they cannot choose; if they are imprisoned by living on the margin of subsistence with no education and no skills. The advantage of material development is that it expands the range of human choice open to individuals and societies at large.

These three core components are interrelated. Lack of self-esteem and freedom result from low levels of life sustenance, and both lack of self-esteem and economic imprisonment become links in a circular, self-perpetuating chain of poverty, by producing a sense of fatalism and acceptance of the established order – the 'accommodation to poverty', as the famous economist J.K. Galbraith (1980) once called it.

Goulet's three core components of development are also related to Amartya Sen's vision of development (Sen, 1981, 1983, 1999), defined in terms of the expansion of people's **entitlements** and **capabilities**, the former giving life sustenance and self-esteem, the latter giving freedom. Sen defines entitlements as the set of alternative commodity bundles that a person can command in a society using the totality of rights and obligations that they face, and entitlements generate the capability to do certain things. According to Sen, the capabilities of a person reflect the alternative combinations of functionings the person can achieve, and from which they can choose one collection. The approach is based on a view of living as a combination of various 'beings and doings', with the quality of life to be assessed in terms of the capabilities to achieve valuable functionings.

Economic development should be thought of in terms of the expansion of entitlements and capabilities, which are not necessarily well captured by aggregate measures of output growth. For most people, entitlements depend on their ability to sell their labour and on the price of commodities. It is not only the market mechanism that determines entitlements, however, but also such factors as power relations in society, the spatial distribution of resources in society, such as schools and healthcare, and what individuals can extract from the state.

In the final analysis, Sen views freedom as the primary objective of development, as well as the principal means of achieving development. Development consists of the removal of various types of 'unfreedoms' that leave people with little choice and opportunity. Major categories of 'unfreedom' include famine and undernourishment, poor health and lack of basic needs, a lack of political liberty and basic civil rights, and economic insecurity. Development should be regarded as a process of expanding the real freedoms that people enjoy. The growth of per capita income is only a means to that end. The ideas and views of Amartya Sen, who won the Nobel Prize for Economics in 1998 for his work on the interface between welfare and development economics, have been enormously influential within the international community and can be seen in the World Bank's *World Development Report 2000/2001*, which is devoted to the topic of how to expand the entitlements, capabilities and freedom of poor people (see Chapter 2).

These concepts and ideas of Goulet and Sen are part of what Qizilbash (1996) calls **ethical development**. Drawing on the work of Griffin (1986) in his book *Well-Being: Its Meaning, Measurement and Moral Importance*, Qizilbash (1996) suggests nine core values by which development should be defined:

- minimum levels of health, nutrition, sanitation, shelter and security
- minimal capacities, including literacy and physical capacities

- self-respect and aspiration
- positive freedom or autonomy
- liberty
- enjoyment
- understanding or knowledge
- significant relations with others and some participation in social life
- accomplishment.

Thus, 'development occurs if and only if there is some overall expansion in human flourishing or the quality of human lives or human well-being consistent with the demands of social justice and freedom' (Qizilbash, 1996).

The new focus and stress on the ethical dimension of development, and the entitlements and capabilities of people (and ultimately freedom), is a natural switch in development thinking away from growth maximization to concern with the structure of production and consumption and distribution of income. As far as entitlements are concerned, Sen's dissent is that income is often a very inadequate measure, which he tries to illustrate with reference to the incidence of famines across the world. He finds that most famines have been associated with a lack of entitlements, not with a lack of food.

Amartya Sen

Born 1933, Santiniketan, West Bengal, India. Professor of Economics, Delhi University, London School of Economics, Oxford, Cambridge and Harvard Universities. Made important contributions to many branches of development economics, including choice of techniques, project appraisal, the measurement of welfare, and the analysis of famines. Foremost economist working on the interface between development and welfare economics. Sees development as 'freedom' – the title of one of his books. Awarded the Nobel Prize for Economics 1998.

In conclusion, therefore, and in answer to the question: 'Development for what?', we can say that **development has occurred when there has been an improvement in basic needs, when economic progress has contributed to a greater sense of self-esteem for the country and individuals within it, and when material advancement has expanded people's entitlements, capabilities and freedoms.** The fact that many of these ingredients of development are not easily measurable does not detract from their importance: the condition of being developed is as much a state of mind as a physical condition measurable by economic indices alone. For an illuminating case study, see Case example 1.1 on Costa Rica.

The challenge of development economics lies in the formulation of economic theory and the application of policy, in order to understand better and meet these core components of development. Clearly, the range of issues that development economics is concerned with is quite

Case example 1.1

Costa Rica: developing in the right way

According to the World Bank and the organization **Social Progress Initiative**, Costa Rica is, in many respects, a development success story. It is classified as an upper-middle income country with a per capita income of $13,000 in 2014, and has experienced steady economic expansion over the past 25 years or so. The country pursues a strategy of outward-oriented, export-led growth, and the attraction of foreign direct investment.

More importantly, it attempts to spread economic and social progress as widely as possible among its 5 million inhabitants. According to the Social Progress Index for 2015, calculated by the Social Progress Initiative based in Washington DC, Costa Rica is the country with most social progress relative to income. Among developing countries, only Chile and Uruguay rank higher, but both these countries have higher levels of per capita income. Costa Rica met six of the eight Millennium Development Goals in 2015. The Social Progress Index is based on such factors as: basic human needs; foundations of well-being; opportunity; nutrition and medical care; water and sanitation; shelter; personal safety; access to basic knowledge and information; personal rights, freedom and choice; tolerance and inclusiveness; and economic sustainability. The country scores highly on freedom of life choices, tolerance, lack of corruption and health, with a life expectancy of 80 years, which is higher than in the USA.

Elementary education has been compulsory since 1869; women in Costa Rica have more schooling than men, and the adult literacy rate is close to 100%. A welfare state was created in 1941. Democracy was established in 1948 and the army was abolished at the same time, saving millions of dollars on the military. Costa Rica's social expenditure on education and health is over 20% of GDP, much higher than the Latin American average. There is still some poverty, particularly among those of African descent, but attempts are being made to redress this inequality. The country takes seriously the public provision of leisure facilities and gives priority to the environment. **The Happy Planet Index**, constructed by the New Economics Foundation, ranks Costa Rica as the top country based on measures of subjective well-being, life expectancy and ecological footprint (care of the environment).

The country has moved close in recent years to the true meaning of development as defined by Goulet and Sen. Development is not just about a rise in the average level of per capita income; it is about the expansion of entitlements and capabilities, and ultimately personal freedom.

distinctive and because of this the subject has developed its own *modus vivendi* (way of doing things), although drawing liberally on economic theory, as do other branches of economics.

If it is to be useful, however, a great deal of conventional economic theory must be adapted to suit the conditions prevailing in developing countries, and many of the assumptions that underlie conventional economic models have to be modified, if not abandoned, if they are to yield fruitful insights into the development process. Static equilibrium theory, for example, is ill-suited to the analysis of growth and change and of growing inequalities in the distribution of income between individuals and countries. It is probably also true, as Todaro and Smith (2015) strongly argue, that economics needs to be viewed in the much broader perspective of the overall social system of a country (which includes values, beliefs, attitudes towards effort and risk-taking, religion and the class system) if development mistakes are to be avoided that stem from implementing policy based on pure economic theory alone.

The perpetuation of underdevelopment

The study of economic development helps us to understand the nature and causes of poverty in low-income countries, and the transformation of societies from being primarily rural to primarily industrial, with the vast bulk of resources utilized in industrial activities and in service activities that serve the industrial sector. But why have some countries hardly participated in this process or have been left behind? The first Industrial Revolution gave the present developed countries an initial advantage, which they then sustained through the existence of various cumulative forces against those left behind (see Chang, 2002; Reinert, 2007). Since the 1960s, there has been a second industrial revolution, which has propelled the so-called 'newly industrialized countries' of Southeast Asia and Latin America into industrialized states, and many others into semi-industrialized states. But many countries, particularly in Africa, are still left behind in a semi-feudal state, including the very poorest, which have now become the prime focus of concern of the World Bank and other development agencies.

There are many theories of the perpetuation of underdevelopment but none seems to have universal validity. The condition of agriculture is of foremost importance. It was, first of all, settled agriculture that laid the basis for the great civilizations of the past, and it was the increase in agricultural productivity in England in the eighteenth century that laid the basis for, and sustained, the first Industrial Revolution. If there is one overriding factor that explains why some countries developed before others, and why some countries are still backward without a significant industrial sector, it lies in the condition of agriculture, which, in the early stages of development, is the sector that must release factors of production for other activities and provide the purchasing power over industrial goods (see Chapter 5).

The condition of agriculture depends on many factors, institutional as well as economic, and physical conditions are also of key importance. Climate particularly affects the conditions of production. Heat debilitates human beings. Extremes of heat and humidity also reduce the quality of the soil and contribute to the low productivity of certain crops. It cannot be a coincidence that almost all developing countries are situated in tropical or subtropical climatic regions and that development 'took off' in the temperate zones. The condition of agriculture has not been helped by what Lipton (1977) called 'urban bias', which in many countries has starved agriculture of resources. This has happened because ruling elites generally originate from, or identify with, the non-rural environment, and because policy-makers have been led astray both by empirical evidence that shows a high correlation between levels of development and industrialization, and by early development models that stressed investment in industry.

Many other internal conditions have acted as barriers to progress in poor countries; barriers that interacted in a vicious circle. In some countries, population size and growth presents a problem, combined with low levels of human capital formation. The latter in turn perpetuates poverty, which is associated with high birth rates and large family size. This is a form of 'accommodation to poverty' (Galbraith, 1980), which then perpetuates low living standards in a circular process. Other countries may lack the psychological conditions required for modernization, built on individualism and the competitive spirit, coupled with a strong work ethic, rationalism and scientific thought, which characterized the Industrial Revolutions of eighteenth- and nineteenth-century Europe, and which played a large part in the emergence of the newly industrialized Southeast Asian countries in the latter half of the twentieth century.

External relations between countries also play a part in the process of poverty perpetuation, and this has given rise to **structuralist** and **dependency** theories of underdevelopment. It seems to be the general lesson of history that once one set of countries gains an economic advantage, the advantage will be sustained through a process of what Myrdal (1957) has called 'circular and cumulative causation', working through the media of factor mobility and trade. (For a full discussion, see Chapter 10.) Favoured regions denude the backward regions of capital and skilled labour, and they trade in commodities whose characteristics guarantee that the gains from trade accrue to them. **Colonialism** was an extreme form of dependency, and many of the countries exploited during the colonial era are still poor today. On the other hand, a number of countries that were never colonized, such as Ethiopia and Thailand, are equally backward.

Dependence can take more subtle forms, however, based on the international division of labour, for example, which leads to unequal exchange relations between rich and poor, with the poor dependent on the rich for capital and technology to equip their industrial sectors. The current indebtedness of the less developed countries, and the 'increasing price' they have to pay for development inputs, relative to the price they receive for their exports, are, in the long run, manifestations of this dependency. There are exceptions to the thesis of 'circular and cumulative causation', but in most cases it requires a strong exogenous shock to break out of a vicious circle of poverty and dependency.

Some of these issues will be discussed in Part 3 of this book, but first, Chapter 2 focuses attention on the magnitude of poverty in developing countries and the world distribution of income.

Summary

- Development economics is a challenging and exciting subdiscipline of economics, which addresses the fundamental issues of why some countries are poor and others rich, why some countries grow faster than others over long periods, and what is the best way to tackle poverty in poor countries.
- Interest in the progress of nations is not new. It was the fundamental preoccupation of all the great classical economists such as Adam Smith, Thomas Malthus, David Ricardo, John Stuart Mill and Karl Marx – but the subject matter of development economics has witnessed a revival since the Second World War.
- Revival of interest in development economics has been the result of several factors such as: increased awareness of world poverty; developing countries asking for a fairer deal from the functioning of the world economy; the call for a new international economic order; and the increased globalization and interdependence of the world economy. The Millennium Development Goals set out explicit targets for poverty reduction, education and health (among other things) to be achieved by 2015 and the new Sustainable Development Goals to be achieved by 2030 do the same.
- Economic development means more than a rise in the average level of income per head of a country. A definition of economic (and social) development must embrace a variety of goals and values that societies strive for, particularly self-esteem and freedom for people based on their entitlements and capabilities (to use the terminology of Amartya Sen).
- Economic development presents a major challenge to development economists and policymakers. This is because there are structural forces at work within countries and in the world economy, which tend to perpetuate underdevelopment and poverty and cause countries to get caught in 'vicious circles' related to unequal trade between countries and the dependence of poor countries on the rich for aid and investment.

Chapter 1 Discussion questions

1. What constitutes the study of development economics?
2. Do you think there is a case for a separate subject of development economics, and what are the arguments against it?
3. What accounts for the political and academic interest in poorer countries' development?
4. Why was the status of the discipline of development economics called into question in the 1980s?
5. How would you define the process of economic development?
6. What do the developing countries want from a 'new international economic order'?
7. Do you think that the Sustainable Development Goals are achievable?
8. What forces perpetuate underdevelopment?
9. What lessons, if any, can poor countries learn from the development experience of today's developed countries?
10. What is meant by 'globalization' and the mutual interdependence between rich and poor countries?
11. What do you see as the major challenges confronting development economics and the developing countries?

Websites

The study of development economics requires a good deal of reading and familiarity with case study material, as well as access to statistical sources. Below is a list of general internet sites that can be accessed with links to topics, countries, regions and international organizations. Other sites on specific topics will be given at the end of other chapters.

Institutes of Development Studies

Institute of Development Studies, University of Sussex www.ids.ac.uk
School of Development Studies, University of East Anglia www.uea.ac.uk/international-development

International organizations

World Bank www.worldbank.org
International Monetary Fund www.imf.org
United Nations Conference on Trade and Development (UNCTAD) www.unctad.org
United Nations Development Programme (UNDP) www.undp.org
Food and Agricultural Organization (FAO) www.fao.org
World Trade Organization (WTO) www.wto.org
World Health Organization (WHO) www.who.int

United Nations Industrial Development Organization (UNIDO) www.unido.org
International Labour Organization (ILO) www.ilo.org
African Development Bank www.afdb.org
Asian Development Bank www.adb.org
Inter-American Development Bank www.iadb.org
Center for Global Development (Washington) www.cgdev.org
NGO Global Network www.ngo.org
Heritage Foundation www.heritage.org
Sustainable Development Goals https://sustainabledevelopment.un.org/sdgs and www.un.org/sustainabledevelopment/sustainable-development-goals

Databases

Penn World Tables 8.1 http://knoema.com/PWT2015/penn-world-table-8-1
World Bank http://data.worldbank.org
World Bank, World Development Indicators http://data.worldbank.org/data-catalog/world-development-indicators
International Monetary Fund http://data.imf.org/
Gapminder www.gapminder.org/
World Health Organization, Global Health Observatory www.who.int/gho/en/
UN Comtrade http://comtrade.un.org/
UNIDO https://stat.unido.org/
UNU-WIDER www.wider.unu.edu/project/wiid-%E2%80%93-world-income-inequality-database

Globalization

Centre for Research on Globalization www.globalresearch.ca
Peterson Institute for International Economics http://piie.com
New Economics Foundation www.neweconomics.org

2

THE DEVELOPMENT GAP AND THE MEASUREMENT OF POVERTY

Introduction

This chapter focuses on three major topics: first, the development gap in the world economy and the measurement of the world distribution of income; second, the measurement of global poverty and the problems associated with the use of per capita income as a measure of development; and third, the construction of alternative measures of economic and social development, including the Human Development Index (HDI) and the Multidimensional Poverty Index (MPI) developed by the Oxford Poverty and Human Development Initiative, and both published in the *Human Development Report* of the United Nations Development Programme (UNDP).

To measure the development gap, and the degree of income inequality across countries of the world, we consider:

- the absolute gap between the richest and poorest country (the range)
- the relative gap between the richest and poorest countries
- the dispersion of income per capita around the average level of per capita income for all countries
- the Gini ratio, which is derived from the Lorenz curve of the income distribution.

Using the Gini ratio, we distinguish between **international inequality**, which takes each country's per capita income as just one observation (regardless of the distribution of income within countries) and **global inequality**, which takes account not only of the distribution of income between countries but also within countries (using household survey data). We show that international and global inequality have both risen since the beginning of the nineteenth century, but the major cause of global inequality today is inequality between nations, not inequality within nations.

It is important to recognize, however, that when measuring income inequality and poverty, the measures of income per head in US$ at official exchange rates are not necessarily a good measure of the purchasing power of local currencies (or what is called **purchasing power parity, PPP**), because official exchange rates do not take account of the much cheaper price of non-traded goods in poor countries relative to richer countries. We show how PPP is measured, and discuss in general the comparability of per capita incomes between countries, and the use of per capita income as an index of development.

Turning to the measurement of poverty, we discuss the World Bank's criterion of absolute poverty, which is $1.90 a day at PPP, and give the **headcount index** of the numbers living below this level of income across different regions of the world. The concept of the **poverty gap** is also discussed, because the headcount index does not take account of how far below the poverty line people live. Another method of measuring poverty is the **food energy method**, which measures the income necessary to buy a certain nutritional intake in different countries.

The World Bank claims that it puts poverty reduction at the heart of all the work that it does, and in its *World Development Report 2000/2001* (World Bank, 2000a), it proposed a three-pronged strategy for poverty reduction: promoting opportunity, facilitating empowerment and enhancing security. The meaning of these concepts is discussed in this chapter. Growth is, of course, central to poverty reduction, but how fast the poverty rate falls with growth (to meet the Sustainable Development Goal, for example) depends on the elasticity of the poverty rate with respect to growth.

To overcome the limitations of taking a single measure of per capita income as an index of development, the UNDP annually constructs a Human Development Index (HDI) and also publishes a Multidimensional Poverty Index (MPI). The HDI is based on three variables: life expectancy at birth, educational attainment (measured as the geometric mean of the average and expected years of schooling), and the standard of living measured at PPP. The MPI is also based on three dimensions of poverty: education, health, and standard of living, but with several sub-dimensions of poverty as well. The rankings of countries by their level of per capita income are not the same as the rankings of countries by the HDI or MPI indices, because some countries devote more resources to social expenditure than others, particularly on education and health.

Finally, we consider the question of whether poor countries are ever likely to catch up with the rich, and we reach the pessimistic conclusion that it will take the average poor country at least 100 years to achieve the current living standards in developed countries and probably 300 years for poor countries to equalize living standards with developed countries if they manage to grow, say, 1% faster than the rich countries. But this, of course, cannot be taken for granted.

The development gap and income distribution in the world economy

By any measure one cares to take, the evidence is unequivocal that the world's income is distributed extremely unequally between nations and people. There are many ways of classifying these divisions in the world economy. First, at a very basic level, there is the division between rich industrialized countries, mainly concentrated in the northern hemisphere, and poorer non-industrialized (or semi-industrialized) countries in the southern hemisphere – often referred to in the development literature as the 'North–South divide'.

Second, there is the division between continents: between the developed continents of Europe and North America on the one hand, and the continents of Asia, Africa and Latin America on the other. But the countries of Asia, Africa and Latin America are by no means homogeneous. They have many characteristics, and obstacles to development, in common, but there is also much that divides them, not least their economic performance since the 1960s, with Southeast Asia, China and India forging ahead, Africa left behind, and Latin America in the middle (often prone to financial crises).

Third, the World Bank, which was established by the Bretton Woods Agreement in 1944 as a development agency to lend to poor countries, classifies countries in its annual *World Development Report* into three broad categories: low-income, middle-income and high-income countries, with the middle-income countries split into lower middle-income and upper middle-income.

Table 2.1 lists the low-income and lower middle-income countries, and these are the countries normally thought of as developing countries. There are 36 low-income countries mainly concentrated in Africa, and 48 lower middle-income countries spread across the different continents. Table 2.2 gives the population and average level of per capita income in current dollars measured at the official exchange rate, and at PPP for 2014. We see that for low-income countries with a population of 622 million, the average level of income per head is only $629 at current dollars and $1,570 at PPP (or roughly $5 a day). For lower middle-income countries, with a population of nearly 3 billion, the average level of per capita income is $2,012 at current dollars and $6,000 at PPP (or roughly $16 a day). Compare these figures with an average income per head in high-income countries of roughly $40,000 (or just over $100 day). The discrepancies are huge. The richest country in the world is currently Norway, with an income per head of $66,330 at PPP, and the poorest countries are Democratic Republic of the Congo, with an income per head of $650, and Burundi with $770.

Measures of inequality and historical trends

1. One measure of dispersion is **the range or absolute income gap** between the richest and poorest countries. This gap is almost bound to grow over time if both the rich and poorest countries

Table 2.1 List of low-income and lower middle-income countries

Low-income countries		
Afghanistan	Gambia, The	Myanmar
Bangladesh	Guinea	Nepal
Benin	Guinea-Bissau	Niger
Burkina Faso	Haiti	Rwanda
Burundi	Kenya	Sierra Leone
Cambodia	Korea, Dem. Rep.	Somalia
Central African Republic	Kyrgyz Republic	South Sudan
Chad	Liberia	Tajikistan
Comoros	Madagascar	Tanzania
Congo, Dem. Rep.	Malawi	Togo
Eritrea	Mali	Uganda
Ethiopia	Mozambique	Zimbabwe
Lower middle-income countries		
Armenia	India	Samoa
Bhutan	Kiribati	São Tomé and Príncipe
Bolivia	Kosovo	Senegal
Cameroon	Lao PDR	Solomon Islands
Cape Verde	Lesotho	Sri Lanka
Congo, Rep.	Mauritania	Sudan
Cote d'Ivoire	Micronesia, Fed. Sts.	Swaziland
Djibouti	Moldova	Syrian Arab Republic
Egypt, Arab Rep.	Mongolia	Timor-Leste
El Salvador	Morocco	Ukraine
Georgia	Nigeria	Vanuatu
Guatemala	Pakistan	Vietnam
Guyana	Papua New Guinea	West Bank and Gaza
Honduras	Paraguay	Yemen, Rep.
Indonesia	Philippines	Zambia

Source: World Bank, website.

experience positive growth. For example, if the richest country, Norway, grows at 1%, this adds roughly $700 to the level of per capita income in Norway, while the same growth rate adds only $6–$7 dollars to the per capita incomes of the Democratic Republic of the Congo or Burundi. These countries would have to grow at 700% for the absolute gap between themselves and Norway to be narrowed. But even the gap between the richest and poorest country is an understatement of the degree of income inequality in the world economy because it compares only the *average* income for poor and rich countries. If the income per head of the poorest people in poor countries is compared with the income per head of the richest people in rich countries, the absolute gap is even wider.

2. A second measure of dispersion, or division in the world economy, is the **relative income gap**, which is the ratio of the richest country (or group of countries) to the poorest country (or

Table 2.2 Population and income per capita, 2014

	Population, millions	Gross national income per capita, $	PPP gross national income per capita, $
World	7,261	10,787	14,931
Low income	622	629	1,570
Middle income	5,240	4,666	9,673
Lower middle income	2,879	2,012	6,000
Upper middle income	2,361	7,901	14,179
Low and middle income	5,862	4,238	8,811
East Asia and Pacific	2,021	6,156	11,872
Europe and Central Asia	264	6,892	13,580
Latin America and Caribbean	525	8,990	14,053
Middle East and North Africa	357	4.222	11.834
South Asia	1,721	1,496	5,299
Sub-Saharan Africa	973	1,638	3,382
High income	1,399	38,274	40,749

Source: World Bank, 2015.

group of countries). At present, the ratio of income per head of the richest to the poorest country is approximately 700:1, and the ratio of income per head in the low-income countries to the high-income countries is approximately 60:1 at current exchange rates. This relative income gap is unprecedented historically. A necessary condition for the relative income gap to narrow is that the poorest countries grow faster than the richest.

3. A well-known statistical measure of dispersion is the **standard deviation (SD)**, or the square root of the variance, which measures the average sum of the squared deviations of each country's per capita income from the average (or mean) income for all countries. Formally, the SD is measured as:

$$SD = \sqrt{\frac{\sum_{i=1}^{n}(Y_i - \overline{Y})^2}{n}}$$

where Y_i is the per capita income of country i; $\overline{Y}$ is the average level of per capita income of the whole sample, and n is the number of countries. In the growth and development literature, movements in this ratio, up or down, are referred to as 'sigma (σ) divergence or convergence', respectively.

4. There is the **coefficient of variation**, which is the SD divided by the mean of the sample ($\overline{Y}$). This normalizes the SD because there is a positive correlation between the mean and the SD.
5. But the most widely used measure of income inequality is the so-called **Gini ratio**, derived from the **Lorenz curve**, which in this field of enquiry relates to the distribution of income in relation to the distribution of population across countries or groups of countries. Three

measures or concepts of inequality need to be clearly distinguished in using the Gini ratio. First, there is **international inequality**, with each country treated as a single unit and given equal weight in the measure. Second, there is weighted international inequality, with each country treated as a single unit but **weighted by its size of population**. Third, there is **world** or **global inequality**, which takes the individual person (or household), not the country, as the unit of measurement, and therefore takes into account not only differences in income *between* countries, but also between people *within* countries. Each measure has its own purpose, and there is no theoretical reason why the measures should move together (although, in practice, they tend to, taking a long historical perspective).

Before describing how the Lorenz curve is constructed and the Gini ratio is measured, however, it needs to be said in advance that a single statistic does not say what is happening *within* the distribution, and, in particular, what is happening at the extremes of the distribution. Ratios of extremes, such as the income of the poorest 10% of the world's population compared with the richest 10% (often called the **Kuznets ratio**), or income of the poorest countries compared with the richest, can say as much, if not more, about income inequality and social justice than any integral measure. In fact, the Gini ratio may indicate convergence or less inequality, while the ratio of extremes is increasing. For discussion of the conceptual problems relating to analysis of the world distribution of income, see Atkinson and Brandolini (2010).

Consider now Figure 2.1. On the vertical axis is measured the percentage of income, and on the horizontal axis is measured the percentage of population. To draw the distribution of income (the Lorenz curve) first rank each country, groups of countries, or groups of individuals in ascending order according to the ratio of the percentage of income they receive and the percentage of population they represent; then cumulate the observations, and plot them on the diagram. To give a

Figure 2.1 Lorenz curve diagram

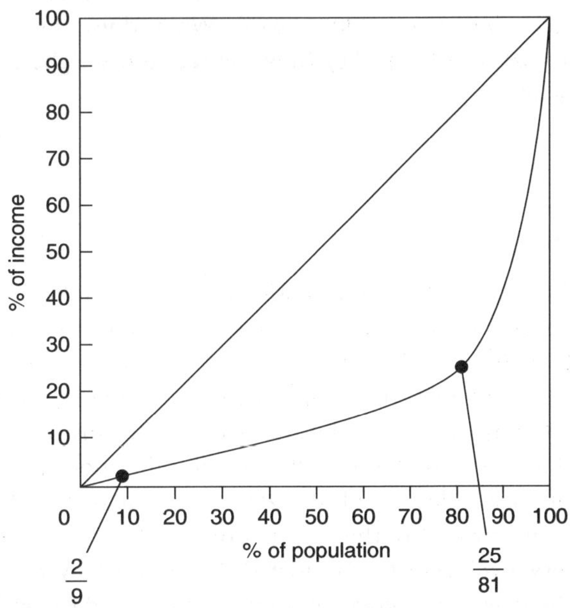

simple example, suppose we take the World Bank's division of countries into low, middle and high income, and that low-income countries contain 9% of the world's population and receive only 2% of world income, middle-income countries contain 72% of the world's population and receive 23% of world income, and rich countries contain 19% of the world's population and receive 75% of world income. The cumulative distribution of income in relation to population would then be 2/9, then 25/81 (when middle-income country figures are added), and finally 100/100 when the rich countries are added.

These points are plotted in Figure 2.1 and the curve joining them is the Lorenz curve. The diagonal 45⁰ line on the diagram shows an equal distribution of income. The position of the Lorenz curve in relation to the 45⁰ line therefore gives a visual impression of the degree of inequality. The closer the Lorenz curve, the more equal the distribution, and the more 'bowed' the curve, the more unequal the distribution.

The Gini ratio is calculated as the area between the Lorenz curve and the 45° line divided by the area of the triangle it lies within. If the Lorenz curve is coincident with the 45° line, the Gini coefficient would be zero – complete equality. If one person received all the world's income, the Lorenz curve would follow the horizontal and vertical axes and the Gini coefficient would be one. When we examine international and global inequality, what we find is that through time, at least since the early 1900s, the Lorenz curve has been shifting outwards, and the Gini ratio has been rising, although according to some investigators, it may recently have levelled off, albeit at a high level. A central estimate for the current level of international inequality would be a Gini ratio of 0.54, and for global inequality a Gini ratio of 0.67. But, as we shall come to see, estimates vary depending on factors such as the sample of countries taken, how income is measured – whether by per capita income or household income – and whether income is measured at official exchange rates or at PPP rates.

There have been many recent studies measuring and summarizing what has been happening to international and global inequality historically (e.g. Milanovic, 2005, 2016; Bourguignon and Morrisson, 2002), and particularly since the 1950s (e.g. Norwegian Institute of Economic Affairs, 2000; Sala-í-Martin, 2002; Maddison, 2003; Ghose, 2004; Wade, 2004; Sutcliffe, 2004; Svedberg, 2004; Milanovic, 2005, 2016). What does the evidence show? We distinguish between international inequality (unweighted and weighted by population) and global (or world) inequality.

International inequality (unweighted and population weighted)

The unweighted Gini ratio of international inequality takes each country as one unit, regardless of population size, and assumes that each person within the country has the same average income. The distribution of income within the country is not considered. It is countries that are the focus, not people. The ratio is basically, therefore, a measure of whether or not countries are converging with each other, not whether the distribution of income across individuals in the world is becoming more or less equal. What does the evidence show? Using the best historical data available (Maddison, 2001; Bourguignon and Morrisson, 2002) for 26 countries covering nearly 80% of the world's population, the Gini ratio in 1820 was approximately 0.2. This is very low by current standards. Two hundred years ago, international differences in income per head were not great. Maddison (2003) and Easterlin (2000) show that the ratio of per capita income of the richest to the poorest country in 1820 was only 3:1, compared with nearly 700:1 today.

Table 2.3 shows the evolution of the unweighted Gini ratio through time, rising consistently to 0.54 in 2013 – a more than doubling of income inequality in the space of nearly 200 years. Some of the increase may be spurious due to the larger sample of countries used to calculate the ratio, but Milanovic (2005, 2016) shows that for the same 26 countries as used for the 1820 calculations, the Gini ratio still rises to just over 0.5 in 2000. For the period since the Second World War, the Gini ratio shows an increase for a consistent set of over 100 countries from 0.45 in 1952 to a peak of 0.58 in 2002. Since then, it has been falling slightly due to the fast growth of China and India, and some African countries because of the rise in commodity prices (Bourguignon, 2015).

Turning now to the population-weighted measure of international inequality, Table 2.3 tells a slightly different story. It shows the Gini ratio peaking at 0.6 in 1988 and falling consistently to 0.47 in 2013. This implies that poor countries with large populations must have been growing faster on average than richer countries with smaller populations. In the 1950s and 1960s, this was due to the fast growth of some of the big Latin American countries, such as Brazil and Mexico, and Japan and South Korea, all using trade protection of one form or another. In the 1990s and 2000s, the decline in the weighted Gini ratio has been largely due to the rapid growth of a small number of poor populous Asian countries, especially India and China. Ghose (2004), in his study of 96 countries over the period 1981 to 1997, finds that the weighted Gini ratio fell by 0.7% per annum,

Table 2.3 A comparison of Gini ratios

	International inequality		Global (or world) inequality		
Year	Unweighted	Population weighted	Milanovic (2005, 2016)	Bourguignon and Morrisson (2002)	Sala-i-Martin (2002)
1820	0.20	0.12		0.50	
1870	0.29	0.26		0.56	
1890	0.31	0.30		0.59	
1913	0.37	0.37		0.61	
1929	0.35	0.40		0.62	
1938	0.35	0.40			
1952	0.45	0.57		0.64	
1960	0.46	0.55		0.64	
1978	0.47	0.54		0.66	0.66 (1970)
1988	0.53	0.60	0.68		0.65
1993	0.56	0.59	0.70	0.66 (1992)	0.64
1998	0.56	0.57	0.69		0.63
2002	0.58	0.56	0.71		0.63 (2000)
2005	0.57	0.54	0.70		
2008	0.55	0.51	0.69		
2011	0.54	0.48	0.67		
2013	0.54	0.47			

Sources: Adapted from Milanovic, 2005, Table 11.1; Milanovic, 2016.

but only 17 of the 76 developing countries in the sample converged on the per capita income of the 20 developed countries. The majority of poor developing countries diverged. Despite the fall in the ratio since 1988, it is still high and much higher than the estimate of 0.12 in 1820. In other words, for a large part of the past two centuries, the world's poorest and most populous countries have fared badly compared with the smaller, rich countries of the world. China and India are now reversing the trend, but for how long remains to be seen.

Global (or world) inequality

The Gini ratio of global (or world) inequality takes into account not only differences in average per capita income between countries, but also differences in income per capita within countries. Because internal income distributions are never equal, the measure of global inequality is bound to be higher than the unweighted measure of international inequality. It also means that changes in the global distribution of income are an amalgam of forces, including what is happening to the distribution of income between countries, what is happening to population growth in rich and poor countries, and what is happening to the distribution of income within countries. What does the evidence show? As far as the historical record is concerned, Bourguignon and Morrisson (2002) have tried to measure inequality among world citizens back to 1820 using a sample of 33 countries (or groups of countries) and measuring domestic income inequality by taking decile income shares (with the top decile of income earners divided into two). The results are shown in Table 2.3 above. It can be seen that the global Gini ratio in 1820 was already 0.5, more than double the level of international inequality, implying that domestic inequality was as great, if not greater, than international inequality. Through time, global inequality has increased, but because of rising international inequality, not because of even greater inequality within countries. On the contrary, domestic income inequality, at least until recently, has shown a decrease historically, particularly in the richer countries of the world. Bourguignon and Morrisson calculate that within-country inequality accounted for 80% of global inequality in the first half of the nineteenth century, when most countries were more or less at the same income level, but by 1950, within-country inequality accounted for 40% of global inequality because of the increase in inequality between countries. Today, the contribution is about 20%. The Gini ratio of global inequality seems to have peaked in the early 2000s at 0.71 and has since declined (Bourguignon, 2015). But conflicting forces are at work. Population-weighted international inequality is falling because of the fast growth of India and China, but income distribution within some countries is widening, such as between the urban and rural sectors of China and India and in some developed countries such as the USA and countries of Europe. If the income distribution within countries was falling, the global Gini ratio would evidence a greater fall.

Sala-í-Martin (2002) covers the period 1970–98, taking the income distribution of 125 countries and aggregating them. Despite the much larger sample, the calculated global Gini ratios are remarkably similar to those of Bourguignon and Morrisson. The estimate for 1970 is 0.66, gradually falling to 0.63 in 2000 (see Table 2.3). The explanation for the slight fall is that the lower 'tail' of the aggregated income distribution has shifted rightwards more dramatically than the upper 'tail', largely due to developments in China and India. Fast growth in these two countries has lifted millions of people above the poverty line, and has reduced the relative income gap with richer countries, and this has been enough to just offset the worsening income distribution within China and India, as mentioned earlier. Still, we have evidence again of global inequality on a vast scale.

Milanovic (2005, 2016) has also undertaken the Herculean task of bringing together 300 household sample surveys of income and expenditure for over 100 countries for selected years from 1988 to 2011, covering 80–90% of the world's population. The calculated global Gini ratio using household income or expenditure measured at PPP is 0.68 in 1988 and 0.67 in 2011 (see Table 2.3). These estimates are remarkably similar to those of Sala-í-Martin, despite the difference in samples and the measure of income. Bourguignon (2015) gives a figure of 0.691 for 2010. These results are confirmed by Edward (2006) using national consumption distributions and collating them into a global distribution measured at PPP in US$ for 1993 and 2001. The global Gini ratio is estimated at 0.610 for 1993 and 0.614 for 2001. Just over 80% of this inequality is the result of between-country differences.

All the evidence and studies show a massive degree of inequality in the world distribution of income, which shows some recent improvement but may not last if growth in China and India slows and the income distribution within countries gets worse. This development gap naturally extends into other aspects of human welfare such as health, nutrition, life expectancy, education, employment opportunities and so on, as we shall come to see later in this chapter and in Chapters 3 and 7. The UNDP (1997) has described the world as 'gargantuan in its excesses and grotesque in its human and economic inequalities'. This is, of course, a normative statement, but economists should not be afraid of making normative statements, as Basu (2006) does when he argues that:

> the hiatus between the richest and the poorest people is too large, and the extent of poverty on earth is unacceptable. I like to believe that there will come a time when, looking back at today's world, human beings will wonder how primitive we were that we tolerated this.

Many other statistics can be given to illustrate the grotesque inequalities that exist. The richest 1% of people in the world receive as much income as the bottom 60%. Or, to put it another way, the 60 million richest people receive as much income as 2.7 billion poor. The total income of the richest 25 million Americans is equal to the total income of 2 billion of the world's poorest people. The assets of the world's 400 billionaires (mostly in rich countries) exceed the total amount of income of nearly one-half of the world's total population.

The most evocative graph comes from Wade (2001), who divides the world's population up into equal 20% shares (quintiles) from poorest to richest, and then shows the percentage of income that each share receives. Interestingly, and ironically, the picture resembles a champagne glass with a very narrow stem in the hands of the poor and a wide open bowl (containing the champagne) in the hands of the rich (Figure 2.2).

Below we discuss some technical problems concerning the measurement and comparability of per capita income across countries, and the measurement of poverty itself.

Figure 2.2 Distribution of world income (percentage of total, with quintiles of population ranked by income)

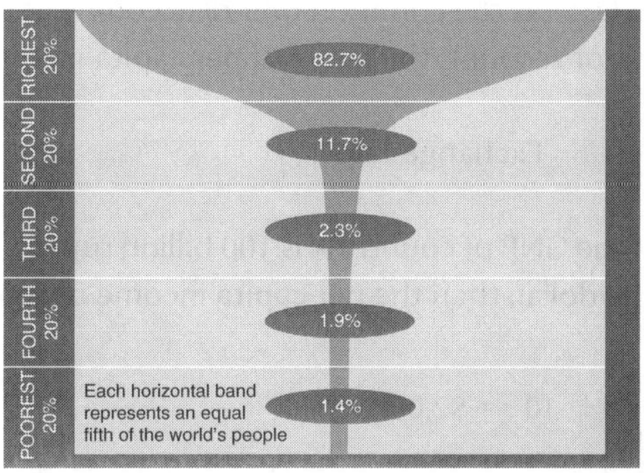

Source: Wade, 2001, based on Figure 3.2 in UNDP, 1992.

The measurement and comparability of per capita income

When using per capita income (PCY) figures to measure poverty, to classify countries into rich and poor, and to compare the rate of development in different countries over time, the difficulties of measuring real per capita income and real living standards between countries must be continually borne in mind. There are two issues to discuss. The first concerns the problems associated with national income accounting, particularly in developing countries. The second is the need to convert each country's per capita income in its own *domestic* currency into a common unit of account (e.g. the US$) so as to be able to make meaningful international comparisons of living standards. This leads to the topic of **purchasing power parity (PPP) estimates of PCY.**

Turning first to national income accounting, the first point to bear in mind is that only goods that are produced and sold at a price in the market are included in the value of national income, measured by either the output or the expenditure method. Much output in developing countries never reaches the market, particularly in the rural sector where production is for subsistence purposes. If no allowance is made for the subsistence sector, this will bias downwards the calculation of national income, and therefore PCY. This point also implies that growth rates will tend to have an upward bias as a result of the extension of the money economy and the shift of economic activities from the household and subsistence sector to the marketplace. Part of the growth in developing countries may be a statistical illusion arising from the changing balance between the informal subsistence sector and the modern exchange sector.

Second, there is the sheer practical difficulty of measuring money national income in a rural economy where communications are bad, illiteracy is rife, and accounting procedures are rudimentary. Differences in the extent of the subsistence economy between developing countries, and differences in the ease and difficulty of collecting data, may markedly influence estimates of national income, and therefore of per capita income differences, between these countries and the rest of the world. Attempts are made in developing countries to make some allowance for production that never reaches the marketplace, but the estimates are likely to be subject to a wide margin of error.

Some testimony to the role that the subsistence sector must play in the economies of most developing countries is provided by the inconceivability that 10% of the world's population could remain alive on less than $1,000 per annum. But this is not the whole story.

Purchasing power parity (PPP)

The other part of the story, and probably the major part, concerns the understatement of living standards in developing countries when their national incomes measured in local currencies are converted into US$ (as the common unit of account) at the official rate of exchange. If the US$ is used as the unit of account, the national per capita income of country X in US$ is given by:

$$\frac{GNP_X}{\text{Population}} \div \text{Exchange rate}$$

For example, if the GNP of country X is 100 billion rupees, its population is 5 million, and there are 10 rupees to the dollar, then the per capita income of country X in dollars is:

$$\frac{100 \text{ billion}}{5 \text{ million}} \div 10 = \$2{,}000$$

But if the living standards of the two countries are to be compared by this method, it must be assumed that 10 rupees in country *X* buys the same living standard as $1 in the USA. It is well known, however, that official exchange rates between two countries' currencies are not good measures of the PPP between countries, especially between countries at different levels of development. The reason is that exchange rates are largely determined by the supply of and demand for currencies based on goods and assets that are traded (the prices of which tend to be equalized internationally) but living standards depend also on the prices of **non-traded goods**, which are largely determined by unit labour costs, and these tend to be lower the poorer the country. As a general rule, it can be said that the lower the level of development and the poorer the country, the lower the price of non-traded goods relative to traded goods and the more the use of the official exchange rate will *understate* the living standards of the developing country measured in US$.

Let us give a simple example. The motor car is an internationally traded good. Suppose that the dollar price of a particular model of car is $10,000 and there are 10 rupees to the dollar. Ignoring transport costs, tariffs and so on, the price of the car in India will be $\$10{,}000 \times 10 = 100{,}000$ rupees, otherwise a profit will be made by dealers buying in the cheapest market and selling in the most expensive. The forces of demand and supply (and arbitrage) will equalize the price of traded goods. But let us now consider a non-traded good such as a haircut. Suppose a haircut in the USA costs $10. At the official exchange rate of 10 rupees to the dollar, a haircut in India should be 100 rupees. But suppose that, in fact, it is only 25 rupees. This would mean that as far as haircuts are concerned, the value of the rupee is underestimated by a factor of four. The PPP rate of exchange for haircuts alone is $\$10 \div 25$ rupees, or $\$1 = 2.5$ rupees. If the national income of country *X* measured in rupees was divided by 2.5 instead of 10, the national income of country *X* in dollars, and therefore PCY in dollars, would now be four times higher: $8,000 per head instead of $2,000 per head, as in the example above.

As development proceeds, the ratio of the price of non-traded goods to traded goods tends to rise as wage levels in the non-traded goods sector rise but productivity growth is slow – slower than in the traded goods sector. **To make meaningful international comparisons of income and living standards, therefore, what is required is a measure of PPP, or a real exchange rate, between countries.**

There are several methods of constructing PPP ratios in order to make binary comparisons (one country with another) or 'multilateral' comparisons, in which the currency of any one of a group of countries can act as the unit of account without altering the ratios of living standards between countries.

The most common way of constructing a PPP ratio between two countries (say, India and the USA) is to take a representative, comparable basket of goods and services in both countries, and then take the weighted average of prices, where the weights (w_i) reflect the proportion of expenditure on each good in total expenditure. The PPP rate of exchange between India and the USA is therefore:

$$PPP = \frac{w_{iI}P_{iI}}{w_{iUS}P_{iUS}},$$

where P_{iI} is the price of the good in India and P_{iUS} is the price of the good in the USA.

The difference between estimates of PCY at the official exchange rate and PPP estimates of PCY for, say, the low-income countries, can be seen in Table 2.2 (p. 30). The difference is quite large. At the official exchange rate, the level of PCY is only $629 per annum, but at PPP it is $1,570, or more than double. In other words, in low-income countries, a person's income would be able to buy more than *twice* the goods and services that the official exchange rate would suggest. Notice that in high-income countries, there is hardly any difference between the two estimates because wage costs per unit of output in the non-traded goods sector match those of the traded goods sector.

Per capita income as an index of development

Now let us turn to the question of the use of per capita income figures as an index of development and for making a distinction between developed and developing countries, as well as between rich and poor. While there may be an association between poverty and underdevelopment and riches and development, there are a number of reasons why some care must be taken when using per capita income figures alone as a measure or indicator of development (unless underdevelopment is *defined* as poverty and development as riches). Apart from the difficulty of measuring income in many countries and the difficulty of making intercountry comparisons, using a single per capita income figure to separate developed from developing countries is inevitably somewhat arbitrary, because it ignores such factors as the distribution of income within countries, differences in development potential and other physical indicators of the quality of life. It is not so much a question of whether or not low-income countries should be labelled 'underdeveloped' or 'developing', but what income level should be used as the criterion for separating the developed from the developing countries, and whether all high-income countries should necessarily be labelled 'developed'. In many ways, it should be the *nature* and *characteristics* of the countries that determine which income level should be used as the dividing line. It also makes sense to categorize separately the oil-rich countries, which have high per capita incomes but cannot be regarded as developed by the criteria discussed in Chapter 1.

Acronyms abound to describe the different stages of development. Perhaps the most amusing set is attributable to the Brazilian economist Roberto Campos, who distinguishes five categories of countries: the HICs, PICs, NICs, MICs and DICs. These stand for hardly industrialized countries, partly industrialized countries, newly industrialized countries, mature industrialized countries and decadent industrialized countries. The HICs and the PICs would certainly cover all the low-income countries and at least the lower half of the middle-income countries. The NICs cover most of the upper half of the middle-income countries – Brazil, Mexico, Hong Kong and Singapore being prime examples. The MICs and DICs cover most of those countries classified as 'industrial market economies', with the exception of New Zealand and Australia, which have become rich through agriculture.

But bearing in mind the arbitrariness of per capita income, it is still very convenient to have a readily available and easily understandable criterion for classifying countries, and perhaps per capita income is the best single index we have. It also has one positive advantage, namely that it focuses on the raison d'être of development: raising living standards and eradicating poverty. And, in the last resort, per capita income is not a bad proxy for the social and economic structure of most societies. If developing countries are defined on the basis of a per capita income level so as to include most of the countries of Asia, Africa and Latin America, striking similarities are found between the characteristics and development obstacles of many of the countries in these continents. These include:

- A high proportion of the labour force engaged in agriculture with low productivity.
- A high proportion of domestic expenditure on food and necessities.

- An export trade dominated by primary products and an import trade dominated by manufactured goods.
- A low level of technology and poor human capital.
- A high birth rate coupled with a falling death rate.
- Savings undertaken by a small percentage of the population.

There are, of course, some countries that on a per capita income basis are classified as developed and possess many of the above-mentioned characteristics (e.g. some oil-producing countries), but the exceptions are few, and the reverse of this situation would be unusual. Also, these countries have many social problems in common, such as growing unemployment in urban areas, inegalitarian income distributions, and poor health and standards of education – about which we shall say more later.

In general, therefore, it can be said that per capita income may be used as a starting point for classifying *levels* of development, and can certainly be used to identify the *need* for development. The only major reservation that we shall have to consider later concerns the case of geographically dual economies, where an aggregate per capita income figure can disguise as great a need for the development of a sizeable region within the country as the need for the development of the country itself.

There is a difference, however, between using per capita income as a guideline for classifying countries into developed or underdeveloped at a point *in time* and using the growth of per capita income as an index of development *over time*. The difficulty of using per capita income for the latter purpose is the obvious one that if, in a particular period, per capita income did not grow because population growth matched the growth of a country's total income, one would be forced into the odd position of denying that a country had developed even though its national product had increased. This is an inherent weakness of linking the concept of development to a measure of living standards.

This leads on to the distinction between **growth** and **development**. Development without growth is hardly conceivable, but growth is possible without development. The upswing of the trade cycle is the most obvious example of the possibility of growth without development; and examples of abortive 'take-offs' are not hard to find where countries have grown rapidly for a short time and then reverted to relative stagnation. Historically, Argentina is a case in point. On the other hand, development is hardly possible without growth; but development is possible, as we have suggested, without a rise in per capita income. It would be a strange, rather purposeless type of development, however, that left per capita income unchanged, unless the stationary per capita income was only temporary and a strong foundation was being laid for progress in the future. The ultimate rationale of development must be to improve living standards and welfare, and while an increase in measured per capita income may not be a sufficient condition for an increase in individual welfare, it is a necessary condition in the absence of a radical redistribution of income and the provision of basic needs to the poor.

Measuring poverty

The World Bank defines poverty as the inability of people to attain a minimum standard of living. The World Bank's 1990 and 2000/2001 *World Development Reports* were devoted to a consideration of the measurement, magnitude and nature of poverty in developing countries, and how to tackle it. This definition gives rise to three questions. How do we measure the standard of living?

What is meant by a *minimum* standard of living? How can we express the overall extent of poverty in a single measure?

The most obvious measure of living standards is an individual's (or household's) real income or expenditure (with an allowance made for output produced for own consumption). The same level of real income and expenditure in different countries, however, may be associated with different levels of nutrition, life expectancy, infant mortality, schooling and so on, which must be considered as an integral part of 'the standard of living'. Measures of living standards based on per capita income, therefore, may need to be supplemented by further measures that include these other variables. Later in this chapter, we discuss the attempt by the UNDP to construct a Human Development Index, and the Oxford Poverty and Human Development Initiative to construct a Multidimensional Poverty Index, which take some of these factors into account.

To separate the poor from the not so poor, an arbitrary per capita income figure has to be taken that is sufficient to provide a minimum acceptable level of consumption. There are two main ways of setting a consumption poverty line in order to measure poverty and make comparison across countries: the **PPP method** and the **food energy method**. As we have seen above, a country's PPP is defined as the number of units of the country's currency required to buy the same amount of goods and services in the domestic market as a dollar in the USA. The World Bank publishes the PPP levels of per capita income for all countries and regions of the world (see Table 2.2 on p. 30). For the measurement of poverty, to give an example, the PPP poverty line could be set at, say, \$60 per month or \$720 per annum. By definition, people on this PPP poverty line in any country have the purchasing power to obtain the same level of consumption of any person on the poverty line in any other country. But the composition of the consumption bundle is very likely to differ. The PPP poverty line is not explicitly linked to nutritional intakes derived from different consumption bundles, so there are likely to be intercountry differences in nutrition on the PPP poverty line.

The **food energy method** of setting a consumption poverty line is one way of dealing with this problem by defining a minimum internationally agreed calorie intake line, and converting consumption bundles into calorie intakes using the nutritional values of consumption goods (with non-food goods having a zero value). The problem here, however, is that consumers in different countries may choose different combinations of food and other goods, which then require different incomes to meet nutritional requirements. Indeed, the nature of the society and the stage of development reached may *require* different combinations. What are regarded as optional extras in some countries may be necessities in others. The UN's Food and Agriculture Organization defines undernourishment as 'food intake that is continuously insufficient to meet dietary energy requirements'.

A consumption-based poverty line can therefore be thought of as comprising two elements: an objective measure of the expenditure necessary to buy a minimum level of nutrition; and a subjective additional amount that varies from country to country, reflecting the cost to individuals of participating in the everyday life of society.

All this is in theory. In practice, to measure the extent of extreme poverty in the world, the World Bank takes \$1.90 a day at PPP at 2011 prices as the cut-off point. This used to be \$1.25 a day at 1995 prices (and before that at approximately \$1 a day), but the revised poverty line was introduced in 2014 to reflect the rising cost of basic food, clothing and shelter. The real value of \$1.90 a day at 2011 prices is the same as \$1.25 a day at 2005 prices.

Given the poverty line, the simplest way to measure the amount of poverty is by the **headcount index**, which simply adds up the number of people who fall below the poverty line, which can also be expressed as a proportion of the total population, giving the **poverty rate**. In 2012, there were just under 900 million, or nearly 13% of humanity, living in extreme poverty. The numbers in poverty and the poverty rates for different areas of the world are shown in Table 2.4. Sub-Saharan

Africa has by far the highest incidence of extreme poverty, with 43% of the population living on less than \$1.90 a day – a staggering figure. Students reading this book might like to try the experiment of living on such a meagre sum, and see how they fare.

Paul Collier (2007) once called those living on less than \$1 a day **the bottom billion**. On the new estimates of absolute poverty, the 'bottom billion' have become the 'bottom 900 million' caught in the four 'poverty traps' he identifies: the conflict trap (civil wars); the natural resources trap (the curse of natural resources – see Chapter 3); the trap of being landlocked with bad neighbours; and the trap of bad governance in a small country.

One weakness of the headcount index, however, is that it ignores the *extent* to which the poor fall *below* the poverty line, so that comparisons between countries, or over time, using only the headcount index or the poverty rate, do not tell the full story. To overcome this weakness, the concept of the **poverty gap** is used and measured. This measures the proportionate gap between the average level of income below the poverty line and the poverty line itself. For example, if the poverty line is \$1.90 a day and the average income for the poor below the poverty line is \$1.50 a day, then the poverty gap is (\$1.90 − \$1.50)/\$1.90 = 0.21 or 21%. The poverty gap for different regions of the world is shown in Table 2.5. It can be seen that the poverty gap is by far the highest in sub-Saharan Africa at 16.47%.

Table 2.4 Absolute poverty and poverty rates, 1990 and 2012

Global and regional poverty at the poverty line of \$1.90 per day (at 2011 PPP)				
Region	**Number of poor in millions**		**Poverty rate, % of population**	
	1990	**2012**	**1990**	**2012**
East Asia and Pacific	996	147	60.6	7.2
Europe and Central Asia	9	10	1.9	2.1
Latin America and the Caribbean	78	34	17.8	5.6
Middle East and North Africa	14		6.0	
South Asia	575	309	50.6	18.8
Sub-Saharan Africa	288	389	56.8	42.7
World	1,959	897	37.1	12.7

Source: World Bank, 2015.

Table 2.5 Poverty gap at \$1.90 a day (2011 PPP) (%)

	2012
East Asia and Pacific (developing only)	1.47
Europe and Central Asia (developing only)	0.58
Latin America and Caribbean (developing only)	2.64
Low income	18.6
Lower middle income	4,69
Low and middle income	4.35
Middle East and North Africa (developing)	
Sub-Saharan Africa (developing only)	16.47

Source: World Bank, 2015.

The difference for every individual could also be summed and expressed as a proportion of total GDP. This would give the proportion of total income that would have to be redistributed to raise everyone above the poverty line.

The focus of the World Bank is now very much on poverty eradication. When Robert McNamara was president of the World Bank in the 1970s, he defined absolute poverty as 'a condition of life so degraded by disease, illiteracy, and malnutrition and squalor, as to deny its victims basic human necessities – [a condition] so limited as to prevent the realisation of the potential of the genes with which one was born'. In May 1992, Lewis Preston, the then president of the World Bank, declared that poverty reduction will be 'the benchmark by which our performance as a development institution will be measured'. And in the *World Development Report 2000/2001*, James Wolfensohn, the then president, wrote: 'Poverty amidst plenty is the world's greatest challenge. We at the Bank have made it our mission to fight poverty with passion and professionalism, putting it at the centre of all the work that we do' (World Bank, 2000a). Jim Yong Kim, the current president, has said: 'I want to eradicate poverty. I think there is a tremendous passion for that in the World Bank.' As Collier (2007) writes: 'an impoverished ghetto of 1 billion people [is] increasingly impossible for a comfortable world to tolerate'.

Meeting the Sustainable Development Goal of poverty reduction

To meet the Sustainable Development Goal of reducing extreme poverty to 1% of the world's population by 2030 will require high sustained growth in the poorest countries. To calculate the growth required to go from the 2015 poverty rate to 1%, the elasticity of the poverty rate with respect to the growth of per capita income needs to be determined. As a rough guide, it is estimated by the World Bank (see Ravallion, 2013) that every 1% increase in per capita income leads to a 1.7% reduction in the poverty rate. This calculation, however, also depends on the distribution of income within countries. More equal countries cut poverty further and faster than unequal ones. In the most unequal countries, a 1% increase in income cuts the poverty rate by less than 1%, while in more equal countries a 1% increase in income reduces the poverty rate by as much as 4%. Ravallion (2013) calculates that if developing countries maintain their post-2000 growth performance, the number of extremely poor people will fall from the current level of 900 million to 200 million by 2030, or 3% of the world's population. This would be a remarkable achievement. To reach the 1% poverty target, however, would require an increase in household consumption of 7.6% per annum – an unrealistically high level.

Tackling poverty from the 'grass roots'

Poverty not only means low income and consumption, and low levels of human development in terms of education and healthcare, but also feelings of powerlessness, vulnerability and fear, because poor people are not free, and are exposed to greater risk, living on the margin of subsistence.

What it means to be poor is well illustrated in the World Bank's study *The Voices of the Poor* (World Bank, 2000b), which asked 60,000 poor people in 60 countries to articulate their feelings about their physical and mental state. Some of the answers are contained in Case example 2.1, which are both moving and revealing. Feelings of helplessness, humiliation and lack of self-esteem are paramount.

Case example 2.1

The voices of the poor

Poor people in 60 countries were asked to analyse and share their ideas of well-being (a good experience of life) and 'ill-being' (a bad experience of life). Well-being was variously described as happiness, harmony, peace, freedom from anxiety, and peace of mind. In Russia, people say 'well-being is a life free from daily worries about lack of money'. In Bangladesh, 'to have a life free from anxiety'. In Brazil, 'not having to go through so many rough spots'. People describe ill-being as lack of material things, bad experiences, and bad feelings about oneself. A group of young men in Jamaica ranks lack of self-confidence as the second biggest impact of poverty: 'Poverty means we don't believe in self, we hardly travel out of the community – so frustrated, just locked up in a house all day.'

Although the nature of ill-being and poverty varies among locations and people – something that policy responses must take into account – there is a striking commonality across countries. Not surprisingly, material well-being turns out to be very important. Lack of food, shelter and clothing is mentioned everywhere as critical. In Kenya, a man says: 'Don't ask me what poverty is because you have met it outside my house. Look at the house and count the number of holes. Look at my utensils and the clothes I am wearing. Look at everything and write what you see. What you see is poverty.'

Alongside the material, physical well-being features prominently in the characterizations of poverty. And the two meld together when lack of food leads to ill health – or when ill health leads to an inability to earn income. People speak about the importance of looking well fed. In Ethiopia, poor people say, 'We are skinny', 'We are deprived and pale', and speak of a life that 'makes you older than your age'.

Security of income is also closely tied to health. But insecurity extends beyond ill health. Crime and violence are often mentioned by poor people. In Ethiopia, women say, 'We live hour to hour', worrying about whether it will rain. An Argentine man says, 'You have work, and you are fine. If not, you starve. That's how it is.'

Two social aspects of ill-being and poverty also emerged. For many poor people, well-being means freedom of choice and action and the power to control one's life. A young woman in Jamaica says that poverty is 'like living in jail, living in bondage, waiting to be free'.

Linked to these feelings are definitions of well-being as social well-being and comments on the stigma of poverty. As an old woman in Bulgaria says: 'To be well means to see your grandchildren happy and well dressed and to know that your children have settled down; to be able to give them food and money whenever they come to see you, and not to ask them for help and money.' A Somali proverb captures the other side: 'Prolonged sickness and persistent poverty cause people to hate you.'

The following quotations are an illustration of what living in poverty means:

> Certainly our farming is little; all the products, things bought from stores, are expensive; it is hard to live, we work and earn little money, buy few things or products; products are scarce, there is no money and we feel poor.
>
> (from a discussion group of poor men and women, Ecuador)

> We face a calamity when my husband falls ill. Our life comes to a halt until he recovers and goes back to work.
>
> (poor woman, Zawyet Sultan, Egypt)

> Poverty is humiliation, the sense of being dependent on them, and of being forced to accept rudeness, insults, and indifference when we seek help.
>
> (poor woman, Latvia)

Source: World Bank, 2000b.

The World Bank proposes a three-pronged strategy for poverty reduction: **promoting opportunity, facilitating empowerment and enhancing security**.

Promoting opportunity is partly about expanding economic opportunities for poor people through the process of economic growth, and partly about expanding the asset base of poor people and increasing the return on those assets. The major causes of individual poverty can be linked to a lack of assets and/or a low return on assets. Important assets to enable people to grow out of poverty include natural assets, such as land; human assets, such as education and health; financial assets, including access to credit, and social assets, such as networks of contacts. The return on assets once acquired depends on the institutional framework of a country, the performance of the economy, and what is happening in the world economy. The state has a role to play in expanding poor people's assets because markets do not work well for poor people owing to lack of access, power and collateral. The state can help in three major ways: first, by using its power to redistribute resources; second, through institutional reforms to deliver services more effectively, particularly in the fields of health and education; and third, by facilitating the engagement of poor people in programmes that help them to acquire assets, such as land and credit.

A growing economy is absolutely crucial for poverty reduction as emphasized by the World Bank's Commission on Growth and Development headed by the Nobel Prize-winning economist Michael Spence (World Bank, 2008). Poverty cannot be reduced in a stagnant economy. The Commission finds a strong negative association across countries between the average growth of income and consumption and the *share* of people living on less than $1 per day. A 1 percentage point growth of income below the average is associated with a 2 percentage point increase in the share of people living in poverty.

On the other hand, similar rates of growth of countries are associated with different rates of poverty reduction. This is the result of existing inequalities in the distribution of income, assets and access to opportunities. Growth is much more effective in reducing poverty where the income distribution is more equal than where there are big inequalities. The World Bank estimates that when inequality is low, growth reduces poverty by nearly twice as much as when inequality is high.

Facilitating empowerment is a new departure in the thinking of the World Bank compared with its 1990 Report. Empowering poor people means strengthening the participation of poor people in decision-making, eliminating various forms of discrimination – ethnic, religious, sexual – and making state institutions more accountable and responsive to poor people. The great challenge here is to tackle the institutional structures of poor countries that continue to marginalize, discriminate against and disenfranchise vulnerable sections of society. The law, the Church, bureaucrats and local elites, and customs and traditions all play a part. The state has a role to play in helping to empower people by:

1. Curbing corruption and harassment, and using the power of the state to redistribute resources for actions benefiting the poor.
2. Ensuring that the legal system is fair and accessible to the poor.
3. Making sure that the delivery of local services is not captured by local elites.
4. Encouraging the participation of poor people in the political process.
5. Galvanizing political support for public action against poverty.

Enhancing security means reducing poor people's vulnerability to the various forms of insecurity that affect people's lives, such as economic shocks, natural disasters, crop failures, ill health, violence, wars and so on, and helping people to cope with these adverse shocks when they occur. The wide range of risks that poor people are exposed to is highlighted in Case example 2.2. This vulnerability to risk requires a range of insurance mechanisms for managing risk, such as health and

Case example 2.2

Poor people's exposure to risk

Poor people are exposed to a wide range of risks.

Illness and injury

Poor people often live and work in environments that expose them to greater risk of illness or injury, and they have less access to healthcare. Their health risks are strongly connected to the availability of food, which is affected by almost all the risks the poor face (natural disasters, wars, harvest failures and food price fluctuations). Communicable diseases are concentrated among the poor, with respiratory infections the leading cause of death. A recent study of poverty in India found that the poor are 4.5 times as likely to contract tuberculosis as the rich and twice as likely to lose a child before the age of two.

Illness and injury in the household have direct costs (for prevention, care and cure) and opportunity costs (lost income or schooling while ill). The timing, duration and frequency of illness also affect its impact. A study of South India found that households can compensate for an illness during the slack agricultural season, but illness during the peak season leads to a heavy loss of income, especially on small farms, usually necessitating costly informal borrowing.

Old age

Many risks are associated with ageing: illness, social isolation, inability to continue working, and uncertainty about whether transfers will provide an adequate living. The incidence of poverty among the elderly varies significantly. In most Latin American countries, the proportion of people in poverty is lower for the elderly than for the population at large. In contrast, in many countries of the former Soviet Union, the incidence of poverty is above average among the elderly, particularly among people 75 and older. Women, because of their longer life expectancy, constitute the majority of the elderly, and they tend to be more prone to poverty in old age than men. The number of elderly people in the developing world will increase significantly in coming decades with the rapid demographic transition.

Consultations with poor people show that income security is a prime concern of the elderly, followed closely by access to health services, suitable housing and the quality of family and community life. Isolation, loneliness and fear all too often mark old people's lives.

Crime and domestic violence

Crime and domestic violence reduce earnings and make it harder to escape poverty. While the rich can hire private security guards and fortify their homes, the poor have few means to protect themselves against crime. In 1992 in São Paulo, Brazil, the murder rate for adolescent males in poor neighbourhoods was 11 times that in wealthier ones. Poor people frequently voice their fear of violence and the resulting powerlessness: 'I do not know whom to trust, the police or the criminals.'

Crime also hurts poor people indirectly. Children exposed to violence may perform worse in school. A study of urban communities in Ecuador, Hungary, the Philippines and Zambia showed that difficult economic conditions lead to destruction of social capital as involvement in community organizations declines, informal ties among residents weaken, and gang violence, vandalism and crime increase. Violence and crime may thus deprive poor people of two of their best means of reducing vulnerability: human and social capital.

continued overleaf

Case example 2.2 **Poor people's exposure to risk** – *continued*

Unemployment and other labour market risks

Labour market risks include unemployment, falling wages, and having to take up precarious and low-quality jobs in the informal sector as a result of macroeconomic crises or policy reform. The first workers to be laid off during cutbacks in public sector jobs are usually those with low skills, who then join the ranks of the urban poor; a pattern observed in Africa and Latin America during the structural adjustment reforms of the 1980s and early 1990s. The East Asian crisis also had pronounced effects on labour markets, with real wages and non-agricultural employment falling in all affected countries. As state enterprises in Eastern Europe and the countries of the former Soviet Union were privatized, poverty increased among displaced workers with low education and obsolete skills, not qualified to work in emerging industries.

Fluctuations in demand for labour often disproportionately affect women and young workers. Most public sector retrenchment programmes have affected women's employment more than men's, and women are more likely than men to work for small firms, which tend to be more sensitive to demand fluctuations. As incomes fall, poor households try to increase their labour market participation, especially for women and children.

Harvest failure and food price fluctuations

Weather-related uncertainties (mainly rainfall), plant disease and pests create harvest risk for all farmers, but technologies for reducing such risks (irrigation, pesticides, disease-resistant varieties) are less available in poor areas. Between 1994 and 1996, less than 20% of all cropland was irrigated in low- and middle-income countries (only 4% of such land was irrigated in sub-Saharan Africa).

Fluctuations in food prices are a related risk. Since poor households spend a large part of their income on food, even small price increases can severely affect food intake. Households that meet their food needs through subsistence agriculture are less vulnerable than households that have to buy all their food.

Liberalization of markets often boosts the price of staples – a benefit to small farmers if they are net sellers of food. Those hurt are the urban poor and the landless rural poor, as net food buyers, and farmers who engage in seasonal switching, selling food after the harvest when food is plentiful and cheap and buying it when it is scarce and expensive. Where transport facilities are good, traders can step in and equalize prices over the year through arbitrage, but such infrastructure is lacking in many areas.

Source: World Bank, 2000a.

old-age insurance, unemployment insurance and workforce programmes, social funds and cash transfers, microfinance programmes, insurance against crop failures and price instability and so on.

The World Bank points out, however, that promoting opportunities, facilitating empowerment and enhancing security are *necessary* conditions for tackling poverty, but not *sufficient* conditions in an interdependent, global economy. International action is also required to help poor people in at least five ways:

- Promoting global financial stability and reducing the risks of economic crisis.
- Opening up markets (particularly in developed countries) to the goods of poor countries.
- Encouraging the production of international public goods that benefit poor people; for example the control of disease, agricultural research and the dissemination of knowledge.

- More foreign aid and debt relief.
- Giving a greater voice to poor countries and peoples in the global forums and multilateral institutions of the world, such as the World Bank, the IMF and the WTO.

Randomized control trials (RCTs)

One of the most interesting and useful ways to find out which is the most effective way to fight poverty at the micro-level is to conduct **randomized control trials (RCTs)**, which is the approach taken by the Abdul Latif Poverty Action Laboratory set up by Abhijit Banerjee and Esther Duflo at the Massachusetts Institute of Technology in 2003, and described in their bestselling book *Poor Economics: A Radical Rethinking of the Way to Fight Global Poverty* (2011). RCTs enable anti-poverty policies to be based on scientific evidence rather than hunch or custom. As the authors argue: 'ideology, ignorance and inertia often explain why good-intentioned [anti-poverty] policies fail'. Research officers located in five offices around the world have completed, or are engaged in, over 250 experiments in more than forty countries.

The essence of an RCT is to take a random group of people or families to conduct an experiment and then to compare the results of the experiment on the group with another random sample (or control group) not subject to the experiment, and to see whether the experiment leads to a significant change in behaviour or outcome. For example, there was a microcredit experiment in Hyderabad (India) on whether microcredit works to help poor people. Fifty-two neighbourhoods were chosen at random to receive microcredit help and 52 other neighbourhoods were taken as a control group. After eighteen months, there was clear evidence of microcredit working.

In the fields of education and health, RCTs show that financial incentives work. Immunization camps against preventable diseases are very successful where people are rewarded for attending. Free chlorine dispensers next to water sources; free worming pills and free nutritional supplements also 'work'. Conditional cash transfers to families that send children to school have proved effective in Brazil (the Bolsa Familia programme) and Mexico (Oportunidades). In the field of population control, trials show that the provision of family planning services makes very little difference to fertility unless there is a demand for them and women are seen alone for advice. Teenage pregnancies have been reduced where girls have been provided with free school uniforms to stay in school rather than roam the streets.

Poor people live surrounded by huge risks to their livelihoods (see Case example 2.2), and the way they cope by diversifying activities is very inefficient. The challenge here is for governments to assist the development of insurance markets through education and subsidizing insurance premiums.

One way for poor people to expand their asset base is to borrow, but from moneylenders it is expensive, and the formal banking system is not interested in lending to the poor with no collateral. This is the challenge of the microcredit movement (see Chapter 13). The alternative to borrowing for investment is prior saving, and RCTs show the important role that mobile phone banking can play in encouraging small saving and dealing with small accounts.

These are just some of the fields in which RCTs have taken place. While the results can be interesting, there are limitations of such trials; in particular, it may be difficult to generalize the results of RCTs because they are context specific. Evaluation may be conducted on only one specific sample, the trial may be implemented in such a way that it cannot be replicated, and if a *specific* programme is implemented, a slightly different programme may not have the same results. Also, the evaluation of a trial itself may cause both treatment and comparison groups to alter their behaviour for the period of the experiment, leading to false inferences.

Notwithstanding these limitations, and that the trials are generally small scale, RCTs are beginning to make a major contribution to our understanding of the causes of poverty, the solution to poverty (what works and what does not), and what types of incentives poor people need to improve their health, value education and escape from the poverty trap.

Human Development Index (HDI)

To overcome the limitation of taking a single measure of PCY as an index of development and the problems of using PCY as a measure of living standards, the UNDP has developed the **Human Development Index (HDI)**. This index gives a measure of the economic well-being of nations that does not necessarily accord with the usual measure: the level of per capita income. As the UNDP says in its *Human Development Report* (2014): 'although GNP growth is absolutely necessary to meet all essential human objectives, countries differ in the way that they translate growth into human development'. The UNDP defines human development as 'a process of enlarging peoples' choices'. This depends not only on income but also on other social indicators such as life expectancy, health, education and literacy.

Originally, the HDI was based on three variables: life expectancy at birth; educational attainment measured by a combination of adult literacy (two-thirds weight) and combined primary, secondary and tertiary school enrolment ratios (one-third); and the standard of living measured by real PCY at PPP. An arithmetic average was taken of the three indices calculated. In 2010, the construction of the index changed. First, some of the variables changed, and second, the method of aggregation changed from an arithmetic average of the indexes to a geometric mean. The variables for the construction of the HDI are:

- Life expectancy at birth
- Educational attainment measured as the arithmetic mean of the average years of schooling, and expected years of schooling
- Gross national income per head at PPP.

These four variables are shown in columns 2, 3, 4 and 5 of Table 2.6 for 10 countries with very high human development, 10 countries with high human development, 10 countries with medium human development, and 10 countries with the very lowest human development, and also for regions of the world. To construct the index, fixed minimum and maximum values are taken for each of the variables. For life expectancy at birth, the range is 20–85 years. For average years of schooling, the range is from 0–15 years. For expected years of schooling, the range is 0–18 years. For per capita income at PPP, the range is from \$100–\$75,000 (taking logs). For any component of the HDI, the individual indexes can be computed according to the general formula:

$$\text{Index} = \frac{\text{Actual value} - \text{Minimum value}}{\text{Maximum value} - \text{Minimum value}} \tag{2.1}$$

Each index thus ranges from zero to 1. If the actual value of the variable is the minimum, the index is zero. If the actual value of the variable is equal to the maximum value, the index is one. Case example 2.3 shows how the index is calculated for Costa Rica.

There is not always a close correspondence between the ranking of countries by their HDI and their ranking by per capita income. For example, many of the oil-producing countries, such as Qatar, Kuwait, Angola and Equatorial Guinea have much lower HDI rankings than per capita income rankings because they don't use their riches for education and health, while countries

Table 2.6 Human Development Index and its components, 2013

HDI rank	Country	Human Development Index 2013	Life expectancy at birth (years)	Mean years of schooling (years)	Expected years of schooling (years)	Gross national income per capita, PPP$
Very high human development						
1	Norway	0.944	81.5	12.6	17.6	63,909
2	Australia	0.933	82.5	12.8	19.9	41,524
3	Switzerland	0.917	82.6	12.2	15.7	53,762
4	Netherlands	0.915	81.0	11.9	17.9	42,397
5	United States	0.914	78.9	12.9	16.5	52,308
6	Germany	0.911	80.7	12.9	16.3	43,049
7	New Zealand	0.910	81.1	12.5	19.4	32,569
8	Canada	0.902	81.5	12.3	15.9	41,887
9	Singapore	0.901	82.3	10.2	15.4	72,371
10	Denmark	0.900	79.4	12.1	16.9	42,880
High human development						
50	Uruguay	0.790	77.2	8.5	15.5	18,108
51	Bahamas	0.789	75.2	10.9	12.6	21,414
51	Montenegro	0.789	74.8	10.50	15.2	14,710
53	Belarus	0.786	69.9	11.50	15.7	16,403
54	Romania	0.785	73.8	10.7	14.1	17,433
55	Libya	0.784	75.3	7.5	16.1	21,666
56	Oman	0.783	76.6	6.8	13.6	42,191
57	Russian Federation	0.778	68.0	11.7	14.0	22,617
58	Bulgaria	0.777	73.5	10.6	14.3	15,402
59	Barbados	0.776	75.4	9.4	15.4	13,604
60	Palau	0.775	72.4	12.2	13.7	12.823
Medium human development						
103	Maldives	0.698	77.9	5.8 b	12.7	10,074
103	Mongolia	0.698	67.5	8.3	15.0	8,466
103	Turkmenistan	0.698	65.5	9.9 s	12.6 p	11,533
106	Samoa	0.694	73.2	10.3	12.9 t	4,708
107	Palestine, State of	0.686	73.2	8.90	13.2	5,168
108	Indonesia	0.684	70.8	7.5	12.7	8,970
109	Botswana	0.683	64.4	8.8	11.7	14,792
110	Egypt	0.682	71.2	6.4	13.0	10,400
111	Paraguay	0.676	72.3	7.7	11.9	7,580
112	Gabon	0.674	63.5	7.4	12.3	16,977

continued overleaf

Table 2.6 Human Development Index and its components, 2013 – *continued*

HDI rank	Country	Human Development Index 2013	Life expectancy at birth (years)	Mean years of schooling (years)	Expected years of schooling (years)	Gross national income per capita, PPP$
Lowest human development						
178	Mozambique	0.393	50.3	3.2	9.5	1,011
179	Guinea	0.392	56.1	1.6	8.7	1,142
180	Burundi	0.389	54.1	2.7	10.1	749
181	Burkina Faso	0.388	56.3	1.3	7.5	1,602
182	Eritrea	0.381	62.9	3.4	4.1	1,147
183	Sierra Leone	0.374	45.6	2.9	7.5	1,815
184	Chad	0.372	51.2	1.5	7.4	1,622
185	Central African Republic	0.341	50.2	3.5	7.2	588
186	Congo, Democratic Republic of the	0.338	50.0	3.1	9.7	444
187	Niger	0.337	58.4	1.4	5.4	873
	Regions					
	Arab States	0.682	70.2	6.3	11.8	15,817
	East Asia and the Pacific	0.703	74.0	74	12.5	10,499
	Europe and Central Asia	0.738	71.3	9.6	13.6	12,415
	Latin America and the Caribbean	0.740	74.9	7.9	13.7	13,767
	South Asia	0.588	67.2	4.7	11.2	5,195
	Sub-Saharan Africa	0.502	56.8	4.8	9.7	3,152
	Least developed countries	0487	61.5	3.9	94	2,126
	Small island developing states	0.665	70.0	7.5	11.0	9,471
	World	0.702	70.8	7.7	12.2	13,723

Source: UNDP, 2014.

such as Bangladesh, the Philippines, Ghana, Peru, Cuba and some of the Pacific Islands have high HDI rankings compared with per capita income because they invest in human development– education and health.

Multidimensional Poverty Index (MPI)

Poverty is not only about lack of income and low levels of education and health. It has many other dimensions. This is recognized by the **Multidimensional Poverty Index (MPI)**, developed by Alkire and Santos (2010) with the **Oxford Poverty and Human Development Initiative**, and

Case example 2.3

Calculating the HDI for Costa Rica

- Life expectancy at birth in Costa Rica is 79.93 years
- Mean years of schooling is 8.37
- Expected years of schooling is 13.50
- Gross national income per capita at PPP is $13,011.7

Now plug these values into the general formula, equation 2.1 above, to derive an index (I) for each of the variables.

$$\text{Health index} = \frac{79.93 - 20}{85 - 20} = 0.922$$

$$\text{Mean year of schooling index} = \frac{8.37 - 0}{15 - 0} = 0.558$$

$$\text{Expected years of schooling Index} = \frac{13.50}{18} = 0.750$$

$$\text{Education index} = \frac{0.558 + 0.750}{2} = 0.654$$

$$\text{Income index} = \frac{\ln(13{,}011.7) - \ln(100)}{\ln(75{,}000) - \ln(100)} = 0.735$$

The HDI is the geometric mean of each of the three indexes:

$$\textbf{HDI} = (I_{health} \times I_{education} \times I_{income})^{1/3}$$

where the education index is the mean of the two education variables.

The HDI for Costa Rica is therefore:

$$(0.922 \times 0.654 \times 0.735)^{1/3} = 0.763$$

This ranks Costa Rica 68th in the world, which puts it in the high human development category – but as we saw in Case example 1.1, it ranks much higher on other indexes of economic development and happiness. It is brought down by its relatively low level of per capita income compared with its educational performance and life expectancy.

Source: UNDP, 2014.

published by the UNDP's *Human Development Report* since 2010. It represents an internationally comparable measure of acute poverty covering more than one hundred developing countries. Three main dimensions of poverty are identified – education, health and standard of living – and each has various indicators, as shown in Table 2.7. In total, there are 10 indicators with their weights attached. Data on each indicator are collected at the household level and a person is identified as poor if they are deprived of at least one-third of the weighted indices. This is the cut-off point (c). In other words, if c is greater than 33.3%, the household (and everyone in it) is multidimensionally poor. If c is greater than 50%, the household is 'severely poor'.

The MPI index is the product of two measures: the multidimensional headcount ratio (H) and the intensity (or breadth) of poverty (A). The headcount ratio is the proportion of the population that is multidimensionally poor:

$$H = q/n \tag{2.2}$$

where q is the number of people who are multidimensionally poor and n is the total population. The intensity of poverty (A) is the sum (for poor households only) of the household deprivation

Table 2.7 Multidimensional Poverty Index and its components, 2014

Dimensions of poverty	Indicator	Deprived if …	Weight
Education	Year of Schooling	No household member has completed five years of schooling.	1/6
	Child School Attendance	Any school-aged child is not attending school up to class 8.	1/6
Health	Child Mortality	Any child has died in the family	1/6
	Nutrition	Any adult or child for whom there is nutritional information is malnourished.	1/6
Living Standard	Electricity	The household has no electricity.	1/18
	Improved Sanitation	The household's sanitation facility is not improved (according to MDG guidelines), or it is improved but shared with other households.	1/18
	Improved Drinking Water	The household does not have access to improved drinking water (according to MDG guidelines) or safe drinking water is more than a 30-minute walk from home, roundtrip.	1/18
	Flooring	The household has a dirt, sand or dung floor.	1/18
	Cooking Fuel	The household cooks with dung, wood or charcoal.	1/18
	Assets Ownership	The household does not own more than one radio, TV, telephone, bike, motorbike or refrigerator and does not own a car or truck.	1/18

Source: UNDP, 2014.

scores multiplied by the number of people in the household divided by the total number of poor people (q):

$$A = \frac{\sum_h c_{jh} i}{q} \tag{2.3}$$

where c_j is the deprivation score of the household, i is the number of people in the household, and h is the number of households.

Let us give a numerical example. Table 2.8 gives data for four households with different numbers of people in each.

Take household 1 with 4 persons. In only two categories is it 'poor': one or more children have died (weight 0.167), and the household uses only 'dirty' cooking (weight 0.056). The sum of the deprivation scores is 22.2%, which is less than the cut-off of 33.3%, so the household is not poor. By the same calculations, households 2, 3 are 4 are poor. For all these poor households, the head-count ratio (H), applying equation (2.2), is:

$$H = \frac{(7 + 5 + 4)}{(4 + 7 + 5 + 4)} = 0.800$$

The intensity of poverty (A) (for households that are poor) is:

$$A = \frac{(72.2)7 + (38.9)5 + (50.0)4}{(7 + 4 + 5)} = 0.563$$

Table 2.8 Hypothetical household data

		Households			Weights
Indicators	1	2	3	4	
Household size	4	7	5	4	
Education					
No one has completed five years of schooling	0	1	0	1	16.7%
At least one school-age child not enrolled in school	0	1	0	0	16.7%
Health					
At least one member is malnourished	0	0	1	0	16.7%
One or more children have died	1	1	0	1	16.7%
Living conditions					
No electricity	0	1	1	1	5.6%
No access to clean drinking water	0	0	1	0	5.6%
No access to adequate sanitation	0	1	1	0	5.6%
House has dirt floor	0	0	0	0	5.6%
Household uses 'dirty' cooking fuel (dung, firewood or charcoal)	1	1	1	1	5.6%
Household has no car and owns at most one of: bicycle. motorcycle, radio, refrigerator telephone or television	0	1	0	1	5.6%
Results					
Household deprivation score, c (sum of each deprivation multiplied by its weight)	22%	72.2%	38.9%	50.0%	
Is the household poor (c > 33.3%)?	No	Yes	Yes	Yes	

Note: 1 indicates deprivation in the indicator; 0 indicates non-deprivation
Source: UNDP, 2014.

that is, the average poor person is deprived in 56.3% of the weighted indicators. The MPI index ($H \times A$) is therefore: $MPI = 0.8 \times 0.563 = 0.490$.

The index can be compared over time and across countries, and the different contributions of education, health and the standard of living deprivation to the total index can also be calculated. There is a close correlation between the ranking of countries by their MPI and their HDI. Table 2.9 below gives countries where more than 50% of the population live in multidimensional poverty. The total number of people living in multidimensional poverty in the 28 countries listed is nearly 400 million out of a total of nearly 800 million overall. This latter figure is less than the number of individuals living on less than \$1.90 a day because typically a family consists of more than one person so that family income is more than \$1.90 a day. The MPI does not take account of income – only the consequences of a lack of income.

Can poor countries ever catch up?

If living standards are largely determined by the level and growth of productivity, the interesting question is whether developing countries will ever catch up with the performance of rich industrialized countries. There are at least three possible mechanisms by which catch-up may occur:

1. It is sometimes argued that the larger the gap between a poor country's technology, productivity and per capita income and the level of productivity in advanced countries, the greater

Table 2.9 Countries with more than 50% of the population living in multidimensional poverty

Country	% of population	No. of people (000)
Afghanistan	66.2	17,116
Bangladesh	51.2	75,610
Benin	71.8	5,897
Burkina Faso	84.0	12,875
Burundi	80.8	7,553
Central African Republic	77.6	332
D.R. Congo	74.0	46,278
Cote d'Ivoire	58.7	11,772
Ethiopia	87.3	78,887
Gambia	60.4	901
Guinea	82.5	8,278
Guinea-Bissau	77.5	1,168
India	53.7	63,199
Liberia	83.9	2,883
Madagascar	66.9	15,774
Malawi	66.7	10,012
Mali	86.6	10,545
Mauritania	61.7	2,197
Mozambique	69.6	17,246
Niger	89.3	15,408
Rwanda	69.0	7,669
Senegal	74.4	9,247
Sierra Leone	72.5	4,180
Somalia	81.2	7,106
Tanzania	65.6	29,842
Uganda	69.9	24,712
Yemen	52.5	7,714
Zambia	64.2	7,600

Source: UNDP, 2014.

the scope for a poor country to absorb existing technology and catch up with richer countries. Technology is thought of as a public good, so for a given amount of technological investment, a poor country can reap high returns because it has paid none of the development costs. Clearly, there also has to be the willingness and ability to invest and the capability to absorb new technology. A productivity gap is a necessary but not a sufficient condition for catch-up by this means.

2. The process of development is characterized by a shift of resources from low-productivity agriculture to higher productivity industrial and service activities. Other things being equal, this should also produce a move towards convergence, to the extent that the resource shifts are greater in poor countries than in rich countries.
3. Mainstream neoclassical growth theory predicts convergence (see Chapter 4) because of the assumption of diminishing returns to capital. Rich countries with a lot of capital per head will

have a lower productivity of capital than poor countries. Thus, if tastes and preferences are the same, the same amount of saving and investment in poor countries should lead to faster growth than in rich countries.

The standard procedure for testing the convergence hypothesis is to do a simple correlation across countries between the rate of growth of per capita income (y) as the dependent variable and the *initial* level of per capita income (or productivity) as the independent variable, and to see whether the relation is significantly negative. If it is, this means that per capita income is growing faster in poor countries than in rich countries, which is a necessary condition for convergence to take place (often called **beta convergence** in the literature). One of the earliest studies of this type (Baumol, 1986) showed a strong inverse correlation between a country's productivity level and its average productivity growth among industrial countries and those at an intermediate stage of development, but no evidence of convergence as far as the poorer countries are concerned.

Zind (1991) focused on 89 developing countries and regressed the rate of growth of per capita income on the level of per capita income in 1960. He could find no evidence of overall convergence, but there was some evidence of convergence taking place between countries with relatively high per capita incomes. One reason appears to be that in these latter countries, there was a positive relation between per capita income and the rate of growth of investment per capita.

Another study by Dowrick (1992) across 113 countries showed that while there was some evidence of catch-up in the 1970s and 1980s, in the sense that growth rates were negatively related to initial levels of productivity, other factors caused per capita income growth to be faster the higher the level of per capita income, producing a *divergence* of living standards across the world.

Similarly, Pritchett (1997) takes 117 countries over the period 1960–88 and regresses the rate of growth of per capita income on the initial level of per capita income relative to the leading country and finds no evidence of unconditional convergence. It is interesting to note, however, that when differences in investment and schooling between countries are allowed for, the coefficient becomes negative, indicating conditional convergence. The problem is, however, that rich countries are able to save and invest more, and they devote more resources to education, which perpetuates their growth advantage.

It has been argued by some (see Eichengreen et al., 2011) that when poor countries reach middle-income status, they may get caught in a so-called **middle-income trap**, meaning that they exhaust the potential for fast growth which leads to middle-income status, and then they lack the capability to make the next step to high-income status. The fast growth stage is associated with the shift of resources from agriculture to higher productivity sectors, and then growth slows down because of a fall in total productivity growth, and countries lack the capability to produce higher value-added goods necessary to achieve developed country status. It is true that economies are unlikely to sustain growth rates of 6–10% per annum, as China has done over the past 30 years, but as long as per capita income growth is positive, poor countries will ultimately become rich, and if the growth of per capita income exceeds that of developed countries, there will ultimately be convergence. It is debatable, therefore, whether a middle-income trap exists in practice.

But an interesting question then arises: How long it will take for poor countries to catch up with the rich? Let us consider two issues:

1. Given the recent growth experience of the poor countries of roughly 3% per annum, how long will it take for the average poor country to reach the current average living standards of rich developed countries?
2. How long will it take for poor countries to catch up with rich countries, assuming that rich countries grow at 3% per annum and poor countries were to raise their per capita growth to

4% per annum. (Clearly, a necessary condition for catch-up is that poor countries do grow faster than rich countries, otherwise convergence is impossible.)

We can answer both questions using the simple compound interest formula:

$$S = P(1 + r)^n$$

where P is the 'initial' income level, and S is the sum to which the income level grows at an annual compound rate of interest, r, over n years.

The answer to the first question, assuming that the current level of per capita income in poor countries (P) is \$1,200 per annum, and in rich countries (S) it is \$25,000, and the recent growth performance of poor countries (r) has been 2% per annum, is that it would take 153 years for poor countries to reach the current standard of living of rich countries.[1]

The answer to the second question is that it would take nearly 300 years for the average poor country growing at 4% per annum to catch up with the rich country growing at 3% per annum, given the initial difference in the level of per capita incomes.[2]

The above calculations are sensitive to the initial income levels taken and the assumed future growth rates of poor and rich countries, but it is difficult not to reach the conclusion that the timescale of catch-up will be extremely prolonged.

It can be argued, of course, that world income equality is an impracticable ideal, and that the primary aim is not equality of living standards throughout the world but 'tolerable' living standards in all countries, which is a very different matter. This seems to be the position of the World Bank, which argued in its *World Development Report 2000/2001* that rising income inequality 'should not be seen as a negative', provided that incomes at the bottom do not fall, and the number of people in poverty falls or does not rise (World Bank, 2000a). The problem is defining 'tolerable' living standards, and specifying an acceptable income distribution at that average level of real income. The timescale involved to reach 'tolerable' living standards is clearly less than that required to eliminate the income gap entirely, but even so, if the average level of per capita income now enjoyed in rich developed countries is regarded as the tolerable level, we estimate it will take over a century for the average poor country to attain it on current performance. Can these countries wait that long?

On the other hand, it is easily forgotten that the rich–poor country divide in the world economy is a relatively recent phenomenon. All countries were once at subsistence level, and as recently as 200 years ago, at the advent of the British Industrial Revolution, the absolute differences in living standards between countries cannot have been great. The average per capita income of low-income countries today is approximately \$1,500 per annum at PPP, and this is not far below the average level of real per capita income in Western Europe in the mid-nineteenth century, measured at current prices. If we regard \$1,500 as only barely above subsistence, the major part of the present income disparities between developed and developing countries must have arisen over the twentieth century. Some countries, through a combination of fortune and design, have managed to grow much faster than others. The overriding influence has been industrialization and the technological progress associated with it. The close association between industrialization and living standards spells out the clear policy message that to base a development policy on agricultural activities *alone* would be misguided, however attractive such aphorisms as 'back to the land' and 'small is beautiful' may sound.

The concentrated impact of industrialization on living standards in the Western world is dramatically emphasized by the observation that if 6,000 years of 'civilized' human existence prior to 1850 is viewed as a day, the last century or so represents little more than half an hour; yet in this 'half-hour', more real output has been produced in developed countries than in the preceding period. It is true that living standards in most developing countries have risen faster since 1950 than at any time in the past; but so too have the living standards in developed countries, and the gap between rich and poor countries continues to widen. Although development consists of more than a rise in per capita incomes, income disparities are the essence of the so-called 'development gap'.

Summary

- The development gap between rich and poor countries is huge. The absolute gap between the per capita income (PCY) of rich and poor countries is growing, and the ratio of the PCY of high-income developed countries to low-income developing countries is currently at a historical high of 60:1.
- The Gini ratio for international inequality has risen from 0.2 in 1820 to over 0.5. The Gini ratio for global inequality has risen from 0.5 in 1820 to over 0.6 today.
- This income gap and income inequality in the world economy manifests itself in other aspects of human welfare such as health, nutrition, life expectancy, education and employment opportunities (see Chapter 7). No wonder the UNDP (1997) has described the world as 'gargantuan in its excesses and grotesque in its human and economic inequalities'.
- The number of people living in the world on less than US$1.90 at PPP is 900 million. In Africa, nearly one-half of the population live on less than $1.90 a day.
- The average PCY of countries, even converted into PPP, is not always a good indicator of the development of a country, because it ignores the distribution of income and various aspects of human development such as education and health.
- Alternative measures of economic development and progress can be constructed such as the HDI and the MPI, which include measures of schooling, literacy, health, life expectancy and so on. Countries rank differently by PCY, HDI and MPI.
- The World Bank attempts to tackle poverty from the 'grass roots' by promoting opportunity, facilitating empowerment and enhancing economic security.
- At current rates of PCY growth in poor countries, it will take at least 100 years for the average poor country to reach the current living standards enjoyed by developed countries, and 300 years for living standards to be equalized. This is some measure of the development 'gap'.

Chapter 2 **Discussion questions**

1. How would you measure the development gap in the world economy?
2. How would you construct a Lorenz curve and calculate the Gini ratio for the measurement of income inequality?
3. What has been happening to the international and global distribution of income over time?
4. What difficulties arise in measuring and comparing the per capita incomes of poor countries using the US$ as the unit of account?
5. What do you understand by the concept of purchasing power parity (PPP), and how would you make PPP calculations of per capita income across countries?

Chapter 2 **Discussion questions** – *continued*

6. What difficulties are encountered in the measurement of poverty?
7. What is the World Bank's 'grass roots' thinking concerning the attack on world poverty?
8. What are the strengths and weaknesses of randomized control trials (RCTs)?
9. What is the rationale for the UNDP to construct the Human Development Index (HDI)?
10. What variables are included in the Multidimensional Poverty Index (MPI)?
11. Are there any theoretical reasons for supposing that poor countries might catch up with the rich countries?
12. How would you analyse how fast poor countries have to grow to catch up with the rich countries?

Notes

1. Rearranging the formula for compound interest gives:

$$n = \frac{\log (S/P)}{\log (1 + r)}$$

and applying the assumed values gives:

$$n = \frac{\log (\$25{,}000/\$1{,}200)}{\log (1.02)} = 153 \text{ years}$$

2. The solution is obtained from the expression:

$$S_r(1 + r_r)^n = P_p(1 + r_p)^n$$

where S_r is the initial income of rich countries; P_p is the initial income of poor countries; r_r is the assumed growth rate of the rich country (= 3%) and r_p is the assumed growth rate of the poor country (= 4%). Therefore:

$$n = \frac{\log (\$25{,}000/\$1{,}200)}{\log (1.04) - \log(1.03)} = 287 \text{ years}$$

Websites on poverty and income distribution

World Bank www.worldbank.org/en/topic/poverty
UNDP (Human Development Report) http://hdr.undp.org
Oxford Poverty and Human Development Initiative www.ophi.org.uk/
Oxfam www.oxfam.org.uk
War on Want www.waronwant.org
UNU-WIDER www.wider.unu.edu/project/wiid-%E2%80%93-world-income-inequality-database
Stone Center on Socio-economic Inequality www.gc.cuny.edu/stonecenter
University of Texas, Inequality Project utip.lbj.utexas.edu

3

THE CHARACTERISTICS OF UNDERDEVELOPMENT AND STRUCTURAL CHANGE

Introduction

This chapter is about the distinguishing characteristics of poor developing countries, and the process of structural change necessary for a rise in living standards. There cannot be an increase in living standards and a reduction in poverty without an increase in output per head of the working population or an increase in labour productivity. This is the sine qua non of development. Rich countries have high levels of labour productivity, poor countries have low levels of productivity. Why is productivity low in poor countries, and what are the major sources of productivity growth?

The major distinguishing characteristics of poor countries that contribute to low levels of productivity and poor economic performance are: the dominance of low-productivity agriculture and petty service activities in the economic structure; low levels of capital formation, physical and human (education); rapid population growth; and exports dominated by primary commodities. Some of these major characteristics of underdevelopment are both causes and effects of poverty; for example, low savings and investment, poor education, and rapid population growth can be causes of poverty but also symptoms.

In addition to these major distinguishing features of poor countries, some suffer from what is called 'the curse of natural resources', which refers to the detrimental effects that high dependence on natural resource exploitation and exports can have on an economy, because of an overvalued exchange rate (the Dutch disease), corruption and rent-seeking behaviour.

Many poor countries possess weak institutional structures such as lack of property rights, absence of the rule of law and political instability, all of which act as disincentives to investment.

In this chapter we also discuss many other dimensions of poverty in poor countries such as unemployment, income inequality, and the basic needs of people.

The chapter ends with a discussion of the **stages of growth** and development that countries go through, and the strong association that seems to exist between the progress of nations and the shift of resources from agriculture into industry and sophisticated service activities, known in the literature as **Kaldor's growth laws**. The fastest growing developing countries today are those where the share of industry in GDP is rising the fastest; and this is no accident, because manufactured goods have production and demand characteristics that make them the 'engine of growth'.

The dominance of agriculture and petty services

One of the major distinguishing characteristics of poor developing countries is the fact that their economies are dominated by agriculture and petty service activities. There is very little manufacturing industry in many of the poorest countries. Table 3.1 shows the distribution of employment by sectors of the economy in low-, middle- and high-income countries in different continents. It can be seen that in low-income countries, a large proportion of the labour force still relies on agriculture to make a living: 71% in sub-Saharan Africa and 67% in South Asia. By contrast, the proportion engaged in agriculture in high-income countries is less than 5%. The proportion employed in industry in low-income countries is very low – only 7% in sub-Saharan Africa. In high-income countries, employment is dominated by high-productivity service activities.

Most of those working on the land in poor countries are either subsistence farmers (producing only for themselves), tenant farmers (with no land rights and no incentive to increase output) or landless labourers (selling their labour in a daily labour market). Some high-productivity commercial agriculture does exist, but it forms a small proportion of total agricultural activity. The dominance of agriculture has a number of implications and poses a number of problems for developing

Table 3.1 Distribution of employment, by sector (percentage)

	Region	Agriculture (%)	Industry (%)	Services (%)
Lower income	Asia and the Pacific	53.7	17.9	28.4
	Eastern Asia	34.8	23.8	41.4
	Latin America and the Caribbean	43.3	10.8	45.9
	South-Eastern Asia and the Pacific	50.1	16.8	33.1
	Southern Asia	67.5	14.6	17.9
	Sub-Saharan Africa	71.2	7.1	21.7
Lower middle income	Asia and the Pacific	43.8	21.8	34.4
	Latin America and the Caribbean	28.7	18.2	53.1
	South-Eastern Asia and the Pacific	38.1	19.0	42.9
	Southern Asia	46.0	23 .0	31.0
	Sub-Saharan Africa	49.0	10.9	40.2
Upper middle income	Asia and the Pacific	24.5	25.7	49.8
	Eastern Asia	24.0	25.7	50.3
	Latin America and the Caribbean	15.2	21.2	63.6
	South-Eastern Asia and the Pacific	34.3	22.0	43.7
	Southern Asia	19.8	32.0	48.2
	Sub-Saharan Africa	18.8	16.1	65.1
High income	Asia and the Pacific	4.0	25.5	70.5
	Eastern Asia	4.2	26.2	69.6
	Latin America and the Caribbean	4.9	22.5	72.7
	South-Eastern Asia and the Pacific	2.9	21.2	75.9

Source: ILO, 2015, Table R4.

countries. First, agriculture is a **diminishing returns** activity because cultivatable land is ultimately a fixed factor of production. There are only a few incontrovertible laws in economics, but one is that if a variable factor is added to a fixed factor, its marginal product will eventually fall: **the law of diminishing returns**. This principle is illustrated in Figure 3.1.

As labour is added to the land, the marginal product of labour first rises because land requires a certain amount of labour for each unit of labour to work with maximum efficiency, but then the marginal product declines and could become zero (or even negative in extreme cases where

Figure 3.1 The law of diminishing returns

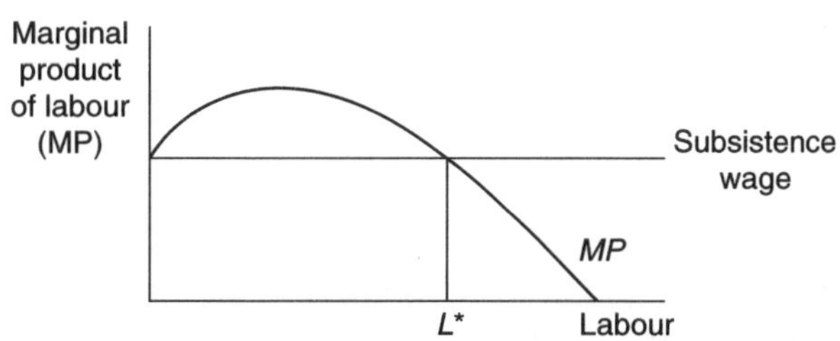

there is so much labour on a fixed piece of land that everyone gets in each other's way, reducing total output).

If the marginal product of labour falls below the subsistence level, the unit of labour will not be able to survive unless total output is shared. This may characterize family farms. If labour is hired, however, or works on commercial farms, no (profit-maximizing) employer will pay a wage above the marginal product of labour. We reach the conclusion that in a diminishing returns activity, such as agriculture, there is always a limit to employment set by the minimum subsistence wage. This can lead to unemployment, open or disguised (see Chapter 5), particularly in a society where the population is growing rapidly and there are limited alternative employment opportunities.

Second, on the demand side, the demand for most agricultural products (and other primary products derived from the land) is **income inelastic**. This means that the rise in demand is proportionately less than the rise in income, and the growth of demand for agricultural output is less than the growth of supply potential determined by the growth of the labour force plus the growth of labour productivity. For example, suppose that the agricultural labour force is growing at 2% and labour productivity is growing at 1%, so that the growth of productive potential in agriculture is 3%. Now suppose that income growth in the economy is 3% but the income elasticity of demand for agricultural products is only one-half (0.5). The demand for output therefore grows by only 1.5%. The gap between the growth of potential supply and demand is 1.5%, which will manifest itself in unemployment.

There are thus two major causes of surplus labour in agriculture: one arises from the low income elasticity of demand for agricultural output; the other arises from the fact that agriculture is a diminishing returns activity, so that there is a limit to the employment of (paid) labour set by the minimum subsistence wage. What happens to this surplus labour? First, it may stay in the rural sector and work is spread, with each unit of labour working a suboptimal day. This is described as **disguised unemployment** (see Chapter 5). This, of course, depresses labour productivity and therefore per capita income. Second, the surplus agricultural labour may migrate to the towns to find alternative work. If work cannot be found in the formal sector of the economy, the labour attempts to make a living in the informal sector by providing petty services of various kinds: street trading, haircutting, shoe-shining, transport and so on. These are also very low-productivity activities.

Industry has very different characteristics from agriculture. First, it is not a diminishing returns activity. If anything, it is an increasing returns activity. All factors of production are variable, and no limit to employment is set by the marginal product of labour falling below the minimum (subsistence) wage. Second, the demand for most industrial goods is income elastic so that the demand for labour may rise faster than labour productivity, leading to increases in employment – at least in the early stages of industrialization. Also, there is greater scope for capital accumulation in industry, which enhances labour productivity. Overall, the productivity of labour in industry is much higher. As discussed later, there is a strong association across countries between the level of per capita income, and the share of resources devoted to industrial activities, and between the growth of industry and the growth of economies as a whole.

Low level of capital accumulation

A second major distinguishing characteristic of developing countries is their low level of capital accumulation – both physical and human. Physical capital refers to the plant, machinery and equipment used in the production of output. Human capital refers to the skills and expertise embodied in the labour force through education and training. (The role of education in the development process will be discussed in Chapter 7.) Low levels of capital accumulation are a cause of low productivity and poverty, but are also a *function* of poverty, because capital accumulation requires investment and saving and it is not easy for poor societies to save. The process of development can be described as a generalized process of capital accumulation, but the levels and rates of capital accumulation in poor countries are low. The amount of physical capital that labour has to work with in a typical developing country is no more than one-twentieth of the level in Europe and North America. This reflects the cumulative effect over time of much higher savings and investment ratios in rich countries.

The saving and investment ratios for various regions are shown in Table 3.2. Domestic investment can differ from domestic saving owing to capital inflows from abroad. This can be seen in Table 3.2 for the low-income countries where domestic saving is only 16% but gross capital formation is 28%. Notice the high ratios of savings and investment in East Asia and the Pacific region. In general, savings and investment rise with development and then fall, as shown by the figures for the high-income countries. If we exclude China, the savings ratio of low-income countries is less than half that of the middle- and high-income countries, although their investment ratio is still relatively high because of capital inflows from abroad. These are not always stable, however.

Sir Arthur Lewis, distinguished development economist, once described development as the process of transforming a country from a net 5% saver and investor to a 12% saver and investor.[1] Walt Rostow, in his well-known book *The Stages of Economic Growth* (1960), defines the take-off stage of self-sustaining growth in terms of a critical ratio of savings and investment to national income of 10–12% (see below for a discussion of Rostow's model). What is the significance of this ratio? It has to do with a very simple growth formula, which originally came from the growth model of British economist (Sir) Roy Harrod (see Chapter 4). The formula is:

$$g = s/c \tag{3.1}$$

where g is the growth of output ($\Delta Y/Y$), s is the savings ratio (S/Y) and c is the incremental capital–output ratio – that is, how much investment is associated with an increase in the flow of

Table 3.2 Savings and investment as a percentage of GDP, 2014

	Gross capital formation	Gross savings
Low income	28	16
Middle income	31	31
Lower middle income	27	29
Upper middle income	32	32
Low and middle income	31	31
East Asia and Pacific	42	45
Europe and Central Asia	21	16
Latin America and Caribbean	21	18
Middle East and North Africa	30	–
South Asia	30	31
Sub-Saharan Africa	22	16
High income	20	21

Source: World Bank, 2015.

output by one unit ($I/\Delta Y$). Substituting these definitions of s and c into equation (3.1) shows that, in an accounting sense, the formula is an identity since in the national accounts $S = I$

$$\Delta Y/Y = (S/Y)/(I/\Delta Y) \tag{3.2}$$

That is, if $S = I$, then $g = s/c$.

Now, for the level of per capita income to rise, output growth must exceed population growth. If population growth is 2% per annum, output growth must exceed 2% per annum. It can be seen from equation (3.1) that how much saving and investment as a proportion of national income is required for growth depends on the value of the incremental capital–output ratio (c). If 4 units of capital investment are required to produce a 1 unit flow of output year by year over the life of the investment, then $c = 4$, so s must exceed 8% for the growth of output to exceed 2%. A net rate of saving and investment to national income of at least 8% or more is therefore necessary if there is to be sustained growth of per capita income. In most developing countries, the net savings and investment ratio is above this critical magnitude, but the fact remains that a major cause of low productivity and poverty in developing countries is the low level of capital that labour has to work with. In Case example 3.1, the interrelationship between saving, investment and growth is discussed.

Rapid population growth

A third distinguishing feature of most developing countries is that they have a much faster rate of population growth than developed countries – in fact, their population is growing faster than at any time in the world's history (see Chapter 11 for a full discussion). This can confer advantages, but

Case example 3.1 **The interrelationship between savings, investment and growth**

The relationship between savings, investment and growth is complex, with causality running in several different directions, but recent research suggests two important conclusions: first, saving often seems to follow, rather than precede, investment and growth (contrary to orthodox theory); and second, investment and innovation are the centrepieces of growth.

Saving may not be the chief driving force behind growth, but ensuring an adequate savings level must remain a central policy concern – to ensure enough financing for capital accumulation and to prevent inflationary pressures or balance of payments disequilibrium, or both. And encouraging private saving may be essential to expand investment, considering capital market imperfections and liquidity constraints on firms and households in many developing countries. Four main policy conclusions emerge:

1 Public saving does not crowd out private savings one to one, so increasing public saving is an effective direct way to raise national saving
2 Foreign saving should be allowed to support domestic investment
3 Higher private saving should not be expected in response to the liberalization of interest rates. Pension reform may be a better way to raise domestic savings
4 The best way to promote investment and growth is a supportive policy and institutional environment ensuring macroeconomic stability, social consensus, and a low cost of doing business.

Source: Schmidt-Hebbel et al., 1994.

it also imposes acute problems. Population growth in the developing countries as a whole averages 1.3% per annum, resulting from a birth rate of 24 per 1,000 population (or 2.4%) and a death rate of 11 per 1,000 population (or 1.1%). The rapid acceleration of population growth compared with its historical trend is the result of a dramatic fall in the death rate without a commensurate fall in the birth rate. Population growth in developed countries averages no more than 0. 6% per annum. The population growth rate in low-, middle- and high-income countries is shown in Table 3.3. Population growth in low-income countries is over four times higher than in high-income countries.

Table 3.3 Population growth (average % per annum)

	2000-05	2005–10	2010–15
Low income	2.72	2.69	2.69
Middle income	1.28	1.21	1.18
High income	0.59	0.69	0.52

Source: UN DESA, 2015.

Rapid population growth, like low capital accumulation, may be considered as both a cause and a consequence of poverty. High birth rates are themselves a function of poverty because child mortality is high in poor societies and parents wish to have large families to provide insurance in old age. High birth rates also go hand in hand with poor education, a lack of employment opportunities for women, and ignorance of birth control techniques. Population growth, in turn, helps to perpetuate poverty if it reduces saving, dilutes capital per head, and reduces the marginal product of labour in agriculture. The pressure of numbers may also put a strain on government expenditure, lead to congestion and overcrowding, impair the environment, and put pressure on food supplies – all of which retard the development process, at least in the short run. In the longer run, population growth may stimulate investment and technical progress, and may not pose such a problem if there are complementary resources and factors of production available, but the short-run costs may outweigh the advantages for a considerable time.

Exports dominated by primary commodities

A fourth distinguishing characteristic of developing countries is that their trade tends to be dominated by the export of primary commodities and the import of manufactured goods. This has consequences for the terms of trade of developing countries, the distribution of the gains from trade between developed and developing countries, and the balance of payments situation – all of which may adversely affect real income per head. Table 3.4 shows primary commodities as a percentage of the total exports of different continents. The trade of Africa, the Middle East, Latin

Table 3.4 Primary commodities as a percentage of total exports, 2014

East Asia and Pacific	13
Latin America and Caribbean	43
Middle East and North Africa	84 (2006)
South Asia	35
Sub-Saharan Africa	73

Source: World Bank, 2015, Table 4.4.

America and the Caribbean is still dominated by primary commodities. Only Asia and the Pacific region have made headway in reducing dependence on commodity exports.

The **barter terms of trade** measures the ratio of export prices to import prices. There has been a historical tendency for the terms of trade of primary goods relative to manufactured goods to deteriorate over the past 100 years or so – by about 0.5% per annum on average. This tendency is known in the literature as the 'Prebisch–Singer thesis' (see Chapter 15). The falling price of exports relative to imports reduces the real income of a country because more exports have to be exchanged to obtain a given quantity of imports.

A second point to note is that the income elasticity of demand for primary commodities in world trade is less than unity, while the income elasticity of demand for manufactured goods is greater than unity. This means that as world income grows, the demand for primary commodities grows at a slower rate, but if developing countries grow at the same rate as the world economy, their demand for manufactured imports grows at a faster rate. As a consequence, developing countries specializing in the production and export of primary commodities suffer acute balance of payments difficulties. Often, the only means available to developing countries to adjust the balance of payments is to slow down their economies in order to reduce the growth of imports.

The prices of primary commodities are also more cyclically volatile than the prices of manufactured goods. This can also cause havoc with a country's balance of payments and its tax revenues if it relies heavily on trade taxes. The resulting instability makes planning difficult and may deter private domestic investment and investment from overseas.

For all these reasons, the structure of trade poses severe problems for many developing countries and may keep countries poorer than they would be if they were able to produce and export more industrial goods. It is not possible to understand the growth and development process – and the perpetuation of divisions in the world economy – without reference to the unequal trading relations between rich and poor countries and the balance of payments consequences of specializing in primary commodities.

The curse of natural resources

In general, it seems to be the case that the more natural resources a country has, the worse it performs. This phenomenon is referred to in the literature as the **curse of natural resources** (Sachs and Warner, 2001; Gylfason, 2001). This is illustrated in Figure 3.2, which shows a scatter diagram for 105 countries of the relationship between the growth of per capita income over the period 1965–98, and the share of the labour force employed in the primary sector. There is a very strong negative relationship ($R^2 = 0.7218$), and the regression coefficient of –0.0871 indicates that a country with a primary sector share 10 percentage points above the average has experienced a growth of per capita income of nearly 1 percentage point below the average (controlling for the initial level of per capita income). This represents a substantial loss of welfare.

The same negative pattern emerges when the growth of per capita income is regressed against the export of natural resources as a share of GDP; and the negative relation persists even when controlling for other variables, such as differences in the level of investment between countries, and climate and geography (Sachs and Warner, 2001). Most countries that have grown rapidly in recent decades started as resource poor, not resource rich. There are exceptions to this general rule – countries such as Malaysia, Thailand, Indonesia and Botswana, for example – but most of these exceptional countries have grown fast not through the exploitation of natural resources but through diversification into manufacturing industry.

Figure 3.2 Natural resources and economic growth

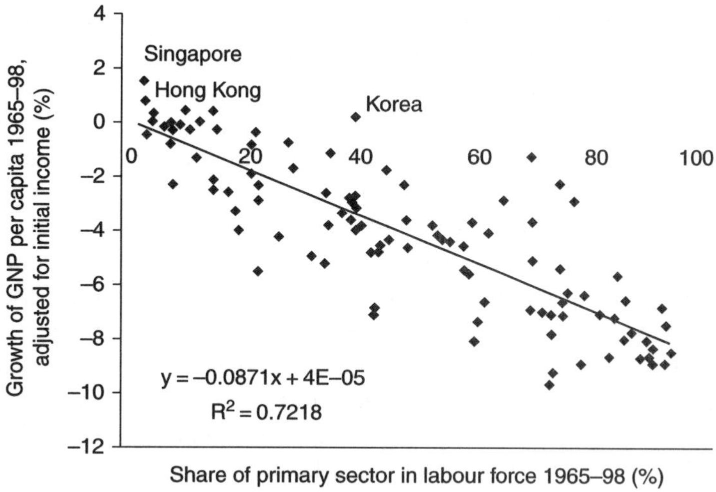

What lies behind this 'curse of natural resources'? A number of interrelated factors can be mentioned that seem to have an adverse effect on many of the important determinants of development. Gylfason (2001) shows a negative relation across countries between the share of the primary sector in the labour force and export performance, domestic and foreign investment and education, and a positive relation with the size of external debt, the level of protection, corruption and income inequality. We have already seen why primary production can lead to poor export performance because many natural resources are income inelastic and suffer terms of trade deterioration, but why should natural resource-abundant countries neglect investment and education, and be more corrupt? There are two major explanations.

First, natural resource abundance may 'crowd out' other activities through two mechanisms: higher wages or earnings in the natural resources sector discouraging entrepreneurial activity and innovation in other sectors; and revenues from natural resource exports keeping the exchange rate artificially high, which makes the rest of the economy uncompetitive. This is known as the **Dutch disease** – so named because of the effect that the discovery of natural gas in Holland in the 1960s had on the exchange rate and other sectors of the economy. Sachs and Warner (2001) test this 'crowding-out' hypothesis across 99 countries and find a positive correlation between natural resource abundance and the domestic price level. The higher relative price level is then found to impede the export growth of manufactured goods. It could also be that a country rich in natural resources simply neglects to develop other sectors of the economy.

A second major explanation why natural resource abundance may lead to poor performance is that the **rents** from natural resources may be misused by politicians and bureaucrats. Democracy and the rule of law seem to be inversely related to natural resource abundance, and Gylfason (2001) shows corruption to be more widespread in natural resource-abundant countries. This is not surprising since limiting access to a resource provides a rent, and where the state owns the resource, bureaucrats will take bribes in return for exploitation rights. Rent earners may not be interested in schooling and education, having lined their own pockets and those of their children, without acquiring an education. Thus, rent-seeking leads to low levels of expenditure on education and school enrolment. It is also the case that the primary sector of an economy does not have the same educational needs as a more diversified economy.

Weak institutional structures

Economies cannot function in an institutional vacuum, otherwise there is economic (and political) chaos. At the very minimum there has to be the rule of law, the protection of property rights, and constraints on power and corruption if private individuals are to be entrepreneurial, to take risks and invest. In many developing countries, the rule of law and the protection of property rights is still rudimentary, and politicians (and bureaucrats) abuse their powers. Many economists (e.g. Acemoglu, 2003; Rodrik, 2007) have argued that it is weak institutional structures that are the fundamental cause of underdevelopment, because the character of institutions is the determinant of all the proximate causes of progress such as investment, technology, education and trade. There are several measures of institutional quality that economists focus on, and they will be discussed in detail in Chapter 8. Three main ones are: the extent of legal protection of private property, the quality of governance (including the strength of the rule of law), and the limits placed on political leaders. Attempts have been made to distinguish econometrically the relative importance of institutions compared with other factors (including geography) in explaining different levels of per capita income across the world, with interesting, but controversial, results. Rodrik et al. (2004) take a large sample of developed and developing countries, measuring the quality of institutions mainly by a composite indicator of a number of elements that capture protection afforded by property rights, and conclude: 'Our results indicate that the quality of institutions overrides everything else. Controlling for institutions, geography has, at best, weak direct effects on income ... similarly trade ... has no direct positive effect on income.' Easterly and Levine (2002) also test the influence of institutions compared with geography and policy variables across 75 rich and poor countries and find that institutions seem to matter most as the determinant of per capita income. Even countries with 'bad policies' do well with good institutions. We will examine the evidence for this in more detail in Chapter 8.

It is recognized, however, that the correlation found between institutions and economic development could reflect reverse causality, or omitted factors. We need to find a source of exogenous variation in institutions where institutions differ or change independently of other factors. Acemoglu et al. (2001) argue that the different experience of **colonization** is one exogenous source where, at one extreme, colonizers set up exclusively extractive institutions (to exploit minerals and other primary products) – such as slavery and forced labour – which neither gave property rights to inhabitants nor constrained the power of elites. This was the experience in Africa and Latin America. At the other extreme, colonizers created settler societies, replicating the European form of institutions protecting private property and controlling elites and politicians, in countries such as Australia, New Zealand and North America. But what determined why some countries were settled and others not? Acemoglu et al. (2001) argue that the major determinant was the mortality rate faced by the early settlers, and that there is a strong negative correlation between past mortality rates and current institutional quality (because institutions persisted) and between past mortality and the current levels of per capita income. In fact, over 50% of the variation in per capita income across the 75 countries is associated with variation in one particular index of institutional quality, which measures 'protection against expropriation'. Acemoglu et al. (2001) conclude:

> There is a high correlation between mortality rates faced by soldiers, bishops and sailors in the colonies and European settlements; between European settlements and early measures of institutions, and between early institutions and institutions today. We estimate large effects of institutions on income per capita using this source of variation. ... this relationship is not driven by outliers, and is robust controlling for latitude, climate, current disease environment, religion, natural resources, soil quality, ethnolinguistic fragmentation, and current racial composition.

But this is where the controversy starts because presumably the mortality rates of the early settlers, which affected the nature of institutions, was strongly influenced by geography because this affects disease. In the same vein, Sachs (2008) argues that Acemoglu et al.'s (2001) finding concerning the negative relation between mortality rates 200 years ago and per capita income today is simply picking up the pernicious effects of malaria (which still persists), not institutions. Development is not simply about good government and institutions. Institutions might make anti-poverty policies more effective, but that is all. Poor countries need resources to fight disease, to provide education and infrastructure, and all the other resource prerequisites of development. Sachs (2008) classifies three types of countries combining institutions and geography, which is a sensible approach:

- Countries where institutions, policies and geography are all reasonably favourable, for example the coastal regions of East Asia.
- Countries with favourable geography, but weak institutions, for example many of the transition economies of Eastern Europe and the former Soviet Union.
- Countries impoverished by a combination of unfavourable geography, such as landlocked countries and those plagued with disease, and poor governance, for example many of the countries of sub-Saharan Africa.

One manifestation of poor governance and weak institutions is **wars** both within countries (civil wars) and between countries. According to Oxfam (2007), conflicts in Africa since 1990 have cost the continent $150 billion, equivalent to the total amount of foreign aid received over the same period. The economic damage to economies is immense. In countries such as the Democratic Republic of the Congo, Burundi and Rwanda, for example, wars have reduced national output by over 20%. This is the 'conflict trap' referred to by Collier (2007) in his book *The Bottom Billion*. In war-torn countries, inflation, debt and unemployment are all higher, public investment in education, health and infrastructure suffer, life expectancy is lower, and people are more prone to disease and malnourishment.

Other dimensions of the development gap

Deprivation in developing countries is not simply a matter of low levels of per capita income. There are many other dimensions to the development gap between rich and poor countries. Developing countries generally experience much higher levels of unemployment – open and disguised – than developed countries. The levels of education, health and nutrition are often abysmally low, and income distribution tends to be much more inegalitarian. Policy in developing countries is increasingly concerned with these other features of the development gap. The **basic needs approach** to development, originally pioneered by the World Bank, is a reflection of this switch of emphasis from exclusive concern with per capita income to these wider development issues. Here, we consider unemployment and the distribution of income. In Chapter 7, we discuss education, health and nutrition.

Unemployment

The developing countries contain a huge reservoir of surplus labour. For a long time, poor countries, particularly since the population explosion, have been characterized by underemployment or disguised unemployment in rural areas (see Chapter 5). What has happened in recent years is that disguised rural unemployment has transferred itself into **disguised** and **open unemployment** in the towns. Unemployment in the urban areas of developing countries is another dimension of the development problem and an increasingly serious one. The rationale for rural–urban migration will be considered later, but first it is appropriate to outline some of the facts on employment and unemployment. According to the International Labour Organization (ILO, 2009) in Geneva, 1 billion people in developing countries are either jobless or underemployed, which amounts to one-third of the total working-age population.

This represents a colossal challenge, particularly as the workforce is expected to grow by another 1.5 billion by the year 2025. The ILO argues for a renewed commitment by developing countries to the goal of employment creation, and not to treat current unemployment levels as natural and the inevitable outcome of market forces, as if nothing can be done. The World Bank devoted its 1995 and 2013 *World Development Reports* to the conditions of employment in developing countries, and it painted a sombre picture (World Bank, 1995, 2012). (See Case example 3.2.) To stop unemployment rising, there has to be employment growth of at least 2% per annum, which requires output growth of at least 4% per annum. Not many countries are able to grow this rapidly and consistently over time.

Case example 3.2

The importance of jobs

Jobs provide higher earnings and better benefits as countries grow, but they are also a driver of development. Poverty falls as people work their way out of hardship and as jobs empowering women lead to a greater investment in children. Efficiency increases as workers get better at what they do, as more productive jobs appear, and less productive ones disappear. Societies flourish as jobs bring together people from different ethnic and social backgrounds and provide alternatives to conflict. Jobs are thus more than a byproduct of economic growth. They are transformational – they are what we earn, what we do, and even who we are.

High unemployment and unmet job expectations among youth are the most immediate concerns. But, in many developing countries, where farming and self-employment are prevalent and safety nets are, at best, modest, unemployment rates can be low. In these countries, growth is seldom jobless. Most of the poor work long hours but simply cannot make ends meet. And the violation of basic rights is not uncommon. Therefore, the number of jobs is not all that matters: jobs with high development payoffs are needed.

Confronted with these challenges, policy-makers ask difficult questions:

- Should countries build their development strategies around growth, or should they focus on jobs?
- Can entrepreneurship be fostered, especially among the many microenterprises in developing countries, or are entrepreneurs born?
- Are greater investments in education and training a prerequisite for employability, or can skills be built through jobs?
- In times of major crises and structural shift, should jobs, not just workers, be protected?
- Is there a risk that policies supporting job creation in one country will be at the expense of jobs in other countries?

Case example 3.2 **The importance of jobs** – *continued*

The *World Development Report 2013: Jobs* offers answers to these and other difficult questions by looking at jobs as drivers of development – not as derived labour demand – and by considering all types of jobs – not just formal wage employment. The report provides a framework that cuts across sectors and shows that the best policy responses vary across countries, depending on their levels of development, endowments, demography and institutions. Policy fundamentals matter in all cases, as they enable a vibrant private sector, the source of most jobs in the world. Labour policies can help as well, even if they are less critical than is often assumed. Development policies, from making smallholder farming viable, to fostering functional cities, to engaging in global markets, hold the key to success.

Source: World Bank, 2012.

All this is a very aggregative analysis. The issue still to be addressed is the emergence of increasing urban unemployment. The problem is not so much one of a deficiency of demand for labour in an aggregate demand sense. The causal factors relate to the incentives for labour to migrate from rural to urban areas, and the incapacity of urban areas to provide employment owing to a lack of other necessary factors of production to work with labour, particularly capital. As far as migration is concerned, there are both push and pull factors at work.

The **push factors** have to do with the limited job opportunities in rural areas and a greater desire and ability to move, fostered by education and improved communications. The **pull factors** relate to the development of urban industrial activities that offer jobs at a higher real wage than can be earned in rural areas, so that even if a migrant is unemployed for part of the year, they may still be better off migrating to the town than working in the rural sector. If there is no work at all in the rural sector, the migrant loses nothing, except friends and the security of the extended family system. The rate of growth of job opportunities in the rural sector depends on the rate of growth of demand for the output of the rural sector and the rate at which jobs are being 'destroyed' by productivity growth.

As we saw earlier, if the demand for agricultural output is growing at 1.5% and productivity is growing at 1%, then the growth of labour demand will be 0.5%. But if the labour force is growing at 2%, there will be a 1.5 percentage point gap between the supply and demand for labour. If the level of disguised unemployment in the rural sector does not increase, this figure constitutes the potential volume of migrants. If the urban labour force is one-half of the size of the rural labour force, a 1.5% migration of rural labour would represent a 3% increase in the urban labour force owing to migration.

On average, this is about the extent of the influx from the rural sector into the urban areas of developing countries. On top of this, there is the natural increase in the workforce in urban areas of 2% to consider. If job opportunities in urban areas are increasing at only 3%, then 2–3% of the urban labour force will be added to the amount of urban unemployment year by year, forcing labour into the informal service sector. In that case, unemployment shows up as poverty.

Historically, the process of development has always been associated with, and characterized by, an exodus from the land, continuing over centuries. The uniqueness of the present situation is not the migration itself, but its magnitude and speed. And the problem is that the urban sector cannot absorb the numbers involved. For any given technology, the rate at which the urban (industrial) sector can absorb migrants largely depends on the rate of capital formation. If labour and capital must be combined in fixed proportions, and the rate of capital accumulation is only 3%, then the rate of increase in job opportunities can be only 3% also. Unfortunately, however, as will be shown in Chapter 5, the problem is not necessarily solved by a faster rate of capital accumulation in the urban sector, because migration is not simply a function of the actual difference in real remuneration between the two sectors, but also of the level of job opportunities in the urban sector. If the rate of job creation increases, this may merely increase the flow of migrants, with no reduction in unemployment. The solution would seem to be to create more job opportunities in the rural sector. This requires, however, not only the redirection of investment but also the extension of education and transport facilities, which, in the past few years, have themselves become powerful push factors in the migration process. Whereas formerly redundant labour might have remained underemployed on the family farm, nowadays education and easy transportation provide the incentive and the means to seek alternative employment opportunities. While education and improved communications are desirable in themselves, and facilitate development, their provision has augmented the flow of migrants from rural to urban areas.

The pull factors behind migration are not hard to identify. The opportunities for work and leisure provided by the industrial, urban environment contrast sharply with the conservatism and stultifying atmosphere of rural village life and naturally act as a magnet for those on low incomes or without work, especially the young. Given the much higher wages in the urban sector, even the prospect of long spells of unemployment in the towns does not detract from the incentive to migrate. Moreover, the choice is not necessarily between remaining in the rural sector and migrating to the urban sector, with the prospect of long periods of unemployment. The unemployed in the urban sector can often find work, or create work for themselves, on the fringes of the industrial sector – in particular in the **informal service sector** of the urban economy. The wages may be low, but some income is better than no income. In other words, unemployment in urban areas may take the form of underemployment, or become disguised, just as in the case of the rural sector – its manifestation being low income. This has led to the notion of an **income measure of unemployment**, which needs to be added to registered unemployment to obtain a true measure of unemployment and the availability of labour supply.

One way of measuring the extent of unemployment disguised in the form of low- productivity/low-income jobs is to take the difference between the actual labour employed at the sub-standard income and the labour that would be required to produce a given level of output or service at an acceptable level of income per head. Before measurement can take place, of course, the acceptable (standard) level of income has to be defined. It could be that the level is set as the 'poverty line', below which health and welfare become seriously impaired. The income measure of unemployment would thus be:

$$U = L - L^* = \frac{O}{O/L} - \frac{O}{O/L^*}$$

where L is the actual labour employed, L^* is the labour consistent with an acceptable level of income per person employed, O/L is the actual level of productivity (or income per head), O/L^* is the acceptable level of income per employed person, and O is output. Let us work an example. Suppose that the annual flow of output of an activity or service, such as haircuts, is \$1 million and that the existing number employed is 5,000, giving a level of productivity of \$200. Now suppose that the acceptable level of productivity to produce an acceptable level of income per person employed is \$500 (roughly the international poverty line of \$1.90 a day). The income measure of unemployment is then:

$$U = \frac{1{,}000{,}000}{200} - \frac{1{,}000{,}000}{500} = 3{,}000$$

that is, over one-half of the existing labour force is disguisedly unemployed, in the sense that the level of output is not sufficient for those who currently work to maintain an adequate standard of living.

The above analysis of employment and unemployment trends in developing countries points to a number of policy implications that were also highlighted by the ILO as long ago as 1969, when it first sponsored missions to several countries to undertake a detailed diagnosis of the employment problem (see Thorbecke, 1973). Certainly, an adequate rate of output growth is required to employ workers entering the labour market for the first time and to absorb the effects of productivity growth, but much more is required. There is a case for the use of more labour-intensive techniques of production (see Chapter 6), and the issue of rural–urban migration needs to be tackled by promoting more employment opportunities outside the urban centres, particularly for young people. Without such measures, unemployment will continue to grow, especially in urban areas. Felipe and Hasan (2006), at the Asian Development Bank, argue that employment creation, and combating unemployment, is the major development challenge facing Asian economies today because unemployment is a major cause of poverty and social unrest.

One way of mitigating the effects of unemployment is through **public employment schemes**. India has a national rural employment guarantee scheme, which was launched in 2006, whereby every rural household is guaranteed up to 100 days of unskilled manual wage employment per year at the statuary minimum wage for agricultural workers. If employment is not provided within 15 days, the worker is entitled to an unemployment allowance. So far, over 5 million public works have been undertaken across India, providing employment to more than 50 million households, and over 3 billion person days of work have been generated on projects such as water conservation, rural connectivity and land development. A beneficial side effect of the scheme is that it raises productivity in agriculture and raises agricultural incomes as the demand for food rises. The scheme costs the Indian government about 0.6% of GDP.

In 2002, Argentina launched a programme for providing a subsistence income to unemployed heads of households with at least one child in return for work for a minimum of 20 hours a week on small projects that improve local infrastructure. About 2 million households have benefited from the scheme, at a cost of 1% of GDP. The impact on unemployment and poverty has been significant, with multiplier effects on the rest of the economy estimated as 2.5 times the amount of initial expenditure.

There is much scope for these programmes to be adopted more widely across developing countries.

Inequality: vertical and horizontal

As well as the average per capita income being low in developing countries, the distribution of income, wealth and power is also typically very unequal, and much more unequal than in developed countries. All too often, the growth and development that takes place in poor countries benefits the richest few, and the vast mass of the population is left untouched. Rural and urban poverty are still widespread, and if anything the degree of income inequality within many developing countries is increasing. The way income is distributed across individuals and households is referred to as **vertical inequality**, and is the traditional measure of inequality that development policy focuses upon. There is also the concept, however, of **horizontal inequality**, which is concerned with how different *groups* in society are treated, based on race, religion, language, class, gender and so on. The well-being of people can be affected as much by horizontal inequality as by vertical inequality. First, we will consider vertical inequality and then horizontal inequality.

It should come as no surprise that the transformation of economies from a primitive subsistence state into industrial societies, within a basically capitalist framework, should be accompanied in the early stages by widening disparities in the personal distribution of income. Some people are more industrious than others and more adept at accumulating wealth. Opportunities cannot, by the very nature of things, be equal for all. In the absence of strong redistributive taxation, income inequality will inevitably accompany industrialization because of the inequality of skills and wealth that differences in individual ability and initiative – and industrialization – produce.

The observation that income inequality increases with the level of development and then declines is often called the **Kuznets curve**, named after the famous development economist Simon Kuznets, who did pioneering research on structural change and income distribution in the 1950s and 1960s (e.g. Kuznets 1955, 1963), which earned him the Nobel Prize for Economics in 1971. Kuznets showed that in many of the present developed countries, the degree of inequality first increased and then decreased in the later stages of industrialization, giving an inverted U-shaped curve. For the developing countries, the pioneering work of Adelman and Morris (1971), extended by Paukert (1973), also showed fairly conclusively that inequality increases up to a certain stage of development and then declines, graphically showing an inverted U-shape similar to the work of Kuznets for developed countries. The greater degree of inequality in developing countries appears largely due to the higher share of income received by the richest 5% of income recipients – nearly 30% of income in developing countries compared with 20% in developed countries.

Deininger and Squire (1996), of the World Bank, have surveyed 682 studies of income distribution in over 100 countries and calculated average Gini ratios for each country, together with the ratio of the share of income received by the top 20% of income earners (top quintile) to that of the bottom 20% of income earners (bottom quintile). Latin America, the Caribbean and Africa have by far the largest degree of income inequality, with the Gini ratio well over 50 in many countries, for example Brazil (57.3), Mexico (53.8) and South Africa (62.3). In contrast, income inequality in Asia, the Pacific region and Eastern Europe appears to be much less. In China and India, the two largest countries in the world measured by population, the Gini ratio is just over 30, much the same as for high-income countries. Generally speaking, the higher the Gini ratio, the greater the ratio of income shares between the top and bottom 20% of income earners. In South Africa that ratio is 32:1 and in Brazil 23:1.

Income inequality has been increasing in most countries since the mid-1980s, supporting the Kuznets curve for developing economies, but defying the Kuznets curve for developed countries. The exception is some Latin American countries, particularly Brazil, Mexico and Argentina, where inequality is still high, but declining. In China and India, inequality is increasing.

The traditional view used to be that inequality was good for growth because investment relied on savings from the rich. This view is now challenged because physical capital accumulation has become less important than human capital (education and skills) for growth, and income inequality is not good for growth if those on low incomes suffer poor health, a lack of education and low productivity. Income inequality can also lead to a lack of social cohesion and damaging political lobbying by rich vested interests. It has been estimated by the World Bank that a 5 point increase in the Gini ratio reduces growth by about 0.5% per annum (Milanovic, 2011).

Redistributing income to reduce inequality can promote growth. Table 3.5 gives some representative figures for the Gini ratio in countries with the highest and lowest levels of inequality.

South Africa has the second highest degree of income inequality as measured by the Gini ratio. This is the legacy of the apartheid policy pursued in South Africa over many years, with a minority white population discriminating against the black and Asian majority with regard to jobs, housing, education and health. Four other African countries stand out – Central African Republic, Zambia, Lesotho and Rwanda. Notice also that many of the countries with the highest degree of inequality are located in South and Central America, but there are no countries in Asia with Gini ratios over 50. Countries with the lowest Gini ratios are either Scandinavian or former territories of the Soviet Union.

There are several formidable barriers to narrowing the income distribution gap:

1. There is the dualistic nature of many economies (see Chapter 10), perpetuated by feudal land tenure systems and urban bias in the allocation of investment resources.
2. There is inequality in the provision of education facilities, and a particular lack of facilities in rural areas where the poorest are concentrated.
3. There is disguised rural unemployment, underemployment and open unemployment in urban areas created by rural–urban migration, a shortage of investment resources and inappropriate production techniques.

Until development policy comes to grips with these problems, there will continue to be large pockets of absolute poverty and a marked degree of inequality in income distribution. When deciding on the allocation of investment resources and the choice of projects, a high weight must be given to projects that raise the income of the poorest if the income distribution is to be narrowed (see Chapter 6).

Now let us turn to horizontal inequality (HI), which is concerned with how economic differences, social demarcations and political power combine to produce differences in entitlements and

Table 3.5 The Gini ratio for high and low inequality countries, 2013

High inequality	Gini ratio	Low inequality	Gini ratio
Namibia	63.9	Sweden	25.0
South Africa	63.1	Ukraine	25.6
Haiti	59.2	Norway	25.8
Zambia	57.5	Slovakia	26.0
Bolivia	56.3	Belarus	26.5
Central African Republic	56.3	Finland	26.9
Colombia	55.9	Romania	27.4
Guatemala	55.7	Afghanistan	27.8
Brazil	54.7	Bulgaria	28.2
Lesotho	52.3	Germany	28.3
Chile	52.1	Montenegro	28.6
Paraguay	52.4	Kazakhstan	29.0
Panama	51.9	Austria	29.2
Rwanda	50.8	Serbia	29.6

Source: World Bank, 2015.

capabilities for different groups in society. Groups may be defined in a number of ways, as already mentioned: race, religion, gender, location, class, language and so on. Stewart (2001) develops the hypothesis that not only is HI responsible for much conflict within societies, but it also affects the development process in a number of ways. For example, some groups may be denied access to public goods such as education and healthcare. This impoverishes not only the group, but the economy at large. Certain regions may be deprived of infrastructure investment because of particular groups located in these regions, which not only damages the region but the progress of the whole economy. To be discriminated against on the basis of a particular group identity has psychological effects, and affects the core goals of development discussed in Chapter 1: life sustenance, self-esteem and freedom. Thus, HI is an important dimension of well-being, and can have economic and political consequences highly detrimental to development. Despite this, international development policy is rarely focused on the narrowing of group divisions. HI would not matter so much if there was mobility between groups, or if individuals were free to choose which group they belonged to, but this is rarely the case in often highly stratified developing countries. Stewart (2001) gives examples of several case studies of the basis and consequences of horizontal inequality, for example, in Mexico, Brazil, Fiji, Malaysia and South Africa. The situation in several countries is given in Case example 3.3. It is clear that development policy needs to tackle horizontal inequality between groups, as well as vertical inequality with respect to income distribution across individuals.

Case example 3.3 **Inequalities between groups can fuel conflict and tension**

The root causes of violent conflict are rarely simple. But as the examples below show, a common theme is emerging from recent research into conflict: the role that socioeconomic and political inequalities between groups can play in causing tensions and violence. Less research has been done on the role that cultural exclusions of groups may play (such as lack of recognition of languages or religious practices), but these are also issues that can lead to mobilization and protests and so may also be important root causes or triggers of conflict.

- Severe rioting against the Chinese in **Malaysia** in the late 1960s has been attributed largely to the animosity felt by the politically dominant but economically sidelined Bumiputera majority towards the economically dominant Chinese minority.
- Civil war in **Sri Lanka** since the early 1980s has been linked to tensions resulting from inequalities between the Tamil minority and Sinhalese majority. Colonial administrators had favoured the Tamil minority economically, but this advantage was sharply reversed once the Sinhalese gained power and increasingly sidelined the Tamil minority in areas such as educational opportunities, civil service recruitment and language policy.
- In **Uganda**, the Bantu-speaking people (largely in the centre and south) have been economically dominant but politically sidelined compared with the non-Bantu-speaking people (largely in the north). These economic and political inequities have played a role in major conflicts, including the violence initiated by Idi Amin (1970s) and by the second Obote regime (1983–85).
- Indigenous people in the state of Chiapas, **Mexico** have long suffered political and socioeconomic deprivation. They have demanded greater political autonomy, improved socioeconomic conditions and protection of their cultural heritage, culminating in uprisings against the Mexican state in four municipalities.

Case example 3.3 **Inequalities between groups can fuel conflict and tension** – *continued*

- In **South Africa** before 1994, the black majority was severely disadvantaged politically and socioeconomically, which led to many uprisings between 1976 and the transfer of power in 1993.
- Catholics in **Northern Ireland** have suffered economic and political deprivation since the sixteenth century. The continuance of Northern Ireland as part of the UK in the 1920s ensured that Protestants would enjoy permanent political and economic dominance – fuelling demands by northern Catholics to become part of the predominantly Catholic Republic of Ireland. Violent conflict started in the late 1960s and began to ease in the 1990s following systematic efforts to reduce these inequalities.
- Constitutional crises and coups have occurred in **Fiji**, notably in 1987 and 1999, as economically sidelined indigenous Fijians have feared losing political control to the economically dominant Indian-origin Fijians.
- Increasing tensions between Muslims and Christians in Poso, Central Sulawesi, **Indonesia** began surfacing in the mid-1990s as the Muslim community increasingly gained more than indigenous Christians from new economic policies.
- Since colonial times, the indigenous people of **Guatemala** have suffered political and economic discrimination, contributing to the country's ongoing conflicts.
- The Maoist insurgency launched in **Nepal** in 1996 may be attributed to deep grievances stemming from the systematic marginalization and exclusion of certain ethnic groups, castes and women.

Source: UNDP, 2004.

Growth and distribution

The observation that income inequality increases with the level of development and then declines is not to say that faster economic growth within a country necessarily worsens the income distribution. Recent international evidence suggests that rapid structural transformation and fast economic growth have benefited the poor as much as the rich. Nor, for that matter, is inequality a necessary condition for growth because it generates more saving, as it is sometimes claimed. Naqvi (1995) looked in detail at 40 developing countries and found that high growth rates and distributive justice (as well as macroeconomic stability) have tended to move together. This is also the conclusion of Dollar and Kraay (2000), who examined the relationship between growth and income distribution across 80 countries over 40 years. They found that the income of the poor (the bottom 20% of the population) rises one to one with overall growth, and the relation is no different in poor countries than in rich ones. Nor has the poverty–growth relationship changed much over time. In other words, growth seems to benefit the poor as much as the rich, so that relative inequality (the Gini ratio) stays the same (although *absolute* inequality still widens, of course, because the same growth of income gives more dollars to a rich person than a poor person).

On the question of whether inequality promotes growth, the answer seems to be 'no'. If the Gini ratio is included in a cross-section equation to explain differences in growth between countries, the coefficient is normally negative, not positive (see Forbes, 2000). In other words, a more equal distribution of income is good for growth. Income equality is probably standing here as a proxy for such growth-inducing factors as good governance, civil society, equal property rights and equality of opportunity. The successful Asian 'tiger economies' have much more equal distributions of income, and better governance, than most other developing economies.

Poverty-weighted growth rates

Whether progress is being made towards achieving the twin objectives of faster growth and a more equal distribution of income can be examined simultaneously by constructing **poverty-weighted indices of growth**.

GNP growth as conventionally measured is a weighted average of the growth of income of different groups of people, where the relevant weights are each group's share of total income. The measured growth rate pays no regard to the distribution of income. A high growth rate may be recorded, but this may have benefited only the rich. For example, suppose the bottom third of the population receive 10% of income, the middle third receive 30% of income, and the top third receive 60% of income. GNP growth would be measured as:

$$\% \text{ growth of GNP} = r_1(0.1) + r_2(0.3) + r_3(0.6),$$

where r_1, r_2 and r_3 are the respective rates of growth of income of the three groups. Suppose $r_1 = 1\%$, $r_2 = 1\%$ and $r_3 = 10\%$. A GNP growth rate of 6.4% would then be recorded, which looks very respectable but the position of the poorest will hardly have changed.

The idea of constructing poverty-weighted indices of growth is to give at least equal weight to all income groups in society, if not a higher weight to the poor, in order to obtain a better measure of the growth of overall welfare combining the growth of income with its distribution.

In the above example, for instance, if each group is given an equal weight of one-third, the measured growth of welfare becomes:

$$\% \text{ growth of 'welfare'} = 1(0.33) + 1(0.33) + 10(0.33) = 4\%$$

which is much less than the rate of growth shown by the conventional measure of GNP growth when distributional considerations are taken into account.

A society could go further and say that it places no value or weight on income growth for the richest third of the population, and places all the weight on the lower income groups with, say, a 60% weight to the bottom third and a 40% weight to the middle third. The growth of 'welfare' would then look derisory:

$$\% \text{ growth of 'welfare'} = 1(0.6) + 1(0.4) + 10(0) = 1\%$$

This approach has been experimented with by economists from the World Bank (see Ahluwalia et al., 1979) to compare countries, giving a 60% weight to the lowest 40% of the population, a 40% weight to the middle 40% and no weight to the top 20%. In countries where the distribution of income had deteriorated, the poverty-weighted measure of the growth of welfare showed less improvement than GNP growth, and where the distribution of income had improved, the poverty-weighted growth rate showed more improvement than GNP growth.

Stages of development and structural change

It is often argued that countries pass through certain phases during the course of development and that by identifying the particular characteristics of these phases, a country can be deemed to have reached a certain stage of development. The simplest stage theory is the sector thesis of Fisher (1939) and Clark (1940), who employed the distinction between primary, secondary and tertiary production as a basis of a theory of development. Countries are assumed to start as **primary** producers and then, as the basic necessities of life are met, resources shift into manufacturing or

secondary activities. Finally, with rising income, more leisure and an increasingly saturated market for manufactured goods, resources move into **service** or **tertiary** activities producing 'commodities' with a high income elasticity of demand.

Naturally enough in this schema, less developed countries are identified with primary production, more developed countries with the production of manufactured goods, and mature developed economies have a high percentage of their resources in the service sector.

There can be no dispute that resource shifts are an integral part of the development process, and that one of the main determinants of these shifts is a difference in the income elasticity of demand for commodities and changes in their elasticity as development proceeds. But just as care must be taken to equate (without qualification) development and welfare with the level of per capita income, caution must also be exercised in identifying different degrees of underdevelopment, industrialization and maturity, with some fairly rigid proportion of resources engaged in different types of activity. Such an association would ignore the doctrine of **comparative advantage**, which holds that countries will specialize in the production of those commodities in which they have a relative cost advantage, as determined by natural or acquired resource endowments. The fact that one country produces predominantly primary products while another produces mainly manufactured goods need not imply that they are at different stages of development, particularly if productivity in the primary sector matches productivity in the industrial sector. Such an association would also ignore the different types of service activities that may exist at different stages of a country's history. There are three broad categories of service activities. Newer service activities linked with the growth of leisure and high mass consumption tend to have a high income elasticity of demand; services linked to the growth of manufacturing also grow, but at a declining rate; and traditional services of pre-industrial times, such as domestic servants, decline. In short, tertiary production is an aggregation of many dissimilar service activities, some of which are related to low per capita incomes and some to high per capita incomes. Thus, the same proportion of total resources devoted to services may be associated with very different levels of development.

Having said all this, however, the fact remains that there is a good deal of empirical support for the Fisher–Clark view that the pattern of development across countries evidences many common characteristics, especially the shift of resources from agriculture to industry.

Figure 3.3 plots the relation between the level of per capita income and the share of employment in agriculture, industry and services across 69 countries using simple regression analysis. The broad thesis of Fisher and Clark is confirmed. On average, in low-income countries, the share of employment in agriculture is approximately 40% (and much higher in the very poorest countries of Africa), while only 15% is employed in industry. By contrast, in high-income countries, less than 5% is employed in agriculture and nearly 30% in industry. The proportion of the labour force employed in services rises inexorably, but the nature of the service activities is different – petty services in low-income countries and sophisticated services in the high-income countries.

What is true of the sectoral distribution of the labour force is also true of the sectoral distribution of output, although the magnitude of the proportions differ in lower income countries because productivity differs between sectors. Figure 3.4 shows the sectoral distribution of output across 141 countries also by regressing the shares on per capita income. In low-income countries, on average, the share of agriculture in total GDP is 30% compared with an employment share of over 40%, because productivity is lower in agriculture than in industry. Industry's share of output in poor countries is 20% compared with an employment share of 15%. The share of output and employment in services is roughly equal.

Figure 3.3 The distribution of the labour force (%)

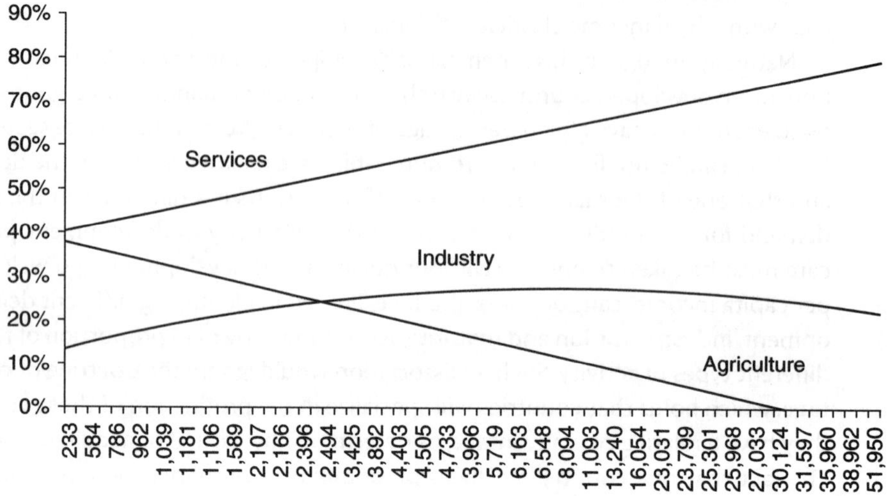

Source: Data from the World Bank, 2009 and the ILO, 2009 for 69 countries.

Figure 3.4 The distribution of output (%)

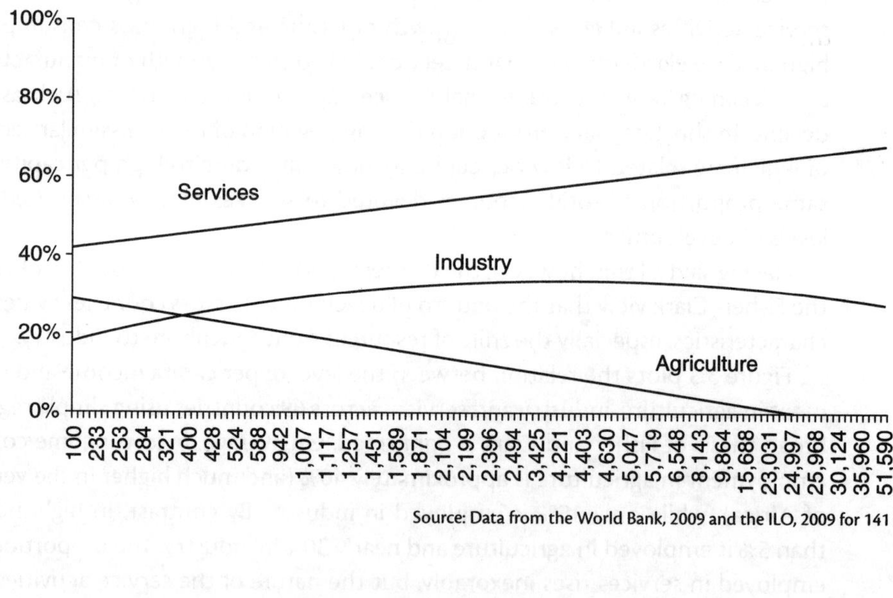

Source: Data from the World Bank, 2009 and the ILO, 2009 for 141 countries.

Notice also that while the share of agriculture falls continually, and the share of services increases continually, the share of employment and output in industry first rises and then falls as countries get richer. The latter is referred to as the process of **deindustrialization**. This process started in developed countries many years ago (see Rowthorn and Ramswamy, 1999), but is now beginning to hit middle-income (and even some low-income) countries (see Pieper, 2003; Tregenna, 2009). The level of per capita income at which the share of industry peaks seems to be falling; a phenomenon referred to as 'premature deindustrialization' or 'premature non-industrialization' (Rodrik, 2016). Some African and Latin American countries seem to be deindustrializing before they have ever been properly industrialized. This is worrying in an open economy where export growth is highly correlated with the growth of manufacturing output (see Pacheco-López and

Thirlwall, 2014). One explanation is that poor countries lack the capabilities and infrastructure to compete in the global marketplace for industrial goods, particularly with freer trade and the free movement of labour and capital. Manufacturers seek locations where wage costs per unit of output (the efficiency wage) are lowest, which are not necessarily the poorest countries. Another explanation would be that the world is becoming more and more saturated with manufactured goods, and there is a continued shift in the purchase of, and trade in, service activities. India has responded to this shift to the neglect of its industrial base. Pakistan, Sri Lanka and Nepal are imitating India and, to a large extent, skipping the stage of industrialization. If countries can acquire an early comparative advantage in tradable service activities, their exports may not suffer, but other countries are likely to get left behind. Also, many service activities, particularly in the information technology sector, require skilled labour, and are increasingly automated, which presents an enormous employment challenge as the labour force continues to grow. Only in East Asia and the Pacific region is the importance of industry increasing.

Table 3.6 gives a summary of output shares of GDP by activity in the different regions of the world. The shares of agriculture can be seen to go down the richer the countries, and the share of services to rise. The share of manufacturing starts very low in low-income countries and reaches a peak in the upper middle-income countries, and then falls again. Notice the very small share of manufacturing output in sub-Saharan Africa.

As already mentioned, the changing structure of output and employment is a function of the different income elasticities of demand for different products. It is possible to make estimates of the income elasticity of demand for different commodities by using an estimating equation of the form: $\log V = \log a + b \log Y$, where V is value-added (or output) per capita for good X, Y is per capita income and b is the income elasticity of demand for good X. An income elasticity less than unity would imply that the share of the good in total output declines as income grows. Conversely, an income elasticity greater than unity means that the good's relative importance in total output will increase. To estimate the income elasticities, the equation is applied to data

Table 3.6 The shares of output in GDP by region

	Agriculture	Industry		Services
	% of GDP	Total % of GDP	Manufacturing % of GDP	% of GDP
World	3	26	16	71
Low income	32	22	9	47
Middle income	10	35	22	56
Lower middle income	17	31	17	52
Upper middle income	10	36	24	57
Low and middle income	10	34	22	55
East Asia and Pacific	10	42	32	48
Europe and Central Asia	8	28	16	63
Latin America and Caribbean	5	30	14	65
Middle East and North Africa	11	37	14	52
South Asia	18	29	17	53
Sub-Saharan Africa	15	27	11	58
High income	2	25	15	74

Source: World Bank, 2015, Table 4.2.

across countries at different stages of development. When this is done, the income elasticity for agricultural products is typically estimated at about 0.5, while the income elasticity for services is significantly above unity. The income elasticity for industries is nonlinear. Up to a certain level of income, the elasticity is above unity, and then it falls below unity (consistent with the share of industrial output first rising and then falling).[2]

Within the industrial sector, there are also differences in the income elasticity of demand for products, which cause the pattern of industry to change as development proceeds. The most notable demand shift is the relative switch from basic necessities and low value-added goods to high value-added consumer durables.

Rostow's stages of growth

Interest in stage theories of development was given a major impetus with the publication of Rostow's *The Stages of Economic Growth* (1960), which represents an attempt to provide an alternative to the Marxist interpretation of history – hence its subtitle, *A Non-Communist Manifesto*. Rostow presents a political theory as well as a descriptive economic study of the pattern of the growth and development of nations.

Walt Rostow

Born 1916, New York, USA. Died 2003. Professor of Economic History, MIT (1950–61) and, after US government service in the 1960s during the Kennedy and Johnson administrations, Emeritus Professor of Political Economy, University of Texas, Austin. Famous for his bestselling, but controversial book *The Stages of Economic Growth: A Non-Communist Manifesto* (1960), in which he identifies several necessary conditions for countries to take off into self-sustaining growth: important among them an agricultural revolution, an investment ratio at least 10% of GDP, and an institutional environment conducive to entrepreneurship.

The essence of Rostow's thesis is that it is logically and practically possible to identify stages of development and to classify societies according to those stages. He distinguishes five such stages: **traditional, transitional, take-off, maturity** and **high mass consumption.**

All we need say about **traditional societies** is that, for Rostow, the whole of the pre-Newtonian world consisted of such societies; for example, the dynasties of China, the civilizations of the Middle East, the Mediterranean and medieval Europe and so on. Traditional societies are characterized by a ceiling on productivity imposed by the limitations of science. Traditional societies are thus recognizable by a very high proportion of the workforce in subsistence agriculture, coupled with very little mobility or social change, great divisions of wealth and decentralized political power. Today, few societies could be classed as traditional, except perhaps some of the primitive tribes of Amazonia or Papua New Guinea. Most societies emerged from the traditional stage some time ago, mainly under the impact of external challenge or the rise of nationalism. The exceptions to the pattern of emergence from the traditional state are those countries that Rostow describes as having been 'born free', such as the USA and certain British dominions. Here, the preconditions of 'take-off' were laid in a more simple fashion by the construction of 'social overhead capital' (growth-promoting institutions) and the introduction of industry from abroad. But, for the rest of the world, change was much more basic and fundamental, consisting not only of economic transformation but also a political and social transition from feudalism.

The stage between feudalism and take-off Rostow calls the **transitional stage**. The main economic requirement in the transition phase is that the level of investment should rise to at least 10% of national income to ensure self-sustaining growth. The main direction of investment must be in transport and other social overhead capital to build up society's infrastructure. The preconditions for a rise in the investment ratio consist of the willingness of people to lend risk capital, the availability of entrepreneurs, and the willingness of society at large to operate an economic system geared to the factory and the principle of the division of labour. But a country shifting resources out of agriculture needs to feed itself, so an agricultural revolution is also necessary.

On the social front, a new elite must emerge to fabricate the industrial society, and it must supersede in authority the land-based elite of the traditional society. Surpluses must be channelled by the new elite from agriculture to industry, and there must be a willingness to take risks and to respond to economic incentives. And because of the enormity of the task of transition, the establishment of an effective modern government is vital. The length of the transition phase depends on the speed with which local talent, energy and resources are devoted to modernization and the overthrow of the established order. In this respect, political leadership has an important part to play.

Then there is the **take-off stage**. The characteristics of take-off are sometimes difficult to distinguish from the characteristics of the transition stage, and this has been a point of contention between Rostow and his critics. Nonetheless, let us describe the take-off stage as Rostow sees it – a 'stage' to which reference is constantly made in the development literature. Since the preconditions of take-off have been met in the transitional stage, the take-off stage is a short stage of development, during which economic growth becomes self-sustaining. Investment must rise to a level in excess of 10% of national income in order for per capita income to rise sufficiently to guarantee adequate future levels of saving and investment. Also important is the establishment of what Rostow calls 'leading growth sectors'. Historically, domestic finance for take-off seems to have come from two main sources. The first was from a diversion of part of the product of agriculture by land reform and other means. The examples of Tsarist Russia and Meiji Japan are quoted, where government bonds were substituted for the landowner's claim to the flow of rent payments. A second source was from enterprising landlords voluntarily ploughing back rents into commerce and industry.

In practice, the development of major export industries has sometimes led to take-off permitting substantial capital imports. Grain in the USA, Russia and Canada, timber in Sweden and, to a lesser extent, textiles in Britain are cited as examples. Countries such as the USA, Russia, Sweden and Canada also benefited during take-off from substantial inflows of foreign capital. The sector or sectors that gave rise to the take-off seem to have varied from country to country, but in many countries railway building seems to have been prominent. Certainly, improvement of the internal means of communication is crucial for an expansion of markets and to facilitate exports, apart from any direct impact on industries such as coal, steel and engineering. But Rostow argues that any industry can play the role of leading sector in the take-off stage, provided four conditions are met:

1. The market for the product is expanding rapidly to provide a firm basis for the growth of output.
2. The leading sector generates secondary expansion.

3. The sector has an adequate and continual supply of capital from ploughed-back profits.
4. New techniques of production can be continually introduced into the sector, leading to increased productivity.

Rostow contends that the beginnings of take-off in most countries can be traced to a particular stimulus. Historically, this has taken many different forms, such as a technological innovation or, more commonly, political revolution, for example Germany in 1848, the Meiji Restoration in Japan in 1868, China in 1949 and Indian independence in 1947. Rostow stresses, however, that there is no one single pattern or sequence of take-off. Thus, there is no need for the developing countries today to repeat the course of events in, say, Britain, Russia or America. The crucial requirement is that the preconditions for take-off are met, otherwise take-off, whatever form it takes, will be abortive. Investment must rise to over 10% of national income; one or more leading sectors must emerge; and there must exist or emerge a political, social and institutional framework that exploits the impulse to expand. The examples are given of the extensive railway building in Argentina before 1914, and in India, China and Canada before 1895, which failed to initiate take-off because the full transition from a traditional society had not been made. The dates of take-off for some of the present developed countries are given as follows: Britain 1783–1802; France 1840–60; the USA 1843–60; Germany 1850–73; Sweden 1868–90; Japan 1878–1900; and Russia 1890–1914.

Then there is the **maturity stage**, which Rostow defines as the period when society has effectively applied the range of modern technology to the bulk of its resources. During the period of maturity, new leading sectors replace the old. By this criterion, Rostow sees the development of the steel industry as one of the symbols of maturity. In this respect, the USA, Germany, France and Britain entered the stage of maturity roughly together.

Accompanying changes in the industrial structure will be structural changes in society, such as changes in the distribution of the workforce, the growth of an urban population, an increase in the proportion of white-collar workers, and a switch in industrial leadership from entrepreneur to manager.

Maturity also has important political features. This is the period when nations grow confident and exert themselves – witness Germany under Bismarck and Russia under Stalin. This is also the period when fundamental political choices have to be made by society on the use to which the greater wealth should be put. Should it be devoted to high mass consumption, the building of a welfare state, or imperialist ends? The balance between these possibilities has varied over time within countries, and between countries. Eventually, however, every nation will reach the stage of **high mass consumption** whatever the balance of choices at the stage of maturity. Since there is no likelihood of developing countries reaching this stage in the foreseeable future, and only a handful of rich countries have reached it already, we shall ignore this fifth stage here.

Instead, let us evaluate Rostow's thesis and consider the usefulness of this type of stage theory, apart from its use in providing a valuable description of the development process and pinpointing some of the key growth variables. Most criticisms have hinged on whether a valid and operationally meaningful distinction can be made between stages of development, especially between the so-called transitional stage and take-off, and between take-off and maturity. Critics have attempted to argue that the characteristics that Rostow distinguishes for his different stages are not unique to those stages. Thus, the demarcation between take-off and transition is blurred because the changes that take place in the transition stage also seem to take place in the take-off phase, and similarly with the demarcation between take-off and maturity.

Despite these points of criticism, Rostow's stage theory still offers valuable insights into the development process. While the concept of a stage may be quibbled with, and stage theory dismissed as a blueprint for development, there are certain features of the development process that do follow a well-ordered sequence. Moreover, there are certain development prerequisites that countries neglect at their peril. The importance of agriculture in the early stages of development cannot be overemphasized, together with the provision of infrastructure and political stability, if the preconditions for take-off into self-sustaining growth are to be met. The role of investment is also highlighted: investment must reach a certain ratio of GDP (at least 10%) if per capita income growth is to be positive. Finally, there is the transition from the rural to the industrial society, with growth based on the development of leading sectors and foreign trade, which propels a society from take-off to the stage of maturity and eventually high mass consumption. The process of industrialization is crucial.

Diversification

Another feature of structural change is that, as well as resource shifts from agriculture to industry and services, the structure of production tends to become more diversified as countries develop, at least up to a fairly high level of per capita income – after which there is evidence that it becomes more specialized again. This is well documented in the work of Imbs and Wacziarg (2003) on 'stages of diversification' (see also Felipe, 2009). They take several different measures of industrial concentration (including the Gini ratio) and, using ILO and the UN Industrial Development Organization (UNIDO) data, show how the concentration of employment and value-added tends to fall as countries get richer up to about \$9,000 per head (at 2000 prices) and then increases, giving a U-shaped curve. Obvious explanations for this pattern are that people's preferences widen as they get richer, and there are more risk-takers willing to undertake new investments, which increases diversification. But at later stages of development, international trade increases the degree of specialization due to agglomeration benefits (increasing returns) and falling transport costs.

Industrialization and growth

From a global perspective, there seems to be a close association across countries between living standards and the share of resources devoted to industrial activities, at least up to a certain point. In very poor countries there is virtually no industrial activity at all, while middle- and high-income countries devote 20–40% of resources to industry. Only three countries in the world have become rich on agriculture alone: Australia, New Zealand and Canada. In all other countries, living standards have risen rapidly only as resources have shifted out of agriculture into industry and sophisticated services (see Szirmai, 2012).

Furthermore, research (see, for example, Szirmai et al., 2013; Thirlwall, 1983; Hansen and Zang, 1996; Guo et al., 2012; Wells and Thirlwall, 2003; Libanio, 2006; Necmi, 1999) also shows a close association across countries between the growth of industry and the growth of GDP; or more precisely, GDP growth is faster, the greater the *excess* of industrial growth relative to GDP growth; that is, when the *share* of industry in total GDP is rising the fastest. Figure 3.5 shows this relationship across 131 developing countries over the period 2000–14, with GDP growth measured on the vertical axis and the growth of industry on the horizontal axis. The scatter points represent the individual country observations. A line through the points with a slope less than unity shows that the greater the excess of industrial growth over GDP growth, the faster GDP growth seems to be. The point where this line cuts the 45° line gives the average growth rate that divides countries into those where the share of industry is falling and are growing slowly, and those where the share of industry is rising and are growing fast. A linear equation fitted to the scatter points in Figure 3.5 gives the following regression result:

$$g = 2.529 + 0.394x \quad r^2 = 0.507$$

The equation says that a country with industrial growth one percentage point above the average for all countries will have GDP growth of 0.394 percentage points above the average; and the point where the regression line cuts the 45° line is approximately 4.5%.[3] This rate of industry growth separates the slow-growing countries from the faster-growing countries.

The structural thesis of the role of manufacturing is supported by the research of Szirmai and Verspagen (2015), who take a panel of 88 countries over the period 1950–2005 and regress the growth of per capita income on the share of manufacturing output and services in total GDP. Their results support the hypothesis of 'manufacturing as the engine of growth'. A 10 percentage point rise in the share of manufacturing is associated with a 0.5 percentage point increase in the growth of per capita income. The impact has got weaker over time, however, as countries have got richer; the impact is stronger in low-income countries than in high-income countries. The significance of the service sector for growth is much weaker, but increases in high-income countries.

The question is: What is special about industry, and particularly manufacturing industry, which accounts for these empirical associations, and which makes industry 'the engine of growth'? Since differences in the growth of GDP are largely accounted for by differences in the rate of growth of labour productivity, there must be an association between the growth of industry and the growth of labour productivity. This is to be expected for two main reasons. First, if there are increasing returns to scale in industry, both static and dynamic, a relation is to be expected between the growth of industrial output and the growth of labour productivity in industry. **Static economies of scale** refer to the economies of large-scale production whereby the mass production of commodities allows them to be produced at a lower average cost. **Dynamic economies of scale** refer to the induced effect that output growth has on capital accumulation and the embodiment of new technical progress in capital. Labour

Figure 3.5 Association between growth of industry and growth of GDP

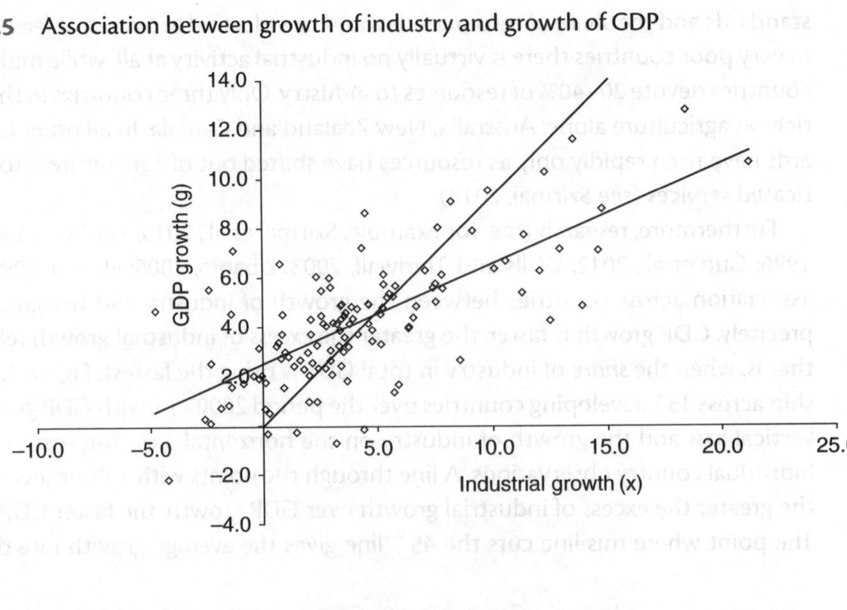

productivity also increases as output grows through **learning by doing**. Second, if activities outside industry, such as agriculture and petty services, are subject to diminishing returns, with the marginal product of labour less than the average product, then if resources are drawn from these activities into industry as industry expands, the average product of labour will rise in non-industrial activities. Case example 3.4 illustrates the role of structural change. These relationships between industrial growth, productivity growth and GDP growth are known in the growth and development literature as **Kaldor's growth laws**, named after the well-known Cambridge economist (Lord) Nicholas Kaldor, who first enunciated them in the 1960s (Kaldor, 1966, 1967).

Case example 3.4

Structural change as the driver of growth: China, South Korea and Indonesia compared

Structural change – as the transition from low-productivity activities with low value-added, such as agriculture and garment production, to high-productivity activities that can absorb surplus labour, generate higher profits and wages, and are most closely associated with technological development and innovation, such as manufacturing – promotes economic growth. The *speed* at which such a transition takes place also has an impact on the rate of economic growth. Countries that quickly climb the ladder towards more technologically advanced economic activities grow more rapidly and are more successful at lifting people out of poverty.

The remarkable economic growth of China and Southeast Asia, for example, is linked to the decline in the significance of the traditional agricultural sector, and rapid expansion of the industrial sector and subsequent higher value-added. When the programme of economic reforms was initiated in China in 1978, 70% of the total labour force was engaged in primary sector activity. This figure declined to 38% in 2009, while the share of the labour force in industry rose from 17% to 28%. Today, China is an economic powerhouse, on account of its profound and planned structural change, spurred by economic reforms, liberalized foreign trade, and high domestic and foreign investment in industry.

Structural change analysis is a powerful tool with which to compare and contrast the development experience of different countries. Looking at how much and how fast countries have diversified their structure as they climbed the stairway of development can reveal useful insights into the sustainability of their growth strategies. A comparison of the development experience of South Korea and Indonesia illustrates this point. Comparing the two countries from the same starting point when their per capita incomes were equivalent, structural change has been much more rapid in South Korea than in Indonesia. As a result, South Korea has become one of the fastest growing manufacturing economies of the world. In Indonesia, by contrast, no profound structural change took place, resulting in much slower growth of the economy.

There is widespread agreement by development economists that structural change is necessary for economic growth, and that the state – and not market forces alone – has a role to play. It is also argued that the government should not attempt to modify the structures of the current economy too quickly or too drastically. Yet, how closely a government's industrial policies should conform to the country's current comparative advantage, or to what extent a country's industrial structure should deviate from it, continue to be debated.

Source: UNIDO, 2012.

Kaldor's growth laws

There are three basic laws that have been widely tested in developed and developing countries using cross-section data (that is, across countries), time-series data, and panel data combining time-series and cross-section data.

The **first law** is that there exists a strong positive correlation between the growth of manufacturing output (g_m) and the growth of GDP (g_{GDP}), that is:

$$g_{GDP} = f_1(g_m) \quad f'_1 > 0 \tag{3.3}$$

where f_1 is the functional relationship that is hypothesized to be positive.

The **second law** is that there exists a strong positive correlation between the growth of manufacturing output and the growth of productivity in manufacturing (p_m), that is:

$$p_m = f_2(g_m) \quad f'_2 > 0 \tag{3.4}$$

where f_2 is the functional relationship that is assumed to be positive. This law is also known as **Verdoorn's law** after the Dutch economist P.J. Verdoorn, who, in the 1940s, first discovered such a relationship across a sample of European countries.

The **third law** is that there exists a strong positive relationship between the growth of manufacturing output and the growth of productivity outside manufacturing (p_{nm}), that is:

$$p_{nm} = f_3(g_m) \quad f'_3 > 0 \tag{3.5}$$

where f_3 is the functional relationship that is assumed to be positive.

The most rigorous test of these laws is to take a cross-section of countries, or a cross-section of regions within a country, and to perform correlation and regression analyses for each equation. We will illustrate this with reference to an interesting study that applies the model across 28 regions of China, taking average data for the period 1965–91 (Hansen and Zhang, 1996). See Case example 3.5 below for an application of the model to the countries of Africa.

Case example 3.5 **Testing Kaldor's growth laws across African countries**

One of the striking features about Africa since the 1980s is that there has been virtually no structural change. This is undoubtedly one of the explanations for its poor growth performance. Over the period 1980–96, the average growth of GDP was 2.09% per annum. The growth of manufacturing output was 2.11%, and the growth of agricultural and service output were both 2.07%. On the other hand, some African countries grew faster than others (e.g. Uganda, Botswana, Mauritius, Equatorial Guinea, Swaziland and Cape Verde grew particularly fast). To what extent can this differential growth performance be explained by the differential performance of manufacturing industries?

Regressing GDP growth against the excess of manufacturing growth (g_m) over non-manufacturing growth (g_{nm}) across 45 countries (the side test of Kaldor's first law) gives:

$$g_{GDP} = 0.021 + 0.408\,(g_m - g_{nm}) \qquad r^2 = 0.188$$

This suggests that a country with excess growth of manufacturing of 1 percentage point has experienced a GDP growth rate of 0.41 percentage point above average.

Case example 3.5 **Testing Kaldor's growth laws across African countries** – *continued*

When GDP growth is regressed against the excess of agricultural growth over non-agricultural growth, there is a strong *negative* correlation.

Estimating Kaldor's second law gives a Verdoorn coefficient of 0.878, which suggests substantial increasing returns in industry.

Estimating Kaldor's third law gives:

$$p_T = 0.020 + 0.524\,(g_i) - 1.606\,(e_{ni}) \qquad r^2 = 0.712$$

This shows that overall productivity growth (p_T) across African countries is positively related to the growth of industry (g_i), but negatively related to the growth of employment outside industry (e_{ni}).

These results support Kaldor's structural thesis that there is something special about industrial activity that makes it the 'engine of growth'.

Source: Wells and Thirlwall, 2003.

Fitting equation (3.3) to the Chinese regional data gives the following regression result:

$$g_{GDP} = 1.79 + 0.56\,(g_m) \qquad r^2 = 0.67$$

The r^2 measures the correlation between the two variables, so this equation says that 67% of the difference in the growth rate of output between the 28 regions in China can be accounted for by variation in the growth of manufacturing output between regions. This is a high degree of explanatory power. The regression coefficient of 0.56 says that a region with manufacturing output growth of 1% above the average for all regions will grow 0.56% above the average for all regions.

But before the equation can be used to support the hypothesis of manufacturing industry as the engine of growth, some words of warning are in order. If manufacturing output is a large fraction of total output, the correlation will, to a certain extent, be spurious because the same variable appears on both sides of the equation. There are ways to overcome this problem, however. One is to regress the growth of output on the *difference* between manufacturing and non-manufacturing output growth. The other is to regress non-manufacturing output growth on manufacturing output growth. Also, for manufacturing industry to be regarded as special, it needs to be shown that there is no significant relationship between total output growth and the growth of other major sectors, such as agriculture or services.[4]

Turning to the second law, fitting equation (3.4) to the regional data for China gave the following result:

$$p_m = -0.009 + 0.71\,g_m \qquad r^2 = 0.73$$

We see again that the correlation is very high, with 73% of the difference in the growth of labour productivity between regions accounted for by differences in the growth of output itself. On average, a 1% difference in the growth rate of output induces a 0.71 percentage point difference in the growth of labour productivity. This coefficient is referred to as the **Verdoorn coefficient**. The coefficient here is higher than typically found in developed countries, which is normally about 0.5, but this may reflect the large economies of scale to be reaped in the early stages of development. Again, for manufacturing industry to be regarded as special, this second law (or Verdoorn's law) should be weaker for other activities, which it will be in the absence of scale economies.

The third law is difficult to test directly because it is not easy to measure productivity growth in many activities outside manufacturing, particularly service activities where output can only be measured by inputs; for example, public services such as teaching, health, defence, the civil service and so on. It can be tested indirectly, however, by taking *overall* productivity growth (p_{GDP}) as the dependent variable to be explained and linking this to employment change in non-manufacturing activities (e_{nm}), holding constant the effect of output growth in manufacturing (g_m). The equation to be estimated is thus:

$$p_{GDP} = a_3 + b_3 (g_m) + c_3 (e_{nm}) \tag{3.6}$$

with the expectation that $c_3 < 0$.

Fitting equation (3.6) across the Chinese regions gives:

$$p_{GDP} = 0.02 + 0.49\, g_m - 0.82\, (e_{nm}) \qquad r^2 = 0.70$$

The coefficient on e_{nm} is significantly negative so that the slower employment growth outside manufacturing industry, the faster overall productivity grows. This study of China is supported by the work of Guo et al. (2012), who conclude: '[our] study validates Kaldor's laws in the regional economies of China ... the strong emphasis on the manufacturing sector has now proven to accelerate the growth of GDP and living standards in regions where the sector is concentrated'.

Kaldor's first and second laws have recently been confirmed in two major studies of a cross-section of 63 middle- and high-income countries over the period 1990–2013 (Marconi et. al., 2016), and a panel of 29 developing countries in Africa, Asia and Latin America over the period 1975–2005 (Di Meglio et al., 2015). In the former study, the relationship between manufacturing growth, productivity growth and GDP growth is particularly strong in middle-income countries, which include the newly industrializing countries of Southeast Asia. The study also confirms the importance of manufacturing exports in driving manufacturing growth and economies as a whole (see also Pacheco-López and Thirlwall, 2014). The latter study also finds that some service sectors, such as business services with their use of knowledge and technology, may also act as an engine of growth where industrialization is faltering, particularly in some Asian countries.

The complete Kaldor model of the relationship between industrial growth and the development process also contains a number of subsidiary propositions. First, as the scope for absorbing labour from diminishing returns activities dries up, the overall growth of GDP will slow down. The successful newly industrializing countries in Southeast Asia will not go on growing at close to 8% per annum forever. Second, there is the question of what determines the rate at which industry grows in the first place. In the early stages of development, it must be demand coming from the agricultural sector because this is what dominates the economy. In the later stages of development, however, it is export demand that drives the system. The internal market is often too small to reap economies of scale, and selling to the home market does not provide the foreign exchange to pay for necessary imported inputs. The most successful developing countries are those that have geared themselves to export markets. The third proposition is that the fast growth of exports and output can set up a **virtuous circle of growth** that other countries will find difficult to break into without exceptional enterprise or protection. This can lead to polarization between countries, which is the essential feature of the centre–periphery models of growth and development, which will be discussed in Chapter 10.

Finally, there is the big policy question of how developing countries bring about structural change in favour of industrial activities if growth and development are to be accelerated. Should everything be left to market forces, or is there a role for government? The late Cambridge development economist Ajit Singh tells the story of when he first went to Cambridge University as a student of Kaldor in the 1960s, Kaldor taught him three things: first, developing countries must industrialize; second, they can industrialize only by protection; and third, anyone who says otherwise is being dishonest. It is indeed worth remembering that none of today's developed countries developed on the basis of free trade. All countries protected and promoted their infant industries in one way or another (see Chang, 2002; Reinert, 2007). And it is a myth, of course, that the highly successful countries of Southeast Asia have developed on the basis of minimalist state intervention and simply allowed markets to work freely (Wade, 1990). In Japan, South Korea, Singapore and other 'Asian tigers', there has been heavy state involvement in the promotion of industry, often working through the banking system. The issue is not *whether* to protect, but *how* to protect and promote industry while preserving efficiency and international competitiveness. These are issues that will be addressed when we turn to the topic of trade and development in Chapter 15.

Summary

- Poverty and underdevelopment of poor countries are associated with many characteristics that combine to keep labour productivity low.
- The economic structure of poor countries tends to be dominated by low-productivity agriculture and petty service activities. Still over 50% of the labour force in many poor countries live and work in the rural sector where value-added per head is barely US$2 a day.
- Levels of saving and investment are low in poor countries because poor people naturally lack the capacity to save, and investment can be risky.
- Poor countries tend to have higher rates of population growth than rich countries and while this can confer some benefits, it can cause major difficulties by depressing saving, putting pressure on food supplies and the environment, and adding to unemployment.
- Some poor countries suffer the 'curse of natural resources'. Mineral and oil production can lead to corruption and rent-seeking behaviour and keep the exchange rate high, making the production and export of other goods uncompetitive.
- Unemployment is high in poor countries because there are limited employment opportunities on the land, and the growth of alternative employment opportunities is constrained by a lack of investment. Rural–urban migration exacerbates unemployment in the cities.
- The distribution of income tends to be more unequal in poor countries than rich, and also in power relations between sections of society. There is very often discrimination on the grounds of gender, religion, race and ethnic origin.
- Countries pass through stages of development – what Rostow describes as traditional, transitional, take-off, maturity, and high mass consumption. Many poor countries are still in the transitional or early take-off stages. Certain preconditions must be met for full take-off including: an agricultural revolution; investment in infrastructure; the emergence of leading sectors in the economy; saving and investment of at least 10% of GDP; and an institutional structure conducive to risk-taking and investment.
- Countries grow fast and living standards rise when resources shift into industrial activities, because manufacturing industry experiences considerable static and dynamic returns to scale. This is the experience of history and the contemporary experience of the fast-growing countries of the world today (Kaldor's growth laws).

Chapter 3 Discussion questions

1. What are the major reasons why some countries are rich and others poor?
2. What is the importance of the distinction between diminishing returns activities and increasing returns activities?
3. Why have economists identified a certain ratio of investment to GDP as a necessary condition for self-sustaining growth?
4. What are the causes of growing urban unemployment in developing countries?
5. What is meant by 'income measure' of unemployment?
6. Why is the distribution of income more unequal in developing countries than in developed countries?
7. What major structural changes take place in a country during the course of development?
8. What contribution does Rostow's stage theory make to an understanding of the development process?
9. What accounts for the fact that a close association exists between industrial growth and the growth of GDP?
10. What is the difference between static and dynamic returns to scale?

Notes

1. 'Net' in the sense of making an allowance for investment to cover depreciation of worn-out plant and machinery.
2. For pioneering studies of structural change, see Chenery and Syrquin (1975) and Chenery et al. (1986). For a more recent assessment, see Naqvi (1995).
3. Setting g = x, and solving for x gives: $2.529/(1 - 0.394) = 4.17\%$.
4. An alternative explanation of Kaldor's first law of growth in an open economy is that export growth drives GDP growth, and export growth is faster, the faster the growth of manufacturing output (Pacheco-López and Thirlwall, 2014). The importance of export growth for overall growth is discussed in Chapter 15.

Websites on structural change and income distribution

Labour market statistics

International Labour Organization http://laborsta.ilo.org

Income distribution

University of Texas, Inequality Project utip.gov.utexas.edu
UNU-WIDER www.wider.unu.edu/project/wiid-%E2%80%93-worldincome-inequality-database
Stone Center on Socio-Economic Inequality www.gc.cuny.edu/stonecenter

4

THEORIES OF ECONOMIC GROWTH: OLD AND NEW

- Introduction
- Classical growth theory
- The Harrod–Domar growth model
- Neoclassical growth theory
- The production function approach to the analysis of growth
- Production function studies of developing countries
- 'New' (endogenous) growth theory and the macrodeterminants of growth
- 'Growth diagnostics' and binding constraints on growth
- Summary
- Discussion questions
- Notes
- Websites on growth theory

Introduction

Growth and development theory is as old as economics itself. The great classical economists of the eighteenth and nineteenth centuries were, in a sense, all development economists writing about forces determining the progress of nations as the countries of Europe embarked on the process of industrialization. The most famous of the early classical economists was Adam Smith, who published a path-breaking book in 1776 entitled *An Inquiry into the Nature and Causes of the Wealth of Nations*. This work is still widely cited today because Smith recognized how specialization in industrial activities could lead to increasing returns and big increases in labour productivity, compared with specialization in agriculture.

In this chapter we examine how theories of growth and development have evolved through time from the classical economists to modern-day thinking about factors that determine the pace of economic growth. Other great classical economists, apart from Smith, were Thomas Malthus, David Ricardo and John Stuart Mill, who were all pessimistic about the growth and development process because of the pressure of population on food supply and diminishing returns in agriculture, which, they argued, would reduce the rate of profit in industry. Eventually, a stationary state would be reached. Even more pessimistic was Karl Marx, who predicted the collapse of capitalism itself.

Modern growth theory started with (Sir) Roy Harrod's well-known 1939 paper, 'An Essay in Dynamic Theory' (Harrod, 1939). His main purpose was to make dynamic Keynes' static theory of income determination. In doing so, he showed how unstable economies can be in the short run, and how, in the long run, it is possible for countries to experience either prolonged periods of secular stagnation if the supply of saving exceeds the demand for it, or structural unemployment if the growth of the labour force exceeds the growth of capital (as it does in most developing countries).

The neoclassical response to the Harrod model was Robert Solow's well-known growth model (Solow, 1956), which attempts to show that if the prices of factors of production are flexible, and labour and capital are substitutable, it is possible for countries to achieve equilibrium growth at the so-called 'natural rate', determined by the growth of the labour force and labour-saving technical progress. What determines labour force growth and technical progress is left unexplained. Because of the assumption of diminishing returns to capital, investment itself does not matter for long-run growth. The model also predicts that capital-scarce countries should grow faster than capital-rich countries, leading to a convergence of per capita incomes across the world, because the marginal product of capital should be higher in poor countries than in rich countries.

As we saw in Chapter 2, however, convergence of living standards across countries is not apparent, and this led in the 1980s to the development of the so-called 'new' growth theory or endogenous growth theory, which relaxes the assumption of diminishing returns to capital by redefining capital to include improvements in human capital and new techniques of production through research and development (R&D) expenditure. In these 'new' models, convergence is only conditional, and investment matters for long-run growth because the marginal product of capital does not decline as more investment takes place.

We not only look at theory, but also empirics, and see how the neoclassical production function has been used to analyse the sources of growth in developing countries, and how 'new' growth theorists treat their models empirically.

An attempt is made to illustrate the contemporary relevance of the theories discussed. We shall, in fact, discover that the wheel has turned full circle, and that the most recent theories of endogenous growth rehabilitate many of the ideas of the old classical economists, particularly Adam Smith's emphasis on **increasing returns** associated with investment in manufacturing industry, and the general emphasis in both classical and Keynesian theory on the role of capital accumulation, and the embodiment of various forms of technical progress associated with it.

The chapter ends with a discussion of the topic of growth diagnostics and identifying binding constraints on growth.

Classical growth theory

The macroeconomic issues of the growth of output, and the distribution of income between wages and profits, were the major preoccupation of all the great classical economists, including Adam Smith, Thomas Malthus, David Ricardo and, last but not least, Karl Marx. This discussion starts with **Adam Smith**, because while Smith had a generally optimistic vision of the growth and development process, the later classical economists tended to have a more gloomy vision. This led historian Thomas Carlyle to describe economics as a 'dismal science' – not a sentiment, we hope, that will be shared by students reading this book.

Adam Smith

Born 1723, Kirkcaldy, Scotland. Died 1790. Professor of Moral Philosophy, University of Glasgow. Often described as the 'father' of modern economics. Famous for two main books: *The Theory of Moral Sentiments* (1759) and *An Inquiry into the Nature and Causes of the Wealth of Nations* (1776). Strong advocate of free markets and free trade, but most important for recognizing the role that increasing returns play in the growth and development process, based on the principle of the division of labour or specialization – a characteristic of manufacturing industry in particular.

Adam Smith and increasing returns

One of Smith's most important contributions was to introduce into economics the notion of **increasing returns**, based on the **division of labour**. He saw the division of labour (or gains from specialization) as the very basis of a social economy, otherwise everyone might as well be their own Robinson Crusoe producing everything they want for themselves. This notion of increasing returns, based on the division of labour, lay at the heart of his optimistic vision of economic progress as a self-generating process, in contrast to later classical economists who believed that economies would end up in a stationary state owing to diminishing returns in agriculture and a falling rate of profit in industry. It was also in contrast to Marx, who believed that capitalism would collapse through its own 'inner contradictions', by which he meant competition between capitalists reducing the rate of profit and the alienation of workers.

Given the central importance of increasing returns, the essence of Smith's model is a simple one, and many of the features he emphasizes will be a recurring theme in this and other chapters. The growth of output and living standards depends first and foremost on investment and capital accumulation. Investment, in turn, depends on savings out of the profits generated by industry and agriculture and the degree of labour specialization (or division of labour). The division of labour determines the level of labour productivity, but **the division of labour is limited by the extent of the market**. The extent of the market, however, depends partly on the division of labour as the determinant of per capita income. We have here a circular cumulative interactive process, although not without constraints, as we shall see later.

The notion of increasing returns may, on the surface, appear to be relatively trivial, but it is of profound significance for the way economic processes are viewed. It is not possible to understand divisions in the world economy and so-called 'centre–periphery' models of growth and development (see Chapter 10) without distinguishing between activities that are subject to increasing returns on the one hand, and diminishing returns on the other. 'Increasing returns' means rising labour productivity and per capita income as output and employment expands, while 'diminishing returns' means falling labour productivity and per capita income and a limit to the employment of labour at the point where the marginal product of labour falls to the level of the subsistence wage. Beyond that point, there will be no more employment opportunities, and there will be disguised unemployment (see Chapters 3 and 5). Increasing returns are prevalent in most industrial activities, while diminishing returns characterize land-based activities such as agriculture and mining, because land is a fixed factor of production – and one of the few incontrovertible laws of economics is that if a variable factor is added to a fixed factor, its marginal product will eventually fall (the law of diminishing returns). Poor developing countries tend to specialize in diminishing returns activities, while rich developed countries tend to specialize in increasing returns activities, and this is one of the basic explanations of the rich country–poor country divide in the world economy. As we see later, it is the concept of increasing returns (or more precisely, non-diminishing returns to capital) that lies at the heart of the new endogenous growth theory.

Adam Smith (1776) gives three sources of the increasing returns to be derived from the division of labour:

> This great increase in the quantity of work, which, in consequence of the division of labour, the same number of people are capable of performing, is owing to three different circumstances; first to the increase of dexterity in every particular workman [what we now call learning by doing]; secondly, to the saving of time which is commonly lost in passing from one species of work to another; and lastly, to the invention of a great number of machines which facilitate and abridge labour, and enable one man to do the work of many.

That is, specialization provides greater scope for capital accumulation by enabling complex processes to be broken up into simpler processes permitting the use of machinery. But the ability to specialize, or the division of labour, depends on the extent of the market. Smith uses the example of the production of pins. There is no point in installing sophisticated machinery to deal with the different processes of pin production if the market for pins is very small. It is only economical to use cost-saving machinery if the market is large. If the market is small, there would be surplus production. To quote Smith (1776) again:

> when the market is very small, no person can have any encouragement to dedicate himself entirely to one employment, for want of power to exchange all that surplus part of the produce of his own labour, which is over and above his own consumption, for such parts of the produce of other men's labour as he has occasion for.

Smith (1776) recognized, however, that increasing returns based on the division of labour were much more a feature of industry than agriculture:

> the nature of agriculture, indeed, does not admit of so many subdivisions of labour, nor of so complete a separation of one business from another, as manufactures. It is impossible to separate so entirely the business of the grazier from that of the corn farmer, as the trade of the carpenter is commonly separated from that of the smith.

This does not mean, of course, that agriculture is unimportant in the development process. On the contrary. Even though industry offers more scope for the division of labour, it would be difficult for industry to develop at all without an agricultural surplus, at least in the absence of imports. Smith recognized that an agricultural surplus is necessary to support an industrial population, and labour released by improved productivity in agriculture can be used for the production of non-agricultural goods. So, agriculture is certainly important for industrialization from the supply side. On the demand side, it is the agricultural surplus that gives rise to the demand for other goods, which can be purchased with the excess supply of agricultural goods. As Smith (1776) put it: 'those, therefore, who have the command of more food than they themselves can consume, are always willing to exchange the surplus – for gratification of this other kind [manufactured goods]'. We have here a model of reciprocal demand between agriculture and industry, with industry demanding food from agriculture to feed workers, and agriculture exchanging its surplus for industrial goods. Balanced growth between agriculture and industry is essential for the growth and development process to proceed without impediment. Many later models of economic development reflect this insight (see Chapters 5 and 9). For a full exposition of Smith's vision of the development process, in which aggregate demand and aggregate supply interact in a cumulative expansionary process, together with structural change, see Kim (2015).

The division of labour is limited by the size of the market. This is a central axiom of Smith's model. The size of the market will be partly limited by restrictions on trade; hence Smith's advocacy of free trade and laissez-faire, internally and externally. Goods must be able to be exchanged freely between industry and agriculture. But demand for industrial goods can also come from abroad, and Smith (1776) recognized the role of exports in the development process:

> without an extensive foreign market, [manufactures] could not well flourish, either in countries so moderately extensive as to afford but a narrow home market; or in countries where the communication between one province and another was so difficult as to render it impossible for the goods of any particular place to enjoy the whole of that home market which the country could afford.

The subject of trade and growth, and models of export-led growth, is discussed in detail in Chapter 15.

Smith's model of development is driven by capital accumulation generated by profits from industry; and the stimulus to invest, as in all classical models, comes from the rate of profit. If the rate of profit falls, the desire to invest diminishes. Smith was somewhat ambiguous about what happens to the rate of profit as development proceeds. On the one hand, he recognized that as the economy's capital stock grows, the profit rate will tend to fall due to competition between capitalists and rising wages. On the other hand, new investment opportunities raise the rate of return. Thus, the rate of profit may rise or fall in the course of development depending on whether investment is in old or new technology. If there is any tendency towards a stationary state, in which the rate of profit falls to zero so that there is no further incentive to invest, it is a long way off in Smith's model, in contrast to the models of Malthus, Ricardo and Marx, in which a fall in the rate of profit is seen as inevitable.

Before turning to these models, which focus on some of the more depressing features inherent in the development process, it needs to be said that Smith's vision of development as a cumulative interactive process based on the division of labour and increasing returns in industry lay effectively dormant until Allyn Young, an American economist, revived it in a profound but neglected article in 1928 entitled 'Increasing Returns and Economic Progress'. As Young (1928) observed:

> Adam Smith's famous theorem [that the division of labour depends on the extent of the market and the extent of the market depends on the division of labour] amounts to saying that the division of labour depends in large part on the division of labour. [But] this is more than mere tautology. It means that the counter forces which are continually defeating the forces which make for equilibrium are more pervasive and more deeply rooted than we commonly realise . . . Change becomes progressive and propagates itself in a cumulative way.

For Young, increasing returns are not simply confined to factors that raise productivity *within* individual industries, but are related to the output of *all* industries, which, he argued, must be viewed as an interrelated whole: what are now sometimes called **macroeconomies of scale**. For example, a larger market for product X may make it profitable to use more machinery in its production, which reduces the cost of X *and* the cost of the machinery, which then makes the use of machinery more profitable in other industries and so on. Under certain conditions, change will become progressive and propagate itself in a cumulative way; the precise conditions being increasing returns and an elastic demand for products so that as their relative price falls, proportionately more is bought. Take the example of steel and textiles, both of which are subject to increasing returns and are price elastic. As the supply of steel increases, its relative price (or exchange value) falls. If demand is price elastic, textile producers demand proportionately more steel, and offer proportionately more textiles in exchange. Textile production increases and its exchange value falls. If demand is price elastic, steel producers demand proportionately more textiles and so on. As Young said: 'under these circumstances there are no limits to the process of expansion except the limits beyond which demand is not elastic and returns do not increase'.

The process described above could not occur with diminishing returns activities with an inelastic price demand, which characterizes most primary products. No wonder rapid development tends to be associated with the process of industrialization. It is true to say, however, that Young's vision was also lost until the 1950s, when economists, such as Gunnar Myrdal, Albert Hirschman and Nicholas Kaldor, started to challenge equilibrium theory and develop non-equilibrium models of the growth and development process, in books such as *Economic Theory and Underdeveloped Regions* (Myrdal, 1957), *Strategy of Economic Development* (Hirschman, 1958), *Strategic Factors in Economic Development* (Kaldor, 1967) and *Economics without Equilibrium* (Kaldor, 1985). Kaldor used to joke that economics went wrong after Chapter 4, Book I of Smith's *Wealth of Nations*, when Smith abandoned the assumption of increasing returns in favour of constant returns, and the foundations for neoclassical general equilibrium theory were laid. In contrast, it is now Smith and Young's emphasis on increasing returns that lies at the heart of the new endogenous growth theory.

The classical pessimists

The prevailing classical view after Smith was very pessimistic about the process of economic development, focusing on the problems of rapid population growth and the effect exerted on the rate of profit in industry by rising food prices owing to diminishing returns and rising costs in agriculture. One of the foremost pessimists was **Thomas Malthus**, and it might be said that the ghost of Malthus still haunts many developing countries today with respect to his views on population. But there are two strands to Malthus's writing: his theory of population, and his focus on the importance for development of maintaining 'effective demand' – a concept later borrowed by Keynes, who acknowledged a debt to Malthus. In fact, Malthus was the only classical economist to emphasize the importance of demand for the determination of output – all others adhered to **Say's law**: that supply creates its *own* demand, so that the level and growth of output are a function of the supply of physical inputs alone. For Malthus, effective demand must grow in line with productive potential if profitability as the stimulus to investment is to be maintained, but there is nothing to guarantee this. Malthus focused on the savings of landlords and the possible imbalance between the supply of saving and the planned investment of capitalists, which might impede development. If landlord saving exceeded the amount that capitalists wished to borrow, Malthus suggested the taxation of landlords as one solution.

Malthus is best known, however, for *An Essay on the Principle of Population* ([1798]1983), in which he claimed that there is a 'constant tendency in all animated life to increase beyond the nourishment prepared for it'. According to Malthus, 'population goes on doubling itself every twenty five years, or increases in a geometrical ratio', whereas 'it may be fairly said ... that the means of subsistence increase in an arithmetical ratio'. Taking the world as a whole, therefore, Malthus ([1798]1983) concluded:

> the human species would increase (if unchecked) as the numbers 1, 2, 4, 8, 16, 32, 64, 128, 256, and subsistence as 1, 2, 3, 4, 5, 6, 7, 8, 9. [This would mean that] in two centuries the population would be to the means of subsistence as 256 to 9; in three centuries as 4096 to 13, and in two thousand years the difference would be incalculable.

If food production only grows at an arithmetic rate, this implies, of course, diminishing returns to agriculture. The imbalance between population growth and growth of the food supply would lead to the per capita income of countries oscillating around the subsistence level, or being caught in what is now sometimes called a **low-level equilibrium trap** (see Chapter 11). Any increases in per capita income brought about by technical progress lead to more births, which then reduce

Thomas Malthus

Born 1766, Surrey, England. Died 1834. Professor of History and Political Economy at the East India Company College. Famous for *An Essay on the Principle of Population* (1798) predicting that population growth will outstrip food supply because of diminishing returns in agriculture. Some communities in developing countries still have Malthusian characteristics, and some 'environmentalists' predict a Malthusian world in the future.

per capita income back to subsistence level. Early development models of the 'big push' were designed to lift economies from this trap. Malthus recognized certain checks to the process, which he divided into 'preventative' and 'positive' checks, some of which still operate today in certain countries. Preventive checks include sexual abstinence or the use of contraception, although Malthus was opposed to the latter. Where preventive checks are weak, positive checks take over in the form of pestilence, disease and famine. Malthus's solution to population growth was the 'postponement of marriage in a viceless society'.

While Malthusian economics may still have relevance in certain parts of Africa and Asia, Malthus's gloomy prognostications have not materialized for the world as a whole, because preventive checks have become stronger and food production has grown not at an arithmetic rate but at a rate faster than the growth of population (see Chapter 5). Technical progress in agriculture has offset diminishing returns. The underestimation of technical progress in agriculture has confounded all the classical pessimists.

David Ricardo was another of the great classical pessimists. In 1817 he published his *Principles of Political Economy and Taxation* (Ricardo, [1817]1992), in which he predicted that capitalist economies would end up in a stationary state, with no growth, also owing to diminishing returns in agriculture. In Ricardo's model, like Smith's, growth and development are a function of capital accumulation, and capital accumulation depends on reinvested profits. However, profits are squeezed between subsistence wages and the payment of rent to landlords, which increases as the price of food rises owing to diminishing returns to land and rising marginal costs. Ricardo thought of the economy as 'one big farm' in which food (or corn) and manufactures are consumed in fixed proportions, so that corn can be used as the unit of account. Figure 4.1 illustrates the model.

With the employment of *L* amount of labour, the total output is *0RZL*. Rent is determined by the difference between the average and marginal product of labour working on the land and is given by the area *PRZY*. Wages are equal to *0WXL*, and profit is the difference between rent and wages, equal to *WPYX*. As output increases and the marginal product of labour falls to the subsistence wage (L_1), profits disappear. In equilibrium, the rate of profit in agriculture must equal the rate of profit in industry. As the profit rate in agriculture falls, capital will shift to industry, causing the rate of profit to decline there. Profits are also squeezed because wages rise in terms of food. But for Ricardo, unlike Malthus, there was no problem of effective demand. Ricardo saw no limit to the amount of capital that could be employed because he accepted Say's law that supply creates its own demand. The villain of the piece is wages. Ricardo ([1817]1992) wrote: 'there is no limit to demand – no limit to the employment of capital while it yields any profit, and that

Figure 4.1 Ricardo's model of the economy

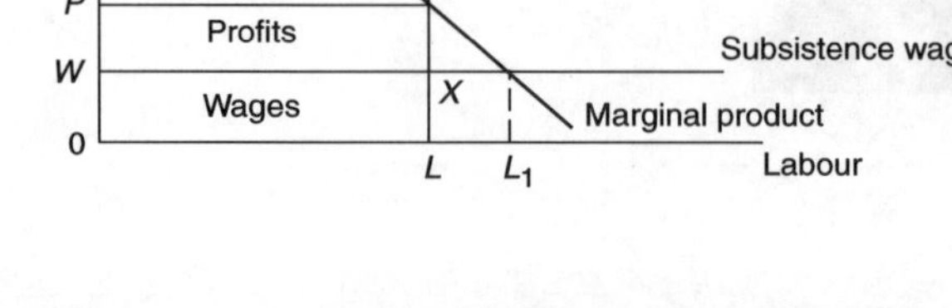

however abundant capital may become, there is no other adequate reason for a fall in profit but a rise in wages'. As profits fall to zero, capital accumulation ceases, heralding the stationary state. As Ricardo ([1817]1992) put it:

> a real rise of wages is necessarily followed by a real fall in profits, and, therefore, when the land of a country is brought to the highest state of cultivation, when more labour employed upon it will not yield in return more food than what is necessary to support the labourer so employed, that country has come to the limit of its increase both of capital and population.

As discussed in Chapter 5, Arthur Lewis's well-known development model, 'economic development with unlimited supplies of labour', is a classical Ricardian model, but wages are assumed to stay the same until disguised unemployment on the land is absorbed.

Given the central importance of capital accumulation in Ricardo's vision of economic progress, anything that reduces capital accumulation (including rises in wages) will slow economic growth. Ricardo was thus opposed to all forms of taxes, levies and tariffs on inputs into the productive system, including tariffs on imported food. Indeed, he believed that the importation of cheap food might delay the predicted stationary state indefinitely by holding down wages measured in terms of food:

> a country could go on for an indefinite time increasing its wealth and population, for the only obstacle to this increase would be the scarcity, and consequent high value, of food and other raw produce. Let these be supplied from abroad in exchange for manufactured goods, and it is difficult to say where the limit is at which you would cease to accumulate wealth and to derive profits from its employment (Ricardo [1817]1992).

It was for this reason that Ricardo campaigned for the abolition of the Corn Laws in Britain in the nineteenth century. These laws were eventually repealed in 1846 – to the benefit of industrialists but the detriment of domestic farmers. In developing countries today, governments often attempt to keep the price of agricultural goods artificially low in order to keep wages low (measured in terms of food). Doing this, however, raises another problem of reducing the incentive of farmers to produce. Determining the equilibrium terms of trade between agriculture and industry, which maximizes the output growth of both sectors, is a difficult empirical issue (see Chapter 5).

David Ricardo

Born 1772, London, England. Died 1823. Led a colourful life as politician, industrialist, speculator and economist. *Principles of Political Economy and Taxation* (1817) made him the foremost classical economist of the first half of the nineteenth century. Predicted that economies will end up in a stationary state through diminishing returns in agriculture reducing the rate of profit in industry. Campaigned for the repeal of the Corn Laws in England to make food cheaper. Most famous for his formulation of the doctrine of **comparative advantage**; one of the few non-trivial theorems in economics.

Finally, we turn to **Karl Marx**, famous for *Das Kapital* ([1867]1967), and his prediction of the collapse of capitalism. All members of the classical school agreed that the rate of profit on capital would fall as the economy grew, but they differed as to the reason for the fall. Adam Smith saw the decline in profits as the result of competition among capitalists. Ricardo saw the fall as the result of diminishing returns to land, and profits being squeezed between rent and wages, leading to a stationary state. For Marx, the economy does not grow forever, but the end comes not from a stationary state but from 'crises' associated with overproduction and social upheaval. But Marx's model bears many similarities to the other classical economists. The capitalist surplus is the source of capital accumulation and the principal mainspring of growth. Population growth responds to wages in Malthusian fashion, keeping wages down, and the rate of profit has a long-run tendency to fall.

Let us briefly consider Marx's model and his prediction of crisis. Gross output consists of three elements:

- Variable capital or the wage bill (v)
- Constant capital (c), that is, plant and machinery and the raw materials used in production
- Surplus value or profit (s).

The wages of labour are determined by the minimum subsistence level (what Marx called the cost of reproducing the working class), and surplus value (which only labour can create) is the difference between output per worker and the minimum wage per worker. The rate of surplus value, or what Marx called the 'degree of exploitation', is given by s/v. The rate of profit is given by the ratio of surplus value to total capital; that is:

$$s/(v + c) = (s/v)/(1 + [c/v]) \tag{4.1}$$

where the ratio of constant capital to variable capital (c/v) is defined as the **organic composition of capital**. As techniques of production become more capital intensive, the organic composition rises through time, and as it does so, the rate of profit falls unless surplus value rises. While there is no limit to the rise in c/v, however, there is a limit to s/v. Marx foresaw no major problem as long as surplus labour exists to keep wages down, but he predicted that as capital accumulation continues, the **reserve army of labour**, as he called it, would disappear, driving wages up and profits down. The capitalist's response is then either to attempt to keep wages down, leading to the **immiserization of workers** and social conflict, or to substitute more capital for labour, which would worsen the problem by raising c/v.

For Marx ([1867]1967), the desire and necessity to invest are inherent in the psychological makeup of the capitalist: 'To accumulate, is to conquer the world of social wealth, to increase the mass of human beings exploited by him, and then to extend both the direct and indirect sway of the capitalist.' Thus the capitalist's motto is 'Accumulate, accumulate! That is Moses and the Prophets.' But as capital is substituted for labour, there is another problem: labour cannot consume all the goods produced, and a **realization crisis** is caused by the failure of effective demand. Capitalism eventually collapses through its own 'inner contradictions', and power passes to the working classes because fewer and fewer people benefit from capitalism. Capitalism is replaced by socialism, whereby workers own the means of production, distribution and exchange, and ultimately the state withers away.

Marx's analysis contains valuable insights into the functioning of capitalism, but his predictions, like those of his predecessors, have not materialized. There seem to be two basic reasons for this. The first is that there is a confusion in Marx's work between *money wages* and *real wages*. A rise in money wages as surplus labour disappears does not necessarily mean a rise in

Karl Marx

Born 1818, Trier, Germany. Died 1883. Settled in England in 1848 and supported by Friedrich Engels. *Das Kapital* (vol. 1, 1867, and three further volumes published posthumously), his major work, has inspired generations of left-wing thinkers in their critiques of the inequalities of capitalism. His prediction that capitalism would collapse through a decline in the rate of profit and the immiserization of workers leading to social revolution has not materialized, because in a growing economy with technical progress, there is no clash between real wages and the rate of profit.

real wages; but in any case, any rise in real wages could be offset by a rise in labour productivity, leaving the rate of profit unchanged. The second and related reason is that just as the other classical economists underestimated the rate of technical progress in agriculture as an offset to diminishing returns, so Marx underestimated the effect of technical progress in industry on the productivity of labour. It can be seen from equation (4.1) that even if c/v is rising, the rate of profit can remain unchanged if technical progress exceeds the rate of wage growth by the same amount. Technical progress also means there is no necessary clash between real wages and the rate of profit. Both can rise.

For nearly 60 years after Marx's death in 1883, growth and development theory lay effectively dormant, as economics came to be dominated by static neoclassical value theory under the influence of Alfred Marshall's *Principles of Economics* (1890). Marshall treated growth and development as more or less a 'natural' phenomenon; an evolutionary process akin to biological developments in the natural world. Modern growth theory started with the classic article by British economist Roy Harrod, 'An Essay in Dynamic Theory' (1939), and American economist Evsey Domar arrived at Harrod's result independently in 1947 (Domar, 1947), which led to the development of what is now called the Harrod–Domar growth model. The model has played a major part in thinking about development issues since the Second World War, and is still widely used in development planning (see Chapter 9).

The Harrod–Domar growth model

Harrod's original model is a dynamic extension of Keynes' static equilibrium analysis. In Keynes' *The General Theory of Employment, Interest and Money* (1936), the condition for income and output to be in equilibrium (in the closed economy) is that plans to invest equal plans to save (or injections into the circular flow of income should equal leakages). The question Harrod asked is: If changes in income induce investment, what must be the *rate of growth of income* for plans to invest to equal plans to save in order to ensure a *moving* equilibrium in a growing economy through time? Moreover, is there any guarantee that this required rate of growth will prevail? If not, what will happen? In static Keynesian theory, if equilibrium between saving and investment is disturbed, the economy corrects itself and a new equilibrium is achieved via the multiplier process. If growth equilibrium is disturbed, will it be self-correcting or self-aggravating? Moreover, will this equilibrium rate be equal to the maximum rate of growth that the economy is able to sustain, given the rate of growth of productive capacity? If not, what will happen? These are fundamental questions for the understanding of the growth performance of any country, be it developed or underdeveloped, and Harrod's place in the history of economic thought was guaranteed by the insight and simplicity with which he answered them.

To consider the questions posed, Harrod distinguished three different growth rates: what he called the **actual growth rate** (g), the **warranted growth rate** (g_w) and the **natural growth rate** (g_n). The actual growth rate is defined as:

$$g = s/c \tag{4.2}$$

where s is the ratio of savings to national income (S/Y) and c is the *actual* incremental capital–output ratio, that is, the ratio of extra capital accumulation or investment to the flow of output ($\Delta K/\Delta Y = I/\Delta Y$). This expression for the actual growth rate ($g = s/c$) is, by definition, true since it expresses the accounting identity that savings equals investment. We can see this if we substitute the expressions for s and c into equation (4.2) – that is, $s/c = (S/Y)/(I/\Delta Y) = \Delta Y/Y$, given $S = I$, where $\Delta Y/Y$ measures the growth of output.

We need more than a definitional equation, however, to know whether the actual growth rate will provide the basis for steady advance in the future, in the sense that it keeps plans to invest and plans to save in line with one another at full employment. This is where the concepts of the warranted rate of growth and the natural rate of growth become important.

Harrod (1939) defined the warranted rate of growth as:

> that rate of growth which, if it occurs, will leave all parties satisfied that they have produced neither more nor less than the right amount. Or, to state matters otherwise, it will put them into a frame of mind which will cause them to give such orders as will maintain the same rate of growth.

In other words, the warranted growth rate is the rate that induces just enough investment to match planned saving and therefore keeps capital fully employed (that is, there is no undercapacity or overcapacity), so that manufacturers are willing to carry on investment in the future at the same rate as in the past. How is this rate determined? Plans to save at any point in time are given by the Keynesian savings function:

$$S = sY \tag{4.3}$$

where s is the propensity to save. This gives the potential supply of investment goods. The demand for investment is given by the **acceleration principle** (or what Harrod calls 'the relation'), where c_r is the accelerator coefficient measured as the *required* amount of extra capital or investment to produce a unit flow of output at a given rate of interest, determined by technological conditions. Thus:

$$c_r = \Delta K_r/\Delta Y = I/\Delta Y \tag{4.4}$$

The demand for investment, given by the accelerator principle, is then:

$$I = c_r\Delta Y \tag{4.5}$$

For planned saving to equal planned investment, therefore, we have:

$$sY = c_r\Delta Y \tag{4.6}$$

and the required rate of growth for a moving equilibrium through time is:

$$\Delta Y/Y = s/c_r = g_w \quad (4.7)$$

This is the warranted rate of growth, g_w. For dynamic equilibrium, output must grow at this rate. At this rate, expenditure on consumption goods will equal the production of consumption goods, and this is the only rate at which entrepreneurs will be satisfied with what they are doing, so that they do not revise their investment plans.

Now, suppose there is a departure from this equilibrium rate. What happens? The condition for equilibrium is that $g = g_w$ or, from equations (4.2) and (4.7), that $gc = g_w c_r$. First, suppose that the actual growth rate exceeds the warranted rate. It is easily seen that if $g > g_w$, then $c < c_r$, which means that actual investment falls below the level required to meet the increase in output. There will be a shortage of equipment, a depletion of stocks and an incentive to invest more. The actual growth rate will then depart even further from the warranted rate. Conversely, if the actual growth rate is less than the warranted rate, $g < g_w$, then $c > c_r$, and there will be a surplus of capital goods and investment will be discouraged, causing the actual growth rate to fall even further below the equilibrium rate. Thus, as Harrod points out, we have in the dynamic field a condition opposite to that in the static field. A departure from equilibrium, instead of being self-righting, will be self-aggravating. This is the short-term trade cycle problem in Harrod's growth model.

Roy Harrod

Born 1900, Norfolk, England. Died 1978. Spent all his academic career in Christ Church College, Oxford. One of Keynes' inner circle; in the late 1930s, made static Keynesian theory dynamic, thus pioneering modern growth theory. One of the most original economists of the twentieth century; made important contributions to the theory of the firm, international economics and economic dynamics. Authored a book on inductive logic as well as the first biography of Keynes.

American economist **Evsey Domar**, working independently of Harrod, arrived at Harrod's central conclusion, although by a slightly different route. Domar recognized that investment is a double-edged sword: it both increases demand via the multiplier, and increases supply via its effect on expanding capacity. The question Domar asked, therefore, was: What rate of growth of investment must prevail in order for supply to grow in line with demand (at full employment)? The crucial rate of growth of investment can be derived in the following way. A change in the level of investment increases demand by:

$$\Delta Y_d = \Delta I/s \quad (4.8)$$

and investment itself increases supply by:

$$\Delta Y_s = I\sigma \quad (4.9)$$

where σ is the productivity of capital or the flow of output per unit of investment ($\Delta Y/I$). For $\Delta Y_d = \Delta Y_s$, we must have:

$$\Delta I/s = I\sigma \tag{4.10}$$

or:

$$\Delta I/I = s\sigma \tag{4.11}$$

In other words, investment must grow at a rate equal to the product of the savings ratio and the productivity of capital. With a constant savings–investment ratio, this also implies output growth at the rate $s\sigma$. If $\sigma = 1/c_r$ (at full employment), then the Harrod–Domar result for equilibrium growth is the same.

But even if growth proceeds at the rate required for full utilization of the capital stock and a moving equilibrium through time, this still does not guarantee the full employment of labour, which depends on the natural rate of growth. The **natural growth rate** is derived from the identity $Y^* = L^*(Y/L)^*$, where Y^* is the potential level of output, L^* is the potential labour force and $(Y/L)^*$ is the potential level of labour productivity. Taking rates of change of the variables gives $y^* = l + \dot{q}$. The natural rate of growth (g_n) is therefore made up of two components: the growth of the potential labour force (l) and the growth of potential labour productivity ($\dot{q}$) (what Harrod called the rate of growth of the labour force in efficiency units) – both exogenously determined in the Harrod model.[1] The natural rate of growth plays an important role in Harrod's growth model in two ways. First, it defines the rate of growth of productive capacity or the long-run full employment equilibrium growth rate. Second, it sets the upper limit to the actual growth rate, which brings cumulative expansion in the Harrod (trade cycle) model to a sticky end. If $g > g_w$, g can continue to diverge from g_w only until it hits g_n, when all available labour has been completely absorbed: g cannot be greater than g_n in the long run. The long-run question for an economy, then, is the relation between g_w and g_n; that is, the relation between the growth of capital and the growth of the labour force (measured in efficiency units). With fixed coefficients of production, the full employment of labour clearly requires $g = g_n$. The full employment of labour *and* capital requires:

$$g = g_w = g_n \tag{4.12}$$

a state of affairs that the well-known Cambridge economist Joan Robinson once called a 'golden age' to emphasize its mythical nature, because there is nothing in the Harrod model that would automatically generate this happy coincidence.

Let us now consider what happens if the warranted growth rate diverges from the natural rate. If $g_w > g_n$, there will be a chronic tendency towards depression because the actual rate of growth will never be sufficient to stimulate investment demand to match the amount of saving at full employment equilibrium. There is too much capital and too much saving. This was the worry that economists had in the 1930s, particularly when it was predicted that the size of the population would fall in developed countries because the net reproduction rate had fallen below one (that is, females were not replacing themselves). If $g_w < g_n$, there will be a tendency towards demand inflation because there will be a tendency for the actual rate of growth to exceed that necessary to induce investment to match saving. Inflationary pressure, however, will be accompanied by growing unemployment of the structural variety, because the growth of capital falls short of the growth of the effective labour force and there is no change in the techniques of production.

Where do developing countries fit into this picture? In most developing countries, the natural growth rate exceeds the warranted rate. If the population growth is, say, 2% and labour productivity is growing at 3%, this gives a rate of growth of the labour force in efficiency units of 5%. If the net savings ratio is, say, 9% and the required incremental capital–output ratio is 3, this gives a warranted growth rate of 3%. This has two main consequences. First, it means that the effective labour force is growing faster than capital accumulation, which is part of the explanation for growing unemployment in developing countries. Second, it implies plans to invest greater than plans to save, and therefore inflationary pressure. If $g_n = 5\%$ and $c_r = 3$, there will be profitable investment opportunities for 15% saving, whereas actual saving is only 9%.

The simultaneous existence of inflation and high unemployment in developing countries is therefore not a paradox. It can easily be explained within the framework and assumptions of the Harrod growth model, as can a great deal of development policy. Given the inequality $g_n \neq g_w$, or $l + \dot{q} \neq s/c_r$, it can be seen that there are basically four ways in which g_n and g_w might be reconciled:

1. If the problem is $g_n > g_w$, the rate of growth of the labour force could be reduced. Measures to control population growth can be justified on these grounds, as a contribution to solving the problem of structural unemployment.
2. A reduction in the rate of growth of labour productivity would help, but this would reduce the growth of living standards of those in work. There is a clash here between employment and efficiency.
3. A rise in the savings ratio could narrow the gap. This is at the heart of monetary and fiscal reform in developing countries (see Chapter 13).
4. The natural and warranted growth rates might be brought into line by a reduction in the required capital–output ratio through the use of more labour-intensive techniques.

There is an active debate in developing countries over the appropriate choice of techniques, and whether developing countries could move towards the use of more labour-intensive techniques without impairing output and sacrificing saving (see Chapter 6). All these adjustment mechanisms are illustrated in Figure 4.2.

Growth is measured on the vertical axis, and the investment and savings ratios on the horizontal axis. Growth and the investment ratio are related through c_r – the required incremental capital–output ratio. The savings ratio is independent of the growth rate. Figure 4.2 depicts a situation in which the natural growth rate (g_n) exceeds the warranted growth rate (g_w). To equalize g_n and g_w, we can bring down g_n to g_w by measures to curb labour force growth; we can shift rightwards the S/Y curve through monetary and fiscal policies (and also by foreign borrowing) to raise g_w to g_n, or we can pivot the I/Y curve inwards by reducing c_r through the use of more labour-intensive techniques of production.

Figure 4.2 Adjustment of g_w and g_n

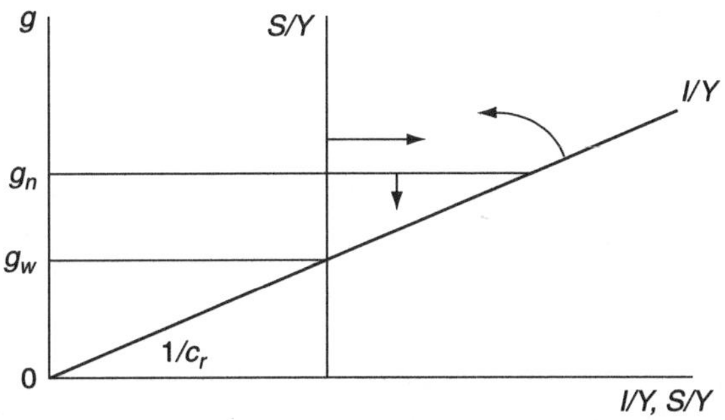

The Harrod framework is not only useful for understanding some of the development difficulties of developing countries, it is also useful for planning purposes. If a country sets a target rate of growth of, say, 5% per annum and the required capital–output ratio is 3, it knows it must save and invest 15% of GDP if the target growth rate is to be achieved. If domestic saving is less than 15% of GDP, there is an investment–savings gap to fill, which might be done by foreign borrowing (see Chapter 14).

At a theoretical level, there has been a great deal of discussion in the literature of whether *automatic* adjustment mechanisms might not come into play to reconcile the divergence between g_n and g_w. In the Harrod model, the parameters and variables that make up the model, l, $\dot{q}$, s and c_r, are all independently determined. Harrod himself recognized that, in the long run the savings ratio may not be fixed, but will adjust. Specifically, in periods of recession, savings may fall, and in periods of demand inflation, savings may rise. One way this may come about is through a change in the functional distribution of income between wages and profits. This is a possible mechanism of adjustment emphasized by the **post-Keynesian economists of Cambridge, England**, represented by Joan Robinson, Nicholas Kaldor, Richard Kahn, Luigi Pasinetti and others. If $g_w > g_n$, and there is a tendency towards depression, this will tend to reduce the share of profits in national income and increase the share of wages, so that if the propensity to save out of profits is higher than the propensity to save out of wages, this change in the distribution of income will lower the overall savings ratio and reduce g_w towards g_n. There is a limit, however, to which the share of profits can fall, given by the minimum rate of profit acceptable to entrepreneurs. Likewise, if $g_w < g_n$, and there is a tendency towards demand inflation, the share of profits in national income will tend to rise, increasing the overall savings ratio and raising g_w towards g_n. There is also a limit, however, to the rise in the profit share, set by the degree to which workers are willing to see their real wages reduced – what Joan Robinson called 'the inflation barrier' (see Chapter 13).

At the same time (the 1950s), in contrast to the Cambridge, England school of post-Keynesian economists, a formidable group of **economists in Cambridge, Massachusetts**, represented by Robert Solow, Paul Samuelson, Franco Modigliani and others, developed the so-called **neoclassical model of growth** as an attack on Harrod and the post-Keynesian school. They pointed out that the gloomy conclusions of Harrod concerning the possibility of achieving steady growth with full employment assume fixed coefficients of production, and that if the capital-labour ratio is allowed to vary, there is the possibility of equilibrium growth at the natural rate. In other words, if capital grows faster than labour ($g_w > g_n$), economies will move smoothly via the price mechanism to more capital-intensive techniques, and growth in the long run will proceed at the exogenously given natural rate. Conversely, if labour grows faster than capital ($g_n > g_w$), the wage rate will fall relative to the price of capital, economies will adopt more labour-intensive techniques, and again growth will proceed at the natural rate.

One central feature of this neoclassical model, which has come under sustained attack in recent years from new growth theory, is that investment does not matter for long-run growth. Any increase in the savings or investment ratio is offset by an increase in the capital–output ratio, because of diminishing returns to capital, leaving the long-run growth rate (at the natural rate) unchanged. The argument depends, however, on the productivity of capital falling (or c_r rising) as the capital–labour ratio rises. This is disputed by the new growth theorists. If there are mechanisms to prevent the productivity of capital from falling as investment increases, then investment does matter for long-run growth and growth is *endogenous* in this sense. But before we turn to new growth theory and the important new studies of the macrodeterminants of growth, we need to consider the assumptions and predictions of neoclassical growth theory, and see how it has been used empirically for understanding the sources of growth in developed and developing countries.

Neoclassical growth theory

There are three basic propositions of neoclassical growth theory:

1. In the long-run steady state, the growth of output is determined by the *rate of growth of the labour force in efficiency units*, that is, by the rate of growth of the labour force plus the rate of growth of labour productivity (exogenously given as in Harrod's natural rate of growth), and is independent of the ratio of saving and investment to GDP. This is so because a higher savings or investment ratio is offset by a higher capital–output ratio or lower productivity of capital, because of the neoclassical assumption of **diminishing returns to capital.**
2. The *level* of per capita income (PCY), however, *does* depend on the ratio of saving and investment to GDP. The level of PCY varies positively with the savings–investment ratio and negatively with the rate of growth of the population.
3. If there is an inverse relation across countries between the capital–labour ratio and the productivity of capital, and tastes (i.e. savings behaviour) and technology are the same across countries, poor countries with a small amount of capital per head should grow faster than rich countries with a lot of capital per head, leading to the *convergence* of per capita incomes and living standards across the world.

Let us now consider how these fundamental propositions are arrived at. The basic **neoclassical growth model** was first developed independently by Robert Solow and Trevor Swan in 1956 and has been very influential in the analysis of growth ever since – particularly the use of the aggregate production function, as we shall see. The model is based on three key assumptions (ignoring technical progress for the moment):

1. The labour force grows at a constant exogenous rate, l.
2. Output is a function of capital and labour: $Y = F(K, L)$; the production function relating output to inputs exhibits constant returns to scale, diminishing returns to individual factors of production, and has a unitary elasticity of substitution between factors (see later).
3. All saving is invested: $S = I = sY$; there is no independent investment function.

What the basic neoclassical growth model is designed to show is that an economy will tend towards a long-run equilibrium capital–labour ratio (k^*) at which output (or income) per head (q^*) is also in equilibrium, so that output, capital and labour all grow at the same rate, l. The model therefore predicts long-run growth equilibrium at the natural rate.

Robert Solow

Born 1924, New York City, USA. Spent all his academic career at the Massachusetts Institute of Technology. Famous for his pioneering work on the theory of economic growth and technical change with his 1956 paper 'A Contribution to the Theory of Economic Growth', which challenged the rigid Harrod model of long-run disequilibrium growth. Also made important contributions to mathematical economics, capital theory and macroeconomics. Received the Nobel Prize for Economics, 1987.

The most commonly used neoclassical production function with constant returns to scale is the so-called **Cobb–Douglas production function**:

$$Y = bK^{\alpha}L^{1-\alpha} \tag{4.13}$$

where α is the elasticity of output with respect to capital, $1-\alpha$ is the elasticity of output with respect to labour, and $\alpha + (1 - \alpha) = 1$, that is, a 1% increase in K and L will lead to a 1% increase in Y, which is what is meant by output exhibiting constant returns to scale.

Equation (4.13) can also be written in 'labour-intensive' form by dividing both sides of the equation by L to give output per head as a function of capital per head:

$$\frac{Y}{L} = \frac{bK^{\alpha}L^{1-\alpha}}{L} = b\left(\frac{K}{L}\right)^{\alpha} \tag{4.14}$$

or, for short:

$$q = b\,(k)^{\alpha} \tag{4.15}$$

This is the 'labour-intensive' form of the neoclassical production function, and can be drawn as in Figure 4.3. The diminishing slope of the function represents the diminishing marginal product of capital.

Now impose a ray from the origin along which the rate of growth of capital is equal to the rate of growth of labour, so that the capital–labour ratio is constant. This is given by:

$$q = (l/s)k \qquad (4.16)^{2}$$

where s is the savings ratio. This straight line from the origin with slope l/s shows the level of q that will keep capital per head constant, and the level of k that will keep output per head constant – given the rate of growth of the labour force, l. Superimposing equation (4.16) on Figure 4.3 gives Figure 4.4.

The slope of the ray from the origin to any point on the production function determines the capital–output ratio at that point. It is clear from Figure 4.4 that only where these two lines cross is an equilibrium capital–labour ratio (k^*) and output per head (q^*) defined. To the left of k^* (at k_1), where $q > (l/s)k$, q is greater than necessary to maintain k constant; that is, there is too much saving and capital accumulation relative to the growth of the labour force, and steady growth requires more capital-intensive techniques. There will be a movement from k_1 towards k^*. The capital–output ratio adjusts to bring the rate of growth of capital and labour (or the warranted and natural growth rates) into line. Similarly, to the right of k^* (at k_2), where $q < (l/s)k$, q is less

Figure 4.3 The 'labour-intensive' form of the neoclassical production function

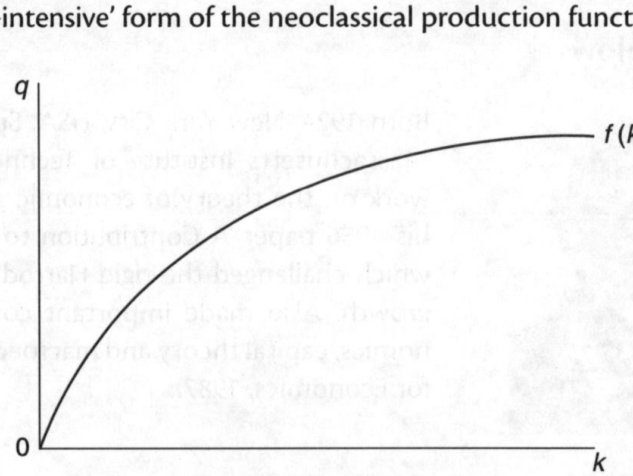

Figure 4.4 Equilibrium capital–labour ratio and output per head

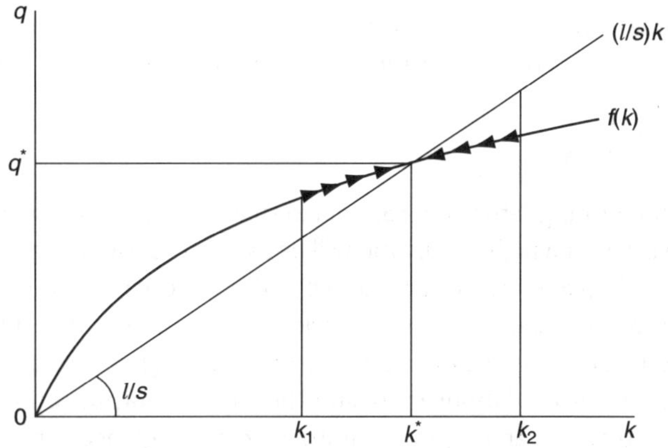

than necessary to maintain k constant; there is too little saving and capital accumulation to keep pace with the rate of growth of the labour force, and steady growth requires more labour-intensive techniques. There will be a movement from k_2 towards k^*. Again, the capital–output ratio adjusts if there is a spectrum of techniques to choose from.

When k reaches an equilibrium, q also reaches an equilibrium, so output must be growing as fast as labour. Thus, output, labour and capital must all be growing at the same rate, l, the natural rate of growth, with the capital–output ratio constant. This is the neoclassical story.

We can now see what happens if there is an increase in the ratio of savings and investment to national income (s). If s rises, this lowers the slope of the l/s line in Figure 4.4, *which increases the equilibrium level of per capita income and the capital–labour ratio, but leaves the equilibrium growth rate unchanged.* This demonstrates formally the first two basic propositions of neoclassical growth theory. The reason a higher savings or investment ratio does not affect the long-run equilibrium growth rate is that a higher savings–investment ratio is ultimately offset by a higher capital–output ratio. The capital–output ratio adjusts 'passively' to keep the growth of capital in line with the growth of the labour force.

None of these conclusions is altered if technical progress is introduced into the model. If technical progress augments the productivity of labour only (so-called Harrod neutral technical progress, which leaves the capital–output ratio unchanged), the *effective* labour force now grows at the rate $l + \dot{q}$, where $\dot{q}$ is the rate of growth of labour productivity. Equilibrium is now defined in terms of output per effective worker and capital per effective worker. Equilibrium capital per worker requires $\Delta K/K = l + \dot{q}$, and equilibrium output per effective worker requires $\Delta Y/Y = l + \dot{q}$, so that capital per head and output per head grow at the same rate $\dot{q}$; that is, by the rate of Harrod neutral technical progress:[3]

$$\Delta Y/Y - l = \Delta K/K - l = \dot{q} \tag{4.17}$$

This is, of course, consistent with what we observe in the real world – output and capital grow faster than the rate of growth of the labour force. But a rise in the ratio of savings and investment to GDP still has no effect on the equilibrium growth of output, unless, of course, a higher level of investment raises the rate of growth of labour-augmenting technical progress, but this is ruled out by assumption in the neoclassical model, because technical progress is assumed to be exogenously determined.

It now only remains to demonstrate the third basic proposition of neoclassical growth theory: that poor countries should grow faster than rich countries, leading to the convergence of per capita incomes because poor countries with a low ratio of capital to labour will have a higher productivity of capital (or lower capital–output ratio). The capital–output ratio may be written as:

$$\frac{K}{Y} = \frac{K}{L} \cdot \frac{L}{Y} \tag{4.18}$$

Given diminishing returns to capital (so that Y/L does not rise in the same proportion as K/L), it can be seen that a higher K/L ratio will be associated with a higher K/Y ratio. This means that if the ratio of savings and investment to GDP is the same across countries, capital-rich countries should grow slower than capital-poor countries. Note, however, that if there are *not* diminishing returns to capital, but, say, constant returns to capital, a higher capital–labour ratio will be exactly offset by a higher output–labour ratio, and the capital–output ratio will not be higher in capital-rich countries than in capital-poor countries, so convergence is not to be expected. If there are not diminishing returns to capital, this also means that the capital–output ratio will not rise as more investment takes place, and therefore **the ratio of saving and investment to GDP does matter for growth. In this sense, growth is endogenously determined**; it is not simply exogenously determined by the rate of growth of the labour force and technical progress. This is the starting point for the new (endogenous) growth theory, which seeks to explain why, in practice, living standards in the world economy have not converged (see Chapter 2), contrary to the predictions of neoclassical theory. The explanation offered by the new growth theory is that there are forces at work that prevent the marginal product of capital from falling (and the capital–output ratio from rising) as more investment takes place as countries get richer. Before turning to the new growth theory, however, let us first consider how the neoclassical production function can be used to analyse the sources of growth. This requires us to look more closely at the concept of the production function and the properties of the Cobb–Douglas production function, which is still widely used in the analysis of growth in developed and developing countries.

The production function approach to the analysis of growth

We have already seen that there are several ways in which the growth of income or output of a country may be expressed, but frequently they consist of identities that tell us very little about the causes or sources of growth. For example, in the Harrod–Domar model, growth can be expressed as the product of the ratio of investment to GDP and the productivity of investment, so that, by definition, slow growth is the product of a low investment ratio and/or a low productivity of capital. By itself, however, this does not further much our understanding of the growth process in different countries. Why do some countries save and invest more than others, and why does the productivity of capital differ? Likewise, we have seen that the growth of output can be expressed as the sum of the rate of growth of the labour force and the rate of growth of labour productivity. By definition, slow growth is attributable to a slow rate of growth of the labour force and/or a slow rate of growth of labour productivity. Again, why does growth in labour productivity differ between countries? Is it because of differences in capital accumulation, or differences in technical progress, broadly defined to include such factors as improvements in the quality of labour, improvements in the quality of capital, economies of scale, advances in knowledge, a better organization of capital and labour in the productive process and so on? Growth identities cannot distinguish between such competing hypotheses.

The production function approach to the analysis of growth is a response to this challenge. It takes the concept of the aggregate production function and attempts to disaggregate the sources of growth into the contribution of labour, capital, technical progress and any other variable included in the production function that is thought to influence the growth process. In this sense, it is a very versatile approach. It is, however, a **supply-oriented** approach. It does not tell us *why* the growth of capital, labour, technical progress and so on differs over time or between countries. The sources of growth are treated as *exogenous*. In practice, however, the supply of most resources to an economic system is endogenous, responding to the demand for them. Capital is a produced means of production and comes from the growth of output itself; labour is very elastic in supply from internal and external sources (migration), and technical progress is itself partly dependent on the growth of output arising from static and dynamic returns to scale.

Thus, while the production function approach can disaggregate any measured growth rate into various constituent growth-inducing sources, and can 'explain' growth rate differences in terms of these sources, it cannot answer the more fundamental question of why labour supply, capital accumulation and technical progress grow at different rates in different countries. The answer to this question must lie in differences in the strength of *demand* for countries' products, which, in the early stages of development, depends largely on the prosperity of agriculture (see Chapter 5), and in the later stages of development depends largely on the country's export performance relative to its import propensity (see Chapter 16).

Having said this, the production function approach can provide a useful **growth accounting** exercise, which is in fact widely used. Apart from deciding which determinants of growth to specify in the production function, and accurately measuring the independent variables, the main problem is a methodological one of fitting the appropriate production function to the data; that is, specifying the function relating output to inputs.

The production function

A desirable property of any macroeconomic hypothesis, apart from being consistent with the observed facts, is that it should be consistent with and derivable from microeconomic theory. What we call the **production function approach to the analysis of growth** in the aggregate possesses, in part, this desirable property, in that it borrows the concept of the production function from the theory of the firm. Just as it can be said that, for a firm, output is a function of the factors of production – land, labour, capital and the level of technology (or factor efficiency) – so aggregate output can be written as a function of factor inputs and the prevailing technology:

$$Y = f(R, K, L, T) \tag{4.19}$$

where R is land, K is capital, L is labour and T is technology.[4]

The question is how to separate empirically the contribution to output growth of the growth of factor inputs from other factors that can lead to higher output, included in T, such as economies of scale (due to technical change and increases in factor supplies), improvements in the quality of factor inputs, advances in knowledge, better organization of factors and so on. The task is to fit an appropriate, correctly specified production function that, if possible, will not only separate the contribution of factor inputs to growth from the contribution of increases in output per unit of inputs (increases in 'total' factor productivity), but will also distinguish between some of the factors that may contribute to increases in the productivity of factors, such as education, improvements in the quality of capital, and economies of scale.

Before going on to discuss the types of function that may be employed, let us examine in a little more detail the properties of a production function. We have established so far that the aggregate production function expresses the functional relation between aggregate output and the stock of inputs. If land is subsumed into capital, and technology is held constant, we are left with two factors, and the production function may be drawn on a two-dimensional diagram, as in Figure 4.5. Capital (*K*) is measured on the vertical axis and labour (*L*) on the horizontal axis, and each function represents a given level of output that can be produced with different combinations of capital and labour. The functions slope negatively from left to right on the assumption that marginal additions of either factor will increase total output – that is, factors have positive marginal products – and they are drawn convex to the origin on the assumption that factors have a diminishing marginal productivity as their supply increases, so that if one unit is withdrawn, it needs to be substituted by more and more of the other factor to keep output constant. The position of the functions broadly reflects the level of technology. The more 'advanced' the technology, the greater the level of output per unit of total inputs, and the closer to the origin will be the production function representing a *given* output.

Figure 4.5 The production function

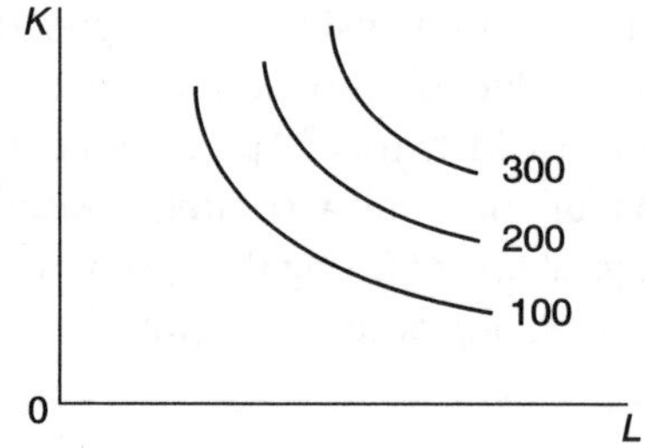

From the simple production function diagram, it is easy to see how output may increase. First, there may be a physical increase in factor inputs, *L* and *K*, permitting a higher level of production. Either or both factors may increase. If only one factor increases, the movement to a higher production function will involve a change in the combination of factors, and output will not be able to increase forever, because ultimately the marginal product of the variable factor will fall to zero. This is illustrated in Figure 4.6, where, with a given stock of capital $0K_1$, output cannot increase beyond 300 with increases in the supply of labour ($0L_1$, $0L_2$ and so on) beyond the limit indicated. The diminishing productivity of the variable factor, labour, with

Figure 4.6 Production function diagram

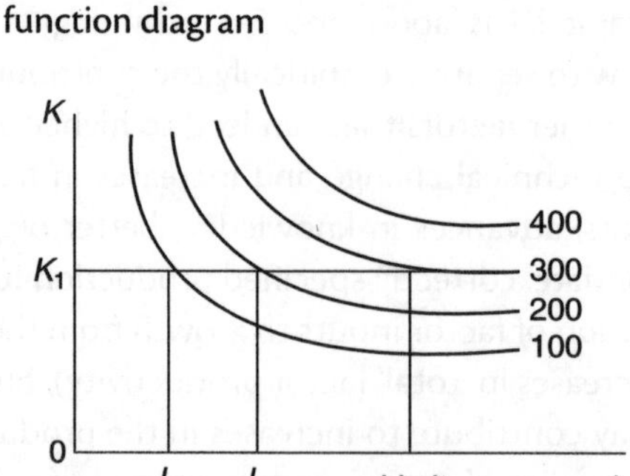

Figure 4.7 The effect of increasing returns

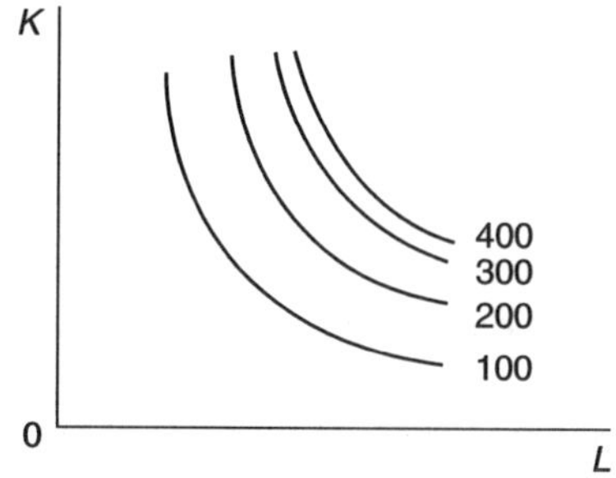

capital fixed, is shown by the flatter and flatter slope of the production functions at successive points, L_1, L_2, until, at the limit, the production function is horizontal and the marginal product of labour is zero.

If both factors increase in supply, however, there is no reason why output should not go on increasing indefinitely. In fact, if both factors increase in supply, there is a possibility that production may be subject to increasing returns, such that output rises more than proportionately to the increase in combined inputs. If this is the case, output per unit of total inputs will increase and the production functions representing equal additional amounts of production, for example 100, 200, 300 and so on, must be drawn closer and closer together, as in Figure 4.7.

In the opposite case of decreasing returns, the functions would be drawn further and further apart. Finally, in the case of production subject to constant returns, the functions would be drawn equidistant from one another.

Increasing returns may also result from advances in technology, irrespective of increases in factor supplies. These are called **technological economies of scale**. In this case, increases in output per unit of input would have to be represented on a production function diagram either by relabelling the functions or relabelling the axes. That is, either the same amount of factor inputs, measured on the axes, would have to be shown to be producing a higher output than before, or the same output could be shown to be produced by lesser amounts of inputs. If the functions are relabelled and not the axes, this is tantamount to a shift in all the production functions towards the origin. Shifts in the production function towards the origin are implied by all forms of technical progress or any factor that increases the productivity of the physical inputs.

In short, three broad sources of growth can be distinguished using the production function framework:

1. Increases in factor supplies
2. Increasing returns
3. Technical progress, interpreted in the wide sense of anything that increases the productivity of factors other than increasing returns.

The Cobb–Douglas production function

The production function most commonly fitted to aggregate data to distinguish empirically between these three broad sources of growth has been the unconstrained form of the **Cobb–Douglas production function**, named after its two American originators, Charles Cobb (a mathematician) and Paul Douglas (an economist), who pioneered research in the area of applied economic growth in the 1920s and 1930s (Cobb and Douglas, 1928). The Cobb–Douglas function may be written as:

$$Y_t = T_t K_t^{\alpha} L_t^{\beta} \tag{4.20}$$

where Y_t is real output at time, t, T_t is an index of technology, or 'total' productivity, K_t is an index of the capital stock, or capital services, at constant prices, L_t is an index of labour input (preferably man-hours), α is the partial elasticity (responsiveness) of output with respect to capital (holding labour constant), and β is the partial elasticity of output with respect to labour (holding capital constant).

It is assumed that changes in technology are exogenous and independent of changes in factor inputs, and that the effect of technical progress is neutral on the factor intensity of production (see Chapter 6 for a definition of neutral technical progress). T_t, α and β are constants to be estimated empirically if the function is unconstrained. If α and β are assigned values in advance of the use of the function for estimating purposes, the function is said to be constrained. Normally, α and β will be less than unity on the assumption of diminishing marginal productivity of factors. The sum of the partial elasticities of output with respect to the factors of production gives the scale of returns, or the degree of homogeneity, of the function: $\alpha + \beta = 1$ represents constant returns, $\alpha + \beta > 1$ represents increasing returns, and $\alpha + \beta < 1$ represents decreasing returns, and the function is said to be homogeneous of degree one, greater than one, and less than one, respectively.

If α and β are not estimated empirically but are assumed to sum to unity, in which case the function will be constrained to constant returns, then increasing or decreasing returns will be reflected in the value of T_t, which is the index of total factor productivity. The existence of increasing returns would bias the value of T_t upwards, and decreasing returns would bias the value of T_t downwards. These points are made because, in practice, the Cobb–Douglas function is often employed in this constrained form with the sum of α and β put equal to unity. Then values are assigned to α and β according to the share of capital and labour in the national income. The underlying assumption is the perfectly competitive one that if production is subject to constant returns and factors are paid the value of their marginal products, then factor shares will reflect the elasticity of output with respect to each factor.[5]

In order to use equation (4.20) to separate the influence of the three broad sources of growth mentioned earlier, we must first make it operational by transforming it into *rate of growth* form. This can be done by taking logarithms of the variables and differentiating with respect to time, which gives:[6]

$$\frac{d \log Y_t}{dt} = \frac{d \log T_t}{dt} + \alpha \frac{d \log K_t}{dt} + \beta \frac{d \log L_t}{dt} \tag{4.21}$$

or:

$$\frac{dY}{dt} \times \frac{1}{Y} = \left(\frac{dT}{dt} \times \frac{1}{T}\right) + \alpha\left(\frac{dK}{dt} \times \frac{1}{K}\right) + \beta\left(\frac{dL}{dt} \times \frac{1}{L}\right)$$

The above equations are in continuous time. The discrete approximation, taking annual rates of change of the variables, may be written as:

$$r_Y = r_T + \alpha r_K + \beta r_L \tag{4.22}$$

where r_Y is the annual rate of growth of output per time period, r_T is the annual rate of growth of total productivity, or technical progress, r_K is the annual rate of growth of capital, r_L is the annual rate of growth of labour, and α and β are the partial elasticities of output with respect to capital and labour, respectively, as before.

In other words, equation (4.22) says that the rate of growth of output is equal to the sum of the rate of growth of 'total' factor productivity, the rate of growth of capital weighted by the partial elasticity of output with respect to capital and the rate of growth of labour weighted by the partial elasticity of output with respect to labour. With knowledge of r_Y, r_K, r_L, α and β, it becomes possible as a first step to separate out the contribution of factor inputs to growth from increases in output per unit of inputs represented by r_T. Now let us give an illustrative example. Suppose $r_Y = 5\%$ per annum, $r_K = 5\%$ per annum, $r_L = 1\%$ per annum, $\alpha = 0.25$ and $\beta = 0.75$ (decided on the basis of factor shares). Substituting in equation (4.22), we have:

$$5.0 = r_T + 0.25\,(5.0) + 0.75\,(1.0) \tag{4.23}$$

The contribution of capital to measured growth is 0.25 (5.0) = 1.25 percentage points; the contribution of labour is 0.75 (1.0) = 0.75 percentage points; and r_T is left as a residual with a contribution of 3.0 percentage points. If α and β were estimated empirically and there happened to be increasing returns ($\alpha + \beta > 1$), the significance of the factor contribution would be enhanced and r_T would be smaller.

On the assumption of constant returns to scale, the production function can also be estimated in its so-called labour-intensive form to analyse the **growth of output per head** (see equation (4.14)). If we subtract r_L from both sides of equation (4.22) and assume $\alpha + \beta = 1$, so that $\beta = 1 - \alpha$, we get:

$$r_Y - r_L = r_T + \alpha\,(r_K - r_L) \tag{4.24}$$

which means that the rate of growth of output per head (or labour productivity) is equal to the sum of the rate of growth of total productivity plus the rate of growth of capital per head times the elasticity of output with respect to capital. Taking the illustrative figures above, if $r_Y = 5\%$ and $r_L = 1\%$, then the rate of labour productivity growth is 4%. Therefore:

$$4.0 = r_T + 0.25\,(5.0 - 1.0) \tag{4.25}$$

The contribution of capital per head (capital deepening) to productivity growth is 1 percentage point, leaving r_T with a contribution of 3 percentage points (as before).

Although r_T has been variously called 'technical progress', 'advances in knowledge' and so on, it is, by definition, that portion of the growth of output not attributable to increases in the factors of production, and includes the effects not only of the multifarious factors that increase the productivity of labour and capital but also any measurement errors in the capital and labour input series. Perhaps r_T is best described as a residual, or, perhaps more appropriately still, a 'coefficient of ignorance' if the analysis proceeds no further.

One important component of r_T, which can be considered the result of measurement errors, is likely to be the effect of **resource shifts** from less productive to more productive activities. Since the analysis is aggregative, there is bound to be a confounding of changes in actual output with changes in the composition of output unless the weights used for aggregating inputs are continually revised. Resource shifts from agriculture to industry can be expected to figure prominently in any production function study of developing countries, as they do for studies of many advanced economies.

Limitations of the Cobb–Douglas function

Before considering some of the results of applying the Cobb–Douglas function to empirical data, we must briefly mention some of its limitations. Its use has come under attack on four main counts. First, since only one combination of factor inputs can be observed at any one time, there is an identification problem in attempting to distinguish shifts in the function (technical progress) from movements along the function (changes in factor intensity), unless the assumption of neutral technical progress is made. But technical progress may not be neutral and therefore the effects of technical progress and changing factor intensity become confused, biasing the results of the contribution of factor inputs and technical progress to growth.

Second, the assumption that technical progress is independent of increases in factor inputs can been questioned. This is not a specification error of the function itself, however, and the Cobb–Douglas function can be used, making technical progress a function of the rate of growth of inputs – so-called 'endogenous models of technical progress'.

Third, the Cobb–Douglas function possesses the restrictive property of constant unitary elasticity of substitution between factors, whatever the factor intensity.[7] The assumption of constant elasticity means that the function cannot represent a change in the ease of substitution between capital and labour. The assumption of unitary elasticity may be serious if the elasticity of substitution of factors differs significantly from unity and there are wide discrepancies in the growth rate of factors. For example, if the elasticity of substitution between capital and labour is significantly less than unity, and capital grows faster than labour, this will result in an overestimate of the contribution of capital to growth and an underestimate of the role of other factors. The intuitive explanation of this bias is that the smaller the elasticity of substitution, the more difficult it is in practice to obtain increased output just by increasing one factor, because diminishing returns set in strongly. By assuming the elasticity is higher than it is, the importance of the fastest growing factor is exaggerated. If elasticity is high, diminishing returns are not a problem, and if both capital and labour expand at the same rate, growth is obviously independent of the elasticity of substitution.[8]

A final criticism relates to the measurement of output and inputs. What, argue some, is the meaning of a function that aggregates so many heterogeneous items; in particular, what is the meaning of an aggregation of capital goods built at different times, at different costs and with varying productivities? How are such capital goods to be equated and added in an aggregate measure of capital?

By and large, most of the above-mentioned criticisms are theoretical worries, the practical significance of which is hard to determine. Studies of the nature of technical progress, at least in advanced countries, suggest that the assumption of neutrality is a fair working hypothesis. The fact that technical progress may be dependent on factor accumulation can be accommodated within the Cobb–Douglas framework. Capital and labour would have to grow at very different rates for the value of the elasticity of substitution to matter very much, but, in any case, studies show that it is quite close to unity. Finally, although the aggregation of heterogeneous outputs and inputs can present severe problems, especially the aggregation of capital, which cannot be measured directly in physical units, there are techniques of aggregation available that various studies have used with some success.

Application of the Cobb–Douglas function

What have been the results of applying the Cobb–Douglas function to empirical data? First, let us consider its application in developed countries and consider the conclusions that emerge. We can start with the pioneering work of Cobb and Douglas themselves. Ironically, the Cobb–Douglas function, as first conceived, was not intended as a device for distinguishing the sources of growth but as a test of neoclassical marginal productivity theory; that is, to see whether elasticities of output with respect to labour and capital corresponded to the shares of factors of production in national income. Douglas had observed that the output curve for US manufacturing industry for the period 1899–1922 lay consistently between the two curves for the factors of production, and he suggested to his mathematician friend Cobb that they should seek to develop a formula that could measure the relative effect of labour and capital on the growth of output over the period in question. This story is described by Douglas (1948 p. 20) in his fascinating review article 'Are There Laws of Production?' As an insight into the inductive method, the relevant passage is worth quoting in full:

> Having computed indexes for American manufacturing of the number of workers employed by years from 1899 to 1922 as well as indexes of the amounts of fixed capital in manufacturing deflated to dollars of approximately constant purchasing power, and then plotting these on a log scale, together with the Day index of physical production for manufacturing, I observed that the product curve lay consistently between the two curves for the factors of production and tended to be approximately one-quarter of the relative distance between the curve of the index for labour, which showed the least increase in the period, and that of the index of capital which showed the most. I suggested to my friend Charles Cobb that we seek to develop a formula which could measure the relative effect of labour and capital upon product during this period. At his suggestion the sum of the exponents was tentatively made equal to unity in the formula $Y = TK^{\alpha}L^{1-\alpha}$ [our notation] . . . The fact that on the basis of fairly wide studies there is an appreciable degree of uniformity, and that the sum of the exponents approximates to unity, fairly clearly suggests that there are laws of production which can be approximated by inductive studies and that we are at least approaching them.

The estimated function derived was $Y = 1.01K^{0.25}L^{0.75}$, which lent support to the neoclassical model of constant returns and marginal product pricing. There was no discussion of the relative importance of factors of production and the T variable in accounting for measured growth. It was not until Abramovitz (1956) and Solow (1957) showed that 80–90% of the growth of output per head in the US economy in the first half of the twentieth century could not be accounted for by increases in capital per head that the production function started to be used in earnest as a technique in the applied economics of growth. Abramovitz (1956, p. 11) remarked that:

> This result is surprising in the lop-sided importance which it appears to give to productivity increase and it should be, in a sense, sobering, if not discouraging to students of economic growth. Since we know little about the causes of productivity increase, the indicated importance of this element may be taken to be some sort of measure of our ignorance about the causes of economic growth in the USA, and some sort of indication of where we need to concentrate our attention.

Abramovitz's findings were supported by Solow, who found, when examining the data for the non-farm sector of the US economy for the period 1919–57, that approximately 90% of the growth of output per head could not be accounted for by increases in capital per head; that is, using the notation in equation (4.24):

$$r_T/(r_Y - r_L) = 0.90 \tag{4.26}$$

The findings of Abramovitz and Solow disturbed economists brought up in the belief that investment and capital accumulation played a crucial role in the growth process. Even allowing for the statistical difficulties of computing a series of the capital stock, and the limitations of the function applied to the data (for example, the assumption of constant returns and neutral technical progress, plus the high degree of aggregation), it was difficult to escape from the conclusion that the growth of the capital stock was of relatively minor importance in accounting for the growth of total output.

It would not be misleading to say that much of the subsequent research effort in this field of growth was designed (even before the advent of new growth theory) to reverse this conclusion, or rather to 'assign back' to the factors of production sources of growth that make up the residual factor but are interrelated with, or dependent on, the growth of factor inputs. Work has proceeded on two fronts. On the one hand, attempts have been made to disaggregate the residual factor, measuring factor inputs in the conventional way; on the other hand, attempts have been made to adjust the labour and capital input series for such things as changes in the *quality* of factors and their composition, so that much more measured growth is seen to be attributable to increases in factor inputs in the first place. For example, the labour input series has been adjusted for improvements in its quality due to the growth of education, and for changes in its composition due to age/sex shifts. Likewise, the capital stock series has been adjusted to reflect changes in its composition and, more importantly, to allow for the fact that new additions to the capital stock in any line of production are likely to be more productive than the existing capital stock as a result of technical advance. This is the notion of **embodied** or **endogenous technical change** as opposed to the exogenous technical change assumption of the original Cobb–Douglas function, which assumes that all vintages of capital share equally in technical progress.

A distinction is made, therefore, between embodied and disembodied technical progress – 'embodied technical progress' refers to technical improvements that can only be introduced into the productive system by new investment, and 'disembodied technical progress' is exogenous and not dependent on capital accumulation. There are several ways in which embodied technical progress can be isolated from the residual factor by appropriate adjustments to the capital stock series to reflect the greater productivity of the latest investments. The net result is to enhance the role of capital accumulation in the growth process.

Efforts have also been made to overcome one of the problems associated with the aggregation of outputs by taking explicit account of shifts of labour and capital from low-productivity to high-productivity sectors. This, too, reduces the significance of the residual factor and makes the role of labour and capital in the growth process look correspondingly more important.

Since Abramovitz and Solow reported their findings in 1956 and 1957, a substantial body of empirical evidence relating to the sources of growth has accumulated, experimenting with different specifications of the aggregate production function. Unfortunately, it is not systematic. The time periods taken, the data used, the sectors of the economy examined, and the methodology employed all vary within and between countries.

Until recently, most of the evidence available pertained to fairly advanced economies and it is largely from this evidence, wisely or not, that conclusions have been drawn on development strategy for developing countries. Research in developing countries has been hampered by a shortage of reliable empirical data and perhaps an even greater suspicion of the aggregate production function, and its implicit assumptions, than in developed countries. The assumption that factor shares can be used as weights to measure the relative contribution of labour and capital to growth is probably more dubious in developing countries than in developed countries. First, the price of labour almost certainly exceeds its marginal product, while the price of capital falls short of it so that the share of income going to labour exceeds the elasticity of output with respect to labour and the share of income going to capital understates the elasticity of output with respect to capital. Second, the aggregation of inputs and outputs is generally more difficult, and there are greater problems of resource underutilization to contend with. The recent past, however, has witnessed a number of production function studies for developing countries.

Production function studies of developing countries

Two of the early production function studies of the sources of growth in developing countries are by Maddison (1970) and Robinson (1971) (surveyed, with others, by Nadiri, 1972). More recent studies include the World Bank (1991), Young (1995), Hu and Khan (1997), Felipe (1999), Senhadji (2000), and Sala-í-Martin (1997) who surveys other studies. Let us consider these studies and bring out their major conclusions, especially any important contrasts with the conclusions from studies of developed countries.

The major conclusions of the early production function studies of developing countries were:

- Capital accumulation is more important as a source of growth than total productivity growth, and more important than in developed countries.
- Improvements in the *quality* of labour are important through better health, nutrition and education.
- Resource shifts are not as important as might have been expected, perhaps due to the general surplus of labour in developing countries and the low capacity to absorb labour into productive employment in the industrial sector.

Now let us turn to the more recent studies. Table 4.1 provides the results of a World Bank study for the period 1960–87, showing the contribution of factor inputs and total productivity growth to the growth of output in various continents. It is clear that the major source of growth is not productivity growth, but the growth of inputs themselves.

Young (1995) has used the production function model to debunk the idea that there has been a 'growth miracle' in the four East Asian countries of Hong Kong, Singapore, South Korea and Taiwan (the so-called 'tigers' or 'little dragons'). Young uses the production function approach and shows that while the growth of output was spectacular over the 1966–90 period, most of the growth can be accounted for by the rapid growth of factor inputs and there was nothing abnormal about the growth of total factor productivity. Table 4.2 presents the figures. Young describes such calculations as 'the tyranny of numbers', by which he means that there is nothing special to explain. On the basis of Young's calculations, Krugman (1994) has described the 'Asian miracle'

Table 4.1 Contribution of factor inputs and total productivity growth to economic growth in 68 developing countries, 1960–87

	GDP growth (% p.a.)	Contribution of labour	Contribution of capital	Total factor productivity
Africa	3.3	1.0	2.3	0.0
East Asia	6.8	1.1	3.8	1.9
Europe, Middle East and North Africa	5.0	0.7	2.9	1.4
Latin America	3.6	1.2	2.4	0.0
South Asia	4.4	0.9	2.9	0.6
68 economies	4.2	1.0	2.6	0.6

Source: World Bank, 1991.

Table 4.2 Growth of output and total factor productivity in the East Asian 'tigers', 1966–90 (%)

	Output growth	Total factor productivity growth
Hong Kong	7.3	2.3
Singapore	8.7	0.2
South Korea	8.5	1.7
Taiwan	8.5	2.1

Source: Compiled from Young, 1995.

as a myth. The spectacular growth of inputs, however, does need explaining. The rapid growth of capital and labour is a function of an internal dynamism fuelled by the relentless and successful drive for export markets, partly engineered by deliberate government intervention. East Asia is not the bastion of free-market enterprise that is often portrayed. The growth of factor inputs may decelerate in the future, but the performance of these four economies up to 1990 was indeed remarkable, notwithstanding the relatively low rate of growth of total factor productivity.

Hu and Khan (1997) use the production function[9] approach to understand the sources of fast growth in China over the period 1953–94, and the acceleration of growth after the economic reforms and 'open door' policy were introduced in 1978. From 1953 to 1978, GDP grew at 5.8% per annum, and then accelerated to 9.3% per annum from 1979 to 1994. Why was this? To estimate the contribution of labour, capital and total factor productivity (TFP) to measured growth over the periods, factor shares of GDP are taken as the elasticities of output with respect to labour and capital, with labour's elasticity approximately 0.4, and capital's elasticity approximately 0.6. The results are shown in Table 4.3.

To give an example, in the pre-reform period 1953–78, the growth of capital was 6.2% per annum. Multiplying 6.2 by 0.6 (capital's elasticity) gives a contribution of capital to growth of 3.72 percentage points, which is approximately 65% of the total growth of output of 5.8%. Capital accumulation was by far the most important contributor to growth in this period. In the post-reform period 1979–94, however, it can be seen that the contribution of productivity growth increases considerably to almost equal importance with capital. The rate of growth of TFP more than triples, from 1.1% per annum to 3.9%, contributing over 40% to measured growth. According to Hu and Khan (1997), the process of reform stimulated productivity growth in a number of ways, including the transfer of resources from agriculture to industry, a reallocation of resources from the public to the private sector, the encouragement of foreign direct investment (FDI), and a faster growth of exports.

Table 4.3 Sources of growth in China, 1953–94 (%)

	1953–94	1953–78	1979–94
Output growth	7.2	5.8	9.3
Capital input growth	6.8	6.2	7.7
Labour input growth	2.6	2.5	2.7
TFP growth	2.1	1.1	3.9
Contribution of capital	55.6	65.2	45.6
Contribution of labour	14.9	16.8	12.8
Contribution of productivity growth	29.5	18.0	41.6

Source: Hu and Khan, 1997.

Felipe (1999) surveys the studies done of TFP growth in the whole of East Asia, most of which use the production function approach. He is critical of many of them, and shows how estimates of TFP can vary according to the time period taken, the estimates made of the growth of factor inputs, and the assumed elasticities of output with respect to labour and capital. Remember that TFP is obtained as a residual after the contribution of the factor inputs has been calculated. The various methodological and conceptual problems associated with the use of production functions discussed earlier are also emphasized, particularly the assumption that technical progress and factor inputs are exogenous and not interrelated.

The most comprehensive recent study of the sources of growth using the aggregate production function comes from Senhadji (2000) at the IMF. He estimates production functions for 66 countries over the period 1960–94 (including 46 developing countries) of the form: $Y = TK^{\alpha}(LH)^{1-\alpha}$, where T is TFP, K is the stock of capital, L is the active population and H is an index of human capital. The function is estimated using both levels of the variables (measured in logarithms) and taking first differences of the log level (i.e. in rate of growth form – see equation (4.21)). The estimates of the elasticity of output with respect to capital (α) vary considerably across countries (and regions) and also according to whether levels or first differences of the variables are used (which is another problem). Using levels, the estimates of (α) range from 0.43 in sub-Saharan Africa to 0.63 in the Middle East and North Africa. Using first differences, the estimates of α range from 0.30 in East Asia to 0.62 in Latin America. Using the mean value of α from the equations estimated in levels gives the sources of growth in different regions shown in Table 4.4.

It can be seen again from Table 4.4 that capital accumulation is by far the most important contributor to measured growth in all the regions. The small contribution of TFP in the fastest growing region of East Asia confirms the conclusions of Young (1995). Notice also, the *negative* contribution of TFP in Africa and Latin America. Human capital formation makes a positive contribution to growth in all regions, but a relatively minor one.

It is satisfying that the conclusions from a wide range of studies using different techniques and dubious data should all point in roughly the same direction:

1. The major source of growth in developing countries is increased factor inputs, aided by improvements in the quality of labour through health improvement and education.
2. The growth of 'total' factor productivity in developing countries is relatively slow compared with that in developed countries, which may be partly a reflection of the different stage of development reached.
3. Resource transfers from agriculture to industry are quite important as a source of growth, but not as important as one might have expected. They will become more important as the ability of the industrial sector to absorb surplus labour increases.

Table 4.4 Sources of growth by region of the world, 1960–94

Region	Output growth (%)	Contribution (percentage points) of:			TFP
		Capital	Labour	Human capital	
East Asia	6.49	4.50	1.27	0.44	0.28
South Asia	4.66	2.87	0.99	0.25	0.55
Sub-Saharan Africa	2.83	1.79	1.39	0.22	−0.56
Middle East & North Africa	5.05	3.99	0.84	0.25	−0.03
Latin America	3.42	2.31	1.22	0.28	−0.39

Source: Senhadji, 2000.

Before ending, it should be said again that the aggregate models that produced the above results are rough tools. They do, however, give an important idea of the forces at work and a rough idea of the likely quantitative significance of different factors. The production function approach is also a versatile tool of analysis. Sala-í-Martin (1997) has surveyed a number of production function studies and found that researchers have included at least 62 different variables in the production function to explain growth, in addition to the growth of capital and labour.

'New' (endogenous) growth theory and the macrodeterminants of growth[10]

Since the mid-1980s there has been an outpouring of literature and research on the applied economics of growth, attempting to understand and explain the differences in the rates of output growth and per capita income growth across the world, many inspired by the so-called 'new' growth theory, or endogenous growth theory. This spate of cross-sectional studies seems to have been prompted by a number of factors:

- Increased concern with the economic performance of the poorer regions of the world, and particularly the striking differences between countries and continents.
- The increased availability of standardized data (e.g. Summers and Heston, 1991; and the World Bank *World Development Indicators*), enabling more reliable econometric work.
- Pioneering studies (e.g. Baumol, 1986) that could find no convergence of per capita incomes in the world economy, contrary to the prediction of neoclassical growth theory based on the assumption of diminishing returns to capital, which, given identical preferences and technology across countries, should lead to faster growth in poor countries than in rich ones.

It is the latter finding (although hardly new, as outlined in Chapter 2) that has been the major inspiration behind the development of the 'new' growth theory, which relaxes the assumption of diminishing returns to capital and shows that, with constant or increasing returns, there can be no presumption of the convergence of per capita incomes across the world, or of individual countries reaching a long-run steady-state growth equilibrium at the natural rate. If there are not diminishing returns to capital, investment is important for long-run growth and growth is endogenous in this sense. In these 'new' models of endogenous growth, pioneered by Robert Lucas (1988) and Paul Romer (1986, 1990), there are assumed to be positive externalities associated with human capital formation (e.g. education and training) and research and development (R&D) that prevent the marginal product of capital from falling and the capital–output ratio from rising. We have a production function in capital of:

$$Y = AK^{\alpha} \tag{4.27}$$

where K is a composite measure of capital (i.e. physical capital plus other types of reproducible capital), and $\alpha = 1$. This is the so-called **AK model** of new growth theory. As Barro and Sala-í-Martin (2003) put it: 'the global absence of diminishing returns may seem unrealistic, but the idea becomes more plausible if we think of K in a broad sense to include [for example] human capital'. It can be seen from the expression for the capital–output ratio, that is:

$$\frac{K}{Y} = \frac{K}{L} . \frac{L}{Y} \tag{4.28}$$

that anything that raises the productivity of labour (Y/L) in the same proportion as K/L will keep the capital–output ratio constant. Learning by doing and embodied technical progress in the spirit of Arrow (1962) and Kaldor (1957), as well as technological spillovers from trade (Grossman and Helpman, 1990, 1991) and FDI (de Mello, 1996), are other possibilities in addition to education and R&D.

The first crude test of the new growth theory is to see whether or not poor countries do grow faster than rich ones, or, in other words, to see whether there is an inverse relation between the growth of output (or output per head) and the *initial* level of per capita income. If there is, this would provide support for the neoclassical model. If there is not, this would support the new growth theory's assertion that the marginal product of capital does not decline. The equation to be estimated is:

$$g_i = a + b_1 (PCY)_i \tag{4.29}$$

where g_i is the average growth of output per head of country i over a number of years and PCY_i is its initial level of per capita income. A significantly negative estimate of b_1 would be evidence of **unconditional convergence**, or **beta (β) convergence** as it is called in the literature; that is, poor countries growing faster than rich without allowing for any other economic, social or political differences between countries. As we saw in Chapter 2, none of the studies taking large samples of developed and developing countries has been able to find evidence of unconditional convergence. The estimate of b_1 is not significantly negative; in fact, it is invariably positive, indicating divergence.[11]

Before jumping to the conclusion that this is a rejection of the neoclassical model, it must be remembered that the neoclassical prediction of convergence assumes that the savings or investment ratio, population growth, technology and all factors that affect the productivity of labour are the same across countries. Since these assumptions are manifestly false, there can never be the presumption of unconditional convergence (even if there are diminishing returns to capital), only **conditional convergence**, holding constant all other factors that influence the growth of per capita income, including population growth (p), the investment ratio (I/Y) and variables that affect the productivity of labour, for example education (ED), research and development expenditure ($R + D$), trade (T) and even non-economic variables such as political stability measured by the number of revolutions and coups (PS). The equation to be estimated is therefore:

$$g_i = a + b_1(PCY)_i + b_2(p)_i + b_3(I/Y)_i + b_4(ED)_i + b_5(R + D)_i + b_6(T)_i + b_7(PS)_i + \ldots \tag{4.30}$$

and the question to be asked is: What happens to the sign of the initial per capita income variable (PCY) when these other variables are introduced into the equation? If the sign turns negative ($b_1 < 0$) when allowance is made for these other factors, this is supposed to represent a rehabilitation of the neoclassical model (see Barro, 1991); that is, there *would be* convergence if it were not for differences between rich and poor countries in all these other important variables in the growth process. New growth theory would be supported by finding that education, R&D expenditure and so on matter, and it is these factors that keep the marginal product of capital from falling, producing actual divergence in the world economy.

Note here that if the model of new growth theory is represented by the AK model, as in equation (4.27), this can be shown to be equivalent to the Harrod–Domar growth equation. Assuming $\alpha = 1$, totally differentiate equation (4.27) and divide by Y. This gives:

$$dY/Y = A(dK/Y) = A(I/Y) \tag{4.31}$$

where dY/Y is the growth rate, I/Y is the investment ratio, and A is the productivity of capital (dY/I), which is the reciprocal of the incremental capital–output ratio. This is the same as the Harrod growth equation $g = s/c$, where s is the savings ratio and c is the incremental capital–output ratio, or the Domar equation $g = s\sigma$, where σ is the productivity of capital.

If the productivity of capital was the same across countries, there would be a perfect correlation between the growth rate of countries and the investment ratio where the slope of the relationship is the reciprocal of the incremental capital–output ratio (c). If there is not a perfect correlation, then, by definition, the productivity of capital, or the capital–output ratio, must differ between countries. New growth theory equations that attempt to explain growth rate differences between countries (such as equation (4.30) – and see empirical studies later) are really asking the question (and hopefully answering it): Why does the productivity of capital differ between countries (assuming I/Y is included in the equations)? (See Nell and Thirlwall, 2016.)

We said above that evidence of conditional convergence delights the neoclassical economists because it is interpreted as a rehabilitation of the neoclassical growth model with diminishing returns, but this may be a hasty judgement. Outside the neoclassical paradigm, there is another distinct body of literature that argues that economic growth *should be* inversely related to the initial level of per capita income because the more backward the country, the greater the scope for **catch-up**; that is, for absorbing a backlog of technology (see Gomulka, 1971, 1990; Abramovitz, 1986; Dowrick and Nguyen, 1989; Dowrick and Gemmell, 1991; Amable, 1993). Thus, the negative sign on the per capita income variable could be picking up the effect of catch-up, and the notion of catch-up is conceptually distinct from the *shape* of the production function and whether or not there are diminishing returns to capital. How are the two effects to be distinguished? As Benhabib and Spiegel (1994) remark in their paper on the role of human capital in development: 'a negative coefficient estimate on initial income levels may not be a sign of convergence due to diminishing returns, but of catch up from adoption of technology from abroad. These two forces may be observationally equivalent in simple cross-section growth accounting exercises'. Also, output growth will be a function of the stage of development because of sectoral differences in the productivity growth rates of agriculture, industry and services, so that convergence may also be partly 'structural', independent of both diminishing returns and catch-up (see Cornwall and Cornwall, 1994). This adds further complications to the interpretation of the coefficient relating country growth rates to the initial level of per capita income.

Now let us turn to the question of the capital–output ratio. Non-diminishing returns to capital, or constancy of the capital–output ratio, lie at the heart of new growth theory, as pioneered by Lucas and Romer, who emphasize externalities to education and research. For the historical record, however, it should be mentioned that, many years ago, Cambridge economist Nicholas Kaldor pointed out the fact that despite continued capital accumulation and increases in capital per head through time, the capital–output ratio remains broadly the same, implying some form of externalities or constant returns to capital. It is worth quoting Kaldor (1961) in full:

> As regards the process of economic change and development in capitalist societies, I suggest the following 'stylised facts' as a starting point for the construction of theoretical models . . . (4) steady capital–output ratios over long periods; at least there are no clear long-term trends, either rising or falling, if differences in the degree of capital utilisation are allowed for. This implies, or reflects, the near identity in the percentage rate of growth of production and of the capital stock i.e. for the economy as a whole, and over long periods, income and capital tend to grow at the same rate.

Kaldor's explanation (as a critique of the neoclassical production function) lay in his innovation of the **technical progress function**, which relates the rate of growth of output per worker $\dot{q}$ to the rate of growth of capital per worker $\dot{k}$, as depicted in Figure 4.8.

Figure 4.8 Kaldor's technical progress function

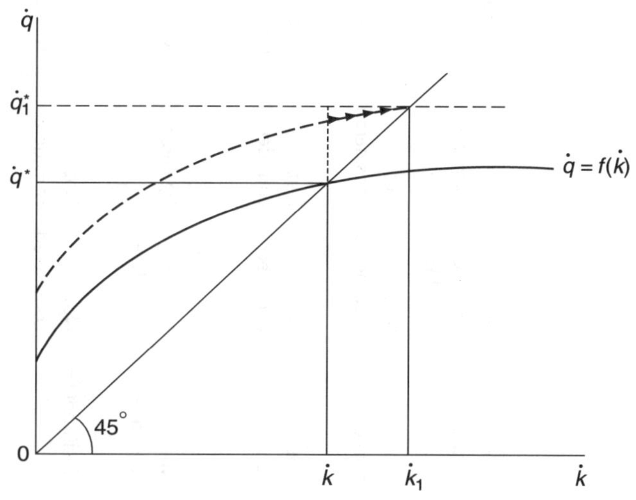

The position of the function depends on the exogenous rate of technical progress, and the slope of the function depends on the extent to which technical progress is embodied in capital. Along the 45° line the capital–output ratio is constant, and the equilibrium growth of output per head will be at $\dot{q}$. An upward shift of the technical progress function – associated, for example, with new discoveries, a technological breakthrough or more education – will shift the curve upwards, causing the growth of output to exceed the growth of capital, raising the rate of profit and inducing more investment to give a new equilibrium growth of output per worker at $\dot{q}_1^*$. An increase in capital accumulation to $\dot{k}_1$ *without* an associated upward shift in the schedule will cause the capital–output ratio to rise. New growth theory is precisely anticipated. Kaldor's technical progress function is the true progenitor of endogenous growth theory.

What applies to countries through time applies, *pari passu*, to different countries at a point in time, with differences in growth rates at the same capital–output ratio being associated with different technical progress functions. To quote Kaldor (1972, emphasis added) again:

> A lower capital–labour ratio does not necessarily imply a lower capital–output ratio – indeed, the reverse is often the case. The countries with the most highly mechanised industries, such as the USA, do not require a higher ratio of capital to output. The capital–output ratio in the USA has been falling over the past 50 years whilst the capital–labour ratio has been steadily rising; *and it is lower in the United States today than in the manufacturing industries of many underdeveloped countries.*

In other words, rich and poor countries are simply not on the same production function.

Empirical studies

In this section we survey six pioneer studies of intercountry growth rate differences that have been inspired by new growth theory. A summary of the studies is given in Table 4.5. Before turning to the individual studies, it may be said from the outset that only four variables seem to be

Table 4.5 The macrodeterminants of growth

Study	Dependent variable	Convergence	Savings–investment ratio	Population growth	Education	Government consumption distortions	Political instability	Monetary and fiscal variables	Trade variables	Inflation
Barro (1991)	Growth of per capita income	Conditional	Significant (+)	Not considered	Significant (+)	Significant (−)	Not considered	Not considered	Not considered	Not considered
Mankiw et al. (1992)	Level and growth of per capita income	Conditional	Significant (+)	Significant (−)	Significant (+)	Not considered	Not considered	Not considered	Not considered	Not considered
Knight et al. (1993)	Growth of output per worker	Conditional	Significant (+)	Significant (−)	Significant (+)	Not considered	Not considered	Not considered	Significant (+)	Not considered
Barro and Lee (1993)	Growth of per capita income	Conditional	Significant (+)	Not considered	Significant (+)	Significant (−)	Significant (−)	Not considered	Not considered	Not considered
Levine and Renelt (1992)	Growth of per capita income	Conditional	Significant (+)	Not robust	Significant (+)	Not robust	Not robust	Not robust	Not robust	Not robust
Levine and Zervos (1993)	Growth of per capita income	Conditional	Not considered	Not considered	Significant (+)	Not considered	Significant (−)	Weak	Weak	Not significant

Note: Barro (1991), Mankiw et al. (1992), Knight et al. (1993) and Levine and Zervos (1993) – 98 countries, 1960–85; Barro and Lee (1993) – 116 countries, 1965–85; and Levine and Renelt (1992) – 119 countries, 1960–89.

robust in the sense that they remain statistically significant regardless of what other variables are included in the equation. Consider an equation of the form:

$$Y = b_i I + b_m M + b_z Z + \mu \qquad (4.32)$$

where I is a set of variables always in the regression, M is the variable of interest, and Z is a subset of variables added to the regression. As a first step, estimate the regression with the I variables (for example, *PCY*) and the variable of interest (say, investment). Then add up to three other variables and observe the significance of the variable of interest. If the variable remains significant without changing its sign, the variable is regarded as robust; otherwise, it is 'fragile'. The only robust variables found in the majority of studies are the ratio of savings and investment to GDP, population growth, the initial level of per capita income, and investment in human capital measured by the secondary school enrolment rate. All other variables are fragile.

The six studies surveyed are Barro (1991), Mankiw et al. (1992), Levine and Renelt (1992), Levine and Zervos (1993), Barro and Lee (1993) and Knight et al. (1993).

Robert Barro has been one of the major investigators of new growth theory. He examines the growth of per capita income across 98 countries over the period 1960–85. He is interested in testing the neoclassical growth model augmented by human capital formation. There is no significant relation between the initial level of *PCY* and the growth rate of *PCY*, which, on the surface, contradicts the neoclassical model and supports the new models of endogenous growth, which assume non-diminishing returns to capital. In the first instance, however, he does not allow for differences in investment ratios and population growth. Instead, he augments the model by allowing for differences in human capital formation, proxied by school enrolment ratios. With this additional variable, *PCY* growth is found to be negatively related to initial levels of *PCY*, which, he argues, supports the neoclassical (conditional) convergence hypothesis.

An interesting difference between 'continents' is apparent. The Pacific Rim countries in 1960 had higher human capital formation than predicted by the level of *PCY* and grew rapidly, while Africa had lower human capital formation than predicted by *PCY* and grew slowly. Countries with high ratios of human capital formation also seem to have lower fertility rates and higher ratios of physical investment to GDP, which means that the human capital variable is likely to be picking up differences in population growth and investment ratios.

Mankiw et al. (1992) take three samples of countries over the period 1960–85: 98 non-oil-producing countries, 76 developing countries (excluding small countries and those where data are doubtful), and 22 OECD countries with a population of more than 1 million. First, they take the *level* of *PCY* as the dependent variable and find that differences in savings rates and population growth account for over 50% of income differences in the large sample of countries, which is support for the second basic proposition of neoclassical growth theory. However, the cross-section regression implies a much higher elasticity of output with respect to capital than capital's share of national income, so that the empirical model overpredicts. The authors thus augment the model for differences in human capital formation, proxied by secondary school enrolment rates, and find that the augmented Solow model 'explains' 80% of differences in *PCY*, and human capital formation is a significant variable in all three samples of countries. Regressing the *growth* of *PCY* on initial *PCY* levels shows no tendency for convergence (except in the OECD sample), but there is evidence for conditional convergence in all three samples if differences in investment ratios and population growth are allowed for. It is therefore claimed by Mankiw et al. (1992) that the data give support to the Solow neoclassical model against the new endogenous growth models, which, because of the assumption of non-diminishing returns to capital, predict that differences in *PCY* between countries will persist indefinitely or even widen.

Knight et al. (1993) extend Mankiw et al.'s study in two ways. First, they use panel data (that is, pooled time-series and cross-section data) to look at country-specific effects. Second, they assume that the rate of technical progress is influenced by the 'outwardness' of trade policy and by the stock of infrastructure investment (proxied by the 'flow' variable, government fixed investment as a proportion of GDP). Trade is assumed to influence technical progress in two ways: through technological transfers, and through greater availability of foreign exchange, which enables countries to purchase technologically superior capital goods. Tests of the model, taking two samples (76 developing countries and 22 OECD countries), show that the growth of output per worker is positively related to the savings ratio, and negatively related to the growth of population and the initial level of *PCY*; that is, there is evidence of conditional convergence. Human capital investment is significant and raises the productivity of physical investment. The tests of trade 'openness', and the role of infrastructure investment, also show significant positive effects and enhance the coefficient on physical capital.

Barro and Lee (1993) analyse 116 countries over the period 1965–85 and find that five factors differentiate reasonably well slow-growing countries from fast-growing countries:

1. The initial level of *PCY* (relative to educational and health attainment), which has a negative effect (that is, there is evidence of conditional convergence).
2. The investment ratio (+).
3. The ratio of government consumption to GDP (−).
4. Market distortions measured by the black market rate of foreign exchange (−).
5. Political instability measured by the number of political 'revolutions' per year (−).

These five variables 'explain' 80% of the growth rate differences between countries. No trade variables are included in the analysis.

Levine and Renelt (1992) show that cross-country regression results are 'fragile' to model selection and datasets, but at least two 'robust' results stand out: the relation between investment and growth, and the relation between the investment ratio and the ratio of international trade to GDP. Levine and Renelt first take 119 countries over the period 1960–89 and use the growth of *PCY* as the dependent variable. The *I* (constant) variables used (see equation (4.32)) are the investment ratio, the initial level of *PCY*, the initial level of secondary school enrolment, and population growth. The pool of *Z* variables used includes government expenditure, exports, inflation, the variance of inflation, domestic credit expansion and its variance, and political instability. When the *Z* variables are added to the *I* variables, the investment ratio remains robust, the initial *PCY* variable remains robust (that is, there is evidence of conditional convergence), the secondary school enrolment rate is robust, but not population growth. None of the *Z* variables themselves are robust, however; they depend on the conditioning variables, that is, which other *Z* variables are introduced. Levine and Renelt repeat the Barro (1991) study and find only the investment ratio and the initial level of *PCY* to be robust. No fiscal or monetary indicators are robust, and no trade variables. Levine and Renelt (1992) suggest that the importance of trade probably works through investment (rather than through improved resource allocation).

Levine and Zervos (1993) report new evidence on the 'robustness' of variables, taking a different set of *I* and *Z* variables. The *I* (constant) variables used are the Barro (1991) variables of initial *PCY*, initial secondary school enrolment rate and the number of political revolutions and coups. The results largely support the earlier findings of Levine and Renelt (1992), but no investment variable is included. Levine and Zervos pay particular attention to financial variables and the role of inflation. Various indicators of financial deepening are robust (which may be standing as a proxy for investment), and apparently there are no *Z* variables that make growth and inflation negatively correlated. Levine and Zervos (1993) comment that: 'given the uncharacteristically unified view among economists and policy analysts that countries with high inflation rates should adopt policies that lower inflation in order to promote economic prosperity, the inability to find simple cross-country regressions supporting this contention is both surprising and troubling' (see Chapter 13 for a discussion of the relation between inflation and growth).

The above studies relate to countries as a whole. Rodrik (2013), however, has found that if just the manufacturing sector of countries is considered, there is evidence of unconditional convergence, taking a sample of over 100 developed and developing countries since 1990. This is, perhaps, not surprising, because manufacturing industries produce tradable goods subject to competitive pressure in a global environment where there is scope for technological transfer and the absorption of new knowledge. Traditional agriculture and non-traded goods do not share these characteristics. This suggests that lack of unconditional convergence across countries has to do with the structural characteristics of countries and particularly the relative shares of traded and non-traded goods.

What have we learned?

These studies (and many others not reported here) have revealed a lot about the sources of intercountry growth rate differences. Interestingly, the variables of significance turn out to be those that have traditionally been at the heart of mainstream growth and development theory, particularly the importance of investment and capital accumulation.

On the other hand, it is often the case that studies reach conflicting conclusions, and a large proportion of intercountry growth rate differences remain unexplained (as much as 40%). Why is this? One set of reasons relate to the availability and quality of data, and the econometric procedures used for testing. Often, data are weak and unreliable, and the econometric methodology used not only differs but is also questionable, because allowance has not been made for lags in the relationship between variables or intercorrelation between variables. A second set of reasons is that countries are much more heterogeneous in their structure and institutions than most studies allow for. As Kenny and Williams (2001) put it: 'it is because countries are so heterogeneous in their make-up and institutions that cross section studies reach contradictory results and produce a lack of robustness'. They argue: 'perhaps more energy should be directed towards understanding the complex and varied inner-workings of actual economies rather than trying to assimilate them into abstract universal models'.

A similar point is made by Putterman (2000), who argues that one of the important reasons why countries have grown at different rates over the past 60 years is that the *preconditions* for development were not equal in terms of institutional structure (the strength of government, for example), the tax system, the state of agriculture, the stock of knowledge and ideas and so on, and these factors are not well captured by the initial level of per capita income. Emphasis on preconditions, and why countries have responded differently to the possibilities of industrialization, goes back to Rostow's ideas of the preconditions for take-off. To put it another way: economic history matters. The question is how to measure the level of 'pre-modern' development. Putterman (2000) concentrates on the conditions prevailing in agriculture such as cultivatable land per head, population density, and the prevalence of irrigation. When these variables are included in regression equations, along with the investment ratio, population growth and education, there is an increase in the proportion of the variance in growth rates that is explained.

Another serious weakness of new growth theory is that many of the models are closed economy models, and there are no demand constraints. It is difficult to imagine how growth rate differences between countries can be explained without reference to trade, and without reference to the balance of payments position of countries, which in most developing economies constitutes a major constraint on the growth of demand and output (see Chapter 16). Where a trade variable is included in the models tested, it is invariably insignificant, or loses its significance when combined with other variables. All this is very puzzling, given the rich theoretical and empirical literature that exists on the relation between trade and growth (see Chapter 15). There are at least two possible explanations. First, it could be that trade works through investment. Indeed, in some studies that look directly at the determinants of investment, trade and exports are found to be very significant. Second, the measure of trade taken is a very static one, usually measured as the share of trade in GDP. This may pick up the static gains from trade but not the dynamic gains. In a growth model, the most obvious trade variable to focus on is the *growth* of exports, which will favourably influence growth from the demand side (particularly by relaxing a balance of payments constraint on domestic demand), and from the supply side by raising import capacity. Nell and Thirlwall (2016) show export growth to be the second most important variable after the investment ratio in explaining differences in the growth performance of 84 countries over the period 1980–2011.

Finally, a more fundamental issue is raised by Pritchett (2000), who argues that it is difficult to characterize the growth of many developing countries by a single time trend because growth is very volatile. Periods of rapid growth are often followed by plateaus and steep declines. Rapid and slow growth are, for the most part, transitory. Very few countries see their success or failure persist from decade to decade. Correlations of country growth rates across periods (e.g. 5–10 years) show very low correlations. Taking 111 countries over a 25-year period, Pritchett shows that in 55 of them, growth either accelerated or decelerated by more than 3 percentage points on at least one occasion over the period. In 40% of developing countries, trying to estimate a time trend for the growth of output gives a correlation coefficient of less than 0.5; and volatility around the trend is much higher for developing countries than developed countries. So Pritchett asks the question: What aspects of a country's growth is growth theory trying to explain when growth is so ephemeral and volatile? If growth is so volatile, it is no wonder that the variance of growth explained by traditional variables is relatively low. What is important is to analyse and explain the determinants of *shifts* in growth rates from one period to another.

Hausmann et al. (2005) try to do this. They take 106 countries over the period 1957–92, defining a 'growth acceleration' as an increase in PCY growth of 2% or more per annum over an eight-year period with a minimum growth rate of 3.5% per annum. Also the post-acceleration output level must exceed the pre-episode peak level of income (to rule out cases of pure recovery from deep depression). They find 83 episodes of growth accelerations, and 60 countries out of the 106 had at least one. The average growth acceleration is 4.7 percentage points. When they look at the causes of accelerations, however, they are struck by their unpredictability. There is only a weak link between conventional determinants of growth and growth accelerations. Investment, trade and real exchange rate depreciation are the strongest links, but there seems to be very little association between standard economic reform packages and growth accelerations. **Only 14% of accelerations were associated with economic liberalization.** Only 18% of reform episodes and 14% of political regime change were followed by growth accelerations. Hausmann et al. (2005) conclude that 'growth accelerations seem to be driven largely by idiosyncratic causes'. This may be because the 'binding constraints' on growth are 'idiosyncratic' and for certain time periods get relieved. This leads us to a brief discussion of the topic of growth diagnostics and binding constraints on growth pioneered by Hausmann et al. (2008).

'Growth diagnostics' and binding constraints on growth

A poor growth and development performance may be caused by a multitude of factors, but a sweeping programme of reforms (à la Washington Consensus), including financial and trade liberalization, the privatization of enterprises and reductions in public expenditure, may not be the solution. This is what Hausmann et al. (2008) call the 'spray gun' approach to economic policy-making, which may not hit hard enough the binding constraints on growth and development that really matter, and which are likely to vary from one country to another. Much better, they argue, is to undertake 'growth diagnostics', which locates the binding constraints on economic performance, and to target them directly, giving the most favourable outcomes from the resources expended. For an overview of the approach, see Rodrik (2010).

The framework of 'growth diagnostics' encompasses all major strategies of development. Its importance is that it clarifies *which* strategies are most likely to be effective. Since investment is the key to long-run growth, the obvious starting point for growth diagnostics is to answer the question: Why is investment low? Is it the high cost or lack of access to finance? Is it an intrinsically low social rate of return to investment, or is it that returns cannot easily be appropriated by private agents? If the problem is the cost and availability of financial resources, this is likely to be associated with low savings rates, high interest rates, and large balance of payments deficits. If the social return is low, this could be due to unfavourable geography, lack of infrastructure, poor education and health, and a lack of technological dynamism. If the ability to appropriate returns is difficult, this could be due to an uncertain economic and political climate, high taxes, absence of the rule of law, and weak property rights. Once the diagnosis is done, certain policy reforms follow and others can be ruled out, saving time and effort. Policy must then be targeted as close to the distortion and binding constraint as possible.

Hausmann et al. (2008) illustrate their methodology by comparing and contrasting three developing economies: Brazil, El Salvador and the Dominican Republic. According to the identification of binding constraints, policy recommendations differ. Brazil, for example, seems to be constrained by a shortage of finance, not by low returns on investment, so the policy message is to raise domestic saving and to attract foreign funds. By contrast, the binding constraint in El Salvador is not a shortage of investment funds, but a low social return associated with a lack of technological dynamism. It needs new (industrial) activities to invest in. The Dominican Republic tells a story of inability to cope with shocks. Here, institutional and political reforms are likely to yield the highest return. Institutions to deal with conflict management are very important to cope with the consequences of shocks and change (see Chapter 8).

The World Bank's Commission on Growth and Development, chaired by the Nobel laureate Michael Spence, and including Robert Solow, identified 13 countries that have grown at more than 7% per annum for at least 25 years since 1950. They are listed in Case example 4.1. The ingredients of their success are also highlighted: commitment to growth, combined with effective governance; high savings and investment rates; rapid export growth; macroeconomic stability; the import of knowledge and technology, and market-friendly policies.

Case example 4.1

Findings of the Commission on Growth and Development

The World Bank's Commission on Growth and Development 2008, headed by Nobel laureate Professor Michael Spence, identified 13 countries that have grown at more than 7% per annum for at least 25 years since 1950. They are listed below.

		Per capita income	
Economy	**Period of high growth**	**At start of growth period**	**2005**
Botswana	1960–2005	210	3,800
Brazil	1950–1980	960	4,000
China	1961–2005	105	1,400
Hong Kong SAR	1960–1997	3,100	29,900
Indonesia	1966–1997	200	900
Japan	1950–1983	3,500	39,600
Korea	1960–2001	1,100	13,200
Malaysia	1967–1997	790	4,400
Malta	1963–1994	1,100	9,600
Oman	1960–1999	950	9,000
Singapore	1967–2002	2,200	25,400
Taiwan (Province of China)	1965–2002	1,500	16,400
Thailand	1960–1997	330	2,400

The commission identified six major ingredients of success:

1. Commitment to growth, combined with effective governance
2. High savings and investment rates
3. Fast export growth
4. Macroeconomic stability
5. Import of knowledge and technology
6. Market-friendly policies.

Source: World Bank, 2008.

Summary

- All the great classical economists of the eighteenth and nineteenth centuries were development economists, in the sense that they were all concerned with the causes and consequences of economic growth during the Industrial Revolution in Europe at this time.
- Adam Smith was optimistic about the growth and development process based on increasing returns in industry.
- Malthus, Ricardo, Mill and Marx were all pessimistic about the development process because of diminishing returns in agriculture and a declining rate of profit in industry. Classical pessimism has been confounded by rapid technical progress in both agriculture (offsetting diminishing returns) and industry (allowing real wages to rise without the rate of profit falling).

- Modern growth theory originated with Harrod's 1939 paper 'An Essay in Dynamic Theory', in which he distinguishes three growth rates: the actual growth rate (g), the warranted growth rate (g_w) and the natural growth rate (g_n). Divergences between g and g_w cause short-run instability. Divergences between g_w and g_n cause secular stagnation if $g_w > g_n$, or growing structural unemployment with inflation if $g_n > g_w$ (which is the case for most developing economies). There were no mechanisms in the Harrod model for equalizing g, g_w and g_n.
- Solow's 1956 neoclassical growth model provided an equilibrating mechanism to bring g_w and g_n together so that all economies in the long run would grow at their natural rate of growth determined by the growth of the labour force and the growth of labour productivity. In Solow's original model, investment did not matter for long-run growth because of the assumption of diminishing returns to capital.
- Solow's model also predicted that poor countries should grow faster than rich countries, leading to a convergence of per capita incomes across the world, but we do not observe a convergence of living standards. 'New' growth theory, or endogenous growth theory, attempts to provide an answer. There are lots of factors that prevent the marginal product of capital from falling as countries get richer and invest more, such as education, R&D expenditure, learning by doing, trade and so on, so that investment does matter for long-run growth and is not simply exogenously determined by the natural rate of growth. The AK model is the simplest new growth theory model, which assumes constant returns to capital.
- The neoclassical Cobb–Douglas production function can be used to decompose the sources of growth into the contribution of labour input, capital input and total factor productivity growth. In fact, any variable can be included in a production function and its contribution to output measured.
- New growth theory uses many of the same variables as the production function approach in analysing the sources of growth, but with particular focus on education, R&D effort and institutional variables, and testing for conditional convergence by including in the estimating equation the initial level of per capita income.
- Cross-country analysis, however, is unable to explain the growth and development experience of individual countries, so growth diagnostics become important in identifying the binding constraints on growth in particular economies, and the factors that are associated with growth accelerations within countries.
- The major determinants of rapid growth and development are: high investment, fast export growth (to pay for imports), macroeconomic stability, high levels of human capital formation, and an institutional framework conducive to growth (e.g. secure property rights, the rule of law and political stability).

Chapter 4 Discussion questions

1. What did Adam Smith mean when he said that the 'division of labour is limited by the extent of the market' and 'the extent of the market is limited by the division of labour'? What is the economic significance of these propositions?
2. Why were the classical economists after Adam Smith pessimistic about the growth and development process?

Chapter 4 **Discussion questions** – *continued*

3. How does Harrod define the warranted growth rate and the natural growth rate? What are the implications for a country if the natural growth rate exceeds the warranted rate?
4. What is the mechanism in neoclassical growth theory by which the warranted rate of growth adjusts to the natural rate? Do you think it is a realistic mechanism?
5. What are the essential assumptions and predictions of neoclassical growth theory, and how is the conclusion reached that investment does not matter for long-run growth?
6. What are the special properties of the Cobb–Douglas production function, and how might the function be used to calculate the sources of growth?
7. What is the difference between exogenous and endogenous technical progress?
8. What factors does the growth of 'total factor productivity' depend on?
9. What have been the major findings of production function studies of the sources of growth in developing countries?
10. Outline the essential propositions of new (endogenous) growth theory.
11. What have we learnt from the major studies of the macrodeterminants of growth in developing countries?
12. How useful is the exercise of growth diagnostics?

Notes

1. In practice, g_n may respond to g. This is the idea of the endogeneity of the natural rate of growth. See Leon-Ledesma and Thirlwall (2002) for a study of developed countries; studies by Vogel (2009) and Libanio (2009) for Latin American countries, and Dray and Thirlwall (2011) for a study of a selection of Southeast Asian countries. Typically, an increase in the actual growth rate of 1 percentage point above the estimated natural rate increases the natural rate by between 0.5 and 0.8 percentage points through increasing the rate of growth of the labour force and labour productivity growth.
2. This can be seen by rearranging the equation to $qs/k = l$, where $q = Y/L$; $s = S/Y = \Delta K/Y$ (since all saving leads to capital accumulation); $k = K/L$, and $l = \Delta L/L$. Therefore $(Y/L)(\Delta K/Y)(L/K) = \Delta L/L$, or $\Delta K/K = \Delta L/L$.
3. To illustrate the effect of a change in technical progress on the steady state, the axes in Figure 4.4 must be changed to 'output per *effective* worker' on the vertical axis and 'capital per *effective* worker' on the horizontal axis.
4. For the time being, the formidable problems associated with an aggregate measure of capital are ignored.
5. The proof is as follows. The elasticity of output with respect to capital, α, is $(dY/Y)/(dK/K) = (dYK)/(dKY)$. Now, if capital is paid its marginal product, then $dY/dK = r$, where r is the rental on capital. Hence, $\alpha = rK/Y$, where rK/Y is capital's share of total output. Thus, under perfectly

competitive assumptions, the elasticity of output with respect to any factor is equal to that factor's share of total output.

6. Alternatively, the total differential of equation (4.20) can be taken and the result divided by output, which will also convert the equation into rate of growth form.
7. The elasticity of substitution (σ) relates the proportional change in relative factor inputs to a proportional change in the marginal rate of substitution between labour and capital (MRS) (or the proportional change in the relative factor–price ratio on the basis of marginal productivity theory). The elasticity of substitution may therefore be written as

$$\sigma = \frac{\partial \log (L/K)}{\partial \log \text{MRS}}$$

The proof that $\sigma = 1$ is very simple:

$$\text{MRS} = \frac{\partial Y}{\partial K} \bigg| \frac{\partial Y}{\partial L} \bigg| = \frac{\alpha L}{\beta K}$$

$$\log \text{MRS} = \log \frac{\alpha}{\beta} + \log \frac{L}{K}$$

Differentiating with respect to log MRS gives

$$1 = \frac{\partial \log (L/K)}{\partial \log MRS} = \sigma$$

8. To overcome the restrictive property of the Cobb–Douglas function when the growth rates of factors differ, it is possible to use the more general constant elasticity of substitution production function, of which the Cobb–Douglas is a special case. We cannot discuss the function here except to say that it, too, is not without its specification errors. There is still the assumption of constancy, which has the drawback that one may be ascribing changes in elasticity to changes in technology that are really due to changes in factor proportions. This limitation can be overcome only with a function possessing the property of variable elasticity of substitution.
9. The production function used here is the translog production function, which allows for the elasticity of substitution between inputs to vary.
10. For a discussion of the origins of endogenous growth theory, and its relevance to developing countries, see Romer (1994), Pack (1994), Ruttan (1998) and Temple (1999). For an advanced textbook treatment of the topic, see Barro and Sala-í-Martin (2003).
11. For an advanced theoretical discussion of convergence issues, see Durlauf (1996); see also Islam (2003).

Websites on growth theory

New School for Social Research (New York) www.newschool.edu/nssr/

Economic Growth Resources run by Jon Temple, Bristol University, UK www.bristol.ac.uk/efm/people/jon-r-temple/overview.html

Overseas Development Institute www.odi.org

Foundation for Advanced Studies on International Development www.fasid.or.jp/english

Institute of Developing Economies: Japan External Trade Organization www.ide.go.jp/English/

Vienna Institute for International Economic Studies www.wiiw.ac.at

Carnegie Endowment for International Peace http://carnegieendowment.org/

II

FACTORS IN THE DEVELOPMENT PROCESS

5

THE ROLE OF AGRICULTURE AND SURPLUS LABOUR FOR INDUSTRIALIZATION

- Introduction
- The role of agriculture in development
- Barriers to agricultural development
- Land reform
- The supply response of agriculture
- Transforming traditional agriculture
- The growth of the money economy
- Finance for traditional agriculture
- The interdependence of agriculture and industry
- Economic development with unlimited supplies of labour
- A model of the complementarity between agriculture and industry
- Rural–urban migration and urban unemployment
- Disguised unemployment: types and measurement
- Incentives and the costs of labour transfer
- Summary
- Appendix: the functioning of markets in agrarian societies
- Discussion questions
- Notes
- Websites on agriculture

Introduction

The task of a true theory of economic growth and development must be to explain why some societies developed sooner than others, why some societies have experienced such rapid increases in living standards while others have lagged behind, and why development has not spread more evenly across the globe.

The answer must be that at different stages of development, different constraints on progress operate. While some of these factors are likely to be sociological and political, the major constraints are likely to be economic. One of the most critical factors in the early stages of development is the health of the agricultural sector, because without a surplus of food production over subsistence needs, little else can be done. There would be no surplus labour, no saving, no investment and no food to feed labour working in alternative activities.

It is no coincidence that the material progress of mankind started 8,000 years ago in the region of Mesopotamia (the cradle of civilization, now Iraq), where, for the first time, agriculture became settled. Unless agriculture is settled, there is no prospect of agricultural productivity increasing to provide the basis for the development of non-agricultural activities, the building of cities and the enjoyment of leisure. Where shifting agriculture is practised, as by nomadic tribes in the Kalahari Desert of Botswana and Namibia, for example, there is no basis for an agricultural surplus.

As the World Bank says in its *World Development Report 2008: Agriculture for Development* (World Bank, 2007):

> agricultural growth was the precursor to the industrial revolutions that spread across the temperate world from England in the mid-18th century to Japan in the late-19th century. More recently, rapid agricultural growth in China, India and Vietnam was the precursor to the rise of industry . . . the special powers of agriculture as the basis for early growth are well established.

In many developing countries today, agriculture is still extremely backward. Low productivity is a major cause of poverty and retards development of the whole economy. Over 3 billion people live in rural areas, and most of them live in households engaged in agriculture earning just a few dollars a day. The World Bank (2007) recognizes 'that agriculture must be a prominent part of the development agenda whether for delivering growth in the agricultural-based countries or for reducing rural poverty'. It also recognizes that the state has a role to play in providing core public goods and incentives for investment in the agricultural sector.

In this chapter, we consider some of the reasons for agricultural backwardness, and why productivity is so low. We look at the process of transforming traditional agriculture and the growth of the money economy, and model the interrelationship between the growth of agriculture and industry. Then, we use Arthur Lewis's (1954) well-known model of economic development with unlimited supplies of labour to illustrate the important role that surplus labour in agriculture (and other sectors) plays in the development process and in fuelling industrial growth. The precise meaning of surplus labour is addressed, as well as the rural–urban migration process. An appendix describes the various markets in agrarian societies – land, labour and credit – and how they interlock.

The role of agriculture in development

Agriculture makes four major contributions to the process of economic development: a **product**, a **factor**, a **market** and a **foreign exchange contribution**.

Product contribution

The product contribution of agriculture refers to the fact that agriculture must supply food above subsistence needs in order to feed labour working in alternative occupations. If other sectors of the economy are to be developed, labour needs to be fed, and this cannot be done by imports until export activities have been developed to provide foreign exchange to pay for the imports. It will be remembered from Chapter 3 that in Rostow's model of economic growth, the take-off stage of development must be preceded by an agricultural revolution. Indeed, as mentioned above in the quote from the World Bank, one of the major reasons why Britain was the first country to industrialize was that it was the first to experience a significant agricultural revolution based on the abolition of serfdom and on the enclosure movement, which raised agricultural productivity and provided surplus labour and food to support industrial expansion.

The difference between total agricultural output and subsistence needs is called the **marketable surplus.** Economic progress in the early stages of development requires an increase in the marketable surplus, which, in turn, requires an increase in labour productivity. If productivity does not increase naturally or 'voluntarily', a marketable surplus can be forcibly extracted, as it was in Japan at the time of the Meiji Restoration in 1868, when landowners were compulsorily taxed, and more dramatically in the Soviet Union in the 1920s, when there was mass genocide of the *kulaks* (small prosperous landowners) during Stalin's collectivization programme.

'Marketable surplus' is an important concept in the neoclassical model of the development process, because unless the marketable surplus rises as the demand for food increases, the price of food will tend to rise. This will turn the terms of trade against industry, higher wages will have to be paid to workers in industry, which will eat into profits and capital accumulation. The marketable surplus therefore becomes the major constraint on industrial growth.

Factor contribution

The factor contribution of agriculture consists of two parts: a labour contribution and a capital contribution. Labour for industry and other activities must come from agriculture, but can be released only if productivity in agriculture rises. The existence of surplus labour (or disguised unemployment) plays a major role in the development process, as we shall see when we consider the Lewis model of economic development with unlimited supplies of labour. The lower the cost of industrial labour, the faster the rate of industrial expansion is likely to be, but this depends on the rate at which the agricultural sector is releasing labour. Industrial development today in many of the rapidly growing countries of Southeast Asia is being fuelled by cheap labour drawn from agriculture. In this respect, China's industrial potential is enormous.

Agriculture is a source of saving and capital accumulation for industrial development. The saving can be voluntary or involuntary. Examples of voluntary saving are rich landlords voluntarily investing in industrial activities (the Industrial Revolution in Britain was partly financed in this way), and peasant farmers investing small savings in rural banks. Involuntary saving could take the form of the government taxing the agricultural sector and using the proceeds for investment, or, more drastically, the forced extraction of the agricultural surplus through expropriation or collectivization (as in Stalinist Russia).

Another traditional way in which governments have taxed the agricultural sector is through the pricing policies of **marketing boards**, established to market agricultural produce. The prices paid to farmers are lower than the prices at which the goods are sold on the market – the difference providing net revenue to the government.

The general policy in developing countries of keeping agricultural prices low used to be justified on two main grounds: that low prices benefit the industrial sector, and that peasant farmers have limited horizons and do not respond to incentives, so if prices are higher, they may actually produce less if all they are interested in is a fixed money income. This is the notion of a **backward-bending supply curve of effort**. It can be said without hesitation that the deliberate policy of keeping agricultural prices low has done enormous damage to the agricultural sector in developing countries. As we shall see later, there is ample evidence that peasant farmers do respond to price incentives. They not only increase supply in response to price rises, but also switch crops as relative prices change.

Market contribution

The market contribution of agriculture refers to the fact that the demand from agriculture must be the major source of autonomous demand for industrial goods. If industry is to grow and prosper, it must be able to sell its goods. In the early stages of development, the agricultural sector is likely to provide the largest market for industrial goods. There is a *complementarity* between agricultural and industrial growth. This is well documented in the historical experience of developed countries, and in the contemporary world economy. In his classic study of Japanese economic development, Lockwood (1954) wrote:

> The growth of primary production was interrelated with industrialization and urbanization at every point . . . As industry developed, it offered a widening market for the food and raw material surpluses of the countryside . . . On the other hand, the increasing productivity of the primary industries created a growing home market for manufactures and services.

The *World Development Report 1979* (World Bank, 1979) noted that 'a stagnant rural economy with low purchasing power holds back industrial growth in many developing countries'. The *World Development Report 1982* (World Bank, 1982) documented the close correspondence across countries between agricultural development and industrial growth: 'fast growth of industry and sluggish agriculture were evident *only* in countries with oil or mineral-based economies, such as Algeria, Ecuador, Mexico, Morocco and Nigeria . . . These were exceptions but they prove the rule.' In other words, a precondition for rapid industrial growth is a rapidly expanding agricultural sector, at least in terms of purchasing power.

This has implications for the pricing of agricultural goods relative to industrial goods, or what is called the agricultural (or industrial) terms of trade. Low farm prices are good for industry from the point of view of supply potential, because this means that industry can obtain cheaper raw material inputs and wage goods, which increases profitability. On the other hand, low farm prices are bad for industry from the demand side, because this means low farm purchasing power and therefore a lower demand for industrial goods. There needs to be an equilibrium terms of trade between the two sectors to achieve balanced growth between the two sectors, so that industrial growth is not constrained from the supply side by agricultural prices being too high or constrained from the demand side by agricultural prices being too low. Later in the chapter, we bring the two sectors together in an equilibrium framework and derive the equilibrium terms of trade that maximizes the growth rate of the economy as a whole.

Foreign exchange contribution

In the early stages of development, the only source of foreign exchange is likely to be primary commodity exports. Agriculture therefore makes an important foreign exchange contribution. Foreign exchange is a resource, just like savings. It provides access to goods that either cannot be produced domestically or can be produced only at higher cost in an opportunity cost sense. Either way, the imports made possible by exporting agricultural products will be very productive – the more so if they are investment-type goods necessary for the development process. There are not many countries in the world that could not grow faster, given the greater availability of foreign exchange. The link between trade, the balance of payments and growth is explored fully in Chapters 15 and 16.

Barriers to agricultural development

For the agricultural sector to supply food, release labour, provide savings, contribute to the market for industrial goods, and earn foreign exchange, it must generate a steadily rising surplus of production in excess of subsistence needs. Since land is relatively fixed in supply, this requires rising agricultural productivity. The 'grassroots' school of economic development, which came into fashion as a reaction against the emphasis on industrialization at any cost, lays stress on policies to raise the level of productivity in agriculture as the most crucial development priority and an indispensable element of a long-run development strategy. Overall, agricultural productivity in developing countries is less than one-twentieth of the level in developed countries, and there are even bigger differences between countries.

Table 5.1 gives figures on agricultural productivity in selected regions of the world in 2013 measured in US dollars at 2005 prices. Notice the huge disparities that exist, which go some way to explaining divisions in world income. In low-income countries, in which over half of the population are engaged in agriculture, value-added per head is only $310, which is less than a dollar a day. In sub-Saharan Africa and South Asia (which includes India, Bangladesh and Pakistan), productivity is less than $2 a day. In East Asia and the Pacific region (which includes China), value-added is just over $2 day. By contrast, in the high-income countries, productivity is over $24,000. Some progress has been made in recent years with particular crops in particular countries, but

Table 5.1 Agricultural productivity, 2013

	Value-added per worker, US$
World	1,406
Low income	310
Middle income	1,053
Lower middle income	939
Upper middle income	1,156
Low and middle income	956
East Asia and Pacific	803
Europe and Central Asia	5,247
Latin America and Caribbean	4,125
Middle East and North Africa	3,264
South Asia	711
Sub-Saharan Africa	706
High income	24,509

Source: World Bank, 2015.

the performance of the agricultural sector is still disappointing, and the lack of marketable surplus still holds back development on a wide front. So what impedes agricultural productivity? There are several factors, particularly related to geography and land–labour ratios, the existence of urban bias in the treatment of agriculture and the allocation of resources, and unfair competition in world markets, but the most important factors of all are the structure of rural societies, the organization of agriculture and the land tenure system that operates.

As far as geographical factors are concerned, climate and terrain determine, to a large degree, what goods a country can produce, the amount of cultivatable land available per inhabitant and the land's fertility. To some extent, the application of capital to land can compensate for unfavourable natural forces, but there are obvious limits. Mountains cannot easily be flattened or deserts readily watered. This is the concept of **geographic determinism**, which can be advanced as a hypothesis of underdevelopment in its own right. Having said this, however, differences in natural conditions and the fertility of the soil can be no more than a partial explanation of low productivity. Poor people are to be found along the highly productive alluvial banks of the Nile, as well as on the barren plateaus of Asia and South America.

Productivity is also affected by land–labour ratios. Low labour productivity may be associated, for example, with a high population density and a high ratio of labour to land. In this case, productivity might be increased substantially with small applications of capital in the form of drainage schemes, fertilizers and so on. On the other hand, low productivity may be associated with the opposite situation of a high ratio of land to labour, in which case the solution to low productivity is likely to involve much larger doses of capital for labour to work with. Most countries in Asia have high ratios of labour to land, while in Latin America and Africa, the reverse is true, as was the case in many of today's richest countries at an equivalent stage in their economic history, for example the USA, Canada and Australia.

Urban bias against agriculture takes many forms:

- The holding down of agricultural prices to favour the industrial/urban sector.
- The concentration of investment in industry.
- Tax incentives and subsidies to industry.
- Overvalued exchange rates, which keep the price of industrial inputs low, and the domestic price of agricultural exports low.
- Tariff and quota protection for industry, which raises the price of fertilizers, seeds and equipment.
- Greater spending in urban areas on education, training, housing, nutrition and medical provision, which all affect productivity and the quality of life.

Unfair competition consists of the subsidies that developed countries give to their farmers, and the tariffs that developed countries impose on imported agricultural products from developing countries. The USA and the European Union (EU) alone spend nearly $150 billion a year on farm subsidies. This has two major consequences. First, it leads to overproduction, and the surpluses are then frequently dumped on the markets of developing countries, impoverishing domestic farmers. Second, farmers in developing countries are not able to compete in their own markets, let alone overseas markets. The situation is made worse by developing countries being forced by international agreements to lower their tariffs against imported agricultural produce, while developed countries continue to protect their own agricultural sectors. The average global tariff on agricultural commodities is 62%. The maize growers of Mexico cannot compete with cheap maize from the USA; nor can the cotton growers of West Africa compete against subsidies of $4 billion a year given to the 20,000 cotton growers in the southern states of America. Unfair competition between developed and developing countries in the markets for agricultural goods is one of the central issues in ongoing world trade talks under the auspices of the World Trade Organization.

Geographic factors, the land–labour ratio, urban bias and competition from developed countries can only explain a small part of the low productivity of agriculture in most developing countries. There are more fundamental forces at work concerned with the structure of rural society, the organization of agriculture, the incentives to produce and the supply of inputs (see Binswanger and Deininger, 1997).

In a typical developing country, rural society consists of rich landowners, peasants, sharecroppers, tenants and labourers. Apart from the landowners, most others in the rural sector are extremely poor. Because they live on the margin of subsistence, they tend to be **risk averse**. In all developing countries, peasant subsistence farming is a traditional way of life, and attempts to raise productivity will alter that way of life and necessarily involve risk. As Theodore Schultz (1980) perceptively remarked in his Nobel Prize-winning lecture:

> Most of the people in the world are poor, so if we knew the economics of being poor we would know much of the economics that really matters. Most of the world's poor people earn their living from agriculture so if we knew the economics of agriculture we would know much of the economics of being poor. People who are rich find it hard to understand the behaviour of poor people. Economists are no exception, for they, too, find it difficult to comprehend the preferences and scarcity constraints that determine the choices that poor people make. We all know that most of the world's people are poor, that they earn a pittance for their labour, that half and more of their meagre income is spent on food, that they reside predominantly in low-income countries and that most of them are earning their livelihood in agriculture. What many economists fail to understand is that poor people are no less concerned about improving their lot and that of their children than rich people are.

Poor people on the margin of subsistence may be reluctant to make the changes necessary to improve productivity because if things go wrong it will spell disaster. But even if poor people wanted to change the traditional ways of doing things, there is the serious constraint of lack of access to credit to finance the purchase of new inputs such as seeds, fertilizers, pesticides, drainage schemes and so on.

Then there is the question of the incentive to change. Where there are tenant farmers, there is little or no security of tenure, and therefore no incentive to invest in improved methods of production. Where there is sharecropping, a certain proportion of output must be relinquished to the landowner, which also reduces the incentive to invest. Any serious programme of agrarian reform must provide greater security of tenure for farmers and give incentives to raise agricultural production, coupled with access to credit, water, fertilizers and extension services for advice.

The appendix to this chapter gives a detailed description of the markets for land, labour and credit in rural societies, how they are interlocked, and the inefficiencies that arise as a result of the structure of the agricultural sector of developing countries.

Land reform

The system by which land is held and farmed is a serious impediment to increased productivity in many developing countries. The structure of peasant agriculture differs between countries, largely for historical reasons, but the structures have many common characteristics that keep productivity low. In many countries, landholding tends to be highly concentrated. The average Gini ratio for the concentration of landholdings in Latin America is 0.8, and in Asia, 0.4. In Latin America, 1% of landowners own roughly 70% of the land. In Brazil, 15% of landowners own 90% of the land. In many parts of Latin America, agriculture is based on a combination of large estates (*latifundios*), owned by a wealthy few, and small farms (*minifundios*), which are often so small that they cannot support a single family. When land is held and worked in the form of large estates, it is frequently underutilized and farmed inefficiently by peasants, who may have no security of tenure and may have to relinquish to the landowner a large fraction of their output. In these circumstances, there is little incentive to increase efficiency and improve productivity.

In Asia, the organization of peasant agriculture is also an important determinant of productivity. Because of the high population density, the major problem is that too many small farms are operated by sharecroppers and tenant farmers, the land being owned by absentee landlords. As families multiply and debts rise, land is continually sold and subdivided, leading to a very inefficient structure.

Land reform has two aspects: first, the redistribution of land in favour of landless or near-landless households, and second, tenancy reform in favour of sharecroppers and other forms of tenant farming. Such reforms involving land rights, and security for tenants, can contribute both to an increased intensity of land use and to improved efficiency and initiative on the part of the tenant farmers, particularly if they are allowed to reap fully the rewards of their own labour.

There is impressive evidence that where a change in the tenure system has permitted the producers themselves to reap the rewards of new techniques, peasant farmers have been ready to break with custom and tradition. The task of persuading producers to adopt more modern methods of production and to purchase improved seeds and fertilizers has been much easier. In a study of China from 1978, Lin (1992) finds that the shift from collective to household farming led to big increases in agricultural productivity related to the acquisition of property and land rights. Likewise, in a study of India, Besley and Burgess (2000) find that rural poverty was reduced by land reform, particularly reforms that strengthened property rights over land. In Vietnam, efficiency has increased and poverty has been reduced since the end of collectivization in the 1990s.

As was first discovered by Amartya Sen (1964), using Indian farm data, small farms are more productive (per hectare) than large farms. This has been shown in many other studies subsequently. The reason is that land tends to be more fertile on small farms, and family labour tends to work the land more intensively. In other words, small farms tend to employ more labour per unit of land than large farms. Thus, land redistribution from owners of large estates to smaller family farms can raise agricultural output and employment simultaneously, helping to reduce poverty.

Land reform may be a necessary condition for increased productivity, but it is clearly not a sufficient condition. It needs to be accompanied by other measures of agrarian reform. New landowners must be given access to credit, water, fertilizers and extension services for advice. Farmers need to be brought within the organized money market to improve access to credit and to reduce the role of village moneylenders, who charge exorbitant interest rates. Improved farm implements, irrigation and new social infrastructure are likely to be important. There needs to be improved dissemination of agricultural research. Too often, the agricultural extension services available are perfunctory and ineffective because the personnel are ill-trained and ill-equipped. Conditions vary from country to country, but in theory at least, agrarian reform, coupled with the application of complementary inputs, offers substantial scope for increased agricultural productivity.[1] See Case example 5.1 on the attempt to raise productivity in Africa, and Case example 5.2 on the approach of the World Bank.

Case example 5.1

Raising agricultural productivity in Africa

African agriculture was often neglected by most governments and donors in the 1980s and 1990s. Now, however, there is a renewed commitment to agriculture centred on the **Comprehensive Africa Agricultural Development Programme**. There is broad agreement that there needs to be more investment in agriculture, particularly in public goods, such as rural roads, agricultural research and extension services, rural schooling, clean water and healthcare. But, often in rural Africa, there are market failures in that farmers cannot get access to credit, insurance and necessary inputs. These failures can be severe and leave small farmers in a poverty trap from which they struggle to escape even when the technology exists for them to produce more.

Subsidies can help overcome poor farmers' inability to obtain credit or take risks and to allow farmers to learn about new agricultural inputs such as new seeds and fertilizers. Subsidies can also be justified, on the grounds of equity, to overcome soil degradation and improve soil quality in the case of fertilizers, and to stimulate production to reduce the cost of food and raise the real incomes of the poor. But subsidies can be costly, with costs rising over time if not targeted properly. Where subsidies are used, they need to be 'smart': targeted to those who need them most, limited in time, and designed to enhance commercial distribution rather than supplant it. Complementary investment in transport and input dealer training can reinforce these programmes and make it easier to reduce or remove subsidies in the future. There are alternatives to subsidies, as Keyna's experience of liberalized fertilizer distribution shows.

Source: Africa Progress Panel, 2010.

Case example 5.2

The World Bank tackles low productivity in agriculture

The World Bank is committed to boosting agricultural productivity and agricultural-related investment. The world needs to produce at least 50% more food by the year 2050 to feed a projected 9 billion people. To help meet this goal, the bank is working with countries to boost the productivity of farms, livestock and fisheries.

To raise yields sustainably, the bank supports 'climate-smart' approaches that have the potential to increase productivity, enhance resilience, promote agricultural innovation through research and education, and facilitate responsible agricultural investment. Gender-specific interventions are important because women account for the majority of smallholder farms – up to 70% in Africa.

Improved land governance can help smallholder farmers increase the productivity of their land and improve their livelihoods. The bank supports government policies that implement systematic land surveying and titling programmes that recognize all forms of land tenure.

The bank is committed to agricultural innovations that boost productivity, as well as better land and water management. It also promotes the use of new livestock breeds, better animal nutrition, improved veterinary services, vaccinations and improved husbandry to sustainably increase livestock productivity for about 1 billion farmers who depend on livestock for their livelihoods. The bank supports work on breeding and animal nutrition in India, grassland management in China, and sustainable aquaculture at coastal fisheries in Tanzania and Vietnam. These are just a few examples of the World Bank's work.

Source: World Bank, 2013.

The supply response of agriculture

What may also be required is a rise in the price of agricultural products relative to industrial products in order to induce extra supply. Traditionally, attempts have been made to 'tax' the agricultural sector by keeping prices low in order to maintain the terms of trade in favour of the industrial sector. This policy was justified by the widespread belief that peasant producers in traditional societies would not respond to price incentives, but this assumption has proved to be wrong. Depressing the agricultural terms of trade has depressed agricultural output and caused problems for the feeding of a growing urban population.

Many countries have had to introduce a positive price policy to act as a stimulus to agricultural output in general and to alter the composition of agricultural output as circumstances warrant. There is, in fact, considerable evidence that producers, especially those in close proximity to large markets with good transport facilities, respond positively to price changes, as economic theory would predict. Schultz (1964) gave early warning that 'the doctrine that farmers in poor countries either are indifferent or respond perversely to changes in prices . . . is patently false and harmful. Price policies based on it always impair the efficiency of agriculture.'

When discussing the supply response of agricultural output to price, however, a distinction needs to be made between three types of response:

- A change in the composition of agricultural output to a change in the relative price of individual agricultural commodities.
- An increase in total agricultural output with respect to an improvement in the relative price of agricultural commodities compared with industrial goods.
- An increase in the marketed surplus in response to an increase in the price of agricultural commodities.

Most of the studies on the supply response in peasant agriculture in developing countries relate to how producers respond to changes in the relative price of different agricultural commodities. But, of course, it would be quite possible for the supply of any individual commodity to be quite elastic with respect to price, yet the total supply of agricultural output and the marketed surplus to be quite inelastic, or even to fall, in response to a change in prices.

Having said this, there are reasons for believing that the other two elasticities are likely to be positive if the supply of individual commodities is positive, especially when crops are grown not just for subsistence purposes. For example, for any crop grown commercially, the elasticity of marketed supply will be virtually equal to the output elasticity, and unless inputs are withdrawn from the production of other commodities, the elasticity of total agricultural supply will also be positive. Only in cases where peasants are content with a fixed money income, or all increased production of a commodity is consumed within the subsistence sector, will the elasticity of marketed supply be zero or negative at the same time as the price elasticity of supply is positive. These conditions are not likely to prevail.

Empirical research on the supply response of agriculture can be divided into four main categories:

1. Cross-country studies that look at output differences in relation to price differences across countries.
2. Time-series studies that examine output movements in relation to price movements within countries over time.
3. Cross-section studies that look at output differences in relation to price differences across farms within a country.

4. Intersectoral general equilibrium models that examine how the output of agriculture varies in response to changes in the prices of agricultural goods relative to the price of other goods in the economy.

The evidence shows that aggregate supply elasticities of agricultural output range from 0.3 to 0.9 (Chhibber, 1988).[2] Long-run elasticity is obviously higher than short-run elasticity, and elasticity tends to be higher in the more advanced and land-abundant developing countries. The supply response of farmers to price changes depends crucially on the ability of farmers to respond to price signals, which, in turn, depends on transport, infrastructure and access to agricultural inputs. In poorer countries with inadequate infrastructure, supply elasticity is low (0.2–0.5). In fact, the supply elasticity of agriculture with respect to non-price factors (e.g., the provision of public goods and services) is much higher than it is with respect to price, especially in poorer developing countries with inadequate infrastructure and marketing facilities. In a study of farm households in Ethiopia, Abrar et al. (2004) find a high supply response of different crops to changes in relative prices, but non-price factors such as access to fertilizers, land, infrastructure and marketing are often more important than prices in determining how much of which crops is produced for market.

The International Monetary Fund (IMF) and the World Bank are naturally concerned with the performance of the agricultural sector in countries to which they lend under various adjustment programmes (see Chapters 14 and 16). Three interrelated issues are typically addressed:

- The terms of trade between agriculture and the rest of the economy.
- The efficiency of the agricultural sector.
- The supply response of agriculture to price changes.

With regard to the agricultural terms of trade, the IMF normally insists that the prices paid by state marketing boards to producers be increased. Traditionally, governments have 'taxed' the agricultural sector through agricultural marketing boards, driving a large wedge between the prices paid to producers and the market prices of the commodities concerned. One implication, therefore, of raising producer prices is that government revenue may fall. This has implications for government expenditure if there is a budget constraint. Only if the elasticity of the supply of output with respect to producer prices is greater than unity will government revenue not fall; but as we saw above, supply elasticity is typically less than unity.

To achieve efficiency within agriculture, the IMF concentrates on factors such as improving storage and transport facilities, increasing the availability of agricultural inputs, improving extension services, insisting on the economic pricing of output and inputs, and privatizing marketing and extension services.

We saw earlier that the supply response of farmers to price changes depends a great deal on the ability to respond, which, in turn, depends on infrastructure, transport, access to inputs and so on. Governments may be in a dilemma here because raising producer prices and reducing their own revenue may impair their ability to spend on infrastructure and other facilities. Given that the elasticity of supply with respect to non-price factors is higher than with respect to price, it would seem unwise to cut public expenditure as far as it affects the agricultural sector.

Transforming traditional agriculture

The task of transforming traditional agriculture is not simply a question of land reform or price policy, however. The transformation of traditional agriculture is also dependent on **new inputs**. The policy issue is to determine the form that the new inputs should take if agriculture is to attract an adequate share of investment resources. New seeds are especially important to raise agricultural productivity (see Lipton and Longhurst, 1989).

The way to transform traditional agriculture into a dynamic source of growth is by investment to produce a supply of new agricultural inputs that will be profitable for farmers to adopt. What is lacking is not so much an unwillingness on the part of the agricultural sector to accept new ideas, but public expenditure and the organization of particular public activities to serve the agricultural sector. Agricultural research, and investment in people to improve human capabilities in agriculture, has been neglected.

The state of agriculture in Africa is particularly dire. Agricultural yields are low and food shortages and undernourishment are rife. Much of the support in place for agriculture in Africa was dismantled in the 1970s by World Bank structural adjustment programmes (see Chapter 14); for example, subsidies for fertilizers and seeds, guaranteed prices for crops, and research and development – all the policies that supported Asia's so-called **Green Revolution** in the 1960s, which tripled and quadrupled yields of crops such as wheat, rice and maize.

The father of the 1960s' Green Revolution (which bypassed Africa) was **Norman Borlaug**, an American biologist working in Mexico, who crossed Japanese dwarf wheat with a disease-resistant local strain to produce a high-yielding hybrid, which came to be known as 'Mexican dwarf wheat'. In countries such as India and Pakistan, yields increased threefold. Borlaug is credited with saving more lives than anyone in history – at least 1 billion in Asia alone. His motto was 'it is impossible to build a peaceful world on empty stomachs'. He was awarded the Nobel Peace Prize in 1970 and died in 2009, aged 95. Borlaug's breakthrough – the result of 30 years' research – is a prime example of the impact that technology can have on the productivity of agriculture.

A similar breakthrough or 'kick-start' is required in Africa. To this end, an Alliance for a Green Revolution in Africa (AGRA) was founded in 2006 with a $150 million grant from the Rockefeller Foundation and the Bill & Melinda Gates Foundation to help raise yields through improved farming methods, new seeds and fertilizers, working with the African Agricultural Technology Foundation based in Nairobi, Kenya. One of the major projects is to develop 'water-efficient' maize to cope with long periods of drought now being experienced in southern Africa.

In general, there is a need for a second Green Revolution in agriculture to follow the first in the 1960s, which has now run its course. Modern science can help. **Biotechnology**, including **genetically modified (GM) technology**, has the potential to raise productivity substantially and to reduce the incidence of famine and malnutrition. A GM crop is any crop variety that has had a gene or genes from a different species or variety inserted into its genetic material using genetic engineering techniques. Currently, about 15% of the world's farmland (approximately 180 million hectares) is devoted to GM crops. Research is being done on many crops, but virtually all planting covers just five crops: soya beans, maize, cotton, rice and oilseed rape (canola). There is, however, strong opposition to GM crops from consumers and environmental groups on the grounds of risk to human health, but GM crops are already in the food chain because they are widely used as processed food ingredients and for animal feed. So far, there is no scientific evidence that they are harmful.

The benefit of GM technology is that it can produce crops that can resist pests, can grow in salty soil, are drought resistant, use nitrogen more efficiently, can be stored for longer, and are more nutritious. Rice is an important staple food for poor people. Over 3 billion people in the world get at least 20% of their calorie intake from rice. The International Rice Research Institute in Manila, Philippines is at the forefront of research to produce different varieties of rice to suit particular environments where the problem may be drought, flooding, heat or salty water. With regard to nutrition, **Ingo Potrykus**, working in Zurich, teamed up with Peter Beyer to genetically engineer a type of rice ('golden rice') to contain beta-carotene, which is the pigment that produces vitamin A. This is an important breakthrough since vitamin A deficiency kills 2 million children a year and blinds many more. This research has been funded not by biotechnology companies, concerned with maximizing returns by patenting and the exercise of intellectual property rights, but by the Swiss government and the Rockefeller Foundation. The plan is for growers to be given the new rice free by national research centres supervised by the International Rice Research Institute. Agricultural innovation cannot flourish without well-resourced agricultural extension services within countries. Research is now under way to cross 'golden rice' with a grain implanted with three genes to boost iron content to combat anaemia, which many people suffer from in developing countries. A quality protein maize has also been developed by Norman Borlaug, containing many important amino acids that could dramatically reduce the number of children who die of malnutrition. GM cotton has increased yields by nearly 100% in India by being more disease resistant.

Some people argue that GM is the only technology that can prevent future world food crises and rising prices of basic foodstuffs. Malnutrition remains a major scourge in developing countries, and by 2030, there will also be 2 billion more mouths to feed. The application of new technology is urgently required.

What matters most are the incentives and associated opportunities that farm people have to augment production by means of investments that include the contribution of agricultural research and the improvement of human skills. We emphasize again that subsistence agriculture is an uncertain activity and therefore risky, particularly when survival is at stake, and this is another factor that breeds conservatism and makes change difficult, even in the face of opportunities. Poor people prefer to be safe than sorry; they tend to prefer an inferior outcome that is relatively certain to the prospect of a higher average return with a greater degree of risk attached. They are **risk averse**. This is clearly not irrational behaviour for poor people living on the margin of subsistence, even if the greater risk is imagined rather than real. To overcome inertia on this score, an integral element of agrarian reform must be policies designed to minimize risk and uncertainty through the provision of various types of insurance (as discussed in Chapter 2).

The growth of the money economy

The question of the willingness to change customs and traditions leads naturally to a consideration of how peasant subsistence economies, producing goods for consumption only, typically transform themselves into money economies with an export and industrial sector. From historical experience (see Chang, 2009), two factors would appear to be crucial for the expansion of the agricultural sector and the eventual production of goods for exchange at home and abroad:

1. The expansion of communications to create outlets and markets for surplus production – and to encourage the production of the surplus itself.
2. The emergence of a class of middlemen or export–import merchants acting as agents between world markets and the domestic agricultural sectors.

If these conditions prevail, purely subsistence farming can develop first into mixed agriculture, where part of the crop is retained for subsistence and part is sold in the market, and then into modern agriculture with production entirely for the market, very often based on one crop. In the transition from subsistence agriculture, cash crops can utilize slack labour and land when the subsistence crops are finished; but the transition into mixed farming is possible only if the farmer has the inputs to raise productivity and the credit to purchase those inputs, as well as the marketing facilities.

Modern agriculture, run on strictly commercial lines for profit and based on one crop, must rely on exports since the size of the domestic market will generally be too small. The system of modern commercialized agriculture, upon which many developing countries depend for their export earnings, is often termed **agribusiness.** This is a catch-all phrase referring not only to the production of the commodity in question, but also to the backward and forward linkages associated with the production process: the provision of finance, machinery, fertilizers, seed and so on at the input end, and the processing, manufacturing and marketing of the product at the output end.

Today, **multinational corporations** have a powerful position and a strong hold over the production and export of major agricultural commodities produced in developing countries. To give just a few examples: three US firms control over one-half of the global banana trade, five European companies control 90% of the tea sold in developed countries, and the two largest coffee companies control 20% of the world market.

The ability to export and the ability to market internally imply surplus production over subsistence needs, and it is the size of this surplus that will largely determine the speed with which the subsistence sector can be drawn into the money economy. Again, we come to the fact that unless productivity in agriculture increases, the expansion of the monetized sector will tend to decelerate as the land for cultivation dries up. When land has been exploited to the full, it acts as a constraint on development unless agricultural productivity increases or non-agricultural activities can be established.

The emergence of an export sector provides a powerful stimulus to the development and extension of the money economy. Exports create the capacity to import, and the very purchase of foreign products can encourage further export specialization. A population that acquires a taste for imported goods provides the impetus to producers to export more. In the case of new goods, as well as new techniques, there is strong evidence that peasant producers respond to incentives, and are not as different from 'Western economic man' as is sometimes claimed. Imports also provide a stimulus to industrialization. If a market for a foreign manufactured good becomes established, it becomes easier and less risky, with the aid of tariff protection, for a domestic manufacturer to set up in business because the market is assured. Imports can also substitute for domestic capital and raise the growth rate directly.

When farmers start to specialize in goods for export, and rely on other producers for goods they previously produced themselves, the money economy will spread from the foreign trade sector to the rest of the domestic economy. This is nothing more than the international division of labour giving rise to the need for a means of exchange within a country as well as between countries.

The emergence of an export sector, the spread of the money economy and the establishment of industries typically occur concurrently. What form industrialization takes will depend, in the first instance, on the initial impetus. One stimulus to industrialization that we have already mentioned is imports creating a market for goods that can be produced domestically without much difficulty. A more obvious factor leading naturally to industrialization is the availability of resources from the land, forming an indigenous industrial base. In this case, industrialization takes the form of the processing of raw materials. There are few countries that do not possess some natural resource or other, and every country will have a comparative advantage in the production of one or other raw material that can be processed. These are the agribusinesses mentioned earlier.

In many of the present developing countries, formerly under colonial rule, the initiating force behind industrialization was the foreign exploitation of resources. Industrial activity took the form of mining operations and plantation agriculture. The establishment of foreign enclave activities undoubtedly exerted a development impact, but it is sometimes argued that development would have been more rapid if countries had been left to their own devices. Some claim that the long-run development of these countries was impaired because the availability of cheap labour from the subsistence sector discouraged the installation of more modern productive machinery, and also that the foreign ownership and exploitation of countries' resources considerably reduced the potential level of investment through the remittance of profits to the host country. This is the argument of dependency theorists, which is discussed more fully in Chapter 10.

Finance for traditional agriculture

For many years, traditional agriculture has been starved of investment resources. While it accounts for approximately 30% of output and 50% of total employment, it attracts little more than 10% of total investment resources. Private capital has no doubt been deterred by the risks involved and the low returns in traditional agriculture. But institutional investment has also been meagre. For example, in the early years of the World Bank, 1947–59, only $124 million was spent on agriculture out of total loans of $4 billion. Official development assistance (ODA) to agriculture from multilateral and bilateral sources rose sharply in the 1970s, but since 1979, the share of ODA going to agriculture decreased from 18% to 3.5% in 2004. In absolute terms, it reached a peak of $8 billion (measured at 2004 US$) in 1984, falling to only £3.4 billion in 2004 (World Bank, 2007).

Within agriculture-based developing economies, the share of public expenditure spent on agriculture has also decreased from 7% in 1980 to 4% in 2004 (World Bank, 2007). This gives some measure of the neglect of agriculture, which was partly responsible for the world food crisis and food price rises in 2007–08.

The public sectors of developing countries, and multilateral institutions such as the World Bank, have a responsibility to invest in agriculture to raise productivity and combat poverty. Some projects will involve increasing the output of traditional crops through the more effective use of seeds, fertilizers and water. Other projects will involve changing the product mix from subsistence crops to the production of high-value crops.

At present, the largest single component of lending to agriculture is irrigation, which permits the expansion of cultivation and makes more intensive cultivation possible by permitting double cropping. Bank-financed irrigation schemes have had a major impact on rice yields and production in Asia. The World Bank has also become the most important source of financial and technical assistance for the construction of fertilizer plants in developing countries, and these have played an important role in increasing yields and output. The World Bank gives credit for rural infrastructure projects, such as roads to reduce marketing and supply bottlenecks, and rural electrification schemes. **Agricultural extension** is another important aspect of the World Bank's assistance to the rural sector. In India, where 'contact' farmers disseminate knowledge to their neighbours of improved techniques learnt from field agents, over 10 million farm families have been helped. The rural poor now have more extensive and easier access to credit financed by the World Bank. In India, much of the credit has been used by small farmers to provide supplementary irrigation.

Finally, the World Bank operates various multipurpose projects that combine a wide range of activities, normally in conjunction with a regional development programme. In Mexico, some 75,000 low-income families have benefited from such a project in about 30 localities through investments in irrigation, soil conservation, electrification, schools, healthcare, water supplies and marketing services. Each dollar the bank invests in rural development is supplemented by local investment, and the bank rightly stresses that its contribution to the total flow of resources can be effective only if appropriate national policies are pursued on pricing, taxation, land reform and so on. The major part of the World Bank's programme to reach the rural poor is still in the process of implementation, and is therefore difficult to assess reliably, but indications suggest that a combination of additional resources, institutional reforms and national government commitment to improvement in the rural sector can have a major impact.

Apart from the World Bank, other multilateral institutions exist to help traditional agriculture, notably the UN's **International Fund for Agricultural Development (IFAD)**, which seeks to integrate small farmers and landless people into the development process. IFAD states that its priority is for 'projects which will have a significant impact on improving food production in developing countries, particularly for the benefit of the poorest sections of the rural population'. Between 1978 and 2014, $15 billion had been dispersed.

In the absence of external institutional investment, the sources of capital for the expansion of agriculture and industry are relatively limited in the early stages of development. In a truly subsistence economy, in the sense of an economy producing only what it needs for itself and no more, everyone is a Robinson Crusoe, supplying their own capital by refraining from present consumption. With specialization in the production of goods for export, and the producer's need for capital to expand productive capacity, mechanisms grow up spontaneously to meet the need for credit. It is a good market maxim that demand will create a supplier at a price. The suppliers are generally village moneylenders, shopkeepers, landlords and, not infrequently, the Church – especially in South America – charging rates of interest that often exceed 50%.

The interdependence of agriculture and industry

Once agriculture emerges from its subsistence state and starts to specialize and produce goods for export, and industry develops under the impact of growth in the agricultural sector, the two sectors of agriculture and industry become interdependent. The industrial sector adds to the demand for goods produced by agriculture and absorbs surplus labour, which may raise productivity in agriculture. In turn, the agricultural sector provides a market for industrial goods out of rising real income, and makes a factor contribution to development through the release of resources if productivity rises faster than the demand for commodities. Adam Smith, in *Wealth of Nations* (1776), clearly recognized this interdependence (Kim, 2015).

Demand coming from agriculture can be a major stimulus to industrialization. Adelman (1984) has described the process as 'agricultural demand-led industrialization'. Taking 27 social accounting matrixes for low- and high-income economies, Vogel (1994) has shown that the impact of agriculture on industry is much higher than the impact of industry on agriculture, and it increases with the level of income. At low levels of income, a $1 expenditure in agriculture generates a $2.75 increase in induced demand for non-agricultural inputs and services, and a $10 increase in high-income countries. It is rural household demand that contributes most to the backward multiplier, which leads Vogel (1994) to conclude: 'the early development theorists failed to articulate a place for rural household demand for consumer goods. Not recognizing the centrality of these institutional feedbacks in agriculture's production linkages in developing economies has been one of the great failures of theories of economic development.' It is true that a stagnant rural sector has held back industrial development in several developing countries. (See section below, A model of the complementarity between agriculture and industry.)

The transfer of resources from agriculture to industry may be in the form of capital or labour or both. Since labour is in abundant supply in most low-income countries, there is generally no difficulty in releasing labour for industry, except during harvest time. In any case, labour will tend to migrate naturally in response to seemingly better opportunities in the industrial sector and higher real incomes. The real earnings of labour in the industrial sector may be more than twice as much as the agricultural wage. If the industrial sector is to be guaranteed an adequate supply of labour, some wage differential is inevitably required to offset the higher real living costs in an urban environment, to compensate for the forfeit of non-monetary benefits of rural life, and to compensate for greater job uncertainty in the industrial sector. Real earnings may also be higher because of genuinely higher productivity in the industrial sector, where labour has more factors of production to work with. Most models of rural–urban migration make migration a positive function of the *expected* urban–rural wage differential, which is the difference between the urban wage, adjusted for the proportion of the total urban labour force employed (as a proxy for the probability of finding work), and the agricultural real wage (see the section below, Rural–urban migration and urban unemployment, for an outline of the model).

Capital may be less 'mobile' than labour, and if there is considered to be insufficient lending from the agricultural sector on a voluntary basis, it may become necessary for a government to extract savings compulsorily from the agricultural sector by taxation. As mentioned already, this method was resorted to in a harsh manner by Japan at the time of the Meiji Restoration and Soviet Russia after the communist revolution. In Japan between 1880 and 1900, the land tax provided approximately 80% of central government tax revenue, and in Russia forced extraction of the agricultural surplus took the form of expropriation of land and the extermination of labour. Industrialization in Western Europe, and particularly in England, was also financed to a large extent by surpluses generated on the land, but transference of these surpluses was, on the whole, voluntary through a rapidly expanding banking system. Today, developing countries, despite their access to foreign sources of capital, must also rely heavily on extracting the surplus from agriculture to finance industrialization. The difficulty is to decide on the best means of extraction without impairing the incentive to produce, or damaging the growth of productivity, on which a growing agricultural surplus depends. The financing of economic development will be discussed more fully in Part IV.

Economic development with unlimited supplies of labour

The process of the emergence of a money economy from a subsistence state was formalized by Sir Arthur Lewis in his classic paper 'Economic Development with Unlimited Supplies of Labour' (1954).[3] There, he presented a 'classical' model of a dual economy with the purpose, as he described it, of seeing what can be made of the classical framework for understanding the issues of distribution, capital accumulation and growth in developing countries. His ultimate aim was to emphasize the crucial role of the capitalist surplus in the development process.

Arthur Lewis

Born 1915, St Lucia, West Indies. Died 1991. Professor of Economics, Manchester University, University of the West Indies and Princeton University. Vice-Chancellor, University of the West Indies; Director of the Caribbean Development Bank. Wrote the first textbook on development economics, *The Theory of Economic Growth* (1955), but most famous for his 1954 paper, 'Economic Development with Unlimited Supplies of Labour', one of the most influential papers in development economics, still widely consulted today. One of the 'fathers' of development economics; awarded the Nobel Prize for Economics, 1979.

The Lewis model therefore starts with the assumption of a dual economy with a modern exchange (capitalist) sector and an indigenous (non-capitalist) subsistence sector, and assumes that there are unlimited supplies of labour in the subsistence sector, in the sense that the supply of labour exceeds the demand for labour at the subsistence wage; that is, the marginal product of workers in the subsistence sector is equal to, or less than, the subsistence or institutional wage.

It has even been argued that the marginal product of labour may be zero or negative in an economy that is still at a fairly low level of development and experiencing a rapid growth of population. Indeed, Lewis (1954) said: 'there are large sectors of [a developing] economy where the marginal productivity of labour is negligible, zero or even negative'.

One of the distinguishing features of agriculture is that it is an activity that is subject to diminishing returns owing to the fixity of the supply of land. If there is rapid population growth and labour has little employment opportunity other than on the land, a stage may be reached where the land cannot provide further workers with a living unless the existing workers drastically reduce their hours of work. These propositions are illustrated in Figure 5.1. The curve drawn represents the marginal product of successive units of labour added to the land. After the employment of X units of labour, the marginal product of labour begins to fall owing to diminishing returns; after X_1 units of labour, labour's marginal contribution to output falls below the subsistence wage; and

Figure 5.1 Marginal product of successive units of labour added to the land

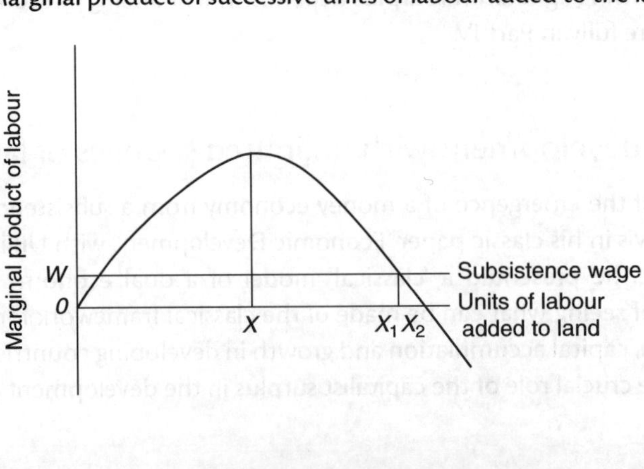

after X_2 units of labour, labour's contribution to output becomes negative and total product will decline with successive additions of labour beyond X_2.

In Lewis's model, labour in excess of X_1 in Figure 5.1 is in completely elastic supply to the industrial sector at whatever the industrial wage.[4] The industrial or capitalist sector is represented in Figure 5.2. The curve *NR* represents the marginal product of labour in the capitalist sector, *W* is the industrial wage and, on the profit-maximizing assumption, labour is employed in the capitalist sector up to the point where the marginal product is equal to the wage rate. That is, *M* will be employed. Workers in excess of *M* earn what they can in the subsistence sector. The industrial wage is assumed to be determined in some relation to the wage that workers can earn in the subsistence sector. The differential (WW_1) between the industrial wage and the subsistence wage will be a function of many factors, some of which were mentioned earlier, for example higher real living costs in the capitalist sector and greater job uncertainty. Given that the industrial wage is based on earnings in the subsistence sector, capitalists have a direct interest in holding down productivity in the subsistence sector, and Lewis commented that the record of every imperial power in Africa in modern times was one of impoverishing the subsistence economy.

In Figure 5.2, the total product of labour, *0NPM*, is split between the payment to labour in the form of wages, *0WPM*, and the capitalist surplus, *WNP*. The expansion of the capitalist sector and the rate of absorption of labour from the subsistence sector depends on the use made of the capitalist surplus. If the surplus is reinvested, leading to greater capital formation, this will increase the total product of labour. The marginal product curve will shift upwards to the right, say N_1R_1, which means that if wages remain constant, the capitalist sector can now afford to employ more labour and will do so by drawing on labour from the subsistence sector to the extent of MM_1 workers. The size of the capitalist surplus will increase from *WNP* to WN_1P_1, which is available for further reinvestment and so the process goes on. For Lewis, this is the essence of the development process. The stimulus to investment in the capitalist sector comes from the rate of profit, which must rise over time because all the benefits of increased productivity accrue to capital if the real wage is constant.[5]

According to Lewis (1954), the share of profits in the national income (*P*/0) will also rise. First, the share of profits in the capitalist sector (*P*/*C*) will increase, and second, the capitalist sector relative to the national income (*C*/0) will tend to expand; that is, if $P/0 = P/C \times C/0$, then *P*/0 will rise as *P*/*C* and *C*/0 increase. For Lewis, the latter is the more important. Lewis (1954) said: 'if we ask why the less developed countries save so little, the answer is not because they are so poor but because their capitalist sector is so small'.

Figure 5.2 Industrial/capitalist sector

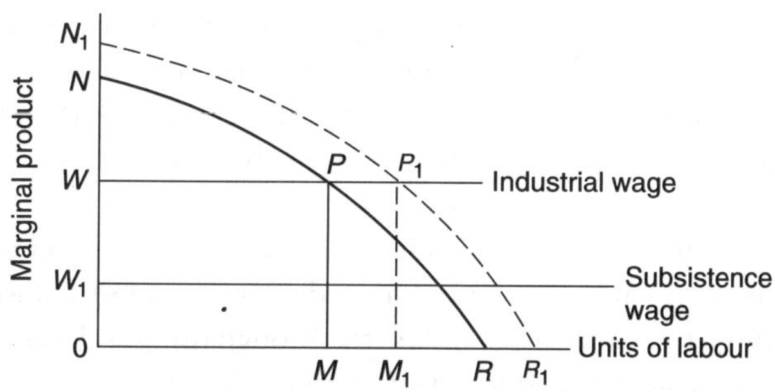

The process outlined by Lewis comes to an end when capital accumulation has caught up with population, so that there is no surplus labour in the subsistence sector left to absorb. When all surplus labour is absorbed, the supply of labour to the industrial sector becomes less than perfectly elastic. It is now in the interests of producers in the subsistence sector to compete for labour, since the marginal product of labour is no longer below the institutional wage. This is the so-called 'Lewis turning point'. This change in producer behaviour in the subsistence sector has also been defined as the end of the take-off stage (Ranis and Fei, 1961). There is a debate in the literature over whether China has reached the Lewis turning point (Islam and Yokota, 2008). Some argue that its arrival can be seen in more assertive workers and wage rises. Others argue, however, that recent wage rises represent an upward shift in the whole labour supply curve, not a turning point, because the reserves of labour in agriculture are still vast and where labour's productivity is less than 20% of the rest of the economy. Lewis gave several reasons why wages may rise before the turning point is reached (see below).

Implicit in the Lewis model is the assumption that employment growth in the capitalist sector will be proportional to the rate of capital formation. If profits are reinvested in labour-saving technology, however, this will not be so, and the rate of growth of employment in the industrial sector, as well as the rate of absorption from the agricultural sector, may be very low.

It is also possible that the process of absorption may end prematurely before surplus labour in the subsistence sector is fully exhausted, owing to checks to the expansion of the capitalist surplus. Capital accumulation and labour absorption may be checked due to the expansion of the capitalist sector itself. For example, as the capitalist sector expands, the terms of trade may turn against it. If the demand for food expands faster than agricultural output, the capitalist sector will be forced to pay higher prices for food in exchange for industrial goods, reducing the size of the capitalist surplus. This will have two effects.

First, if the capitalists are forced to pay higher prices for the goods they buy relative to those they sell, this means less saving for investment. The problem does not arise if productivity in agriculture is expanding rapidly, but Lewis recognized that the failure of peasant agriculture to increase its productivity has probably been the chief factor holding back the expansion of the industrial sector in many developing countries. If this is so, argue Lewis's critics, the growth of non-farm employment can be said to depend on the growth of the agricultural surplus. This is, in fact, the starting point of **neoclassical models of development** (see Jorgenson, 1966), in contrast to classical models with their emphasis on surplus labour.

The second effect arising from the expansion of the capitalist sector if there is a shortage of food is that the real wage may have to rise in industry, further squeezing the capitalist surplus. If labour is needed in agriculture to meet the demand for food, unlimited supplies of labour at a *constant real wage* may be very limited indeed. The assumption of an unlimited supply of labour is the central proposition underlying the classical approach to the theory of development, and Jorgenson has argued that the classical approach stands or falls by this hypothesis. Historically, of course, real wages have risen in agriculture *and* industry, and the capitalist sector has also expanded rapidly, which lends support to a middle view between the classical and neoclassical approaches. Lewis (1954) recognized the importance of both capital accumulation and food supply, and it is this consideration that forms the basis of his argument for the balanced growth of the agricultural and industrial sectors.

Capital accumulation in the industrial sector may also be checked for reasons unrelated to the expansion of the capitalist sector and its demand for food. For example, real wages may be forced up directly by trade unions, or indirectly through rising real wages in the subsistence sector due to increased agricultural productivity. Lewis (1954) states that:

> anything which raises the productivity of the subsistence sector (average product per person) will raise real wages in the capitalist sector, and will therefore reduce the capitalist surplus and the rate of capital accumulation, unless it at the same time more than correspondingly moves the terms of trade against the subsistence sector.

Lewis reached this conclusion because one of the simplifying assumptions of his classical two-sector model is that the expansion of the capitalist sector is limited *only* by a shortage of capital, so that any increase in prices and purchasing power for farmers is not a stimulus to industrialization but an obstacle to the expansion of the capitalist sector. How does this square with the idea of the agricultural sector providing a market for industrial goods, and the view of the World Bank (1979) that 'a stagnant rural economy with low purchasing power holds back industrial growth in many developing countries'? The answer is that there does seem to be a contradiction, because the classical approach emphasizes supply to the exclusion of demand, or rather takes for granted that there will always be a market clearing price for industrial goods. In practice, there will always be a minimum below which the price of industrial goods cannot fall, set by the subsistence level wage in industry.

Johnston and Mellor (1961) recognized this worrying feature of the Lewis model many years ago, when they perceptively remarked: 'there is clearly a conflict between emphasis on agriculture's essential contribution to the capital requirements for overall development, and emphasis on increased farm purchasing power as a stimulus to industrialization. Nor is there any easy reconciliation of the conflict.' The challenge of reconciliation has never been taken up in a satisfactory way, but there is a resolution of the conflict if the **complementarity** between the two sectors is recognized from the outset, and it is remembered that there must be an equilibrium terms of trade that balances supply and demand in both sectors. The basis of a model of reconciliation is provided by Kaldor (1979).

A model of the complementarity between agriculture and industry[6]

We have seen that agriculture provides the potential for capital accumulation in industry by providing a marketable surplus. The greater the surplus, the cheaper industry can obtain food and the more saving and capital accumulation can be undertaken. This is the supply side. But industry also needs a market for its industrial goods, which, in the early stages of development, must largely come from agriculture. This is the demand side, and the higher the price of agricultural goods, the greater agricultural purchasing power will be. Given this conflict between low food prices being good for industrial supply and high food prices being good for industrial demand, what is required is a simple model that brings together agriculture and industry in an equilibrium framework, where the terms of trade between agriculture and industry provide the equilibrating mechanism, ensuring that supply and demand grow at the same rate in each sector.

Let us first model growth in the agricultural sector in relation to the terms of trade, then growth in the industrial sector, and then bring the two sectors together. Agriculture's growth rate will be a function of how much it invests relative to output and of the productivity of investment. How much investment goods it obtains from industry in exchange for food that it 'saves' depends on the price of industrial goods relative to food; that is, on the terms of trade between industry and agriculture. The higher the price of investment goods, the lower the possible investment for a given amount of food and the lower the growth of supply capacity. This inverse relation between the industrial terms of trade (the price of industrial goods relative to the price of food) and the agricultural growth rate (g_A) is shown in Figure 5.3.

Figure 5.3 Industrial terms of trade and agricultural growth rate

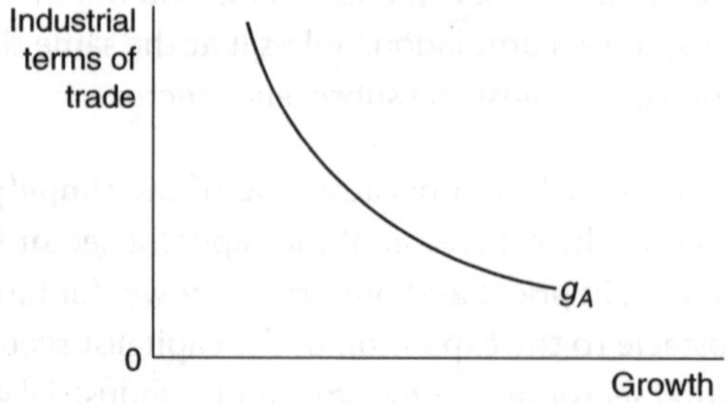

Industry's growth rate will also be a function of its investment ratio and the productivity of investment. But there is a certain minimum to the terms of trade, below which industry would not be able to invest anything because all output would be required to pay for workers' wage goods (food). If all wages are consumed, the cost of food input per unit of output in industry will depend on the real wage rate in industry divided by the productivity of labour, that is $w/(O/L) = (W/O)$, where w is the real wage and W is the wage bill. Industrial prices must cover W/O, and this sets the lower limit to industrial prices relative to food prices. At the other extreme, industrial growth cannot exceed a certain maximum where the price of food is so low relative to industrial goods that all industrial goods are retained for investment in industry. The investment ratio approaches, in effect, 100%, and the upper limit to growth is given by the productivity of investment. The positive relation between the industrial terms of trade and the industrial growth rate (g_I) is shown in Figure 5.4.

If we now assume for simplicity (although without loss of generality) that the income elasticity of demand for agricultural and industrial goods is unity, then at a given terms of trade, the rate of growth of agricultural output represents the rate of growth of demand for industrial goods, and the rate of growth of industrial output represents the rate of growth of demand for agricultural output, and where g_A and g_I cross, there will be balanced growth of agriculture and industry (g^*) at equilibrium terms of trade (p^*), as shown in Figure 5.5.[7] In this model of the complementarity between agriculture and industry, we can see the implications of what happens if the terms of trade are not in equilibrium, as well as the checks to the expansion of industry that Lewis mentioned.

Figure 5.4 Industrial terms of trade and industrial growth rate

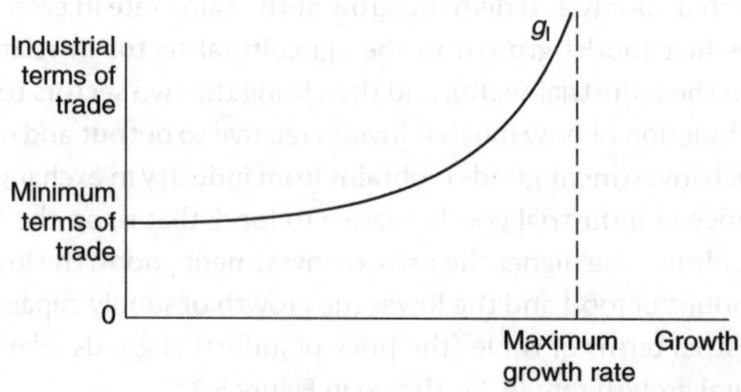

Figure 5.5 Growth equilibrium and disequilibrium

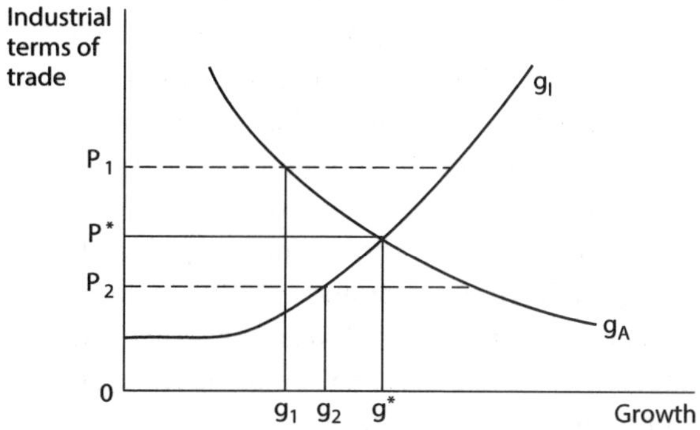

If the terms of trade are not in equilibrium – if the price of food is 'too low' or 'too high' in relation to industrial goods – then industrial growth is either demand constrained or supply constrained. For example, if in Figure 5.5, the terms of trade were at P_1, because the price of food was 'too low', industrial growth would be demand constrained to g_1 by a lack of agricultural purchasing power over industrial goods. Industry could accumulate capital, but it could not sell its goods. Alternatively, if the terms of trade were below equilibrium at P_2, industrial growth would be supply constrained to g_2 because the price of food would be 'too high', impairing capital accumulation in industry. Agriculture could buy, but industry could not supply. Growth is maximized at P*

We can now examine what happens if there are shifts in the curves. Clearly, shifts in the curves will cause both the growth rates and the equilibrium terms of trade to vary. An improvement in agricultural productivity that shifts g_A outwards will mean both higher industrial growth and an improvement in the industrial terms of trade. The importance of agricultural productivity improvement could not be better illustrated. An improvement in industrial productivity will shift g_I outwards, which will also mean higher industrial growth but at the expense of worse terms of trade for industry.[8] If there is a tendency for real wages in industry to rise commensurately with productivity increases, however, the g_I curve will remain stable and the terms of trade will never move against industry in favour of agriculture unless agricultural productivity falls and the g_A curve shifts inwards.

The checks to industrial expansion in Lewis's model are easily illustrated. A rise in the real wage in industry will shift the g_I curve inwards, which will choke industrial expansion unless an equivalent increase in agricultural productivity shifts the g_A curve outwards (see the earlier quote from Lewis).

A final implication of the model is that if, through time, agriculture is subject to diminishing returns, productivity in agriculture will fall, shifting inwards the g_A curve and reducing the rate of industrial growth. If the g_I curve is relatively stable, industrial growth depends fundamentally on the rate of land-saving innovations (technical progress) in agriculture to offset the effect of diminishing returns.

Rural–urban migration and urban unemployment

Lewis (1954) spoke of an urban–rural wage differential of approximately 30% to attract labour to the industrial sector. What has happened in recent years, however, is that the urban–rural wage differential has widened considerably beyond this level – there has been rural–urban migration on an unprecedented scale, but the expansion of the industrial sector has not generated sufficient employment for all those available to work. The urban–rural wage differential in China is over 300%, in Guatemala 300%, and in Vietnam 210% (World Bank, 2007). Migration has thus served to transfer unemployment from rural to urban areas, as described in Chapter 3. In 2008, for the first time in human history, the number of people living in urban areas exceeded those living in the rural sector. The **informal economy** of the urban sector harbours the bulk of unemployed labour in transition from the rural sector into industrial employment. The conclusion to be drawn is that the *expected* value of the urban wage, notwithstanding the probability of long spells of unemployment, still exceeds the wage in the rural sector, and as long as it does so, the process of migration will continue.

In these changed circumstances, development theory has focused its attention in recent years on **urban unemployment** and policies to combat it. Most of the models of the rural–urban migration process are pessimistic about reducing the level of urban unemployment by conventional means such as subsidies to labour or public works programmes in the urban areas. The reason is that migration from the land is made to be a function not only of the *actual* urban–rural wage differential but also of the level of employment opportunities. More employment opportunities reduce unemployment immediately but encourage more migration. It thus becomes an empirical question whether increasing the rate of growth of employment in urban areas will actually reduce unemployment. New migrants may exceed the number of new jobs created. The very real possibility exists that urban areas may be caught in a 'high level unemployment equilibrium trap' as long as surplus labour on the land remains and development policy concentrates new activity in established urban (industrial) centres.

One of the earliest and simplest models of the rural–urban migration process, which is also operational in the sense of being testable, is that of Todaro (1969, 1971). Let us consider its main features and implications.

The supply of labour to the urban sector is assumed to be a function of the *expected* urban–rural wage differential (*d*), where the expected urban–rural wage differential is equal to the actual urban wage times the probability of obtaining a job in the urban sector minus the average rural wage. Thus:

$$S = f_s(d) \tag{5.1}$$

where S is the supply of labour to the urban sector and:

$$d = w\pi - r \tag{5.2}$$

where *w* is the urban real wage, *r* is the average rural wage, and π is the probability of obtaining a job in the urban sector.

The probability of obtaining a job in the urban sector is assumed to be directly related to the rate of new job creation and inversely related to the ratio of unemployed jobseekers to the number of existing job opportunities,[9] that is:

$$\pi = \frac{\gamma N}{W - N} = \frac{\gamma N}{U} \tag{5.3}$$

where γ is the net rate of new urban job creation, *N* is the level of urban employment, *W* is the total urban labour force,[10] and *U* is the level of urban unemployment. Substituting equation (5.3) into equation (5.2) gives:

$$d = \frac{w\gamma N}{U} - r \tag{5.4}$$

If it is assumed that migration will come to a stop when the *expected* urban wage equals the rural wage (that is, when $d = 0$), we can derive from equation (5.4) the equilibrium level of unemployment as:

$$U^e = \frac{w\gamma N}{r} \tag{5.5}$$

It can be seen from equation (5.5) that a reduction in the *actual* urban wage will reduce the equilibrium level of unemployment, and a rise in the rural wage will also reduce it, but (paradoxically) an increase in the rate of new job creation will *raise* the equilibrium level of unemployment by increasing the probability of obtaining a job and encouraging migration. Whether policies such as wage subsidies can reduce unemployment therefore depends on whether the increase in the demand for labour as a result is greater or less than the induced supply.

From equation (5.5), we can solve for the equilibrium ratio of unemployment to employment and give some quantitative content to the model. Dividing both sides by N gives $U^e/N = w\gamma/r$. Thus, for example, if the industrial wage is twice as high as the rural wage ($w/r = 2$), and $\gamma = 0.05$, the equilibrium ratio of unemployment to employment will be 10%.

To consider the policy implications more fully, and to answer the question: Under what conditions will the actual level of urban unemployment rise?, let us suppose that the rate of urban job creation is a function of the urban wage, w, and a policy parameter, a (e.g., a government policy variable to increase employment). Thus:

$$\gamma = f_d(w,a) \qquad \frac{\partial \gamma}{\partial a} > 0 \tag{5.6}$$

If the growth of urban labour demand is increased, the response of labour supply can be written as:

$$\frac{\partial S}{\partial a} = \frac{\partial S}{\partial d}\frac{\partial d}{\partial \gamma}\frac{\partial \gamma}{\partial a} \tag{5.7}$$

Now, from equation (5.4) by partial differentiation, we have:

$$\frac{\partial d}{\partial \gamma} = w\frac{N}{U} \tag{5.8}$$

Substituting equation (5.8) into equation (5.7) gives:

$$\frac{\partial S}{\partial a} = \frac{\partial S}{\partial d}\frac{wN}{U}\frac{\partial \gamma}{\partial a} \tag{5.9}$$

There will be an increase in the absolute level of urban unemployment if the increase in supply in response to a policy change exceeds the increase in the absolute number of new jobs created, that is, if:

$$\frac{\partial S}{\partial d}\frac{wN}{U}\frac{\partial \gamma}{\partial a} > N\frac{\partial \gamma}{\partial a} \tag{5.10}$$

Now, cancelling N and $\partial\gamma/\partial a$ from both sides and multiplying both sides by d/w and U/W, the condition for unemployment to increase becomes:

$$\frac{\partial S/W}{\partial d/d} > \frac{d}{w}\frac{U}{W} \tag{5.11}$$

or substituting equation (5.2) into equation (5.11):

$$\frac{\partial S/W}{\partial d/d} > \frac{w\pi - r}{w}\frac{U}{W} \tag{5.12}$$

In words, equation (5.12) says that unemployment will increase in the urban sector as a result of a policy change to increase employment if the elasticity of the urban labour supply (by migration) with respect to the urban–rural wage differential exceeds the expected urban–rural wage differential as a proportion of the urban wage times the unemployment rate. Equation (5.12) is clearly testable. It transpires, in fact, that equation (5.12) is satisfied with a very low elasticity. For example, suppose that the actual urban wage is twice the rural wage,[11] that the probability of obtaining a job in the urban sector is 0.8 and that the unemployment rate is 10%, then the level of unemployment will increase if the elasticity of the urban labour supply with respect to the expected urban–rural wage differential is 0.03.

Note that the growth of total labour supply as a result of migration ($\partial S/W$) is not the same thing as the rate of growth of migration ($\partial S/S$), so that the elasticity of *supply* with respect to a change in job opportunities is not the same as the elasticity of *migration* with respect to a change in job opportunities. We could, however, convert equation (5.12) into the elasticity of migration with respect to $\partial d/\partial$ by multiplying both sides of equation (5.10) by U/S instead of U/W. This would give:

$$\frac{\partial S/S}{\partial d/d} > \frac{w\pi - r}{w}\frac{U}{S} \tag{5.13}$$

Since the ratio of unemployment to migration (U/S) is much higher than U/W, the elasticity of migration itself would have to be higher than the elasticity of labour supply for unemployment to increase following a job expansion programme. If, as before, we assume that $w/r = 2$, $\pi = 0.8$ and, say, $U/S = 2$, the migration elasticity would have to exceed 0.6 for unemployment to rise. In principle, this elasticity is easy to estimate by specifying a migration function in which migration is a function of the expected urban–rural wage differential, holding constant other factors affecting migration. For an interesting case study on Tanzania, see Barnum and Sabot (1977), who estimate an elasticity of migration with respect to the urban wage itself, holding other things constant, of between 0.7 and 2.0.[12]

Disguised unemployment: types and measurement

We must now examine more critically the classical assumption of unlimited supplies of labour, defined as labour's marginal product below the subsistence wage.

If the marginal product of labour in the rural sector is positive (which is not precluded in Lewis's model as long as it is below the subsistence wage), the withdrawal of labour from the subsistence sector will reduce total output. To argue that development via unlimited supplies of labour is feasible and relatively painless, one must implicitly assume that the marginal product of labour is virtually zero. The term **disguised unemployment** is usually defined loosely in this way. But the question arises of how workers can survive on the land if their marginal product is zero, or even positive but below subsistence. Who would employ such labour? Would output in the subsistence sector really remain unaffected if substantial quantities of labour migrated? In short, what precisely is meant by the term 'disguised unemployment'? Can it be quantified, and what are we to make of the argument that industrial development in surplus labour economies is a relatively painless process?

Let us redraw Figure 5.1 from the point of diminishing returns and describe more formally three possible interpretations of the concept of disguised unemployment that are commonly found in the literature. Let *A* in Figure 5.6 be the actual number of workers employable. One possible measure of disguised unemployment is the difference between *A* and *S*, or the gap between the number of workers available for work and the amount of employment that equates the marginal product of labour and the subsistence wage. This is the definition of unlimited supplies of labour in Lewis's model where, if the marginal product of labour is below the subsistence wage, landowners have no interest in retaining these workers and therefore do not compete for them with the industrial sector.

A second possible measure of disguised unemployment is the difference between *A* and *D*, or the gap between the actual number of workers available for employment and the level of employment at which the marginal product of labour is zero, which is sometimes referred to as the **static surplus**. This surplus is clearly less than if disguised unemployment is defined as labour with a marginal product below the subsistence wage.

A third measure of disguised unemployment is the difference between the actual number of workers available and the level of employment at which the marginal product of labour would be zero if some change occurred that enabled the same level of output to be produced with fewer workers. This is represented by a pivoting of the marginal product curve to MP_1. Disguised unemployment is now measured by the difference between *A* and *U*, which is sometimes referred to as the **dynamic surplus**. The dynamic surplus clearly embraces many 'types' of disguised unemployment because there are many reasons, particularly in developing countries, why labour productivity may be low and why small changes in technique and organization of production may release substantial quantities of labour.

There are three main ways of ascertaining whether surplus labour exists in the sense that labour's marginal product is zero. The first is to examine instances where substantial numbers of

Figure 5.6 Disguised unemployment

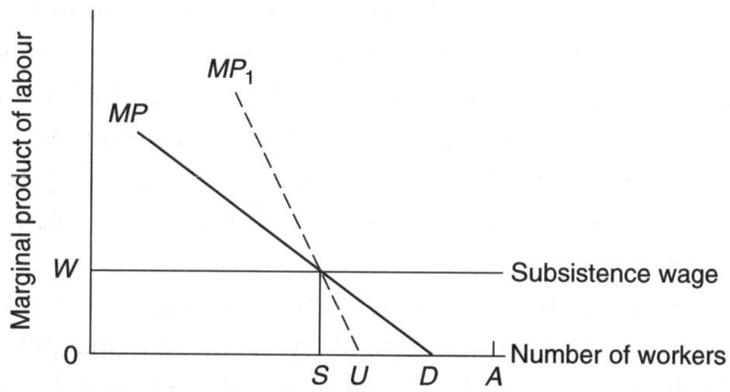

the agricultural labour force have been withdrawn from the land, either to work on some industrialization project or as the result of illness, and to observe whether agricultural output falls or not.

This method was followed by Schultz (1964), who examined the effect of the influenza epidemic in India in 1918–19, which killed approximately 8% of the agricultural labour force. He found that acreage and output during the following year declined, and concluded from this that surplus labour in Indian agriculture did not exist. An important criticism of Schultz's study, however, is that he failed to distinguish between the summer and winter season of the year following the epidemic. Mehra (1966) has shown that summer production, which just followed the epidemic, was not in fact reduced and that the decline in agricultural production in 1919–20 found by Schultz was entirely due to a reduction in the winter crop, which could have resulted from low rainfall. Notwithstanding the criticism, this is one method of approach.

A second method of estimating the static surplus is to take the difference between the labour available and the labour required to produce the current level of agricultural output *with given techniques*, making due allowance for the seasonality of production. The estimate of the magnitude of surplus labour in this case will vary with local conditions, and what is regarded as a normal working day.

A third approach is to estimate agricultural production functions (see Chapter 4) to test whether the elasticity of output with respect to labour input is significantly different from zero. This approach indicates whether or not there is surplus labour, but does not measure its magnitude.

When discussing labour's marginal product in agriculture and the extent of disguised unemployment, two important distinctions need to be made: between harvest and non-harvest time; and between farms that hire labour and those that do not. Within the production function approach, this distinction is easily made explicit and is a fruitful approach for that reason. As far as the distinction between hired and non-hired labour is concerned, the marginal product of family labour is unlikely to be zero if workers are hired, nor can the marginal product of the hired workers be zero if they are paid.

We now turn to the measurement of the **dynamic surplus**, which is the difference between the actual labour employed and the labour required, given some small change in technique (including an increase in the number of hours worked per day).

Unfortunately, those investigators who have measured the dynamic surplus have generally not distinguished between the causes of the surplus, nor made explicit the assumptions on which their estimates of labour requirements are based, and this is a major reason why estimates and opinions differ on the extent and existence of disguised unemployment. If the surplus is measured simply by the difference between the amount of labour that, in the investigator's opinion, should be necessary to produce a given output and the amount of labour that there actually is, this does not distinguish between the different causes of low productivity, such as poor health, lack of incentive, primitive technology or institutional factors. One interesting case study is by Foster and Rosenzweig (2010), who calculate that approximately 20% of the Indian agricultural workforce could be in dynamic surplus based on estimates of the minimum efficient scale of farms measured by the land–labour ratio. Increasing efficiency by expanding farm size could release substantial quantities of labour. The dynamic surplus in this case is related to unspecified barriers to land consolidation.

The simplest reconciliation between those who argue that there is such a phenomenon of disguised unemployment, in the sense of a very low marginal product of labour in agriculture, and those who disagree, is provided by the distinction between **the amount of labour time employed**

and the number of persons employed. In a wage payment system, it is extremely unlikely that labour would be used up to the point where its marginal product is zero. If the wage is positive, the marginal product will be positive too. But profit-maximizing behaviour is quite consistent with redundant labour. Labour is employed up to the point where the marginal product of a unit of *labour time* is equal to the wage, and **disguised unemployment takes the form of a small number of hours worked per person.** It is not that there is too much labour time but too many labourers spending it. Total output would fall if workers were drawn from the land, unless those remaining worked longer hours to compensate. How much disguised unemployment is estimated to exist depends on what is regarded as a normal working day. Estimates may be subjective, but unlimited supplies of labour exist in the classical sense provided those remaining on the land work harder or longer. Let us illustrate these points diagrammatically.

In Figure 5.7, total output is measured on the vertical axis above the origin, and the amount of labour time on the horizontal axis. Let L_1 be the point where the marginal product of labour time is equal to the subsistence wage corresponding to total output, Q. The number of workers is measured on the vertical axis below the origin, so that the tangent of the angle $0YL_1$ (tan *a*) gives the average number of hours worked by each unit of labour. If the tangent of the angle $0XL_1$ is regarded as the normal length of a working day so that the same output, Q, could be produced by X labour instead of Y, the amount of disguised unemployment would be equal to XY. It can easily be seen that if there was a reduction in the labour force from Y to *t* and the number of hours worked per worker remained the same (that is, tan $0tS$ = tan $0YL_1$), total output would fall from Q to P. If the normal working day is considered to be longer or shorter than the hours given by tan *b*, the amount of disguised unemployment will be greater or less than XY.

Let us now give a practical example. Suppose a producer employs 10 workers ($Y = 10$), each doing 5 hours' work a day ($\tan a = 5$), and the marginal product of the 50th hour is equal to the subsistence wage ($L_1 = 50$). If one worker leaves (say, *Yt*), total output will fall from Q to P unless the 9 workers now do the 50 hours' work previously done by 10 workers; that is, the working day must be increased by five-ninths of an hour. The amount of disguised unemployment depends on what is considered to be a full day's work. If 10 hours is considered normal, then only 5 workers would be required to do 50 hours' work and 5 could be regarded as disguised unemployed.

The precise conditions under which the remaining labour force would supply more work effort have been formalized by Sen (1966). If workers are rational, they will work up to the point

Figure 5.7 The dynamic surplus

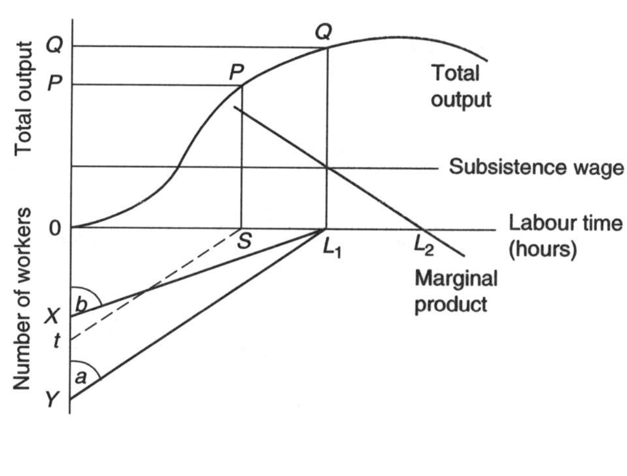

where the marginal utility of income from work (dU/dL) is equal to the marginal disutility of work (dV/dL). Now the marginal utility of income from work can be expressed as:

$$\frac{dU}{dL} = \frac{dY}{dL} \cdot \frac{dU}{dY} \tag{5.14}$$

where dY/dL is the marginal product of labour and dU/dY is the marginal utility of income. Welfare maximization therefore implies that:

$$\frac{dY}{dL} \cdot \frac{dU}{dY} = \frac{dV}{dL} \tag{5.15}$$

or:

$$\frac{dY}{dL} = \frac{dV}{dY} \div \frac{dU}{dY} = \frac{\text{Marginal disutility of work}}{\text{Marginal utility of income}} \tag{5.16}$$

Sen (1966) defines the ratio of the marginal disutility of work to the marginal utility of income as the **real cost of labour**.

Now consider Figure 5.8. Equilibrium is at N where the marginal product is equal to the real cost of labour. The removal of one worker reduces total output from $0PXN$ to $0PX_1N_1$, and marginal product rises from X to X_1. Equilibrium will be restored again at N if the real cost of labour remains constant – that is, if the ratio of the marginal disutility of work to the marginal utility of income does not increase. If the real cost of labour rises, there will not be full compensation for output lost. In other words, disguised unemployment in the sense of *zero* marginal product (or full compensation for lost output) implies a **non-increasing marginal disutility of work and a non-diminishing marginal utility of income**. Sen (1966) gives a number of reasons why this may be the case for people near subsistence with little work and a lot of leisure; for example, rising aspirations and more public expenditure on things such as education may prevent the marginal utility of income from falling, and higher incomes may prevent the marginal disutility of work from increasing if people are better fed.

The amount of underutilized labour is likely to be greater, the less capitalistic the organization of agriculture. In fact, in the extreme situation of no wage payment system with no competitive

Figure 5.8 Effect of labour withdrawal

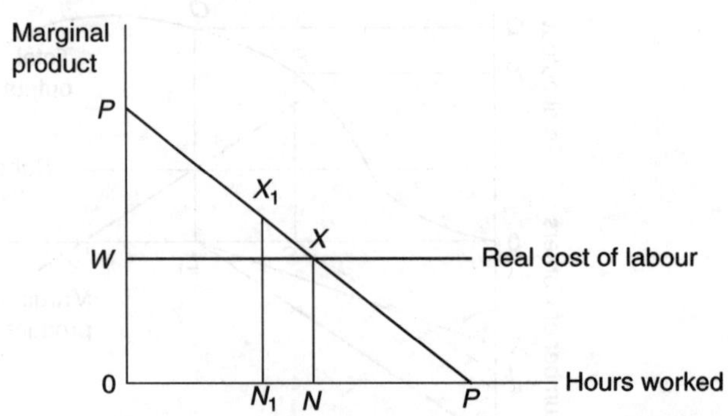

pressure and little desire to maximize, the distinction between a unit of labour and a unit of labour time becomes largely redundant, as in the classical model. It is perhaps this type of environment that the originators of the classical model mainly had in mind. In an extended family-type system, for example, the marginal product of both workers and labour time may be below the subsistence wage. It is the *average* product that matters for the group as a whole, not the product of the last worker or hour, and the average product may still be above the subsistence level when the marginal product of labour time is below it. It is difficult to represent both cases on the same diagram, but if the marginal product of labour is zero, the marginal product of labour time is bound to be zero (and probably negative), so we may continue to illustrate the argument in terms of labour time, as in Figure 5.9.

The basis of Figure 5.9 is the same as Figure 5.7. When the marginal product of labour time is zero at L_2, the average product of labour time is P_1, or PP_1 in excess of the subsistence wage P. The amount of labour time could be extended to L_3 without the average product of labour time falling below subsistence, and the amount of labour time could be made up of any combination of workers and hours worked. If the number of workers was Y_1, they could work hours equal to the tangent of $0Y_1L_3$ without the average product of labour time falling below subsistence. Even though the marginal product of labour time, L_2L_3, is negative, all workers can subsist if the total product is equally shared. A zero or negative marginal product of labour time is not inconsistent with rational worker behaviour if positive utility is attached to work, regardless of the effect on output.

Suppose, as in Figure 5.10, that the marginal product of a unit of labour time is zero after 4 hours' work but the marginal disutility of leisure is still negative at this point. The worker may substitute work for leisure, working, say, 6 hours, despite the fact that the marginal product of labour time is negative after the fourth hour. If such behaviour is observed, the presumption must be that the marginal utility attached to working exceeds the loss of utility resulting from a lower average product. The fact that people receive positive utility from work may partly explain why, in some societies, the time taken to do specific tasks seems to be much longer than in others.

Figure 5.9 Maximum sustainable labour

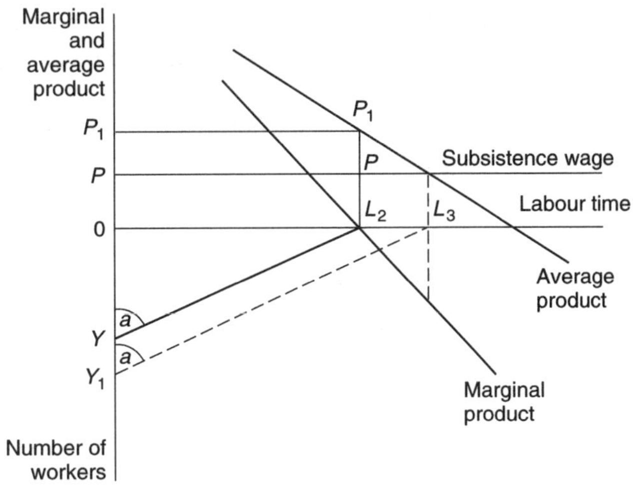

Figure 5.10 The possibility of negative marginal product

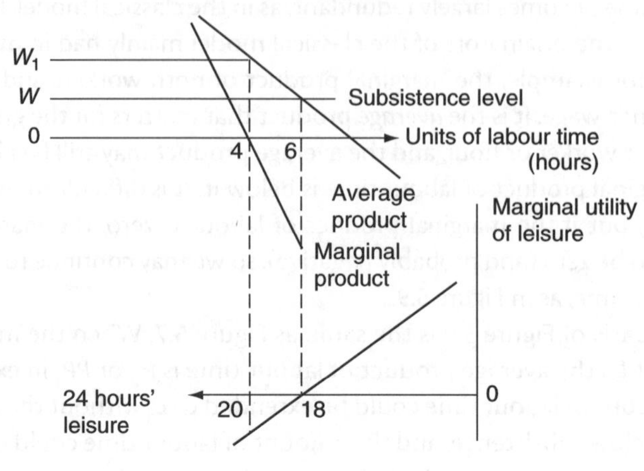

Incentives and the costs of labour transfer

Whether workers are willing to work more intensively to compensate for lost production as labour migrates, or whether capital is substituted for labour to raise productivity, requires some discussion of worker motivation and attitudes towards industrialization in general in a predominantly rural society.

Some economic incentive will almost certainly be required to induce agricultural labour to work extra hours. At the least, there will need to be goods with which to exchange their surplus production. It is sometimes argued, however, that peasant producers, accustomed to a traditional way of life, may not respond to such incentives – that their horizons are so limited that they have no desire to increase their surplus either by investing in capital or by working longer hours. The corollary of this argument is that as labour productivity increases, workers will ultimately reduce the number of hours they work. This is the notion of the **backward-bending supply curve of effort**, illustrated in Figure 5.11. *SS* is the supply curve of effort relating hours worked to the wage, determined by productivity. Total income is equal to the product of hours worked and the wage. Up to income level *SWZX*, supply responds positively to the wage. Beyond the wage *SW*, however, fewer hours will be offered. This is the point where the positive substitution effect of work for leisure (leisure is more 'expensive' the higher the wage) is offset by a negative income effect because of low aspirations.

A backward-bending supply curve of effort is not necessarily indicative, however, that peasants work for a fixed income and no more. The total income from work effort will still increase as long

Figure 5.11 Backward-bending supply curve

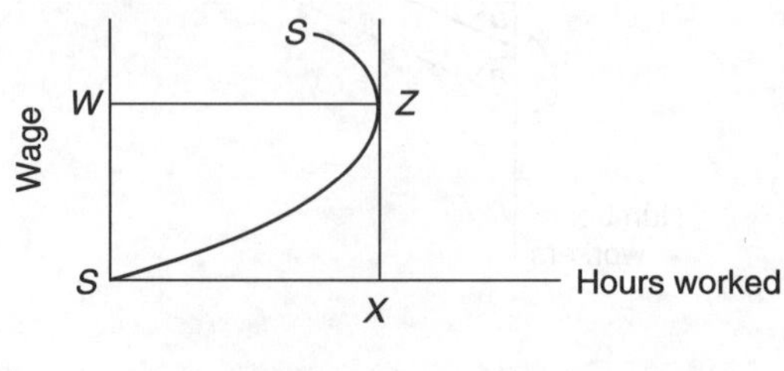

as the number of hours worked falls less than in proportion to the increased wage. But the need for incentives implies a claim on the community's real resources, which creates added difficulties for the argument that a pool of disguised unemployment can be used to build up 'productive' goods and expand the industrial sector in a 'costless' way. Not only may the opportunity cost of agricultural labour not be zero, but resource costs will also be involved in providing incentives to increase effort and productivity in order for resources to be released from agriculture in the first place. The resource costs will include the provision of investment goods in agriculture, consumer goods for peasant producers to buy, and social capital in the industrial sector to cater for migrants.

All this has an important bearing on the question of the valuation of labour in surplus labour economies when planning the social optimum allocation of resources and deciding on the degree to which activities in the industrial sector should be labour intensive. Even if labour's opportunity cost is negligible, the resource costs of labour transference must be considered as a cost to the community in expanding the industrial sector.

There is also the question of increased consumption to consider. If the objective of a surplus labour economy is to maximize growth, as opposed to the level of current consumption, the transference of labour will also involve a further 'cost' in terms of increased consumption because there will be a reduction in the size of the capitalist surplus if labour is valued at its opportunity cost. Consider Figure 5.12, which represents the capitalist sector of the economy. On the normal assumption of profit maximization, labour will be employed up to the point where the marginal product of labour is equal to the industrial wage. The capitalist surplus is equal to *WNX*. But suppose the supply of labour to the industrial sector is assumed to be 'costless' to society and is given, by the planners, a notional (or shadow) wage of zero. In this planned system, labour would be employed up to the point L_1. Given the industrial wage, *W*, and assuming the propensity to consume out of wages is unity, each additional unit of labour employed beyond *L* will involve consumption in excess of production. If LL_1 additional labour is employed, the size of the investible surplus would be reduced by XX_1L_1. It follows that in an economy geared to growth, the relationship between the consumption and production of migrant labour must also be taken into account when estimating the costs to society of industrial expansion with surplus labour from agriculture. If, at the margin, additional saving is valued more than an additional unit of consumption, the cost of a unit of labour transferred from agriculture to industry must include an allowance for increased consumption.

Figure 5.12 The social valuation of labour

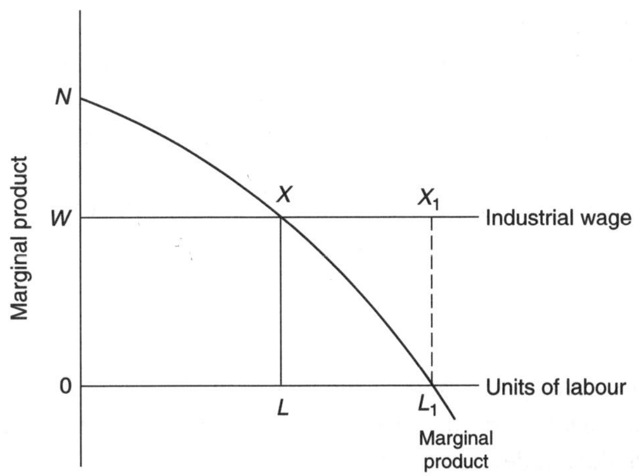

Summary

- Agriculture plays a crucial role in the early stages of a country's economic development. A surplus of agricultural output over subsistence needs – a marketable surplus – is required to feed labour in alternative activities, to release labour and to provide capital for investment in industry, to buy other domestically produced goods, and to provide foreign exchange to buy imports.
- A necessary condition for agriculture to make these various contributions to economic development is an increase of productivity in agriculture. Agricultural productivity is extremely low in most developing countries, which accounts for why so many people are so poor.
- There are several reasons for low agricultural productivity, including poor geographic and climatic conditions, a lack of investment and knowledge, the land tenure system, and urban bias in the allocation of resources for health, education and infrastructure.
- Land reform is needed in many countries in order to break up large inefficient estates, and to provide tenants with security of tenure so that they have the incentive to invest in new inputs.
- Attention needs to be paid to the pricing of agricultural goods to encourage a supply response in agriculture.
- The transformation of traditional agriculture requires new inputs such as new varieties of seeds and proper irrigation. Genetically modified (GM) food is a matter for debate. Finance for the purchase of new inputs is crucial.
- As productivity in agriculture rises, the agricultural sector and other sectors of the economy become more and more interdependent. Industrial growth can be fuelled by the release of cheap labour from agriculture. This is the essence of Arthur Lewis's model of 'economic development with unlimited supplies of labour'. The reinvestment of industrial profits drives industrial expansion.
- But industry needs a market for its goods, so the purchasing power of the agricultural sector is important. It is vital to get the terms of trade right between agricultural and industrial goods, if the growth of the economy is not to be demand constrained if the prices of agricultural goods are too low, or supply constrained because the prices are too high.
- Surplus labour on the land has led to a vast rural–urban migration process, which is swelling the amount of unemployment and underemployment in the cities of developing countries. Todaro's model of rural–urban migration explains why migration is still so high despite the low probability of getting a job in the urban area.
- There are many different definitions of surplus labour, or different measures of so-called 'disguised unemployment'. The most important distinction is between the static surplus, which assumes that the marginal product of labour is zero, and the dynamic surplus, which is the amount of labour that could be released without agricultural output falling, providing some small compensating changes take place such as the remaining labour working longer hours or small improvements in techniques of production, which raise labour productivity.
- The transfer of labour from agriculture to industry or from rural to urban areas is not a costless process either for individuals or society at large. The economic and social costs of congestion and overcrowding in urban areas are particularly acute.

Appendix: the functioning of markets in agrarian societies[13]

In mature developed countries, markets tend to be specialized; the markets for land, labour and credit are segmented. Each market has its own set of institutions, which have their own specialized function. In developing countries, at least in poor rural communities, markets are different;

transactions of all kinds are interlinked, with the terms of one transaction contingent on another. **The land, labour and credit markets are interlocked**. For example, landlords might provide credit to tenants and labourers in the slack season, when there is no income being generated, in return for a specific amount of labour in the peak season; or traders may grant credit to farmers in return for a specific amount of their crop at a pre-agreed discount price. These interlinked transactions make many of the markets very imperfect, not least because they create serious barriers to the entry of new agents, and inefficiency in one market may be the cause, or consequence, of imperfections in another. Inefficiencies arise through lack of information, lack of incentives, the inability to enforce contracts and so on. Imperfect and inefficient markets are a characteristic feature of the economic functioning of poor developing economies, and they are the basis of informal institutional arrangements that govern economic behaviour in rural societies.

Below, there are separate discussions on the markets for land, labour and credit, but as we go along, we will see how they interlock. What we shall find is that the contract choices made by peasant farmers depend on the technological, economic and social conditions that exist in different environments, which determine risks and transaction costs. Agricultural production has three distinguishing features: production is subject to uncertainty, production is seasonal and hired labour is required, and the costs of supervising labour are high. These all play a part in determining the institutional arrangements and types of contracts reached in different markets.

The land market

One of the characteristics of the market for land is that the volume of land transactions (buying and selling) relative to the stock of land is low. This has to do with the very inegalitarian ownership of land in poor countries, and a lack of property rights for a large number of people who work on the land. The high concentration of land ownership in a few hands, and lack of access to land, can have serious consequences for the overall development of an economy. Land may not be used efficiently, large tracts of land may not be fully utilized, food production is likely to be below potential, and those who might want to farm and work the land become migrants to already overcrowded cities.

The concentration of land, and the size distribution of farms, differ across continents. Latin America has by far the highest concentration of land ownership, with Gini ratios of over 0.8 in countries such as Brazil, Peru, Uruguay, Colombia and Venezuela. In Asia, the concentration is less, but still high – with a Gini ratio in excess of 0.4 in Bangladesh, India, Thailand, Indonesia and Nepal. Latin America, unsurprisingly, also has the largest farms. The proportion of small farms of less than 5 hectares is less than 50% on average, and covers only 2% of the total land area. Ninety per cent of land is cultivated on farms in excess of 50 hectares. In Asia, by contrast, 90% of farms are less than 5 hectares, occupying over 50% of farmland. The figures on land concentration and farm size are summarized in Table A5.1. In Africa, the situation differs because much of the land is communally owned. The predominant form of farming is subsistence agriculture based on the village. On large tracts of land, there is also shifting cultivation, although this type of farming is now on the decline because of increased pressure of population on food supplies. It has been replaced by small owner-occupied plots. There is virtually no sharecropping with large landlords.

There are not many economies of scale in farm production. In fact, it turns out that small farms produce a higher output per hectare than large farms (see Sen, 1964; Ray, 1998). One explanation is that labour is used more intensively on small (family-owned) farms because the opportunity cost of using labour is very low, whereas large farms hire labour and pay a market wage, which leads to a lower input of labour per unit of land. Owner-occupied farms using family labour are always found to be more productive than large mechanized farms using hired labour, or tenant farms with no property rights, because the incentive to be efficient is greater (see Binswanger and Deininger, 1997).

If small owner-occupied farms are more productive than large farms, there would be an efficiency or productivity gain if large landowners were to sell their land to small family units and appropriate the surplus. But the market for land doesn't work in this rational way. First, land confers power, and can be used as collateral for other purposes. Second, in practice, most land sales are not from rich to poor, but from poor to rich because the poor often have to sell land in order to pay debts and survive, and they are credit constrained (see later). This matters for efficiency if tenants and sharecroppers replace owner-operated family farms. This is a collective action problem and the only solution is state involvement in **land reform**, which transfers land compulsorily from rich to poor.

Land reform can take three main forms:

1. The transfer of land from landowners to tenants who already work the land, as happened historically in South Korea, Japan and Taiwan. South Korea is an interesting case where land reform took place when the country ceased to be a Japanese colony in 1949. Over one-half of agricultural land owned by Japanese and large domestic landowners was transferred to over 60% of the rural population comprising tenant farmers.
2. The transfer of large estates to smaller farms, as happened in Mexico after the revolution in 1917.
3. The expropriation and break-up of large estates for new settlements, as in some countries in Africa in recent times, but often with disastrous results, as in Kenya and Zimbabwe.

Table A5.1 Land concentration and farm size in Asia and Latin America

Countries	Gini ratio of land concentration	Percentage of farms and farmland				Percentage of sharecroppers or tenants
		Below 5 hectares		Above 50 hectares		
Asia		Farms	Area	Farms	Area	
Bangladesh	0.42	90.6	62.6	–	–	91
India	0.62	88.7	46.7	0.1	3.7	48
Indonesia	0.56	92.9	68.7	0	13.6	60
Nepal	0.56	97.2	72.1	0	0.8	48.3
Philippines	0.51	84.8	47.8	0.2	13.9	79.3
Thailand	0.45	72.3	39.4	0	0.9	29
Latin America						
Brazil	0.84	36.8	1.3	16.3	84.6	–
Costa Rica	0.82	48.9	1.9	14.5	79.7	9.4
Colombia	0.86	59.6	3.7	8.4	77.7	49.4
Peru	0.91	78	8.9	1.9	79.1	0
Uruguay	0.82	14.3	0.2	37.6	95.8	4.7
Venezuela	0.91	43.8	0.9	13.6	92.5	–

Source: Otsuka et al., 1992.

Historically, most land reforms have taken place at the same time as political change, which has transferred power from corrupt elites to 'the people' through the creation of democratic institutions. Land reform is an important institutional change conferring property rights and providing incentives to invest.

Where tenant farmers exist, arrangements between tenants and landlords vary in different parts of the world. In Latin America, tenants tend to pay a fixed rent to the landlord for the right to cultivate, but retain 100% of the output. In Asia, tenants tend to be **sharecroppers**, sharing output with the landlord on an agreed percentage basis, depending on circumstances, usually 50:50. With fixed rent contracts, the tenant bears the risk of fluctuations in output. Poor farmers, however, are risk averse, and so they tend to be sharecroppers, sharing the risk with the landlord. It is often argued that sharecropping is inefficient compared with fixed rent tenancies because work incentives are weaker. With fixed rents, tenant farmers keep any extra output produced, whereas sharecroppers have to relinquish a certain share, and thus there will be a tendency for sharecroppers to undersupply effort (unless, of course, their work can be costlessly observed and enforced by the landlord). The empirical evidence shows (see Ray, 1998), however, that productivity on tenant-owned land is higher than on sharecropped land, controlling for other factors.

The question then arises: If sharecropping is inefficient, why is it so widely practised? The answer is that it can be beneficial to landowner and farmer by reducing the risks and costs to both. Stiglitz (1974) was the first to show formally that sharecropping reflects a compromise between risk-sharing and work incentives. From the landlord's point of view, they can use a sharecropping contract as a screening device to choose between more wealthy, high-productivity tenants and poorer, lower productivity tenants – the former receiving the fixed rent contracts and the latter receiving the sharecropping contracts. Also sharecropping is cheaper, compared with self-cultivation using hired labour. Labour recruitment, and the supervision of labour effort, can be costly. This is a classic **principal–agent** example, where the interests of the landowner and the worker differ. The principal (the landowner) naturally wants as much effort and output as possible, but work effort generates disutility and the worker may shirk. The landowner has no way of knowing how much of a worker's output is dependent on their effort and how much on exogenous factors. The principal cannot easily monitor and enforce the work effort they want without employing supervisory staff. Sharecropping may also be the preferred contract if input costs are being shared between landlord and tenant. Cost-sharing inputs is a way of offsetting disincentive effects of applying inputs under output-sharing contracts (Otsuka et al., 1992). Cost-sharing can be thought of as production loans to the tenant, which are repaid with the output, which is deducted from total output before the output is shared.

From the tenants' point of view, not paying a fixed rent considerably reduces risk because in the event of a bad harvest, tenants could find themselves in considerable difficulties, with their livelihood threatened. Landlords also know this. For the landlords, they can vary the share they get in order to get the same income as a fixed rent, taking good and bad years together. In fact, in recent years, the tenant's share has been falling because landlords have been bearing the cost of increased mechanization. But greater overall efficiency will only come with giving sharecroppers a greater share of output, to induce more effort, and providing security of tenure on the land to provide tenants themselves with the incentive to invest.

The labour market

There are two main types of labour working in the rural sector of developing countries. The first is **casual labour**, hired on a daily basis and paid either a daily wage or 'piece rates' for specific tasks. Large landowners need more than family labour to work on their large estates, and if people are landless, or possess only very small farms, they need to earn extra income for nutrition and survival. The second type of labour is **permanent labour** hired by landlords on long-term contracts. The function of the two types of labour is different. Casual labour is used for routine tasks that are easily monitored. It will need a minimum income in order to have enough nutrition and energy to work productively – the so-called **efficiency wage**. If the labour is landless and has no other source of income, this is the minimum wage that will be paid. If the labour has other sources of income, however, either from a small farm or other assets, it can supply labour at a lower threshold wage because the other income buys the nutrition it needs. On the other hand, as non-labour income rises, the minimum at which labour is willing to work rises because it values leisure more highly. Thus, there are conflicting forces working in the labour market (Ray, 1998). At low levels of non-labour income, the availability to work for a lower wage rate dominates, while at higher levels of non-labour income, the willingness to work dominates. This gives rise to two types of unemployment, or categories of surplus labour, in rural areas. The first category is 'voluntary' unemployment among labour able to work but who do not want to because of high non-labour income. The second category is 'involuntary' because the wage rate is not high enough to enable labour to work productively. In these circumstances, land reform and income distribution would increase total agricultural output, because if the landless are given land, the increase in their non-labour income will increase their ability to work, and a lower level of income for the previously more 'wealthy' will increase the incentive to work. The necessity to pay a minimum efficiency wage is one of the reasons why wages tend to be rigid downwards in rural economies, despite unemployment. Another explanation is the phenomenon of **segmented labour markets**, with village employers hiring local labour even when it is cheaper outside. Institutions and social norms often determine economic outcomes, not the free forces of the marketplace.

The main drawback of the casual labour market from the point of view of economic development is that employers of labour (landlords) have no interest in improving the working conditions of workers or investing in them by way of health or education, because there is no guarantee that they will reap the benefits. Ray (1998) commented, 'a casual labour market creates a deterioration in the nutritional status of the workforce'. The function of permanent labour, and the argument for more permanent labour contracts, is that a lot of agricultural work needs supervising and large landowners require people to supervise and monitor work. One facet of permanent labour is **labour-tying**, which, because of the seasonal nature of production, suits employer and employee. The employer is guaranteed labour in the busy season and the worker is guaranteed work in the off-season. The wage paid to permanent labour will be some margin above the casual wage to provide the incentive to monitor and supervise tasks properly. The premium must be just enough to prevent 'shirking', and also to compensate for the threat of dismissal.

Another way of enforcing work effort is to offer long-term contracts, so that a party not honouring a contract will suffer **loss of reputation**, and find it difficult to work in the future. In small rural communities, reputation matters. If long-term fixed wage contracts can elicit loyal effort from permanent workers, they may also receive fringe benefits and subsidized credit in return.

According to Ray (1998), however, the amount of permanent labour used on farms relative to casual labour has been falling in recent years. One reason may be that because of multiple cropping, the seasonality of production has decreased, and therefore there is less need to offer permanent contracts to ensure labour is available in the harvest season. Second, if the casual wage in the harvest season is above the contracted income for permanent labour, it is difficult to enforce 'tied contracts'.

We can summarize this section on labour contracts by saying that when work effort is unenforceable, there are three basic predictions from a standard model of landlord and workers both attempting to maximize their utility in the face of production uncertainty and risk (Otsuka et al., 1992):

- If production is uncertain and the worker is risk averse, the share contract will be optimal. (If the worker is risk neutral, which is highly unlikely, the fixed rent contract would be chosen.)
- A share or fixed rent tenancy is superior to a fixed wage permanent labour contract because the latter is costly, but long-term and interlinked contracts may be observed because they can help to enforce contracts through reputation effects. Permanent labour contracts will also be observed if land tenancy is illegal.
- A share tenancy is less efficient than a fixed rent tenancy and owner cultivation because of reduced work incentives (unless labour can be monitored costlessly).

Where work effort is perfectly enforceable, optimal contracts are, in general, indeterminate. If the worker is risk neutral and contract enforcement is costless, all forms of contract become equally efficient. If both landlord and workers are risk averse, the share contract will be chosen to share production risk.

Credit markets

Farmers need credit for three main reasons: first, for fixed capital investment; second, to bridge the gap between financing production (seeds, fertilizers, pesticides) and sales receipts from the harvest (in other words, they need working capital); and third, to smooth consumption before the harvest.

Credit markets in the rural sector of developing countries are not well developed, however, for two main reasons. First, due to lack of information, it is difficult for lenders to monitor loans, to know how risky they are, and whether they are going to be used productively. Second, credit contracts are difficult to enforce because the legal system is weak, therefore there is the risk of default. This makes the formal banking sector reluctant to lend to the rural sector. The risk of default means that the formal sector only lends to richer farmers with collateral. The poor may have some collateral in the form of a plot of land, but the formal banking system wants something more.

This means that the rural credit market is dominated by **informal moneylenders**, charging high interest rates either explicit in the form of high money rates of interest, or implicit because the loan is given in return for a share of the borrower's output at a discount price, or an agreed amount of labour service at a lower-than-market wage. The rural credit market is also very segmented. Because moneylenders have much more knowledge of borrowers within a local community, moneylenders tend to become very specialized, dealing with a particular clientele within a village or serving a particular type of person. Segmentation often takes place on occupational lines. Because of these links, lenders in informal markets do not like their borrowers borrowing from another lender, so the existence of many lenders does not necessarily mean there is competition. Rather, the credit market is more like a series of local monopolies, and because of this segmentation, interest rates on loans in the informal market are not only high but can also vary considerably. There is little chance of arbitrage.

High interest rates largely reflect lenders' risk; that is, the risk that the borrowers might not repay either because of adverse circumstance, such as a bad harvest, or because of the difficulties of collecting bad debts. Potential default exists, but in practice, it turns out to be quite low. One reason is that in rural communities where everybody knows each other, if someone defaults, everybody knows and no one else will lend to them. There is 'peer' pressure to repay. The second reason is that moneylenders devise contracts that minimize the risk of default, which also makes the implicit interest rate high. If the lender is a large landowner, and the landowner knows the farmer, they can minimize the risk of default by making the first claim on the borrower's output, or insist that the borrower supplies labour at a lower-than-market wage (**bonded labour**). If the lender is a trader, they can minimize risk by contracting to buy the output of the borrower at a discount price. Udry (1994) found that over 90% of loans to the rural sector in Northern Nigeria came from the informal sector. Research in the Punjab and Sindh regions of Pakistan shows that landlords are the major source of credit for tenant farmers, while traders are the major source of credit for owner-cultivators (Ray, 1998).

Even though risk of default can be minimized by various practices, credit-rationing still exists because high interest rates may attract too many high-risk customers, and high interest rates, which would equilibrate the supply and demand for loans, would themselves increase the risk of default. Lenders therefore prefer to ration credit instead.

There is also the issue of risk and insurance to consider. Agricultural production is risky because of the vagaries of the weather, the incidence of disease and many other factors. Peasant farmers somehow need to be able to smooth their income and consumption, so as not to suffer unduly in bad times. This is where insurance mechanisms are important. Self-insurance is one possibility, smoothing consumption using one's own resources; for example, saving grain in good times for use in bad. Mutual insurance is another possibility. If farmers produce different products, and good and bad harvests for different crops are negatively correlated, producers can help each other out in what are bad times for some and good times for others. But mutual insurance may not be easily enforceable. There could be risk pooling within a community through formal insurance markets, but these are not well developed. If there is not risk pooling or mutual insurance, saving and credit have to be used for consumption smoothing. There is evidence from a wide variety of studies (see Bardhan and Udry, 1999) that households in poor, risky agricultural environments engage in risk pooling and consumption smoothing, although not always successfully because of informational and enforcement difficulties.

Interlinked markets

As we have indicated above, the markets for land, labour and credit in the rural sector of developing countries are closely interlinked. Inefficiency in one market may be both the cause and consequence of inefficiencies in others. The markets for land and labour are interlinked because an imbalance in the market for land (with both large and small holdings) leads to imbalances in the market for labour. If people are landless, or have only very small holdings, they need to sell their labour to large landowners who need more than just family labour.

The markets for land and credit are linked because, as we have outlined before, landlords are a major source of credit for farmers, and their labour or output is used as collateral. Also crop-traders are the main source of credit for cultivators who own land, and loans are provided in advance of crop production. In Muslim countries, where charging interest is against Sharia law, credit contracts, which take part of the output of the borrower, or specify the sale of the output at a certain discount, are a substitute for charging interest.

Floro and Yotopoulos (1991), in their study of the Philippines, identify five types of credit market interlinkages:

1. Credit in return for the procurement of output.
2. Credit in return for the sale of output to the lender.

3. Credit tied to the purchase of inputs or leasing machinery from the lender.
4. Credit in return for provision of labour to the lender.
5. Transfer of rights over the usufruct (profits) of the land to the lender.

Floro and Yotopoulous (1991) find that the first three types of interlinkages are most common among trader lenders, while the last two are most prevalent among farmer lenders.

In conclusion, in rural communities where formal lending is limited by lack of proper collateral, interlinked contracts in the informal money market make sense because the lender has more control over the borrower and saves the cost of monitoring, and reduces the risk of non-repayment. Landlords, or traders, in effect, get their 'interest' immediately if loans are conditional on work for lower wages or output at lower prices.

Institutions and decision-making in agriculture

Agriculture is a neglected sector of the economy in many developing countries, and governments pursue policies that discriminate against agriculture in favour of industry. The explanation is partly historical, but mainly institutional and political. The agricultural sector's potential for collective action is weak because of the unequal relation between landlords and workers and the weak bargaining power that the agricultural sector has vis-à-vis other groups in society due to history and initial conditions. It is difficult for owner-operated family farms to act collectively to change things because farmers are dispersed and lack political clout. If peasant farmers lack education and cannot vote, they lack the means to promote change. Only by enhancing the poor's potential for collective action, by increasing their potential participation, will there be increased efficiency and sustained and equitable growth in the rural sector (Binswanger and Deininger, 1997).

Chapter 5 Discussion questions

1. What is the importance to economic development of rapid productivity growth in agriculture?
2. What factors hold back productivity growth in agriculture?
3. How could land reform help to raise agricultural productivity?
4. What is meant by 'marketable surplus'?
5. Explain why poor people tend to be risk averse and reluctant to innovate.
6. In what sense is there disguised unemployment on the land?
7. Does disguised unemployment on the land mean that development using surplus labour is a relatively painless and costless process?
8. Compare and contrast the main features of Lewis's classical model of development with the neoclassical model.
9. Explain the continued process of rural–urban migration despite growing unemployment in urban areas.
10. In what ways do the agricultural and industrial sectors of an economy complement one another?

Chapter 5 **Discussion questions** – *continued*

11. **What are the major characteristics of the market for land in the rural sector of developing countries?**
12. **What is the principal-agent problem facing landlords in the rural sector of poor countries?**
13. **Why is sharecropping so common in the agricultural sector of many poor countries?**
14. **In what ways is the credit market linked to the land and labour markets in the rural sector of poor countries?**

Notes

1. For excellent surveys of the issues, see Bardhan (1984), Binswanger and Deininger (1997), Dorner (1992), Otsuka et al. (1992) and Lipton (2011).
2. See also Askari and Cummings (1976) and Schiff and Montenegro (1997).
3. See also the symposium on the Lewis model to celebrate its 25th anniversary in the *Manchester School*, September 1979, Kirkpatrick and Barrientos (2004); the symposium on the Lewis model after 50 years, *Manchester School*, December 2004, and Gollin's 60 retrospective in *Journal of Economic Perspectives*, Summer 2014.
4. The capitalist sector is not synonymous with the industrial sector, but it is convenient to think of it in this way. Agribusiness, for example, is also capitalist.
5. The profit rate can be expressed as

$$P/K = \frac{(O/L - w/p)}{(K/L)}$$

where P is profits, K is the quantity of capital, O/L is the productivity of labour, w/p is the real wage and K/L is the capital–labour ratio. The profit rate will rise if O/L rises and w/p remains the same (assuming no offsetting rise in K/L).

6. A formal algebraic model, with various extensions, can be found in Thirlwall (1986).
7. If the income elasticity of demand for industrial goods is greater than unity, and for agricultural goods less than unity, then the equilibrium growth rate for industry will exceed that for agriculture.
8. See Weisdorf (2006) for historical evidence on how industrial growth promoted agriculture by lowering the relative price of industrial goods and buying more goods commercially rather than producing 'non-agricultural' goods within the agricultural sector itself.
9. This is not a statistical probability, since π is not bounded between zero and unity. The 'chance' of getting a job would be a better word to use.
10. Todaro (1971) uses the same notation, S, for the total urban labour force as for the supply of migrants. This can be confusing. We therefore use W for the total urban labour force and S for the supply of migrants.
11. Any values can be substituted as long as $w/r = 2$.
12. Other early studies of the rural–urban migration process include Knight (1972). For a survey of studies, see Todaro (1976), Yap (1977) and Stark (1991). Todaro gives an alternative way of evaluating whether urban unemployment will rise or not. It can be shown that the *level* of unemploy-

ment will rise if $\eta > g \times N/S$, where η is the period elasticity of induced migration with respect to the change in modern sector job probabilities, g is the growth of urban employment prior to the increase in job opportunities, N is the level of urban employment and S is the existing level of rural–urban migration. It can also be shown that the rate of urban unemployment will rise if $\eta > g \times W/S$, where W is the urban workforce.

13. This section relies heavily on the works of Otsuka et al. (1992), Binswanger and Deininger (1997), Ray (1998) and Bardhan and Udry (1999).

Websites on agriculture

Food and Agricultural Organization www.fao.org/home/en/
International Food Policy Research Institute www.ifpri.org
Consultative Group on International Agricultural Research www.cgiar.org
Inter-American Institute for Cooperation on Agriculture www.iica.int/en
International Rice Research Institute www.irri.org
International Maize and Wheat Improvement Center www.cimmyt.org

6

CAPITAL ACCUMULATION, TECHNICAL PROGRESS AND TECHNIQUES OF PRODUCTION

Introduction

Economic growth and development are impossible without capital accumulation. If all the output produced by an economy was consumed, there would be no saving, no investment, and the economy would grind to a halt. In this chapter, we discuss the role of physical capital and infrastructure investment in the development process, leaving the role of human capital formation (education and health) to Chapter 7.

Growth depends not only on the quantity of capital invested but also its productivity, which largely depends on the technical progress embodied in it. We identify the different meanings of technical progress and the types of technical progress that take place – whether it is labour-saving, capital-saving or neutral – which has implications for employment and the distribution of income between wages and profits. The process of learning by doing is a form of technical progress, because it improves the productivity of factors of production.

We then explore how societies progress technologically by acquiring the capabilities to invest, innovate, undertake R&D and absorb new ideas. Some evidence is given of how backward technology is in poor countries and the challenge of the magnitude of 'catch-up'. Finally, we discuss the important issue of the choice of techniques of production in developing countries and whether labour-abundant economies could move towards the use of more labour-intensive techniques without jeopardizing the level of output and saving for future growth. Theory and evidence suggest that the potential clash between employment and output and employment and saving in the choice of *new* techniques is exaggerated.

The role of capital in development

The capital stock of a country increases through the process of net investment, which is the difference between a country's net income in an accounting period (that is, gross income minus depreciation) and how much it consumes out of that income in the same period. The essence of capital accumulation is that it enhances a country's capacity to produce goods in the future and enables it to grow faster.

There are many types of capital goods:

1. There are **plant and machinery** used in factories and offices, which yield no utility directly but produce consumption goods and services that do.
2. There is **infrastructure investment**, which partly provides goods and services directly, and at the same time makes other forms of investment more productive; for example transport facilities, telecommunications, power generation, the provision of water facilities and so on.
3. There is expenditure on **research and development (R&D)**, which may improve the productivity of labour or capital, or both. R&D can lead to new inventions and then to innovation – either **process innovation** or **product innovation**. Process innovations make the production of existing products more efficient; product innovations involve the creation of new products that not only add to utility but also enhance productivity by enabling new ways of doing things, for example information technology.
4. If capital is defined as any asset that generates an additional future stream of measurable income to society, many goods and services that might be thought of as primarily consumption goods ought strictly to be included as part of a country's capital stock. If cars, for example, or other consumer durable goods save time and make people more efficient, part of the expenditure on them should be considered as an investment. Expenditure on housing is another

example where private expenditure may be partly considered as consumption and partly investment; and the public provision of housing might be put in the category of **social capital**. Similarly, if certain types of consumption goods are necessary as incentives to induce peasant producers in the agricultural sector, or workers elsewhere, to increase their productivity, they too ought to be considered as part of the capital stock.

If it is agreed, therefore, that the only way to build up a country's productive potential and to raise per capita income is to expand the capacity for producing goods, this need not refer simply to the provision of physical capital such as plant and machinery, but also to roads, railways, power lines, water pipes, schools, hospitals, houses and even 'incentive' consumer goods such as consumer durables – all of which can contribute to increased productivity and higher living standards.

When using the production function approach to the study of the sources of growth or the macrodeterminants of growth, as described in Chapter 4, it is important to define capital as broadly as possible if the relation between capital accumulation and growth is to be properly understood. This is in addition to the point, which was also emphasized in Chapter 4, that capital is likely to be the main vehicle for the introduction of technical progress in the productive system. In other words, capital accumulation is not only important in its own right, but is the major conduit for advances in knowledge, which, in turn, are also a major determinant of productivity growth.

Developing economies lay great emphasis on the importance of capital accumulation, and stress the need to raise the level of investment as a proportion of national output. A glance at any national development plan will testify to this. Development is associated with industrialization and industrialization with capital accumulation. Many famous development economists in the past have picked out investment as the most important single factor in the growth process. As we saw in Chapter 3, Rostow (1960) defines the process of 'take-off' into sustained growth in terms of a critical ratio of investment to national product, and Arthur Lewis (1955) has described the process of development as one of transforming a country from being a 5% saver and investor to a 12% saver and investor. It is common, in fact, for countries to calculate fairly precise ratios of investment to national income that will be required to achieve a particular rate of growth. These calculations involve assumptions about the normal relation between capital and output, a relation that is formally expressed in the concept of the **capital–output ratio**, which measures how much capital stock is required to produce a unit flow of output over an accounting period (normally one year). If 300 units of capital (from new investment) are required to produce an annual flow of 100 units of output, the capital–output ratio is 3.

The returns to investment in developing countries are potentially much higher than in developed countries, which already have large quantities of capital per head. In countries where specialization (the division of labour) is minimal, the scope for capital to permit more roundabout methods of production and increase productivity will be greater than where specialization has already reached a high level of sophistication. Moreover, in technologically backward countries, the rate of growth of capital required to absorb new technology is likely to be greater than in advanced countries. By definition, technologically backward countries also have a backlog of technology to make up. Furthermore, in a labour-abundant economy with a low capital–labour ratio, the very act of *capital deepening* – giving each worker a little more capital to work with – may make a substantial difference to total product, much more so than in countries where the process of capital deepening has been a continuing process for some length of time. All these factors represent important contributions that capital can make to economic progress, which may be relatively more important, the smaller the initial capital stock of a country relative to its population. It is a familiar proposition in economics that the scarcer one factor of production is in relation to another, the higher its productivity is likely to be, all other things being equal.

Capital accumulation is also seen as an escape from the so-called 'vicious circle of poverty' – a circle of low productivity, leading to low per capita income, leading to a low level of saving per head, leading to a low level of capital accumulation per head, leading to low productivity. Low productivity is seen as the source of the vicious circle of poverty, and the point where the circle must be broken by capital accumulation (see Chapters 10 and 11).

According to research by Hulten and Isaksson (2007), the amount of capital per head of the working population in high-income developed countries is \$150,000 (in 2000) compared with \$3,000 in low-income countries, and this difference is one of the major explanations of why labour productivity is \$52,000 in rich countries and only \$2,300 in poor countries.

These huge differences in the amount of capital per head are the cumulative effect of much higher levels of savings and investment in rich countries than in poorer countries that cannot, or prefer not to, save and invest. A precondition for raising the level of capital per head in poor countries is a higher level of investment. There needs to be greater incentives for investment. Case example 6.1 contains the conclusions of the World Bank's *World Development Report 2005: A Better Investment Climate for Everyone* (World Bank, 2004).

Case example 6.1 **Main messages from *World Development Report 2005* on investment**

The investment climate is central to growth and poverty reduction

Improving the opportunities and incentives for firms of all types to invest productively, create jobs and expand should be a top priority for governments. It is not just about increasing the volume of investment but also spurring productivity improvements that are the keys to sustainable growth:

- The goal is to create a better investment climate for everyone. A good investment climate benefits society as a whole, not just firms. And it embraces all firms, not just large or politically connected firms.
- Expanding opportunities for young people is a pressing concern for developing countries, where 53% of people live on less than US\$2 a day, youths have more than double the average unemployment rate, and populations are growing rapidly.

Reducing unjustified costs is critical, but policy-related risks and barriers to competition also need to be tackled

Costs, risks and barriers to competition all matter for firms and thus for growth and poverty reduction:

- Costs associated with weak contract enforcement, inadequate infrastructure, crime, corruption and regulation can amount to over 25% of sales – or more than three times what firms typically pay in taxes.
- Firms in developing countries rate policy uncertainty as their top concern. This and other sources of policy-related risk – such as insecure property rights, macroeconomic instability and arbitrary regulation– chill incentives to invest. Improving policy predictability can increase the likelihood of new investment by over 30%.
- Barriers to competition benefit some firms but deny opportunities and increase costs to other firms and consumers. They also weaken incentives for protected firms to innovate and improve their productivity. Increasing competitive pressure can increase the probability of firm innovation by more than 50%.

continued overleaf

Case example 6.1 **Main messages from *World Development Report 2005* on investment** – *continued*

Progress requires more than changes to formal policies

Over 90% of firms claim gaps between formal rules and what happens in practice, and the informal economy accounts for more than half of output in many developing countries. Creating a better investment climate requires governments to bridge these gaps and to tackle the deeper sources of policy failure that undermine a sound investment climate. This requires efforts to:

- Restrain corruption and other forms of rent-seeking that increase costs and distort policies
- Build policy credibility to give firms the confidence to invest
- Foster the public trust required to enable and sustain policy improvements
- Ensure policy responses are crafted to fit local conditions.

Investment climate improvements are a process, not an event

Government policies and behaviours influencing the investment climate cover a wide field. But everything does not have to be fixed at once, and perfection on even a single policy dimension is not required. Significant progress can be made by addressing the important constraints facing firms in a way that gives them the confidence to invest – and by sustaining a process of ongoing improvements.

Because constraints differ widely across and even within countries, priorities need to be assessed in each case. Reform processes benefit from effective public communication and other measures to build consensus and maintain momentum.

Source: World Bank, 2004.

Technical progress

The term 'technical progress' is used in several different senses to describe a variety of phenomena, but three in particular can be singled out:

1. Economists use the term to refer to the *effects* of changes in technology, and specifically to the role of technical change in the growth process. It is in this sense that the term was used in Chapter 4; that is, as an umbrella term to cover all those factors that contribute to the growth of 'total' factor productivity.
2. Technical progress is used by economists in a narrow specialist sense to describe the *character* of technical improvements, and is often prefaced for this purpose by the adjectives 'labour-saving', 'capital-saving' or 'neutral'.
3. Technical progress is used more literally to refer to *changes* in technology itself, defining technology as useful knowledge pertaining to the art of production. Used in this sense, the emphasis is on describing improvements in the design, sophistication and performance of plant and machinery, and the economic activities through which improvements come about – by R&D, invention and innovation.

Having already discussed technical progress in the first sense in Chapter 4, we concentrate here on the narrow specialist descriptions of technical progress, and on how societies progress technologically.

Capital- and labour-saving technical progress

The classification of technical progress as to whether it is capital-saving, labour-saving or neutral owes its origins primarily to the work of Harrod (1948) and Hicks (1932). Their criteria of classification differ, however. **Harrod's classification of technical progress** employs the concept of the capital–output ratio. Given the rate of profit, technical change is said to be capital-saving if it lowers the capital–output ratio, labour-saving if it raises the capital–output ratio, and neutral if it leaves the capital–output ratio unchanged.

The nature of technical progress by this criterion will be an amalgam of the effect of 'pure' technical change on factor combinations on the one hand and the effect of the substitution of capital for labour on the other (as, for example, relative factor prices change). As such, Harrod neutrality at the aggregate level is quite consistent with capital-saving technical progress at the industry level. In fact, most of the evidence for advanced countries suggests that *if* technical progress is neutral in the aggregate in the Harrod sense, this must be due to substitution of capital for labour because 'pure' technical advance has saved capital. The substitution of capital for labour takes place because as countries become richer, the price of labour relative to capital tends to rise, which not only induces a 'pure' substitution effect but also encourages inventive effort towards saving labour, which is becoming relatively expensive (and scarce).

Hicks's classification of technical progress takes the concept of the marginal rate of substitution between factors, which is the rate at which one factor must be substituted for another, leaving output unchanged. The marginal rate of substitution is given by the ratio of the marginal products of factors. Holding constant the ratio of labour to capital, technical progress is said to be:

- **capital-saving** if it raises the marginal product of labour in greater proportion than the marginal product of capital
- **labour-saving** if it raises the marginal product of capital in greater proportion than the marginal product of labour
- **neutral** if it leaves unchanged the ratio of marginal products.

These definitions are illustrated in Figures 6.1, 6.2 and 6.3, respectively.

It will be recalled from Chapter 4 that technical progress on a production function map is represented by shifts in the function towards the origin, showing that the same output can be produced with fewer inputs, or that the same volume of inputs can produce a greater output. According to the shape of the new production function, fewer of either one or both factors will be required to produce the same output. In the case of neutral technical progress, a quantity of both factors can be dispensed with. In the case of non-neutral technical progress, if only one factor is

Figure 6.1 Capital-saving technical progress

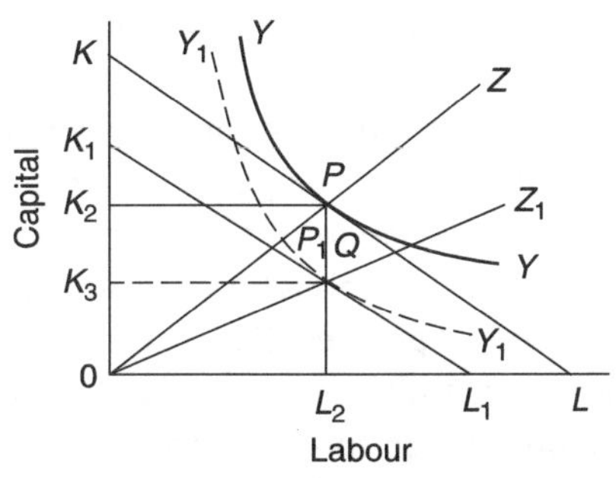

Figure 6.2 Labour-saving technical progress

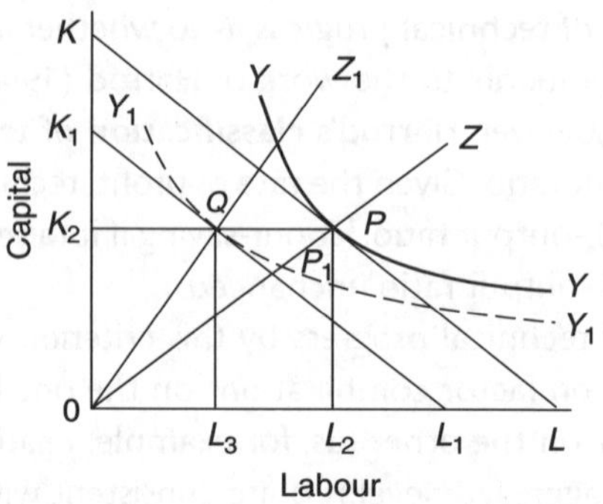

Figure 6.3 Neutral technical progress

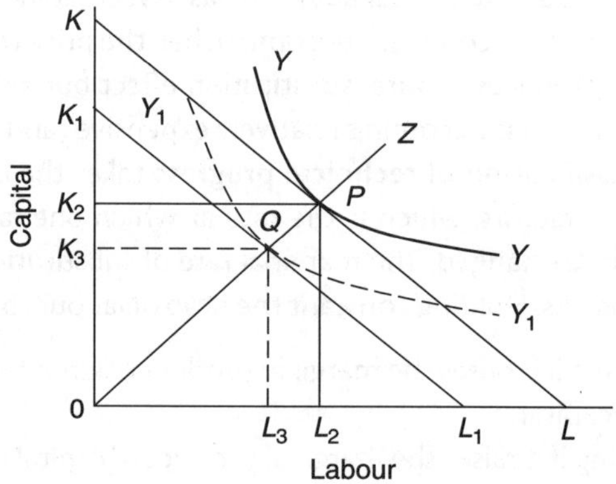

saved, technical progress is said to be *absolutely* labour- or capital-saving. If fewer of both factors are required, technical progress is said to be *relatively* labour- or capital-saving.

Consider first **neutral technical progress** (Figure 6.3). The ray from the origin, or expansion path, 0Z, goes through the minimum cost point of tangency between the production function YY and the factor–price ratio line KL. With neutral technical progress the production function shifts to Y_1Y_1 such that the new point of tangency at the same factor–price ratio lies on the same expansion path. This means that the ratio of marginal products is the same at the same capital–labour ratio, and equal proportionate amounts of the two factors are saved. The condition for neutral technical progress is simply that the new production function is parallel to the old.

With **labour-saving technical change** (Figure 6.2) the ratio of the marginal product of capital to the marginal product of labour rises so as to shift the minimum cost point of tangency from the old expansion path 0Z to a new expansion path $0Z_1$. At P_1, where the new production function (Y_1Y_1) cuts the old expansion path, the ratio of the marginal product of labour to capital is lower than at *P*. P_1 is not an equilibrium point and it will pay producers to move to point *Q*, substituting capital for labour. The ratio of marginal products has not remained unchanged at a constant labour–capital ratio, and L_2L_3 labour is saved. The isoquants have been so drawn as to keep the volume of capital the same, but this is for expositional purposes only.

Capital-saving technical progress (Figure 6.1) may be described in an exactly analogous fashion. In this case, the ratio of the marginal product of labour to the marginal product of capital rises and the shift in the production function (to Y_1Y_1) is such that the minimum cost point of tangency now lies to the right of the old expansion path. At P_1, where the new production function cuts the old expansion path, the ratio of the marginal product of labour to capital is higher than at P. Again, P_1 is not an equilibrium point and it will pay producers to move to point Q, substituting labour for capital. The ratio of marginal products has not remained unchanged at a constant labour–capital ratio, and in this case K_2K_3 capital is saved.

As with Harrod technical progress, it is difficult to know what form Hicks technical progress takes in practice, largely because of identification problems. While the classification is analytically distinct, how does one distinguish empirically between a change in factor proportions due to a shift in the production function and a change in factor proportions due to a change in relative prices? Hicks himself seemed to be of the view that technical progress is relatively labour-saving, but the indirect evidence we have for this is slight. For example, given the magnitude of the rise in the price of labour relative to capital and an elasticity of substitution close to unity, labour could not have maintained or increased its share of the national income (as it has done slightly in some advanced countries) if technical progress was markedly biased in the labour-saving direction. If technical progress is biased in one direction or another, its major impact will be on factor utilization if the price of factors is not flexible. The type of technology employed, and the factor proportions it entails, must bear a major responsibility for the high level of unemployment and underemployment in developing countries, as described in Chapter 3. We examine the case for the use of more labour-intensive techniques of production later in this chapter.

How societies progress technologically

Improvements in the art of production, which is the most literal interpretation of technical progress, result from a combination of **R&D, invention** and **innovation**. R&D and invention are the activities that 'create' knowledge, and innovation is the activity that applies new knowledge to the task of production. These are all basically economic activities. But the study of the way in which societies progress technologically, and the speed of progress, is not only the preserve of the economist.

The economist can identify the mainsprings of progress, but their pervasiveness and acceptance in societies is not a purely economic matter. The spread of new knowledge, for example, depends on its rate of *adoption* and *diffusion* and this raises questions of individual motivation, the willingness of societies to assimilate new ideas and to break with custom and tradition, which impinge heavily on territory occupied by development sociologists. The relative importance of different factors contributing to progress, and the speed of progress itself, will vary from country to country according to the stage of development and a whole complex of socioeconomic forces. Moreover, many of the mainsprings of technological progress are not mutually exclusive. At the risk of excessive simplification, attention here will be confined to four main sources of progress that are of potential significance to any society.

One major source of improvement in technology and progress is the **inventive and innovative activity** of the population. All societies are endowed to some degree with a potential supply of inventors, innovators and risk-takers, and in the absence of imported technology and personnel, it is on the emergence of this class of person that technological progress will primarily depend during the early stages of development. Economic backwardness in many countries may quite legitimately be traced back to a relative shortage of inventors, innovators and risk-takers. It is fairly well established that some cultures and some environments are more amenable to change than others, and have, in the past, produced a greater supply of entrepreneurs. One of the major sources of growth during Britain's Industrial Revolution was technological progress fostered by an abundant supply of inventors, innovators, entrepreneurs and risk-takers. The great Austrian economist **Joseph Schumpeter** (1934, 1943) laid great stress on the role of the entrepreneur and innovation in the development process. Ultimately, however, it is the lag between the creation of knowledge and its adoption, and the rate of dissemination of new knowledge, that most directly affects the rate of measured technical progress between countries; and these two facets of innovation are influenced by the attitudes of society to change.

For Schumpeter, progress results from what he called the **process of creative destruction,** which is bound up with innovation and instigated by competition. Innovation, in turn, is the driving force behind competition. But innovation requires decision-takers and hence his complementary stress on the role of the entrepreneur. A characteristic of many poor countries is a shortage of decision-takers, a relative lack of competitive spirit, and a general aversion to risk-taking. These may be partly cultural traits and also partly, if not mainly, a function of the stage of development itself. The characteristics commonly associated with business dynamism are themselves a function of business and, more particularly, the form of organization we call 'capitalism'.

There is an enormous technological divide in the world economy, which acts as a serious barrier to narrowing the gap between rich and poor countries. A small number of countries (accounting for about 15% of the world's population) produce nearly 50% of the world's technological innovations. A number of other countries (containing 50% of the world's population) are able to adopt some or all of these technologies. The remaining countries (containing one-third of the world's poorest people) are almost entirely excluded from technological progress. These latter countries are also the areas of the world most affected by low agricultural productivity, malnutrition and disease. They need technology to raise productivity and to improve health, but cannot afford or assimilate it.

The major channels of technical diffusion across countries are trade (see Grossman and Helpman, 1991) and foreign direct investment (FDI) (see Keller, 2004, for a survey of the impact of these channels on economic performance). Countries can import technology embodied in intermediate imports or final goods, they can obtain it on licence from patent holders, or they can attract FDI, which brings technology with it. The spread of technology and ideas may also be expected to come about naturally in the general process of commercial intercourse and the exchange of information through trade. This is one of the dynamic gains from trade (see Chapter 15). But not all countries have equal access to technology. Geography, culture, institutions and the quality of human capital matter. The speed with which modern technology is absorbed by economically backward countries will depend on the same class of factors as the diffusion of knowledge within countries, which, in the final analysis, amounts to the receptiveness of all sections of the community to change, and the ability to assimilate new ways of doing things. Some economists argue that the World Bank should focus more of its lending to countries specifically for knowledge creation and assimilation.

New technology and its diffusion could lead to greater divergence in the world economy if richer countries are more adept at adopting foreign technology than poorer countries. This underlines the importance of identifying the major determinants of technical diffusion. The two most important variables are human capital and R&D, which determine absorptive capacity. According to a study by Fagerberg et al. (2007), of 90 countries over the period 1980–2002, the superior growth of innovative activity is the main factor behind the difference in economic performance between the newly industrializing countries of Asia on the one hand, and Latin America and Africa on the other. Growth rate differences between open economies can be explained in terms of technological competitiveness, which is the capacity to absorb technology and to exploit knowledge from elsewhere; price competitiveness, which is a function of new technologies that reduce costs; and non-price competitiveness, which largely depends on product innovation.

Learning

A third means by which societies progress technologically, gradually raising their efficiency and productivity, is through the process of **learning by doing**, which refers to the accumulation of experience by workers, managers and owners of capital in the course of production, which enables productive efficiency to be improved in the future. It is a learning process that Adam Smith referred to when discussing the benefits of **division of labour** (see Chapter 4). Smith stressed the importance of the division of labour for three main reasons: as a means of improving the dexterity of workers, to save the time lost in the absence of specialization, and to encourage the invention of machines that facilitate and abridge labour to improve the productivity of labour. All these advantages of the division of labour are part of a learning process. Labour improves its skill through specialization and work experience, and becomes more adept at the job in hand. Managers see deficiencies in organization, which can subsequently be remedied; and on the basis of accumulated knowledge, they are also able to embody more productive techniques in the capital stock.

Learning may be regarded as either endogenous or exogenous, or both, depending on the factor of production considered. If existing labour and existing capital are subject to a learning process, then learning by doing may be regarded as exogenous and part of disembodied technical progress. If, however, it is assumed that learning enters the productive system only through the addition of new factors, then learning by doing must be regarded as endogenous. This is the basis of Kenneth Arrow's capital model (1962), from which the term 'learning by doing' originates. His hypothesis with respect to capital is that, at any moment of time, new capital goods incorporate all the knowledge then available, based on accumulated experience, but once built, their productive efficiency cannot be altered by subsequent learning.

The endogenous model may be appropriate in the case of capital but is much less relevant in the case of labour. It is in relation to labour that most research into the learning process has been conducted. The notion of the **learning curve**, or progress function, which has been found in many industries, relates direct labour input per unit of output to cumulative output as the measure of experience. Typically, labour input per unit of output is found to decline by 10–20% for each doubling of cumulative output, with a corresponding rise in the productivity of labour. For any one product, of course, learning cannot go on at the same rate forever, but since product types are constantly changing, it is probably safe to conclude that at the aggregate level, over time, there is no limit to the learning process.

Infrastructure investment

Another major type of investment that is very important to developing countries is infrastructure investment. Just as the productivity of physical capital depends on investment in human capital, so it also depends on the existence of infrastructure investment, for example in transport and power facilities. Good infrastructure improves productivity and reduces production costs in the private sector. Apart from this obvious benefit, the adequacy of infrastructure can make a crucial difference to a country's development programme in a number of ways, such as diversifying production, expanding trade, improving environmental conditions, and reducing poverty.

For poor farmers, improved infrastructure will reduce input costs, increase agricultural output and reduce traders' monopoly by improving access to markets. Over half of African farmers are cut off from national and world markets because of poor infrastructure and market access. Better transport means greater access to public services, including schools, hospitals and other health-care facilities. In this way, infrastructure investment can help to meet some of the Sustainable Development Goals in the field of education, health and gender equality that we discussed in Chapter 2. Research at the World Bank (2005) across 73 countries shows that a 10% improvement in a country's infrastructure index is associated with a 5% reduction in child mortality, a 3.5% reduction in infant mortality, and a 7.8% reduction in maternal mortality (linked to safer water supply, sanitation and easier access to hospitals). Piped water promotes gender equality by freeing women who traditionally spend hours a day collecting water from wells.

Research at the macro-level shows a significant positive effect of infrastructure investment on output, productivity and growth. Calderón et al. (2015) take a panel of 88 developed and developing countries over the period 1960–2000 and estimate an output elasticity with respect to a multi-dimensional index of different types of infrastructure of between 0.07 and 0.10. The results are highly significant and robust and mean that, on average, a doubling of infrastructure investment would increase total output (GDP) by about 10%. Likewise, Arslanalp et al. (2011) of the World Bank have studied the impact of public investment (mainly infrastructure) on economic growth across 48 developed and developing countries over the period 1960–2001 and find a significant positive impact, allowing the responsiveness of output to public capital to vary with the initial stock of public capital itself. The elasticity of growth tends to be higher, the lower the initial level of public capital, rising to nearly 0.2 and then falling close to zero.

Currently, developing countries spend nearly a $1 trillion a year on new infrastructure – transport, power, water, sanitation, telecommunications, irrigation and so on, equal to 20% of total investment and approximately 5% of GDP – and the need for such investment is still huge. One billion people still lack access to clean water, 2 billion people lack access to sanitation (including 500 million in India alone) and electric power, and transport facilities are still rudimentary in many developing countries. The Asian Development Bank has estimated that $8 trillion of investment is needed between 2010 and 2020, mainly for roads, electricity and telecommunications. To meet this need in Asia, China announced in 2015 the establishment of a new **Asian Infrastructure Investment Bank (AIIB)**, based in Beijing, with 57 founding member countries and initial capital of £50 billion, expected to rise to over $100 billion. It is seen by the USA as a rival to the World Bank (largely controlled by the USA) and so has not joined; neither has Japan, which has a hold on the Asian Development Bank. Given the need for infrastructure investment, however, none of these banks should see themselves as rivals, but as complements.

Most infrastructure investment is undertaken by governments. The public sector owns, operates and finances virtually all infrastructure because it is either regarded as a natural monopoly or a public good. Without competition and accountability, however, there can be a great deal of inefficiency and waste. The underutilization of capacity can be a major problem in transport and power because of lack of maintenance. The World Bank (1994) calculates that raising operating efficiency to best-practice levels could save over $50 billion a year, and that the greater private provision of infrastructure and the recoupment of costs from users could reduce government subsidies by over $100 billion.

The World Bank (1994) has called for a shift of emphasis 'from increasing the quantity of infrastructure stocks to improving the quality of infrastructure services', and a change of thinking from the view that infrastructure services can only be provided by government. It makes three major recommendations:

1. The wider application of commercial principles, including managerial autonomy and the setting of performance targets.
2. The introduction of more competition, for example arranging for suppliers to compete for an entire market.
3. The increased involvement of users so that suppliers respond to user needs.

Technology and the developing countries

Most technological improvement originates from developed countries. The Organisation for Economic Co-operation and Development (OECD) countries spend over $800 billion a year on R&D, and account for more than 90% of patents issued. If developing countries are to develop their own technology, there needs to be the right institutional environment, including an incentive structure through patents, sound infrastructure, political stability to attract investment funds, and the availability of credit. Some of the technological leaders among developing countries include Singapore, Taiwan, India, South Korea, Malaysia, China, Mexico, Thailand, Philippines and Brazil, measured by the share of medium- and high-technology manufactures in total manufacturing value-added.

Technology is currently making a contribution to development in three major fields: agriculture, health, and information and communications technology (ICT). In agriculture, the impact of the Green Revolution in the 1960s and 1970s has now diminished, but on the horizon is biotechnology with the potential to end world hunger through the use of genetically modified (GM) foods and crops. The advantage of GM technology is that it allows the transfer of traits between unrelated species. For example, a gene in one species associated with the ability to resist drought can be directly transferred into the genetic code of another species. We now have GM crops more resistant to viruses and insects and more tolerant of herbicides; in the future, we could have food with extra vitamins and protein, and even vaccines to combat malnutrition and disease. In the late 1990s, China gave 26 approvals for GM crops, including transgenic peppers, tomatoes, rice and cotton. China has the advantage of being an authoritarian regime. Other countries – including India, China's main economic rival – have had to deal with public protests against GM technology, with invasion of field trials and burning of GM crops.

In health, new technology and advances in medicine have been the biggest single factor in reducing mortality and increasing life expectancy in developing countries. Important discoveries include vaccines against influenza, smallpox, polio, measles, tuberculosis, antibiotics (penicillin), and oral rehydration therapy – which was originally developed in Bangladesh and has saved millions of babies from dying from diarrhoea. Biotechnology and genomics offer new ways to cure disease by altering genes that contribute to cancer, or boosting genes that might fight it.

ICT can provide enormous benefits to developing countries, both as consumers and producers. Any task that can be digitized can now be done at a distance, which gives the opportunity for low-cost countries to develop ICT industries. India's software industry now employs nearly 2 million people. Call centres are one of the fastest-growing industries in the subcontinent. For consumers, access to information through the internet can be of benefit in almost any field – for weather information in agriculture, the dissemination of knowledge in healthcare and the tracking of diseases, and for distance learning in education. Telephone banking is revolutionizing access to finance and credit in African countries.

Case example 6.2 describes the World Bank's views on bridging the technology divide between rich and poor countries.

Case example 6.2

Bridging the technology divide

Technological progress – improvements in the ways that goods and services are produced, marketed, and brought to market – is at the very heart of human advancement and development. It has helped reduce the share of people living in absolute poverty in developing countries from 29% in 1990 to 18% in 2004. As a result, the technology gap between rich and poor countries has narrowed, although it remains wide. Low-income countries employ only one-fourth the technology used in high-income countries.

Technological progress in developing countries (that is, low-income, lower middle-income, and upper middle-income countries) outstripped progress in high-income countries between the early 1990s and 2000s. Of course, the initial level of technology in lower income countries was much lower to begin with.

The very strong technological progress developing countries have enjoyed has come mainly from adopting and absorbing existing technologies. Compared with the size of their economies, they perform relatively little new-to-the-world innovation.

The diffusion of technology across developing countries has been facilitated by their increased exposure to foreign technologies. Over the past 15 years, FDI levels and imports of high-tech and capital goods have doubled as a percentage of GDP – in part because of contacts with well-educated migrant populations living abroad.

Slow diffusion within countries means that, although individual cities may be technology leaders, the use of technology in a country as a whole may be low. For instance, while more than one in two urban Indian families has mobile phone access, only one in 10 in the rural sector does.

Partly as a result of this increased exposure, newer technology – such as mobile phones, computers and the internet – now spreads much more quickly. In the early 1900s, new technology took more than 50 years to reach most countries; today it takes about 16 years. But technology tends to spread slowly within countries because many developing countries lack the technical skills necessary to master new, or even older, technologies.

Although better macroeconomic and educational policies, as well as the spread of older enabling technologies – such as electrical networks, road infrastructure, telephone land lines, and sanitation networks – have advanced the spread of technology in developing countries, progress has been slow and the capacity to absorb new ideas and techniques remains weak.

Closing the gap

To continue catching up with high-income countries, developing countries need to:

- Maintain exposure to foreign technologies through trade openness, foreign direct investment, and the participation of migrant populations.
- Further improve the investment climate to allow innovative firms to grow.
- Invest in enabling technologies and basic infrastructure, such as roads, electricity and telephones.
- Improve the quality and increase the quantity of education throughout the economy – not just in major centres.
- Emphasize technology diffusion by reinforcing dissemination systems and the market orientation of R&D programmes.

Source: Burns, 2008.

Techniques of production

If labour is more abundant and capital is scarcer in developing countries than in developed countries, we might expect to observe the use of more labour-intensive techniques of production in the industrial sector of developing countries, reflecting a lower price of labour relative to capital. Figure 6.4 shows this. Assuming the same production function in the two sets of countries, labelled '1', and holding everything else constant, the lower relative price of labour in the developing country, given by the price line (or isocost curve), *cb*, gives a more labour-intensive choice of technique than in the developed country, where the relative price of labour is given by the steeper line *ad*.

In the developed country, the capital–labour ratio is given by the ray from the origin, *DC*, while in the less-developed country, the capital–labour ratio is given by the ray *LDC*; both rays pass through the point of tangency between the price line and production function – *A* and *B*, respectively.

In practice, however, it is often the case that for the same outputs produced, the capital intensity of techniques is not very different between the two sets of countries, and that the capital–labour ratio differs between developed and developing countries in the aggregate only to the extent that the composition of output differs; that is, because there are large sectors in developing countries' economies where very little capital is employed at all, as in subsistence farming and petty service activities. In the modern sectors of developing countries, however, techniques are much more capital-intensive than would be predicted on the basis of knowledge of factor endowments. Given the supply of labour available, and given the rate of investment, the more capital-intensive the techniques, the less employment and the more unemployment there will be.

Unemployment and underemployment are major preoccupations in developing countries, and are one reason why the prevailing techniques of production might be regarded as 'inappropriate'.

But what accounts for this relative capital intensity of modern sector techniques, and would developing countries be better off using more labour-intensive techniques? There are a number of reasons why technological choice sometimes appears to be little different in developing countries than in technologically advanced societies.

First, for a large number of commodities, there may not be a spectrum of techniques to choose from; that is, in practice, the production function in Figure 6.4 may not be smooth, and a country cannot move from point *A* to *B* in accordance with differences in relative factor endowments and

Figure 6.4 Optimal choice of technique

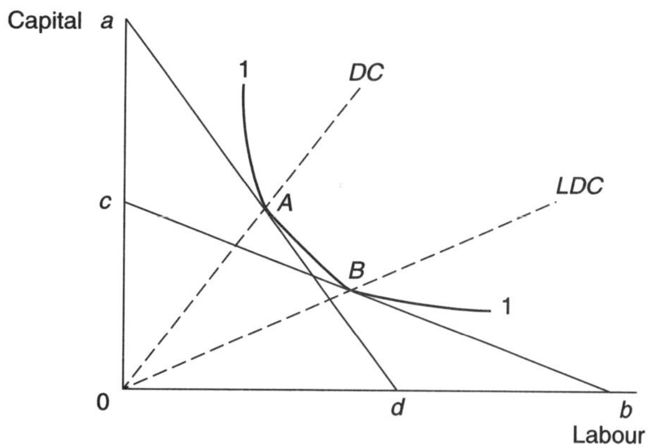

relative factor prices. We are talking here, of course, about techniques that are profitable. There may always be more labour-intensive techniques using more labour and capital, but then the output would not be competitively saleable. If there is not a spectrum of profitable techniques of production, and the coefficients of production are fixed, the production function is L-shaped (sometimes called a **Leontief production function**, after Wassily Leontief, the 'father' of input–output analysis, which assumes no substitutability between capital and labour). Whether technology is such that there is only one profitable technique, or whether there are many but developing countries do not have access to them, is an empirical question we shall consider later in the chapter.

A second reason for the relative capital intensity of production in developing countries is that the market prices of factors of production frequently do not reflect relative abundance or scarcity. This tendency is often exacerbated by developing countries themselves, which give generous subsidies to scarce capital and encourage high wages in the modern manufacturing sector by the government paying high wages to its own employees. The old justification for using capital-intensive techniques, which governments used to believe in and still do to some extent, was that they are necessary to maximize output and saving, and that more labour-intensive techniques would reduce the level of output and saving because of their relative inefficiency and higher wage bills. Later in the chapter, we shall examine these contentions; but, clearly, the cheaper that capital is made by subsidies, and the higher wages are above their 'shadow' price, the more capital-intensive the techniques will tend to be.

A third factor to bear in mind is that although labour may be abundant and the money wage may be lower than in developed countries, it is not necessarily 'cheaper' or less 'costly' to employ, because its productivity may be lower. In other words, the so-called **efficiency wage** (that is, the wage rate divided by the productivity of labour), or wage costs per unit of output, may differ very little between developing and developed countries. This means that the production function for the developing country in Figure 6.4 above will lie outside the production function for the developed country in such a way that even if the relative money wage of labour is lower in the developing country, it is profitable to choose a relatively capital-intensive technique. Figure 6.5 shows this. The production function for the developing country is labelled '2'. Even though labour is cheaper relative to capital in the developing country (slope of *cb* < slope of *ad*), nonetheless the most profitable capital–labour ratio will be the same in both countries (given by the ray from the origin, *DC* = *LDC*). It is probably because abundant labour is not necessarily 'cheap', in a cost per unit of output sense, that accounts for the observation that, in trade, developing countries' exports are sometimes as capital-intensive as in developed countries, contrary to the prediction of certain trade theories. This apparent paradox (sometimes called the **Leontief paradox**) can be explained

Figure 6.5 Different wages: same technique

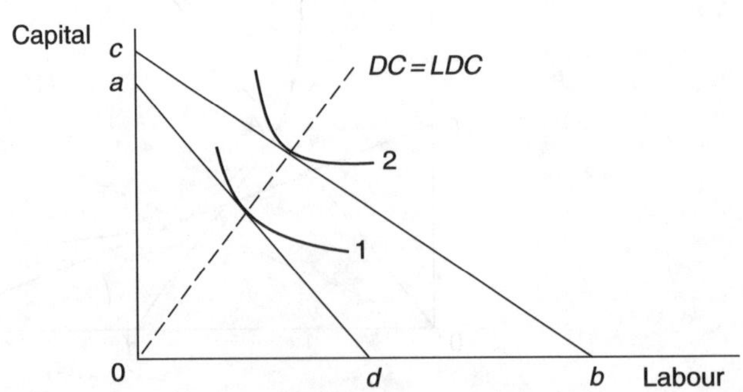

by the fact that it is the 'efficiency' wage that matters, not the money wage, and while the money wage may be low in developing countries, the 'efficiency' wage is relatively high.

Fourth, in certain instances, capital intensity may be explained by a skill constraint. Typically, labour-intensive techniques require a great deal of skilled labour, compared with capital-intensive techniques which mainly require a preponderance of semi-skilled labour to undertake routine tasks. In developing countries that are short of skilled manpower, capital may substitute for skills and constitute a rational response on the part of decision-makers, whoever they may be.

But perhaps the overriding factor that accounts for the relative capital intensity of the modern sector of developing countries is that many, if not most, of the techniques of production are imported from abroad, with a heavy bias in the labour-saving direction. The techniques may either be employed by indigenous firms or, as increasingly seems to be the case, by large foreign-owned **multinational corporations**, which invest in the country and bring their technology with them. In this case, the technology may be 'inappropriate' not because there is not a spectrum of techniques to choose from or an inappropriate selection is made, but because the technology available is circumscribed by the global profit-maximizing motives of the companies investing in the developing country concerned. The labour-saving bias of the technology is to be explained by the labour-saving bias of technical progress in advanced countries where labour is relatively scarce and expensive. As we saw earlier (Figure 6.2), labour-saving bias on a production function diagram is represented by a non-uniform inward shift in the production function, causing capital to be substituted for labour at the same ratio of relative factor prices.

If developed countries have designed labour-saving technologies that, through the process of international investment, are now being widely used in developing countries, it might well be asked: Why have developing countries not invented capital-saving technologies to economize on scarce capital? The answer is that if a country is to develop technology to save capital, it must have a capital goods industry, but typically the capital goods sector of developing countries is rudimentary or non-existent. With a large fraction of investment goods coming from abroad, coupled with a lack of domestic knowhow, there has been very little incentive for developing countries to establish their own capital goods industries.

Capital goods production is characterized by the ability to specialize, but to do this economically requires a large market – a much larger market than for homogeneous consumer products that can reap economies of scale. Capital saving also comes from improvement in the efficiency of capital goods production itself, but without a capital goods sector there cannot be innovations, and an important source of capital saving and technical progress in the economy as a whole is lost. It is widely recognized that a capital goods sector is essential for innovatory activity in the economy as a whole, and if developing countries are to reduce their dependence on imported technology, priority must be given to the establishment and nurture of an indigenous capital goods sector (for a lucid discussion of these issues, see Stewart, 1977, especially Chapter 6).

The empirical evidence on multinational corporations and the choice of techniques is mixed. Lall (1978) distinguishes three separate issues:

1. Whether the technologies used by multinationals are adaptable to abundant labour and low wage conditions in developing countries.
2. Whether multinationals do adapt the technologies they transfer.
3. Whether multinationals adapt better or worse than local firms.

Regarding the first question, the technologies used by multinationals are unlikely to be very flexible because the companies tend to predominate in modern industries where processes are complex, continuous and, by their very nature, capital-intensive. Outside processing, however, ancillary activities, such as the handling of materials and packaging, may be amenable to substitution. On the second issue, it is unlikely that multinationals will undertake major, expensive alterations to technology simply to suit local conditions, and there is not much evidence that they do so.

With regard to the third matter, however, in comparison with local firms, the experience of the multinationals seems to be mixed. The problem here is that when making comparisons, like must be compared with like; that is, local and foreign firms must be compared in the same market, producing similar products with equal access to technology. Studies must therefore be treated with caution. It is easy to reach the conclusion that multinationals are more capital-intensive than local firms if they operate in different industries producing different products. This is, in fact, often the case, as they tend to be concentrated in activities that are intrinsically more capital-intensive such as heavy industries and extractive industries. We shall say more about the empirical evidence below, and more about multinational corporations in Chapter 14, where we consider the role of FDI in the development process.

We turn now to the potential conflict between moving towards the use of more labour-intensive techniques of production and output on the one hand, and saving on the other.

The conflict between employment and output and employment and saving in the choice of techniques

Developing countries have three broad objectives: to raise the level of *present* consumption, to raise the level of *future* consumption (by saving now), and to raise the level of *employment*. In the choice of *new* techniques, a conflict between objectives may arise. First, a technique that maximizes employment may involve a sacrifice of output. Second, a technique that maximizes employment may involve a sacrifice of saving. As we have mentioned already, certainly one of the justifications for the use of modern capital-intensive technology used to be that labour-intensive techniques would reduce output and the investible surplus. We need to look at this matter theoretically and empirically. We shall argue that while, in theory, there may be a conflict, the assumptions on which a potential conflict is based are either invalid or too extreme, and that, in practice, developing countries could move towards the use of more labour-intensive techniques without sacrificing the level of present or future consumption. Some of the empirical evidence would seem to bear this out.

Employment versus output

A potential conflict between employment and output exists in the choice of new techniques because methods that employ high labour–capital ratios may involve high capital–output ratios because labour productivity is lower.[1] Assume that a fixed amount of capital, £1,000, is to be invested. Technique I employs 100 persons with an incremental capital–output ratio of 5, giving an annual flow of output of £200. Technique II employs 50 persons with an incremental capital–output ratio of 4, giving an annual flow of output of £250. Therefore the technique that maximizes employment has a lower flow of current output.

It should be said straight away that there is very little evidence, if any, to support the view that labour-intensive techniques have higher capital–output ratios than capital-intensive techniques. On the contrary, there is growing evidence that labour can be substituted for capital, provided cooperating factors are available, without the level of output being impaired. One interesting pioneer study is that by Pack (1974), using UN data on capital per unit of output (K/O) and labour

Figure 6.6 Efficiency frontier

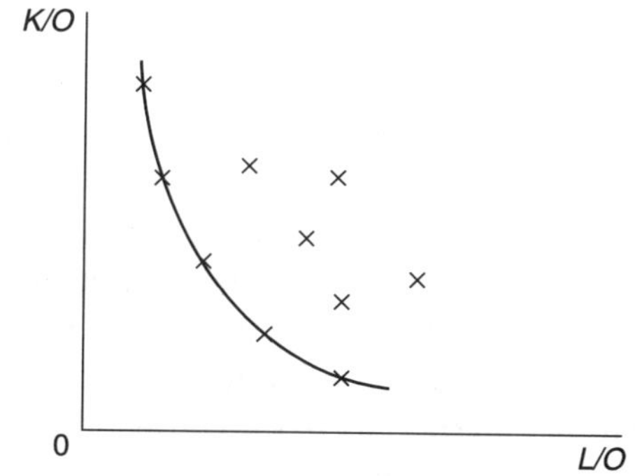

per unit of output (*L/O*) for 6 commodities in 16 firms across 10 countries. Pack plots the observations of (*K/O*) and (*L/O*) (as in Figure 6.6) for each commodity from the cross-section data, and then defines the efficiency frontier to estimate the elasticity of substitution along it.

Each scatter point in Figure 6.6 represents country observations for one industry, say cotton textiles, of the relative amounts of capital and labour employed per unit of output. The **efficiency frontier** (or unit isoquant) is drawn through the points closest to the origin and the elasticity of substitution is calculated as:

$$\frac{(K/L)_i}{(K/L)_j} = \left[\frac{(w/r)_i}{(w/r)_j}\right]^{\sigma}$$

where w/r is the wage-rental ratio, i and j are the two observations closest to the origin, and σ is the elasticity of substitution. For five of the six commodities, there is a large difference in the amount of capital per worker year used by countries on the efficiency frontier and a fairly high elasticity of substitution. The results are shown in Table 6.1.

Table 6.1 Capital–labour substitution possibilities

Industry	Countries on the efficiency frontier	Capital per worker year ($)	Elasticity of substitution (σ)
Bicycles	India	400	0.24
	Japan	520	
Grain milling	Japan	280	3.70
	Israel	6,410	
Paints	India	214	1.60
	Middle Europe	2,790	
Tyres	Iran	6,240	1.50
	Mexico	10,600	
Cotton textiles	India	1,100	2.00
	Mexico	8,240	
Woollen textiles	India	260	1.20
	Japan	4,600	

The results suggest that for countries using large amounts of capital per unit of labour, there are more labour-intensive techniques available (as used by other countries) that could be adopted without sacrificing output, unless the cooperating factors associated with the increased labour intensity are not available. One interesting observation from Pack's work is that India is invariably either on or close to the efficiency frontier, and hence is using labour-intensive techniques effectively.

Pack's study (1976) of 42 plants in Kenyan manufacturing also suggests that there appears to be considerable *ex ante* choice of capital intensity in most industries, particularly outside the processing sector in the auxiliary activities of material receiving, material handling among processes, packaging and storage of the finished products. In fact, many auxiliary activities are already very labour-intensive, and contrary to the conventional wisdom, it was found that foreign-owned firms generally used more labour-intensive techniques than indigenous firms. Pack ascribes this to the better managerial expertise and technical training of personnel in foreign firms. Forsyth and Solomon (1977), in a study of Ghana, also found scope for capital/labour substitution and could find no conclusive evidence that foreign firms are more capital-intensive than resident expatriate or private indigenous firms. The situation varies from industry to industry. Helleiner (1975) concludes his survey of multinational corporations and technological choice by saying:

> In particular industrial sectors, the multinational firm has often proven more responsive and adaptable in its factor and input use, especially in the ancillary activities associated with the basic production processes, than local firms, and so it perhaps should be with its wide range of experience on which to draw.

Even if more labour-intensive techniques can be used without a sacrifice of output, there is still the question of whether the investible surplus, and therefore future output, will be impaired. Pack's work suggests otherwise, but let us now consider in more detail the potential conflict between employment and saving, as the traditional argument has it.

Employment versus saving

The potential conflict between employment and saving can be illustrated in its starkest form using a simple production function diagram, first used in this context by Dobb (1955) and Sen (1968).

Consider the use of a given amount of investible resources, *K*, and the possibility of employing those resources with varying amounts of labour to produce output. In Figure 6.7, 0O is the production function in the consumption sector, exhibiting diminishing returns to labour. Now take the standard traditional (although not necessarily correct) assumption that in the industrial sector, labour is paid a fixed wage that is all consumed, so that a ray from the origin (0C) with a constant slope (*w*) shows the level of the wage bill and consumption at each level of employment. The difference between 0O and 0C is profit, and if all profits are saved, the difference also shows the level of saving at each capital–labour ratio. Saving is maximized where a line drawn parallel to 0C is tangential to the production function – at employment level *L* in Figure 6.7. Beyond this point, further employment generation would diminish the level of saving and investible surplus.

The potential clash between increasing employment and maximizing saving can be seen, however, to be based on several assumptions, the validity of which may be questioned:

Figure 6.7 Employment versus saving

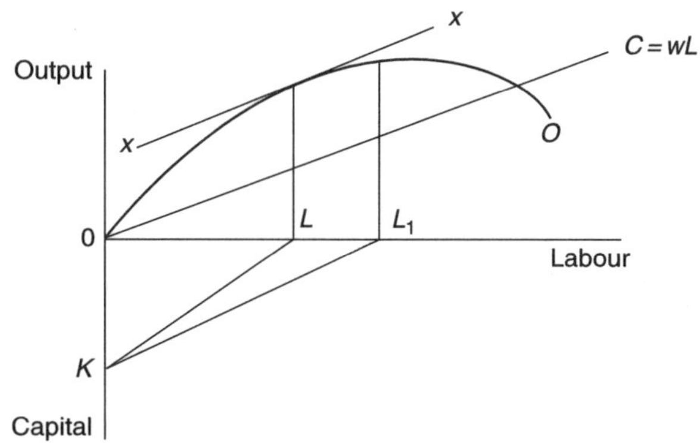

- The wage rate is given and invariant with respect to the technique of production. This assumption would seem to be a hangover from Lewis's influential model of the development process (discussed in Chapter 5), which assumes an elastic supply of labour to the industrial sector at a *constant* wage. If this wage is above the minimum necessary, several other implications ensue.
- All profits are saved and all wages are consumed.
- Unemployment resulting from the use of capital-intensive techniques does not reduce community saving by at least as much as with more employment and a higher wage bill.
- Consumption is not productive (that is, it has no investment component), or that present consumption is no more productive than future consumption.
- Governments lack the ability to tax and to subsidize labour to reconcile the potential conflict.

Let us relax these assumptions and see what difference is made.

Wages and the capital intensity of production

Let us first relax the assumption that the wage rate is given and the same for all techniques, regardless of capital intensity. There are two fundamental points to be made here in the context of a developing country. The first is that a great deal of the technology, at least in the modern industrial sector, is not indigenous but imported. In this case, the wage structure is set by the *skill mix* demanded by the technology and the need to keep the labour force well nourished and contented if the capital equipment is to be worked productively and profitably. By and large it may be expected that the greater the degree of capital intensity, the higher the average wage paid.

The second point is that with large amounts of disguised and open unemployment in the urban sector of developing countries, there is likely to be a big difference between the wage that is being paid with the use of existing technology (imported or indigenous) and the wage at which labour would be willing to work, given the opportunity, with the use of more labour-intensive technology. If more labour-intensive technology could be developed and applied, there is no reason why the wage rate should not be lower with the use of these techniques, unless there is strong trade union resistance in certain sectors.

If the wage is not assumed to be given, but may vary with the technique of production for the reasons outlined above, the conclusion of a conflict between employment and saving in the choice of new techniques is affected considerably. Indeed, if the marginal product of labour declines with the labour intensity of production, and the wage is equal to the marginal product, the conflict disappears entirely. The surplus increases in line with increases in the amount of employment because the surplus on *intra-marginal* units of labour increases.

Wages cannot fall to zero, however – there must be some minimum below which wages cannot fall. This gives the conclusion that there is no necessary conflict between employment and saving up to the point where the marginal product equals the *minimum* wage. Beyond that point there will be a conflict.

Different classes' propensity to consume

The alleged conflict between employment and saving also depends on the assumption that the propensity to save out of profits is higher than the propensity to save out of wages. In Figure 6.7 above, the difference between employment levels L (which maximizes saving) and L_1 (which maximizes employment) depends on the extreme assumption that all profits are saved and all wages are spent. No one would dispute that the propensity to save out of profits (s_p) is higher than the propensity to save out of wages (s_w) (indeed, there is plenty of empirical evidence to support the assertion), but it would be unrealistic to argue that there is no saving out of wages and no consumption out of profits. Both consumption out of profits and saving out of wages will reduce the conflict between employment and saving and move the point of maximum surplus away from L towards L_1.

The narrower the difference between s_w and s_p, the higher the level of employment before a conflict sets in, until at the limit, if $s_w = s_p$, there is no conflict at all. The distribution of income between wages and profits will not affect the aggregate level of saving.

Support of the unemployed

If a particular choice of technology, which is designed to maximize the reinvestible surplus, causes unemployment and the unemployed make claims on society's investible resources, the surplus may ultimately be less than if more labour-intensive techniques had been chosen. There are three main ways in which the unemployed may reduce the investible surplus:

- If the unemployed remain in the agricultural sector, they may depress average product and consume more than they produce, thus reducing the agricultural surplus.
- If the unemployed remain in the industrial sector, they will absorb family savings to support themselves.
- There may be public support for the unemployed through unemployment insurance programmes, in which case, public saving will be reduced below what it otherwise might be.

If 'compensation' to the unemployed in any of the forms outlined above exceeds the difference between the industrial wage and the marginal product using more labour-intensive techniques, it would pay to create extra employment because the difference between consumption and production as a result of expanding employment would be less than the reduction in saving caused by the unemployment. At the limit, of course, if the unemployed 'consumed' resources equal to the value of the industrial wage, it would make no difference if labour was employed up to the point where the marginal product of labour is zero. There is clearly no difference from the point of view of saving between an unemployed person consuming the equivalent of an industrial wage and an employed man with zero marginal product receiving an industrial wage. As long as unemployment absorbs saving, therefore, in whatever form, employment can be higher without reducing the investible surplus to below what it would otherwise have been. Thus, as a general proposition, it may be said that the extent of the conflict between employment and saving will also depend on the amount of compensation to the unemployed out of the total investible surplus.

Are consumption and investment distinct?

The alleged conflict between employment and saving also assumes either that consumption has no investment component or that present and future consumption are equally productive. Those who argue for techniques to maximize the investible surplus at the expense of employment place no value on present consumption at the margin, and those who argue for techniques to maximize employment are indifferent at the margin between an extra unit of consumption and saving (investment). It can be shown, however, that if consumption has an investment content, and the productivity of consumption falls as the level of consumption increases, the relative valuation of present consumption increases, favouring more labour-intensive techniques (Thirlwall, 1977). 'Productive' consumption refers to consumption that improves the efficiency of labour, thereby raising the level of income in the same way as normal additions to the capital stock. As long as consumption is productive, therefore, an increase in employment and consumption need not be at the expense of 'investment' for future output.

All too little is known about the precise extent to which low levels of consumption, and particularly food intake, impair working efficiency and productivity. But we do know that the food requirements considered by nutritionists to be necessary for efficient working and healthy living are far greater than the levels achieved by a large minority of the population in developing countries (see Dasgupta, 1993). Calorie deficiency causes loss of body weight, tiredness, listlessness and a deterioration of mental faculties. Protein deficiency causes such conditions as kwashiorkor, and may cause death in children. Vitamin A deficiency causes blindness, and iodine deficiency is a cause of goitre, which leads to cretinism and deaf-mutism. Altogether, it has been estimated by the UN Food and Agriculture Organization that at least 1 billion people in the world suffer from various degrees of malnutrition. To the extent that this impairs efficiency and output, and is caused by a lack of consumption, an increase in employment and present consumption may be as valuable at the margin as an extra unit of saving from the point of view of future welfare. The more equal the relative valuation of consumption and saving at the margin, the less the conflict between employment generation in the present and the level of future output.

Taxes and subsidies

It has been assumed so far that savings and employment depend exclusively on the choice of technique. In practice, of course, governments can tax and subsidize to achieve desired ends, and this they can do to reconcile the conflict between employment and saving. As Sen (1969) has remarked:

> the total amount of income to be saved can be determined by the planner in any way he likes... If this is true then the link snaps between the choice of techniques and the proportion of income saved. The technical choice may be made with the main purpose of maximising the amount of output, and the proportion of the output to be invested can be decided at a separate stage.

Consider again Figure 6.7, which is redrawn here as Figure 6.8. By the choice of techniques alone, maximization of the surplus XY means a sacrifice of employment L_1L. Or employment L_1 means a sacrifice of savings equal to Y_1Y_2. Now suppose that the government possesses the power to tax and subsidize. To employ L_1 requires a shadow wage of zero: that is, a subsidy to employers equal to the full value of the wage. The employers' surplus will now be X_1L_1, but since workers receive the market wage and all wages are consumed, consumption will still be Y_1L_1, and the investible surplus, X_1Y_1. The question is: Can tax policy in the new situation preserve the level of the surplus XY generated by the more capital-intensive technology? The answer must be yes, provided the

Figure 6.8 Preserving the level of saving through taxation

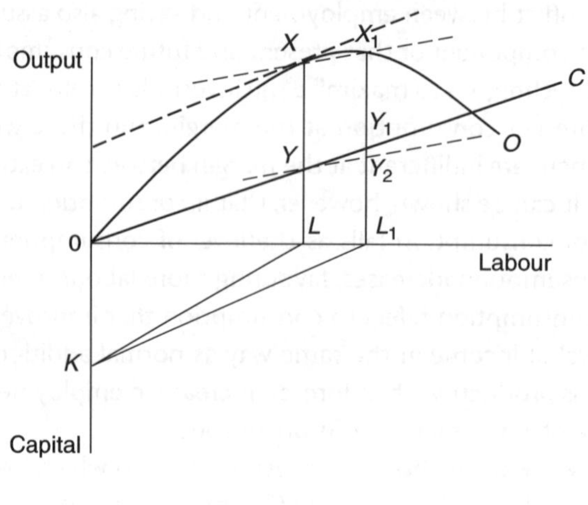

propensity to consume is greater than zero. The total wage bill is Y_1L_1 and it is desired to reduce consumption out of the wage bill by Y_1Y_2. Consumption will fall by the amount of tax times the propensity to consume (c). Hence, the level of tax raised must be $T = (Y_1Y_2)/c$. If the wage bill is, say, £1,000, Y_1Y_2 is £100 and c is 0.8, then the tax raised must be £100/0.8 = £125.

In this example, the preservation of the level of saving is quite easily accomplished while moving from the more capital-intensive to labour-intensive techniques. If, of course, a fairly high level of taxation already exists, and there is no scope for further taxation, subsidization and taxation will not be a feasible means of reconciliation. In practice, however, the presumption must be that developing countries are not yet at their taxable capacity, and that the subsidization of labour, coupled with appropriate tax policy, is a possible policy.

Some care must be taken, however, over the form of taxation. For example, if the wage is fixed in real terms, then indirect taxes that raise prices will reduce the real wage, and the money wage will have to rise to compensate. Since the money wage is the cost to the employer, subsidies will then have to be increased. The imposition of indirect taxes to finance subsidies may lead to a spiral of increased taxation, inflation and subsidization. Direct taxes on workers' incomes may also be counterproductive if workers bid for money wage increases to maintain disposable income. The only feasible taxes to finance subsidies may be on exports or luxury consumption goods, which will not affect the real income of the broad mass of the population. While theoretically, therefore, a policy of labour subsidization financed by taxation may reconcile the conflict between employment and saving, it may run into a number of practical difficulties.

All the factors that may lead to an increase in the labour intensity of production without impairing the investible surplus may either be thought of as additive, or any one of them by itself may be powerful enough to push employment close to L_1 in Figure 6.7 above without loss of saving or its benefits.

Future policy

It has become part of conventional wisdom, and there may be a good deal of truth in the assertion, that a major cause of the growth of urban unemployment in developing countries lies in the application of 'inappropriate' production techniques because of the limited choice of techniques available, from within the countries and from outside. The choice is limited from within owing to the absence of a domestic capital goods sector, and it is limited from without because the techniques imported reflect the labour-saving bias of technical progress in the developed countries from which they come. The application of 'inappropriate' technology not only exacerbates unemployment, but perpetuates the dualistic structure of developing countries, increases income inequality, may worsen the foreign exchange position, and, in general, produces a distorted economy, while increasing the dependence of developing countries on developed countries.

There is now a strong movement throughout the developing countries in support of the creation of an **intermediate technology** using more labour per unit of capital and fewer foreign inputs. What is required is a whole spectrum of techniques to suit different circumstances, from which developing countries can choose. For this to happen, developing countries need to encourage the establishment of their own capital goods industries, and more R&D is required both within, and on behalf of, poor countries. An **international technology bank** would be a useful starting point, giving countries access to technological blueprints from different sources.

The capital intensity of production is also a function of the composition of output. There are often many ways of meeting a given need, some of which may be more labour-intensive than others. Where this is so, such as in transport, nutrition, housing and so on, serious consideration should be given to the most labour-intensive way of meeting such needs, consistent with other objectives.

Finally, the location of activity needs to be considered. Whatever technology is applied in the modern sector, it will have implications for the rural sector that will rebound on the modern sector. We saw in Chapter 5 that the creation of more modern sector jobs may encourage more migrants than the number of jobs created, thus increasing urban unemployment. This would seem to call for the location of new labour-intensive industries in the rural sector, to curb the flow of migrants and ease urban unemployment.

To conclude our analysis, we have seen that there are many reasons for believing that the potential conflicts inherent in the choice of new techniques between employment and saving on the one hand and between employment and output on the other have been exaggerated, and that techniques can be more labour-intensive without impairing the level of the investible surplus or the level of output. **It is in the direction of more rural-based, labour-intensive projects that development strategy ought to move for the maximization of general welfare.**

Summary

- There can be no economic growth unless economies invest a proportion of their output. The amount of capital per worker in developing countries is much lower than in developed countries, which partly accounts for the lower productivity of labour in developing countries.
- There are many different types of capital: physical plant and machinery, infrastructure, human capital and social capital, including health expenditure, which makes labour more productive (see Chapter 7).
- The productivity of capital depends to a large extent on the amount of technical progress embodied in it.
- The pace of technical progress depends on the willingness and capacity of societies to be inventive, to innovate, and to devote resources to human capital formation, skills training and R&D expenditure.
- There is a huge technological divide between rich and poor countries, which will take time and effort to bridge.

- The choice of techniques of production is an important issue in developing countries – whether to choose relatively labour-intensive techniques to create more employment, or relatively capital-intensive techniques, which embody more technology.
- Theory and evidence suggests that developing countries can move towards the use of more labour-intensive technologies without sacrificing future growth.

Chapter 6 Discussion questions

1. What is meant by the process of capital accumulation?
2. Distinguish between the various forms of investment and capital accumulation that can raise per capita income.
3. Why do developing countries, and many development economists, lay great stress on the role of capital accumulation in the development process?
4. What is meant by the following terms: neutral, capital-saving, and labour-saving technical progress?
5. What are the main means by which societies progress technologically?
6. What is 'learning by doing'?
7. In what sense is infrastructure investment complementary to investment in plant and machinery, and does it have to be provided publicly?
8. What are the major factors that dictate the choice of techniques in the industrial sector in developing countries?
9. Why did early development theory tend to stress the importance of capital-intensive techniques for rapid economic development?
10. Would the use of more labour-intensive techniques necessarily reduce the size of the investible surplus?
11. What do you understand by the 'efficiency wage' of labour, and how does this concept help to explain the relative capital intensity of production and goods traded?

Note

1. The capital–output ratio (K/O) may be expressed as the product of the capital–labour ratio and labour requirements per unit of output, that is, $K/O = (K/L)(L/O)$. Techniques with a low K/L may nonetheless have a high K/O because L/O is high – that is, the productivity of labour is low.

Websites on technology and investment

Economic Growth Resources run by Jon Temple, Bristol University, UK www.bristol.ac.uk/efm/people/jon-r-temple/overview.html
International Institute for Communication www.iicd.org
World Intellectual Property Organization www.wipo.int
United Nations Industrial Development Organization www.unido.org

7

HUMAN CAPITAL: EDUCATION, THE ROLE OF WOMEN, NUTRITION AND HEALTH

- Introduction
- Education
- Estimating the rate of return to education
- Measuring the contribution of education to economic growth
- The role of women in economic development
- Women's education
- Women's health
- Mothers' Index
- Policies to reduce gender gap
- Nutrition
- Water
- Health
- Killer diseases
- Other diseases and health expenditure
- The impact of ill health on growth and development
- Summary
- Discussion questions
- Notes
- Websites on education, women, nutrition and health

Introduction

This chapter focuses on human capital formation in developing countries, and discusses the effects of education, the role of women, nutrition and health on the process of economic and social development. For a poor country to experience a faster pace of economic and social development, it requires educated and literate people, an equitable participation of women and men in the labour force, and, above all, well-nourished, healthy people free from the debilitating diseases that adversely affect the lives and productivity of so many people in poor countries.

Investment in human capital takes many different forms, including expenditure on formally organized education (both public and private expenditure), on-the-job and institutional training and retraining, study programmes and adult education, publicly funded nutrition programmes to keep people healthy and productive during their working lives, and expenditure on health facilities for the prevention and treatment of illness.

First, we consider the participation in education at the primary, secondary and tertiary levels, and expenditure on education as a proportion of total government expenditure and gross domestic product (GDP). Primary school enrolment is virtually universal across regions of the world, but at the secondary level, enrolment is less than half the age group in low-income countries (particularly in sub-Saharan Africa), and tertiary enrolment is less than 10% of the age group. The ratios of educational expenditure to total government expenditure and GDP are similar across regions, but per capita expenditure is much lower in low-income countries: only \$100 compared to nearly \$7,000 per head in high-income countries.

Second, we look at the rates of return to education and show that the private returns exceed 10% for males and even higher for females (because the opportunity cost of education is lower). The highest returns come from investment in tertiary education. Third, we show the different ways in which the contribution of education to economic growth can be measured. With regard to the role of women in the development process, we highlight how women are disadvantaged as far as educational and employment opportunities are concerned, and the discrimination and burden they face in many developing countries.

Finally, we focus on nutrition and health, and highlight the link between poor nutrition and poor health. Evidence is provided on the benefits of improved nutrition in terms of improved productivity and reduction in the number of working days lost, and on how poor health hurts the functioning of economies. The three major 'killer' diseases in poor countries are malaria, tuberculosis and HIV/AIDS, and we discuss the various campaigns that exist to combat these and other diseases.

Education

The education of a population, male and female, from primary through secondary to tertiary education can overcome many of the characteristics of the labour force that act as impediments to social and economic progress, such as illiteracy, fear of change, unreceptiveness to new knowledge, a lack of incentive, and immobility. Improvements in the education and skills of labour can considerably increase the productivity and earnings of labour, and may be preconditions for the introduction of more sophisticated, advanced technology applied to production. The capacity to absorb and use physical capital may be limited by, among other things, investment in human capital. It is in this respect that there may be a close association between education and the mainsprings of technical progress.

Table 7.1 Education for All 2000–15: goals and their assessment

Goal	Assessment
Goal 1: Expanding and improving comprehensive early childhood care and education, especially for the most vulnerable and disadvantaged children	Progress in early childhood care and education was rapid but from a low base and highly inequitable
Goal 2: Access to and complete free primary education of good quality	Universal primary education was not reached in 2015
Goal 3: Equitable access to appropriate learning and life skills programmes	More adolescents received secondary education but measuring skill acquisition among youths and adults remains limited
Goal 4: Achieving a 50 per cent improvement in levels of adult literacy by 2015, especially for women, and equitable access to basic and continuing education for all adults	Progress in adult literacy was below the target
Goal 5: Eliminating gender disparities in primary and secondary education by 2005, and achieving gender equality in education by 2015, with a focus on girls' full and equal access to and achievement in basic education of good quality	Many countries have not achieved gender parity and obstacles to equality remain
Goal 6: Improving all aspects of the quality of education and ensuring excellence of all so that recognized and measurable learning outcomes are achieved by all, especially in literacy, numeracy and essential life skills	There has been increased attention to issues of quality

Source: UNESCO, 2015.

Two main international bodies have recognized education as a basic human right: the UN's **Convention on the Rights of the Child** in 1989 and UNESCO's **World Declaration on Education for All** in 1990. Then, in 2000, representatives of the international community met at the World Education Forum in Dakar, Senegal, under the auspices of UNESCO, and produced what is called the **Dakar Framework for Action**, comprising six goals to be achieved by 2015. The goals, and a brief assessment of each of these, are presented in Table 7.1. It can be seen from Table 7.1 that some progress has been made towards the goals set down, but still some poor countries have been unable to guarantee primary education to all school-age children, gender disparities still exist, and progress in adult literacy has been below target. The poor quality of education has effects on the well-being of children, their families and communities.

Table 7.2 shows clearly the underprovision of educational facilities and opportunities in many poor countries, and the low rate of literacy in the poorest countries. In low-income countries, the secondary school enrolment rate is less than 50%, and the tertiary enrolment rate is only 9%. The figures mirror the statistics for sub-Saharan African countries, which constitute the majority of low-income countries. Literacy rates are correspondingly low in low-income countries and Africa, barely reaching 50% for females. Note that for primary education, the enrolment ratio exceeds 100% in all regions. This is because the ratio is *total* enrolment, regardless of age, as a percentage of the population of the age group that corresponds to that level of education. So, the primary school age group may be 5–11 years, but children older than that are attending. Also note that the enrolment rate is not the same as the completion rate, which is only 71% in low-income countries, and 69% in Africa. Moreover, enrolment and completion do not necessarily mean receiving a good education. For economic development, it is not just the quantity of education that is important, but also its quality. Case example 7.1 provides a study of primary education in India, which highlights this fundamental difference.

Table 7.2 Participation in education, 2010 and 2013

	School gross enrolment ratio % of relevant age group			Adult literacy rate % ages 15 and older	
	Primary 2013	**Secondary 2013**	**Tertiary 2013**	**Female 2010**	**Male 2010**
World	108	75	33	80	89
Low income	107	45	9	54	68
Middle income	109	77	29	78	88
Lower middle income	106	67	23	62	79
Upper middle income	116	92	37	92	96
Low and middle income	109	71	26	75	86
East Asia and Pacific	118	85	30	92	97
Europe and Central Asia	102	99	55	97	99
Latin America and Caribbean	105	93	43	92	93
Middle East and North Africa	110	76	35	70	85
South Asia	111	66	21	50	73
Sub-Saharan Africa	100	43	9	51	68
High income	102	104	73	–	–

Source: World Bank, 2010, 2013.

Case example 7.1

Primary education in India

During the period 2005–15, 350,000 new primary schools were built in India. Today, over 95% of villages have a state primary school and enrolment is universal. A 2002 constitutional amendment established primary education as a 'fundamental right' for every child aged 6–14. However, teaching and learning standards are very poor. Although the facilities have been provided, the quality of the teaching and learning process has been neglected. Over the past decade, 100 million children completed primary school but without attaining basic reading and maths skills. Many rural primary schools have just one or two teachers running mixed classrooms, with students of all ages and competency levels sitting together in a single room. Most teachers end up focusing on the students best able to keep pace, while the rest are left behind. Pupil and teacher absenteeism is very high. Children leave school during the harvest season, when they have to help their families. Whatever they have learnt, they forget. Attendance at government primary schools averages about 70%, but it is less than 35% in many states. Also, high teacher absenteeism (15–25% of appointed teachers are absent on any given day) hinders the performance of pupils. State governments request teachers for large-scale tasks such as surveys and elections.

The difference between the targets and the results is a consequence of an ambitious national curriculum. It expects that students will read fluently by the end of the first year of school, without considering their limited exposure to books or written material. Teachers are expected to transfer vast quantities of factual information to students, regardless of their comprehension.

This situation in Indian education acts as a serious constraint on the performance of individuals and on Indian society. Most newly created jobs are in services, which require basic literacy and numeracy. Young people who lack these fundamental skills are likely to get jobs that don't pay enough to raise them out of poverty.

Table 7.3 Public spending on education, by region and income level, 1999 and 2012

Region	Public education spending				
	% of GNP		% of government expenditure on education		Per capita, primary education, PPP constant 2011 prices, US$
	1999	2012	1999	2012	2012
World	4.5	5.0	13.8	13.7	1,337
Low Income	3.2	4.0	14.7	14.9	100
Lower middle income	4.4	4.9	15.0	15.6	467
Upper middle income	5.0	5.1	14.8	14.9	–
High income	4.9	5.4	12.4	12.3	6,805
Arab States	5.3	–	16.9	–	–
Central and Eastern Europe	4.4	4.9	12.7	11.7	4,478
Central Asia	4.0	3.4	–	13.0	–
East Asia and the Pacific	5.1	3.4	13.8	17.5	–
Latin America and Western Europe	4.5	4.9	14.8	–	1,187
North America and Western Europe	5.2	6.0	12.3	12.5	7,943
South and West Asia	3.6	3.9	16.6	12.6	240
Sub-Saharan Africa	3.9	4.9	14.8	18.4	136

Source: UNESCO, 2015.

Developing countries neglect educational provision at their peril. Research shows a strong association across countries between levels of human capital formation, growth performance and poverty reduction. For example, Baldacci et al. (2005) find, using a panel dataset of 120 developing countries over the period 1975–2000, that an increase in education spending of 1% of GDP is associated, on average, with three years of extra schooling and an increase in annual GDP growth of 1.5 percentage points after 15 years. This reduces the poverty head count by 17%.

Table 7.3 gives information on educational spending as a proportion of total government expenditure and GDP.

It can be seen that these ratios of educational expenditure in poor countries are not much different from rich countries, but because government expenditure and GDP are much lower in poor countries, the expenditure per capita is much less. In sub-Saharan Africa and South and West Asia, expenditure is particularly low, which is reflected in the very poor educational facilities for teaching and learning; large class sizes; lack of equipment; lack of books and other learning media; and often the poor quality of teachers. Moreover, it is clear from comparing figures between 1999 and 2012 that not much progress, if any, has been made in shifting resources towards education.

Estimating the rate of return to education

The main way of estimating the private rate of return to education is the method originally adopted by Mincer (1974), where the log of earnings ($\text{Ln } w_i$) is regressed on the number of years schooling (S_i), controlling for the potential experience of an individual (X_i)

(estimated as $age_i - S_i - 6$) and potential experience squared $(X_i)^2$ (to allow for the diminishing returns to experience). Therefore:

$$\text{Ln } w_i = a + b_1 (S_i) + b_2 (X_i) + b_3 (X_i)^2 + \mu_i \quad (7.1)$$

where μ_i is a random disturbance term reflecting unobserved abilities and b_1 is the average monetary return to years of schooling.

This earnings function method can be used to estimate returns to different levels of schooling by converting the continuous years of schooling variable (S_i) into a series of dummy variables, say D_P, D_S, D_T, where D_P is primary schooling, D_S is secondary schooling, and D_T is tertiary education, that is:

$$\text{Ln } w_i = a + b_P (D_{Pi}) + b_S (D_{Si}) + b_T (D_{Ti}) + b_2 (X_i) + b_3 (X_i)^2 + \mu_i \quad (7.2)$$

The returns to primary (r_p), secondary (r_s), and tertiary (r_t) education are then:

$$r_p = b_p/S_p; \quad r_s = (b_s - b_p)(S_S - S_P) \text{ and } r_t = (b_T - b_S)(S_T - S_S)$$

where S_P, S_S and S_T stand for the total number of years of schooling for each educational level.

The costs of education at different levels are the opportunity cost of not earning, tuition fees (if any), and expenses incurred in going to school.

The traditional consistent findings on rates of return to education when extra earnings and costs are considered are:

- private returns are positive, averaging 10% a year
- returns are higher in low- and middle-income countries than high-income countries
- returns are higher for primary schooling than for secondary education
- returns are higher for women than for men
- returns to education have declined slightly over time because, despite rising levels of average school attainment, the supply of schooling and educated people has responded to demand.

A new meta-study by Montenegro and Patrinos (2014) for the World Bank confirms all these conclusions, except that they find that the return to tertiary education is now the highest, and not the return to primary education. The new study uses data for 139 countries, with a total of 819 harmonized household surveys over the period 1970–2013 (with 75% of estimates coming from the period 2000–13), covering 92% of world population.

The basic earnings functions in equations (7.1) and (7.2) are first applied to three different groups: the total sample, males, and females. The results are shown in Table 7.4. The average private rate of return to another year of schooling is 10.1%. For males, the return is 9.6%, and for females it is higher at 11.7%. The returns are also estimated for levels of schooling, as shown in Table 7.4. The rate of return to primary education is 10.6%, while for secondary education it is 7.2% and for tertiary it is the highest at 15.2%. At all stages of education, the return for females is higher than for males because foregone earnings (opportunity costs) are less.

Montenegro and Patrinos also calculate rates of return to education across different regions of the world. Table 7.5 shows the results, and also the average years of schooling in different regions.

The returns do not differ much across regions, but are clearly highest in sub-Saharan Africa for both males and females. This is also true when the rates of return are estimated according to the level of education, shown in Table 7.6. The returns to primary, secondary and tertiary education in

Table 7.4 Summary statistics of the returns to schooling

Variable	Mean (%)	Standard deviation	Number
Years of schooling total	10.1	(3.3)	819
Years of schooling male	9.6	(3.2)	819
Years of schooling female	11.7	(3.3)	819
Primary schooling total	10.6	(6.4)	547
Secondary schooling total	7.2	(3.6)	619
Tertiary schooling total	15.2	(5.8)	762
Primary schooling male	10.0	(6.6)	543
Secondary schooling male	7.1	(3.8)	614
Tertiary schooling male	15.2	(5.8)	745
Primary schooling female	10.9	(7.6)	519
Secondary schooling female	8.7	(4.6)	607
Tertiary schooling female	16.8	(6.1)	738

Source: Montenegro and Patrinos, 2014.

Table 7.5 Average returns to schooling (latest period for each country)

Region	Average returns to schooling (%)			Average years of schooling			
	Total	Male	Female	Total	Male	Female	N
High Income economies	10.0	9.5	11.1	12.9	12.7	13.1	33
East Asia & Pacific	9.4	9.2	10.1	10.4	10.2	10.7	13
Europe & Central Asia	7.4	6.9	9.4	12.4	12.2	12.7	20
Latin America & Caribbean	9.2	8.8	10.7	10.1	9.5	10.9	23
Middle East & North Africa	7.3	6.5	11.1	9.4	9.2	11.0	10
South Asia	7.7	6.9	10.2	6.5	6.5	6.4	7
Sub-Saharan Africa	12.4	11.3	14.5	8.0	8.1	8.1	33
All economies	9.7	9.1	11.4	10.4	10.2	10.8	139

Source: Montenegro and Patrinos (2014).

Africa are higher than in many other regions. There is only one conclusion, which is that there is massive underinvestment in education in Africa – the poorest continent on the planet.

Finally, we can look at the rates of return to education over time. Since 1980, there has been a big expansion in school attainment. In the early 1980s, the average years of schooling was only 6.6 compared to 11.6 in 2011–13. As schooling increases, the return to schooling tends to decrease, as Table 7.7 shows. In the period 1980–85, the return was 13.3 and fell to 10.0 in 2011–13. The returns have declined by 3.3 percentage points over a 30-year period; in other words, another year of schooling leads to a reduction in the returns to schooling by 0.1 percentage point.

The statistics and discussion above relate to the private return to education. The return to society, or social return, also depends on the costs to government of providing schools and teachers,

Table 7.6 Average returns to schooling by levels

Region	Total (%)			Male (%)			Female (%)		
	Primary	Secondary	Tertiary	Primary	Secondary	Tertiary	Primary	Secondary	Tertiary
High Income	4.9	6.6	11.1	3.3	7.5	10.7	7.2	5.2	12.3
East Asia	13.6	5.3	14.8	12.6	5.8	15.0	9.5	6.4	15.8
Europe/Central Asia	13.9	4.7	10.3	12.1	4.2	9.8	11.9	6.4	12.2
Latin America	7.8	5.4	15.9	7.9	5.3	15.7	8.7	6.5	17.4
Middle East/N. Africa	16.0	4.5	10.5	12.7	4.3	10.2	21.4	7.4	13.5
South Asia	6.0	5.0	17.3	4.7	3.9	16.6	4.8	6.2	23.3
Sub-Saharan Africa	14.4	10.6	21.0	12.5	10.1	21.0	17.5	12.7	21.3
All economies	11.5	6.8	14.6	10.1	6.7	14.4	13.2	8.2	16.1

Source: Montenegro and Patrinos (2014).

Table 7.7 Returns to schooling and average years of schooling by period

	Returns to schooling (%)	Average years of schooling	Number of surveys
1980–85	13.3	6.6	12
1986–90	12.7	8.1	23
1991–95	11.0	8.0	58
1996–2000	10.1	8.8	109
2001–05	9.9	10.1	228
2006–10	9.6	10.9	238
2011–13	10.0	11.6	149

Source: Montenegro and Patrinos, 2014.

and on the positive externalities to society that education provides. There are two main types of positive benefits or externalities that can be distinguished:

1. the effect of human capital on current productivity (static externalities)
2. the effect of learning and technological change (dynamic externalities).

The primary static human capital externality is that an individual's human capital enhances the productivity of other factors of production, such as physical capital and the human capital of others. The main dynamic externalities relate to learning by doing and the adoption of new technologies being more effective at higher levels of education. Whether the social return to investment in education is higher or lower than the private return depends on the balance between the costs to governments of providing educational facilities and the various static and dynamic externalities. Empirical evidence is scarce, but an early study by Pascharoupolos (1994) shows social returns to primary, secondary and tertiary education lower than private returns but still positive.

Likewise, Ram (1996) has fitted the Mincer equations (7.1 and 7.2) to pooled time-series and cross-section data for 45 countries using real GDP per worker (not earnings) as the dependent variable, so that the coefficient on the years of schooling per person variable measures the social returns to education rather than simply the private returns. Separate regressions are run for the full sample of countries – developed, developing low-income and middle-income countries. The average rate of return is 13%, which is higher than the private returns estimated by Montenegro and Patrinos (2014). The highest social return is 16.2% in the middle-income countries.

Measuring the contribution of education to economic growth

There are three main ways in which education can improve growth performance:

1. Education improves the quality of labour, and also the quality of physical capital through the application of knowledge.
2. Education has spillover effects (externalities) on other sections of society, which offset diminishing returns to physical capital.
3. Education is one of the most important inputs into R&D and for attracting FDI.

There are three main methods of estimating the contribution of education to growth:

1. Measuring the contribution that education makes to the difference in earnings of individuals.
2. The production function approach.
3. The use of macrodeterminants of growth equations.

The first method involves constructing a quality-weighted index of the labour force, where quality is measured by the contribution that education makes to the difference in the earnings of individuals as a measure of productivity. The approach, pioneered by Denison (1962), involves two steps. The first entails gathering information on the distribution of the labour force by amounts of schooling at different dates. The second step involves collecting information on income differences between education cohorts with different amounts of schooling embodied in them, which are then used as weights to derive an index of the improvements in the *quality* of labour due to education, on the assumption that a certain percentage of differences in earnings is due to differences in the amount of education.

Suppose, for instance, that the earnings differential between those with eight years' schooling and those with ten years' schooling is 20%, that one-half of the difference is assumed to be due to the extra two years' schooling, and that a person with eight years' schooling is treated as one unit; then the person with ten years' education counts as $1 + (0.5 \times 0.2) = 1.1$ units. The growth of the quality of labour due to education over a given period can then be estimated and its contribution to measured growth calculated. For example, suppose that the growth in the quality of labour is estimated to be 1% per annum, the elasticity of output with respect to labour is 0.7, and the annual average growth rate of the economy is 3%. This gives a contribution of education to measured growth of 23%, that is, $(0.7 \times 1.0)/3.0 = 0.23$.

The approach is not without its difficulties. The proportion of earnings differences assumed to be due to differences in the amounts of education between individuals is arbitrary, and if the figure is too high, this will give an upward bias to the contribution of education. On the other hand, there are other reasons why the approach underestimates the contribution of education:

- The methodology employed ignores the role of education in maintaining the *average* quality of the labour force.
- No allowance is made for improvements in the quality of education.
- There are the externalities or 'spillovers' from education to consider, such as the contribution of education to knowledge and its diffusion throughout society.

The second method for estimating the contribution of education to growth, and also the rate of return to educational expenditure, is to use the production function approach outlined in Chapter 4 (see equation (4.22)). All that is required is a measure of education expansion to include in the production function. The contribution of education to measured growth is then the rate of growth of the education variable multiplied by the elasticity of output with respect to the education variable. In estimating form, the production function with the growth of education included is written as:

$$r_y = r_T + ar_k + \beta r_L + \gamma r_E. \tag{7.3}$$

where r_E is the rate of growth of education, and γ is the elasticity of output with respect to education. Suppose, for example, that the growth of educational expenditure ($r_E = \Delta E/E$) is 10% per annum and the elasticity of output with respect to education (γ) is 0.01, then the contribution of education to measured growth would be (10)(0.01) $=$ 0.1 percentage point. If the average growth of GDP is 2% per annum, the contribution of education to economic growth would be $0.1/2 = 5\%$.

The average social rate of return to education can also be measured independently using equation (7.3). Since $\gamma = (\Delta Y/Y)/(\Delta E/E)$, we can write:

$$\frac{\Delta Y}{\Delta E} = \gamma \frac{\overline{Y}}{\overline{E}}. \tag{7.4}$$

where $\overline{Y}$ and $\overline{E}$ are the mean levels of output and the education variable, respectively. For example, suppose that the mean level of output over a period was £100 million, the mean level of expenditure on education was £5 million, and the elasticity of output with respect to education (γ) was 0.01. The rate of return would then be 0.2 or 20%, that is, $(0.01)(100/5) = 0.2$ or 20%.

The third method for estimating the contribution of education to growth comes from new growth theory, discussed in Chapter 4, in which the stock of education (measured by enrolment rates, or number of years of schooling) is included as a variable to explain differences in growth rates between countries using large samples of countries. A simple cross-section estimating equation would be of the form:

$$g = a + b\,(PCY) + c\,(education). \tag{7.5}$$

where *g* is the average growth rate of countries over, say, a 20-year period; *PCY* is the initial level of per capita income of countries, and (*education*) measures the proportion of the age group enrolled in primary or secondary schools in each country, or the average years of schooling. The coefficient, *c*, then measures the contribution of a 1 percentage point difference in school enrolment rates, or years of schooling, to the difference in growth rates between countries. Barro's (1991) pioneer study using this approach, and adopted by others (see Table 4.5), suggested that each additional year of schooling was associated with a 0.3 percentage point faster growth of per capita income over the period 1960–85. These so-called 'macrodeterminants of growth' studies also include a number of other variables, and the contribution of education to growth sometimes remains a significant variable and sometimes not. The fast growth of the East Asian economies in recent decades is often attributed to their heavy investment in education.

But highlighting the role of education in the growth process predates new growth theory. In the postwar years, it was Denison and T.W. Schultz (1961), in his presidential address to the American Economic Association in 1961, who first drew attention to the importance of education for growth with quantitative evidence. According to Schultz, the stock of education in the USA rose by approximately 850% between 1900 and 1956 compared with an increase in reproducible capital of 450%. He acknowledged the difficulties of estimating the rate of return to education, but argued that even when every conceivable cost is considered, and all expenditure is treated as investment and none as consumption,[1] the return on investment in education is at least as high as, if not higher than, the return on investment in non-human capital. Denison estimated a contribution of education to the growth of per capita income of 40%.

It is the apparent importance of education in the historical growth process of developed countries that has invoked the response that investment in human capital may be as important as investment in physical capital in developing countries. The empirical evidence seems to support this view. A World Bank (1980) survey concluded that 'studies have shown that economic returns on investment in education seem, in most instances, to exceed returns on alternative kinds of investment, and that developing countries often have higher returns than the developed ones'. The figures presented in Tables 7.4–7.6 certainly suggest that investment in education yields a rate of return as high, if not higher, as investment in alternative assets. This is, of course, in addition to the intrinsic satisfaction to the individual of education itself.

The role of women in economic development

Women play a vital role in the development process as mothers, workers, entrepreneurs and agents for change; but in many poor developing countries, their role is not fully utilized and appreciated, and they face discrimination in many areas of life, such as in education, in the workforce and in the ability to express their voice. **Gender equality** should be an integral part of the process of economic development. Gender equality can enhance the overall productivity of an economy, improve development outcomes for future generations, and make institutions more representative. Both men and women benefit when women's welfare is improved. Women now account for 40% of the global labour force. However, the increased participation of women in the labour market has not been accompanied by equal employment opportunities or earnings with men. Women are more likely than men to engage in low-productivity activities, and, on average, women earn 10–30% less than men for the same work/responsibilities. There exists a serious gender pay gap. Likewise in the field of education, there are far fewer women in secondary and tertiary education, which is reflected in much lower literacy rates for females than men. Many factors explain the discrimination against women in poor countries, which differ from country to country, but the major factors would include: cultural traditions and the perception of women's role in everyday life; gender differences in time use; unequal access to credit and assets; and institutional discrimination in the private and public sector (see Klugman et al., 2014; UN Women, 2015).

The World Bank's (2012) *World Development Report 2012* was devoted to the topic of gender equality. The report is evidence-based, drawing on qualitative field research covering over 4,000 men and women in 98 communities from nineteen developing countries, exploring how gender affects the everyday lives of women, as well as their aspirations, education, job choices, decision-making, and other aspects of welfare. The report argues that gender equality matters for two types of reasons. First, it matters *intrinsically* because it gives equal freedom to both women and men, and freedom is the ultimate goal of development (Sen, 1999). Second, it matters *instrumentally* because it contributes to economic efficiency and the achievement of other development goals. Three main channels are identified through which gender equality promotes development:

- A more efficient allocation of resources by reducing barriers to women accessing education and skills, thereby raising productivity.
- Improving women's opportunities, human capital and voice has positive externalities for children by increasing investment in their health, nutrition and education.
- Improving women's voice can improve the quality and effectiveness of institutions that benefit the economy and society as a whole. For example, where women have greater power, there is less corruption in public life. Giving power to women often increases the supply of public goods such as water supply and sanitation.

Some gender gaps have shrunk in recent years, but others have not. Most progress has been made in the following areas:

- Life expectancy is now as high for women as it is for men in all regions of the world.
- Fertility has declined dramatically (see Chapter 11).
- Primary school enrolment rates are equal for girls and boys.
- Participation of women in the labour force has increased.

But many gender gaps still persist and are rooted in deeply entrenched gender roles and social norms relating to who is responsible for the household, and what it is acceptable for girls and women to study. In general, the poorer the country, the greater the gender gap. Forms of horizontal inequality such as ethnicity, race, religion and disability all adversely affect gender equality.

There are three main areas in which gender inequality still exists:

1. The mortality rate for girls and women is higher than for men. This gap is often referred to as the **missing girls and women**. Globally, it is estimated that 4 million females below the age of 60 are 'missing': 40% are never born (because of the preference for males); 20% go missing in infancy and childhood; and 40% go 'missing' in the 15–59 age group because maternal mortality is much higher in poor countries than in rich.
2. There is a serious gender gap in earnings and asset ownership. Women are still concentrated in low-productivity activities where earnings are lower. In agriculture, women tend to operate smaller plots of land. In more dynamic sectors of the economy, there are fewer females in positions of responsibility and fewer entrepreneurs. Household duties still predominate for most women. Women have less access to credit because they lack collateral, and they possess far fewer assets. The IMF addresses this issue of women and work in its 2015 Annual Report (see Case example 7.2).
3. Women have much less agency or voice; that is, they are less represented in politics, law and the judiciary. They also suffer domestic violence.

Gender inequality tends to get reproduced over time. Attitudes are passed on from generation to generation, or change only slowly. If women as mothers do not work outside the home, the daughters are less likely to work. All institutions have inertia, where norms, customs and traditions prevail.

Now let us consider in more detail the current situation with regard to the education and health of women.

Case example 7.2 **Women and work**

A crucial element of jobs and inclusive growth is the role of women in the workplace. Women make up more than half the world's population, but their contributions to measured activity, growth and well-being fall short of potential. This has serious consequences in terms of losses to an individual country's GDP.

Despite significant progress in recent decades, labour markets across the world remain divided along gender lines and progress towards gender equality seems to have stalled. In a keynote speech in Tokyo in September 2014 on 'The Economic Power of Women's Empowerment', Christine Lagarde, IMF managing director, described the barriers working women face worldwide: 'When women do participate, they tend to be stuck in low-paying, low-status jobs. Globally, women earn only three-quarters as much as men – this is true even with the same level of education and in the same occupation.'

Building on the Working Paper 'Can Women Save Japan?' (Steinberg and Nakane, 2012), analysis on women and work has expanded rapidly. Area departments of the IMF have put in place pilot assessments of the issues related to working women in the context of Article IV consultations across a range of countries, with the goal of building expertise, facilitating collaborations with other institutions and sharing knowledge.

Source: IMF, 2015.

Women's education

Women's education brings a wide range of benefits not only for women themselves but also for their families and communities, and hence for society at large. There are many positive externalities to female education. More educated women tend to be healthier, participate more in the formal labour market, earn more income, have fewer children, and provide better education and healthcare for their offspring. The **United Nations Girls' Education Initiative**, launched in 2000, was the first global partnership to specifically promote girls' education and raise awareness of gender equality issues in education. Providing essential educational infrastructure attracts girls to school. Building schools in underserved communities has helped overcome barriers to girls' education. For example, a study in Ghor, Afghanistan, where villages were randomly selected to receive a primary school building, found that girls' enrolment increased by 17 percentage points more than boys, eliminating an existing gender gap (Burde and Linden, 2012). Target 4 of the MDGs laid down in 2000 was to eliminate gender disparities in primary and secondary education, and Table 7.8 gives the data for enrolment in 2013 compared to 1990. It can be seen that substantial progress has been made, although there is still some disparity between boys and girls in secondary school enrolment in sub-Saharan Africa. Two of the new Sustainable Development Goals (SDGs: see Chapter 1), to be achieved by 2030, are 'Ensure inclusive and equitable quality education and promote lifelong learning opportunities for all' (Goal 4) and 'Achieve gender equality and empower all women and girls' (Goal 5).

Table 7.8 Contrasting enrolment in primary and secondary schools between female and male pupils, 1990 and 2013

Region	Primary (%)				Secondary (%)			
	Female		Male		Female		Male	
	1990	2013	1990	2013	1990	2013	1990	2013
Arab world	74.9	96.1	91.7	103.2	45.1	68.7	60.3	73.4
East Asia and Pacific	115.1	117.1	124.9	118.3	34.4	85.6	43.6	84.6
Europe & Central Asia	100.7	101.8	104.5	102.2	82.4	98.0	87.9	100.3
Latin America and Caribbean	115.0	103.3	116.2	105.8	76.1	95.8	71.4	90.0
Least developed countries	59.3	101.2	75.3	108.5	13.5	39.1	23.0	44.5
South Asia	73.2	111.7	100.3	111.3	25.9	63.4	44.8	67.5
Sub-Saharan Africa	65.9	95.9	79.4	103.2	20.3	39.5	26.7	46.1
Small states	100.9	106.0	102.2	109.0	48.1	68.6	47.3	66.3

Note: Gross enrolment ratio can exceed 100% due to the inclusion of over-aged students relative to the age group of primary students.

Source: World Bank, 1990, 2013.

Women's health

Women's health is best analysed according to their age group. The World Health Organization (WHO) refers to four main age groups and their main causes of ill health and the fatal consequences of deaths:

1. **Infancy and childhood (0–9 years)**: The main causes of deaths are birth asphyxia, infections and diarrhoea. Nearly half of deaths in children aged under five is attributed to malnutrition.
2. **Adolescent girls (10–19 years)**: This group suffers from depressive disorders, the leading cause of ill health. Globally, adolescent girls and young women are twice as likely to be at risk of HIV infection compared to young men in the same age group. Pregnant adolescents are more likely than adults to have unsafe abortions, leading to lasting health problems and maternal deaths. Alcohol and tobacco use endangers young women's health in later life. In half of the countries with available data, over a third of girls aged 16–19 years are anaemic. Girls and women are most vulnerable to anaemia due to insufficient iron in their diets, menstrual blood loss and growth spurts.
3. **Reproductive age (15–44 years) and adult women (20–59 years)**: Depression is the leading cause of ill health for women. Depression following childbirth affects 20% of mothers in low- and lower middle-income countries. Women who have been physically or sexually abused have higher rates of mental ill health, unintended pregnancies, abortions and miscarriages than non-abused women. For women aged 15–44, HIV/AIDS is the leading cause of death worldwide (see below). Maternal deaths are the second biggest killer of women of reproductive age. Tuberculosis is among the five leading causes of death. Cervical cancer is the second most common type of cancer in women. Due to poor access to screening and treatment services, more than 90% of deaths occur in women living in low- and middle-income countries. One-third of chronic obstructive pulmonary disease in women is caused by exposure to indoor smoke from cooking with open fires or inefficient stoves.
4. **Older women (60 years and over)**: This group is affected by cardiovascular diseases and cancers and, to a lesser extent, by chronic respiratory conditions. It is important to highlight that much of

Table 7.9 Maternal mortality ratio (number of deaths due to pregnancy-related causes per 100,000 live births)

Regions	2010
Arab states	164
East Asia and the Pacific	72
Europe and Central Asia	31
Latin America and the Caribbean	74
South Asia	202
Sub-Saharan Africa	474
Least developed countries	389
Small island developing states	195

Source: UNDP, 2014.

the poor health faced by women in older age is the result of exposure to risk factors in adolescence and adulthood, such as smoking, sedentary lifestyles and unbalanced diets. Older women experience more disability than men, reflecting broader factors contributing to poor health through their lifetime, such as the unequal treatment of women in the household and the workplace.

The state of women's health in poor countries is most clearly reflected in the maternal mortality rates across the world. Table 7.9 gives the maternal mortality ratios measured as the number of deaths due to pregnancy-related causes per 100,000 live births. It can be seen that the mortality rate is highest in sub-Saharan Africa, followed by the least developed countries (which includes many African countries) and South Asia. In countries such as Afghanistan, Chad, Guinea-Bissau, Liberia, Mali, Niger, Sierra Leone and Somalia, at least 1 out of every 25 women die from complications relating to pregnancy and childbirth. A larger fraction of women also suffer adverse long-term health consequences from giving birth. Target 6 of the Millennium Development Goals (MDGs; see Chapter 1) was to 'reduce by three-quarters between 1990 and 2015, the maternal mortality ratio'. The goal was not met. A number of measures can still be taken to improve the situation, including new maternity clinics, training more maternal health nurses and providing poor women with cash transfers conditional on seeking pre- and postnatal care. Transport facilities also need improving to facilitate the process of getting pregnant women to hospital.

Mothers' Index

State of the World's Mothers (Save the Children, 2015) shows that one of the worst places to be a mother is in an urban slum. Poverty, and the social exclusion that goes with it, leaves the urban poor trapped in overcrowded, makeshift or decrepit housing. Pregnancies occur too early in life and too often. Save the Children, a charitable organization, publishes a **Mothers' Index**, which assesses the well-being of mothers and children. Five indicators are taken into account to construct the index:

- maternal health – lifetime risk of maternal death
- children's well-being – under-five mortality rate
- educational status – expected number of years of formal schooling
- economic status – GDP per capita
- political status – participation of women in national government.

Table 7.10 Mothers' Index rankings, 2015

Top 10		Middle 10		Bottom 10	
Rank	**Country**	**Rank**	**Country**	**Rank**	**Country**
1	Norway	84	Iran	169	Haiti/Sierra Leone
2	Finland	85	Cape Verde	171	Guinea-Bissau
3	Iceland	86	Georgia/St. Vincent and the Grenadines	172	Chad
4	Denmark	88	Belize/Bolivia	173	Cote d'Ivoire
5	Sweden	90	Azerbaijan	174	Gambia
6	Netherlands	91	Namibia	175	Niger
7	Spain	92	Jamaica/Maldives/Sri Lanka	176	Mali
8	Germany	93	Dominican Republic	177	Central African Republic
9	Australia	96	Fiji	178	DR Congo
10	Belgium	97	Mongolia	179	Somalia

Source: Save the Children, 2015.

In 2015, 179 countries were ranked. The top, middle and bottom ten countries are given in Table 7.10. The Nordic countries of Norway, Finland, Iceland, Denmark and Sweden come top, where mothers and children attain very high scores in health, educational, economic and political status.

By contrast, the condition of mothers and children in the bottom ranked countries (all in Africa except Haiti) is grim. On average, 1 woman in 30 dies from pregnancy-related causes, and one child in eight dies before their fifth birthday. There are, however, interesting anomalies. Rwanda, for example, is the top country for political status, with the highest proportion of women in parliament (57.5%), yet it ranks only 121 when the other four indicators are taken into account.

Another measure of the gender gap is the **Gender Inequality Index**, published by the UNDP (United Nations Development Programme), which considers three indicators: maternal mortality ratio (deaths per 100,000 live births); adolescent birth rate (births per 1,000 women aged 15–19); and share of seats in parliament held by women. The top, middle and bottom ten are shown in Table 7.11, out of a total of 151 countries. Again, all the countries in the bottom ten are African.

Table 7.11 Gender Inequality Index rankings, 2013

Top 10		Middle 10		Bottom 10	
Rank	**Country**	**Rank**	**Country**	**Rank**	**Country**
1	Slovenia	63	Costa Rica	142	Mauritania
2	Switzerland	64	Kyrgyzstan	143	Cote d'Ivoire
3	Germany	66	Barbados	144	Central African Republic
4	Sweden	68	Chile	145	Liberia
5	Denmark/Austria	69	Turkey	146	Mozambique
7	Netherlands	70	Uruguay/Thailand	147	Congo
8	Italy	72	Mauritius	148	Mali
9	Norway	73	Mexico	149	Afghanistan
10	Belgium	74	Argentina	150	Chad
				151	Niger

Source: UNDP, 2014.

Policies to reduce gender gap

Let us now turn to policies that could be implemented to help reduce the gender gap. The *World Development Report 2012* (World Bank, 2012) argues for increasing women's individual and collective agency, that is, the ability of women to make choices and transform them into desired actions and outcomes. Empowering women as political and social actors can change policy choices and make institutions more representative. The report identifies five priority areas:

1. Reducing maternal mortality and closing education gaps where they remain.
2. Improving economic opportunities for women.
3. Closing earnings and productivity gaps between men and women.
4. Increasing women's voice and agency in the household and in society.
5. Limiting the transmission of gender inequality across generations.

Reducing maternal mortality requires not only more clinics and trained nurses, but also health-related policies, such as the provision of clean water at the point of use and sanitation, waste disposal and drainage; in other words, a cleaner, safer environment in which to live and raise a family. Closing the education gap requires getting girls into school and staying there. Conditional cash transfers can help. Evidence from a range of countries shows that increasing the share of household income controlled by women through cash transfers or their own earnings change spending in ways that benefit children. Policies that discourage child marriage and school-related, gender-based violence also need to be strengthened.

In terms of improving access to economic opportunities for women, and closing the earnings gap, female farmers and entrepreneurs have less access to land and credit than their male counterparts. It is necessary to improve the functioning of credit markets, in the way that some microcredit schemes have helped women to access small-scale credits and build up a track record of borrower performance (e.g. the Grameen Bank, see Chapter 13). Differences in access to opportunities for women also partly arise from differences in time available because women have responsibility for the care of children and housework. Anything that saves time for women will improve their economic opportunities.

Increasing women's voice and agency in the household and society requires a change in attitude towards women, and removing discriminatory laws and regulations. In over 120 developing countries, the law treats men and women differently, making it impossible, for example, for a woman to obtain independently an identity card or to own property and have access to credit. Control of fertility is also important, which requires family planning services to suit women.

Finally, limiting the transmission of gender inequality across generations must be addressed, and tackled early in life before ideas and norms of behaviour are moulded. The culture and education in households and schools must shift towards empowering women. Everyday tasks such as carrying water or caring can be redistributed within the family to give more time to women.

All these reforms and changes are more likely to succeed if there is broad-based support, particularly support from men. This is where the challenge lies. Discrimination against women is a waste of human capital.

Nutrition

For individuals to achieve their full potential and lead healthy and productive lives, they need the right nutrition from birth. The sad fact is, however, that millions of people in the poorest developing countries are malnourished and may have been from birth. This has serious consequences for the individual and for society at large, which has to cope with the health consequences of malnourishment and proneness to disease. It has been estimated by the UN's Food and Agriculture Organization (FAO), which is based in Rome, that over 3 billion people worldwide suffer from various types of malnutrition, including over half the world's 1.5 billion children. One billion people suffer protein-energy malnutrition, 1.3 billion suffer from anaemia (iron deficiency), 1 billion people have iodine deficiency, and 30 million children have vitamin A deficiency, causing blindness and death. Nearly 1 billion people have no reliable access to safe drinking water, and nearly 2 billion people have no access to proper toilet facilities, including half the population of India (Drèze and Sen, 2013). Nearly half the population of poor countries suffer from water-related diseases. Diarrhoea caused by unclean water claims the lives of 1.5 million children a year. This weakens the body, and the weaker and more undernourished children are, the more prone they are to infection and disease; and the more infections, the greater the undernourishment due to loss of appetite, the difficulties of eating and the low absorption rate of food during digestion. Malnutrition among children is particularly serious because it stunts growth and mental development, and adds another twist to the vicious circle of poverty. Malnutrition is also a major cause of infant mortality, the rate of which is almost ten times higher in developing countries than in developed countries.

In his monumental, path-breaking book *An Inquiry into Well-Being and Destitution* (1993), well-known Indian economist Partha Dasgupta attempts to understand the common circumstances in which people are born in poor countries and in which they live and die in rural communities in these countries. He pays a lot of attention to the question of nutrition and its effects on health and work effort. The relation between low income and food intake is, of course, a two-way one. Low income is the major cause of malnutrition, which, in turn, is a cause of low income as it impairs work efficiency and productivity. Indices or measures of malnutrition can be based either on **nutritional requirements**, in terms of different kinds of food, or on **food energy**. Both affect labour productivity. The food requirements that nutritionists consider necessary for efficient working and healthy living are far greater than the levels achieved by the vast mass of the population living in developing countries. Calorie deficiency causes loss of body weight, tiredness, listlessness and a deterioration of mental faculties. Calories are also required for the absorption of protein: if the calorie requirement is met, the protein requirement is normally met too, but not always. Kwashiorkor – a condition associated with the bloated stomachs and staring eyes of the starving or malnourished children we often see on our television screens – arises from protein deficiency because the calorie intake is in the form of low-protein tubers such as cassavas and yams. Protein is particularly important for brain development in the first three years of life, during which time the brain grows to 90% of its full size. Maternal nutrition is crucial for the health of babies. Once babies are born, the damage that malnutrition does in the first 1,000 days of life is irreversible. According to research published in the *Lancet* (Utzinger and Tanner, 2013), malnourished children are less likely to go to school, less likely to remain at school, and more likely to struggle academically. The consequences go beyond school performance. They earn less than their well-nourished peers over their lifetime, marry poorer spouses and die earlier. Malnutrition is responsible for the deaths of some 3 million children a year (te Lintelo and Nisbett, 2015).

Of the 40 nutrients people need, four are in chronically short supply: iron, zinc, iodine and vitamin A. Lack of vitamin A causes half a million children to go blind every year. Zinc deficiency impairs brain and motor function and causes some 400,000 deaths a year. Shortage of iron weakens the immune system and can badly affect women of childbearing age. Iodine deficiency causes goitre and mental retardation.

When it comes to the relation between nutrition and the capacity for physical effort, nutrition is generally defined in terms of the energy requirement. In this context, Dasgupta (1993)

Figure 7.1 Relation between productivity and energy intake

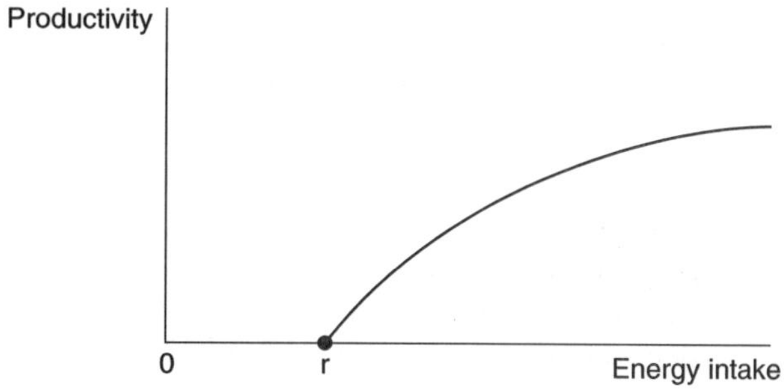

defines undernourishment as 'a state in which the physical functioning of a person is impaired to the point where she cannot maintain an adequate level of performance at physical work, or at resisting or recovering from the effects of any of a ... variety of diseases'. The minimum amount of energy or maintenance requirement (r) is the daily calorie requirement when a person is engaged in the minimal activities of eating and maintaining essential hygiene, with no allowance for work and play. According to nutritionists, r is 1.4 times the basal metabolic rate. The relation between productivity and energy intake is shown in Figure 7.1.

The interesting thing in Figure 7.1 is that the slope of the line is decreasing, but it could be linear or even increasing over certain ranges. When Bliss and Stern (1978) surveyed the literature, they found the line to be linear in the region slightly to the right of r. More recent research confirms this (see Behrman, 1993, for a comprehensive survey) and shows substantial economic and social returns to investment in nutrition and health, in terms of increased productivity on the job, increased productivity of time spent in school, and cost savings from treating the consequences of malnutrition and poor health. The costs of treating various forms of malnutrition are trivial relative to the tangible benefits and the costs of treating the consequences. To prevent malnutrition in children from the age of six months to three years, which is a child's most vulnerable period, can cost as little as $100 at current prices. The annual cost of preventing malnutrition is no more than the daily cost of treating its effects. Vitamin A deficiency is a cause of blindness. The annual cost of supporting a blind person is at least 1,000 times the annual ingredient cost of the vitamin A needed for prevention. Iodine deficiency is a cause of hypothyroidism (goitre), which leads to cretinism and deaf-mutism. The cost of iodized salt to prevent this is less than $0.02 per person per year. And so one could go on. Prevention is better than cure not only for the individual but also in a very real economic sense for the welfare of society as a whole.

The FAO is the major international organization concerned with ensuring food and nutrition security for the people of the world. Case example 7.3 gives its mission statement.

Case example 7.3 **Food and Agricultural Organization (FAO) mission statement**

FAO's mission is to ensure food and nutrition security for all people, to improve diets and to combat micronutrient deficiencies and all forms of malnutrition. It works to protect, promote and improve food systems – the way we produce, collect, store, transport, transform and distribute foods – as the sustainable solution to hunger and

continued overleaf

Case example 7.3 **Food and Agricultural Organization (FAO) mission statement** – *continued*

malnutrition. It ensures that agricultural development is people-centred and leads to improve availability, access to and consumption of safe and diverse foods for better nutrition. To improve nutrition, the FAO:

- Facilitates high-level dialogue between sectors and nations seeking a common agenda on nutrition, agriculture, sustainable food systems and healthy diets.
- Helps countries to devise policies and run programmes that will improve nutrition.
- Shares knowledge to help implement food-based nutrition policies through nutrition education and consumer awareness.
- Reviews evidence, offers guidance and scientific advice on all aspects of nutrition.

Source: www.fao.org/nutrition.

The member states of the WHO have endorsed a comprehensive implementation plan on maternal, infant and young child nutrition, which includes six global nutrition targets to be achieved by 2025 (WHO, 2014a). The six targets are:

1. **Stunting**: 40% reduction in the number of children under-five who are stunted. Childhood stunting is one of the most significant impediments to human development, globally affecting approximately 162 million children under the age of five. Estimates indicate that stunting can reduce a country's GDP by up to 3% a year (see Case example 7.4).
2. **Anaemia**: 50% reduction of anaemia in women of reproductive age. Anaemia affects half a billion women of reproductive age worldwide. The highest prevalence of anaemia is in Asia and Central and West Africa. Improvements have been seen around the world; for example, Burundi (64.4% down to 28% in 20 years), Nepal (65% down to 34% in 8 years) and Nicaragua (36.3% down to 16% in 10 years).
3. **Low birth weight**: 30% reduction in low birth weight. It is estimated that 15–20% of all births worldwide have low birth weight. Affordable, accessible and appropriate healthcare is critical for preventing and treating low birth weight.
4. **Childhood overweight**: No increase in childhood overweight. The prevalence of childhood overweight is increasing in all regions of the world, particularly in Africa and Asia. It is predicted that the prevalence of overweight children under 5 years old will rise to 11% worldwide by 2025, up from 7% in 2012.
5. **Breastfeeding**: Increase the rate of exclusive breastfeeding in the first six months up to at least 50%. Exclusive breastfeeding has the single largest potential impact on reducing child mortality of any preventive intervention. Globally, only 38% of infants aged 0–6 months are exclusively breastfed. Sri Lanka, Cambodia and Malawi have all seen dramatic increases in rates of exclusive breastfeeding.
6. **Wasting**: Reduce and maintain childhood wasting to less than 5%. Wasting is a reduction of body weight in relation to height. It is estimated that 52 million children under 5 years old are wasted, with 17 million of those estimated to be severely wasted. The majority of wasted children live in Asia. India accounts for approximately one-half of the global burden of wasting.

There are links between the global nutrition targets. For example, stunting is linked with anaemia in women of reproductive age, low birth weight, childhood overweight, not enough exclusive breastfeeding and wasting.

Nutrition offers one of the best returns on investment. It has been estimated that every US$1 invested in nutrition generates US$138 in better health and increased productivity. Conversely, not investing in nutrition perpetuates economic losses, at an estimated cost of up to 11% of annual GDP in lost production. On average, governments and donors spend 1–2% of their budgets on nutrition. They need to double the resources devoted to improve nutrition if global nutrition targets are to be met by 2025 (IFPRI, 2015).

Case example 7.4

Childhood stunting

Stunting is an enormous drain on economic productivity and growth. Economists estimate that it can reduce a country's GDP by up to 3% a year. Among many other international organizations, the WHO has been making efforts to ameliorate the problems related to malnutrition. In 2012, the WHO's Assembly endorsed a comprehensive implementation plan on maternal, infant and young child nutrition, which stated six global nutrition targets for 2025. The first target is to reduce by 40% the number of stunted children under 5 years. Childhood stunting is one of the most significant impediments to human development. It has long-term effects on people, including: diminished cognitive and physical development; poor health and reduced productive capacity, and an increased risk of degenerative diseases such as diabetes. Currently, it affects about 162 million children under the age of 5 years, and the target is to decrease it to 100 million by 2025.

There is a suggested framework for action to achieve the stunting target, which focuses on tackling the causes of stunting. It focuses on the 1,000-day window from a woman's pregnancy to her child's second birthday. Policy-makers should consider the following actions:

- improve the identification, measurement and understanding of stunting and scale up coverage of stunting-prevention activities;
- enact policies and/or strengthen interventions to improve maternal nutrition and health, beginning with adolescent girls;
- implement interventions for improved exclusive breastfeeding and complementary feeding practices;
- strengthen community-based interventions, including improved water, sanitation and hygiene (WASH).

Bolivia, Brazil, India and Peru are examples of countries that have implemented successful multisectoral approaches to effectively address stunting; for example, education policies that keep girls at school throughout adolescence; laws curtailing the marketing of breast milk substitutes; labour laws that provide maternity protection in support of exclusive and continued breastfeeding; and agriculture and food policies designed to improve household food security.

Source: WHO, 2014b.

Some countries have made significant progress in reducing the incidence of malnutrition: examples are Bangladesh, Brazil, Colombia, Peru, Vietnam, Egypt, Ethiopia, Kenya and Tanzania. These countries have made progress by creating a political environment conducive to nutrition-improving action, investing in high-impact, cost-effective nutrition intervention, and adopting policies in a wide range of economic and social sectors.

Political commitment to reducing malnutrition is so important that the Institute of Development Studies at the University of Sussex now produces a **Hunger and Nutrition Commitment Index (HANCI)**, which ranks governments on their political commitment to tackling hunger and malnutrition. The HANCI compares 45 developing countries for their performance on 22 indicators relating to three areas of action: legal framework, policies and programmes, and public expenditure. In 2014, Peru topped the index followed by Guatemala. Sudan, Angola and Guinea-Bissau were at the bottom of the ranking (te Lintelo and Lakshman, 2015).

The MDG Target 1c of halving the share of the chronically undernourished of the world's population by the end of 2015 was almost met. Goal 2 of the new SDGs is to 'end hunger, achieve food security and improve nutrition, and promote sustainable agriculture', with the aim of ending malnutrition by 2030. Interestingly, out of the 17 goals, with 169 targets between them, this is the *only* one that mentions nutrition, with no reference to obesity at all. To downplay the role of nutrition is a mistake.

Water

Water is a basic 'nutrient', essential for human existence. Access to clean water at the point of use should be considered as a basic human right, yet three-quarters of a billion people are denied it. Fresh water is extremely important for health. The biggest single cause of child deaths is diarrhoea and other waterborne diseases. Acknowledging the importance of access to clean water for health and sanitation, one of the UN's MDGs was to halve by 2015 the proportion of people without sustainable access to safe drinking water and basic sanitation. In 2012, 748 million people remained without access to safe drinking water. Dirty water and poor sanitation kill over 500,000 children a year.

Women bear the brunt of providing fresh water for their families in many of the poorest countries of the world. In sub-Saharan Africa, only half of households are within 15 minutes of a water source. Women and girls are the primary water carriers for their families. Where rural water sources are distant, women may walk up to two hours a day to collect it. Where urban water is obtained from shared standpipes, they may wait in line for over an hour. Case studies from around the world show that water-related 'time poverty' translates into lost income for women and lost schooling for girls. Constantly fetching and carrying water in heavy containers also has severe health implications. In extreme cases, curved spines and pelvic deformities can result, causing problems in childbirth.

Singapore has been recognized as the best country in the world to manage its water. Little water is wasted. Used water is treated and then safely disposed of, reused for industrial purposes or air-conditioning, or mixed with reservoir water for drinking. Recycled waste and desalinated water are expected to meet 25–30% of demand. There are lessons to be learned from Singapore.

In Africa, the eThekwini and Sharm El-Sheikh Declarations in 2008 committed countries to spending 0.5% of GDP on sanitation and hygiene, but this has gone almost universally unobserved. Countries have a responsibility to provide fresh water for their citizens with the help of the international community.

Water Aid is a leading international charity committed to improve access to safe water, sanitation and hygiene for the poorest and most marginalized people and operates in 26 poor countries. In 2013–14, Water Aid provided 2 million people with safe water: 71% in rural areas, 21% in urban areas and 8% in small towns.

Water is not evenly distributed. Nine countries account for 60% of all available supplies, and among them only Brazil, Canada, Colombia, Congo, Indonesia and Russia have an abundance of it. China and India, with over a third of the world's population between them, have less than 10% of the world's water. Africa has 35 of the 45 most 'water-stressed' countries.

Water is not only required for human survival but also for many activities, including farming, cattle breeding, manufacturing goods, and as a means of transport, among many others. Fresh water management represents a huge challenge, mainly due to its increasing demand by a growing world population and changes in the climate. Of all the activities that need water, agriculture uses almost 70% of the world's supply, while industry takes about 22%, and domestic activities account for 8%. There are options to overcome the growing demand for clean water. Desalination is one possibility. Although it is still an expensive alternative, there are various techniques and technologies available. The prospect is that solar power will make desalination economic in the future.

Health

Human survival depends not only on nutrition but also freedom from infection and disease. This brings us to the topic of the health of people in poor countries, the various diseases that poor people suffer from, and the effect that poor health has on the economies of developing countries in terms of work days lost through illness and low productivity.

Angus Deaton, the Nobel Prize-winning economist, argues in his masterly book, *The Great Escape: Health, Wealth, and the Origins of Inequality* (2013), that improvement in the health of humans is the most important measure of economic and social progress and that although mankind has experienced an improvement in health through time, many people have missed out – notably the poor. There is a vicious circle between poverty and ill health. Poverty leads to illness because of poor nutrition, lack of sanitation and clean water. Poor health then leads to poverty by reducing an individual's productivity and by the potential reduction of assets used to cover the cost of treatment. For Deaton, health is one of the most important components of well-being, and he believes that inequalities in health (between rich and poor countries and rich and poor people) are 'one of the greatest injustices in the world today'. He takes a moral stance when he says: 'those of us who are fortunate enough to have been born in the "right countries" have a moral obligation to help reduce poverty and ill health in the world'. Here, we are going to discuss the various diseases that are prevalent in poor countries, and which still kill millions of children and adults, and the international campaigns that exist to combat them. We shall also consider the research that attempts to measure the effect of ill health on the economic performance of countries.

Angus Deaton

Born in Scotland, 1945. Professor of Economics at Princeton University; one of the foremost economists working in development economics, with particular focus on the analysis of poverty, the consumption choices of poor people, and their nutrition and health. Latest book is *The Great Escape: Health, Wealth, and the Origins of Inequality* (2013). Awarded the Nobel Prize for Economics in 2015, with the citation: 'for his analysis of consumption, poverty and welfare'.

Killer diseases

There are three main killer diseases in poor countries that affect their development potential – malaria, tuberculosis (TB) and HIV/AIDS. These diseases are preventable, and the first two are curable. In 2013, together they killed over 3.5 million people. Their symptoms while people are alive include high temperature, weight loss, muscle pain and fatigue, all of which affect the quality of life and the ability to work productively. Goal 6 of the MDGs was to reverse and then halt the spread of malaria, TB and HIV/AIDS. At the international level, there is a **Global Fund to Fight AIDS, Tuberculosis and Malaria.**[2] This is a private foundation, which raises, manages and disburses private and public funding to support countries in their fight against the three diseases. The Global Fund is complemented by disease-specific targets set by UNAIDS, the WHO, the Stop TB Partnership and the Roll Back Malaria (RBM) Partnership. The Global Fund spent $8 billion between 2002 and 2013, and it is estimated that total eradication of these diseases by 2040 will cost $100 billion – but the total economic benefit would be $2 trillion, which is a very high benefit–cost ratio. Each disease has been assigned a day to raise international awareness: 25 April for malaria, 24 March for TB and 1 December for HIV/AIDS. Table 7.12 provides a summary of the number of people newly infected with malaria, TB and HIV/AIDS, deaths, and progress in prevention.

SDG 3 continues from MDG 6 and aims to 'ensure healthy lives and promote well-being for all at all ages'. Specifically, it aims to end the epidemics of malaria, TB and AIDS, and other contagious diseases, by 2030.

Malaria

Malaria is a preventable and treatable infectious disease transmitted by mosquitoes, which kills more than half a million people a year, most of them (90%) in sub-Saharan Africa, where malaria is the leading cause of death for children under five. The key interventions to prevent malaria – insecticide-treated nets (ITNs), insecticide spraying, and access to treatments – are well known, but eliminating the disease requires a broader range of actions. Efforts to improve housing and infrastructure development, sanitation, agricultural practices, mobility, and nutrition are also needed.

Malaria transmission continues to affect 97 countries and territories worldwide, inflicting a tremendous burden on countries. Nearly 300 million people in sub-Saharan Africa still lack access to a protective ITN, and at least 15 million pregnant women do not receive the protective treatment they need to keep themselves and their unborn child safe. The Democratic Republic of

Table 7.12 Comparing malaria, TB and HIV/AIDS

	People newly infected	Mortality	Prevention
Malaria	198 million cases in 2013	584,000 people in 2013; 90% of malaria deaths occur in sub-Saharan Africa and 78% in children under five years	49% of at-risk population had access to an insecticide treated net in 2013 compared to 3% in 2004
TB	9 million cases in 2013	1.5 million people in 2013; 45% decline between 1990 and 2013	37 million lives saved between 2000 and 2013 through effective diagnosis and treatment
HIV/AIDS	2 million people infected with HIV in 2014	1.5 million people in 2013; 35% fewer than when the number peaked in 2005	143,000 health facilities in 2011 provided HIV testing and counselling, 21% increase from 2007

Source: Based on WHO, www.who.int/en.

the Congo and Nigeria account for over 40% of global deaths from malaria. In Southeast Asia, the second most affected region of the world, India has the highest malaria burden, followed by Indonesia and Myanmar.

Malaria takes a high toll on households and healthcare systems, and impedes economic development in endemic countries. A cross-country regression analysis for a 25-year period (1965–90) estimated annual rates of economic growth to be 1.3% lower in countries with a serious malaria burden than in countries with less malaria (Gallup and Sachs, 2001). Malaria also discourages foreign investment, increases people's out-of-pocket spending on healthcare, and impairs children's ability to learn for those who survive the illness.

The **Roll Back Malaria (RBM) Partnership** was launched in 1998 by WHO, UNICEF, UNDP and the World Bank in an effort to provide a coordinated global response to the disease. The RBM and UNDP convened a Consultation on Developing a Multisectoral Approach to Malaria in July 2013. Participants agreed on the development of an action framework and a roadmap to identify ways forward for better addressing the socio-environmental determinants of malaria and to engage agencies from non-health sectors. The **Multisectoral Action Framework for Malaria** was launched alongside the 68th Session of the UN General Assembly in New York in September 2013 (RBM and UNDP, 2013). The year 2015 marked a turning point in the treatment of malaria. A global framework **Action and Investment to Defeat Malaria** (2016–30) organized by RBM placed the management of the disease as a development issue. It complements the WHO's **Global Technical Strategy for Malaria 2016–2030**. Today, malaria can be diagnosed, treated and prevented with a combination of available tools. However, global estimates indicate that US$4.2 billion is needed each year to fully fund the fight against malaria. There is hope for the future. Scientists working on the global genome project have unlocked the genetic code of the malaria parasite and the mosquito species that transmits it. This paves the way for a new generation of vaccines, insecticides and repellents to combat malaria – provided, of course, that it is profitable for drug companies to develop them.

Tuberculosis

Tuberculosis (TB), like malaria, is also preventable and curable. TB is transmitted by air, through coughing and sneezing. Persons with weak immune systems, such as those living with HIV, malnutrition or diabetes, or people who smoke tobacco, have a much higher risk of getting infected. TB remains a leading cause of death among people living with HIV, accounting for one in five AIDS-related deaths globally. Over 95% of cases and deaths are in developing countries. Brazil, Russia, India, China and South Africa account for almost 50% of global TB cases.[3] In 2013, there were an estimated 9 million new TB cases and 1.5 million TB deaths (including 400,000 people with HIV). Although most TB cases and deaths occur among men, the burden of the disease among women and children is also high. In 2013, there were an estimated 3.3 million cases and 510,000 TB deaths among women, and 550,000 cases and 80,000 deaths among children. Although the TB mortality rate has decreased by 45% since 1990, it is still regarded as serious, given that most deaths are preventable if people can access healthcare for diagnosis and treatment.

Access to TB care has expanded substantially since 2000. Between 2000 and 2013, 37 million lives were saved through effective diagnosis and treatment. However, there remains a huge gap in services. Of the nearly 9 million people who developed TB in 2012, 3 million of them were not diagnosed and thus not treated. Diagnosis can be difficult, particularly in cases of multi-drug resistant forms of the disease. Treatment is also difficult; standard TB involves six months of daily medication, whereas multidrug-resistant (MDR) TB requires up to two years of treatment.

Table 7.13 The post-2015 global TB strategy

Vision	A TB-free world: zero deaths, other diseases and suffering due to TB
Goal	End the global TB epidemic
Milestones for 2025	75% reduction in TB deaths (compared to 2015) 50% reduction in TB incidence rate (less than 55 TB cases per 100,000 people) No affected families facing catastrophic costs due to TB
Targets for 2035	95% reduction in TB deaths (compared with 2015) 90% reduction in TB incidence rate (less than 10 TB cases per 100,000 people) No affected families facing catastrophic costs due to TB

Source: WHO, 2014b.

The cost per patient treated for drug-susceptible TB in 2013 was in the range US$100–500. The cost per patient treated for MDR TB ranged from an average of US$9,235 in low-income countries to US$48,553 in upper middle-income countries. Many TB-endemic countries cannot afford to treat their patients; their national healthcare systems are overburdened with the disease, and the infrastructure necessary for TB treatment is extremely costly. The World Bank estimates that, for some countries, the loss of output attributable to TB is 4–7% of their GDP.

The Millennium Development Goal to reverse the tuberculosis epidemic by 2015 was achieved globally. In 2013, the TB mortality rate had fallen by 45% compared to 1990. The WHO has developed a post-2015 global TB strategy – **The End TB Strategy.** Its goal is to end the global TB epidemic by 2035, with corresponding global targets for a 95% reduction in the number of TB deaths and a 90% reduction in the number of cases compared with the baseline of 2015 (see Table 7.13).

HIV/AIDS

In 2014, 1.2 million people died from **Human Immunodeficiency Virus (HIV)**-related causes. Although there is no cure for HIV, there are effective treatments that can control the virus so that infected people can still lead healthy and productive lives. The most advanced stage of HIV is **Acquired Immunodeficiency Syndrome (AIDS)**. HIV/AIDS has destroyed families, communities and affected the economy of entire nations. As Kofi Annan, former secretary-general of the UN, said when addressing the International AIDS Conference in July 2004 in Bangkok, Thailand: 'AIDS is far more than a health crisis. It is a threat to development itself.' Since 2000, when the outlook was dire, the AIDS epidemic has been taken seriously. The Millennium Development Goal 6 played a crucial role in targeting the epidemic. In 2015, the world achieved the AIDS targets of MDG 6 – halting and reversing the spread of HIV – according to a comprehensive report published by the Joint United Nations Programme on HIV/AIDS (UNAIDS, 2015). In 2000, fewer than 700,000 people were receiving antiretroviral medicines; in 2015, 15 million accessed them. Over the same period, new HIV infections declined by 35%. Table 7.14 summarizes three aspects of HIV/AIDS – people living with HIV, new HIV infections, and AIDS-related deaths, for seven regions in 2014.

New HIV infections declined steadily between 2000 and 2014. The number of newly infected people in 2014 was 35% lower than in 2000. Likewise, since 2004, when the number of AIDS deaths peaked, the annual number of AIDS-related deaths declined by 42% (see Figure 7.2). In 2014, an estimated 1.2 million people died of AIDS-related causes globally. However, the number of people living with HIV continues to increase. This is because more people have access to antiretroviral treatment and as a result are living longer, and there is still a high number of new HIV infections each year.

The most significant gains in reversing the epidemic have been among children under the age of 15. Since 2000, new HIV infections among children have declined by 58%; however, still in 2014, 2.6 million children were living with HIV (see Table 7.14 for a regional breakdown). The epidemic

Table 7.14 Regional HIV/AIDS data, 2014

Region	People living with HIV		New HIV infections		AIDS-related deaths
	Total	Children	Total	Children	Total
Sub-Saharan Africa	25.8 million	2.3 million	1.4 million	190,000	790,000
Asia and the Pacific	5.0 million	200,000	340,000	21,000	240,000
Latin America	1.7 million	33,000	87,000	2,000	41,000
Caribbean	280,000	13,000	13,000	<500	8,800
Middle East and North Africa	240,000	13,000	22,000	2,400	12,000
Eastern Europe and Central Asia	1.5 million	17,000	140,000	1,200	62,000
Western and Central Europe and North America	2.4 million	3,300	85,000	<500	26,000
Global	36.9 million	2.6 million	2.0 million	220,000	1.2 million

Source: UNAIDS, 2015.

among children stems from HIV transmission during pregnancy, childbirth or breastfeeding. In 2015, Cuba became the first country to be certified by the WHO as having eliminated new HIV infections among children and ending mother-to-child transmission.

Although 70% of people living with HIV live in only 17 countries, the HIV epidemic remains global, affecting virtually every country in the world and adding substantially to health burdens. Sub-Saharan Africa has been the most affected region, with 25.8 million people living with HIV. In 2014, South Africa alone accounted for 18% of all the people living with HIV in the world; followed by Nigeria (9%), Zimbabwe (4%), Mozambique (4%), Tanzania (4%), Uganda (4%) and Kenya (4%).

Figure 7.2 People affected by HIV/AIDS (all ages), 1990–2014

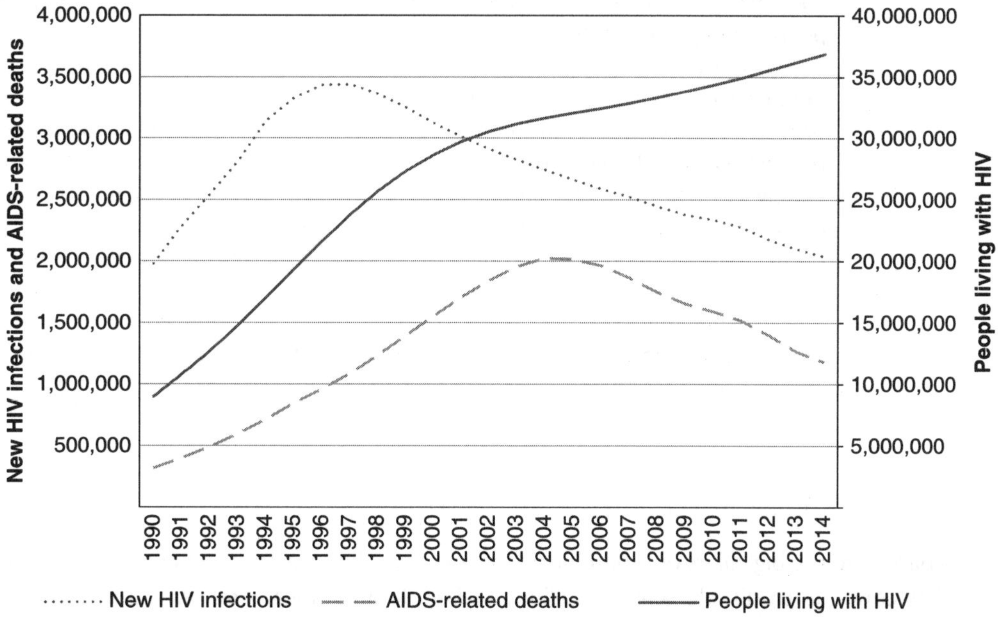

Source: AIDSinfo, http://aidsinfo.unaids.org/#.

When countries are ranked by the incidence of HIV (ratio of people living with HIV to the country's population), in 2014, the following sub-Saharan countries came top: Botswana (18%), South Africa (13%), Zimbabwe (11%), Zambia (8%), Malawi (7%), Mozambique (6%), Uganda (4%), Kenya and Tanzania (3%), and Ivory Coast and Nigeria (2%).

The global response to HIV is estimated to have averted 30 million new HIV infections and nearly 8 million AIDS-related deaths since 2000, when the MDGs were set. Everyone living with HIV needs access to HIV treatment: this is the promise that world leaders committed to in 2015 with the Sustainable Development Goal to end the epidemic by 2030. Two success stories against AIDS are highlighted in Case example 7.5.

Case example 7.5 **Two success stories against AIDS: Senegal and Rwanda**

Senegal

In 2014, Senegal registered 2,400 AIDS-related deaths and 44,000 people living with HIV. It has made major efforts in the past five years to scale up access to HIV prevention, treatment, care and support services for its population, with a focus on key, higher risk groups. It is one of the few countries in the western and central African region that has collected robust data on hard-to-reach populations, such as sex workers, men who have sex with men and people who use drugs. The country has scaled up access to antiretroviral therapy, and treatment is now widely available in many parts of Senegal. The number of people receiving antiretroviral therapy increased from 5,500 in 2006 to nearly 18,000 in 2011. The combination of efforts is having positive results. According to UNAIDS, HIV prevalence among the general population remains stable at 0.7%, while HIV prevalence among sex workers has decreased from 19.8% in 2006 to 18.5% in 2011, and new HIV infections among youth have decreased. The Global Fund highlights Senegal as a model for the response to HIV in the western and central African region.

Rwanda

AIDS-related deaths of all ages in Rwanda have decreased significantly since a peak in 2002–03, when there were 21,000 deaths, compared to 3,000 in 2014. The number of people living with HIV has fallen moderately from 270,000 in 1999 to 210,000 in 2014. The government of Rwanda continues to scale up HIV services: by the end of 2013, 493 out of 495 health facilities in the country provided testing and counselling services, 488 provided services to prevent mother-to-child transmission, and 465 provided antiretroviral therapy. TB-related deaths among people living with HIV declined by approximately 45% between 2000 and 2010, accompanied by a 70% decline in child mortality and a 60% decline in maternal mortality. This achievement provides a sound example of the way that the benefits of investment in AIDS prevention and other chronic diseases can extend far beyond the treatment of AIDS itself. Rwanda is piloting an innovative financing mechanism in partnership with the Global Fund, where grant funds will be used to implement Rwanda's National Strategic Plan for HIV (2013–18) and TB/HIV.

Source: UNAIDS, 2015.

Other diseases and health expenditure

Apart from the big killers of tuberculosis, malaria and AIDS, there are many other tropical diseases that continue to disable tens of millions of people in tropical Asia, Africa and Latin America, such as leprosy, river blindness, Chagas disease and lymphatic filariasis. With modern medicine and antibiotics, there is now the opportunity to eliminate these diseases. The global registered prevalence of leprosy at the beginning of 2013 stood at 189,018 cases. During 2014, 22 countries reported that more than 112 million people were treated with ivermectin to treat river blindness (onchocerciasis), which is transmitted to humans through bites of infected blackflies. Infected people live in 31 sub-Saharan Africa countries and in some particular places in Latin America and Yemen. Chagas disease is spread by bloodsucking bugs and infects 6 to 7 million people worldwide, mostly in Latin America. Lymphatic filariasis, commonly known as 'elephantiasis', is a neglected tropical disease, and 1.1 billion people in 55 countries remain threatened by the disease and require preventive chemotherapy to stop the spread of this infection. In addition, there are waterborne diseases, which include cholera, dysentery, typhoid and worm infection. There are about 1.7 billion cases of diarrhoeal disease every year. It kills around 760,000 children a year under the age of five (for all diseases, see WHO, *Global Health Observatory data*, www.who.int/gho/database/en).

Table 7.15 presents some health-related statistics for 2013, including total expenditure on health as a percentage of GDP, health expenditure per head of the population, life expectancy at birth, and the infant mortality rate. Notice the colossal difference in health expenditure per capita in rich and poor countries. While in high-income countries, expenditure is $4,456, in the low-income countries it is only $37. The low expenditure and lack of access to basic health facilities in poor countries is reflected in the much lower life expectancy of only 61 years in low-income countries (and 58 years in Africa) compared to 79 years in high-income countries. There is also a big difference in infant mortality rates, with 53 deaths per 1,000 live births in low-income countries compared with only 6 deaths in high-income countries. Baldacci et al. (2005) calculate that an increase in health expenditure of 1% of GDP is associated with an increase of 0.5 percentage points in the survival rate of children under 5 and a 0.5 percentage point increase in per capita income growth.

Table 7.15 Health indicators

	Health expenditure		Life expectancy at birth	Infant mortality rate
	Total	Per capita		
	% of GDP	$	years	per 1,000 live births
	2013	2013	2013	2015
World	10	1,042	71	32
Low income	6.4	37	61	53
Middle income	5.8	256	70	31
Lower middle income	4.2	82	67	40
Upper middle income	6.3	466	74	15
Low and middle income	5.8	235	69	35
East Asia and Pacific	5.3	293	74	15
Europe and Central Asia	5.9	413	72	18
Latin America and Caribbean	8.1	729	74	16
Middle East and North Africa	6	258	72	21
South Asia	3.9	56	68	42
Sub-Saharan Africa	5.7	101	58	56
High income	11.9	4,456	79	6

Source: World Bank, 2015, Tables 2.15 and 2.21.

The provision of education, nutrition, health services, water supply, housing and sanitation came to be known in development circles in the 1970s (and supported by the World Bank) as the **basic needs approach** to economic development. The rationale of the approach was that the direct provision of such goods and services was likely to relieve absolute poverty more immediately than alternative strategies, which would simply attempt to accelerate growth or rely on raising the incomes and productivity of the poor. Five arguments were used to support this change in strategy:

1. Growth strategies usually fail to benefit those intended.
2. The productivity and incomes of the poor depend in the first place on the direct provision of health and education facilities.
3. It may take a long time to increase the incomes of the poor so that they can afford basic needs.
4. The poor tend not to spend their income wisely, and certain facilities such as water supply and sanitation can only be provided publicly.
5. It is difficult to help all the poor in a uniform way in the absence of the provision of basic needs.

The basic needs approach has lost none of its rationale in the direct fight against poverty and disease in the world's poorest countries.

The impact of ill health on growth and development

There are several channels through which better health may impact on the economic growth and development of countries:

- Healthier people are more productive. They can work harder, longer and they can think more clearly.
- Health improves educational outcomes through better attendance at school and improved cognitive functioning.
- Lower mortality and higher life expectancy encourage savings for retirement and release resources for investment.

Cole and Neumayer (2006) have conducted a major study of the impact of poor health on total factor productivity growth (TFP), taking a panel of 52 developed and developing countries over the period 1965–95. They estimate TFP from a standard neoclassical production function (see equation 4.22) and then relate differences between countries to malnutrition, malaria and waterborne diseases. Malnutrition impacts on productivity by sapping the energy of workers and making them more susceptible to infection and disease. Malnutrition used as a causal variable in the analysis is measured by the percentage of the population undernourished. Malaria similarly makes workers feel weak, and impairs cognitive ability. Malaria is measured by an index, which combines the percentage of land area affected and the percentage number of malaria cases. Waterborne diseases are a great health risk in poor countries and include dysentery, cholera and typhoid fever. This also impacts on energy at work, and on school attendance. This is measured for empirical analysis by the percentage of the population without access to safe water. The function estimated is therefore:

$$\text{TFP} = a + b_1\,(\text{incidence of malnutrition}) + b_2\,(\text{incidence of malaria}) + b_3\,(\text{lack of access to safe water}) + \varepsilon \qquad (7.6)$$

where the coefficients b_1, b_2 and b_3 measure the effect of these three health variables on the growth of TFP across countries, and ε is an error term. The results are significant and striking. The coefficients on all the health variables are negative. Malnutrition reduces TFP growth by 0.17 percentage points (p.p.), malaria by 0.58 p.p. and lack of access to safe water by 0.1 p.p.

Another way of estimating the effect of poor health on the macroeconomic performance of countries is to calculate the number of working days lost through ill health. This is the preferred approach of the World Health Organization (WHO, 2008), which calculates what they call **disability-adjusted life years (DALYs),** which adds up the number of years lost as a result of poor health or disability, and is measured as the difference between an individual's current health status and an ideal health situation where the entire population lives to an advanced age, free of disease and disability.[4]

Table 7.16 gives the 20 leading causes of work years lost through ill health. Heart disease (which is not infectious) comes top, but malaria, TB, HIV/AIDS and waterborne disease also figure prominently. Once total DALYs have been calculated for each country, they can be included in a cross-country growth regression of the form:

$$y = a + b_1 (DALY) + b_2 X + \varepsilon \tag{7.7}$$

Table 7.16 Leading causes of DALYs, 2012

Rank	Cause	DALYs (000s)	% DALYs	DALYs per 100,000 population
0	**All Causes**	**2,743,857**	**100.0**	**38780**
1	Ischaemic heart disease	165,717	6.0	2342
2	Lower respiratory infections	146,864	5.4	2076
3	Stroke	141,348	5.2	1998
4	Preterm birth complications	107,210	3.9	1515
5	Diarrhoeal diseases	99,728	3.6	1409
6	Chronic obstructive pulmonary disease	92,377	3.4	1306
7	HIV/AIDS	91,907	3.4	1299
8	Road injury	78,724	2.9	1113
9	Unipolar depressive disorders	76,500	2.8	1081
10	Birth asphyxia and birth trauma	74,600	2.7	1054
11	Diabetes mellitus	59,258	2.2	838
12	Malaria	55,111	2.0	779
13	Back and neck pain	53,920	2.0	762
14	Congenital anomalies	52,532	1.9	742
15	Iron-deficiency anaemia	47,627	1.7	673
16	Tuberculosis	43,650	1.6	617
17	Falls	42,466	1.6	600
18	Neonatal sepsis and infections	39,646	1.4	560
19	Self-harm	39,358	1.4	556
20	Trachea, bronchus, lung cancers	38,535	1.4	545

Source: WHO, 2012.

where y is the growth of per capita income and X is a vector of control variables. The coefficient b_1 measures the impact of days lost through ill health on the growth of living standards. Murray and Lopez (1996) estimate the per capita disability-adjusted life years (DALYs) lost in various regions of the world in 1990 due to premature mortality and years lived with disability adjusted for severity. The estimated impact on per capita income is lower in developed countries at about 0.17 p.p. The impact ranges from 0.2 to 0.4 p.p. in various regions of the developing world, and reaches close to 0.6 p.p. in sub-Saharan Africa. Specific disease variables can also be included in equation (7.7). Malaria, for example, has a strong negative effect of 0.36 p.p. (similar to that found by Gallup and Sachs, 2001).

Summary

- The economic and social development of poor countries requires educated and literate people; an equitable participation of men and women in the labour force; and well-nourished, healthy people free from the debilitating diseases that affect work effort and productivity.
- Investment in human capital takes the form of expenditure on formal education; on-the-job and institutional training; study programmes and adult education; nutrition programmes; and expenditure on health facilities.
- There is serious underprovision of education facilities and opportunities in many poor countries – particularly with regard to secondary and tertiary education. Literacy rates are low.
- Private rates of return to education are high in poor countries, averaging 10%.
- Investment in education can add substantially to the growth performance of countries.
- There is serious discrimination against women in developing countries. Gender equality in education, employment opportunities, voice in society, and access to credit should be an integral part of the development process.
- Women's health has been neglected in poor countries and needs urgent attention.
- For individuals to achieve their potential and lead healthy and productive lives, they need the right nutrition from birth – but millions remain malnourished throughout their lives.
- The WHO has a comprehensive plan to tackle maternal, infant and young children malnutrition, targeting child stunting; anaemia; low birth weight; child overweight; breast feeding; and wasting.
- Good health requires clean water, but three-quarters of a billion people lack access.
- There is a vicious circle between poverty and ill health. Ill health means incapacity to work effectively, and low productivity means poverty.
- The three killer diseases in poor countries are malaria, TB and HIV/AIDS, plus various water-borne diseases such as cholera, typhoid and dysentery.
- There are many international campaigns, such as the Global Fund, to eradicate malaria, TB and Aids –and their eradication is one of the Sustainable Development Goals to be achieved by 2030.
- Health expenditure in poor countries is rudimentary, and needs to be given greater priority.
- Ill health has an adverse effect on the growth of total factor productivity of countries and the growth of per capita income when individual diseases are considered or total working days lost through ill health (DALYs).

Chapter 7 Discussion questions

1. What are the main forms of human capital formation?
2. Why is human capital formation essential for the economic and social progress of countries?
3. What is the specific role of education in the growth and development process?
4. How can the rate of return to education be measured, and the contribution of education to economic growth?
5. What form does gender inequality take in many poor countries?
6. Why are women discriminated against in education, employment and participation in civil society?
7. What policies might be implemented to reduce the gender gap?
8. What is the importance of nutrition for economic and social progress?
9. What are the major health challenges confronting poor countries?
10. How does poor nutrition and health impact on the growth performance of countries?

Notes

1. The greater the proportion of expenditure treated as consumption, the higher the rate of return on the investment component.
2. The Global Fund relies on voluntary financial contributions from all sectors of society – governments, private sector, social enterprises, philanthropic foundations and individuals. The Bill & Melinda Gates Foundation has been a key partner of the Global Fund, providing cash contributions, active participation on its board and committees, and substantial funding to related advocacy and fundraising efforts. To date, the foundation has contributed or pledged a total of US$1.4 billion to the Global Fund.
3. The WHO classifies 22 countries as high TB burden countries: Afghanistan, Bangladesh, Brazil, Cambodia, China, D.R. Congo, Ethiopia, India, Indonesia, Kenya, Mozambique, Myanmar, Nigeria, Pakistan, Philippines, Russia, South Africa, Thailand, Uganda, Tanzania, Vietnam and Zimbabwe.
4. DALYs for a particular disease or health condition are calculated as the sum of the years of life lost (YLL), which corresponds to the number of deaths multiplied by the standard life expectancy at the age at which death occurs. So, $YLL = N \times L$, where N is the number of deaths and L is the standard life expectation at age of death in years.

Websites on education, women, nutrition and health

Education

UNESCO www.unesco.org
World Bank Education Data www.worldbank.org/education/edstats/
UNICEF Girl's Education www.unicef.org/girlseducation/

UNESCO eAtlas of Out-of-School Children http://tellmaps.com/uis/oosc/
Barro-Lee Educational Attainment Dataset www.barrolee.com/
UN Girls Education Initiative www.ungei.org
Global Partnership for Education www.globalpartnership.org

Women

UN Women www.unwomen.org/en
International Center for Research on Women www.icrw.org
UNDP Women's Empowerment www.undp.org/content/undp/en/home/ourwork/womenempowerment/overview.html
UN Gender Statistics Manual http://unstats.un.org/unsd/genderstatmanual/
UN Girls Education Initiative www.ungei.org/

Nutrition

United Nations System Standing Committee on Nutrition www.unscn.org
Food and Agricultural Organization (FAO) www.fao.org
International Food Policy Research Institute www.ifpri.org
World Food Programme www.wfp.org
Hunger and Nutrition Commitment Index www.hancindex.org

Health

World Health Organization www.who.int/en
AIDS www.unaids.org; www.who.int/hiv/en
Pan American Health Organization www.paho.org
The Micronutrient Initiative http://micronutrient.org/
The Global Fund to Fight AIDS, Tuberculosis and Malaria www.theglobalfund.org
Roll Back Malaria www.rollbackmalaria.org
Malaria No More www.malarianomore.org
World Health Organization, Tuberculosis www.who.int/tb
Stop TB www.stoptb.org/
TB Alliance www.tballiance.org/

8

THE ROLE OF INSTITUTIONS IN ECONOMIC DEVELOPMENT

Introduction

Growth and development cannot take place in an institutional vacuum. Economic maturity and the growth of markets require an institutional framework that allows transactions to take place in an orderly manner and in which agents know that the decisions they take and the contracts they make will be protected by law, and enforced. Savers, investors, consumers, entrepreneurs, workers and risk-takers of all kinds need a framework of rules if rational, optimizing decisions are to be made. They also need some guarantee of economic stability and certainty, which can be provided only by good governance and sound economic policy-making. The alternative to property rights, law and order and political stability is economic anarchy – and failed states (see Chapter 9).

This chapter deals with the role of formal institutions in general in providing an economic, political and social environment in which economies can flourish and prosper, and it considers some of the empirical evidence on the relationship between institutional development and economic development.

The role of institutions

Nobel Prize-winning economist Douglass North first brought to the fore the role of institutions in economic development. The modern exponents of the **primacy of institutions** are Dani Rodrik of Harvard University and Daron Acemoglu, Simon Johnson and James Robinson of the Massachusetts Institute of Technology. In his well-known book, *Institutions, Institutional Change and Economic Performance* (1990), North said:

> I wish to assert a fundamental role for institutions in societies: they are the underlying determinants of the long-run performance of economies – Third World countries are poor because the institutional constraints define a set of pay-offs to political/economic activity that do not encourage productive activity.

North (1990) also said that 'the inability of societies to develop effective low-cost enforcement of contracts is the most important source of both historical stagnation and contemporary underdevelopment in the Third World', because the absence of secure property and contractual rights discourages investment and specialization. Mancur Olson (1982) makes the same point in his classic book, *The Rise and Decline of Nations*.

It is possible to give both general and narrower, more formal, definitions of institutions. North (1990) describes institutions very broadly as the 'formal and informal rules [or norms] governing human behaviour'. A similar broad definition is given by Lin and Nugent (1995): 'a set of humanly devised behavioural rules that govern and shape the interaction of human beings, in part by helping them to form expectations of what other people do'. At a more formal, precise, level, institutions can be defined in terms of:

- the extent of property rights' protection
- the degree to which laws and regulations are fairly enforced
- the ability of government to protect the individual against economic shocks and provide social protection
- the extent of political corruption.

Without inclusive economic and political institutions, nations will fail, which is the central message of the path-breaking book by Acemoglu and Robinson (2012), *Why Nations Fail*. Inclusive institutions are necessary to challenge and constrain the political power of the elite, otherwise the elite use political power to protect the status quo and preserve extractive economic rents, which diminishes the incentive to innovate and invest. Inclusive political institutions lead to inclusive economic institutions and this is the basis for prosperity – a virtuous circle is started. Similarly, extractive rules are reinforcing in the opposite direction – plunder further empowers the elite. Countries differ in their economic success because of their different institutions; the rules influence how the economy works and the incentives that motivate people. Institutions explain why growth took off earlier in Europe than Africa, Latin America and Asia, and why there are many failed states today, particularly in Africa where autocracy is rife and the benefits of natural resources are siphoned off to an elite.

Incentives and price signals, so vital for a market economy, cannot function properly without institutional structures and rules of behaviour. As Rodrik (2008) says: 'markets require institutions because they are not self-creating, self-regulating, self-stabilising, or self-legitimising'. Which institutions are important and which are not will differ across space and time according to the history of a country, its geography, stage of development and its political aspirations, that is, what sort of society its people want. In small rural communities where everyone knows each other, the scope for cheating, fraud and not honouring contracts is limited. Transaction costs associated with the costs of information, negotiation, monitoring, coordination and enforcement of contracts are low, and communities survive by adhering to norms of behaviour; but economic development is limited through a lack of specialization. In contrast, in large, modern, industrial societies, where transactions are impersonal, there is widespread scope for opportunistic behaviour (Bardhan and Udry, 1999). Transactions (and therefore production) costs may be very high without institutional structures that curtail such behaviour, such as the enforcement of property rights and the rule of law, the provision of limited liability, the guarantee of contracts, patent protection and so on. With low transaction costs, firms and markets can concentrate on the job of investment in the knowledge that property rights are secure.

When economists undertake empirical work on the relation between institutional structure and economic performance, it is, of course, necessary to have quantitative measures of the important institutions being discussed and evaluated. Lumping all institutions together in a single index of 'institutional quality' would obscure the different channels through which institutions work.

There is no one set of institutions that will suit all countries, but there is a consensus among development economists that at least five main types of market-supporting institutions are necessary, if not sufficient, conditions for rapid economic progress (see Rodrik, 2000, 2008; Rodrik and Subramanian, 2008):

- property rights and legally binding contracts: market-creating institutions
- regulatory institutions: market-regulating institutions
- institutions for macroeconomic stability: market-stabilizing institutions
- social insurance institutions: market-legitimizing institutions
- institutions of conflict management: market-legitimizing institutions.

Rodrik (2000) highlights the following institutional arrangements that are conspicuously absent in poor countries:

- a clearly defined system of property rights
- a regulatory apparatus curbing the worst forms of fraud, anti-competitive behaviour and moral hazard
- a moderately cohesive society exhibiting trust and social cooperation

- social and political institutions that mitigate risk and manage social conflict
- the rule of law and clean government.

These five main prerequisites of a sound institutional structure for economic development are described briefly below:

1. **Property rights and legally binding contracts**: These are important because agents lack the incentive to invest and innovate if they do not have control over the return on the assets they accumulate. Intellectual property rights are particularly important to encourage invention. Control is more important than ownership. Formal property rights do not mean very much if there are not control rights; but control rights can spur entrepreneurial activity without clearly defined property rights (witness China).
2. **Regulatory institutions**: Markets fail if there is fraud or anti-competitive behaviour. Regulatory institutions are needed if markets are to function properly. When markets are liberalized, a regulatory framework is also required to avoid the consequences of risky behaviour, such as financial crises if the banking system is not properly regulated (as the world economy witnessed in 2008). Institutions to compensate for capital market imperfections and coordination failures must also be an integral part of a 'regulatory' framework for promoting innovation and growth. A good example of this is the way the state intervened to promote industrial development in South Korea and Taiwan in the 1960s and 1970s. All successful economies have an array of regulatory institutions that oversee different markets, such as the product market, financial markets and the labour market. Developing countries may need more regulatory institutions because market failures are more pervasive than in developed countries.
3. **Institutions for macroeconomic stability**: Monetary and fiscal policy institutions are necessary to provide an enabling environment in which private investment can flourish. Market economies are not self-regulating, and macroeconomic instability creates risk and uncertainty. The minimization of risk is vital if entrepreneurs are to take informed, long-term investment decisions. Financial markets are inherently unstable, which can have damaging real effects, and they need careful supervision. A central bank, a responsible banking system and fiscal prudence are all important ingredients of macroeconomic stability.
4. **Social insurance institutions**: These are necessary if individuals are to accept change. In rural, peasant societies on the margins of subsistence, change may spell disaster, but progress (particularly in agriculture) requires a willingness to take risks. Insurance against unemployment, crop failures and price fluctuations for agricultural commodities are all important if traditional agriculture is to be transformed. Economic reforms of any type, particularly in the process of liberalizing markets, will meet resistance if not enough attention is paid to creating social security institutions to protect the vulnerable. Social stability and cohesion within a market economy in the process of structural change require social insurance and safety nets.
5. **Institutions of conflict management**: Many developing countries have deep ethnic, tribal and religious divisions. Social conflict damages economies because it diverts resources from directly productive activities and creates uncertainty, which deters investment. To minimize conflict requires a full range of institutions – the rule of law, a fair legal system, a political voice for minority groups – which make it clear that the potential winners of social conflict will not benefit and potential losers will be properly safeguarded.

The question is: How are good institutions acquired? Because of history and the diversity of countries, there is no one unique set of institutions that can be prescribed for every country: 'there is no single mapping between the market and the set of non-market institutions required to sustain it' (Rodrik, 2000). Rodrik likens institutions to technical progress that allows countries to transform inputs into higher levels of output, shifting outwards a country's production possibility frontier. But technological blueprints that operate well in one context may not be appropriate in another – and so it is with institutions. A 'market economy' cannot simply be transposed from one country to another, at least not without some adaptation. As Rodrik and Subramanian (2008) put it: 'there is growing evidence that desirable institutional arrangements have a large element of context specificity arising from differences in historical trajectories, geography, political economy and other initial conditions ... institutional innovations do not necessarily travel well'.

Nor is it easy to bring about institutional change. There is a **collective action problem** that limits potential gainers from bringing about change in opposition to vested interests (Bardhan and Udry, 1999). One is the **free-rider problem** about sharing the cost of change; the other is the **bargaining problem** relating to sharing the potential benefits of change. It can be difficult for potential gainers to compensate potential losers, as in the case of land reform, for example. In these circumstances, the state has a role to play in fostering institutional change and development without destroying markets, or allowing itself to be influenced by special interest groups or corrupted by rent-seeking behaviour on the part of politicians and bureaucrats.

Rodrik (2000) argues forcefully that 'institutions need to be developed locally, relying on hands-on experience, local knowledge and experimentation'. Some institutional blueprints for some specific purposes may be borrowed (e.g. forms of financial regulation) because they are straightforward to implement and save costs, but others need to be built from scratch. Building from the 'bottom up' requires **participatory political institutions** that can use and assess local knowledge, so that the institutions created have consent and legitimacy. Institutions imposed from the 'top down' usually fail. Rodrik (2000) finds an association across countries between democratic political structures and economic success; but other studies are more agnostic.

Measuring institutions and the debate on institutions versus geography

To do serious empirical work on the impact of institutions on growth and development requires a measure of institutional development. But some care needs to be taken because if measures of institutional *quality* are used, a correlation with economic performance is almost certain to be found because the measures themselves are partly a function of the stage of development and economic success. Institutional measures are required that are devoid of 'quality'. The statistical way of putting the same point is that the institutional variables used should be strictly *exogenous*; but we know in practice that institutional development is partly a function of growth and development itself, making many institutional variables *endogenous*. To cope with this difficulty, one can either find instruments to proxy for present-day institutions (see below), or take the initial (or base) level of institutions as the independent variable, rather than the contemporaneous level. There are also other econometric difficulties in determining the impact of institutions. Many institutional variables are highly correlated with one another, so it is difficult to measure the separate influence of each, and many institutional measures are ordinal (they simply rank countries) rather than cardinal, which means that they do not measure the *magnitude* of the difference in the institutional variables between one country and another. Several different measures of institutions have been used in empirical work:

- **An aggregate governance index**, which is an average of six measures of institutions developed by Kaufman et al. (1999). These measures include:
  - *voice and accountability*: the extent to which citizens can choose their government and enjoy political rights, civil liberties and an independent press

- *political stability and absence of violence*: the likelihood that the government will not be overthrown by unconstitutional or violent means
- *government effectiveness*: the quality of public service delivery and competence and political independence of the civil service
- *regulatory burden*: the relative absence of government controls on goods markets, banking systems and international trade
- *rule of law*: the protection of persons and property against violence and theft, independent and effective judges, and contract enforcement
- *freedom from graft*: public power is not abused for private gain or corruption.

Each of these measures can be taken individually.

- **A measure of property rights and risk of expropriation** using the International Country Risk Guide (ICRG) and Business Environmental Risk Intelligence (BERI). These indices are used by Keefer and Knack (1995). The ICRG index includes a measure of expropriation risk, rule of law, repudiation of contracts by governments, corruption in government and quality of bureaucracy. The BERI index includes contract enforceability, nationalization potential and bureaucratic delays.
- **An index of democracy, political rights and civil liberties**, for example the Freedom House index of political rights and civil liberties (Gastil, 1983, 1986).
- **Political instability**, as measured by the number of revolutions and coups, and the number of assassinations (Barro, 1991).
- **An index of corruption** (Transparency International).
- **Economic freedom** (Heritage Foundation).
- **An index of social division**, for example, ethnic diversity.

Apart from Rodrik, Acemoglu et al. (2001, 2002) are the other foremost modern exponents of the view that institutions are of primary importance in understanding the development process, and why some countries are rich today and others poor. Acemoglu (2008) identifies three important characteristics of good institutions:

1. The enforcement of property rights and the rule of law, so that individuals have the incentive to save, invest and take risks (as argued above).
2. Constraints on those in positions of power so that they cannot expropriate the resources of a country for their own benefit.
3. Equal opportunities for all, so that everyone has the incentive to better themselves and to participate productively in society.

Acemoglu and his colleagues believe that the fundamental cause of differences in the levels of development across countries of the world lies in differences in the evolution of institutions (in particular, property rights), which has historical roots, and that it is possible to find an *exogenous* cause of variations in institutions today that is unrelated to the level of development itself (or geography); namely the way in which colonizers settled in countries in the seventeenth and eighteenth centuries. This is determined by the mortality rates of soldiers, sailors and missionaries in various parts of the world.

The model of institutional development proposed by Acemoglu et al. (2001) is that (potential) settler mortality determined the degree of settlement, the degree of settlement determined the type of early institutions, and that early institutions have determined current institutions and can explain current economic performance. In other words, mortality rates in countries during early colonial times can be used for predicting institutions and the level of per capita income across countries today.

Let us consider the theory in more detail, and then some of the evidence. The model is based on three basic premises:

1. There were different colonization policies, which created different types of institutions. At one extreme, in some countries (mainly in Africa), 'extractive states' were created with the main purpose of transferring as many resources as possible from the colony. Private property rights were not established and colonizers did not settle in large numbers. At the other extreme, in countries such as the USA and Australia, Europeans settled in large numbers and tried to replicate European institutions, with a strong emphasis on private property and checking the power of elites – political and vested interests.
2. The colonization strategy depended, to a large extent, on the feasibility of settlement, and particularly the incidence of disease and mortality.
3. The institutions created during the colonial period persisted after the colonies became independent.

Acemoglu et al. (2001) present a mass of evidence of how mortality rates affected the willingness to settle in the various colonies, and how the presence or absence of European settlers was a key determinant of the form colonization took. A great deal of historical evidence is also presented that the control structures set up during the colonial period in the 'extractive states' that were not settled, such as in Africa and parts of Latin America, have persisted to this day, while the institutions of protecting private property rights and law and order, which were established in settler countries such as Australia, Canada, the USA, Hong Kong and Singapore, have also persisted.

The measure of institutions today, used by Acemoglu et al. (2001) is a 'risk expropriation' index first used by Keefer and Knack (1995).[1] The index goes from 0 (lowest protection of property rights) to 10 (highest), measured for each country for each year. They test their model using 64 former colonies for which there are data on settler mortality in the nineteenth century, current protection against expropriation risk, and living standards for the period 1985–95. Using simple two-variable regressions shows:

1. A strong negative correlation between per capita income (PCY) today and settler mortality rates per 1,000 of population.
2. A strong positive relation between PCY and protection against expropriation risk today (the correlation coefficient exceeds 50%).
3. That the settler mortality rate explains 25% of the variation in the expropriation risk index.

When the endogeneity of the expropriation risk index (as the measure of institutional quality) is instrumented by the settler mortality variable, a significant negative effect on the current level of per capita income of countries is found, even controlling for other variables that might be correlated with settler mortality, such as the identity of the colonial power, natural resource endowments, soil quality, religion, temperature and humidity. In fact, Acemoglu et al. (2001) dismiss the effect of geography altogether (see below). Moreover, the strong results are not dependent on the heavily settled countries with good institutions, such as the USA, Canada, Australia and New Zealand, nor if African countries are excluded from the sample. When a dummy variable for Africa is used in the equation, it is not statistically significant, which leads Acemoglu et al. (2001) to conclude that Africa is poor not because of geography but because of poor institutions, inherited from the past because the colonial powers established 'extractive states'.

In a separate analysis, Acemoglu et al. (2002) try to support their theory by showing how the fortunes of countries between the sixteenth century and the present have changed because of **institutional reversal**. It is a fact that those countries that were relatively rich in the year 1500 are now relatively poor, and vice versa, and this is attributed to the two different types of institutional structures, discussed above, that were imposed on countries during colonial times. Economic prosperity in 1500 is measured by the rate of urbanization and population density. With either measure, there is a negative relation between prosperity in 1500 and the level of PCY today. The explanation given is that in previously poor areas, European colonialism led to the development of institutions of private property because the regions were sparsely populated, which enabled Europeans to settle in large numbers and develop new institutions to the benefit of all. By contrast, in previously prosperous areas, already more densely populated with powerful ruling elites, colonizers found it easier and more profitable to maintain or introduce extractive institutions. There was a ready workforce available and taxation was relatively easy. Besides, in the more densely populated regions, there was more disease and mortality rates were higher. The reversal of relative incomes took place in the eighteenth and nineteenth centuries, with societies with good institutions taking advantage of the opportunity to industrialize: 'the interaction between institutions and the opportunity to industrialise during the 19th century played a central role in the long-run development of the former colonies' (Acemoglu et al., 2002). The authors find a negative relation between measures of prosperity in 1500 and the risk of expropriation (insecure property rights) today. Some basic econometric results are:

- a 10 percentage point lower rate of urbanization in 1500 is associated with double the level of PCY today
- a 10% higher population density in 1500 is associated with a 4% lower PCY today.

Acemoglu et al. (2002) again dismiss the role of geography because geography is a 'constant' and predicts the persistence of economic outcomes. If geography is the most important factor in development, the most (least) prosperous areas prior to colonization should have continued to be the most (least) prosperous, but this is not the case. Geography cannot explain the reversal of fortunes. Acemoglu et al. (2002) recognize what they call a 'sophisticated version' of the geography hypothesis; that certain geographic characteristics that were inimical to successful economic performance in 1500 became less important later on when new crops and new technologies made temperate zones more productive than the more prosperous tropical zones (where civilization started), and transport costs fell. But they argue that there is no evidence that the reversal of economic fortunes between sets of countries in the eighteenth and nineteenth centuries was associated with agriculture or a more favourable transport environment. Reversal was most closely related to industrialization. Acemoglu et al. (2002) conclude: 'if you want to understand why a country is poor today, you have to look at institutions rather than its geography'.

But institutions and geography cannot be separated so easily. Geography, and its effects on disease, affects the type of colonization and therefore the character of institutions. Acemoglu (2008) effectively concedes this when he says: 'geographic factors also likely influenced the institutions that Europeans introduced'. Rodrik et al. (2004) attempt to tackle this issue empirically (see also Rodrik and Subramanian, 2008). They estimate a series of regressions relating the income levels of countries to measures of geography, institutions (and also the degree of economic integration), taking account of the endogeneity of institutions. Institutional development is measured by a composite indicator of the strength of property rights and the rule of law. Rodrik et al. (2004) reach the conclusion that:

> Quality of institutions is the only positive and significant determinant of income levels. Once institutions are controlled for, integration has no direct effect on income, while geography has but weak direct effects. These results are very robust.

Rodrik et al. (2004) claim that the quality of institutions overrides everything else, but also concede, like Acemoglu, that 'geography has a strong indirect effect through institutions by influencing their quality'. Thus, geography may be the ultimate determinant after all.

In fact, Sachs (2008) points out that the incidence of malaria itself is enough to account for the negative relation between the mortality rates of British soldiers in various parts of the world in the nineteenth century and low levels of per capita income today. Sachs is critical of the almost exclusive emphasis on institutions in explaining differences in economic performance between countries, as if nothing else matters: 'the barriers to economic development in the poorest countries today are more complex than institutional shortcomings ... both institutions and resource endowments are critical, not just one or the other'.

Another critic is Bardhan (2005a), who argues that there are other institutions that matter besides property rights and the rule of law, particularly **coordinating institutions** to overcome the coordination failures that are endemic in poor countries and require institutions to cope with them. They would remain important even if property rights were secure. In Bardhan's view: 'this preoccupation of the literature with the institutions of security and property rights, often to the exclusion of other important institutions, severely limits our understanding of the development process'. Bardhan doubts whether the mortality rate of colonial settlers really captures the major historical forces that determined the economic and social structure of colonies.

Think of the *differences* between countries today all with similar disease environments, such as Brazil, India or the Congo in Africa, let alone the countries that were never colonized, such as Ethiopia and Thailand. Countries had a history before colonization: Bardhan (2005a) calls this **state antiquity**, a term that refers to whether a country had a unified state structure or not. By this criterion, Asia ranks higher than Latin America and Africa, and in the latter, as a result of colonial rule, the postcolonial state was often incongruent with the precolonial political structures and geographic boundaries. This has been a major source of political turmoil and instability. In statistical analysis, Bardhan finds the state antiquity variable a significant determinant of differences in per capita income today (as well as settler mortality rates).

The role of democracy

Apart from the institutions versus geography debate, most empirical work on the role of institutions in economic development has been conducted on political instability and the impact of political structures and the role of democracy. The challenge for any government, whatever its structure, is to provide leadership in resolving collective action problems (Bardhan, 1993), which means a commitment to formulating and implementing development policies in the interests of all the people, to prevent groups going their own separate ways. Democracy can make this more difficult because politicians can succumb to vested interest groups and take short-term decisions. On the other hand, dictatorships may have no interest in maximizing total output, and may allocate resources very inefficiently. Democracy makes life difficult for corrupt elites. In the discussion of democracy and growth, it is also important to distinguish between democracy defined as free, multiparty elections on the one hand and civil and economic liberties on the other (Alesina and Perotti, 1994). Some non-democratic regimes in the first sense (e.g. China) give their citizens a lot of economic rights, and vice versa.

Early work by Barro (1991) measured institutional quality by the number of revolutions and coups in countries and the number of political assassinations. A negative relation was found between these measures and economic growth across a sample of 98 countries, controlling for other variables (see Chapter 4).

But political instability is not the same as the nature of the political system. Here, we shall highlight two major studies on the role of democracy by Rodrik (2000) and Barro (1996a, 2008). Rodrik examines data for 90 countries over the period 1970–89, using the Freedom House index of political rights and civil liberties (the Gastil index) as a measure of democracy, which ranks countries on a scale of zero to one. Rodrik draws four important conclusions:

- democracies deliver more predictable long-run growth rates
- democracies produce greater short-term stability
- democracies handle adverse shocks much better
- democracies promote a fairer distribution of income.

Democracies produce better outcomes in these ways because they produce superior institutions better suited to local conditions. There is little evidence that the average growth rate is higher in democracies than in more autocratic regimes, but the variance around the average is significantly lower in democracies. One reason for this is because adjustment to shocks requires managing social conflict, and democratic institutions are more efficient institutions for conflict management. Democracies deliver better institutional outcomes because they tend to create more equal opportunities for people, especially in the fields of health, education and employment opportunity, which manifests itself in a higher share of wages in national income. In general, therefore, democracy helps to build better institutions based on local knowledge: 'participatory and decentralised political systems are the most effective ones we have for processing and aggregating local knowledge. We can think of democracy as a meta-institution for building other good institutions' (Rodrik, 2000).

Barro (2008), on the other hand, is more circumspect about the impact of democracy. Most agree that democracy tends to follow economic development, rather than precede it; what is debated is the role of democracy in sustaining development once it has started. Barro argues that democracy can hamper growth in the early stages of development by the tendency of majority voting to support programmes that redistribute income from the rich to the poor, involving tax increases and other distortions that reduce incentives. Also, democracies may give in to pressure groups that redistribute resources to themselves; for example, agricultural lobbies, defence contractors and trade unions. On the other hand, and very importantly, democracy is a check on corrupt autocracies (dictators). In statistical work that examines the link between democracy and growth, Barro (2008) measures the degree of democracy using the Gastil index of political rights found in Gastil's publication, *Freedom in the World* (1983, 1986). The definition of political rights is: 'rights to participate meaningfully in the political process. In a democracy this means the right of all adults to vote and compete for public office, and for elected representatives to have a decisive vote on public policies.'

Barro's (2008) results suggest that the relationship between democracy and growth across countries is weakly negative, but not statistically significant. The most interesting finding is that there is evidence of nonlinearity; that is, more democracy increases growth when political freedoms are weak, but depresses growth when a moderate degree of freedom has been achieved (perhaps because, as said above, democracies give in to pressure groups and engage in more redistribution). Barro (2008) concludes that:

> democracy is not the key to economic growth ... advanced Western countries would contribute more to the welfare of poor nations by exporting their economic systems, notably property rights and free markets, rather than their political systems, which typically developed after reasonable standards of living had been attained.

Barro's conclusion concurs with that of Alesina and Perotti (1994) in their early survey of the political economy of growth, when they say: 'growth is influenced not so much by the nature of the political regime (democracy or dictatorship) as by the stability of the political regime ... transitions from dictatorship to democracy, being associated with socio-economic instability, should be typically periods of low growth' (see Case example 8.1).

Case example 8.1

Institutions and African economies

The current evidence for Africa is that the structure of political institutions influences the performance of economies, and that Africa's shift towards a greater degree of democracy has paid off in terms of improved economic outcomes. The democracy–growth relationship may, however, be nonlinear. For African economies, the initial transition to democracy can be fraught with risks of political disorder. It is only when African countries have reached 'advanced-level' democracy that we can expect increasing democratization to be growth-enhancing.

Resource rents have become a curse for many African economies. Research shows that large resource rents lead to more corruption, but that the effect is lower for more democratic countries. Nigeria presents a good illustration of the resource curse challenge. Despite the huge rents that have flowed from oil, there has been little economic development; instead, these rents have served to undermine the quality of institutions and to lower growth. To avoid institutions themselves becoming corroded by resource rents and undermining democracy, oil revenues could be distributed directly to the public. Nigeria has become more democratic since 2000, and there has been improvement in government effectiveness, regulatory quality, the rule of law, and the control of corruption, but, unfortunately, political stability and the absence of violence have deteriorated significantly, consistent with the observation that greater democracy may be associated with a higher risk of conflict – at least in the short-term.

Source: Based on Fosu, 2013.

The historical evidence for the now-developed countries, as documented by Chang (2003), would seem to support this broad conclusion. He considers six categories of institutions as they were in nineteenth-century developed countries – democracy, bureaucracy (including the judiciary), property rights, corporate governance institutions, financial institutions, and welfare and labour institutions – and reaches the following conclusions:

1. The now-developed countries did not develop on the basis of democracy. Universal suffrage only came in the twentieth century. Poor developing countries today are adopting suffrage at much lower levels of income than in now-developed countries.
2. Public offices and the judiciary were historically corrupt. Appointments were made not on merit, but through class or political connections, and the judiciary often lacked independence, dispensing justice according to class and race.
3. Property rights, such as contract law, company law, bankruptcy law, tax law and land law, were all lax historically. So, too, were intellectual property rights. Chang remarks with respect to patents, copyrights and trademarks: 'the protection fell well short of what is demanded in developing countries today'.

4. In most now-developed countries, modern corporate governance structures emerged after, rather than before, industrial development. There was no proper auditing of companies and no bankruptcy law, and competition laws did not properly exist until the twentieth century.
5. Banking regulation in the nineteenth century was very perfunctory, and banks only became professional lending institutions, serving all the people, in the early twentieth century.
6. Social security institutions to protect against change were virtually nonexistent.

The lessons of history are that many institutions deemed to be important for poor developing countries today emerged after, not before, economic development was taking place, and it took a long time for them to emerge in fully fledged form from the time of their perceived need. Chang (2003) is right to conclude, however, that this does not mean 'the clock should be turned back'; rather, that institutional development is not the sine qua non of economic development, and institutional reforms in developing countries should not be imposed from outside, but should be allowed to evolve naturally, internally.

This would accord with the central conclusion of Rodrik (2000), namely everything we know about economic growth indicates that large-scale institutional transformation is not so necessary for getting growth started, but that it is very important for sustaining it. This conclusion is based on the pioneering research by Hausmann et al. (2005) on 'growth accelerations'. The secret of economic success in the early stages of development is to find the 'binding constraints' on growth using 'growth diagnostics' (see Chapter 4). This does not require wholesale institutional reform.

Summary

- Institutional structures and rules of behaviour are a necessary condition for economic activity to flourish because incentives and price signals in a market economy cannot function properly without them.
- There are at least five main types of market-supporting institutions that are necessary, if not sufficient, conditions for rapid economic progress: property rights and legally binding contracts; regulatory institutions; social insurance institutions; institutions for conflict management; and institutions to secure macroeconomic stability.
- Poor countries are often characterized by a lack of trust and the rule of law; weak institutions to mitigate risk and manage social conflict; no clearly defined system of property rights; an inadequate regulatory apparatus to curb fraud and anti-competitive behaviour; and a lack of clean government.
- Without property rights and the rule of law, the incentive to invest, on which economic growth ultimately depends, is very weak.
- It is not easy to bring about institutional change. There is a collective action problem, which limits potential gainers from bringing about change in opposition to vested interests, including the free-rider problem and the bargaining problem of distributing the gains.
- It is not easy to measure institutional development and its impact on economic performance because institutional development itself is endogenous to economic development. An exogenous measure of institutions is required.
- Several different measures of institutions have been used in empirical work, such as a measure of property rights and risk of expropriation; an aggregate governance index; an index of

democracy, political rights and civil liberties; an index of political instability; an index of corruption; an index of economic freedom; and an index of social division.

- The economists Acemoglu, Johnson and Robinson believe that the fundamental cause of differences in the level of development across countries in the world today is the historical evolution of institutions, and that in those parts of the world where conditions were harsh, in Africa for example, colonizers created 'extractive states' with no firm property rights, while in other parts (e.g. the USA and Australia) colonizers settled in large numbers and built institutions conducive to development. Disease and mortality rates in the nineteenth century are taken as an exogenous institutional variable. The role of geography (a constant) is dismissed.
- If geography was the most important factor in development, the most (least) prosperous areas prior to colonization should have continued to be the most (least) prosperous, but this is not the case. On the other hand, geography, and its effects on disease and mortality, affected the type of colonization and thus the character of institutions. The role of geography is therefore controversial.
- Apart from the debate on institutions versus geography, most of the empirical work on the role of institutions in economic development has been conducted on the influence of democracy and political stability on economic performance.
- Rodrik finds that democracies deliver more predictable long-run growth rates, produce greater short-term stability, handle adverse shocks better, and promote a fairer distribution of income than non-democratic states.
- Chang shows, however, that the lessons of history are that many of the institutions that are argued to be important for developing countries today emerged *after*, not before, economic development was taking place; for example, democracy and property rights, contract law, company law, bankruptcy law and tax law. His message is that institutions should be allowed to evolve naturally, internally, and not be imposed from outside.

Chapter 8 Discussion questions

1. Why are institutional structures and rules of behaviour a necessary condition for economic activity to flourish?
2. What institutions do you think are the most important for encouraging investment in developing countries?
3. What is the importance of local knowledge in building appropriate institutions?
4. What are the major empirical problems of testing the relationship between institutions and economic development?
5. Briefly describe the Acemoglu, Johnson and Robinson theory of the link between colonialism, institutions and economic development.
6. Is it possible to distinguish the role of institutions and geography in explaining differences in the level of development between countries?
7. In what ways can democracy help and hinder economic development?

Note

1. Keefer and Knack's (1995) early study examined the impact of property rights on economic growth across countries in the period 1974–89, using composite indices of contract enforceability and risk of expropriation, and found a strong positive effect of property rights; stronger than the effect of political instability or measures of civil liberties.

Websites on institutions and market behaviour

Transparency International www.transparency.org
Heritage Foundation www.heritage.org
Center for Global Development www.cgdev.org
Freedom House https://freedomhouse.org/

9

THE ROLE OF THE STATE IN ECONOMIC DEVELOPMENT

- **Introduction**
- **The market mechanism and market failures**
- **The role of the state**
- **Corruption**
- **Failed states, conflict and violence**
- **Development plans**
- **The allocation of resources: the broad policy choices**
- **Industry versus agriculture**
- **The comparative cost doctrine**
- **Present versus future consumption**
- **Choice of techniques**
- **Balanced versus unbalanced growth**
- **Investment criteria**
- **Summary**
- **Discussion questions**
- **Notes**
- **Websites on government and corruption**

Introduction

The central issue facing all economies is how to allocate resources among competing uses. This question takes on more significance in developing countries than in developed countries because resources are scarcer, the basic needs of people are greater, and the market mechanism as a device for resource allocation has many more imperfections. In this chapter, we first review the role of the market mechanism as an efficient device for resource allocation, and the various imperfections and failures that markets may suffer from, which might be corrected by the state. Four roles for the state are identified: to provide public goods, to eliminate divergences between private and social costs and benefits (which arise because market prices do not reflect the social costs and benefits of goods and factors of production), to protect the vulnerable because the market mechanism does not guarantee an equitable distribution of income, and to provide an institutional environment in which markets can flourish.

But there can be state failures as well as market failures. Corruption is endemic in many poor countries, and there are at least 50 countries in the world classified as **failed states** that hardly function at all, politically or economically.

Finally, the role of planning in developing countries is discussed and some of the broader policy issues confronting decision-makers, including types of planning, the balance between agriculture and industry, the choice between consumption today and consumption tomorrow, pursuing (or not) the law of comparative advantage, techniques of production, and the debate over whether growth should be balanced or deliberately 'unbalanced'.

The market mechanism and market failures

In free-market economies, resources are allocated by Adam Smith's 'invisible hand' of the market in accordance with consumer demand. The market is the organizational framework that brings together those who supply and those who demand a product, who then trade at an agreed price. In a completely free market, the price will clear the market so there are no unsatisfied buyers and sellers. Decision-making about what is produced is decentralized and left to the market, comprising the decisions of myriad private individuals. If the demand for a good increases, the price will rise and producers will be induced to supply more; if demand falls, the price will fall and producers will supply less. Market prices act as **signals** to producers to supply more or less of a commodity according to the changing profitability of production. The efficiency of markets relies on prices acting as signals, on suppliers responding, and on the mobility of the factors of production enabling supply to be forthcoming.

This brings us to one of the most important theorems in welfare economics: if consumers consume to the point where the marginal utility of consumption is equal to the price of a good, and producers produce to the point where the marginal cost of production is equal to price, then resources will be optimally allocated, since the marginal utility of production will just equal the marginal cost. Society will have reached its highest level of utility consistent with its production possibilities. This is illustrated in Figure 9.1.

The curve I_1I_1 is society's indifference curve between two goods, *A* and *B*, representing the highest utility attainable, and X_1X_1 is a country's production possibility curve between the two goods, *A* and *B*. Point 1 represents the optimum allocation of resources between the two goods. Any point to the left or right of point 1, or inside the production possibility curve, would represent a lower level of utility.

Figure 9.1 Welfare maximization

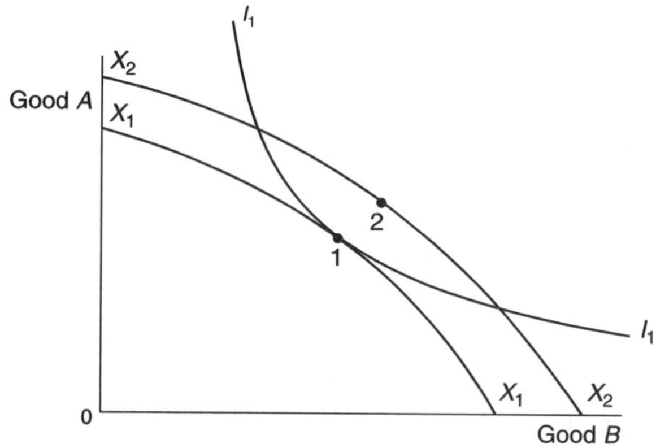

The allocation role of markets is, however, only one of the functions of the market mechanism. To use a distinction introduced by Kaldor (1972), the market also has a *creative* function, to provide an environment for change that expands production possibilities – that is, which shifts the production possibility curve outwards to X_2X_2, enabling a higher level of utility at point 2. An environment for change means all the dynamic forces that lead to technical progress, innovation and, ultimately, investment. In the early stages of development, the creative function of markets, producing new opportunities for growth, may be just as important as the allocative function of markets.

The conditions required for markets to perform their allocative and creative functions in an optimal manner are very stringent, and are unlikely to be satisfied in any economy, let alone developing countries. The true benefit of output may not be reflected in price because of **externalities**; price may not reflect marginal cost because of **market imperfections**; and many developmental goods and services may not be produced at all because **markets are incomplete or missing** entirely, and therefore cannot perform their creative function. In other words, there are likely to be **market failures**.

In addition, there is the problem that there is nothing in the market mechanism that guarantees an equitable distribution of income in society, or that will direct adequate resources away from present consumption to build up the means of production for a higher level of consumption in the future.

In the past, all these types of market failure have led development economists to argue for government intervention in the development process, as well as leading most developing countries to interfere with the market mechanism and to adopt various forms of planning for the allocation of resources. In the former Soviet Union and the countries of Eastern Europe, planning superseded the market mechanism entirely, and output and resource allocation was decided by bureaucrats, not by consumers. In other countries, governments produced plans for the sectoral allocation of resources and took on more and more functions. In the latter half of the twentieth century, there was an explosion of government expenditure in developing countries, rising to over 30% of national income on average and to over 50% in some countries.[1]

In recent years, however, there has been disillusion with planning, and the role of the state has come under increased scrutiny for a number of reasons:

1. There was the collapse of the former state-planned, communist countries of the Soviet Union and Eastern Europe. What to put in their place? Most of these former command economies

have swung to the other extreme, embracing the market mechanism almost unconditionally, with other damaging consequences relating to growing income inequality and unemployment.

2. In many developing countries, the state has failed to deliver even the most fundamental public goods, such as law and order and property rights, and essential social capital and infrastructure, such as education, health facilities and transport.
3. Civil strife has caused the collapse of the state in a number of countries, particularly in Africa, leaving markets to operate in an institutional vacuum.
4. Many countries have found themselves in fiscal crisis – associated with mounting expenditure on the welfare state in developed countries, and huge public enterprise deficits in developing countries.
5. There is a fascination with the enabling role that the state has played in the successful developing countries of Southeast Asia – in Japan and the Asian tigers of Hong Kong, Singapore, Taiwan and South Korea. Can the East Asian model be copied?

Surveying the experience of developed and developing countries in the years since 1945, the message would seem to be that the state has a vital role to play in economic development, but not so much as a direct provider of goods and services; rather as the agency through which market failures can be rectified and as the architect of a framework in which markets can flourish and evolve. History shows that markets can come into existence without government intervention, but markets work incrementally. It takes time for price signals to be recognized, for people to respond to incentives, and for resources to be (re)allocated efficiently. This does not mean that the state should step in and do everything. There is a middle way between state-led, central planning on the one hand, and the minimal state espoused by extreme free-marketeers on the other. The bad experience of government planning in Eastern Europe should not blind us to the market failures mentioned earlier. The way forward in most developing countries must be a judicious mix of market capitalism combined with state intervention. Let us now consider in more detail the role the state can play in correcting these market failures.

The role of the state

The state has four key roles to play in the development process:

1. To provide public goods.
2. To correct market imperfections.
3. To protect the vulnerable and ensure an equitable distribution of income, both intra-temporally (between people at a point in time) and inter-temporally (between generations over time).
4. To provide an institutional environment in which markets can flourish, including the maintenance of macroeconomic stability.

Public goods are goods that have certain characteristics that make it difficult, if not impossible, to charge for them, and therefore private suppliers will not provide them. These characteristics are:

1. Consumption by one user does not reduce the supply available for others – the good is **non-rival**.
2. Users cannot be prevented from consuming the good – the good is **non-excludable**.

There are not many *pure* public goods (air is perhaps the purest of all) but there are others that come close and are important for economic development, such as defence, law and order, and the provision of basic infrastructure such as roads, railways, power supply, sewers and clean water.

A market in defence, or laws governing property rights that benefit the whole nation, is not conceivable. Markets in some infrastructural facilities are conceivable, but not very likely because of the high fixed costs. Also, the providers might have difficulty in charging for, and capturing, the externalities. The market would either not provide at all, or it would underprovide.

Market imperfections refer to three important phenomena. First, market prices may provide a very imperfect guide to the *social* optimum allocation of resources, because they do not reflect the opportunity costs to society of using factors of production, or the value to society of the production of commodities. The price of labour may be above its opportunity cost and therefore used too little. The price of capital and foreign exchange may be below the opportunity cost and therefore used too much from a social point of view. Likewise, the price of goods may not reflect the marginal cost of production. Monopolies, tariffs, subsidies and other imperfections in the market all distort free-market prices, on which private producers base their production decisions.

Second, there is the existence of **externalities**, both positive and negative, which means that some goods may be underprovided and others overprovided from a social point of view because the positive or negative externality is not reflected in the price. Most infrastructure projects, such as transport facilities, power generation, irrigation schemes and so on, and social capital, such as education and health facilities, will have greater social returns than the private return and will therefore be underprovided from a social point of view unless private suppliers in the market are compensated or subsidized. Other activities may produce negative externalities by imposing costs on society that are not paid for by the provider, and therefore the market oversupplies from a social point of view. Governments can curb negative externalities through regulation or taxation, and promote positive externalities through subsidies or providing the output itself, as with education and healthcare.

Third, markets may be incomplete or missing altogether. One good reason why markets may be missing in the case of public goods is the inability of suppliers to exclude **free-riders**, that is, to exclude people from consuming the good once it is provided. But there are other important reasons for incomplete or missing markets. For example, high transaction costs can prevent markets from developing, particularly in developing countries, where poor communications make information costs high and there is an absence of futures markets to compensate for risk in conditions of uncertainty. The actual cost of providing a good or service may be less than individuals are willing to pay, but imperfect information on the part of consumers leads to an undervaluation of the product and therefore restricted supply, for example preventive healthcare. In this sense, the market is incomplete.

Asymmetric information, adverse selection and **moral hazard** can also lead to market inefficiency. 'Asymmetric information' refers to the imbalance of knowledge in a market between buyers and sellers. In the market for bank loans, for example, the borrowers know more about their own circumstances than the lenders. Banks could make bad loans ('adverse selection'), which makes them cautious and leads to credit rationing. It would be very costly for banks to obtain all the information they require on high-risk customers. The informal money market compensates by charging very high interest rates for all. Another example would be the health insurance market, where individuals know more about their health than the suppliers of insurance. Those who know they are prone to illness are more likely to take out insurance, and more likely to be turned down. 'Moral hazard' is present when the possession of insurance encourages the activity that is insured against, leading to resource waste and higher costs (and higher insurance premiums for all). Governments may step in by regulating private insurance, or providing the service themselves at lower cost.

As far as **equity** is concerned, the state has an important role to play in protecting the vulnerable and ensuring an equitable distribution of income between people, between groups in society, between regions and across generations. There is not only a moral case for the state to help those in absolute poverty, but also a strong political and economic one. Poor, vulnerable and disaffected people can be a major cause of civil unrest and political instability (Stewart, 2001). This deters investment and growth. It is also important for the state to keep an eye on the welfare of future generations, which may require altering the balance between consumption and investment in the present. There are a number of ways in which governments can intervene to discourage present consumption and raise the level of investment for higher future consumption; examples are taxation, subsidized interest rates and public investment on society's behalf.

Finally, the state is essential for providing the appropriate **institutional environment** for markets to flourish and operate efficiently (see Chapter 8). In this sense, markets and government intervention are complementary. The World Bank's (1997) *World Development Report 1997: The State in a Changing World* conveys three principal messages:

1. Development (economic, social and sustainable) without an effective state is impossible. It is increasingly recognized that an effective state – not a minimal one – is central to economic and social development, but more as partner and facilitator than director. States should work to complement markets, not replace them.
2. A rich body of evidence shows the importance of good economic policies (including the promotion of macroeconomic stability), well-developed human capital, and openness to the world economy for broad-based, sustainable growth and the reduction of poverty. But, as our understanding of the ingredients of development improves, a deeper set of questions emerges: Why have some societies pursued these actions with greater success than others, and how precisely did the state contribute to these differing outcomes?
3. The historical record suggests the importance of building on the relative strengths of the market, the state and civil society to improve the state's effectiveness. This suggests a two-part strategy of matching the role of the state to its capability, and then improving that capability.

The *World Development Report 1997* (World Bank, 1997) argues that many developing countries are not performing their core functions properly. They are failing to protect property, to ensure law and order, and to protect the vulnerable, all of which causes unrest and leads to a lack of government **credibility**. Its survey of 69 countries shows that government credibility is highest in South and Southeast Asia, and lowest in sub-Saharan Africa and the states of the former Soviet Union (World Bank, 1997). Investment and growth are positively related to credibility. The report says of Africa that many countries are 'trapped in a vicious circle of declining state capability and thus declining credibility in the eyes of their citizens – leading to increased crime and an absence of security affecting investment and growth' (World Bank, 1997). It refers to a 'crisis of statehood' in Africa, and a lower 'state capability' than 50 years ago. In contrast, it praises the countries of Southeast Asia because they have paid attention to the institutional framework for markets to fulfil their various roles in allocating and augmenting resources. State credibility is particularly important if developing countries are to attract private foreign investment.

The World Bank (1997) outlines a two-pronged strategy for governments to increase their credibility and the effectiveness of the state: first, governments must match the role of the state to its capabilities and not try to do too much, and second, they must try to improve capabilities by reinvigorating state institutions. With regard to the first prong of the strategy, the state should concentrate on getting the basics right, such as safeguarding property rights and guaranteeing the rule of law, rather than trying to do too much. In many countries, there is overregulation and excessive state consumption. Governments should decide more carefully what to do and how to do it. The basics should be:

- law and order
- maintaining macroeconomic stability
- investing in basic social services and infrastructure
- protecting the vulnerable
- protecting the environment.

But the state does not have to be the *sole* provider of all infrastructure and social services. It can contract these services out to the private sector and introduce competition into their provision, coupled with a regulatory framework to protect consumers and workers. Neither does the state have to be the monopoly supplier of public utilities such as electricity, gas and telecommunications. These activities can be **privatized** with state supervision. Privatization has gathered pace throughout the world in recent years. There have been thousands of divestitures of state companies in developing countries and in the former communist countries of Eastern Europe. The motivation has been the generally poor economic performance of state-owned companies, the large deficits of public enterprises, and the promotion of competition to improve the delivery of services.

Beyond the basics, the state may want to intervene strategically – in industrial policy, for example, if it has the capability, as the successful Asian tiger economies have done. The past success of Hong Kong, Singapore, Taiwan and South Korea has depended on the state and the private sector working in harmony with each other, with the state providing the economic and legal environment for markets to flourish but with the government taking an entrepreneurial role and intervening where it thought necessary. In Hong Kong, the state took a leading role in planning infrastructure and providing subsidized housing to maintain social stability and to reduce the cost of labour. Singapore, Taiwan and South Korea targeted financial assistance to specific industries and even specific companies (with an emphasis on exports), with spectacular success.

On the second strategy of improving the capabilities of the state and reinvigorating state institutions, the task is to provide incentives for public officials to perform better and reduce the scope for arbitrary action that could lead to poor decision-making and corruption.

Corruption

Corruption is a serious issue in many developing countries. An organization based in Germany called **Transparency International** publishes a yearly Corruption Perceptions Index based on surveys of businesspeople, risk analysts and perceptions of the general public, ranked on a scale 0–10 (the lower the index, the more corrupt). The results for 168 countries in 2015 are shown in Table 9.1.

Developing countries appear to be the most corrupt, although the same level of income (or development) is often associated with different levels of corruption. In general, poverty breeds corruption, and corruption can lead to severe inefficiencies in the functioning of economies (for a comprehensive survey, see Abed and Gupta (2002).

Daniel Kaufmann (2005) at the World Bank reckons that a country that improves its governance from a low average level (and reduces corruption) could triple its average per capita income in the long run, and effectively tackle illiteracy and infant mortality at the same time.

The World Bank (1997) defines corruption as 'the abuse of public office for private gain', including bribery, threats and 'kickbacks'. These are all aspects of **rent-seeking behaviour** that arise primarily because decisions over the allocation of resources are in the hands of politicians

Table 9.1 Transparency International's Corruption Perceptions Index, 2015

Rank	Index	Country	Rank	Index	Country	Rank	Index	Country
1	9.1	Denmark	37	5.6	Malta	76	3.8	Brazil
2	9.0	Finland	40	5.5	Cape Verde	76	3.8	Burkina Faso
3	8.9	Sweden	40	5.5	Costa Rica	76	3.8	India
4	8.8	New Zealand	40	5.5	Latvia	76	3.8	Thailand
5	8.7	Netherlands	40	5.5	Seychelles	76	3.8	Tunisia
5	8.7	Norway	44	5.4	Rwanda	76	3.8	Zambia
7	8.6	Switzerland	45	5.3	Jordan	83	3.7	Benin
8	8.5	Singapore	45	5.3	Mauritius	83	3.7	China
9	8.3	Canada	45	5.3	Namibia	83	3.7	Colombia
10	8.1	Germany	48	5.2	Georgia	83	3.7	Liberia
10	8.1	Luxembourg	48	5.2	Saudi Arabia	83	3.7	Sri Lanka
10	8.1	United Kingdom	50	5.1	Bahrain	88	3.6	Albania
13	7.9	Australia	50	5.1	Croatia	88	3.6	Algeria
13	7.9	Iceland	50	5.1	Hungary	88	3.6	Egypt
15	7.7	Belgium	50	5.1	Slovakia	88	3.6	Indonesia
16	7.6	Austria	54	5.0	Malaysia	88	3.6	Morocco
16	7.6	United States of America	55	4.9	Kuwait	88	3.6	Peru
18	7.5	Hong Kong	56	4.7	Cuba	88	3.6	Suriname
18	7.5	Ireland	56	4.7	Ghana	95	3.5	Armenia
18	7.5	Japan	58	4.6	Greece	95	3.5	Mali
21	7.4	Uruguay	58	4.6	Romania	95	3.5	Mexico
22	7.1	Qatar	60	4.5	Oman	95	3.5	Philippines
23	7.0	Chile	61	4.4	Italy	99	3.4	Bolivia
23	7.0	Estonia	61	4.4	Lesotho	99	3.4	Djibouti
23	7.0	France	61	4.4	Montenegro	99	3.4	Gabon
23	7.0	United Arab Emirates	61	4.4	Senegal	99	3.4	Niger
27	6.5	Bhutan	61	4.4	South Africa	103	3.3	Dominican Republic
28	6.3	Botswana	66	4.2	São Tomé and Principe	103	3.3	Ethiopia
28	6.3	Portugal	66	4.2	The FYR of Macedonia	103	3.3	Kosovo
30	6.2	Poland	66	4.2	Turkey	103	3.3	Moldova
30	6.2	Taiwan	69	4.1	Bulgaria	107	3.2	Argentina
32	6.1	Cyprus	69	4.1	Jamaica	107	3.2	Belarus
32	6.1	Israel	71	4.0	Serbia	107	3.2	Côte d'Ivoire
32	6.1	Lithuania	72	3.9	El Salvador	107	3.2	Ecuador
35	6.0	Slovenia	72	3.9	Mongolia	107	3.2	Togo
36	5.8	Spain	72	3.9	Panama	112	3.1	Honduras
37	5.6	Czech Republic	72	3.9	Trinidad and Tobago	112	3.1	Malawi
37	5.6	South Korea	76	3.8	Bosnia and Herzegovina	112	3.1	Mauritania

Table 9.1 Transparency International's Corruption Perceptions Index, 2015 – *continued*

Rank	Index	Country	Rank	Index	Country	Rank	Index	Country
112	3.1	Mozambique	130	2.7	Nicaragua	150	2.1	Cambodia
112	3.1	Vietnam	130	2.7	Paraguay	150	2.1	Zimbabwe
117	3.0	Pakistan	130	2.7	Ukraine	153	1.9	Uzbekistan
117	3.0	Tanzania	136	2.6	Comoros	154	1.8	Eritrea
119	2.9	Azerbaijan	136	2.6	Nigeria	154	1.8	Syria
119	2.9	Guyana	136	2.6	Tajikistan	154	1.8	Turkmenistan
119	2.9	Russia	139	2.5	Bangladesh	154	1.8	Yemen
119	2.9	Sierra Leone	139	2.5	Guinea	158	1.7	Haiti
123	2.8	Gambia	139	2.5	Kenya	158	1.7	Guinea-Bissau
123	2.8	Guatemala	139	2.5	Laos	158	1.7	Venezuela
123	2.8	Kazakhstan	139	2.5	Papua New Guinea	161	1.6	Iraq
123	2.8	Kyrgyzstan	139	2.5	Uganda	161	1.6	Libya
123	2.8	Lebanon	145	2.4	Central African Republic	163	1.5	Angola
123	2.8	Madagascar	146	2.3	Congo Republic	163	1.5	South Sudan
123	2.8	Timor-Leste	147	2.2	Chad	165	1.2	Sudan
130	2.7	Cameroon	147	2.2	Democratic Republic of the Congo	166	1.1	Afghanistan
130	2.7	Iran	147	2.2	Myanmar	167	0.8	North Korea
130	2.7	Nepal	150	2.1	Burundi	167	0.8	Somalia

Source: Transparency International, 2015.

and government officials. The existence of licences, permits, regulations, subsidies and, of course, taxes all offer scope for corruption. Corruption not only leads to inefficiency – particularly the discouragement of investment – but can undermine the legitimacy of government itself. Where corruption is endemic, policy-making in other areas is less effective and it makes it more difficult for governments to enforce laws in areas such as taxation or control of environmental damage (see Elliott (1997), Tanzi (1998) and Bardhan (1997) for case studies on corruption).

The International Monetary Fund (IMF) now specifies anti-corruption measures as one of the conditions for loan support. For example, the IMF recently got tough with the Kenyan government, insisting first on a 'wealth declaration law' that all government ministers and senior civil servants declare the full range of their assets and liabilities every year, and, second, on a weekly inspection by IMF officials in Washington of the Central Bank of Kenya's balance sheet to prevent foreign aid being used for private gain.

Removing unnecessary regulations and bureaucracy, increasing transparency, and paying officials higher salaries reduce the scope for corruption, but vested interests involved in corruption make the reform process more difficult. The *World Development Report 1997* (World Bank, 1997) outlines three essential ingredients for improving the capabilities of the state (and rooting out corruption):

1. There must be effective rules and restraints to check public authority and prevent corruption. Independence of the judiciary is important, and an independent commission against corruption would be helpful.

2. Public officials should be appointed on merit, not on the basis of political patronage, and can be encouraged to perform effectively through a merit-based promotion system and adequate remuneration. Opening up competition in employment in the delivery of services is necessary to reduce the discretionary power of state officials to minimize rent-seeking behaviour, which is the basis of bribery and corruption.
3. Decision-making needs to be brought closer to the people so that they have more confidence in the state. All government programmes are likely to work better if there is democracy, if power is devolved, and if users are consulted.

Figure 9.2 shows the functions of the state in tabular form, distinguishing between the roles of addressing market failure and improving equity on the one hand, and the provision of minimal functions through to activist functions on the other, according to capability.

Countries with a low state capability should concentrate first on basic functions, such as the provision of pure public goods, macroeconomic stability and anti-poverty programmes. Going beyond these basic services are intermediate functions, such as the management of externalities, regulating monopoly, improving information and providing social insurance. Finally, states with a strong capability can take on more active functions, as mentioned above in the case of the Asian tigers, particularly promoting new markets through active industrial and financial policy.

The state also has a duty to reduce bureaucracy and regulation to allow markets to flourish. According to a World Bank (2004) study of laws and regulations in 133 countries, the costs in time, effort and money in setting up businesses in developing countries are colossal compared with developed countries because of bureaucratic delays and institutional inefficiencies. In Indonesia, it takes 168 days to set up a business and 152 days in Brazil, but it takes only 2 days in New Zealand. In some developing countries, the average bureaucratic cost of setting up a business can be four times the average income per head; in developed countries it is as little as 1% of average income per head. The consequences of poor and inappropriate regulations are that business is discouraged; a higher proportion of businesses operates outside the law, so the tax base is lower and corruption is more widespread. It is estimated that excessive regulations, inadequate enforcement of contracts, corruption and crime reduce the sales of firms by at least 25%.

Figure 9.2 Functions of the state

	Addressing market failure			**Improving equity**
Minimal functions	*Providing pure public goods:* Defence Law and order Property rights Macroeconomic management Public health			*Protecting the poor:* Antipoverty programmes Disaster relief
Intermediate functions	*Addressing externalities:* Basic education Environmental protection	*Regulating monopoly:* Utility regulation Antitrust policy	*Overcoming imperfect information:* Insurance (health, life, pensions) Financial regulation Consumer protection	*Providing social insurance:* Redistributive pensions Family allowances Unemployment insurance
Activist functions	*Coordinating private activity:* Fostering markets Cluster initiatives			*Redistribution:* Asset redistribution

Source: World Bank, 1997.

Failed states, conflict and violence

There are some 40–50 countries in the world, many in Africa, that hardly function at all, politically or economically, because their institutions and the rule of law have broken down. These are **failed states**, or what Paul Collier (2007) has coined **fragile states** caught in a conflict trap and prone to violence. Examples in recent years would be countries such as Somalia, Democratic Republic of Congo, Afghanistan, Yemen, Sudan, Zimbabwe, Sierra Leone, Rwanda, Guinea, Chad, Haiti and many others. Within such countries, people are disenfranchised and trapped in poverty at the mercy of vicious networks of criminality, violence and drugs. In these countries, the state has effectively collapsed, the government has lost control and is unable to provide even the most basic services and protection for its people. Moreover, conflict and violence can spread from one failed state to another – witness the contagion of failed states that we see in the Middle East today. Failed states contain approximately 1.5 billion people or 20% of the world's population. They account for 30% of people living on less than $1.90 a day, and poverty rates in these countries are over 20% higher than in other low-income countries

A major cause and characteristic of failed states is civil war, violence and the breakdown of security. The World Bank's *World Development Report 2011* (World Bank, 2011) was subtitled *Conflict, Security and Development*, and Paul Collier, one of the world's experts on failed states, addresses some of these issues in his book, *Wars, Guns and Votes* (2009). Thirty-nine countries have experienced civil wars since the year 2000, and the cost is huge. The World Bank estimates that civil conflict costs the average developing country approximately 30 years of growth of GDP. The total cost of Sri Lanka's civil war between 1983 and 1996 was about $4 billion or twice the size of its GDP in 1996. Civil conflict not only affects GDP directly but also indirectly by reducing investment, raising inflation, and reducing government revenues and expenditures in fields such as education, health and other productive activities. At the same time, infrastructure is destroyed, human capital is lost, and tourism and trade can be badly affected, thus reducing foreign exchange earnings. Gupta et al. (2002) document these effects, taking 20 conflict-affected countries over the period 1985–99. They look at variables three years before conflict started and three years after conflict, and also test the effect of conflict in a wider study of 45 countries (including countries not affected by conflict) using an index of conflict and terrorism compiled by International Country Risk Guide, and a separate index of conflict compiled by the Stockholm International Peace Research Institute. They estimate strong significant adverse impacts on GDP growth, inflation and tax revenues, with the prospect of a substantial peace dividend once the conflict ends and security is restored. Collier (2007) reckons that 'civil wars tend to reduce growth by 2.3 percent per year, so the typical seven-year war leaves a country around 15 percent poorer than it would have been'.

The World Bank (2011) writes: 'the central aspect of conflict and failed states is absence of legitimate institutions that provide citizens with security, justice and jobs'. The lessons of experience that it draws are:

1. To make the reform of security and justice systems a priority.
2. To build inclusive institutions (see Chapter 8).
3. To try to deliver early results.
4. To recognize that the process of state-building can be a long one with interruptions on the way.

But reforms must be made. These would include security, recognizing the connection between the police and justice, supporting bottom-up links between the state and civil society, tackling corruption, creating jobs particularly for young men who often form the core of disaffected groups, and social improvements to give people hope.

Ghani and Lockhart (2008), in their powerful book, *Fixing Failed States*, outline ten key functions that the state should perform if its citizens are to survive and thrive, avoiding conflict:

- To make laws, and to enforce the rule of law, to allow all sections of society to live in harmony.
- The control of violence.
- The appointment of uncorrupt administrators to oversee public bodies.
- The sound management of public finances.
- Investment in human capital.
- The creation of citizenship rights through social policy to ensure equal opportunities for all.
- The provision of infrastructure services.
- The creation and expansion of markets.
- The management of public assets, such as land, water rights and other 'natural' capital.
- Effective public borrowing.

If all these functions are performed well, a virtuous circle of growth and development is possible. If some of the functions are performed badly, a vicious circle can start, ultimately ending in the failure of the state and any prospect of sustained economic and social development. As the World Bank (2011) says: 'low incomes, poverty, unemployment, income shocks, rapid urbanization, and inequality between groups all increase the risks of violence'. Violence is as important a factor as civil conflict in keeping countries poor. The World Bank has set up the Low-Income Countries Under Stress fund to help failed states, while the UK government's intention is to spend one-half of its bilateral aid budget on 20 or more countries, mainly in Africa, where the state has virtually collapsed (see Case example 9.1 on Rwanda).

Development plans

In its *World Development Report 1997*, the World Bank (1997) does not address the role of development planning, but almost all developing countries, whatever their political ideology, publish development plans.[2] A **development plan** is an ideal way for a government to set out its development objectives and demonstrate initiative in tackling the country's development problems. A development plan can serve to stimulate effort throughout the country, and also act as a catalyst for foreign investment and loans from international institutions.

Case example 9.1 **Rwanda on the road to recovery**

At the end of 1994, almost a million Rwandans were dead and nearly three million were refugees, following years of decline and conflict capped by a cataclysmic genocide. The UK was the first country to provide direct support to Rwanda to help rebuild state institutions, national infrastructure and people's lives. As a result, schools and hospitals have been rebuilt, equal numbers of boys and girls are at school, and an effective tax system provides revenue for a growing national budget. Land ownership – an issue that helped fuel the genocide – is being addressed through practical reforms. Democracy has been boosted by a strengthened electoral system. Rwanda is the first country in the world with a predominantly female parliament. Rwanda has a long way to go but it is rapidly leaving behind the status of 'fragile state'.

Source: Compiled from https://www.gov.uk/government/organisations/department-for-international-development.

As an example, the Tongan 6th Development Plan (1991–95) stated that:

> The ultimate aim of government policy is to induce improvements in the standard of living of Tongans in an equitable manner with a view to protecting natural resources and preserving cultural assets – Government policy will also pursue an equitable distribution of public investment and services between rural and urban areas, and between the capital [city], islands and outer regions.

Four economic and social objectives were set out:

1. To achieve sustainable economic growth conducive to higher per capita income.
2. To achieve a more equitable distribution of income.
3. To generate more employment opportunities.
4. To restore and control external financial imbalances.

Depending on the politics of a country and its available expertise, a development plan will vary in its ambitiousness from a mere statement of aims to detailed calculations (and proposals for action) of the resources needed, and the amount of output that each sector of the economy must generate, in order to achieve a stipulated target rate of growth of output or per capita income. Anything more than a statement of aims inevitably involves some form of model-building, if only to delineate the relationship between sectors of the economy and between the key variables in the growth process.

Four basic types of model are typically used in development planning:

1. **Macro- or aggregate models** of the economy, which may either be of the simple Harrod–Domar type (see Chapter 4) or of a more econometric nature, consisting of a series of equations that represent the basic structural relations in an economy between, say, factor inputs and product outputs, saving and income, imports and expenditure and so on.
2. **Sector models**, which isolate the major sectors of an economy and give the structural relations within each sector, and also specify the interrelationships between sectors, for example between agriculture and industry, between capital and consumer goods industries, and between the government and the rest of the economy.
3. **Interindustry models**, which show the transactions and interrelationships between producing sectors of an economy, normally in the form of an input–output table.
4. Models and techniques for **project appraisal** to decide on the allocation of resources between activities (see this textbook's website, www.palgravehighered.com/Thirlwall-Econ-Of-Dev-10e).

Models such as these serve a twofold purpose. First, they enable planners to reach decisions on how to achieve specified goals. They highlight the strategic choices open to the policy-maker in the knowledge that not all desirable goals are achievable simultaneously. Only with an understanding of the interrelationship between the different parts of the economy, and a knowledge of the parameters of the economic system, is it possible for meaningful and consistent policy decisions to be reached. Without detailed information on which to base planning (or what has been called 'planning without facts'), the case for decentralized decision-making becomes overwhelming.

Second, models of the type described above can perform an equally valuable function of enabling the future to be projected with a greater degree of certainty than would otherwise be possible, thereby providing some knowledge of what resources are likely to be available in relation to requirements within a stipulated planning period. Various types of model may be classified, therefore, according to whether they are required for policy or decision purposes or for projection and forecasting. The necessary constituents of a plan containing both types of model are a statement of economic goals, a specification of policy instruments, an estimation of structural relationships, historical data, the recognition of exogenous variables, and, last but not least, a set of national accounts for national income and expenditure, foreign trade and even manpower to ensure consistency between demand and the supply of resources available.

The allocation of resources: the broad policy choices

Given the scarcity of resources in developing countries in relation to development needs, one of the central issues in development economics is the allocation of resources among competing ends. For most developing countries, the two major constraints on the growth of output are the ability to invest and the ability to import, and most theories of resource allocation and most public investment criteria reflect this fact. A common starting point in the consideration of resource allocation is how to maximize the level or growth of output with the domestic resources available, and how to minimize the use of foreign exchange.

Apart from the decision of how much to invest, three broad types of allocation decision may be distinguished:

1. Which sectors to invest in.
2. Which projects should receive priority, given the factor endowments of a country and its development goals.
3. Which combination of factors of production should be used to produce a given vector of goods and services, which will determine the technology of production.

While these decisions may look independent, in fact they are not. In practice, interdependence between decisions on output and decisions on technology is inevitable. Deciding which goods to produce will, to a certain extent, dictate factor proportions if technical coefficients are relatively fixed, and decisions about technology will influence the types of goods and services that are produced, insofar as factor proportions cannot be varied. Some goods and services are obviously more labour-intensive than others. The choice of technology will, in turn, be particularly influenced by factor endowments and the price of factors of production, and by the relative valuation given to present versus future consumption and welfare.

Because of the interdependence between the choice of goods and the choice of technology, a country that decides to use relatively labour-intensive techniques within the framework of goods chosen may nonetheless have a greater capital intensity than another country using relatively capital-intensive techniques with a different mix of goods. When discussing resource allocation and the choice of techniques, a distinction needs to be made between investment criteria that relate to the pattern of output on the one hand, and the choice of technology to produce the given vector of outputs on the other.

Investment decisions of the micro-type outlined above will also be influenced to a certain degree by the nature of the development strategy intended – that is, by broader policy issues, such as whether emphasis is to be given to agriculture or industry, whether resources are to be used to build up complementary activities, or whether imbalances are to be deliberately created in order to induce investment and influence decision-making, and whether emphasis is to be on static short-term efficiency in the allocation of resources or on laying the foundations for faster growth in the future. And, in an open economy, the potential clash between efficiency and growth also requires a consideration of the implications of adherence to different versions of the comparative cost doctrine. In short, the question of resource allocation between projects cannot be divorced from consideration of the wider policy issues of industry versus agriculture, balanced versus unbalanced growth, foreign trade strategy and so on. And influencing all these decisions will be the underlying objectives of the development strategy: whether the aim is to maximize *current welfare* or to maximize consumption at *some future point in time.*

The choice of development strategy itself will be subject to political, social and economic constraints. A particular strategy, for example, may conflict with the desired income distribution or other social objectives. Other strategies may involve political repercussions inimical to development. One factor that cannot be ignored is the regional distribution of political power. Spatial considerations of this sort add a further dimension to the allocation problem. The pursuit of balanced growth or massive investment in social overhead capital may imply a large public sector in the economy, which may not be politically possible. Certain development plans may antagonize foreign investors or multilateral aid-giving agencies, such that if the plans are carried out, foreign capital or 'agency' capital dries up. Bearing in mind these constraints, let us first consider some of the broader aspects of development strategy and briefly discuss development goals, before examining a number of specific investment criteria that have been recommended for determining the allocation of resources and the pattern of output.

Industry versus agriculture

The issue of the choice between industry and agriculture, and where the emphasis should lie, can be discussed very quickly because, as we saw in Chapter 5, the two sectors are very much complementary to each other. In practice, the fortunes of agriculture and industry are closely interwoven, in that the expansion of industry depends to a large extent on improvements in agricultural productivity, and improvements in agricultural productivity depend on adequate supplies of industrial 'inputs', including the provision of consumer goods acting as incentives to peasant farmers to increase the agricultural surplus. It is worth mentioning, however, that the emphasis on *balance* between industry and agriculture is of fairly recent origin. On the one hand, it represents a shift of emphasis away from the 'modern' view of an all-out drive for industrialization by developing countries, and on the other hand, it represents a reaction against the traditional doctrine of comparative cost advantage, which, when applied to many developing countries, may lead to the production of primary commodities and a pattern of trade that puts these countries at a relative development disadvantage (see Chapter 15).

The comparative cost doctrine

Whether the static comparative cost doctrine should be adhered to is itself a question of development strategy, which is closely bound up with the goals of developing countries (that is, what they are trying to maximize), and with the controversy over whether trade should be looked at more from the point of view of the balance of payments than from that of the allocation of real resources. Assuming the full employment of resources, and that the price of a commodity reflects its opportunity cost (admittedly bold assumptions in any country), adherence to the comparative cost doctrine will produce the optimum pattern of production and trade for a country (see Chapter 15). Efficiency will be maximized when no commodity is produced that could be imported at a lower cost, measured by the resources that would have to be sacrificed to produce it at home.

In a free trade world, this would rule out the production of a wide range of industrial commodities in developing countries.

If the objective is faster economic *growth*, however, as opposed to static efficiency, the theory of growth suggests investment criteria that are quite different from those derived from the theory of comparative advantage. If growth depends on increases in investment, for example, it may not be wise to channel resources into activities that are too labour-intensive, where the income generated is all consumed and none is saved, or where there is no scope for increasing returns. Similarly, if growth is constrained by the balance of payments, it may be equally unwise to develop activities that produce goods with a low price and income elasticity of demand in world markets, such as primary commodities. A low price elasticity of demand can cause fluctuations in export earnings with shifts in supply, and cause the terms of trade to move adversely. A low income elasticity of demand will mean that, for any given growth of world income, countries producing these commodities will be put at a permanent balance of payments disadvantage compared with other countries producing goods with a higher income elasticity of demand (see Chapters 15 and 16).

The question ultimately boils down to one of the relative valuation of present versus future output and consumption (or welfare) – between consumption today and consumption tomorrow. Efficiency in resource allocation will maximize present output and consumption from a given amount of resources, but may impair growth and future consumption. Focusing on growth may lower present welfare but provide greater output and welfare in the future.

Present versus future consumption

The choice between present and future consumption is the same as the choice between consumption and investment in the present. How much investment should be undertaken in the present depends on the time interval over which society wants to maximize consumption and what value it places on consumption in the future compared with consumption in the present – that is, on the rate at which it discounts future consumption gains. Time affects both the accumulation of consumption gains and the effect that discounting has. Investment should take place so as to maximize consumption over the planning period. The investment ratio that maximizes consumption will vary according to the planning period, with and without discounting.

Let us illustrate this with a numerical example. Consider three different investment ratios – 0%, 10% and 50% of national income – and three different planning periods – three years, six years and ten years. Further assume that the capital–output ratio is 2, and that, for simplicity, there is no depreciation and no discounting. Let the initial capital stock equal 200, producing 100 units of output. The time paths of output, consumption, investment and the capital stock for the three different investment strategies and three different planning horizons can now be shown, as in Table 9.2. Over the three-year planning period, the first policy of no investment maximizes consumption. Over the six-year planning period, the second policy of a 10% investment ratio maximizes consumption, and over the ten-year planning period, the third policy of a 50% investment ratio maximizes consumption.

The calculations in Table 9.2, and the conclusions drawn from them about the time period over which consumption will be maximized, will be affected by discounting and the discount rate chosen, because the present value of future consumption gains becomes less and less the further into the future they accrue, and their value is also lower the higher the discount rate chosen. What we illustrate, then, is that the answer to the question of how much to invest depends crucially on the *planning horizon* taken and the *discount rate* chosen. The longer the planning horizon and the

Table 9.2 Consumption benefits with different investment ratios over different planning horizons

Time	Policy 1, no investment				Policy 2, 10% investment				Policy 3, 50% investment			
	K	Y	I	C	K	Y	I	C	K	Y	I	C
1	200	100	0	00	200.00	100.00	10.00	90.00	200.00	100.00	50.00	50.00
2	200	100	0	100	210.00	105.00	10.50	94.50	250.00	125.00	62.50	62.50
3	200	100	0	100	220.50	110.25	11.03	99.22	312.50	156.25	78.12	78.12
4	200	100	0	100	231.53	115.76	11.57	104.19	390.62	195.31	97.65	97.65
5	200	100	0	100	243.10	121.55	12.15	109.40	488.27	244.13	122.07	122.07
6	200	100	0	100	255.25	127.62	12.76	114.86	610.34	305.17	152.58	152.58
7	200	100	0	100	268.01	134.00	13.40	120.60	762.92	381.46	190.73	190.73
8	200	100	0	100	281.41	140.70	14.07	126.61	953.65	476.82	238.41	238.41
9	200	100	0	100	295.48	147.74	14.77	132.97	1192.06	596.03	298.01	298.01
10	200	100	0	100	310.25	155.12	15.51	139.61	1490.07	745.03	372.51	372.51

Key: K = capital stock; Y = output; I = the level of investment; C = consumption.

less the stream of future consumption benefits is discounted, the more investment there should be in the present. The shorter the planning horizon and the higher the discount rate, the less investment there will be.

We also illustrate that countries with low initial stocks of capital and low levels of consumption must invest heavily if high future living standards are to be attained. But to invest heavily, countries must take long planning horizons. One of the arguments for planning is, in fact, to lengthen the planning horizon beyond that chosen by individuals maximizing privately. Any finite planning horizon, however, only takes care of the people living within the planning period. To take account of generations living beyond the horizon, certain constraints must be built into the investment model such that, for example, the level of consumption at the end of the period should not be above a specified level, otherwise maximization of consumption within the horizon would mean consuming all income at the end of the horizon, leaving no saving for future investment and consumption.

Choice of techniques

In a planning framework, the valuation of present versus future welfare is also the central issue regarding the choice of technology – whether techniques should be capital- or labour-intensive. At first sight, it would seem sensible, in a labour-abundant economy, to use labour-intensive techniques of production, and to encourage activities that use factors of production that are in abundance. Doing so, however, may lead to a conflict between efficiency and growth; a clash between the maximization of present consumption and the level of consumption in the future. The problem is that if the wage rate is given, and invariant with respect to the technique of production, the more labour-intensive the technique, the less saving that is likely to be generated for future reinvestment. Specifically, if workers' propensity to consume is higher than that of the owners of capital, the total surplus, and the surplus per unit of capital invested, left for reinvestment, will be smaller than if the technology were more capital-intensive. On the other hand, the more capital-intensive the technology, the lower the level of consumption and employment in the present.[3] In general, we reach the conclusion that the higher the valuation placed on raising the present level of employment and consumption as compared with future output, the more that labour-intensive techniques should be favoured. At the same time, the greater the valuation placed on future output in relation to present welfare, the more that capital-intensive methods of production should be favoured.

There is not only a potential conflict between employment and saving in the choice of techniques, but also a conflict between employment and output. The conflict arises not in the utilization of existing equipment but in the choice of *new* techniques. Labour-intensive techniques of production may have higher capital–output ratios than more capital-intensive techniques. A simple example will illustrate the point. Assume a fixed amount of capital to be invested of £1,000. One technique of production could employ 100 units of labour with £1,000 of capital, but the capital–output ratio is 5. This would give a flow of output of 200 with the employment of 100 persons. A second technique of production employs 50 units of labour but has a capital–output ratio of 4. This would give a flow of output of 250 with the employment of 50 persons. Thus, maximizing both the current level of employment and output are consistent only if the more labour-intensive techniques also have the lowest capital–output ratios. These issues are discussed fully in Chapter 6.

Balanced versus unbalanced growth

Another broad choice of development strategy is between so-called 'balanced and unbalanced growth'. The term 'balanced growth' is used in many different senses, but the original exponents of the balanced growth doctrine had in mind the scale of investment necessary to overcome indivisibilities on both the supply and demand side of the development process (see, e.g., Rosenstein-Rodan, 1943; Nurkse, 1953). Indivisibilities on the supply side refer to the 'lumpiness' of capital (especially social overhead capital), and the fact that only investment in a large number of activities simultaneously can take advantage of various external economies of scale. Indivisibilities on the demand side refer to the limitations imposed by the size of the market on the profitability, and hence feasibility, of economic activities. This was the original interpretation of the doctrine of balanced growth: that the large-scale expansion of activities or **big push** was necessary to overcome divergences between the private and social returns to investment. The doctrine was later extended, however, to refer to the *path* of economic development and the *pattern* of investment necessary to keep the different sectors of the economy in balance, so that lack of development in one sector does not impede development in others; for example, the necessity to strike a balance between sectors such as agriculture and industry, between the capital goods and consumer goods industries, and between social capital and directly productive activities (see also Lewis, 1955).

On the demand side, the argument is akin to Adam Smith's famous dictum that specialization, or the division of labour, is limited by the extent of the market, and that if the market is limited, certain activities may not be economically viable (see Chapter 4). If, however, several activities are established simultaneously, each could provide a market for the other's products, so that activities that are not profitable when considered in isolation would become profitable when considered in the context of a large-scale development programme.

On the supply side, the argument for a 'big push' is related to the existence of **external economies of scale**, whereby the production function of one activity may be favourably altered by the existence of other activities (e.g. those in close proximity), so that the social return of an activity will exceed the private return. The way to eliminate this divergence is to make each activity part of an overall programme of investment expansion. Enterprises that are not, or do not appear to be, profitable in isolation become profitable when considered as part of an overall plan for industrial expansion embracing several activities.

A major criticism of the balanced growth doctrine, however, is that it fails to come to grips with one of the fundamental obstacles to development in developing countries, namely a shortage of resources of all kinds. Critics of balanced growth do not deny the importance of a large-scale investment programme and the expansion of complementary activities. Their argument is that in the absence of sufficient resources, especially capital, entrepreneurs and decision-makers, the striving for balanced growth may not provide sufficient stimulus to the spontaneous mobilization of resources or the inducement to invest, and will certainly not economize on decision-taking if planning is required.

One of the most provocative books ever written on development strategy is that by Hirschman (1958), whose argument is along the above lines. Hirschman was then the foremost exponent of the doctrine of **unbalanced growth**, and we must briefly consider his views as these are still relevant today. The question he attempts to answer is this: Given a limited amount of investment resources and a series of proposed investment projects whose total cost exceeds the available resources, how do we pick out the projects that will make the greatest contribution to development relative to their cost? And how should 'contribution' be measured?

Albert Hirschman

Born 1915, Berlin, Germany. Died 2012. Appointed Professor of Social Science, Institute for Advanced Study, Princeton, in 1974. Best known for his book *Strategy of Economic Development* (1958), which challenges the conventional view that developing countries should strive for balanced growth. Imbalances create incentives and economize on the decision-making process. Governments should deliberately target activities with high backward and forward linkages. Also an expert on Latin American economies and economic history, with such books as *Journeys Towards Progress: Studies of Economic Policy-Making in Latin America* (1963) and *A Basis for Hope: Essays on Development and Latin America* (1971).

Hirschman (1958) distinguishes two types of investment choices – *substitution choices* and *postponement choices*. Substitution choices are those that involve a decision as to whether project *A* or *B* should be undertaken. Postponement choices are those that involve a decision as to the *sequence* of projects *A* and *B* – that is, which should precede the other. Hirschman is mainly concerned with postponement choices and how they are made. His fundamental thesis is that the question of priority must be resolved on the basis of a comparative appraisal of the strength with which progress in one area will induce progress in another. The efficient sequence of projects will necessarily vary from region to region and from country to country, depending on the nature of the obstacles to development, but the basic case for the approach remains the same – that is, to economize on decision-making. In Hirschman's view, the real scarcity in developing countries is not the resources themselves but the means and ability to bring them into play. Preference should be given to that sequence of projects that maximizes **induced decision-making**.

Hirschman (1958) illustrates his argument by considering the relation between social capital (SC) and directly productive activities (DPA). The case in which SC precedes DPA he calls 'development via excess capacity', and the case in which DPA precedes SC he labels 'development via shortages'.

Both sequences create inducements and pressures conducive to development; the question is: Which sequence should be adopted (if it is not possible to pursue a 'balanced' growth path) to produce DPA output at minimum cost in terms of inputs into both DPA and SC? The question can be made clearer with the aid of a diagram (see Figure 9.3).

If the total cost of DPA output is measured on the vertical axis, and the availability and cost of SC is measured on the horizontal axis, curves can be drawn (*a*, *b*, *c*) showing the cost of producing a given full capacity output of DPA from a given amount of investment in DPA, as a function of the availability of SC. The successive curves, *a*, *b*, *c*, represent different levels of DPA output from successively higher investment in DPA. The curves are negatively sloped and convex to the origin because DPA costs will decrease the greater the availability of social capital, but there is a minimum amount of SC necessary for any level of DPA output (for example, OS_1, corresponding to curve *a*), and as SC increases, its impact on the cost of DPA output becomes less and less.

Now assume that the objective of the economy is to obtain increasing outputs of DPA with the minimum use of resources devoted to both DPA and SC. On each curve, *a*, *b*, *c*, the point where the sum of the coordinates is smallest will represent the most desirable combination of DPA and SC on this criterion. The line 0X connects the optimal points on the different curves and this represents the most 'efficient' expansion path, or 'balanced' growth path, between SC and DPA.

But suppose that 'optimal' amounts of SC and DPA cannot be expanded simultaneously to keep in balance with one another. On what criteria is that postponement choice made? One possibility is the sequence AA_1BB_2C, where the initial expansionary step is always taken by social capital. This sequence is called 'development via excess capacity'. The other (opposite) possibility is the sequence AB_1BC_1C, where the initial expansionary step is taken by DPA. This sequence is called 'development via shortages'. According to Hirschman, the preference should go to the sequence of expansion that maximizes 'induced decision-making'. It is difficult to tell *a priori* which sequence this is likely to be. If SC is expanded, existing DPA becomes less costly, encouraging further DPA. If DPA is expanded first, costs will rise but pressures will arise for SC facilities to be provided. Both sequences set up incentives and pressures and, ultimately, in Hirschman's view, the sequence chosen must depend on the relative strength of entrepreneurial motivations on the one hand, and on the response to public pressure of the authorities responsible for social capital on the other.

Hirschman applies the same criterion of 'induced decision-making' to the choice and sequence of projects *within* the directly productive sector. Here, inducements stem from interdependencies between activities, or what Hirschman (1958) calls **backward and forward linkage effects**. Backward linkages measure the proportion of an activity's output that represents purchases from

Figure 9.3 Induced decision-making

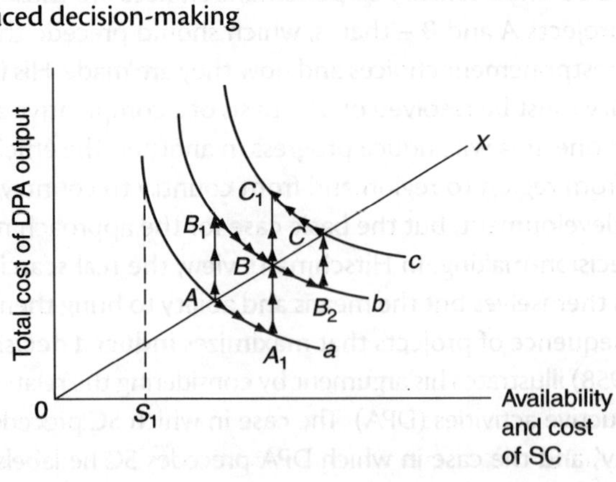

other domestic activities. Forward linkages measure the proportion of an activity's output that does not go to meet final demand but is used as an input into other activities. With knowledge of interindustry flows in an economy, with the help of an **input–output table**, it is possible to rank activities according to the magnitude of their combined linkage effects. Hirschman is suggesting that, within the directly productive sector, a useful development strategy would be to encourage those activities with the potentially highest combined linkages, because this will provide the greatest inducement and incentive to other activities to develop.

Unfortunately, one of the typical characteristics of developing countries is a lack of interdependence between activities. Primary product production has only limited backward linkages with other activities, while forward linkages, although potentially greater, also tend to be limited in practice. Agriculture's demands on other sectors are minimal, and only a comparatively small fraction of total agricultural output in developing countries is processed domestically – most is exported. The fact that manufacturing activities possess greater backward and forward linkages, strengthening the cumulative nature of development, is another powerful argument for industrialization. Hirschman advocates the expansion of industry through the transformation of semi-manufactures into goods required for final demand, or what he calls 'enclave import' industries.

In general, Hirschman (1958) lays great stress on the role of imports in the development process, seeing imports as part of the inducement mechanism. For not only can semi-manufactured imports be processed into goods for final demand, but final demand imports themselves can then be readily produced at home once the market has attained a certain size (or production threshold). If one of the major obstacles to development is a shortage of decision-makers, coupled with uncertainty and a limited market, the existence of imports provides conclusive proof that the market is there. As imports increase, so too do the chances that domestic production will one day be profitable. Hirschman criticizes developing countries for restricting imports prematurely, and argues that infant industry protection should only be given after imports have reached such a level as to guarantee domestic producers a market for their goods.

Investment criteria

Traditional micro-theory teaches that under perfect competition, resources will be optimally allocated when each factor of production is employed up to the point where its marginal product is equal to its price, and that society's output (welfare) will be maximized when the marginal products of factors are equated in all their uses. This is the so-called 'marginal rule' for resource allocation and implies 'efficiency', in the sense that a society's total output of goods and services could not be increased by any redistribution of resources between activities because each factor of production is equally productive in existing activities. In static analysis, therefore, 'efficiency' in resource allocation implies maximizing the national product, which is achieved when the marginal products of factors are equated in their different uses.

If the application of the marginal rule leads to an efficient allocation of resources, what is the allocation 'problem' in developing countries? Why seek other criteria to decide on the allocation of resources? One good reason is that the assumptions of traditional micro-theory do not accord with the realities or aspirations of developing countries. Two major drawbacks of the application of the marginal rule may be cited. One is that the marginal rule is a static criterion, and as we have said before, it is by no means certain that the aim of developing countries is, or ought to be, the maximization of the *present* level of output, consumption or welfare. Second, traditional static theory ignores many factors that may have a bearing on the *social* optimum allocation of resources. In countries characterized by fundamental structural disequilibria and extreme imperfections in the market, it cannot be assumed that the market prices of goods and factors of production reflect the social costs and benefits of production. The application of the marginal rule will only lead to a *socially* optimal allocation of resources in the absence of divergences between market prices and social costs and benefits, or if market prices are corrected to reflect social values.

Several factors can lead to divergences between market prices and the social valuation of goods and factors of production. First, if external economies and increasing returns are attached to some projects, their social value will exceed their private value, and the application of the marginal rule must make allowances for this, if output is to be maximized from a given endowment of factors.

Second, if perfect competition does not prevail in the product market, product prices will not reflect society's valuation of those products, and market prices must somehow be adjusted to achieve a social optimum. Similarly, if perfect competition does not prevail in the factor market, the price of factors will not reflect their opportunity cost to society, so that employing factors up to the point where their marginal product equals their price will not produce a social optimum. Underemployed resources such as labour will be overvalued, and scarce resources such as capital and foreign exchange will be undervalued, and market prices must therefore be corrected to reflect the value of these resources to society.

Third, static analysis ignores the future structure of product and factor prices arising from the choice of projects in the present. An optimum resource allocation in the present may not produce an optimal allocation of resources in the future. The only way of coping with this difficulty is through what is called the **programming approach to resource allocation**, by which the repercussions of one activity on others are explicitly considered and due allowance is made for time.

Finally, the application of the marginal rule can only lead to optimal resource allocation if income distribution is 'optimal' and remains unaffected by whatever programme is decided on. If a new pattern of resource allocation alters income distribution, output may be maximized but welfare diminished because of 'undesirable' changes in the distribution of income gains. To say anything concrete on this score requires an explicit statement of societal objectives, or a **social welfare function**, if interpersonal comparisons of utility are to be avoided. Presumably, there might be a fair degree of consensus that an income distribution that leaves half the population unemployed and starving is 'inferior' to one that does not. Only the conditions for Pareto optimality would deny it (a situation is said to be Pareto optimal only if a change that benefits some does not harm others).

For all the above reasons, there has been a prolonged debate for many years over the most appropriate criterion for resource allocation in the light of the development obstacles of developing countries and their aspirations. The different criteria that have been suggested reflect, by and large, differences of opinion as to what developing countries ought to attempt to maximize, the broad choice being between present and future levels of output and consumption. Most of the criteria discussed by early writers in this field refer to the allocation of capital, reflecting the view of domestic saving as the primary scarce resource. Increasingly, however, attention has been paid to the effects of resource allocation decisions on the balance of payments, in recognition of foreign exchange as an equally scarce resource.

Summary

- In free-market economies, the market mechanism allocates resources among competing ends, but markets in developing countries have many imperfections that need correcting for a social optimum allocation of resources.

- Prices of goods and factors of production may not reflect their social benefit and social cost, respectively, because of positive and negative externalities. Markets may be incomplete or missing entirely. This provides a role for the state.
- The state has four key functions: to correct market imperfections; to provide public goods (such as health and education); to protect the vulnerable; and to provide an institutional environment in which markets can flourish.
- The state may also fail through corruption and rent-seeking behaviour. There are many 'failed states' in the world in which institutions and the rule of law have broken down.
- Many developing countries practise development planning, with various degrees of success.
- The central question facing all developing countries is how to allocate resources to maximize the level or growth of per capita output with the domestic resources available, and how to minimize the use of foreign exchange (which is a scarce resource).
- Apart from the decision of how much to invest, there are three broad types of allocation decisions: which sectors to invest in, which projects should receive priority, and which combination of factors of production should be used, which will determine the technology of production.
- In addition, countries need to decide on the balance between agriculture and industry, the extent to which static comparative advantage is allowed to dictate production, the balance between present and future consumption, and whether growth should be 'balanced' (between sectors) or deliberately unbalanced.

Chapter 9 Discussion questions

1. What is the role of markets in the development process?
2. Distinguish the different types of market failure, and the role that governments can play in rectifying market failures.
3. According to the World Bank (1997), what are the key roles of the state in developing countries, and how can the role of the state be made more effective?
4. What causes corruption, and how can it be reduced?
5. What are the major causes of divergences between the market prices of goods and the value of those goods to society?
6. What are the characteristics of failed states?
7. What are the major causes of divergences between the market prices of factors of production and their cost to society?
8. Why do developing countries construct development plans?
9. Why is there a potential clash between present and future consumption, and how can it be reconciled?
10. What do you understand by the concept of 'balanced growth'?
11. What is Hirschman's major criticism of the doctrine of balanced growth?

Notes

1. In many developed countries, the state is even more pervasive in terms of expenditure, although a much higher proportion represents social security transfer payments, not expenditure on real resources.
2. Students should familiarize themselves with a plan for a country of their choosing.
3. This conclusion depends on, among other things, the wage rate being invariant with respect to the technique of production. If the wage is higher the more capital-intensive the technique, this conclusion would have to be modified. For a discussion of this point, and other considerations that may lessen the conflict between employment and saving in the choice of techniques, see Chapter 6.

Websites on government and corruption

Role of the state

World Bank www.worldbank.org/en/topic/governance

International Development Department (University of Birmingham) www.birmingham.ac.uk/schools/government-society/departments/international-development/index.aspx

Corruption

Transparency International www.transparency.org

Internet Center for Corruption Research www.icgg.org

III

THE PERPETUATION OF UNDERDEVELOPMENT

10

DUALISM, CENTRE–PERIPHERY MODELS AND THE PROCESS OF CUMULATIVE CAUSATION

Introduction

It is easy to argue that poverty and backwardness are due to a general shortage and inefficient use of the key factors of production; it is much harder to determine precisely why there should be a dearth of some factors and an abundance of others, and why development may be a slow and lengthy process. It is certainly impossible to explain current international discrepancies in the level of development with reference to *initial* differences in factor endowments. The present development gap in the world economy has arisen largely through industrial development in certain selected areas of the world, which, in turn, has generated its *own* factor endowments. The purpose here, however, is not to consider why some countries were able to industrialize sooner than others, but rather to consider some of the mechanisms through which divisions in the world economy, and unequal advantage between developed and developing countries, are perpetuated.

First, the **dualistic structure** of developing countries will be considered. Then we shall examine Gunnar Myrdal's model of the process of **circular and cumulative causation**, which can be applied to regions and countries alike (Myrdal, [1957] 1963). We shall see that Myrdal's model is one of many that can be used to understand the perpetuation of the development gap and divergences between North and South or between the 'centre' (industrialized) countries and the 'periphery' (primary producing) countries.

The pioneering models of Raúl Prebisch and Nicholas Kaldor will be examined in this context, and their similarities emphasized. We will then discuss the **new economic geography**, which has links with the model of cumulative causation, and the role of geographic factors that seem to be associated with divisions in the world economy. Finally, we shall briefly discuss models of **unequal exchange** and **dependency**, which emphasize alternative institutional and economic mechanisms making for international inequality in the world economy.

Dualism

The term 'dualism' describes a condition in which developing countries usually find themselves in the early stages of development, which can have implications for the future pattern and pace of development. There are a number of possible definitions and interpretations of 'dualism', but the term is used mainly to refer to the economic and social divisions in an economy, such as differences in the level of technology between sectors or regions, differences in the degree of geographic development, and differences in social customs and attitudes between the rural and urban sectors of developing countries.

Dualism in all its aspects is a concomitant of the growth of a money economy, which, as we saw in Chapter 5, may either arise naturally as a result of specialization or be imposed from outside. Basically, therefore, a dual economy is characterized by a difference in social customs between the subsistence and exchange sectors of the economy, by a gap between the levels of technology in the rural subsistence sector and the industrial monetized sector, and often by a gap in the level of per capita income between regions of a country if the money economy and industrial development are geographically concentrated. In fact, it is not unusual for **geographic**, **social** and **technological dualism** to occur together, with each type of dualism tending to reinforce the other. Also, the more 'progressive' sectors typically have favourable access to scarce factors of production, which is a major cause of the persistence of dualism. **Urban bias** plays an important part in this process (Lipton, 1977).

The first question to ask is: What development problems does the existence of dualism pose for an economy, and how can dualism impede and retard development? As far as **social dualism** is concerned, the obstacles are similar to those presented by a traditional society with no modern exchange sector at all. The task is one of providing incentives in the subsistence sector and drawing the subsistence sector into the money economy. The fact that the indigenous subsistence sector may be reluctant to alter its traditional way of life and respond to incentives is not peculiar to a dual economy. It is therefore true that underdevelopment tends to be associated with social dualism, but it would be misleading to regard social dualism as an underlying *cause* of backwardness and poverty. It is difficult to argue that development would be more rapid in the absence of a monetary sector, from which the existence of dualism stems. Even if the growth of the exchange sector makes little impact on attitudes in the indigenous sector, it is difficult to envisage any progress without the growth of the money economy. In short, it seems more realistic to regard social dualism as an inevitable consequence of development rather than as a basic cause of underdevelopment itself.

Similar reservations can be raised over whether it is accurate to describe **technological dualism** as a cause of underdevelopment. As with social dualism, it is probably more realistic to regard it as an inevitable feature of the development process. Two disadvantages are commonly associated with technological dualism. The first is that where technological dualism is the result of a foreign enclave, a proportion of the profits generated in the industrial sector will be remitted to the home country, reducing the level of saving and investment below what it might have been. The second disadvantage is more fundamental, but difficult to avoid. If in the rural, or non-monetized, sector of the economy, production processes are characterized by labour-intensive techniques and variable technical coefficients of production, while production processes in the industrial, technologically advanced sector are capital-intensive and possess relatively fixed technical coefficients, it is possible that the technology of the industrial sector may impede the progress of the rural agricultural sector. First, relatively fixed technical coefficients (that is, a low elasticity of substitution between factors) means that labour can be absorbed from agriculture into industry only as fast as the growth of capital, and second, capital intensity itself will restrict employment opportunities in the industrial sector, contributing to urban unemployment and perpetuating underdevelopment in the rural sector. Hence, productivity growth in the agricultural sector, which is recognized as being necessary to establish a secure basis for take-off into sustained growth, may be slowed down.

It is true that if the technology of the modern sector (imported or otherwise) does embody fixed technological coefficients, it may be difficult for an economy to use the socially optimum combination of factors, but this disadvantage must be weighed against the favourable impact on productivity stemming from the more advanced technology. If capital accumulation and technical progress, and the development of an industrial sector – in addition to agricultural development – are essential for raising the level of per capita income, it is difficult to see how technological dualism can be avoided, at least in the early stages of development. The best that can be done is, first, to encourage the widespread application and rapid assimilation of technical progress throughout all sectors of the economy, and, second, to ensure the 'proper' pricing of factors of production to prevent the introduction of a technology that may be profitable to private individuals but does not maximize the returns to society at large because factor prices do not adequately reflect relative factor endowments. But even a technology that is socially optimal in this sense may not be the technology that provides the soundest basis for sustained growth in the long run. The question of the choice of techniques was discussed in detail in Chapter 6, and the issue of the 'social' pricing of factors of production can be found on this book's website (www.palgravehighered.com/Thirlwall-Econ-Of-Dev-10e).

The process of cumulative causation

The hypothesis of cumulative causation as an explanation of the backwardness of developing nations is associated with Gunnar Myrdal ([1957] 1963), the well-known Swedish economist who won the Nobel Prize for Economics in 1974. Basically, it is a hypothesis of **geographic dualism**, applicable to nations and regions within nations, which can be advanced to account for the persistence of spatial differences in a wide variety of development indices, including wage rates, per capita income, employment growth rates and levels of unemployment. As such, the process of cumulative causation is a direct challenge to static equilibrium theory, which predicts that the working of economic and social forces will cause spatial differences to narrow.

Myrdal ([1957] 1963) contends that, in the context of development, economic and social forces produce tendencies towards *disequilibrium*, and that the assumption in economic theory that disequilibrium situations tend towards equilibrium is false. If this were not so, how can we explain the tendency for international and regional differences in living standards to widen? Thus, Myrdal replaces the assumption of stable equilibrium with what he calls the hypothesis of **circular and cumulative causation**, arguing that the use of this hypothesis can go a long way towards explaining why international differences in levels of development, and interregional differences in development within nations, may persist and even widen over time.

Myrdal ([1957] 1963) first considers the hypothesis in the context of a geographically dual economy, describing how, through the mechanisms of **labour migration, capital movements** and **trade**, the existence of dualism not only retards the development of backward regions but can also slow up the development of the whole economy. To describe the process of circular and cumulative causation, let us start off with a country in which all regions have attained the same stage of development, as measured by the same level of per capita income, or by similar levels of productivity and wages in the same occupations. Then assume that an exogenous shock produces a disequilibrium situation, with development proceeding more rapidly in one region than another. The proposition is that economic and social forces will tend to strengthen the disequilibrium situation by leading to cumulative expansion in the favoured region at the expense of other regions, which then become comparatively worse off, retarding their future development.

Gunnar Myrdal

Born 1898, Skattungbyn, Sweden. Died 1987. Politician, economist and prolific writer in several fields of economics. One of the architects of the Swedish welfare state in the 1930s. His early work in macroeconomics anticipated Keynes' *General Theory*. In development economics, best known for his challenge to equilibrium theory, and the notion of 'circular and cumulative causation', in books such as *An American Dilemma: The Negro Problem and Modern Democracy* (1944) and *Economic Theory and Underdeveloped Regions* (1957). Also wrote a massive three-volume tome, *Asian Drama: An Inquiry into the Poverty of Nations* (1968). Awarded the Nobel Prize for Economics, 1974.

This contrasts with neoclassical equilibrium theory, which assumes that, through the process of factor mobility, wage rates and the rate of profit will equalize across regions. According to neoclassical theory, in places where labour is scarce and capital is abundant, labour will flow in and capital will flow out, thus reducing wages and raising the rate of profit, while in less prosperous areas where labour is abundant, labour will flow out and capital will flow in, raising wages and reducing the rate of profit.

In contrast, what Myrdal ([1957] 1963) has in mind is a type of multiplier–accelerator mechanism producing increasing returns in the favoured region. Instead of leading to equality, the forces of supply and demand interact with each other to produce cumulative movements away from spatial equilibrium. Since the wage level is the basic determinant of per capita income, let us take the example of wages and wage differences to illustrate the kind of process that Myrdal has in mind. Take two regions, *A* and *B* (for example, northern and southern Italy), and assume that wages are determined by supply and demand, as in Figures 10.1 and 10.2.

Suppose to start with that wage levels are identical in the two regions, that is, $W_A = W_B$. Then assume that a stimulus of some sort causes the demand for labour, and therefore wages, to rise in region *A* relative to region *B*; that is, the demand curve for labour in region *A* shifts to D_1D_1, causing wages to rise to W_{A1}. Since labour tends to respond to differences in economic opportunities of this sort, the wage discrepancy may be assumed to induce labour migration from region *B* to region *A*. Equilibrium theory then predicts that there will be a tendency for wage levels to be equalized once more through a *reduction* in labour supply in region *B* from *SS* to S_1S_1 and an

Figure 10.1 Region *A*

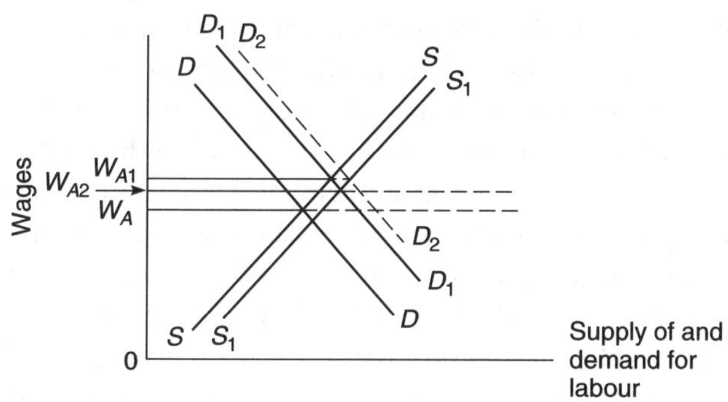

Figure 10.2 Region *B*

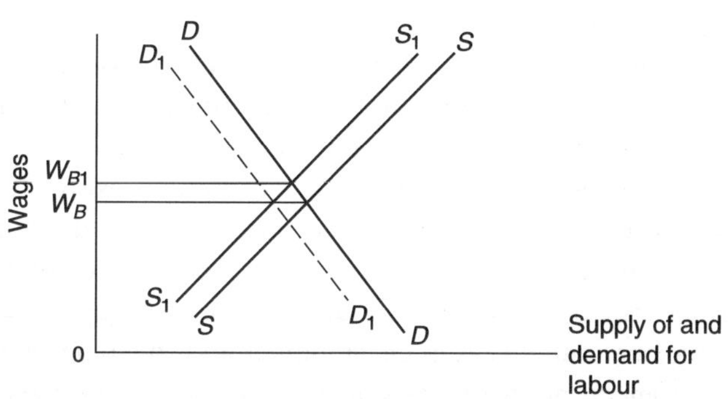

increase in labour supply in region *A* from *SS* to S_1S_1, giving a wage in region *A* of W_{A2}, equal to a wage in *B* of W_{B1}.

According to the hypothesis of cumulative causation, however, changes in supply may be expected to react on demand in such a way as to counteract the tendency towards equilibrium. Migration from region *B* denudes the area of human capital and entrepreneurs, and depresses the local demand for goods and services and factors of production, while movements into region *A*, on the other hand, will tend to stimulate enterprise and the demand for products, adding to the demand for factors of production. In short, migration from region *B* will cause the demand curve for labour to shift to the left, say to D_1D_1, and migration into region A will cause the demand curve for labour to shift further to the right, say to D_2D_2, causing the initial wage discrepancy at least to persist, if not widen (if the shifts in demand are greater than those assumed). Thus, once development differences appear, a chain of cumulative expansion in the favoured region is set in motion, and this has what Myrdal ([1957] 1963) calls a **backwash effect** on other regions, causing development differences in general to persist or even diverge.

Capital movements and **trade** also play a part in the process of cumulative causation. In a free market, capital, like labour, will tend to move to where the prospective return is highest, and this will be to the region where demand is buoyant (not necessarily the region where the wage is lowest, as in neoclassical theory). Capital, labour and entrepreneurship will tend to migrate together. The benefits of trade will also accrue to the host region. Regions within a nation using a common currency cannot have balance of payments difficulties in the normal sense, but the maintenance of employment depends on the ability to export, otherwise unemployment will appear. If production is subject to increasing returns, the region experiencing the rapid growth of factor supplies will be able to increase its competitive advantage over the relatively lagging regions containing smaller scale industries, and increase its real income accordingly. In this same way, the general freeing and widening of international markets and the expansion of world trade will tend to favour the more rapidly growing regions within nation-states.

The impact of immigration into the expanding region is also likely to induce improvements in transport and communications and education and health facilities, improving efficiency and productivity and widening still further the competitive advantage of the growing region over the lagging regions experiencing emigration of the factors of production.

Such is the potential strength of the backwash effects of the process of circular and cumulative causation that Albert Hirschman (1958), eminent development economist, once suggested that lagging regions may possibly be better off if they became sovereign political states. If a lagging area was an independent 'country', the mobility of factors of production could be more easily controlled, competition between the leading and lagging regions could be reduced, each region could more easily concentrate on producing goods in which it possessed a comparative cost advantage, separate exchange rates could be fixed for the two regions, and regions could more easily protect themselves.

Despite these potential advantages of nationhood for a backward region, Hirschman (1958) argues against sovereignty because he believes that the forces making for the interregional transmission of growth are likely to be more powerful than those making for 'international' transmission.

Hirschman (1958) recognizes, however, the continued existence of backwash effects and argues that, to offset them, a nation that is concerned with developing its backward regions should provide certain equivalents of sovereignty, such as a separate tax system and the right to protect certain activities. Policies must be designed to reduce what he calls the **polarization effects** of interregional differences in development and to strengthen the **trickle-down effects**. The 'trickle-down' effects are the favourable repercussions on backward regions emanating from expanding regions, which Myrdal ([1957] 1963) calls **spread effects**. These trickle-down or spread effects consist mainly of an increased demand for the backward areas' products and the diffusion of technology and knowledge. In Myrdal's view, the spread effects are weaker than the backwash effects, and if interregional differences are to be narrowed, nations must rely on state intervention through regional policies. The only alternative is to wait for a natural end to the process of cumulative causation.

A time must eventually come when increasing costs in the expanding region will halt expansion. The higher costs of living, and the external diseconomies produced by congestion, will ultimately outweigh the benefits of greater efficiency and higher money returns to the factors of production. The process of migration will then be halted, and possibly reversed. This stage has now been reached in some developed countries. The question for governments with certain growth and welfare objectives is whether they can afford to let the process take its natural course, and to tolerate the inequalities that may arise before the process ends. High levels of inequality can lead to negative social, economic and political consequences that have a destabilizing effect on societies, causing insecurity and social unrest. In practice, governments in many advanced countries have taken active steps for many years to redress regional imbalances, and this is one reason why regional disparities tend to be less in advanced countries than in developing countries. In developing countries, however, Myrdal ([1957] 1963) was of the view that, far from lessening regional inequalities, the state has been a positive force in their persistence: 'In many of the poorer countries the natural drift towards inequalities has been supported and magnified by built-in feudal and other inegalitarian institutions and power structures which aid the rich in exploiting the poor.' This is still true in many poor countries today.

Regional inequalities

The international cross-section evidence on regional inequalities, and time-series evidence for individual countries, suggests that the degree of inequality follows an inverted U-shaped curve; that is, regional inequalities first rise with the level of development and then decrease. This pattern is not hard to explain. Very poor countries are uniformly poor. Regional differences then first emerge as a result of some favourable shock to one region or set of regions – for example an export enclave or the establishment of industrial activities. Once a difference has emerged, it will tend to be widened by the processes already described. In the early stages of development, migration from poor to richer regions will tend to be selective because only those with skills and education will be able to afford to migrate. Capital will tend to locate in the more dynamic region(s). Spread effects emanating from prosperous regions will be weak, owing to a general lack of political and economic integration.

The factors that accentuate differences in the early stages of development, however, will tend to weaken with time as countries get richer:

- migration will become less selective
- the spread effects will become more powerful
- industrialization will tend to spread and the size of the agricultural sector shrink
- external diseconomies of expansion and congestion in expanding regions will worsen, curbing capital and labour migration from poor to rich regions
- governments may also attempt to rectify imbalances through the implementation of regional policies.

The empirical evidence shows that regional disparities in output and income per head are much more unequal in developing countries than in developed countries.

Shankar and Shah (2003) look at trends in regional inequality over time in 14 developing countries and find inequalities increasing – or moving up an inverted U-shaped curve. Rodriguez-Pose and Gill (2006) also show this in a study of India, China and Mexico since 1980, and find that the growth of regional inequalities is significantly related to the shift of trade from primary to manufactured exports. This trade effect is greater, the larger the share of trade in GDP and the greater the shift. Regional inequalities continue to rise in India – see Case example 10.1.

Case example 10.1 **Regional disparities in per capita income in India**

India comprises 28 states and 4 union territories. There are huge regional differences in living standards measured by per capita income, ranging from 12,000 rupees a year in Bihar (the poorest state) to nearly 100,000 rupees per capita in Goa. These are the product of history and past growth experience.

Regional differences in living standards can have serious implications for the economic and political functioning of national economies. Inflationary pressure in prosperous regions can spread to poorer regions reducing real living standards. Political resentment can arise and disillusionment with the political process, leading to social unrest.

Over the period 1999–2011, regional disparities in India have widened, as measured by the standard deviation of per capita incomes, from 0.18 to 0.23 (see Chapter 2 for how standard deviation is measured). The growth of these divisions is related mainly to the higher share of agriculture in the poorer regions, the faster growth of population, and the lower rate of investment in physical and human capital. What is happening in India is supportive of Myrdal's model of circular and cumulative causation, and bodes ill for the large percentage of the Indian population that lives in the poorest states where life is already wretched.

Source: Cherodian and Thirlwall, 2015.

The experience of developing countries contrasts with what is happening in most developed countries, including the USA and the European Union. In the USA, Barro and Sala-í-Martin (1992) show that a process of regional per capita income convergence has been going on over the past 100 years. Taking personal income data, they find an inverse relation across US states between the average growth of per capita income over the period 1880–1988 and the initial (1880) level of per capita income. Only two subperiods, 1920–30 and 1980–88, show evidence of divergence.

In Europe, the evidence is more mixed. Across the regions of Europe, there is some evidence of per capita income convergence in the postwar years up to 1980, but not thereafter. Regional unemployment rate differences, however, both within Europe as a whole and within industrial countries, have remained very stubborn. Fagerberg and Verspagen (1996) took 70 regions in six EU countries and showed income convergence up to 1980, but not since. The authors argued that the scope for convergence is not exhausted, but other factors in the 1980s pushed towards divergence, particularly differences in unemployment and the R&D effort between industrial and agricultural regions.

Indeed, it appears to be the case from a further study by Fagerberg et al. (1996) that regional differences in per capita income are systematically related to differences in unemployment rates. They took 64 regions in Germany, France, Italy and Spain over the period 1980–90 and found that the growth in poor regions was hampered by unfavourable industrial structure and weak R&D effort. There was evidence of convergence, but only after allowing for differences in industrial structure, R&D effort, population density and migration. Interestingly, labour migration was found to have a strong positive impact on per capita income growth, indicating that migration was disequilibrating during this period. The policy implications are that the predominance of agriculture is a barrier to growth in poor regions, mainly because the scope for scale economies and R&D is less than in industry. Greater regional balance requires structural change in favour of industrial activities, but this, in turn, requires an appropriate physical infrastructure and the provision of human capital.

International inequality and centre–periphery models

The process of circular and cumulative causation is also used by Myrdal ([1957] 1963) in an attempt to explain **widening international differences** in the level of development from similar initial conditions. Through the mechanisms of labour migration, capital movements and trade, international inequalities are perpetuated in exactly the same way as regional inequalities within nations. Myrdal argues that, through trade, the developing countries have been forced into the production of goods, notably primary products, with inelastic demand with respect to both price and income. This has put developing countries at a grave disadvantage compared with developed countries with respect to balance of payments and availability of foreign exchange. Moreover, with the tendency for the efficiency wage (that is, the money wage in relation to labour productivity) to fall in faster-growing areas relative to other areas, developed countries have gained a cumulative competitive trading advantage, especially in manufactured commodities. Myrdal, of course, is not alone in this view, and we shall elaborate below on other models that stress the unequal gains and balance of payments effects of trade as the main mechanisms through which international differences in development are perpetuated, including the contribution of the new economic geography pioneered by Krugman (1991).

Williamson argues, in his book *Trade and Poverty: Why the Third World Fell Behind* (2013), that divergence in the world economy between 'centre' and 'periphery' coincided with globalization in the nineteenth century that led to increased specialization of manufacturing industry in Europe and the USA, combined with increased specialization in primary products in the rest of the world. In the periphery, industrialization was thwarted by the rent-seeking behaviour of landowners, and price and income volatility slowed its growth compared to the 'centre'. Trade benefited the centre at the expense of the periphery.

In the case of capital movements, Myrdal ([1957] 1963) argues in the same vein; because the risks associated with investment tend to be higher in developing countries, the natural tendency will be for developing countries to be net exporters of capital. In practice, because of the large volume of capital from international lending organizations, and the favourable tax treatment of foreign direct investment, developing countries are generally net importers of long-term capital, although the short-term capital account tends to be adverse. The fact remains, however, as Lucas (1990) points out, that capital flows mainly to regions already rich. With regard to foreign direct investment, the richest countries receive over 80% of flows, while the poorest countries (excluding China) receive less than 5%.

The potential weakness of Myrdal's hypothesis at the international level concerns the effects of labour migration. The international migration of labour from developing to developed countries can have beneficial as well as harmful effects on backward economies. The greatest deleterious effect on backward economies is the obvious one of possible loss of human capital, although even here, if the human capital is unemployed, migration may not be a serious loss. But it is not only the skilled and educated that may be induced to leave their native lands. Unskilled labour may also respond to the existence of better employment opportunities elsewhere. If it is argued that developing countries suffer from underemployment, and that productivity is low owing to surplus labour, the emigration of unskilled labour could be a substantial benefit to developing countries. It is possible, for example, that emigration has helped to raise per capita income in some countries, such as Mexico, Pakistan and Bangladesh, while improving the balance of payments through remittances by emigrants to their home countries. Migrant remittances now amount to over $500 billion a year, exceeding the level of official development assistance to developing countries (see Chapter 15). In this important respect, generous immigration policies in developed countries can provide a valuable means of development assistance.

Even so, any potential gain from unrestricted labour mobility is unlikely to offset the international backwash effects arising from trade and international capital movements. Even with unrestricted migration, therefore, there would still be a tendency for international differences in the level of development to widen through trade and the free movement of capital. The existence of international spread effects gives no reason for modifying this conclusion. International spread effects are relatively weak – certainly weaker than the spread effects within nations.

What, then, should be our verdict on the hypothesis of cumulative causation? Given that the hypothesis assumes free trade and free mobility of the factors of production, it perhaps contains more force with respect to interregional differences in development within countries than international differences between countries. On the other hand, it cannot be dismissed lightly when discussing the development gap in the world economy. In view of the fact that there has been no tendency in the recent past for international per capita income levels to converge (see Chapters 2 and 4), the hypothesis is not refuted by the evidence. In particular, the present international trading and payments position of developing countries does not inspire confidence that the total gains from trade between developed and developing countries are distributed equitably (see Chapters 15 and 16).

The contribution of the hypothesis of cumulative causation to an understanding of development and underdevelopment is its emphasis on economic and social development as a cumulative phenomenon and, more important, its challenge to static equilibrium theory; that is, that regions or nations that gain an initial advantage may maintain that advantage to the detriment of development elsewhere. At its root is the phenomenon of increasing returns, defined broadly as the accumulation of productive advantages of the type discussed in Chapter 6 relating to how societies progress technologically.

Two models of 'regional' growth rate differences: Prebisch and Kaldor

While the Myrdal model of centre and periphery emphasizes the process of cumulative causation working through increasing returns and competitiveness in favoured regions, other centre–periphery models stress the balance of payments implications of the particular pattern of production and trade between rich and poor countries, which arise from the fact that industrial goods produced and traded by rich countries have a higher income elasticity of demand than goods produced and traded by poor countries. One of the earliest models, powerful in its simplicity, is that of Raúl Prebisch, well-known Argentinian economist (1901–86).

Raúl Prebisch

Born 1901, Tucuan, Argentina. Died 1986. Argentina's most famous economist; mixed economics and politics on the national and international stage. Architect and first president of the Central Bank of Argentina in his early thirties; first director of the Economic Commission for Latin America, 1948, and first secretary-general of UNCTAD, 1964. 'Father' of Latin American structuralist thinking; worked tirelessly for a fairer deal for poor countries in the world trading system. First to document, with Hans Singer, the historical decline in terms of trade of primary commodities: the Prebisch–Singer thesis.

The Prebisch model[1]

Consider a two-country, two-commodity model in which the advanced centre produces and exports manufactured goods with an **income elasticity of demand**[2] greater than unity, and the backward periphery produces and exports primary commodities with an income elasticity of demand less than unity. Let us suppose that the income elasticity of demand for manufactures (e_m) is 1.3, and the income elasticity of demand for primary commodities (e_p) is 0.8. Assume to start with that the growth rates of income of both centre and periphery are equal to 3%, that is, $g_c = g_p = 3.0$. What will be the growth of exports (x) and imports (m) in the centre and periphery? For the centre, we have:

$$x_c = g_p \times e_m = 3.0 \times 1.3 = 3.9\%$$

$$m_c = g_c \times e_p = 3.0 \times 0.8 = 2.4\%$$

and for the periphery, we have:

$$x_p = g_c \times e_p = 3.0 \times 0.8 = 2.4\%$$

$$m_p = g_p \times e_m = 3.0 \times 1.3 = 3.9\%$$

With imports growing faster than exports in the periphery, this is not a sustainable position, unless the periphery can finance an ever-growing balance of payments deficit on the current account by capital inflows. If it cannot, and balance of payments equilibrium on the current account is a requirement, there must be some adjustment to raise the rate of growth of exports or reduce the rate of growth of imports. Now suppose we rule out the possibility that relative prices measured in a common currency (or real exchange rate) can change as an adjustment mechanism, the only adjustment mechanism left (barring protection) is a reduction in the periphery's growth rate to reduce the rate of growth of imports in line with the rate of growth of exports. From the model, we can solve for the necessary growth rate of the periphery to keep trade balanced. On the assumptions outlined, we must have $m_p = x_p$ or $g_p e_m = x_p$ and therefore:

$$g_p = \frac{x_p}{e_m} = \frac{2.4}{1.3} = 1.846$$

Thus, the growth rate of the periphery is constrained to 1.846%, compared with 3% in the centre. In these circumstances, both the relative and the absolute gap in income between periphery and centre will widen. Notice, in fact, that since the growth of the periphery's exports is equal to $g_c \times e_p$, we can write the above equation as:

$$g_p = \frac{g_c \times e_p}{e_m}$$

and dividing through by g_c, we reach the interesting result that the relative growth rates of the periphery and centre will equal the ratio of the income elasticity of demand for the two countries' commodities:

$$\frac{g_p}{g_c} = \frac{e_p}{e_m}$$

This result will hold as long as current account equilibrium on the balance of payments is a requirement, and relative price adjustment in international trade is either ruled out as an adjustment mechanism to rectify balance of payments disequilibrium or does not work. To avoid the consequences of this model, Prebisch (1959) argued the case for protection and import substitution, which, in effect, is a policy to reduce e_m, which for the periphery is the propensity to import manufactured goods. We reserve discussion of the relative merits of protection until Chapter 15 on trade policy.

Kaldor's model of regional growth rate differences

It is possible to combine the ideas of Myrdal with the insights of Prebisch in a single model, which focuses on the role of export growth in the development process in an open economy and in which the Prebisch result emerges as a special case if relative prices are fixed and trade is balanced. Kaldor's model (1970) is applicable to regions and open developing economies alike.[3] It takes as its starting point the not unreasonable assumption that the output of an open economy is demand-determined, not supply-constrained, and that it is the long-run growth of autonomous demand that governs the long-run rate of growth of output. The main component of autonomous demand in an open economy is, in turn, demand coming from outside the region; that is, the demand for the region's exports. The model is a variant of **export-base models of development**, which stress the importance of exports as a leading sector. The hypothesis is that once a region obtains a growth advantage, it will tend to sustain it at the expense of other regions because faster growth leads to faster productivity growth (the so-called **Verdoorn effect**, see Chapter 3), which keeps the region competitive in the export of goods that gave the region its growth advantage in the first place. Success breeds success, and failure breeds failure. In this section, attention will be confined to outlining the model. An examination of the international evidence of the relation between the growth of exports and the growth of output in developing countries will be left until Chapter 15.

Let:

$$g_t = \gamma(x_t) \tag{10.1}$$

where g_t is the rate of growth of output in time t, x_t is the rate of growth of exports in time t, γ is the (constant) elasticity of output with respect to export growth (= 1 if exports are a constant proportion of output) and t is time. Apart from the theoretical considerations underlying the specification of equation (10.1), that the rate of growth of the economy as a whole will be governed by the rate of growth of autonomous demand, there are a number of practical considerations that make export demand for highly specialized regions (or countries) extremely important for demand and supply. For most industries in a region, local demand is likely to be trivial compared with the optimum production capacity of the industries. The viability of regional enterprise must largely depend on the strength of demand from outside the region.

There are also a number of important reasons why export demand may be a more potent growth-inducing force than other elements of demand, especially in open, backward areas – regions or countries:

1. Exports allow regional specialization, which may bring dynamic as well as static gains.
2. Exports permit imports, and imports may be important in developing areas that lack the capacity to produce development goods themselves.
3. If the exchange of information and technical knowledge is linked to trade, exporting facilitates the flow of technical knowledge, which can improve the area's supply capacity.

Now let us consider the determinants of export demand and the form of the export demand function. It is conventional to specify exports as a multiplicative (or constant elasticity) function of relative prices measured in a common currency and foreign income. Thus:

$$X_t = \left(\frac{P_{dt}}{P_{ft}}\right)^{\eta} Z_t^{\epsilon} \tag{10.2}$$

where X is the quantity of exports in time t, P_d is the domestic price in time t, P_f is the foreign price measured in domestic currency in time t, Z is foreign income in time t, η is the price elasticity of demand for exports (< 0) and ε is the income elasticity of demand for exports (> 0). Taking logarithms of the variables and differentiating with respect to time gives:

$$x_t = \eta(p_{dt} - p_{ft}) + \varepsilon(z_t) \tag{10.3}$$

where the lower-case letters represent the rates of growth of the variables. The rate of growth of income outside the region (z) and the rate of change of competitors' prices (p_f) may both be taken as exogenous to the region. The rate of growth of domestic (export) prices will be endogenous, however. Let us assume that prices are formed on the basis of a constant 'mark-up' on unit labour costs, so that:

$$P_{dt} = \left(\frac{W}{R}\right)_t (T_t) \tag{10.4}$$

where P_d is the domestic price, W is the level of money wages, R is the average product of labour and T is 1+ percentage mark-up on unit labour costs. From equation (10.4), we can write:

$$p_{dt} = w_t - r_t + \tau_t \tag{10.5}$$

where the lower-case letters stand for the rates of change of the variables.

The model becomes 'circular and cumulative' by specifying the growth of labour productivity (r) as partly a function of the growth output itself (Verdoorn's law). If the function is linear, we may write:

$$r_t = r_{at} + \lambda g_t \tag{10.6}$$

where r_{at} is the rate of autonomous productivity growth at time t, and λ is the Verdoorn coefficient (> 0). Equation (10.6) provides the link between exports and growth via productivity growth and prices. Fast export growth leads to fast output growth, and fast output growth leads to fast export growth by making goods more competitive. Combining equations (10.1), (10.3), (10.5) and (10.6) to obtain an expression for the equilibrium growth rate gives:

$$g_t = \frac{\gamma[\eta(w_t - r_{at} + \tau_t - p_{ft}) + \epsilon(z_t)]}{1 + \gamma\eta\lambda} \tag{10.7}$$

Remembering that $\eta < 0$, the growth rate is shown to vary positively with r_a, z, ε, p_f, z and γ, and negatively with w and τ. The effect of η is ambiguous since it appears in both the numerator and the denominator of the equation. It is clear that it is the assumed dependence of productivity growth on the growth of output that gives rise to the possibility that once a region obtains a growth advantage, it will keep it. Suppose, for example, that a region obtains an advantage in the production of goods with a high income elasticity of demand (ε), which causes its growth rate to rise above that of another region. Through the so-called 'Verdoorn effect', productivity growth will be higher, the rate of change of prices lower (other things being the same) and the rate of growth of exports (and hence the rate of growth of output) higher and so on. Moreover, the fact that the region with the initial advantage will obtain a competitive advantage in the produc-

Figure 10.3 Convergent–divergent growth

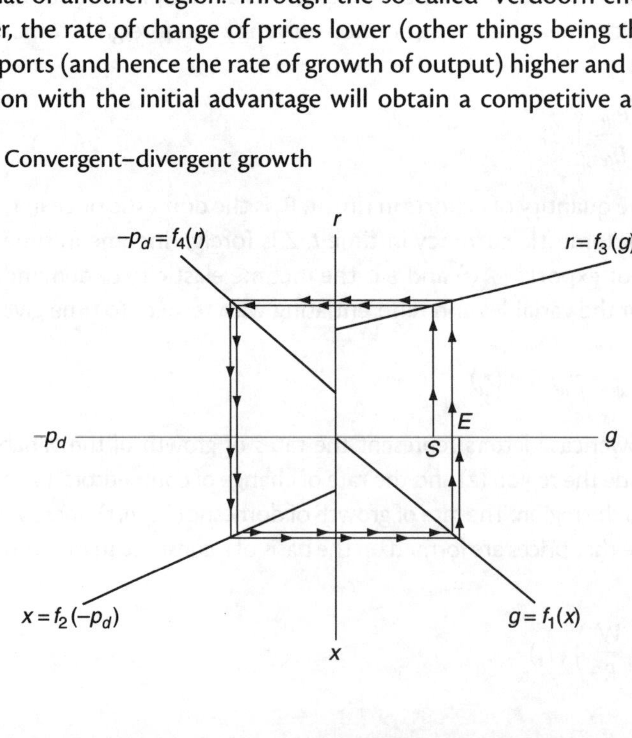

tion of goods with a high income elasticity of demand will mean that it will be difficult for other regions to establish the same activities. This is the essence of the theory of cumulative causation, of divergence between 'centre' and 'periphery' and between industrial (developed) and agricultural (developing) regions (countries). Figure 10.3 illustrates the model graphically.

The distance of each of the linear functions from the origin reflects factors affecting each variable other than the variable specified in the functional relation. From the initial condition, *S*, the growth rate is shown converging to its equilibrium value *E*, as determined in equation (10.7).[4] The link that the Verdoorn relation provides between exports and growth via productivity and prices, and its sustaining influence, is clearly seen. And the greater the dependence of productivity growth on the growth of output (that is, the higher λ), the higher the equilibrium growth rate will be and the greater the divergence between regional growth rates for given differences between regions in the other variables and parameters.

An important implication of the model we have developed is that an autonomous shock will not be sufficient to raise a lagging region's growth rate *permanently* unless the autonomous shock favourably affects the parameters and variables of the model, or is a sustained shock. On these grounds, the relevance of policies of devaluation in a national context, or wage subsidies in a regional context, for improving a region's growth rate may be called into question. What is likely to be required is **structural change**, in particular structural change to improve the demand characteristics of exports. It is recognition of this point that accounts, among other things, for the emphasis placed by developing countries on industrialization and the restructuring of world trade to provide their manufactured goods with easier access to world markets (see Chapter 15).

Note that it is also a property of the model that if relative prices measured in a common currency do not change (that is, $p_{dt} - p_{ft} = 0$), then export growth is determined solely by income growth outside the region or country, and equation (10.7) would reduce to:

$$g_t = \gamma\varepsilon(z_t) \tag{10.8}$$

and if balanced trade is a requirement so that the growth of imports (m) is equal to the growth of exports ($m = x$), we have:

$$g_t\pi = \varepsilon(z_t) \tag{10.9}$$

where π is the income elasticity of demand for imports.

Thus, with relative prices fixed, the growth elasticity with respect to exports (γ) in equation (10.1) must equal the reciprocal of the income elasticity of demand for imports (π) in a balanced trade model such as Prebisch's. Again, we end up with the simple rule that one country's growth rate (g) relative to that of others (z) depends on the ratio of the income elasticity of demand for the country's exports relative to its imports (or the other country's exports in a two-country model), that is, from equation (10.9):

$$\frac{g_t}{z_t} = \frac{\varepsilon}{\pi} \tag{10.10}$$

At the country level, there is substantial empirical support for this simple growth rule, which is discussed more fully in Chapter 16 in connection with the balance of payments and economic development. This growth rule is also known in the literature as **Thirlwall's**

Nicholas Kaldor

Born 1908, Budapest, Hungary. Died 1986. Lecturer and Reader at the London School of Economics 1931–49; then a Fellow of King's College, Cambridge from 1950 and Professor of Economics from 1966. Economic adviser to three British chancellors of the exchequer between 1964 and 1979; tax adviser to many developing countries. Joint architect with Joan Robinson, Richard Kahn and Luigi Pasinetti of post-Keynesian growth and distribution theory, and strong critic of neoclassical equilibrium economics. Famous for his sectoral approach to explaining why growth rates differ between countries. Given a peerage in 1974 as Baron Kaldor of Newham in the city of Cambridge.

law, and **Krugman's 45-degree rule**, after Thirlwall first showed how well the model fitted the growth experience of many countries in the postwar years, and Paul Krugman (1989) showed independently that relative price changes have not been an efficient balance of payments adjustment mechanism and that countries' growth rates relative to others have been equiproportional to the ratio of the income elasticities of demand for imports and exports.[5]

The new economic geography

The **new economic geography**, pioneered by Krugman (1991, 1995, 1998), who received the Nobel Prize in Economics for his contribution, is also an attempt to explain the geographic pattern of economic development between countries, and between regions within countries, in terms of **centripetal forces**, which lead to industrial concentration, and **centrifugal forces**, which lead to industrial dispersal. In this sense, there is an affinity with the cumulative causation model of Myrdal, but in the new economic geography, distance and transport costs play a key role.

There is always a tug of war between centripetal forces, which promote geographic concentration of activities, and centrifugal forces, which oppose it. The centripetal forces, acting as magnets for activity, are mainly the different types of external economies associated with the size of markets and linkages between activities, labour market externalities (pools of skilled labour) and pure externalities such as knowledge spillovers. The centrifugal forces, resisting concentration, are factors such as the immobility of factors of production, high rents in concentrated areas, and pure external diseconomies, such as congestion costs.

Within this framework, the emergence of a 'centre' and 'periphery', and shifts in the geographic pattern of development, can be explained in terms of the changing balance between the pull of the market on the one hand and transport costs on the other. As in the Myrdal model, consider first two identical regions. If transport costs are very high, each region will be more or less self-sufficient. Activity will be widely dispersed serving local markets because it is too costly to transport inputs and outputs elsewhere.

Now suppose that transport costs start to fall. It becomes more economical for some regions to supply the needs of others. Those regions with some small initial advantage, as a result of geography or historical accident, will tend to capitalize on that advantage, exporting to the less favoured region and driving out business. Activity becomes concentrated in a core (or centre), leaving a run-down 'periphery' with only agricultural and service-type activities. A small initial difference between regions leads to a much larger difference in outcomes through the forces of cumulative causation based on external economies associated particularly with market size (**agglomeration economies**). At the regional level, Italy is a good case study. When the railway was introduced and transport costs fell, this made it possible for the factories of northern Italy to supply the needs of less competitive southern Italy, causing the heavy concentration of industrial activity in the north and deindustrialization of the south.

The periphery, however, will tend to have low production costs, particularly low wage costs because of high unemployment and underemployment. At some point, if transport costs fall even more, it may become economical to shift production from the centre to the periphery because low production costs now outweigh the cost of transport to the market. This is one important reason why, in recent years, there has been a major shift of the world's manufacturing base from the core of Europe and North America to the periphery of Southeast Asia.

This set of ideas outlined above helps to explain the historical evolution of divisions between regions and countries of the world, which can spontaneously emerge with better communications, and then go into reverse when transport costs fall even lower (Krugman and Venables, 1995). It is not, however, an equilibrium world; it is an ever-changing world in which economic development in some regions or countries may be precluded altogether.

The World Bank's (2009) *World Development Report 2009: Reshaping Economic Geography* is devoted to this topic and argues that even though in the present circumstances of the world economy, economic growth will be unbalanced (leading to divergence), development can still be inclusive but governments must promote integration through spatially connective infrastructure, spatially targeted incentives and appropriate institutions. The disadvantaged regions (countries) are those that are too small to reap internal and external economies of scale and to attract investment in labour-intensive manufacturing specializing in some part of the productive chain.

Attempts have been made to quantify the impact of distance and transport costs on the level and growth of per capita income of countries across the world, as well as the effect of other geographic variables (e.g. Gallup et al., 1998). Looking at a map of the world by income, two striking relationships are apparent:

1. Countries located close to the sea have higher per capita incomes (PCY) than landlocked countries.
2. Countries located in the tropics are poorer than countries outside the tropics.
3. A third fact (although not visible) is that the coastal, temperate regions of the northern hemisphere have the highest income per square kilometre (km) of land (i.e. PCY × population density).

The regions of North America, Western Europe (and parts of East Asia) that lie within 100 km of the sea contain 13% of the world's population and produce 32% of the world's output of goods and services. The explanation lies in the factors discussed above. Regions near the sea have lower transport costs so they can benefit from greater trade and specialization, and the greater densities of population lead to agglomeration economies and increasing returns. Today, the fastest-growing developing countries have based their growth on labour-intensive manufactured exports located in coastal regions.

Gallup et al. (1998) run regressions across a large sample of countries of the level and growth of PCY against several geographic variables, including:

- the percentage of land in the tropics
- the proportion of the population within 100 km of the coast
- the minimum distance of a country to one of three core 'regions' (New York, Rotterdam and Tokyo)
- the incidence of malaria

- transport costs of a country, measured (imperfectly) as the difference between the cost of imports free on board and their cost including insurance and freight charges.

The level of PCY is found to be negatively related to location in the tropics, malaria, distance and transport costs; and positively related to the proportion of the population close to the sea. The growth of income (holding other variables constant such as education, trade openness) is shown to be 0.9 percentage points (p.p.) less in tropical countries than non-tropical countries; 1.2 p.p. less in countries severely affected by malaria; and 1.0 p.p. less in landlocked countries compared with coastal countries. Distance also significantly reduces growth if the trade openness variable is excluded from the equations.

Given these findings, it is hardly surprising that Africa has some of the poorest and most stagnant economies in the world. Geography is stacked against it.

Theories of dependence and unequal exchange

Apart from the ideas of circular and cumulative causation and balance of payments constrained growth, there are also a number of theories and models in the Marxist tradition (many originating from Latin America and France) concerned with **dependency, exploitation** and **unequal exchange**. These theories attempt to explain the perpetuation and widening of the differences between centre and periphery, and may be regarded as complementary to, and an integral part of, the mechanisms we have been discussing. For example, part of the dependency and unequal exchange relation is related to the characteristics of trade; but there are many other important dimensions to the argument:

- the dependence of the periphery on foreign capital and the expropriation of the surplus by the centre
- the dependence on foreign technology
- terms of trade deterioration
- mechanisms that reduce real wages in developing countries to below what they would otherwise be
- various sociocultural aspects of neocolonialism that thwart the drive for independence and self-reliance.

Pioneer Marxist writers in this tradition include Theotonio dos Santos, Paul Baran, Gunder Frank, Samir Amin and Arghiri Emmanuel. It should be emphasized at the outset that dependency theory cannot easily be tested empirically; rather, it is designed to provide a framework of ideas to accommodate the many aspects and features of the functioning of the world capitalist economy and the many types of dominance and dependency.

Dos Santos (1970) defines dependence thus:

> by dependence we mean a situation in which the economy of certain countries is conditioned by the development and expansion of another economy to which the former is subjected. [The relation is such that] some countries (the dominant ones) can expand and can be self-sustaining, while others (the dependent ones) can do this only as a reflection of expansion, which can have either a positive or a negative effect on their intermediate development.

Unequal development must be seen as an integral part of the world capitalist system. Inequality is inevitable because development of some parts of the system occurs at the expense of others. The monopoly power over trade that is exercised by the centre leads to the transfer of the economic surplus from the dependent countries to the centre, and financial relations that are based on loans and the export of capital by the centre ultimately lead to reverse flows and strengthen the position of the dominant country in the dependent country.

Different forms of dependence can be distinguished, as they have evolved historically:

1. **Colonial dependence**, based on trade and the exploitation of natural resources.
2. **Financial–industrial dependence**, which consolidated itself at the end of the nineteenth century and has geared the economic structure of dependent nations to the needs of the centre.
3. **Technological–industrial dependence**, a new type of dependence that emerged from 1945 based on multinational corporations, which began to invest in industries geared to the internal market of developing countries.

Dos Santos (1970) argues that each of these forms of dependence has so conditioned the internal structure of peripheral countries, that this itself has become part of the dependency relation; for example, the highly dualistic structure, the income inequality and conspicuous consumption of the wealthy classes, a dependency mentality and the ingrained habit of seeking outside help, and the unholy alliance between the domestic ruling elite and foreign interests all conspire to impede internal development. Thus, dos Santos (1973) maintains that dependency is not simply an external phenomenon; it also has to do with the supportive power groups within the poor countries themselves who find the status quo profitable:

> if dependency defines the internal situation and is structurally linked to it, a country cannot break out of it simply by isolating herself from external influence; such action would simply provoke chaos in a society which is of its essence dependent. The only solution therefore would be to change its internal structure; a course which necessarily leads to confrontation with the existing international structure.

Baran (1957), Frank (1967) and Amin (1974) focus their attention more squarely on the traditional Marxist mechanisms by which capitalism in general, and international capitalism in particular, aid the rich in exploiting the poor. Emphasis is placed on the expropriation and transfer of the surplus produced by labour to the owners of capital, which operates at different levels. Think of a cone, the base of which represents the rural poor producing a surplus from their labours in the fields or down the mines. This surplus is first siphoned off by those in the provincial towns, by small employers and merchants. In turn, the wealth of these towns is sapped by the capital cities, and finally, part of this wealth is siphoned away by foreign investors, who repatriate it to the apex of the cone – the rich world. The multinational corporations are seen as the modern instrument for the expropriation of surplus value. Neo-Marxists allow for a residue of surplus, but argue that if it is reinvested in the periphery or left in the hands of local elites, it will not be used appropriately for development purposes. As in dos Santos's model, the system hinges on the collaboration of the governing elite who live in the capital city, who think like, and identify with, their ex-colonial masters. So, poor countries, despite formal political independence, remain locked into an old system of economic dependence that perpetuates underdevelopment.

For Frank (1967), like dos Santos, underdevelopment is a natural outcome of the world capitalist system since the development of some countries inevitably means the distorted development or underdevelopment of others. Development itself perpetuates underdevelopment, a process that Frank has called **the development of underdevelopment**. Frank sees the origins of the process in colonization, which started as a form of economic exploitation and has distorted the economic structure of developing countries ever since. Developing countries were forced into the position of being suppliers of raw materials to industrial countries, thus effectively blocking industrial development in the primary producing countries themselves. The whole export orientation and foreign dominance of these countries has limited the growth of the domestic market and the establishment of basic national industries for widespread development throughout the whole economy. The international, national and local capitalist systems alike generate economic development for the few and underdevelopment for the many. The solution would appear to be nothing short of social and political revolution.

Unequal exchange

The theory of unequal exchange owes its name to Arghiri Emmanuel (1972). Exchange is unequal between rich and poor countries because wages are lower in poor countries, and lower than if the rate of profit in poor countries was not as high as in rich countries. In other words, exchange is unequal in relation to a situation where wages would be equalized: 'Inequality of wages as such, all other things being equal, is alone the cause of the inequality of exchange' (Emmanuel, 1972). Let us illustrate the model diagrammatically and show its affinity with the ideas of those who stress the terms of trade as the main mechanism through which the gains from exchange are unequally distributed. Let us take two countries and call them 'centre' (*c*) and 'periphery' (*p*). Assume that prices in the two countries are based on a percentage mark-up (*r*) on unit labour costs, so that:

$$P_c = w_c\left(\frac{L}{O}\right)_c\left(1 + r_c\right)$$

and:

$$P_p = w_p\left(\frac{L}{O}\right)_p\left(1 + r_p\right)$$

where w is the money wage rate, and wL/O is wage costs per unit of output. Now assume that for institutional reasons $w_c > w_p$ and that the mark-up or rate of profit equalizes between the two countries. The theory of unequal exchange says that because of this, the terms of trade will be worse for the periphery than if wages in the periphery were higher and the rate of profit lower. This can be illustrated diagrammatically, taking the price of the centre's goods as the *numéraire*, so that $P_c = 1$ (see Figure 10.4).

In the centre, the given rate of profit ($\bar{r}$) and wage rate (w_c) give a constant price (P_c), which acts as *numéraire* (hence the horizontal line, w_c). In the periphery, at a given wage (w_p), there is a positive relation

Figure 10.4 The theory of unequal exchange

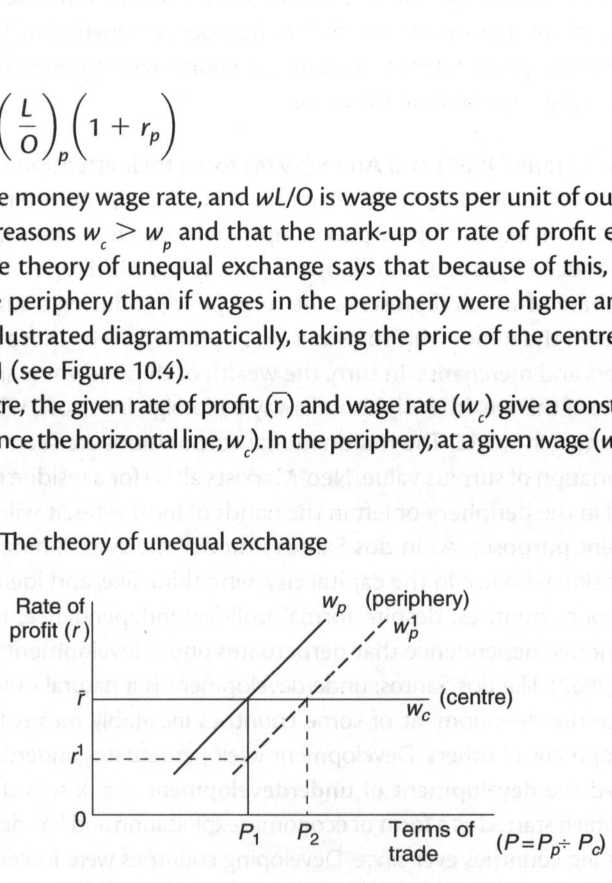

between the rate of profit and terms of trade (P), given by the upward-sloping line w_p. The equilibrium terms of trade is given at P_1. An increase in periphery wages shifts the periphery curve rightwards to w_p^1, giving a new terms of trade, P_2, at the same rate of profit. Unequal exchange is measured as the difference between the actual terms of trade (P_1) and what it would be if wages were higher in the periphery and the rate of profit was lower at r^1. The 'explanation' of unequal exchange is unequal wage rates.

The model does not get us very far, however, without understanding why there are wage differences between centre and periphery. In Emmanuel's model, the wage differences are institutionally determined outside the model, whereas in practice, there are many factors that impinge on wage differences within the model itself that need consideration. Moreover, money wage differences may not be the only factor leading to unequal exchange. If money wage differences between centre and periphery reflect differences in labour productivity, the terms of trade between periphery and centre will not be nearly as bad as suggested by money wage differences alone. Indeed, if differences in money wages are exactly matched by differences in productivity, there will be no difference in money wage costs per unit of output and no difference in relative prices 'caused' by differences in money wages. There can still be unequal exchange in the Emmanuel sense by virtue of the way Emmanuel (1972) defines the concept, but if the cause of low wages is low productivity, it is not a simple institutional matter to raise them.[6]

On the other side of the coin, if there is no good reason why the rate of profit should equalize between the two countries, a higher rate of profit in the centre could be an independent source of unequal exchange between centre and periphery, and also an explanation of why wages are depressed in the periphery. If account is taken of the characteristics of the goods produced by the centre and periphery – manufactured goods in the centre subject to decreasing costs, and primary commodities in the periphery subject to increasing costs – we can predict that oligopolistic structures will develop in the centre, while competitive structures will prevail in the periphery, with a tendency, therefore, for the rate of profit to be higher in the centre. The lower rate of profit in the periphery, and the attempt by capitalists to keep up the rate of profit in the face of competition, leads to the depression of wages in classic Marxist style.

Summary

- Disparities in living standards between countries of the world cannot be explained by initial (God-given) differences in factor endowments (natural resources) between countries. Through time, the process of growth has generated its own factor endowments favouring some countries more than others.
- Geographic differences in living standards between countries and between regions within countries are referred to as 'geographic dualism'.
- Within most developing countries, there are other forms of dualism. There is 'social dualism' between how individuals behave and how markets function in the rural subsistence sector on the one hand and the modern capitalist sector on the other. There is 'technological dualism', relating to differences in the level of technology and differences in techniques of production between the rural and modern sectors of the economy.
- Orthodox theory argues that when economic and social differences arise between sectors or regions, forces will come into play to narrow the differences. That is the equilibrium story.
- Myrdal's theory of circular and cumulative causation is a challenge to static equilibrium theory. In particular, in the case of geographic dualism, he argues that the process of labour migration, capital movements and trade tend to widen regional and country differences in income and welfare, by benefiting the already prosperous regions at the expense of the poorer regions.

- Structural differences between regions and between countries play a big part in the process of cumulative causation. The basis of Prebisch's centre–periphery model is that the periphery specializes in primary products with unfavourable demand characteristics in world markets and declining terms of trade, while the centre specializes in higher value-added industrial and service activities.
- The export-led growth model of Kaldor has cumulative features, which shows how once a region or country gets an advantage in the production and export of particular goods with favourable characteristics, it will sustain it through the impact that growth has on induced productivity growth and competitiveness (Verdoorn's law).
- The new economic geography pioneered by Krugman shows how centripetal forces (which work towards the spatial concentration of industrial activities) and centrifugal forces (which work towards dispersal) depend on the balance between transport costs of importing inputs and exporting output on the one hand, and increasing returns to geographic specialization (agglomeration economies) on the other.
- The dependence of poor countries on the rich is another explanation given for divisions in the world economy. Dependency theorists focus on various forms of exploitation of poor countries by rich ones: in the old days by colonialism, and today by industrial and financial imperialism. Multinational corporations are criticized for siphoning off profits from the periphery to the centre, and the world's banking system is attacked for serving the needs of global finance rather than global development. Trade can also lead to unequal exchange through a deterioration in the terms of trade between primary commodities and industrial goods.

Chapter 10 Discussion questions

1. What do you understand by the terms 'technological dualism', 'social dualism' and 'geographic dualism'?
2. Is dualism avoidable in the development process?
3. In what ways might dualism impede the functioning of the total economy?
4. In what senses is Myrdal's theory of circular and cumulative causation a challenge to static equilibrium theory?
5. What are the mechanisms through which the process of circular and cumulative causation work?
6. If backward regions suffer 'backwash' effects from regions of expansion, would they be better off as sovereign states?
7. What is the so-called 'Verdoorn effect' and what is its importance in the process of circular and cumulative causation?
8. What do the centre–periphery (or North–South) models by Prebisch, Dixon and Thirlwall, and Kaldor all have in common?
9. How does distance, and transport costs, affect the geographical pattern of economic development?
10. What are the various 'Marxist' explanations of the divergence between rich and poor countries?
11. What do you understand by the theory of unequal exchange?

Notes

1. First hinted at in Prebisch (1950) and developed in Prebisch (1959).
2. The income elasticity of demand for goods measures the proportionate change in demand for a good with respect to a proportionate change in income, holding other things constant.
3. The model is discussed more fully in Dixon and Thirlwall (1975) and Thirlwall (2014).
4. Under certain circumstances, the growth rate may not converge to its equilibrium level. This depends on the behaviour of the model out of equilibrium. See Dixon and Thirlwall (1975).
5. Krugman, however, reverses the direction of causation. In the model presented here, it is differences in income elasticities that determine differences in growth rates, while in Krugman, it is unexplained differences in growth rates that cause divergences in income elasticities. For a comprehensive review and discussion of the models, see McCombie and Thirlwall (1994, 2004) and Soukiakis and Cerqueira (2012).
6. Within this framework, movements in the terms of trade can be seen as the outcome of differences in the movement of productivity on the one hand and whether money wage changes fully match productivity changes on the other. If money wage increases fail to match productivity increases in the periphery, for example, so that real wages do not rise as fast as productivity, whereas they do in the centre, there will be a steady deterioration in the terms of trade of the periphery. This is the essence of the Prebisch argument (see Chapter 15).

11

POPULATION AND DEVELOPMENT

Introduction

The relation between population growth and economic development is a complex one and the historical quantitative evidence is ambiguous, particularly concerning what is cause and what is effect. Does economic development precede population growth, or is population growth a necessary condition for economic development to take place? Is population growth an impediment or a stimulus to economic development? Many people consider rapid population growth in developing countries to be a major obstacle to development, yet there are several ways in which population growth may be a stimulus to progress, and there are several rational reasons why families in developing countries choose to have many children.

In this chapter, we first consider the facts on world population, which has grown at unprecedented rates in the years since the Second World War, particularly in developing countries, although the growth is now slowing down.

Then we turn to the question of family size and the determinants of fertility. There is a rationale for poor families to have several children, and it is clear that fertility declines as people and countries get richer. This is the theory of **demographic transition**. The evidence also shows that fertility is heavily influenced by female education and the opportunity for women to work.

The costs to society of rapid population growth are considered, especially the effect of a high young dependency ratio on saving and capital accumulation. The potential benefits of rapid population growth are also considered, including how population pressure can be a stimulus to technical progress, and the fact that young people are more receptive to change and new ideas and ways of doing things. It turns out that the empirical evidence across countries shows no statistically significant relation (positive or negative) between the growth of population and the growth of living standards.

The question then arises of what is the optimum population of countries? This can be defined in a number of ways; and it is argued that the claim that a country is 'overpopulated' or 'underpopulated' needs to be viewed with some caution unless a precise definition of terms is given. The resource base of a country, the size of the country, and the level of technology are crucial to any calculations.

The chapter ends with an exposition of Nelson's well-known model of the **low-level equilibrium trap**, which shows how a poor region or country may get stuck in a situation where its population growth exceeds its output growth, pushing income per capita down to its minimum subsistence level, and how a 'big push' or 'critical minimum effort' may be necessary to get per capita income to a level where the growth of per capita income becomes self-sustaining. The Nelson 'trap' model is similar to the Malthusian trap in which some communities in developing countries still find themselves, with large families and living standards oscillating around subsistence level.

Facts about world population

The pertinent facts about the level and growth of world population are shown in Table 11.1. Today, the world's population is nearly 7.5 billion, of which more than two-thirds live in developing countries and nearly one-half reside in Asia. This level compares with approximately 179 million at the time of Christ, and fewer than 1,000 million as recently as AD 1800. The current rate of growth of the world population is 1.1% per annum, which has no precedent historically. From AD 1 to 1750 the rate was no more than 0.05% per annum; from 1750 to 1850 it was 0.5% per annum; and even between 1900 and 1950 it was only 0.8% per annum (see Kremer (1993) for a history of world population).

Table 11.1 Population statistics

			Dependency ratio			
	Population millions	Average annual population growth %	young, % of working-age population	old, % of working-age population	Crude death rate per 1,000 people	Crude birth rate per 1,000 people
	2014	2000-14	2014	2014	2013	2013
World	7,261	1.23	40	12	8	19
Low income	622	2.73	79	6	9	36
Middle income	5,240	1.25	40	10	7	19
Lower middle income	2,879	1.60	49	8	8	23
Upper middle income	2,361	0.84	29	12	7	15
Low and middle income	5,862	1.39	43	10	8	21
East Asia and Pacific	2,021	0.77	28	11	7	14
Europe and Central Asia	264	0.54	33	15	9	16
Latin America and Caribbean	525	1.28	40	10	6	18
Middle East and North Africa	357	1.81	49	8	5	25
South Asia	1,721	1.55	47	8	7	22
Sub-Saharan Africa	973	2.74	80	6	10	38
High income	1,399	0.62	26	24	9	12

Source: World Bank, 2015.

At the present rate of increase, the world population will double every 65 years. The current projection from the UN is that, by the year 2050, the population will rise to 8 billion if birth rates continue to fall dramatically, or 12 billion if birth rates come down only slowly. Figure 11.1 gives the recent and projected growth rates for various regions of the world up to 2100. All the regions show the rates of population growth slowing down, but with Africa and Oceania still above the world average. In Europe, the population growth rate is already close to zero and forecast to be negative from 2020. In Asia, and Latin America and the Caribbean, population is forecast to fall from 2060.

The country with the largest population is China, with an estimated current population of 1,400 million, followed by India, the USA, Indonesia, Brazil, Pakistan, Nigeria, Bangladesh, Russia, Japan, Mexico and the Philippines, all with populations in excess of 100 million. China and India alone currently add 25 million people to the world's population every year. In the last minute, approximately 300 babies have been born and 150 people have died, increasing the world's population by 150 persons, giving a yearly increase of 80 million.

The rate of growth of population is the difference between the number of live births per thousand of the population and the number of deaths per thousand. In a country where the birth rate is 40 per 1,000 and the death rate is 20 per 1,000, the rate of population growth will therefore be $(40 - 20)/1{,}000 = 20$ per 1,000, or 2% per annum. If (in normal circumstances) a birth rate of 60 per 1,000 is considered to be a 'biological' maximum, and a death rate of 10 per 1,000 is considered a 'medical' minimum, the maximum possible growth rate of population, ignoring immigration, would be about 5% per annum. The current maximum birth rates recorded are 40 per 1,000 in some African countries. For low-income countries, the average birth rate is about 36 per 1,000 and

Figure 11.1 Average annual rate of population change by major area, estimates, 2000–15, and projection, 2015–2100

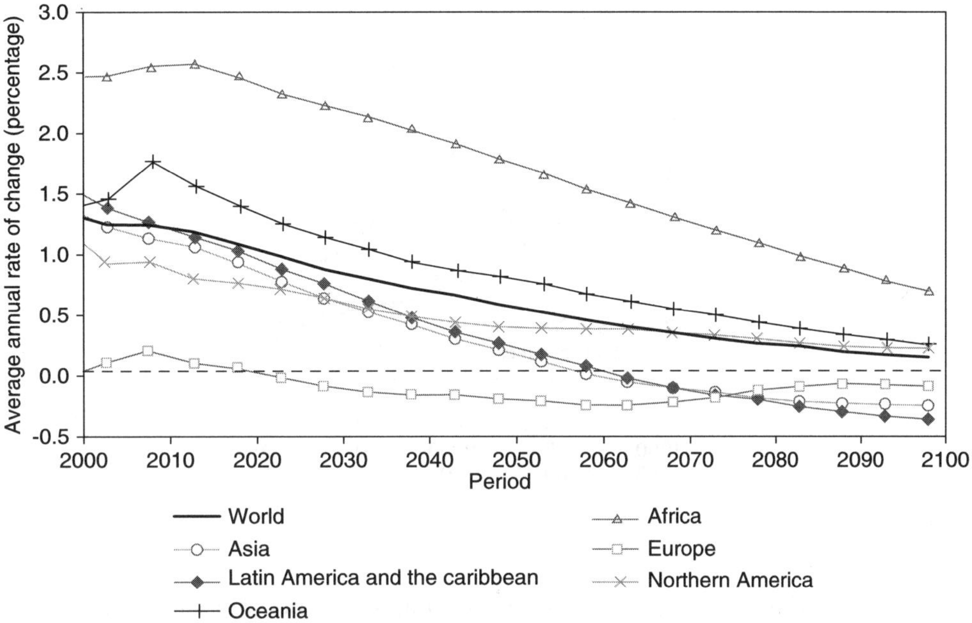

Source: UN DESA, 2015.

the average death rate is now about 9 per 1,000, giving an average rate of population increase of approximately 2.7% per annum (see Table 11.1). This rapid rate of population growth, compared with advanced countries (and also in relation to the growth of national income), is the result of relatively high birth rates coupled with death rates that are as low as in advanced countries. If population growth is a 'problem' in developing countries, this is the simple source of the difficulty and the long-run solution is plain: there must be a reduction in fertility.

The determinants of fertility[1]

The vital questions are: Can high birth rates be expected to fall naturally with development, and if so, what is the crucial level of development and per capita income (PCY) at which the adjustment will take place and how long does the process take? The conventional wisdom used to be that fertility decline would come only with rising levels of per capita income, urbanization and industrialization. This is the theory of **demographic transition**.

If the fertility rate of countries, that is, the number of children per woman, is plotted against the level of PCY, a definite negative relationship is observable. It is also true that through time, the fertility rate decreases at a given level of PCY, and that there are big differences in the fertility rate between countries at the same level of income. Clearly, there are important factors, other than the level of PCY, that affect the level of fertility through time and across countries.

Past and projected fertility rates are shown in Figure 11.2. The data show fertility declining in all regions of the world, with the world fertility rate falling to 2.0 children per woman by the year 2050. The number of children per woman required for the population to replace itself is 2.1. In developed countries, fertility has already fallen below this critical level, with an average of 1.6 children per woman.

Figure 11.2 Past and projected fertility

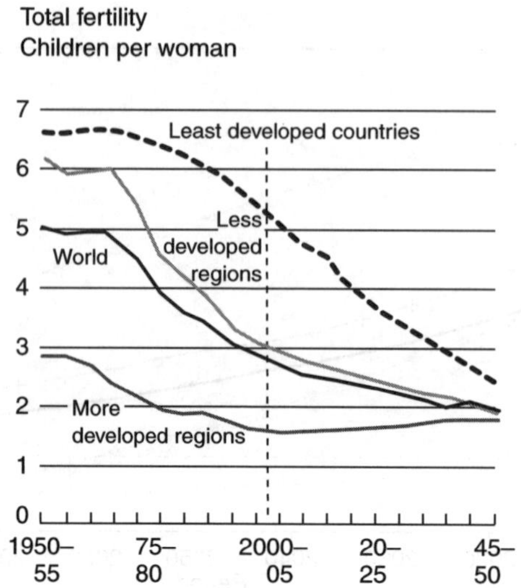

Source: UN DESA, Population Division (2003).

Reductions in fertility can occur with improvements in a wide range of socioeconomic conditions, such as access to family planning services, the provision of healthcare and a reduction in child mortality, greater employment opportunities for women, and, above all, the education of women and the promotion of female literacy. Where women are excluded from secondary education, the average number of children per woman is six. In countries where half of women go to secondary school, the average number of children is three. Figure 11.3 shows the strong negative relationship between female literacy and the reduction in fertility across 93 countries.

There are a number of reasons why women's education lowers fertility:

- Education improves work opportunities for women, which makes having children more costly in terms of income forgone.
- Educated women want their own children to be educated, which raises the cost of having children.
- Education and literacy make women more receptive to information about contraception.
- Education and employment delay marriage and the time available to rear children.
- Education improves the status, bargaining power and independence of women, encouraging and enabling them to make their own choices.

From a **vicious circle** of no education, high fertility, poor health of children and low productivity, the education of women can lead to a **virtuous circle** of lower fertility, better care of children, more educational opportunity and higher productivity. The countries where fertility is declining most rapidly are those with the highest levels of female schooling, the lowest levels of child mortality and the widest availability of family planning services. Bangladesh is a prime example where the fertility rate has fallen to 2.2 births per woman (see Case example 11.1).

The reductions in fertility in different parts of the world over the past two decades are shown in Table 11.2. In developing countries as a whole, the reduction has been 30%, from 3.8 children per fertile woman in 1990 to 2.6 in 2014. In low-income countries, however, the number of

Figure 11.3 Fertility rate and female literacy, 2010

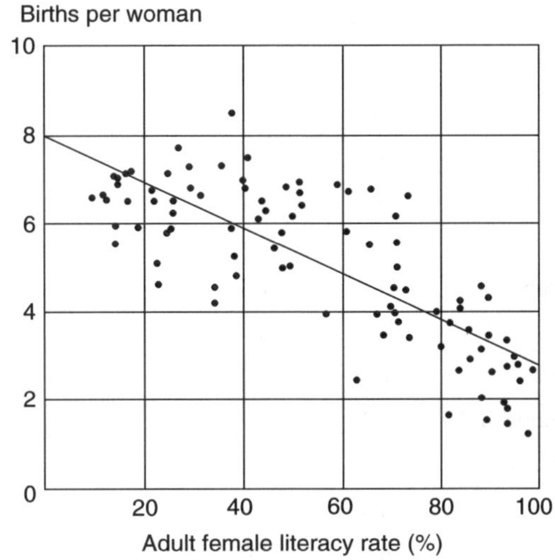

Source: Authors' compilation based on World Bank 2014.

Case example 11.1

Reducing fertility in Bangladesh

Bangladesh provides an excellent case study of the impact that a government-led family planning policy can have on fertility in a poor country. In the mid-1970s, the fertility rate for a Bangladeshi woman was more than six children. This high fertility rate not only jeopardized the health of the woman and children but also acted as a major constraint on the country's economic development and social progress. The Bangladesh family planning programme, launched in the 1980s, relies on a large cadre of female outreach workers going door to door to provide information, motivate clients, and provide contraceptives. The programme has also used the mass media to stimulate a change in attitudes about family size, promoting the merits of smaller families. As a result, virtually all women in Bangladesh are aware of modern family planning methods. The fertility rate has decreased from six children per woman to less than three today. The programme is estimated to have cost between \$100 million and \$150 million a year, but the benefit–cost ratio is high. The cost-effectiveness is estimated at \$13–18 per birth averted.

Source: Center for Global Development, Washington, DC.

children is still nearly 5. Sub-Saharan Africa has the highest fertility rate and Europe and Central Asia the lowest.

The birth rate of a country is equal to its fertility rate multiplied by the ratio of fertile women to the total population. Even though fertility rates decline, birth rates do not necessarily decline in the same proportion because of the young age structure of the population produced by high fertility levels in the past. Thus, even if fertility continues to decline substantially, it will still take decades for the population level to stabilize because of the sheer number of couples having families. There is a **population momentum** built into the present age structure of the population of most developing countries. It is estimated that even if fertility rates were reduced immediately

Table 11.2 Total fertility rate (births per woman), 1990 and 2014

	1990	2014
World	3.3	2.5
Low income	6.3	4.9
Middle income	3.5	2.4
Lower middle income	4.3	2.9
Upper middle income	2.8	1.9
Low and middle income	3.7	2.6
East Asia and Pacific	2.7	1.9
Europe and Central Asia	2.6	2.0
Latin America and Caribbean	3.3	2.1
Middle East and North Africa	4.9	2.8
South Asia	4.3	2.6
Sub-Saharan Africa	6.4	5.0
High income	1.9	1.7

Source: World Bank, 2015.

to the level of replacement (that is, one daughter per woman, which means approximately 2.1 children per family), the population of developing countries will not stabilize until 2050, at a level of about 9 billion.

Given that there may be a time lag between the death rate falling and a subsequent decline in the birth rate, rapid population growth may be considered a transitional or more enduring 'problem' for a country depending on the currently prevailing level of the rate of births and deaths. This proposition is best illustrated by means of a simple diagram (Figure 11.4).

The curves *RB* and *RD* represent the time paths of the birth rate and death rate, respectively. Population growth is determined by the gap between the two curves. To save drawing more diagrams, let us suppose that points *X* and *Y* in Figure 11.4 represent two countries with the same current rate of population growth ($Pq = St$). In the case of country *Y*, population growth will soon slow down since the death rate has reached its minimum and the birth rate is falling. In the case of country *X*, however, which has the same *current* population growth, the population growth rate can be expected to increase in the future as the gap between the birth and

Figure 11.4 Population momentum

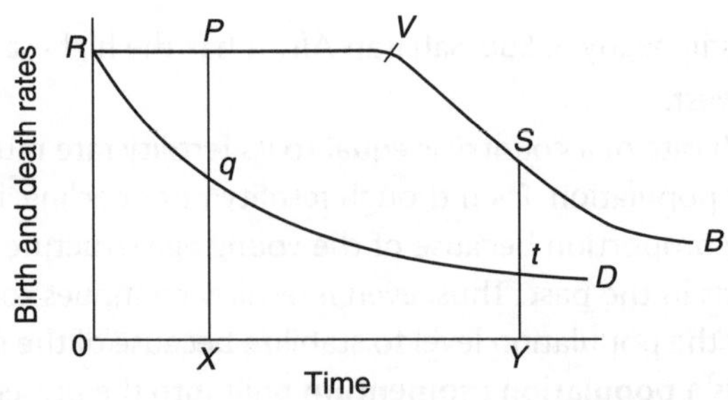

death rates widens. The death rate is falling but the birth rate remains constant to the point *V*; only after this point will population growth decrease. Here, then, are two countries with the same observed population growth at present but with radically different future prospects. When comparing countries, and their population 'problems', the time profile of countries must be borne in mind. But the crucial questions, as we suggested earlier, are: What is the length of the time lag between the death rate falling and the downturn of the birth rate? What is the length of the **demographic transition**? It is the length of this time lag that determines the short-run prospects of countries emerging from a transitional state and attempting to take-off into self-sustaining growth.

The experience of developing countries today has no historical parallel, at least in Western Europe. In nineteenth-century Europe, the birth and death rates tended to fall together and population growth never exceeded 1% per annum. It could almost be argued that the 'balance of nature' has been upset in today's developing countries. The introduction of public health measures and medical advances reduced death rates suddenly and dramatically, but the means and know-how to effect an equally dramatic fall in the birth rate were not provided at the same time. Modern science and public health improvements have contributed to the ending of premature death, but, until recently, have not exerted a significant impact on births.

Costs and benefits of population growth

Population growth plays a conflicting role in the development process. It can act as a stimulus and an impediment to growth and development. The question, to which there is no easy answer, is: At what point do the economic disadvantages begin to outweigh the advantages? Where does the balance lie?

The conventional view is that high levels and rates of growth of population constitute a problem for the world as a whole and for developing countries in particular. Population growth, it is argued, depresses human welfare because it:

- Uses up scarce (non-renewable) resources and causes environmental degradation.
- Puts pressure on food supplies.
- Leads to overcrowding and congestion in cities.
- Adds to the employment problem.
- Reduces the savings ratio and dilutes the quantity of capital per person employed.

There are elements of truth in all these arguments, especially in parts of the world where there are particularly heavy concentrations of population in relation to habitable land. Asia, for example, contains over one-half of the world's population and over 2 billion people live in big cities, which already suffer the highest levels of air pollution in the world, not to mention the congestion. Asia is now the biggest source of greenhouse gases. As we shall see later in the chapter, however, there are also arguments to be put on the other side. See Case example 11.2 for the challenge of population growth in the Philippines.

The pessimistic view of population originated with Malthus (see Chapter 4), and in recent years it has been revived by ecologists, environmentalists and various eco-doomsters of different persuasions. The pessimism of Malthus stemmed from the pervasive classical belief

Case example 11.2

The challenge of population growth in the Philippines

The population of the Philippines is now over 100 million. The country is home to one of Asia's youngest and fastest-growing populations. The country is not expected to reach its demographic peak until around 2077, well after China, South Korea and other powerful economies in the region. But the Philippines may never enjoy its demographic dividend if poverty, unemployment and inflation aren't addressed. Unemployment has remained stubbornly high even as the economy has grown an average of 5% per year over the past decade. The country's economic growth has largely benefited the top 20% of the income distribution. Almost a quarter of the population lives below the poverty line, earning less than $386 a year or just over $1 a day. Although the percentage of Filipinos living in poverty has declined slightly over the past few years, it has increased among youth and urban residents – the two segments of the population that are growing the fastest. A growing population and labour force is not good for unemployment. About 1 million Filipinos enter the labour force every year, but only one-quarter of them find stable jobs. As much as 75% of workers are employed in the informal sector, which means that they have no protection from job losses – a figure that is likely to increase as the population surges. There is urgent need to reduce fertility through expanding female education and employment opportunities.

in the law of diminishing returns, and the underestimation of humankind's response to the challenge of diminishing productivity with the expansion of numbers through invention and innovation.

According to Malthus ([1798]1983), there is a 'constant tendency in all animated life to increase beyond the nourishment prepared for it'. Thus, every mouth is accompanied by a pair of hands, but every pair of hands produces less and less additional output. Technological progress (always grossly underestimated by pessimists in general and by classical economists in particular) would not be rapid enough, it was thought, to offset the tendency. However, Malthus became much less pessimistic between the first and fifth editions of his book, and at one point conceded that, if it were not for population increase: 'no motive would be sufficiently strong to overcome the acknowledged indolence of man and make him proceed to the cultivation of the soil'.

The main argument of the pessimistic school regarding rapid population growth is that it leads to a high **dependency ratio** and reduces an economy's savings because the young spend more than they produce, so that capital accumulation per worker is lower than it would otherwise be, which leads to a lower level of productivity and therefore living standards. This traditional argument, however, ignores the fact that many young children in developing countries do, in fact, work (see Dasgupta, 1995). It must also be remembered that many of the older members of a community also consume without producing and that the proportion of retired members of the community to total population will rise as population growth slows. Thus, what happens to the aggregate savings ratio as the population growth rate changes will depend on how the composition of the *total* dependency ratio alters, and on the propensity to save (or dissave) of the two groups of dependents. For example, if the propensity of the retired to dissave was greater than that of the inactive young, the aggregate savings ratio might fall with a reduction in the birth rate as the retired dependency ratio rose.

It should also be noted that the effect of children on a society's total savings works primarily through the family as a unit and depends on how the family reacts to the increase in the number of children. There may just be a substitution of one form of expenditure (on children) for another. Alternatively, the family may work harder to provide for the children, in which case there may be no adverse effect on saving at all. Saving in some families may even increase if there is a sufficient increase in output and a high degree of substitution. The degree of substitution between one form of expenditure and another will depend on the ability to substitute, determined by living standards and the level of saving already achieved.

The question of an output response to population pressure comes back to the point made earlier of the possibility of a positive relation between population growth and total productivity growth. It may well be that the sheer increase in numbers creates work and production incentives that affect output and productivity favourably. In fact, there is a good deal of theory and empirical evidence to suggest a positive relation between population growth and the growth of output per unit of labour, especially in the manufacturing sector, assuming some growth in employment as the population expands. This is **Verdoorn's law** (discussed in Chapter 3), which hypothesizes a positive relation between the growth of the population, employment and output on the one hand and the growth of labour productivity on the other.

The possible explanations for such a relation are numerous:

1. It has been argued (see Chapter 6) that an economy with a faster rate of growth of employment and output may be able to learn more quickly and hence raise its rate of technical progress.
2. If there are internal and external economies of scale in production, increased employment and output will lead to a faster rate of growth of labour productivity.
3. There are likely to be economies of scale in the use of capital. Capital requirements, in most cases, do not increase in the same proportion as population. There are many important indivisibilities in the provision of capital, especially in the field of transport and other social overhead capital.

It is also possible that population pressure can favourably affect individual motivation and lead to changes in production techniques that can overcome the negative consequences of population growth. In this connection, it has been argued that a major stimulus to the Green Revolution in Asia in the 1960s and 1970s came from the pressure of population on food supply. The young age structure of a country also makes it more amenable to change, more receptive to new ideas, more willing to shift resources from low-productivity to high-productivity sectors and so on, all of which may raise income per head. In Hirschman's model of development (see Chapter 9), population growth increases the supply of potential decision-makers, expands markets and leads to development via shortages.

It must not be forgotten that the world as a whole has grown progressively richer while the population has expanded. Would the world be as rich today if the population had remained static? Would Britain have been the first country to industrialize if its population had not grown? Would the USA have become the richest country in the world without the great influx of people from beyond its shores to exploit its abundant natural resources?

All that has really been said so far is that population growth presents a paradox. On the one hand, increases in population may reduce living standards owing to the adverse effect of population growth on savings and capital per head. On the other hand, increases in population and the labour force can raise living standards through the learning, specialization and scale economies that larger numbers, wider markets and a higher volume of output make possible. What may be called the **paradox of labour** can be seen more easily by taking the identity $O = P(O/P)$, or in differential form, $(\Delta O/O) = \Delta P/P + \Delta(O/P)/(O/P)$, where O is output, P is population and O/P is output per head of population (and a constant fraction of the population is assumed to work). Decreasing amounts of capital per worker (and possibly diminishing returns to land) imply a negative relation between the terms on the right-hand side of the equations, so that output per head and living standards are lower than they would otherwise be as the population increases. On the other hand, the possibility of increasing returns, due to the factors mentioned, implies a positive relation between the two terms, so that living standards rise as the population increases.

The question is: Which forces predominate? The debate as to whether population growth acts as a stimulus or an impediment to the growth of living standards is largely a question of whether the relation between $\Delta P/P$ and $\Delta(O/P)/(O/P)$ is significantly positive or negative. If the relation is negative, then population growth is an impediment to rising living standards. If the relation is positive, then the effect of population growth on the growth of output and output per head is unambiguously favourable. Evidence across countries suggests that population growth and the rate of capital accumulation are inversely related, which decreases the growth of labour productivity, but population growth and technical progress are positively related, which increases the growth of labour productivity. The two effects offset each other, leaving the total effect of population growth on the growth of per capita income roughly neutral (see Thirlwall (1972) for an early study).

This is indeed the conclusion of studies that examine *directly* the relation between population growth and the growth of living standards by correlating the two variables for a cross-section of countries to see whether the relation is positive or negative. When this is done, there is very little systematic relation to be found between intercountry rates of population growth and rates of growth of per capita income. This does not take account of the environmental degradation associated with population growth and the use of non-renewable resources, which are not measured as a cost in the calculation of GDP.

The fact that the international cross-section evidence lends very little support to the notion that curbing population growth will have much impact, if any, on the growth of income per head is not to deny, of course, that curbing population growth may be desirable for other reasons, such as to relieve overcrowding, to relieve pressure on food supplies and, in general, to improve the distribution of income. To be sceptical of an inverse relation between population growth and per capita income growth is not to pour cold water on population control programmes. On the contrary, given the uncertainty of the population growth/living standards relation, and the force of other arguments for limiting numbers, the most sensible strategy is to pursue programmes on the hypothesis that population control increases PCY. In simulation studies of the gains from population control that use the effect on PCY as the criterion for success, however, it is important that explicit account should be taken of the positive relation between population growth and technical progress if the gains from population control are not to be exaggerated. See Case example 11.3 for a general discussion of the concern over population growth.

Case example 11.3 **Population concern**

Population concern is fundamentally about the balance between human needs and the resources available to meet those needs now and in the future. From the period of Confucius and Aristotle, observers throughout history have noted the consequences of unsustainable population growth. The most famous writer on population was Thomas Malthus (1776–1834), who wrote when the human population was 900 million and observed that 'population when left unchecked increases in a geometric ratio [while] subsistence grows in an arithmetic ratio'. The

Case example 11.3 **Population concern** – *continued*

famines that Malthus predicted were averted by the agricultural and industrial revolutions that followed his lifetime, which facilitated a dramatic increase in food productivity.

Following the Second World War, the population reached 2,500 million and improvements in public health spread to the developing world and population numbers took a huge leap forward. Robert McNamara, then president of the World Bank said: 'Short of nuclear war itself, population growth is the greatest issue the world faces. If we do not act, the problem will be solved by famine, riots, insurrection and war.' These views were shared by such diverse people as Albert Einstein, Martin Luther King and Lynden Johnson. Concerned nations and international organizations accelerated support for family planning programmes. In 1968, world population had climbed to 3,600 million. Paul Ehrlich, US biologist, warned in his book *Population Bomb* (1968) that population growth was again raising the spectre of widespread famine. However, another development occurred at this time, the Green Revolution, which transformed agricultural productivity in many developing countries through the introduction of high yield crop variants and the use of modern high input farming methods. Ehrlich reissued his book in 1990 as the world population reached 5,200 million. The predicted famine never took place, although in 2009 the UN estimated that up to 1 billion in the world were undernourished.

In 2010, the global population reached 6,800 million, Some countries continue to limit their population growth by providing reproductive health services and adopting a variety of approaches to limit family size. Pressure on individuals is firmly rejected by international bodies and NGOs, who emphasize the importance of a rights-based approach, such that couples freely make their own reproductive choices. As we look ahead to the middle of this century, world population is projected to reach 8–11 billion, and increasing numbers of people are voicing concern about population numbers, in the context of biodiversity loss, climate change and rapid depletion of oil, fresh water, land, habitat and wildlife resources.

For more on the subject, go to www.populationmatters.org/the-issue/overview.

Population and the growth of cities

One of the major consequences of population growth, and the process of rural–urban migration, is the rapid growth of cities in developing countries. At present, just over one-half of the world's population lives in cities, and this is predicted to rise to two-thirds by 2025. In fact, virtually all the predicted increase in world population will live in cities. The urban population of developing countries is already increasing by almost 700 million a year, which puts huge pressure on resources. While cities only occupy 2% of the land's earth surface, they absorb 75% of natural resources – food, energy and water (Reader, 2005).

Currently, the top ten cities in the world (by population) are Tokyo (35.7m), Mexico City (19m), New York (19m), São Paulo (19m), Mumbai (18.8m), Delhi (15.9m), Shanghai (15m), Kolkata (14.8m), Dhaka (13.5m) and Buenos Aires (12.8m). By 2025, it is predicted that there will be 30 cities in developing countries with more than 10 million people, and 400 cities with more than 1 million.

Living conditions in the cities of developing countries are often extremely poor. One-third of city dwellers live in slums, and many are very insecure because of lack of land rights. There is overcrowding, poor sanitation, lack of clean water, pollution and disease. Over 500 million people lack access to clean water and 2 million die each year as a result.

Simon's challenge

The most concerted challenge to the view that population growth is uniformly depressing for the material well-being of mankind has come from the economist Julian Simon (1992, 1996). Simon's major thesis is that 'the ultimate resource is people – skilled, spirited and hopeful people – who will exert their wills and imaginations for their own benefit, and so, inevitably, for the benefit of us all'. William Petty, seventeenth-century English political economist, was making the same point when he said: 'it is more likely that one ingenious, curious man may rather be found among 4 million than among 400 persons' (Petty, 1682). Simon brings together the theoretical arguments and empirical evidence on both sides of the population debate and presents simulation results on the relation between population growth and living standards. He finds that the initial effects of population increase on per capita income are negative, but that, in the longer term, the positive feedback effects resulting from the stimulus of population growth to technological progress, and other factors that improve the rate of productivity growth, outweigh the negative effects. Simulations suggest that, for countries already industrialized, the initial negative effect of population is offset within 50 years. For less developed countries, the conclusion is that moderate population growth is more favourable to the growth of living standards than either a stationary population or very rapid population growth.

An overall judgement of population growth, and whether it is beneficial or not, therefore depends very much on weighing the balance between the present and the future. In economic analysis, the present and the future are made comparable using the concept of a discount rate. Whether the positive long-run benefits of population growth are considered to outweigh the short-run negative effects depends on the discount rate and the time period taken. The less future benefits are discounted and the longer the time period taken, the more beneficial (less detrimental) population growth appears, and the shorter the time period considered and the more future benefits are discounted, the less beneficial (more detrimental) population growth appears. There will be some time period and some discount rate at which additional population is exactly on the borderline of having a negative or positive value.

What are the positive feedback effects that population increase can have on economic progress that vitiate the classical prediction that population growth is uniformly depressing on living standards? In his simulation model of the relationship between population growth and per capita income in advanced countries, Simon attempts to capture the effect of additional children on factors such as the savings ratio, labour supplied by the parents, scale economies and technical progress. In his simulation model for developing countries, Simon (1992) considers the following important feedback mechanisms:

- the stimulus to new methods in agriculture
- the supply response of families
- the provision of social infrastructure (particularly transport)
- scale economies
- demand-induced investment.

Let us briefly consider some of these factors.

A society under pressure from population growth may be expected to respond by finding new and more efficient ways of meeting given needs. In agriculture, the Malthusian view would be that improvement in agricultural techniques is independent of population and that improvements simply induce population expansion. Others would argue that even if population pressure does not induce the production of new techniques, it certainly induces the *adoption* of new techniques. It is difficult to see how the Green Revolution in Asia in the 1970s would have occurred without the pressure of numbers on food supply.

Agricultural families may respond to the needs of additional children by changing methods, working harder and producing more. Studies suggest that the elasticity of output to increases in the number of children is about 0.5; that is, an increase in family size, say, from four to five (25%) would result in a 12.5% increase in output. Simon argues that population growth also has a large positive effect on agricultural saving, which tends to be overlooked because a large fraction is non-monetized.

Population pressure provides a stimulus to develop social infrastructure, transport and communication facilities, which have far-reaching external repercussions, extending beyond the additional numbers they are designed to serve. Population growth also makes these facilities more economical to provide because of the scale economies involved in their provision. Simon (1992) argues: 'if there is a single key element in economic development other than culture and institutions and psychological make-up, that single key element is transportation together with communications'. Adam Smith (1776), an early contemporary of Malthus and much more optimistic about the development process, was impressed by the benefits of communications:

> good roads, canals and navigable rivers, by diminishing the expense of carriage, put the remote parts of the country more nearly upon a level with those in the neighbourhood of the town. They are upon that account the greatest of all improvements – they break down monopolies ... they open new markets.

To the extent that population growth exerts pressure for these facilities to be provided, a significant output response is to be expected.

Increased population has many other productivity effects that are subtle and indirect, yet nonetheless important. It is very difficult, for example, to improve health and sanitation in sparsely populated areas, but once sanitation and health improvements become feasible and economical with greater numbers, substantial benefits may result – more than in proportion to the increase in population. A growing population also facilitates change without disrupting the organization and positions of those already established. Thus, government and administration may be expected to improve and become more in keeping with the needs of development. Youth itself has positive advantages. Young people are more receptive to change and modernization than older people. The younger a population, the more education (or human capital) per head of the population. Young people tend to be more mobile, which is an asset when structural change is required. With a growing population, investment is less risky. Many economists are of the view that one of the major obstacles to development is not a shortage of savings but a lack of willingness to invest. An expanding market resulting from population growth provides an incentive to investment.

The great difference between the results of Simon and those of the pessimists is that all the beneficial feedback effects of population on output mentioned above are not considered. But any of the feedback factors referred to may partially or fully offset the capital dilution effect of greater numbers in the short run, which is the factor that the predictions of conventional models reflect.

A complete analysis of the relation between population and living standards must have due regard to the longer term benefits that population expansion can confer on societies, as well as the short-term costs. Indeed, only when the benefits are considered, is it possible to comprehend why societies are infinitely wealthier today than centuries ago, despite population expansion.

The 'optimum' population

What is the 'optimum' population? The term **optimum population** is used in several different senses, but four in particular are commonly employed. First, it is sometimes used to refer to the size of population that *maximizes the average product or income per head*. It is in this situation that a society's savings ratio is likely to be maximized. Thus, if the total product curve for an economy is drawn as in Figure 11.5, the optimum population is *P*, where a ray from the origin is tangential to the total product curve. At *P*, total product (*Y*) divided by population (*P*), or average product per head of population, is at its maximum. The condition for maximum average product per head is that the marginal and average product per head should be equal. If the marginal product of an addition to the population is above the average, the average product could be increased by an expansion of the population. Conversely, if the marginal product is below the average, a further increase in population will reduce the average product and the population will exceed the optimum level in the way defined. If there was no saving, the maximization of product per head would maximize welfare per head because consumption per head would then also be at a maximum.

On the surface, this concept of optimum population seems an attractive one upon which to base a population policy. It provides the greatest scope for maximizing savings per head if desired or, in the absence of forced or compulsory saving, it will lead to the maximization of welfare per head. Yet, a population policy based on maximizing per capita income has frightening implications (not entirely fanciful) for all submarginal groups in society that may be deemed to be depressing the average standard of life.

A second approach to the concept of 'optimum' population adopts the criterion of *total welfare maximization*. This is the utilitarian approach, adopted by Henry Sidgwick, English economist cum philosopher, in his *Methods of Ethics*, originally published in 1874. Sidgwick argues:

> If the additional population enjoy on the whole positive happiness, we ought to weigh the amount of happiness gained by the extra numbers against the amount lost by the remained. So that, strictly conceived, the point up to which, on utilitarian principles, population ought to be encouraged to increase is not that at which *average* happiness is the greatest possible – as appears to be often assumed by political economists of the school of Malthus – but at which

Figure 11.5 Maximization of average product

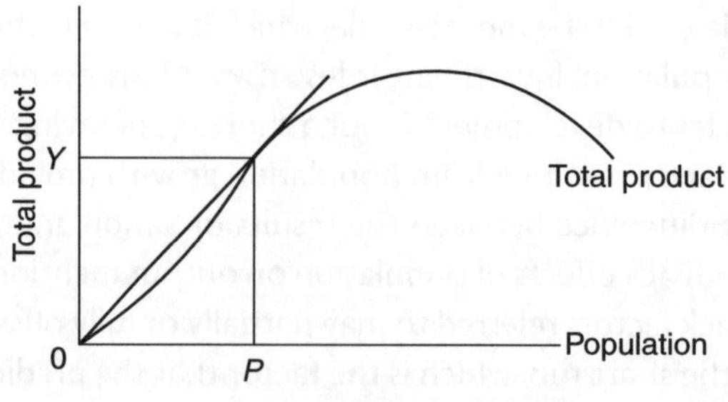

> the product formed by multiplying the number of persons living into the amount of average happiness reaches its maximum (emphasis added).

According to this criterion, the population would be suboptimal if the marginal product of labour was above some notional welfare subsistence level, and would reach the optimum when all incomes were equalized at the welfare subsistence level (assuming a diminishing marginal utility of income). But in conditions of poverty, if increments to population reduce the average standard of living still further, it seems perverse to call this an improvement in welfare simply because the number of people 'enjoying' such an impoverished state has risen. As Rawls (1972) argues in his *Theory of Justice*, if a rational observer was asked to choose membership of one or other society from behind a veil of ignorance, they would undoubtedly reject the maximization of total welfare and choose the society with the prospect of a higher per capita income.

A third definition of optimum population refers to the level of population beyond which the average product in an economy falls below the level necessary for subsistence, on the assumption that the total product is equally shared. In this case, the term 'optimum' simply refers to the maximum population that can be supported with existing resources, and is the point of Malthusian equilibrium. In Figure 11.6, a population beyond P_1 could not be supported because the average product of the population would be below the level of subsistence. If total product was not equally shared, a total population of P_1 would not be supportable, for some would have more income than necessary for subsistence and others less. But note that if the product is equally shared, a much larger population can be maintained than the population at which the marginal product falls below subsistence, that is, P. In fact, the optimum population, P_1, is consistent with a negative marginal product.

This last point leads us to the fourth sense in which the term 'optimum' population is sometimes used, which is to describe a state of affairs where a country's population is so large that further increases lead to a fall in total output, implying a negative marginal product. The population is optimal in this sense when total product is maximized, at P_2 in Figure 11.6. This definition of optimum population is closely linked with the notion of population density, and attempts to define underpopulation and overpopulation in terms of the relation between population and resources and, in particular, land. Since resources such as land vary considerably in quality, however, intercountry comparisons of ratios of population to resources must be treated with great care. One country may be regarded as 'underpopulated' in relation to another country even though it has a higher population–resource ratio, simply because the technology it uses to exploit

Figure 11.6 The 'optimum' population

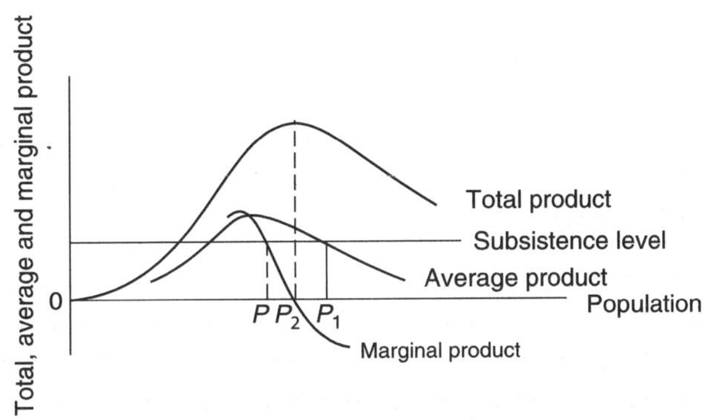

its resources is superior. Technology will influence the position and shape of the total product curve – and hence the optimum population – for any given ratio of population to resources. In view of the variety of interpretations of the concept of optimum population, the claim that a country is 'overpopulated' or 'underpopulated' needs to be viewed with some scepticism unless a precise definition of the terms is given.

Where does all this leave the welfare basis for population control programmes? A firmer basis than whether or not there are diminishing or increasing returns to population growth is to consider the divergences between the private and social benefits that arise from large numbers of children. For example, individual families may prefer to have fewer children if they know that all other families will have fewer children, but, in isolation, they are not willing to limit the number of children they have. This is an example of what is known in welfare economics as the **isolation paradox**, and it establishes a case for public intervention. It is the young who suffer from there being more children because most of the costs arise in the future. Present parents may enjoy their children, but their children may wish their parents had had fewer, and they probably would have had fewer if they could have been sure that everybody else would have had fewer too. A further reason for public intervention in the field of population control may be market failure, if it can be shown that families have more children than they actually want and that there is an unmet need for family planning services.

It is interesting to note that surveys of desired family size in developing countries consistently put the figure at one or two lower than the actual family size. Apart from this, it could be argued that it is a basic human right to be able to choose freely and responsibly the number of children to have and how far apart to have them. This indeed was the resolution endorsed by the first UN World Population Conference in Bucharest in 1974, which laid the foundation for the World Bank's increased support for population control programmes throughout developing countries, and was reiterated by the last UN Conference on Population and Development in Cairo in 1994. The Cairo conference emphasized the right of women to control the number and timing of their children and urged countries to provide universal access to family planning services. It is estimated that only 50% of married women in developing countries use any form of birth control. As we saw earlier, however, the education of women is the major determinant of fertility, and a necessary condition for a reduction in fertility is the expansion of educational and work opportunities for women.

A model of the low-level equilibrium trap

To repeat, there are two main interrelated reasons why rapid population growth may be regarded as a retarding influence on development:

1. Rapid population growth may not permit a sufficiently large rise in per capita incomes to provide the savings necessary for the required amount of capital formation for growth.
2. If population growth outstrips the capacity of industry to absorb new labour, either urban unemployment will develop or rural underemployment will be exacerbated, depressing productivity in the agricultural sector.

It is not inconceivable, moreover, that rises in per capita income (PCY) in the early stages of development may be accompanied by, or even induce, population growth in excess of income growth, holding down PCY to a subsistence level. Today's falling death rates (associated with development) are contributing to population pressure; and presumably for centuries past the

Figure 11.7 Low-level equilibrium trap

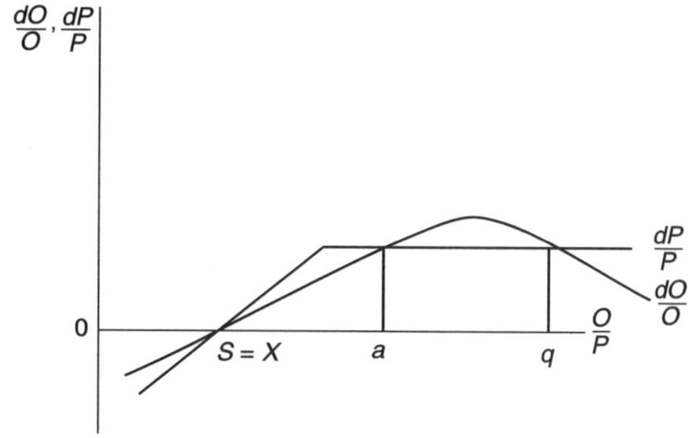

population of most countries has been oscillating around the subsistence level, with small gains in living standards (due to 'technical progress') being wiped out either by higher birth rates or factors such as disease, famine and war. This is the notion of a **low-level equilibrium trap**, illustrated in Figure 11.7.

Figure 11.7 shows the relationship between the growth of population (dP/P) and the growth of output (dO/O) on the one hand (measured on the vertical axis), against the level of per capita income (O/P) on the other (measured on the horizontal axis). $S = X$ represents the subsistence level of PCY at which population growth is zero and output growth is also zero because at the subsistence level there is no saving and investment. Population growth rises with PCY and then levels off at a biological maximum. Output growth rises with PCY because the savings ratio also rises with PCY, but then levels off (and even declines). Output growth eventually falls as the capital–labour ratio falls. If the output growth curve cuts the population growth curve from above at point $S = X$, it can be seen that any increase in PCY above the subsistence level up to a point *a* will lead to population growth in excess of output growth, pushing income per head back to the subsistence level. Conversely, any PCY level beyond *a* will mean a sustained rise in PCY until the two curves cut again at *q*. This would be a new stable equilibrium, with the output growth curve again cutting the population growth curve from above.

To escape from the low-level equilibrium trap, PCY must either be raised to *a*, or the dO/O and dP/P curves must be shifted favourably. The origin of **big push** theories of development (see Chapter 9), and the concept of a **critical minimum effort**, was the belief that to escape from the 'trap', it would be necessary to raise PCY to *a* in one go through a massive investment programme. If countries are in a trap situation, however, much greater hope probably lies in the dO/O curve drifting upwards over time, through technical progress, or in a sudden drop in the dP/P curve from a reduction in the birth rate. Capital from abroad, raising the dO/O curve, and emigration, lowering the dP/P curve, could also free an economy from such a trap.

To take account of factors other than population growth that may depress PCY, and factors other than increases in capital per head that may raise PCY, the low-level equilibrium trap model can be extended and generalized by adopting Leibenstein's terminology of 'income-depressing' forces and 'income-raising' forces (Leibenstein, 1957). Leibenstein's approach is illustrated in Figure 11.8. The curve representing income-depressing forces, *Z*, is measured horizontally from the 45° line, and the curve representing income-raising forces, *X*, is measured vertically from the 45° line. Per capita income level *a* is the only point of stable equilibrium. Between *a* and *q*, income-depressing

Figure 11.8 Leibenstein's approach

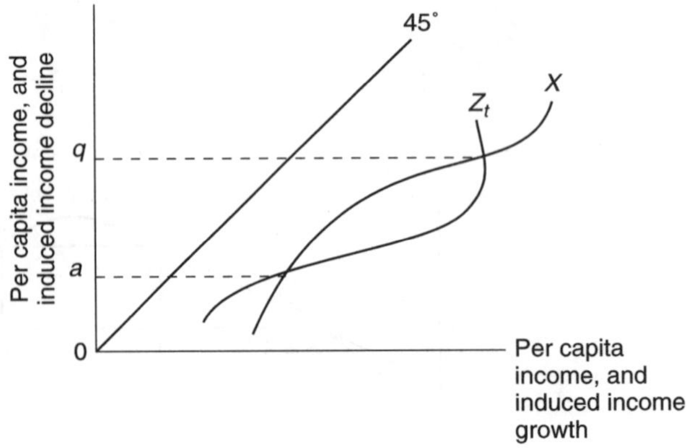

forces are greater than income-raising forces and PCY will slip back to *a*. Only beyond *q* are income-raising forces greater than income-depressing forces, such that a sustained increase in PCY becomes possible. *q* is the critical PCY level necessary to escape from the low-level equilibrium trap.

Most developing countries in the world today are experiencing income growth faster than population growth. Whether income growth would be faster if population growth was reduced is an open question. It is possible to conceive of a low-level equilibrium trap, but its level almost certainly rises over time owing largely to technical progress before a reduction in birth rates sets in (see Cassen (1976), Kelley (1988), Simon (1997), Dasgupta (1995) and Bloom (2016) for surveys of many of the issues discussed in this chapter).

Summary

- Since the 1950s, the world's population has grown at an unprecedented rate, more than doubling from just over 3 billion in 1950 to over 7 billion today. The pace of growth is slowing but population growth in developing countries is still three times faster than in developed countries (1.8% compared with 0.6% per annum). The world's population is forecast to stabilize at around 11 billion in 2050.
- The cause of this population explosion has been a dramatic fall in the death rate due to advances in medical knowledge and improved sanitation, without a commensurate fall in the birth rate (until recently).
- Fertility rates are high in poor countries, but decline with the level of per capita income. This is the theory of demographic transition. Fertility also declines with the years of education women receive and with female employment opportunities.
- The costs of rapid population growth include pressure on food supplies, urban congestion, environmental degradation, the depletion of non-renewable resources, and a reduction in the savings ratio of countries.
- The potential benefits of population growth include the stimulus to new agricultural methods to raise output (e.g. the Green Revolution of the 1960s and 1970s), demand-induced investment, scale economies, and the provision of social infrastructure, which confers positive externalities (e.g. transport).

- There is no statistically significant correlation (negative or positive) between the growth of population and the growth of living standards across countries.
- The term 'optimum' population is used in four different senses: maximizing income per head; maximizing total welfare; the maximum population that can be supported with existing resources; and the population level that maximizes total output. The terms 'overpopulation' and 'underpopulation' need to be treated with caution without knowing the precise basis of the calculations.
- It is possible for countries to get caught in a 'low-level equilibrium trap' with population growth exceeding income growth and income per head oscillating around subsistence level. A 'big push' or 'critical minimum effort' in terms of investment may be necessary to launch communities in this state on to a self-sustaining growth path.

Chapter 11 Discussion questions

1. What accounts for the population explosion in developing countries since the 1970s?
2. Why do poor people have large families?
3. What are the major determinants of fertility?
4. It has been said that 'affluence is its own prophylactic'. Does this mean that it is futile to attempt to control the size of the population before living standards rise?
5. Why will the population continue to grow rapidly even if fertility rates in developing countries fall rapidly?
6. In what ways may rapid population growth impair development?
7. What are the stimuli that rapid population growth might give to development?
8. How would you do a cost–benefit analysis of population growth?
9. What do you understand by the concept of the 'low-level equilibrium trap'?
10. Is it possible to define an 'optimum' population?

Note

1. For an extensive survey of the determinants of fertility relating to the microeconomic behaviour of households, see Dasgupta (1995).

Websites on population

World Bank, World Development Indicators http://data.worldbank.org/data-catalog/world-development-indicators
United Nations www.un.org/popin/wdtrends
UN Population Division www.un.org/en/development/desa/population/
UN Population Fund www.unfpa.org
UN Population Information Network www.un.org/popin/

12

DEVELOPMENT AND THE ENVIRONMENT*

---

* This chapter has been written by our colleague, Professor Iain Fraser.

Introduction

The environment is vital to supporting life, absorbing waste and providing inputs for production. Since the 1960s, there has been increasing concern about the effects of economic activity on the environment. In particular, it has been argued that economic growth has caused serious environmental damage and that the current state of the environment will constrain future economic development. For example, it is now widely, but not universally, accepted that recent economic development has led to climate changes, and that changes will, unless adapted to, seriously disrupt economic activity and society in the future. The poor in developing countries are often dependent on the natural environment for their livelihood and even their continued existence. Thus, damage to the environment and the relationship between the environment and the economy are often thought to be of more importance to developing than developed countries.

Table 12.1 shows how a range of selected environmental indicators vary by economic regions globally. For example, there are significant differences between Africa and Europe in terms of forest net change and access to sanitation. This chapter provides an introduction to the economic analysis of the relationship between the environment (including the climate), development and the economy.

A simple model is developed that explains the services the environment provides for economic activity and the effects of the economy on the environment. Next, the market-based approach to analysing the interactions of the environment and the economy is examined. This approach emphasizes the efficient use of the environment and considers market failures to be the main, and perhaps the only, cause of market economies' difficulties in allowing for environmental concerns in economic development. It is shown how this approach can be used to provide valuations of environmental services and improve the efficient use of the environment. The neoclassical analysis of equity within and between generations is considered and its importance in the context of the environment is examined.

The concept of **sustainable development** is then explained. This idea defines forms of development that meet the needs of the present generation while maintaining the potential to meet the needs of future generations. This is followed by a discussion of the recent **Stern Review on climate change** and the effect of climate change on the poor. Finally, there is a brief review of how environmentalists, economists and international agencies have approached the analysis of the environment, climate change and the economy.

A model of the environment and economic activity

There are many different models of the relationship between the environment and the economy. The model depicted in Figure 12.1 illustrates the four functions of the environment in supporting economic activity and the effects of this activity on the environment. (This discussion of the relationships between the environment and the economy is very general and simple; see Tarbuck et al. (2008) for an introduction to earth sciences and the interaction of humans and the environment.) These four functions are life support, supply of natural resources, absorption of waste products, and supply of amenity services. The economy is represented in Figure 12.1 by households consuming goods and services, and firms producing, using natural resources provided by the environment, and labour and man-made capital provided by households.

The environment provides a **biological, chemical and physical system** that enables human life to exist. This life support system includes the atmosphere, river systems, the fertility of the

Table 12.1 Key environmental indicators data

Key environmental indicator	Latest year on record	World	Africa	Asia and the Pacific	Europe	Latin America and the Caribbean	North America	West Asia	Unit of measurement
Consumption of ozone-depleting substances	2010	43 292	2 559	29 971	103	5 199	2 165	3 295	Million tonnes ODP
HFCs emissions – all gases	2008	651 748	2 146	237 395	140 251	14 882	255 602	1 471	Gigagrams
Carbon dioxide emissions	2008	32.11	1.14	13.69	6.61	1.65	6.01	1.04	Billion tonnes of CO_2
Carbon dioxide emissions per capita	2008	4.8	1.2	3.5	8.0	2.9	17.4	8.3	Tonnes of CO_2 per capita
Forest net change	2005–2010	5.6	-3.4	0.5	0.9	-3.9	0.4		Million hectares per year
Area protected to maintain biological diversity to surface area	2010	12.0	10.1	9.9	10.2	19.3	9.5	17.1	Per cent of total territorial area
Municipal waste collection	2000–2007			271.2	537.9	130.8		20.2	Million tonnes
Total water footprint per capita of national production – blue	1996–2005	167	94	181	109	110	380	345	m^3 per year per person
Total water footprint per capita of national production – green	1996–2005	1 087	1 167	780	1 259	1 924	2 689	426	m^3 per year per person
Access to sanitation	2010	61.0	39.9	57.4	90.9	80.1	100.0	78.3	Per cent of total population
Number of certifications of the ISO 14001 standard	2010	251 000	1 700	131 700	103 700	7 231	5 500	1 200	Number of certifications

Source: UNEP, 2012.

Figure 12.1 A simple model of the relationship between the economy and the environment

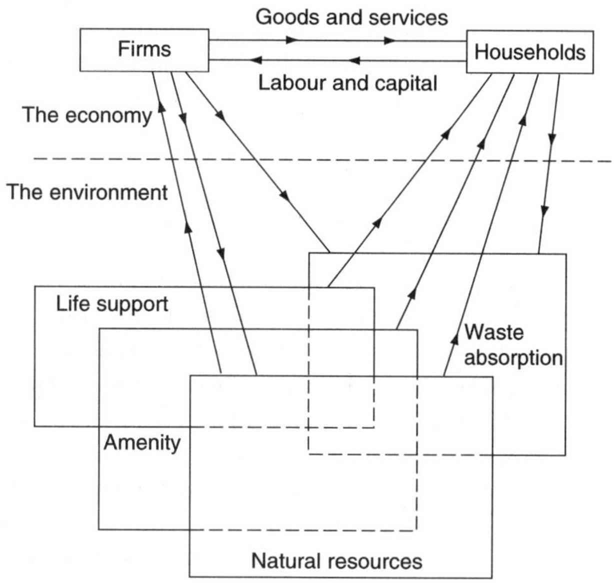

soil, and the diversity of plant and animal life. These environmental services are consumed by households and are essential to life. Large reductions in these services, for example through major climate change, would have catastrophic consequences for life.

The environment provides **raw materials and energy** for economic production and household activity. These natural resources are either renewable, as in forests and fisheries, or non-renewable, as in minerals. Renewable resources can be used in a sustainable manner, although excessive use or mismanagement can result in the complete loss of the resources, for example desertification following deforestation. The ability to use renewable resources sustainably and increase the stock of renewable resources is represented in Figure 12.1 by the flow from firms to natural resources. However, the use of a non-renewable resource reduces the finite stock of the resource forever.

The **waste products** of economic and household activity are absorbed by the environment. This waste absorption function allows some of such waste to be disposed of safely. However, there are certain wastes that are difficult or impossible for the environment to dispose of safely. For example, the global warming gas carbon dioxide (CO_2) is captured through the growth of forests and absorption in the oceans. Deforestation and physical limits to absorption in the oceans mean that the absorptive capacity of these processes has been reduced. Consequently, because of the effect of rising levels of carbon dioxide on climate change, it has been argued that the world economy has to change through reducing carbon dioxide emissions, seeking alternative means of capturing these emissions and adapting to climate change.

The environment also provides **amenity services**, such as natural beauty and space for outdoor pursuits, which are consumed, but are not crucial to the continued existence of life.

Parts of the environment may serve more than one function. The oceans, for example, are important in determining the life support systems provided by the global climate and microclimates, they are sources of many minerals and other resources, they assimilate many different wastes, and they provide the space and opportunity for marine pastimes. Thus, in Figure 12.1 above, the four blocks representing the different functions of the environment overlap. The functions of the environment may be competitive; excessive discharges of waste materials into the oceans will, for example, reduce their capacity to provide a habitat for fish stocks. Alternatively, environmental functions can be complementary; as when appropriate forestry policies can provide a sustainable source of timber (a natural resource function), reduce soil erosion (an improvement in the life support function) and capture CO_2 emissions (a waste absorption function).

The market-based approach to environmental analysis

The market-based approach to environmental analysis has probably been the dominant view of the relationship between the environment and the economy (for an introduction to this subject, see Common, 1996). In particular, many environmental policies and much analysis are based on the view that markets may not function efficiently with regard to the environment and that the state has a duty to intervene and correct market failures. The underlying assumptions of the market-based approach are examined and various applications to the environment are considered.

The market or neoclassical approach to economics is concerned with how scarce resources are allocated in a market economy (explanations of the neoclassical approach to economics can be found in most intermediate microeconomics textbooks: see Varian, 2005). Allocation is assumed to take place on the basis of consumers' preferences, the distribution of economic assets and the costs of production. It is assumed that each consumer is rational and decides to purchase goods and services on the basis of prices and economic assets, which include labour income. It is assumed that the value a consumer places on additional units of consumption declines with increasing consumption. Economic rationality dictates that consumption of a good continues up to the point at which the value placed on an additional unit is just equal to the price. Further expenditure on the good would be inefficient as greater value could be obtained from using the additional expenditure to purchase more preferred goods and services. Similarly, less expenditure is inefficient, as greater value could be obtained by purchasing more of the good and fewer less preferred goods and services. Thus, the neoclassical model assumes that economic rationality gives efficiency in consumption.

The neoclassical view also assumes that firms are profit maximizers. This implies that firms minimize costs. This gives efficiency in production. Finally, it is assumed that competition among firms forces them to charge prices that are equal to their marginal costs of production. As consumption decisions are based on prices, the equality between prices and marginal costs means that these decisions are based on the marginal costs of production. This ensures efficiency between consumption and production.

The neoclassical view has various important implications for the analysis of the relationship between the environment and the economy:

1. It is implicitly assumed that the value of consumption is determined by the individual consuming the good. The value of consumption is not determined by the state or some other authority. Additionally, it is assumed that individual consumers and producers do not consider the effects of their decisions on other economic agents. Consequently, there is no difference between private and social costs or private and social benefits.
2. Economic rationality implies that the value of the marginal consumption of a good or service can be measured by price.
3. The neoclassical analysis of the market is based on considering small changes in consumption and production. This extends to the neoclassical view of the environment.

4. The outcome of a market economy, in terms of prices, quantities and the distribution of economic welfare, depends on the initial distribution of economic assets. Different distributions or reallocations of assets give different outcomes. It is frequently pointed out that under certain conditions, the operation of the market may be efficient, but it may not be equitable. It may be possible to assess the efficiency of a market economy in an objective manner, but evaluation of the equity of a market outcome is a value judgement.

Externalities

The idea of externalities can be used to analyse many, but not all, types of environmental degradation. Externalities occur when the actions of one economic agent affect other economic agents and the actions are not controlled through the operation of the market. Externalities have two related causes: lack of individual property rights, and jointness in either production or consumption (Baumol and Oates, 1988). Individual property rights are exercised over goods, services and factors of production and allow markets to function efficiently. With a complete set of individual property rights, all the effects of an action are controlled by the market, since consumption of a good or service and use of a factor require payment to the owner. Beneficial or positive externalities are likely to be undersupplied by a market, and negative externalities are likely to be oversupplied. For an externality to continue to exist, it is usually presumed that jointness in either production or consumption is involved.

An example of negative environmental externalities and economic development can be seen in the building and operation of the Manantali and Diama hydroelectric dams in Mali (see Bond et al. (2001) for details and evaluation of the external effects of these hydroelectric dams). These dams generate cheap electricity, which has been distributed to Mali, Senegal and Mauritania since 2001. Downstream from the dams, the annual floods have been reduced and this has decreased agricultural productivity. Additionally, the elimination of salt water intrusion through the building of these dams has led to an increased incidence of bilharzia and other health problems. Thus, the building and operation of these hydroelectric dams has imposed external costs on those living and working downstream of the dams.

These (negative) externalities are caused by jointness in production of electricity. At the same time as electricity is being generated, the water system is being altered and this causes health and productivity effects. The economic cause of the externalities is that no markets exist in the management of water systems. In particular, there are not clear, legally enforceable rights to the ownership and services of the water system downstream. A simple model is developed in Figure 12.2 of the interests of the electricity generators and the downstream population.

The downstream environmental degradation by the generators produces a benefit to the economy as it allows the production of electricity. This is denoted by the marginal benefit MB curve (measured in dollars) and is assumed to be downward sloping. The downward slope can be justified by a lower price being obtained for the sale of electricity as more is produced. The environmental effects are mostly negative and are represented by an upward sloping curve, the marginal cost MC of environmental degradation. There is a threshold effect below which there is no environmental damage as the environment can absorb a minor change in the water system without any cost. The curve then slopes upwards as the environment has difficulty in coping with the increased environmental degradation.

The neoclassical view is that there is an optimal level of environmental degradation at which the marginal benefit is equal to the marginal cost, point X in Figure 12.2. Whether this level of degradation is small or large depends on the shape of the marginal benefit and cost functions. This conclusion considers environmental effects purely from the point of view of efficiency. However,

Figure 12.2 Marginal benefits and environmental costs of a dam

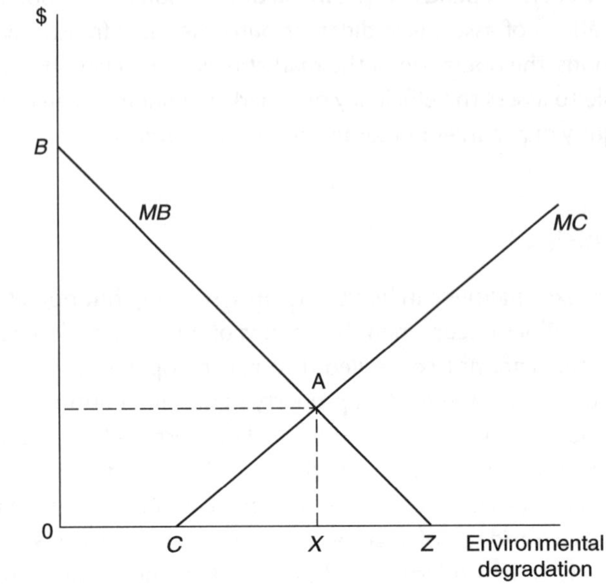

it should be remembered that outcome X may be efficient, but if the costs imposed on the inhabitants are relatively large, the resulting distribution of welfare may not be desirable.

The operation of a market economy is unlikely to lead to an efficient outcome. The downstream inhabitants' environment is being degraded by the actions of the generators. In an economy with a complete set of individual property rights over all economic assets, the inhabitants or the generators would own the property rights to the environment. If the inhabitants owned the rights, the generators would have to pay to be allowed to degrade the environment. In the case of the generators owning the rights, the inhabitants would have to pay the generators to restrict environmental degradation. In reality, such property rights are likely to be ill-defined, particularly across national boundaries. It might be expected that no market controls this environmental degradation. Generators are likely to continue to degrade the environment until the marginal benefit to them of degradation is zero, point Z in Figure 12.2.

This analysis is one of **market failure.** A conventional reaction to market failure is to suggest the intervention of the state to secure a more efficient outcome. There are four feasible policies that have been suggested as solutions to this type of externality problem: **Pigovian taxes and subsidies,** named after A.C. Pigou, well-known Cambridge economist; **Coasian bargains,** named after Ronald Coase, Nobel Prize-winning economist; **marketable permits**; and **administrative action and legislation** (see Perman et al., 2011).

The **Pigovian tax solution** imposes an environmental use tax on the generators of the value of the marginal cost of degradation at the point of the optimal outcome X. This forces the generators to take account of the costs they impose on the inhabitants. This is shown in Figure 12.3, where the generators face a new marginal benefit *MB*′ of environmental degradation schedule that includes the tax (t).

Generators will, out of self-interest, choose the efficient level of degradation. Examples of Pigovian taxes have recently been observed in several countries that have started to charge for plastic shopping bags in an effort to reduce the associated pollution caused by plastic in the environment.

Figure 12.3 Taxation, marginal benefits and costs of a dam

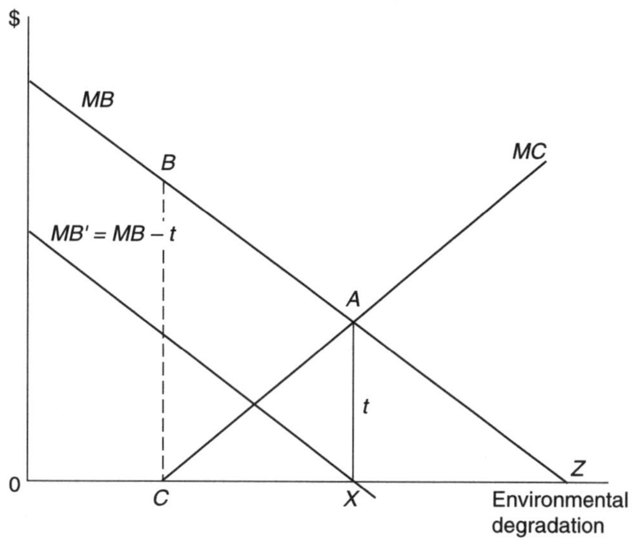

A Pigovian subsidy could alternatively be given to generators to reduce environmental degradation and a similar solution occurs. An example of such a subsidy is the payment made to generators of carbon emissions in Australia under the Emissions Reduction Fund introduced in 2014.

When attempting to increase the supply of positive externalities, it has become widely accepted that payments to correct market failure are legitimate. In this case, the **provider gets principle** as opposed to the **polluters pay principle** is applied. An example of this approach that has gained much attention by policy-makers is the **payment for ecosystem services** approach (Pagiola et al., 2005). This policy mechanism rewards farmers and landowners for maintaining and producing environmental goods and services that are typically undersupplied because of classic market failure. However, the Pigovian solution suffers from a number of problems.

Let us consider the dam example again. First, it is difficult to quantify and value the costs and benefits of environmental degradation (this point is returned to later). The benefits and costs are not likely to be uniform across different dams, which implies the complication of different tax rates. Second, many of the downstream inhabitants are not part of the cash economy and the state is unlikely to be able to tax and regulate generators or afford the cost of subsidies.

The **Coasian bargain solution** assumes that individual property rights are established and economic agents bargain an efficient outcome. If individual property rights over the environment are given to inhabitants, then generators have an incentive to bargain and pay to be allowed the right to degrade the environment, as their marginal benefit exceeds inhabitants' marginal cost at the origin in Figure 12.3 above. The potential efficiency gains of this bargaining are represented by the area *ABC*. Similarly, if the generators are given the property right, there are incentives for the inhabitants to pay the generators to reduce degradation from the point *Z*. The Coasian solution suffers from the major problem of how property rights are established. Additionally, there are incentives for individuals to **free ride** on the contributions that others make to reduce externalities. It is difficult to see how bargains can be enforced when there are many inhabitants. Finally, in many cases, the transaction costs of negotiating a Coasian bargain may be high and are likely to prevent such solutions from emerging.

In the real world, it is rare for Coasian bargains to occur as solutions to environmental problems. The **Global Environment Facility (GEF**, www.thegef.org), which was established in 1991, could be interpreted as such an example. The GEF is a partnership of many countries and international organizations that addresses global environmental issues, and receives donations from many sources, including countries, research institutions and so on. The GEF provides grants to countries to address global problems such as climate changes and pollution of international waters, and was charged with funding mechanisms to help achieve the three Rio Conventions (climate change, biodiversity and desertification) of the 1992 Rio Earth Summit.

The issuing of **marketable permits** that give the bearers the right to pollute is a potentially elegant and efficient means of solving the problem of pollution and externalities such as global warming and gas emissions. The size of the issue of permits directly controls the level of total pollution. Potential polluters have to decide whether to reduce their pollution or use their own or purchased permits. This should result in the set level of pollution being obtained at the least cost. Tietenberg and Johnstone's review (2004) shows that the use of different types of tradable permit schemes have increased and are often regarded as a valuable policy tool. A tradable permit 'cap and trade' scheme lay behind the operation of the **Kyoto Protocol** to reduce global warming gas emissions, and it is also an available policy instrument for the new global policy approach that is attempting to reduce carbon emissions. The operation of tradable permit schemes does not have universal support. There has been little investigation of the use of schemes by developing countries, and experience suggests problems with their operation and outcomes; for example, in 2008 the European Commission responded to criticism of the EU Emissions Trading Scheme (EU ETS) by implementing major changes. However, as policy-makers continue to gain experience, the introduction of tradeable permit-type schemes has increased; one important example being California's Cap-and-Trade Program, which began in 2013, and is second in size after the EU ETS. Ellerman et al. (2016) provide an overview of how the EU ETS has evolved and attempted to deal with the various challenges it has faced in practice.

The fourth solution to the externality problem is **command and control**. This approach takes action to ensure that the externality is reduced to a lower level. The usual examples of this solution are fixed standards backed up by legal sanctions, for example maximum allowable levels of environmental degradation. The actions taken by the Mali government to deal with the environmental problems caused by the previously mentioned Manantali energy project have taken many forms. The government enforced standards and monitored the building of the project. A reservoir management plan was developed to help irrigate downstream areas, affected land was purchased, people were resettled, and health programmes were implemented. These measures are practical, but do not have the theoretical elegance of the three previous solutions.

The one major problem facing all solutions to the problem of dealing with externalities is assessing their physical nature and calculating their economic value. This is discussed later in the section on the Stern Review (Stern, 2006) on the costs and benefits of preventing climate change. In particular, the uncertainties surrounding environmental effects and their economic value are discussed.

Common property rights

The common ownership of a renewable resource is likely to lead to an important externality. Such circumstances are frequently referred to as the **tragedy of the commons.** However, Dasgupta (1982) has forcefully argued that there has been considerable confusion over the economic analysis of this problem. In many cases, the confusion stems from describing something as being common property when, in fact, it is open access. With open access, anybody can access the resource in question. An example would be the oceans. In contrast, 'common property' refers to a situation in which a closed group of individuals have access to a resource, such as a grazing common or an area of forestry. The analysis is frequently considered in terms of the example of cattle farmers grazing their animals on commonly owned land. The rational individual farmer will use common land without regard to the cost this use imposes on all other farmers. This behaviour is a negative externality and is inefficient. The cost imposed on other farmers is the exhaustion of the fertility of the soil. This effect will decrease the future value of the resource to farmers. In this sense, the problem of the commons is an **intertemporal externality**. However, it is not the case that use of the common property resource of grazing land necessarily destroys the usefulness of the land. The extent of overgrazing depends on the private cost of rearing animals, their market value, and the ability of the land to support a large number of animals. Nevertheless, appropriate cooperative action by farmers to reduce overgrazing would increase the economic welfare of the farmers as a group.

The negative implications that stem from the tragedy of the commons were challenged by Elinor Ostrom (1990). The importance of her work resulted in her being awarded the Nobel Prize for Economics in 2009.

Elinor Ostrom

Born 7 August 1933. Died 12 June 2012. Taught for most of her life at the University of Indiana, USA, where she established, with her husband, the Workshop in Political Theory and Policy Analysis to study how institutional arrangements affect behaviour and policy outcomes in diverse settings, particularly the efficient management of natural resources. Awarded the Nobel Prize in Economics in 2009 for showing how the problem of the tragedy of the commons can be 'solved' by appropriate action.

Ostrom's analysis of common property resources was based on a series of studies that explained that the tragedy of the commons did not always result simply because of an absence of property rights. (see Case example 12.1 for an example of such an institutional arrangement). This was because, as she identified, in many different circumstances, a set of institutional arrangements can emerge that allow the common property to be efficiently managed and, as a result, the negative externalities that are forecast to remain are nothing but a theoretical possibility. Her work also showed that voluntary arrangements, that is, institutional structures that do not need the direct involvement of the state, could bring about these alternative forms of resource management, such that voluntary management yields a more sustainable resource management outcome than that achieved by state intervention. In addition, her research also explained when the necessary conditions for the voluntary arrangements will begin to unravel and potentially fail. In particular, she identified that voluntary arrangements struggle to work when confronted with ever-increasing numbers of parties, when there is lack of social capital that exists between the economic parties, such that trust cannot be taken as a given (see Ostrom, 2000).

Case example 12.1 **The tragedy of the commons: southern bluefin tuna**

The phrase 'tragedy of the commons' can be traced back to Hardin (1968) and his classic paper on the inappropriate management of many types of natural resource. Fisheries in the open oceans are an example, as there are an unconstrained number of potential fishers that have no limits on access to the resource and the rate at which the resource is harvested. In such a world, no one fisher has an incentive to reduce effort as somebody else will simply harvest the fish that are not taken.

A well-documented example of this problem is the impact of open access fishing on the southern bluefin tuna. Tuna in general and this species in particular have been heavily overfished by a number of countries. Southern bluefin tuna are a migratory species of pelagic (live in the open oceans) fish that attract a high price because of demand from the Japanese sashimi market. As anticipated by Hardin, the value attached to this species and the fact that they are pelagic have led to excessive fishing that resulted in serious population decline, especially in mature adult fish. In an effort to manage these effects, the existing voluntary management arrangement between Australia, Japan and New Zealand was formalized in 1993 by, first, the Convention for the Conservation of Southern Bluefin Tuna and then, in 1994, the Commission for the Conservation of Southern Bluefin Tuna (www.ccsbt.org). Since 1994, more countries have agreed to abide by the management rules implemented by the commission; for example, South Africa joined in 2016.

Although the spawning biomass of the southern bluefin tuna is very low by historical levels, estimates in 2014 indicated a small improvement compared to 2011. This shows that the problems of resource management identified by Hardin can be resolved if economic agents are willing to cooperate and not simply view a natural resource as an asset to be used without thought for the future.

The discount rate

The degradation of the environment reduces the supply of environmental services in the future. Economic analysis of the environment requires a means of comparing the benefits and costs of environmental effects in the present and the future. This comparison is usually made through a weighting device called the **discount factor**. The practice of discounting environmental costs and benefits has caused much confusion and dispute.

In a neoclassical model of the behaviour of individual economic agents with finite lives, the discount rate is simply the market rate of interest. The level of the market rate of interest is the outcome of the preferences of individuals for present consumption over future consumption and the physical possibilities of transforming present consumption into future consumption. However, even with a set of perfect capital markets, the resulting intertemporal allocation of resources is unlikely to be socially efficient for a number of reasons.

First, the outcome of perfect capital markets reflects the preferences and actions of those presently alive. All individuals will eventually die and presumably value their own consumption more highly than that of their descendants. This implies the market outcome may underweight the consumption of future generations. It might be argued that the state should decide on a distribution of economic welfare over time that favours future generations more. Alternatively, it has been argued that technical progress will increase future incomes, and fairness requires redistribution from future generations to the present. However, it is unclear how the state can easily decide which distribution should be preferred (see Pearce et al., 2006).

Second, even with regard to the preferences of the present generation, the market outcome may be inefficient. The present generation may wish to save for the benefit of future generations. This can lead to two types of market failure, the **assurance problem** and the **isolation paradox** (Sen, 1967). Both phenomena are examples of externalities. The assurance problem concerns saving by one individual for future generations, which benefits all other individuals in the present who place a value on the consumption of future generations. Thus, the market aggregate level of saving is inefficient and the market rate of interest undervalues future consumption. Aggregate saving would be increased if individuals were assured that their additional savings would be matched by other altruistic individuals.

The isolation paradox concerns the value individuals place on their descendants' consumption compared with that of the rest of future generations. If the return from saving for the benefit of future generations cannot be captured entirely by an individual's descendants, then it is likely that even perfect capital markets will provide an inefficient level of saving.

Imperfections in the capital market are widespread and there is no unique interest rate or discount rate. Instead of the use of an observed market interest rate, the 'social opportunity cost of capital' has been used as a measure to discount the future. The social opportunity cost of capital measures the social value of a loss of one unit of capital in the economy to fund the proposed investment. If resources to fund a project displace other investments, rather than consumption, the social opportunity cost of capital is the correct measure of the cost of capital. However, there are practical difficulties in calculating the social opportunity cost of capital.

The effect of the discount rate on environmental degradation is unclear. A low discount rate weights future consumption more heavily and might be thought to give a better future environment than a higher rate. However, most investments have costs at the beginning of their life and benefits thereafter. Thus, a lower discount rate will make these investments appear more attractive as weighted future benefits will increase relative to present costs. Increased investment and the consequent economic growth may lead to more environmental degradation.

The harvesting of renewable resources

Renewable resources are those whose stock is capable of growth as well as depletion. Renewable resources are usually thought of as experiencing growth and regeneration through a biological process. Fisheries, forests and the previous example of common pasture land are all examples of renewable resources. The neoclassical analysis of renewable resources considers efficient harvesting, while biologists are often concerned with the **maximum sustainable yield** (MSY) that can be obtained from the resource. These two ideas are examined in the context of a fisheries example.

The growth of the stock of fish, ΔX, depends on the stock, X. This relationship is shown in Figure 12.4. Below a critical level, X_c, the stock is in danger of terminal decline as it is not capable of replication. The existence of a critical level may be explained by difficulties in reproduction. Above this level, growth is positive. Eventually, the growth declines because of competition for food supplies or the effects of predators. The MSY occurs at the point of greatest absolute growth.

The efficient use of the fish stock is examined by considering a simple model in which harvesting is costless. The objective is to maximize the social value of the stock over time. The social gain is examined in connection with reducing the harvesting of fish and allowing the present stock to increase by one unit. The present marginal social value of one unit of fish is denoted by v.

Figure 12.4 Relation between the growth and stock of a renewable resource

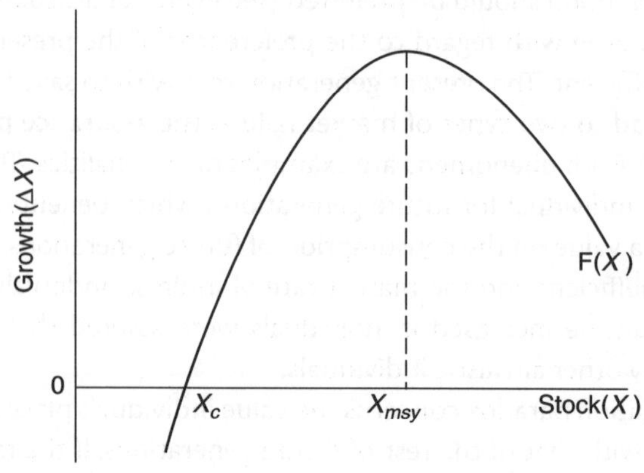

The marginal productivity of the stock, $F'(X)$, represents the change in growth from increasing the stock by one unit. The social value of this gain is $\nu F'(X)$. The marginal social value of an additional unit of fish in the second period is $(\nu + \Delta\nu)$, where $\Delta\nu$ is the change in social value between the first and second periods. With a discount rate of r, the present value of an additional unit of stock in the next period is:

$$\frac{\nu F'(X) + (\nu + \Delta\nu)}{1 + r} \tag{12.1}$$

The marginal social value of consuming one unit of fish in the present period is ν. Thus, if equation (12.1) exceeds ν, an increase in social welfare can be obtained by reducing the level of harvesting. This condition can be written more simply as:

$$F'(X) + \Delta\nu/\nu > r \tag{12.2}$$

This condition has a simple interpretation. If the marginal productivity of the stock plus the proportionate gain in the value of the stock over time exceeds the discount rate, then it is efficient to reduce harvesting. A reduction in the harvest increases the stock, which is likely to decrease $F'(X)$ (see Figure 12.4). A reduction in the harvest means consumption will fall and the marginal social value of present compared with future consumption will increase. These two effects may be expected eventually to give equality in equation (12.2), and thus efficiency.

Equation (12.2) has two important implications. First, the efficient outcome is not the same as the MSY, as the latter is given by $F'(X) = 0$. Second, for species that have a low marginal productivity of stock and whose value does not increase appreciably with decreasing stock, extinction may be an efficient outcome.

The present analysis is concerned with maximizing the social value of the fish stock over time. It is appropriate to consider whether the efficient outcome can be achieved through a market system. The fisheries example is another case of common property rights. In the discussion of common property rights, it was seen that it can be difficult to establish individual property rights for renewable resources such as fisheries, forests and pasture land. Thus, the market use of such renewable resources is likely to be inefficient.

If the property rights for the resource are given to a few individuals, this will affect the distribution of economic welfare and will result in monopoly power. Private monopoly control of a renewable resource may result in its inefficient use, as marginal (private) revenue rather than social value would appear in equation (12.2) and, in order to maximize profits, the monopolist may restrict the use of the resource below the efficient level (see Hanley et al., 2013).

Non-renewable resources

Non-renewable resources cannot be regenerated over time. The present use of one unit of such a resource prevents it from being used in the future. The finite levels of these resources means that they are often referred to as 'exhaustible resources'. This suggests that non-renewable resources should be used with care.

There are many estimates of the stocks of non-renewable resources. Calculation of the known reserves of a non-renewable resource has to be made in the context of the extraction cost and the price of the resource. It is considered inappropriate to include in estimates of reserves sources for which the cost of recovery exceeds the current price or for which there is no proven extraction technology. 'Proven reserves' refer to those sources that are presently known. It is likely that there are sources yet to be discovered. However, uncertainty means that it is difficult to calculate meaningful estimates for unproven reserves.

The depletion of a non-renewable resource can be analysed in terms of the objective of maximizing the social value of the stock. Figure 12.5 considers a one-period model and the maximization of the economic rent from extracting a mineral that has a price *P*. The economic rent is the area between the price and the marginal cost curve. If the price is equal to the marginal social value of consumption, a perfectly competitive industry will extract the resource up to the point Q_0, which is a socially efficient outcome. A monopoly faced with a downward sloping demand curve is likely to restrict output below Q_0, which is inefficient.

The **optimal depletion** of a non-renewable resource over time can be analysed in a similar manner to the harvesting of a renewable resource. Again, the objective is maximization of the social value of the stock over time. The decision to extract a non-renewable resource is simpler, in

Figure 12.5 Economic rent and the use of a non-renewable resource

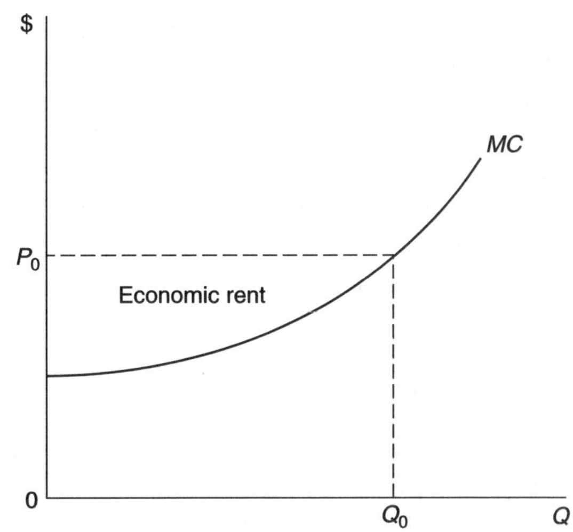

that there is no marginal productivity of the stock to consider. It is assumed that the extraction of the resource is costless. The resource should be further conserved if:

$$\frac{\Delta \nu}{\nu} > r \tag{12.3}$$

Equation (12.3) has a simple interpretation. If the relative appreciation of the social value of the resource is greater than the discount rate, then more of the resource should be saved for the future.

For an efficient outcome, the social value of marginal consumption should be increasing at the rate r. This implies (through integration) that ν is given by the function $\nu_0 e^{rt}$, where ν_0 is the social value at time zero. If a constant marginal cost of extraction (mc) is introduced into the analysis, the efficient outcome gives the equation:

$$\nu(t) = mc + \nu_0 e^{rt} \tag{12.4}$$

Equation (12.4) reflects the optimal depletion path. It is possible for a perfect market to give this outcome. In this case, the optimal price path is given by:

$$p(t) = mc + r_0 e^{rt} \tag{12.5}$$

The $r_0 e^{rt}$ term is referred to as the **discounted rental premium**. It may be interpreted as the social cost of consuming the resource in the present rather than in the future.

As before, if the price is equal to the marginal social value of consumption, a perfectly competitive market will maximize social welfare across time. A monopoly may restrict the use of the resource below the efficient level and the price path will be inefficient (see Hanley et al., 2013).

It has been pointed out by Kay and Mirrlees (1975) that, for reasonable discount rates, one would expect the optimal price to be close to marginal cost for most of the lifetime of a non-renewable resource.

Other environmental values

It is a central tenet of neoclassical economics that prices should reflect the marginal costs of production. In a competitive economy, prices may reflect private marginal costs, but there are a number of other types of social costs that should be taken into consideration (see Garrod and Willis, 1999). First, the external costs imposed on other individuals should be taken into account. (The remaining values could strictly be classified as private or external costs, but for the purpose of exposition they are separated into different categories.)

Second, the economic rent in the use of non-renewable resources should be included in social marginal costs. As noted before, the economic rent may be regarded as a premium that has to be paid for the use of the resource in the present rather than in the future.

There are four other types of value that have not yet been considered: **option**, **quasi-option**, **existence** and **bequest values**:

1. An **option value** is the value placed on an option that allows use to be made of the environment in the future. Option values depend on attitudes to uncertainty, such as risk averseness. The option is not necessarily taken up, but it gives value. An example of an option value is

biodiversity. The protection of species of animals and plants may be desired in order to allow possible future uses of these species as inputs to production, and because many individuals may wish to have the opportunity of seeing these species in the future.

2. **Quasi-option values** are the values placed on an option given an expectation that there will be increases in knowledge. For example, the value of certain plant species may depend on the development of knowledge of new uses of the plants.
3. **Existence value** is the value placed on a good or service independent of any actual or possible future consumption. This value is different from the other types of value in that it is unrelated to use. An example of existence value is the concern expressed by many individuals for the preservation of elephants, even though they are unlikely ever to see them at first hand, or use this resource.
4. **Bequest value**, as the name suggests, is when an economic agent wishes to pass on resources to members of future generations.

Thus, the total social cost comprises seven components:

$$\text{social cost} = \text{private cost} + \text{external cost} + \text{rental premium} + \\ \text{option value} + \text{quasi-option value} + \text{existence value} + \text{bequest value} \qquad (12.6)$$

Efficient allocation requires consideration of all seven components of social costs.

Measuring environmental values

The analysis of this chapter suggests that a market economy will not value all aspects of the environment appropriately. This view is widely held and has led to much intellectual and practical effort being applied to the problem of how to introduce appropriate environmental values into economic decision-making. The following discussion considers the introduction of environmental considerations into social cost–benefit analysis and national income accounting.

Appraisals of many investment projects in developing countries now include **environmental impact assessments** (EIAs) that estimate the environmental effects of the projects. This should be the first stage of the introduction of the environmental effects of a project into social cost–benefit analysis. Often, it is very difficult to assess a project's physical effects on the environment. For example, the British government argued that the Stern Review (Stern, 2006) had underestimated the physical impacts of climate change. EIAs can rarely firmly establish the type and extent of environmental effects of projects. Thus, the introduction of previously unconsidered environmental effects into economic decision-making should take account of this uncertainty.

Once the environmental effects of a project have been estimated, there are four approaches to placing economic values on the effects (more precise details and discussion of economic valuation can be found in Garrod and Willis, 1999). First, the basic valuation technique in social cost–benefit analysis is to use market prices. This is justified by the neoclassical assumption that prices reflect the social value of goods and services. In the case of environmental effects in developing countries, markets and prices may not exist for many of the effects that require valuation. For large environmental effects, the project may actually alter prices. In this case, the changes in the values placed on environmental effects should be modelled. In practice, this is often impossible.

If we are unable to employ market prices, then it is necessary to employ one or more of the large number of valuation methodologies developed by economists. These methodologies have been developed using varying degrees of economic theory and statistical methods. Figure 12.6

Figure 12.6 An overview of economic valuation methodologies

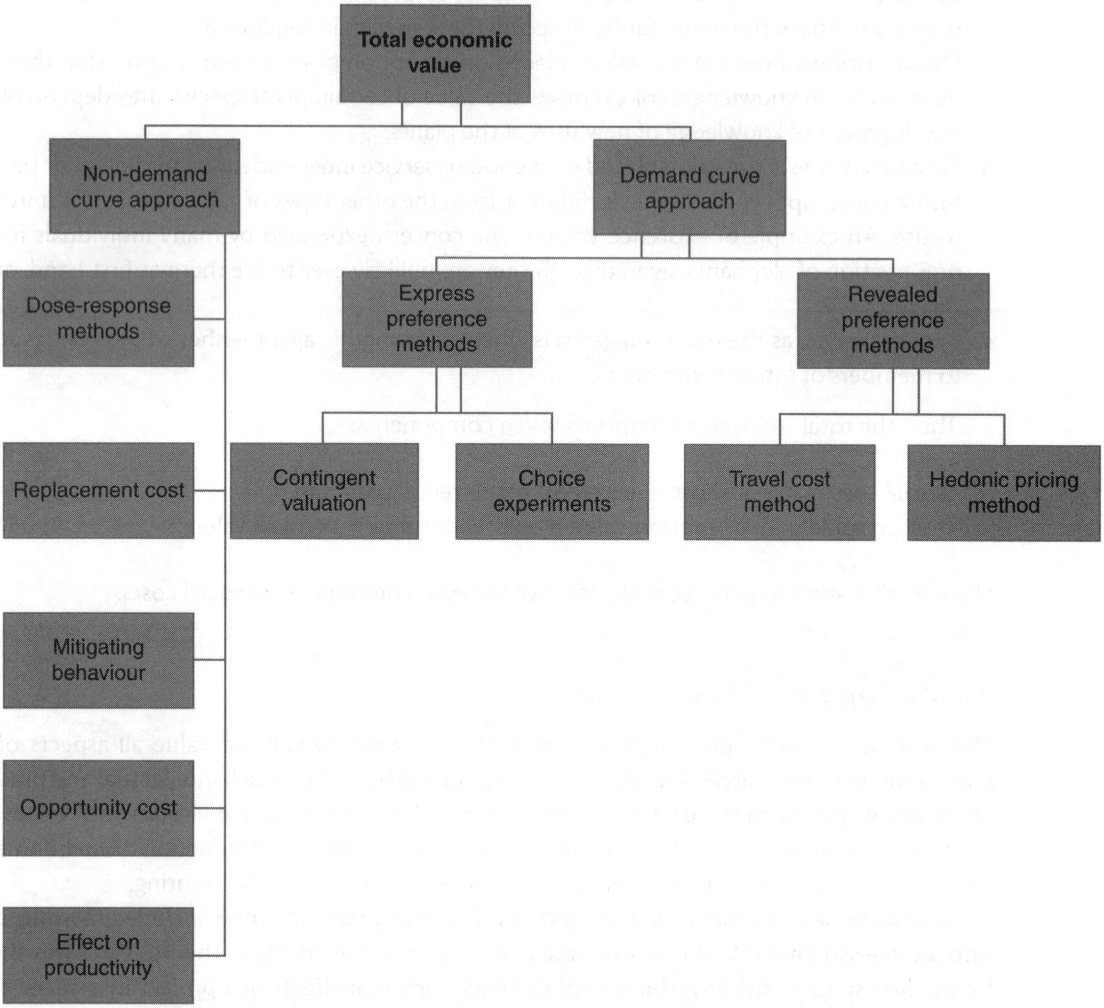

gives an overview of these methods. In this context, economic value is referred to as 'total economic value', which can be estimated in part or full by either employing non-demand (a theoretical) curve approaches or demand (theoretically consistent) curve approaches.

Thus, the second approach calculates the value of environmental effects indirectly through observed economic behaviour; this set of methods is shown on the left-hand side of Figure 12.6. Within this approach, there are a number of different techniques. One is the **mitigating behaviour approach**, which takes the expenditure that people are prepared to undertake to prevent degradation as a measure of the value of the environmental effects. Another is the **replacement cost technique**, which estimates the expenditure people are prepared to undertake to restore the environment to its previous state after degradation has occurred. (These expenditures and costs may be difficult to observe and both techniques often require experts to estimate them.) The full long-term consequences of environmental effects may not be understood. Not all environmental effects can be fully offset by preventive expenditure and the environment cannot always be restored after degradation. Such problems may be particularly important for large changes in the environment, for example changes in the ecology of a large watershed, and climate change. The ability of individuals to fund these expenditures may be limited by imperfect capital markets. For these reasons, it is usually thought that the two techniques may underestimate environmental costs.

The **production function approach** (or **effect on productivity approach**) values environmental impacts by their effects on production. Thus, part of the environmental impact of a change in climate conditions could be valued through the effects on agricultural output. Another example is the valuation of environmental health effects by estimating changes in the productivity of affected individuals. This implies that the value of life is only determined by production and there are no psychic costs to ill health and early death.

The third approach is typically referred to as the **revealed preference approach** and these methods are shown on the right-hand side of Figure 12.6. Why revealed preference? In the absence of a market for an environmental effect, it is sometimes possible to derive the value placed on the effect by the prices paid for other goods and services that implicitly value the effect. For example, property values vary with location, and this may, in part, reflect differences in the environment. The **hedonic prices method** can produce estimates of the contribution of differences in the environment to the prices of property. This can be used to give an estimate of the implied value of certain environmental qualities. In developing countries, there are often significant imperfections in markets, for example rent controls, which affect the validity of the technique. The hedonic price method requires large amounts of data. It is often difficult to measure the environmental quality that is being considered. The importance of the environmental variable may not be properly understood by individuals. These problems limit the usefulness of this technique, particularly in developing countries.

In contrast, the **travel cost method** values the time and costs that people are willing to incur in travelling to areas with more pleasant environments. Thus, the method gives an implied value of environmental quality. The formal assumptions of the model and its applicability to developing countries have been criticized (see Garrod and Willis, 1999). The method implicitly considers the environment in terms of the provision of recreational services rather than basic life support services.

The fourth approach to valuing environmental effects is referred to as the **stated** or **expressed preference approach** and these methods are shown in the middle of Figure 12.6. In this case, survey instruments are developed that are used to directly ask the public how much they might be willing to pay for a specific environmental outcome. The original stated preference approach is **contingent valuation**. A subset of the population is surveyed and asked for their valuation of the environment. There are two ways in which this question can be asked. Individuals can be asked about either their willingness to pay for an environmental benefit or their willingness to accept compensation for a loss of environmental quality. Economic theory suggests that the answers to the two types of question should be similar. In many surveys, willingness to accept compensation questions receive much higher responses. The questions asked are hypothetical and those surveyed may not be familiar with the environmental effect/resource being surveyed. Respondents may respond to questions strategically, and there is evidence of other forms of bias in the replies to surveys. The responses of individuals may reflect the context of the survey question. Thus, for example, individuals could, with appropriate questions, be induced to respond as citizens concerned with the public interest rather than as consumers pursuing their own self-interest. It is not always clear how to gross up the response from a survey to represent the general population's valuation of an environmental effect.

More recently, **choice experiments** have become a popular stated preference methodology. Like contingent valuation, they also make use of a survey but they do not directly ask what a specific environmental good or service is worth. Instead, by drawing on Lancaster's (1966) theory of demand, they frame economic choices in terms of the attributes of a good or service that a consumer will consider when making a choice (Hensher et al., 2015).

Finally, **benefit transfer** is an alternative approach to all the above. As the name implies, benefit transfer takes existing benefit estimates and uses them in related or similar contexts. In recent years, this practice has become much more straightforward with the development of databases containing the results of many earlier valuation studies, such as the Environmental Valuation Reference Inventory (www.evri.ca). This approach can be useful if primary valuation research has not or cannot be conducted. However, there are potentially many biases that can occur in undertaking this approach and, as such, much of the research and application of this approach is directed at attempting to minimize biases that can occur in practice.

In summary, the valuation of environmental benefits and costs is essential to improving economic decision-making on the environment, and social cost–benefit analysis has developed various techniques to this end. However, there remain theoretical and practical problems with the use of all these techniques (IPCC, 2014a).

National income accounting

The neoclassical approach to economic analysis assumes that consumption in its widest sense is, and should be, the objective of economic activity. The ethical issues concerning whose consumption should be considered were examined in Chapter 8. The conventional approach is to measure economic welfare in terms of per capita income. This approach has been widely criticized and alternative measures have been proposed, many of which emphasize the importance of accounting for the environment.

Measures of economic welfare have to be judged in terms of their theoretical definition and practical application. The most obvious measure of current economic welfare is per capita current consumption. Current consumption can be increased by reducing investment and thus future consumption. This suggests that economic welfare in one period should be defined relative to a fixed capital stock. So, additions to capital stock, although not increasing current consumption, should be reflected in a measure of economic welfare as they allow increases in future consumption. This idea underlies the conventional definition of income (see Hicks, 1946): 'A person's income is what he can consume during the week and still expect to be as well off at the end of the week as he was at the beginning.'

There are many conceptual and practical problems with the definition of income, so only those directly concerned with accounting for the environment are examined here. Environmental degradation can be mitigated by the actions of economic agents, for example soil erosion can be reduced by planting forests. In national income accounts, such **defensive expenditures** are taken as giving rise to increases in economic welfare rather than as attempts to maintain the environment. It is commonly argued that these expenditures should be excluded from measures of economic welfare and account be taken of the environmental effects that give rise to these expenditures.

Environmental degradation affects economic welfare as individuals directly consume environmental services, for example unpolluted air. As there is not always a market in such services, or only an indirect one, they are not recorded in national income accounts. Degradation also reduces the productive potential of the environment, for example non-natural causes of soil erosion and reductions in the ability of the environment to absorb waste products. Reductions in the productive potential of the environment are examples of the depreciation of the stock of natural capital. These types of change are not recorded in national income accounts.

The use of non-renewable resources, for example fossil fuels, is not allowed for in a correct manner in national income accounts. These resources are part of the natural capital of the environment. Their use in the present reduces the supply available for future generations. National income accounts consider the use of non-renewable resources as a simple productive activity. It should also be considered as a depreciation of natural capital. (A similar analysis applies in the case of renewable resources, as regeneration can require time and investment, and thus present consumption of renewable resources can impose costs on future generations.)

At the international level, there is the London Group on Environmental Accounting, a UN research group that has attempted to update and modify the System of National Accounts (SNA) to take account of environmental issues in a manner consistent with the SNA. The result was the development in 1993 of the System of Environmental-Economic Accounting (SEEA) (unstats.un.org/unsd/envaccounting/seea.asp). The SEEA has adopted some of the ideas that have been developed by economists to extend the SNA but there are limits to the modifications that are considered, as there is the need to maintain consistency with the SNA.

There have been four general responses to the failure of national income measures to account for the environment, some of which have been adopted within the SEEA, but many of which have not and go far beyond the modifications considered by the London Group. The first method follows Nordhaus and Tobin's (1972) calculations of **measures of economic welfare**, which attempt to recalculate national income accounts to allow for environmental effects. Progress on developing measures of national income that allow for the use of natural capital and environmental degradation has been slow for most developing countries, although the World Bank now reports the value of natural capital in many developing countries. A report in *Nature* (1998) suggested that adjusting for environmental effects may have reduced national income for Brazil, India and Indonesia by 12–17% in the mid-1990s, but a more recent estimate using World Bank data on adjusted national income for Taiwan suggests a reduction of only 1%. Allowing for the environment can often give quite different estimates of economic welfare and economic growth.

The second method of accounting for the environment follows the weak sustainability view that total capital should be at least maintained. In this approach, the level of saving is calculated and the depreciation of natural, man-made and other forms of capital is deducted. If the resulting number is negative, this may be taken as evidence of unsustainable development. The method is explained in World Bank (2002). **Genuine savings** (or adjusted net saving allowing for changes in environmental capital stocks) are reported for many developing countries and are sometimes negative. At the global level, genuine savings do not tend to evolve in a linear or constantly increasing manner. Figure 12.7 indicates that there is a rising trend in genuine savings globally but there can be significant year-on-year variations that indicate the problems faced in constantly being able to achieve even weak sustainability.

A third method of accounting for the environment in economic growth is to construct *physical*, rather than monetary, accounts of the environment. These accounts divide up the environment into different sectors and estimate the changes that have taken place over time. For example, the use and discovery of mineral and energy resources would be recorded. The World Bank (2011) has argued for the collection of physical indicators across time of the effect of human activities on the environment and the effect of the environment on human activities (see www.worldbank.org).

A fourth set of methods starts with national accounts and then makes a series of modifications, many of which remove the underlying theoretical consistency of the accounts. However, the motivation for making these changes is not to remain consistent with national accounting procedures but to yield a measure of economic activity that better reflects economic, environmental and societal policy objectives. An example that has attracted much attention is the **ecological**

Figure 12.7 Global genuine savings, 1990–2014

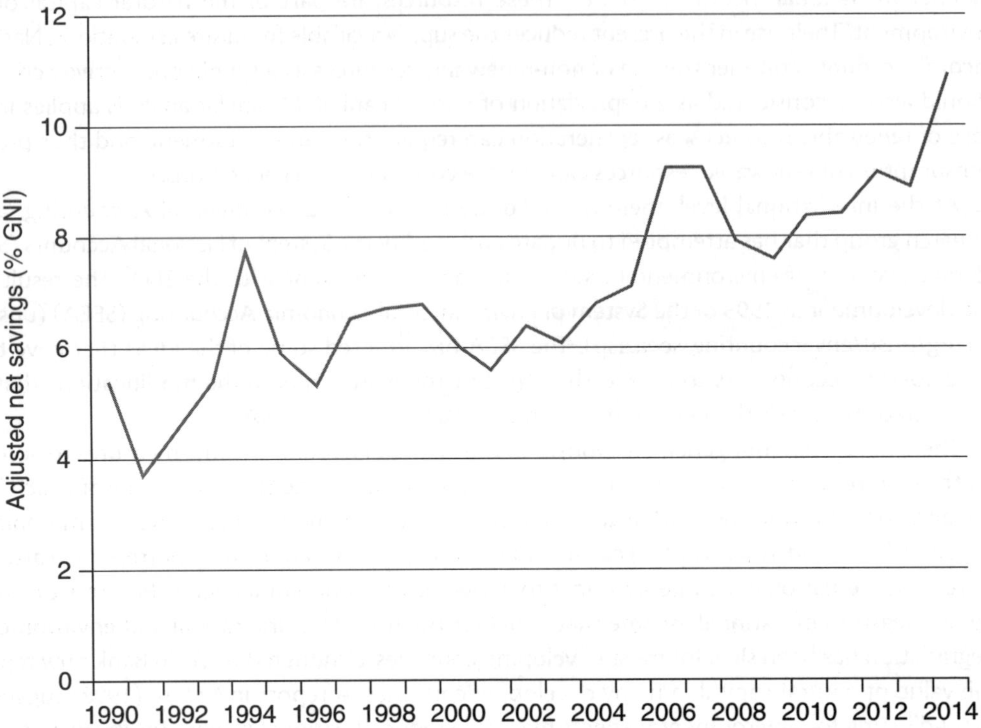

Source: World Bank staff estimates based on World Bank, 2011.

Note: Adjusted net savings equals net national savings plus education expenditure minus energy depletion, mineral depletion, net forest depletion and carbon dioxide and particulate emissions damage.

footprint method. This approach has proved popular with environmentalists who do not feel comfortable with simply relying on monetary measures of sustainability. The ecological footprint has also proved useful as a way for environmentalists to highlight what they consider to be excessive levels of human consumption and use of the environment. For example, Edward O. Wilson (2002), in his book *The Future of Life*, observes that if all individuals consume resources at the same level as the average individual in the USA, then with the current state of technology, we will require four additional planets. This powerful statistic is arrived at by converting all forms of consumption into a land use equivalent measure. Unsurprisingly, it has added another dimension to the ongoing debate about whether or not current levels of consumption are sustainable.

Importantly, the four methods of accounting for the environment are not substitutes. The monetary approach of the first of the two methods also requires the calculation of physical accounts. Physical environmental accounts are useful for considering ecological and environmental issues. Monetary environmental accounts are useful as they reduce all effects to a common measure and estimate a net figure for the use of the environment. However, because of the difficulty of doing this, they have been criticized on theoretical and practical grounds (see Perman et al., 2011).

Risk and uncertainty

Risk exists where there is doubt about a future outcome and it is possible to estimate objective probabilities of the occurrence of different possible future outcomes. The outcome of a throw of a dice is an example of risk. Uncertainty exists where there is doubt about the outcome and it is not possible to estimate probabilities of the occurrence of the different possible future outcomes. It is difficult to analyse uncertain events and most environmental analysis that considers risk and uncertainty assumes, either explicitly or implicitly, that it is possible to estimate probabilities with some degree of objectivity, that is, the circumstances are assumed to be those of risk rather than uncertainty.

Uncertainty about the relationship between the environment and the economy complicates analysis. As previous examples have shown, there is scientific dispute about many important environmental effects. In the analysis of environmental policies, it is possible to distinguish two approaches to managing this uncertainty.

First, the different possible outcomes of a policy are predicted. Then probabilities are estimated for these different outcomes, although these probabilities are necessarily subjective. It could be argued that the notion of estimating probabilities for events such as global warming is not appropriate, as they cannot be considered as repeated probabilistic events like the throwing of a dice. However, recent studies have attempted to provide probability estimates of different levels of global warming and Stern (2006) suggests that there is a 63–99% chance of warming exceeding 2°C after a doubling of greenhouse gas concentrations. Notwithstanding this, policy analysis could proceed by selecting the most preferred policy on the basis of the probabilities of the different outcomes of the policies. If society is averse to taking risks, it can be shown that uncertain costs should be given more weight than the expected value of costs, and uncertain benefits should be given less weight than their expected value.

The alternative procedure is to select the mean estimates of the effects of different environmental policies. These estimates are then used to decide the most preferred policy. This procedure is often used. The choice of the mean estimates is highly subjective. More importantly, this approach does not take account of either risk or uncertainty.

The potential importance of uncertainty in the area of environmental economics has been highlighted by Pindyck (2007), who argues that the uncertainty society faces in the area of environmental economics is far more complicated than in any other area of economics for three reasons:

1. The cost and benefit functions that describe the relationship between the economy and the environment might be highly nonlinear, meaning that we struggle to understand the consequences of our actions.
2. It is highly likely that there are important irreversibilities that exist in terms of policy choices and decisions as well as environmental damages.
3. Many of the most important environmental issues we confront have long time horizons, which conventional project and policy appraisal techniques do not deal with very well.

Economic growth and the environment

Figure 12.1 above indicates that the environment is essential for economic activity and growth, and shows the importance of the effects of economic growth on the environment. Environmentalists have argued that unconstrained economic growth will lead to the exhaustion of non-renewable resources and to levels of environmental degradation and climate change that will seriously affect economic production and the quality and existence of life (Meadows et al., 1972; Forrester, 1971). Economists who believe in the effectiveness of market-based policy instruments have responded to these arguments (see Sterner, 2003).

If markets operate effectively, the increased scarcity of non-renewable resources will increase their prices. These higher prices will give incentives for changes in economic behaviour:

- The direct consumption of these resources may fall: for example, lower consumption of scarce fossil fuels.

- There will be incentives to search for new supplies of these resources: for example, the level of exploration for new oilfields will increase.
- The use of higher priced non-renewable resources in production will decline through substitution with production techniques that are less intensive in these inputs: for example, production will become less fossil fuel-intensive.
- Higher prices will encourage the development of new technologies that provide substitutes for scarce resources: for example, non-fossil fuels such as 'biomass' or wind power – or utilize it more efficiently: for example, fuel-efficient cars.

Thus, efficient markets may provide a solution to the running down of non-renewable resources.

Supporters of economic growth often argue that its contribution to environmental degradation has been overestimated. Alternatively, there is a common view of the existence of opportunities for simultaneous economic development and improvement in the environment, as argued by the World Bank (2001). However, the pursuit of these twin goals is usually assumed to require the state to intervene and improve the operation of markets with regard to the environment.

It has been argued by Grossman and Krueger (1995) that in the early stages of economic development, the level of environmental degradation increases, but after this phase, the environment improves with economic development, but it is important to note that CO_2 emissions increase with the level of development (see Table 12.1 above). This proposition is in line with the World Bank (1992) and the results that are reported at the beginning of this chapter. However, there is an extensive debate on the relationship between the environment and economic growth and development. In particular, the relationship has been characterized by an inverted U-shaped relationship, referred to as the **environmental Kuznets curve** (see Hanley et al., 2013). The shape of this relationship between the environment and economic activity could be explained by changes in the mix of output at different levels of development, changes in the demand for the environment at different levels of income and the policy responses to these demands, and the availability and use of more environmentally friendly technologies in developed countries.

All the different views of economic growth and environmental degradation considered here are likely to be true in part. It is unlikely that the debates on the relationships between the environment and the economy can be resolved through exhaustive scientific and economic investigation. Economic and environmental policies have to be formulated and carried out on the basis of existing uncertain and disputed evidence.

Sustainable development

Much of the vast literature on the environment and the economy could be interpreted as a response to the concern that present patterns of economic growth may seriously degrade the environment and may be unsustainable, as the environment cannot support economic growth forever. This proposition may or may not be substantially true. At its heart lies the view that past and present economic policies have usually been concerned with providing the conditions for equilibrium economic growth, as measured by standard national accounting methods. Many environmentalists are concerned that these policies have not attempted to ensure 'the existence of ecological conditions necessary to support human life at a specified level of well-being through future generations' (Lele, 1991). This concern is of major importance in the concept of **sustainable development**. Sustainable development has perhaps become the most important approach to considering the environment and development.

There is a wide range of definitions and interpretations of the meaning of 'sustainable development'. The term first came to prominence in the *World Conservation Strategy*, presented in 1980 by the International Union for the Conservation of Nature and Natural Resources (IUCN/UNEP/WWF, 1980). It was popularized by the World Commission on Environment and Development's study *Our Common Future* (UN WCED, 1987), which is also known as the Brundtland Report, named in honour of its chairperson, the Norwegian prime minister. These and other studies have defined sustainable development in different ways. The most frequently quoted definition comes from the latter study: **'Sustainable development seeks to meet the needs and aspirations of the present without compromising the ability of future generations to meet their own needs.'**

This definition would appear uncontroversial and is remarkably similar to the neoclassical definition of income given earlier by Hicks (1946). However, the interpretation differs in that *Our Common Future* examined how sustainable development can be achieved (UN WCED, 1987). This inevitably requires making value judgements that link the definition and the operational objectives, which, it has been suggested, will result in the attainment of sustainable development. For this reason, there has been criticism of the connection between the definition and the operational objectives. The objectives are increasing economic growth, meeting basic needs, involving more of the population in decision-making and development, controlling population growth, conserving and improving the environment, accounting for the environment in economic decision-making, changing technology, managing risk, and changing international economic relationships.

The concept of sustainable development has gained wide acceptance and has become a standard model for thinking about the environment, development and the economy. Most countries that attended the Rio Earth Summit in 1992 accepted the general idea of sustainable development, as enshrined in the *Agenda 21* process agreed at that summit (UN, 1993). The UN 2005 World Summit: 'reaffirmed [its] commitment to achieve the goal of sustainable development [and its] three components ... economic development, social development and environmental protection' (UN, 2005). However, as observed above, what the concept of sustainable development should imply for economic and environmental policies is disputed. In particular, the concern for equity between and within generations is central to most interpretations of the concept, but it is unclear how the welfare of individuals can be compared. One of the major controversies concerning the approach of the Stern Review (Stern, 2006) is the low discount rate used to compare costs and benefits for different generations. This is a central problem in neoclassical economics and the concept of sustainable development does not appear to provide a solution to the problem.

The new **Sustainable Development Goals (SDGs)**, which superseded the Millennium Development Goals (MDGs) in 2015, are an important set of policy objectives across a wide range of economic, environmental and social contexts (see Chapter 1). In particular, efforts to deal with climate change are a specific SDG (Goal 13) that articulate several important policy targets. Specifically, this goal argues for the need to integrate climate change policy actions into all national policy decisions. In addition, there is a commitment by all parties to the **UN Framework Convention on Climate Change (UNFCCC)** to have an annual fund of $100 billion by 2020 to ensure that the necessary policy actions are realized. The $100 billion target can be viewed as an explicit test of the willingness of richer nations to help poorer nations tackle climate change. The UNFCCC, which entered into force in 1994, is very important as it provides the primary international intergovernmental forum where global negotiations take place that attempt to deliver policy solutions to issues such as climate change and biodiversity loss.

Natural capital, equity and environmental values

In defining the notion of sustainable development, it is common to require that the stock of capital be non-declining through time. A constant or increasing stock of capital allows consumption levels to be maintained or increased. However, there are major differences of opinion over the capital stock that must be held constant or increased. The weak sustainability view considers all the different forms of capital – man-made, human, natural and social – to be substitutes, which can be aggregated into total capital. Thus, for example, degrading the natural fertility of the soil can be compensated for by using fertilizers and the methods of agricultural science to maintain crop yields. In this example, human capital and man-made capital are used to substitute for natural capital.

The alternative view of strong sustainability takes the position that it is only natural capital that needs to be held constant or increased. In this view, the focus is often on critical natural capital, which is either required for human survival or cannot be substituted for with other forms of capital. Thus, one might take atmospheric global warming gas levels as critical natural capital, as higher levels cannot be offset by other capital. For an economic comparison and analysis of weak and strong sustainability, see Hanley et al. (2013). However, it might be argued that some of the effects of climate change resulting from higher global warming gas levels can be adapted to by additional sea defences and migration of population (see the discussion of the Stern Review later in the chapter).

Underlying the analysis of the environment and development, and the importance of natural capital, are views about environmental values. The study of environmental values suggests three possible ways in which these values could be generated. First, the preferences of individuals give rise to values that with a complete set of perfect markets are reflected in the prices of goods and services. This is the neoclassical approach to valuation, and examples of market failure have already been examined. Market failures suggest that the environment will not be adequately accounted for in the operation of market economies.

The second source of environmental values is that of social preferences. Sagoff (1988) suggested that individuals are capable of considering issues, in particular those concerning the environment, from the point of society. It is not clear how such values could be established in the psyche of individuals. A possible explanation is a sociobiological one, in that individuals behave as social organisms for the benefit of the species (Dawkins, 1976). Environmental choices are so complex that even if social preferences exist, it is difficult to assume that, apart from in a tautological sense, they will result in decisions that improve social welfare. However, it has been suggested that the poor in developing countries are the most dependent on the environment. Thus, if social preferences are to give weight to the circumstances of the poor, the environment should be given greater weight than would occur from simple aggregation of the individual values placed on the environment.

The third source of environmental values follows from the belief that ecological systems have an intrinsic value independent of any value placed on them by humans (see Booth, 1994; Common and Stagl, 2005). The individual preferences basis for values considers only human beings to have rights. The ecological view represents the extension of rights to other species. How these rights can be measured is a difficult problem. The ecological values view suggests that greater weight should be attached to the environment than would be given by taking just social values or simple aggregation of individual values.

Preserving or increasing the stock of natural capital has important effects on intergenerational equity. If it is believed that present levels of environmental degradation and resource use will substantially alter future human economic welfare, then intergenerational equity may be improved by the constraint that the stock of natural capital should be preserved. This is the strong sustainability view. However, the substitution of this constraint by a more flexible approach that allows some use of natural capital could conceivably increase economic welfare measured across all present and future generations. This is the weak sustainability view.

The use of a positive discount rate weights future environmental effects less heavily than those occurring in the present. This has been criticized as underestimating the importance of environmental degradation and resource use. This criticism is misplaced. If the arguments are accepted for the social preference of the present compared with the future, then discounting is appropriate. If it is felt that too little weight is being attached to future environmental effects, their estimated values should be adjusted, but not the discount rate.

Many environmental effects are irreversible, for example the extinction of a species. Irreversibility has been used as an argument for maintaining the natural capital stock. However, the dislike of irreversible losses in natural capital can be captured by the concepts of option, quasi-option and existence values.

The resilience of an ecosystem is its ability to maintain its normal functions after an external disturbance (Common and Stagl, 2005). It has been suggested that the larger the stock of natural capital, the more resilient an ecosystem is likely to be. This argument is justified on the basis of the idea that the diversity of the ecosystem increases its resilience. However, the notion of resilience and the related concept of stability have been criticized, as no ecosystem is likely to be globally stable and constant through time. This implies that the size of the external disturbance is important (Norton, 1987).

As discussed earlier, uncertainty is crucial to the analysis of the relation between the environment and the economy. A possible policy response to such uncertainty is to adopt policies that provide insurance against possibly disastrous future outcomes. This risk-averse strategy of emphasizing the worst possible outcome might be justified by, say, the worst forecasts of the disastrous outcomes of global warming. This argument supports the setting of a constraint that keeps the stock of natural capital fixed. Alternatively, it has been argued (see Lomberg, 2001) that the vast expenditure necessary to reduce global warming, the long period before such effects become important, and the lack of absolutely clear scientific proof of the size of these effects suggest that a conservative approach ought to be adopted. It is unclear how uncertainty should be included in environmental decision-making, but it *is* clear that the treatment of uncertainty has a very important effect on the actual decisions that have been or will be taken.

Arguments about weak and strong sustainability, sources of environmental values, discounting, irreversibility, uncertainty and resilience suggest that perhaps a higher value should be placed on the environment than the operation of a market economy would give. Strictly, this is not the same as suggesting that the stock of natural capital should be maintained. However, the complexity of decision-making on the environment might require an approximate constraint on the use of the environment, such as preserving the stock of natural capital.

This critical discussion of the concept of sustainable development suggests that the environment has an important role in economic development and this may not have been fully understood in the past. The concept of sustainable development has won many academic and political adherents. However, there are differences in opinion whether natural capital deserves special protection in economic development or whether it can be traded off against man-made and human capital. These differences are important in determining how the environment enters into economic decision-making.

There are also practical difficulties with the implementation of a constraint that keeps the stock of natural capital fixed. The environment is made up of many different resources and services. Constancy of the stock of natural capital could be interpreted as constancy of all types of natural capital. This interpretation implies that any positive use of non-renewable resources would not be compatible with sustainable development and is difficult to justify.

The alternative interpretation is to consider a single measure of natural capital that appropriately weights the different types of natural capital. The obvious weights are the values of the various types of natural capital. These values may not only reflect the ideas considered in equation (12.6), but also the distributional views that are often associated with the idea of sustainable development. However, placing values on the different types of natural capital would appear to deny the special role of such capital. If different forms of natural capital can be valued so as to give a single measure, this suggests that it can be traded off against man-made and human capital and requires no special protection in the process of development.

It may be the case that a single measure of most types of natural capital would be desirable, with individual measures for the remaining critical types of natural capital, for example atmospheric levels of greenhouse gases.

If the view is taken that the environment must be preserved, then a social cost–benefit analysis of a project should be carried out, subject to the additional constraint that the net effects on the environment are zero or positive. The strength of this additional constraint can be weakened by adding environmentally friendly investments to the project that allow the constraint to be met. If it is considered necessary to preserve the different types of natural stock, then there must be an additional constraint for each type of natural capital.

The constraint of preservation of all aspects of the environment implies that national income accounting methods cannot be altered to allow the calculation of one measure of economic welfare that includes environmental effects. Thus, it has been suggested that measures of economic welfare be presented alongside a set of indicators of the state of the environment.

The less restrictive interpretation of the concept of sustainable development allows substitution between different forms of capital and the simple inclusion of the environment in social cost–benefit analysis and national income accounting (see www.worldbank.org). The inclusion of the environment simply requires the correct valuation of environmental effects.

Economic thought and the environment[1]

Classical economists, such as Malthus ([1798]1983), Ricardo ([1817]1992) and Mill ([1856]1986), were generally pessimistic about the possibility of continued economic progress (see also Chapter 4). These economists assumed that there were diminishing returns to factors of production and the supply of land was fixed. The growth in population, and thus the labour force, would lead to reductions in the marginal product of labour and a declining average product of labour. Malthus and Ricardo assumed a constant technology, with the inevitable result that average agricultural production per unit of labour would decline. Mill considered that technical progress could offset the effect of diminishing returns to a factor, but was unlikely to do so in the long run. Marshall (1890) invented the idea of an externality, which was developed by Pigou (1920). However, in general, environmental externalities were considered to be unimportant.

The start of the debate about the environment and the economy is usually attributed to Rachel Carson and her book *Silent Spring* (1962). Other early contributions to the environmental debate were made by Boulding (1966), Ehrlich and Ehrlich (1970), Goldsmith et al. (1972),

Forrester (1971), Schumacher (1973) and Commoner (1972). A most influential environmental publication was *The Limits to Growth* by Meadows et al. (1972). The basic point of this study was that there is a number of non-renewable resources whose present levels of consumption are such that the known reserves will be exhausted in the not so distant future. The study was heavily criticized for not allowing for the effects of the price mechanism to reduce consumption and provide incentives to explore for new reserves and develop new technologies. A useful summary of the early developments of environmental economics is provided by Sandmo (2015).

These environmental contributions to the debate stimulated economic interest in the relation between the environment and the economy. Barnett and Morse (1963) could find little evidence of resource scarcity in the US economy in the period 1850–1957. Dasgupta and Heal (1979) provided a rigorous neoclassical analysis of the depletion of exhaustible natural resources. Kneese et al.'s (1970) development of the **materials balance approach** changed the view that some economists had of how the economic system dealt with the environment's waste absorption function. This simple principle states that all resources that flow into an economic system must eventually end up as waste products.

The debate about the environment and the economy has changed public views, and, in particular, the views of international agencies have changed.

Climate change, the Stern Review and predicting the future

Climate change occurs because the earth absorbs energy from the sun and re-emits this energy. Some of this energy is absorbed by greenhouse gases and warms the earth. The existence of the greenhouse effect and the warming of the planet since the middle of the twentieth century are universally agreed. The extent of the contribution to climate change from man-made greenhouse gas emissions, however, has been disputed by some scientists and is difficult to prove beyond doubt.

The impacts on nature of global warming are sea level rises, loss of land and species, ecosystem changes in agriculture, relocation of forests and fisheries, changes in water availability and in local climates, and more unpredictable weather episodes. The impacts on humans are increased mortality and morbidity from climate-related diseases, lack of food, air pollution, and weather-related disasters. Climate change also increases costs to society related to human migrations, changes in economic activity, adaptation to climate changes, and measures to reduce greenhouse gas emissions. The **World Meteorological Organization** and the **UN Environment Programme** set up the **Intergovernmental Panel on Climate Change (IPCC)** (www.ipcc), which reports on the scientific and economic research literature on climate change. These reports (including the current 6th report) suggest that global temperatures will rise by 1–6^{0}C during the twenty-first century. The variation in the estimates is due to the differing assumptions concerning the complex mechanisms and feedback systems that cause global warming.

The 2006 **Stern Review** on the economics of climate change was commissioned by the UK government to review the possible impacts of global climate change, to investigate the costs of these impacts, and to advise on policy actions. This review is the most widely quoted report on the economic effects of climate change, and possible policy responses. The review concludes on the scientific evidence that climate change is a serious threat, with many of the impacts being irreversible, and requires an urgent global response. The review estimates that with a 'business as usual' scenario, the overall costs of climate change will be in the region of 5% of GDP for each year over the next two centuries. Stern suggests that with alternative modelling assumptions, the costs may be as high as 20% of GDP for each year.

Stern calculated that a 2°C rise in global temperatures would cost about 1% of GDP. Subsequently, Stern (2008) has increased this estimate to 2% of GDP because of faster than expected climate change. The *World Development Report 2010: Development and Climate Change* puts the cost to Africa at 4% of GDP and India 5% (World Bank, 2010). The Stern Review estimates that greenhouse gas emissions need to be stabilized at 20% of current levels. It argues that the majority of these cuts must be borne by developed countries, but developing countries must also take significant action. It is suggested that such policies can help promote growth and development and, in particular, '[do] not cap the aspirations for the growth of poor countries' (Stern, 2006).

The different sources of global greenhouse gas emissions measured as CO_2 equivalents in 2014 are given in Figure 12.8. As can be seen in Figure 12.8, the biggest polluters are power generators and industry. We can also consider regional estimates of the use of energy and emission of greenhouse gases per capita and per $1,000 of GDP, as shown in Table 12.2.

It is clear from Table 12.2 who are the big energy users and where greenhouse gases come from. The USA uses by far the most energy per capita and is the biggest polluter per capita. Developed countries produce five times more CO_2 emissions per capita than developing countries. This is why poor countries think it is unfair that they should bear as much of the burden of adjustment to global warming as rich countries.

However, energy use and greenhouse gas emission measured relative to GDP are slightly higher for developing countries compared to developed countries, with transition economies

Figure 12.8 Greenhouse gasses by economic sector, 2014

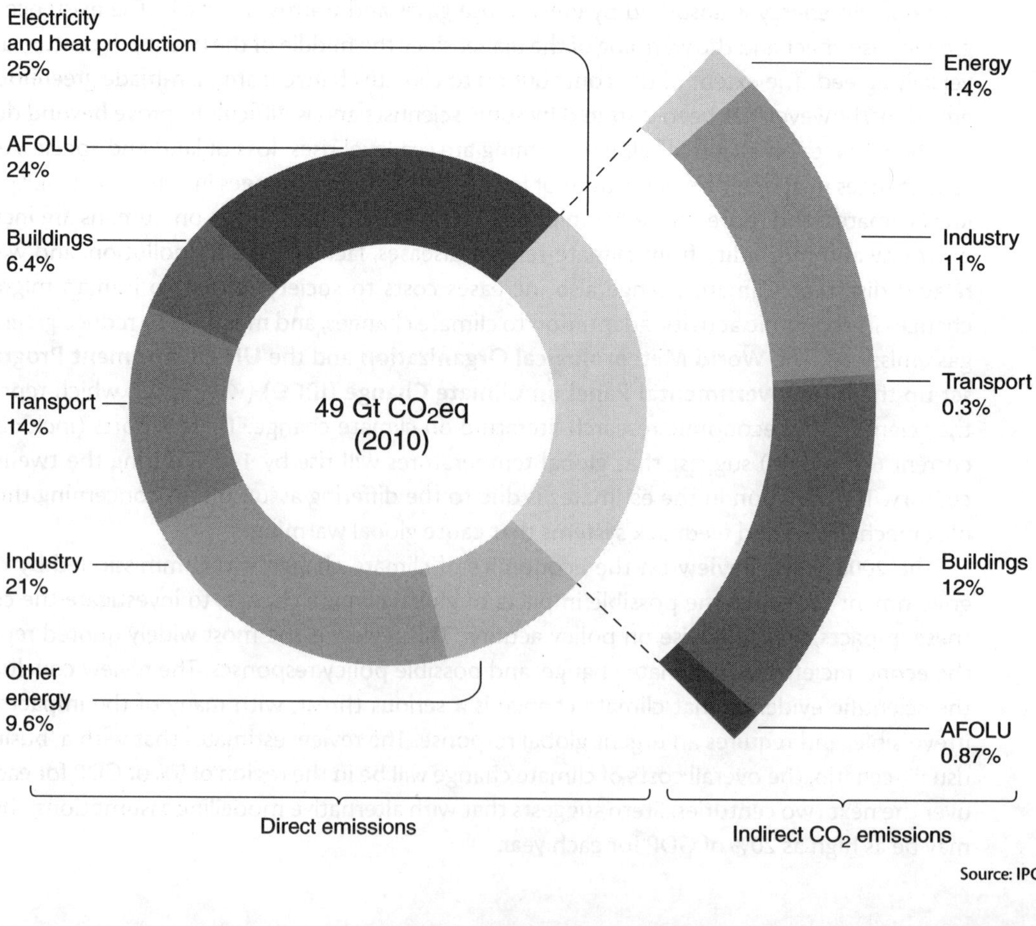

Source: IPCC, 2014a.

Table 12.2 Energy use and CO_2 emissions, 2006

	Energy use per capita (tons of oil equivalent)	Energy use per $1,000 GDP	CO_2 emissions per capita (tons)	CO_2 emissions per $1,000 GDP
World	1.80	0.20	4.4	0.5
Developed countries	4.70	0.18	10.9	0.4
Europe	3.49	0.15	7.6	0.3
Japan	4.13	0.15	9.5	0.3
United States	7.74	0.21	15.2	0.5
Transition economies	3.87	0.48	8.1	1.3
Developing countries	0.97	0.21	2.3	0.5
Africa	0.66	0.28	1.0	0.4
Latin America	1.17	0.15	2.2	0.3
West Asia	2.76	0.36	6.8	0.9
Other Asia, excl. China	0.63	0.17	1.3	0.4
India	0.51	0.15	1.1	0.3
China	1.44	0.21	4.3	0.6

Source: UNCTAD, 2009.

faring the worst. This suggests that economic development is associated with energy and emission-intensive economic activity, which is most apparent in the intermediate and later stages of economic development. Thus, while the higher per capita use of energy and emissions in developed countries indicates that they should bear the major burden of reducing CO_2 emissions, developing and transition economies also need to take significant action to become more energy-efficient.

The Stern Review (Stern, 2006) believes that emissions can be reduced through the trading of emission permits, the pricing of carbon, the development and use of low-carbon technologies such as carbon capture, and action to reduce deforestation. Throughout the review, it is emphasized that the poorest countries are the most vulnerable to climate change. It concludes that it is the duty of rich countries to bear the majority of the emission reductions and provide technical and financial assistance to developing countries to reduce their emissions and adapt to climate change.

The Stern Review has received strong support from a number of experts, including five Nobel Prize-winning economists: Kenneth Arrow, Robert Solow, James Mirrlees, Amartya Sen and Joseph Stiglitz. But it has also been criticized for overestimating the costs of climate change, underestimating the costs of reducing emissions, and, conversely, underestimating the costs of global warming to the environment. These criticisms are important, and, as the range and variety of views in the debate show, it is difficult to evaluate the weight of evidence on this complex subject.

A more technical, but important, criticism of the Stern Review is its use of a low discount rate over time for estimating the present value of the costs of climate change (see Nordhaus, 2007; Dasgupta, 2007). As discussed earlier, the choice of discount rate is a complex technical and ethical issue concerning how to value the future relative to the present. The low values taken by the Stern Review result in greater estimated costs of global warming than may be found in less pessimistic studies (e.g. Nordhaus, 2007).

The Stern Review is undoubtedly the most important report on probably the most pressing economic issue that faces the world in the future. It has many detractors and as many supporters. Either way, the importance of climate change to future economic development requires expensive decisions to be made by the world economic community in the short term. The World Bank (2010) calculates that to keep global warming down to an increase of 2°C by 2050 will cost developing countries alone a minimum of US$140 billion a year (compared with $8 billion they are currently receiving for climate change mitigation). The cost of adapting to global warming (as opposed to trying to stop it) would be $75 billion, compared to the $1 billion now available.

However, it needs to be understood that all these estimates, as well as those contained in the 5th IPCC report (IPCC, 2014b), are generated by complex models that combine science and economics. As recently argued by Stern (2013), many of these models appear to seriously underestimate the risks, which means that achieving the 2°C target is unlikely and that temperature rises of 4°C are potentially plausible. As Stern (2013, p. 839) clearly explains:

> The economic models add further underassessment of risk on top of the underassessment embodied in the science models, in particular because they generally assume exogenous drivers of growth, only modest damages from climate change and narrow distributions of risk.

Therefore, we should treat all the cost estimates presented in the literature with a great deal of caution and be prepared for unanticipated economic shocks that may well result from the impact of climate change in the future.

Climate change and the poor

It is now widely acknowledged that climate change is taking place in a serious way, and that poorer countries are most vulnerable to the impacts of such change (Stern, 2006; World Bank, 2003, 2010; Greenstone and Jack, 2015). This vulnerability results from the close dependence of poor countries and poor people on the natural environment and their limited human, institutional and economic capacity to respond to the effects of climate change. The World Bank (2010), in its *World Development Report 2010: Development and Climate Change*, gives four major reasons why the poor are more vulnerable to climate change than the rich:

1. Natural disasters, such as hurricanes and floods, hurt them more because of poor housing, poor health and inadequate healthcare. In the early 1980s, fewer than 500 million people required international disaster assistance. In the early 2000s, the number was 1.5 billion.
2. Related to the above, global warming increases the chances of catching life-threatening diseases such as malaria, meningitis, dengue fever and diarrhea. It is estimated that by 2030, 90 million extra people in Africa alone may be exposed to malaria as the temperature rises.
3. Poor countries are particularly prone to flooding. Of the fifteen largest cities in the developing world, ten are in low-lying coastal areas, including cities such as Shanghai, Dhaka and Cairo, all with over 10 million inhabitants.
4. Climate change affects agriculture and fishing on which many poor countries still rely for everyday living. The climate, by becoming more extreme, with more drought and more flooding, is starting to affect agricultural productivity. In the short term, some countries may benefit from being able to grow new products, but for most developing countries, agricultural productivity is predicted to fall as a result of climate change. This is likely to lead to greater hunger and famine. The number of malnourished children could rise by 25 million. Warren et al. (2006)

estimate an additional 600 million people in poor countries are at risk from starvation by 2050 if nothing is done. The IPCC (2007) predicts that yields in agriculture may fall by up to 50% by 2050, and the price of staples such as wheat and rice could more than double. Africa is regarded as the most vulnerable continent because of climate variability and its weak capacity to adapt.

As a consequence of the vulnerabilities faced by the poorest nations, it has been suggested that it is critical that developing countries adapt to the consequence of climate change (see Nyong, 2009; Brainard et al., 2009). This adaptation includes increased foreign financial and technical assistance, improved governance, better planning and information, the sharing of information between similar regions and countries, and increasing the resilience of the present types of economic activity and infrastructure to climate change. A particular concern is that climate change will result in substantial migration of population within and between countries and increased pressure on scarce natural resources such as water. Their impacts are likely to result in increased conflict between and within countries (see Bushby (2009) for an analysis of the security implications in developing countries of climate change).

One policy to mitigate fossil fuel CO_2 emissions is to grow biomass (e.g. maize or oil crops) that can be converted into liquid fuels (see IPCC, 2014a). An effect of the shift in the use of land to biomass production can, however, be a reduction in food production, resulting in reductions in supply and finally price increases, especially for the poor. Indeed, it was argued by some that such policy induced changes brought about the price spikes observed in food commodities in 2007/8. Yet, as observed by Wright (2014), biofuel policies adopted in the West are not the typical sources pointed to as causing the price spikes by many of the research agencies that have an agricultural development agenda. Also, Wright (2014) observes that the price increases during this period are far from unprecedented within recent times.

Despite these important policy implications, the IPCC (2014b) has once again argued that agriculture and forestry could become important sectors in mitigating CO_2 emissions via the deployment of bioenergy. If this is to be achieved, it will involve significant adaptation within many farming and forest management systems that will require significant international efforts. And, more importantly, such a policy proposition needs to be sensitive to potential real market effects of government policy, which have, in the past, been ignored by the policy-makers (Wright, 2014).

Of potentially most importance for policy-makers attempting to understand and cope with the issues that arise for the poor as a result of climate change are the Sustainable Development Goals (SDGs). The SDGs of eradicating extreme poverty and hunger and ensuring environmental sustainability are closely linked. Unfortunately: 'the plight of the poor is directly linked to natural resources around them [and as] total emissions continue to grow ... the expected repercussions of climate change will affect [them]' (UN, 2005). As previously noted, given the obvious challenges faced, the SDGs have an explicit action (Goal 13) to deal with climate change and an associated set of targets. It remains to be seen if the SDGs are more successful than the MDGs in helping the poor to deal with the potentially huge impacts that may result from climate change.

Finally, despite the obvious relationship between environmental quality and associated health and productivity consequences, the value that households in many developing countries place on the environment remains low (Greenstone and Jack, 2015). This puzzle has led to more research that attempts to address the following question: Why is environmental quality so poor in developing countries? Greenstone and Jack (2015) identify four possible answers:

1. Society places a low value on environmental quality (this argument is related to the environmental Kuznets curve).
2. The costs of achieving improvements in environmental quality are high so there is a lack of effort.

3. The political economy can be such that the environment is undervalued.
4. There may well be a large number of market failures that have not been corrected and, as such, cause a simple misallocation of resources and economic activity.

This clearly indicates that the nexus between the environment and development is and will remain a key area of research for many years to come.

International agencies, agreements and the environment[2]

Since 1990, international agencies have begun to accept the importance of allowing for the environment in economic development and have started to change their practices.

The World Bank (1992) has accepted that the environment is directly relevant to its mission of supporting development and supports the sustainable development view. There are various aspects to its new policy view. First, it is accepted that there is a need for appropriate valuation of environmental effects. Since 1989, the World Bank has formally required environmental assessments of all projects that are expected to have a significant adverse environmental impact. However, there have been criticisms of whether these assessments contribute to actual project decision-making (see Lawrence, 2003). The World Bank (2001) has also recognized that 'the environment has yet to be fully mainstreamed in to the Bank's operations', but argues that the environment has a 'core task in supporting development and poverty reduction'.

Second, poverty is seen as a major cause of environmental damage and the poor are regarded as being heavily dependent on the environment (see earlier section on climate change and poverty).

Third, it is argued that high-income countries must accept financial responsibility and take the initiative for dealing with major worldwide environmental problems. However, it is also clear that the World Bank disagrees with the view that economic development should take place under the constraint that the stock of natural capital should not be depleted. It does now lend explicitly for environmental projects, and through the Global Environment Facility (GEF) makes grants to protect the environment. (Although the World Bank helped set up the GEF in 1991, at the Earth Summit in 1992, it was restructured to be a separate institution.) To date, the GEF has provided $US14.5 billion in grants and another $US75.4 billion in financing environmental projects (for details, see www.thegef.org). However, the benefits to the environment and native peoples of this lending have been disputed in the past (World Bank, 2001). There are also examples of other international sources of funding directly linked to climate change, such as the Green Climate Fund (see Case example 12.2).

Case example 12.2 **International funding of environmental projects: the Green Climate Fund**

The Green Climate Fund sits within the 2015 Paris Agreement on how to deal with climate change and is an example of a financial mechanism that aims to help support the achievement of the main objectives of the Paris Agreement, especially with regard to developing nations.

An example of the type of funding provided by the fund is the support of vulnerable communities in the Maldives to manage climate change-induced water shortages. In the Maldives, the outer islands are frequently short of water during the dry season. This has an obvious hard impact on the affected communities, in which more than 25% live below the US$2 per day poverty line. This means that some 105,000 people are affected and the majority of these are vulnerable households.

continued overleaf

Case example 12.2 **International funding of environmental projects** – *continued*

The proposed funding to be provided will enable three outcomes to be achieved by:

1. Increasing the scale of the water supply system to include vulnerable households.
2. The adoption and use of cost-effective dry water supply systems.
3. Improvements in groundwater use and management to ensure longer term environmental resilience.

To enable this to happen, the proposed project has a five-year duration, and a budget of almost $US30 million.

Source: www.greenclimate.fund/home.

Similarly, the IMF has slowly begun to recognize the need to take account of the environment in its structural adjustment programmes (SAPs) (see www.imf.org). The IMF has been criticized for only making token and superficial changes in policy (see Friends of the Earth website, www.foe.co.uk). Both the World Bank and the IMF are large international agencies where change is difficult to implement, and whether there is a commitment to implement changes in policies properly to protect the environment and the most disadvantaged persons in developing countries remains to be seen.

The World Trade Organization (WTO, www.wto.org) exists to promote the liberalization of world trade. The WTO's position is that sustainable development and environmental protection are important goals of the organization. WTO rules allow for trade-related measures to be adopted in order to protect the environment. However, the WTO believes that such measures are best managed through multilateral environmental agreements. Although the WTO has a dispute settlement procedure, it has not been used to deal with fundamental environment issues such as climate change. An important environment and trade issue is when developed countries reduce their production of goods that generate high levels of global warming gases and instead import such goods from developing countries. This helps developed countries meet their UN climate change obligations but it is likely to increase total global warming gas emissions. This complex and important subject is only just beginning to be considered by the WTO (see www.wto.org for details). The WTO believes that it is not appropriate for it to set environmental policies and standards. It believes that such issues should be considered by specialist and international negotiation. However, the WTO supports the objective of sustainable development and has been involved in assisting multilateral environmental agreements and increasing the awareness of links between trade and the environment (see Stokke and Thommessen, 2003).

The UN has been responsible for the two reports – *World Conservation Strategy* (IUCN/UNEP/WWF, 1980) and *Our Common Future* (UN WCED, Brundtland Report, 1987) – that have greatly influenced world opinion in favour of sustainable development. The UN Framework Convention on Climate Change (UNFCCC) was signed in June 1992 at the Rio Earth Summit, with the specific objective of stabilizing greenhouse gas concentrations at levels low enough to prevent serious change to the climate system. Subsequently, the Kyoto Protocol of 1997 established legally binding commitments to reduce greenhouse gas emissions. The intention was to reduce by 2012 emissions of industrial countries to an average 5.2% below 1990 levels (the exact targets varied between countries). China, India and other developing countries were not given targets by the Kyoto Protocol but were expected to take responsibility for reducing emissions of greenhouse gases, while their share of global emissions would be allowed to rise in order for them to meet their development needs.

There is general agreement on the Rio Declaration on Environment and Development's support of sustainable global development, and *Agenda 21* considers specific programmes to achieve sustainable development in the twenty-first century (UN, 1993). However, the Rio Earth Summit was criticized for its failure to secure a binding commitment to increase aid, reduce debt and fundamentally shift resources from rich to poor countries. But, since then, the UN has linked the goal of sustainable development to the goal of eradicating extreme poverty and hunger. However, for this to happen, it is necessary for governments and international organizations to intervene and improve the operation of markets with regard to the environment, in particular the impacts of climate change on developing countries.

Finally, the most recent global agreement on how to deal with climate change was achieved by 195 countries at the Paris climate conference (COP21) in 2015, which has become known as the **Paris Agreement**. It builds on the UNFCCC, in that it aims to improve the global response to the potential dangers from climate change, with a specific target of keeping temperature increases to less than 2°C of pre-industrial levels. Furthermore, there is a stated intention to help and support developing nations deal and cope with the challenges that climate change will bring.

The Paris Agreement was reached by the implementation of a novel solution to the complex coordination problem that this issue faces. Specifically, every nation (party to the UNFCCC) was required to submit its proposed best set of activities and efforts to deal with climate change, both domestically and, in some cases, linked to policies that support developing economies' efforts, called **nationally determined contributions (NDCs)**. Importantly, the NDCs make explicit reference to the use of market-based instruments that use economic incentives to change and modify behaviour. In total, by April 2016, there were 161 intended NDCs from 189 parties. Thus, not all parties have provided their intended NDCs but the 161 accounts for 96% of all the parties to the UNFCCC, which covers almost 99% of all global emissions.

Although the Paris Agreement is an important achievement in terms of efforts to deal with climate change, serious questions exist in relation to the NDCs and the ability to limit the temperature increase identified. Current research suggests that the NDCs will reduce global average per capita emissions, but to achieve the temperature target, additional efforts will be required. Thus, although the Paris Agreement is a ground-breaking policy mechanism, the current level of intended actions are insufficient. For this reason, the Paris Agreement, signed in December 2015 and likely to come into effect by 2017, is only the start of global efforts to deal with the consequences of climate change.

Summary

- Economic development in the past has caused serious environmental damage and the current state of the environment will constrain further economic development in developing countries. The environment provides four major functions for the economy and society: life support, amenity, natural resources and waste absorption.
- The neoclassical view of the economy is that markets allocate scarce resources efficiently. Many environmental economists argue that markets fail to allocate efficiently and fairly, and the state should intervene to correct these market failures.
- Externalities occur when the action of one economic agent affects other economic agents and the actions are not controlled through the operation of the market. The burning of fossil fuels and the release of global warming gases is an example of an externality. The effects of

externalities and, in particular, pollution can be corrected to an extent by taxation, subsidization, bargaining, marketable permits and regulation.

- Economic analysis of the environment requires the comparison of the costs and benefits of environmental effects in the present and future, and this is achieved using the device of the discount rate.
- The efficient use of renewable and non-renewable resources across time depends on their social value, the growth of renewable resources, the reserves of non-renewable resources, and the discount rate. The market will not necessarily use renewable and non-renewable resources efficiently.
- Economic analysis of market failures suggests that they can be corrected for in environmental decision-making by estimating and allowing for additional environmental values: external costs, a premium on the prices of non-renewable resources such as oil; value placed on the existence of environmental goods and services by the present generation and its wish to pass on the environment to future generations, and impact of uncertainty on the environment.
- The World Bank and other agencies have attempted to adjust measures of national income for environmental degradation caused by economic activity. The relation between economic development and the environment is complex and the subject disputed.
- The major idea of sustainable development has emerged since the 1980s, in which the well-being of future generations is not compromised by meeting the material needs of the present generation. This idea emphasizes the natural environment supporting economic activity and suggests that the world should be very cautious in depleting natural capital.
- The mitigation of climate change, and global warming, is a major challenge in the twenty-first century.
- The Stern review (2006) is the most comprehensive analysis to date of the costs of climate change and the costs of mitigation.

Chapter 12 Discussion questions

1. What are the functions of the environment in supporting economic activity?
2. What are the different possible solutions to externalities?
3. Explain the causes of 'the tragedy of the commons'.
4. What conditions determine the efficient use of renewable and non-renewable resources?
5. What are the different types of economic value that should be included in social costs?
6. How might one allow for environmental effects in social cost–benefit analysis and national income accounting practices?
7. Define and explain the idea of sustainable development.
8. What are the arguments for and against keeping the stock of natural capital fixed?
9. What are the physical and economic impacts of climate change?
10. How are the poor in developing countries affected by climate change?
11. How have international organizations responded to the ideas of sustainable development and the economic importance of the environment?

Notes

1. See Barbier (1989) for a good survey of the history of economic thought on the environment and development.
2. For a clear summary of the objectives and activities of most international agencies working in the environmental and development fields, see Stokke and Thommessen (2003).

Websites on the environment

International Institute for Environment and Development www.iied.org
World Watch Institute www.worldwatch.org
World Resources Institute www.wri.org
United Nations Environment Program www.unep.org
UN Sustainable Development Knowledge Platform https://sustainabledevelopment.un.org
World Bank www.world bank.org.
Friends of the Earth www.foe.org
Environmental Democracy Index www.environmentaldemocracyindex.org
World Trade Organization www.wto.org
International Monetary Fund www.imf.org

IV

FINANCING ECONOMIC DEVELOPMENT

13

FINANCING DEVELOPMENT FROM DOMESTIC RESOURCES

Introduction

The topic of financing development from domestic resources has two major aspects. The first concerns the ways in which **savings** can be encouraged in developing countries, because only if society is willing to save can resources be devoted to the production of capital goods. Saving is necessary to *fund* investment. In a primitive subsistence economy, without money or monetary assets, saving and investment will tend to be simultaneous acts, in the sense that saving and investment will be done by the same people, and saving will be invested in the sector in which the saving takes place. In a more sophisticated money exchange economy, however, there is no guarantee that saving will necessarily be converted into investment. With the existence of money and monetary assets, the act of saving becomes divorced from the act of investing. Those who want to do the investing may be different from those who want to do the saving, and the process of capital accumulation is likely to require financial and credit mechanisms to 'redistribute' resources from savers to investors. Indeed, with a banking system with the power to create credit, investment can take place *without* prior saving through the process of borrowing. In other words, saving funds investment, but does not necessarily *finance* it. Investment generates its own saving through increases in output and profits. In fact, in the early stages of development, savings may not be the major barrier to capital formation but rather an unwillingness or inability to invest.

Unwillingness to invest may stem from cultural attitudes or simply from a realistic assessment of the risks involved. In Chapter 5, we analysed why poor people may be risk-averse. The inability to invest, on the other hand, may result from shortages of cooperating factors of production (including foreign exchange), or lack of access to credit because of the underdeveloped state of the financial system. The second important aspect of financing development from domestic resources, therefore, has to do with the role of the banking and financial system in promoting and financing investment. **The financial system is important for encouraging saving, financing investment and allocating savings in the most productive manner.**

This chapter starts by distinguishing the different types of saving – voluntary, involuntary and forced – and then distinguishes the different analytical approaches to the finance of development, which have different policy implications. The **prior savings approach** focuses on policies to raise the level of voluntary and involuntary saving as a prerequisite for investment. The **Keynesian approach** focuses on incentives to investment that will generate its own saving. The **quantity theory approach** emphasizes the role of government in appropriating resources for development through monetary expansion and forced saving through inflation (the inflation tax).

Raising the level of voluntary and involuntary saving involves the use of monetary and fiscal policy. The chapter discusses the financial systems of developing countries, including the informal financial sector, which dominates in rural areas; the formal banking system and financial intermediaries, and the various forms of **financial repression** that exist, which, in recent years, have led to extensive programmes of **financial liberalization**. The case for and against financial liberalization, and the empirical evidence, is presented. The role of **microcredit** and **development banks** in helping people out of poverty is also examined.

We then consider fiscal policy and taxation, the tax effort of countries, and the need for fiscal reform to raise tax revenue as a proportion of GDP.

If voluntary and involuntary saving are inadequate for the development effort, inflationary policies that redistribute income between wages and profits, and between the private sector and the government, are alternative possibilities. The former possibility is the Keynesian approach to the finance of development, which argues that stimulating investment can generate its own saving by raising the level of income if the economy is operating below capacity, and by redistributing income from wage earners with a low propensity to save to profit earners with a higher propensity to save if the economy is working at full capacity.

The latter possibility is the quantity theory approach to the finance of development (so named after the quantity theory of money). One of the ways a government can divert more resources to investment is to invest on society's behalf, financing the investment by expanding the money supply. At full employment, monetary expansion will be inflationary. The 'tax' on money consists of a reduction in the real purchasing power of money, and the real resources that holders of money must forgo to restore the real value of their money holdings (forced saving).

The dangers of inflationary finance are recognized, and the extensive empirical research on the relation between inflation and growth is evaluated.

Forms of saving

There are three broad groups in society that save: the household sector, the business sector and the government. The household sector saves out of personal disposable income (personal saving), the business sector saves out of profits, and the government can save out of tax revenues if it spends less than it receives (that is, runs a budget surplus on current account). Household and business saving is sometimes referred to as **private saving**, while government saving is **public saving**. Each of the sectors' motives for saving will differ, and we shall consider the determinants of saving later in this chapter.

As far as the nature of saving is concerned, three broad types may be distinguished: voluntary, involuntary and 'forced'. The nature of these types of saving is fairly self-explanatory:

- **Voluntary savings** are savings that arise through voluntary reductions in consumption out of disposable income. Both the household and the business sector may be a source of voluntary savings.
- **Involuntary savings** are savings brought about through involuntary reductions in consumption. All forms of taxation, social insurance contributions and schemes for compulsory lending to governments are traditional measures involving involuntary reductions in consumption.
- **Forced saving** is when consumption may be reduced because of rising prices (some inflation-induced saving may be voluntary, some involuntary), which may happen for a number of reasons. People may spend the same amount in money terms, but because prices have risen, this means they spend less in *real* terms (money illusion). People may want to keep the *real* value of their holdings of money constant, so they accumulate more money as prices rise – **the real balance effect**. Also, inflation may redistribute income to those with a higher propensity to save, such as profit earners.

For a variety of reasons, which will be considered below, inflation is likely to be a natural concomitant of development, but it can also be deliberately induced by governments financing budget deficits at full employment by monetary expansion. This is the idea of **inflation as a tax on money**. It should also be remembered that if an economy is at less than full employment, there can always be more saving by activating unemployed or underemployed resources, provided not all the increase in output is consumed.

Domestic savings for investment can also be supplemented from abroad. Private foreign investment is a direct source of capital formation and provides a direct addition to domestic investment. It can also be a source of savings by stimulating income and employing previously underutilized resources. Borrowing from abroad also provides resources for investment by enabling imports to exceed exports, which shows up as investment in excess of domestic saving in the national accounts. Foreign assistance may be from multilateral or bilateral sources and may take a variety of forms, ranging from loans at commercial rates of interest to outright gifts of goods and services and technical assistance (see Chapter 14). Remittances from abroad also augment domestic saving.

Finally, a country's commercial policy can stimulate savings and release resources for investment purposes. Trade itself, and an improvement in a country's terms of trade, can provide additional resources for investment if the resulting increase in real income is not fully consumed. Likewise, policies to restrict imports of consumption goods can release additional resources for investment, provided that domestic saving is not reduced by the purchasing power released being switched to home consumption goods.

The amount that countries save and invest as a proportion of their gross domestic product (GDP) differs enormously, affected by differences in the ability and willingness to save and invest. Some countries dissave, consuming more than they produce. Some countries save more than they invest domestically, which means they are investing abroad, and other countries invest more than they save, which means they are net importers of capital. The experience in different areas (continents) of the world is shown in Table 13.1. The first thing to notice is that the savings ratio is much lower in low-income countries than in richer countries, but the savings ratio does not continue to rise for ever as countries grow richer. The ratio peaks in the upper middle-income countries and then declines. The weighted average savings ratio in low-income countries is 16% of GDP compared with 31% in middle-income countries and 21% in high-income countries.

The second important observation is the enormous disparity in savings performance between continents, particularly between the high savings ratios of the highly successful East Asian and Pacific countries (which include China) and the much lower savings ratios in the less successful economies of Latin America, the Caribbean and sub-Saharan Africa. The ratio in East Asia and

Table 13.1 Investment and savings as a percentage of GDP

	Gross capital formation % of GDP 2014	Gross savings % of GDP 2014
Low income	28	16
Middle income	31	31
Lower middle income	27	29
Upper middle income	32	32
Low and middle income	31	31
East Asia and Pacific	42	45
Europe and Central Asia	21	16
Latin America and Caribbean	21	18
Middle East and North Africa	30	..
South Asia	30	31
Sub-Saharan Africa	22	16
High income	20	21

Source: World Bank, 2015.

Pacific (45%) is more than double that of Latin America and the Caribbean (18%) and nearly triple that of sub-Saharan Africa (16%). The question that naturally arises is: Did high savings precede rapid growth in East Asia, or did rapid growth generate its own high savings ratio? Some might argue that it was policies to stimulate saving that were important, including financial liberalization. Some might say it was policies to stimulate investment, partly through control of the banking system, that generated growth and therefore saving. Others might say it was the deliberate involvement of the government in generating and reallocating new resources.

There is no easy answer to the question, but the different replies that might be given highlight the differences in the three broad analytical approaches to the study of financing development from domestic resources, which we will use as the organizing framework for the rest of the chapter. The three approaches are as follows:

- The **prior savings approach** to the financing of development, which stresses the importance of prior savings for investment and the need for policies to raise the level of savings either voluntarily, involuntarily, or both. The approach is classical in conception, emphasizing saving as a prerequisite of investment. The approach is also characterized by a strong aversion to inflation and a belief that saving will readily find investment outlets.
- The **Keynesian approach**, which rejects the idea that saving determines investment and argues instead that the encouragement of investment will generate its own saving, either through increases in output if resources are unemployed, or through income redistribution from groups with a low propensity to save to groups with a higher propensity to save as a result of inflation if resources are fully employed.
- The **quantity theory approach**, which emphasizes the role of government monetary expansion in appropriating resources for development through forced saving or the inflation tax. (The approach gets its name from the quantity theory of money, which predicts that increases in the quantity of money will always lead eventually to increases in the price level.)

If developing countries are characterized as fully employed in the Keynesian sense (with no spare capacity in the consumption goods industries), both the Keynesian and the quantity theory approach to the financing of development will involve inflation. Plans to invest in excess of plans to save at full employment will drive up the price level, and so will monetary expansion by government. In this sense, there is an important practical, as well as a theoretical, difference between the prior savings approach and the other two approaches. In the prior savings approach, the resources released for investment come from voluntary and involuntary saving and no inflation is involved. In the Keynesian and quantity theory approaches, the resources are partly released through the process of inflation, by income redistribution from classes with low propensities to save to those with higher propensities to save, and by inflation as a 'tax' on money, which redistributes resources to government.

The prior savings approach

In classical theory, saving and investment are one and the same thing. All saving finds investment outlets through variations in the rate of interest. Investment and the development process are led by savings. It is this classical view of the development process that underlies such phrases in the development literature as the 'mobilization of savings for development', and also underlies the policy recommendation of high real interest rates to encourage voluntary saving. Lewis's influential classical model of the development process, which was considered in Chapter 5, stresses the importance for development of reinvesting the capitalist surplus.

The level of saving and the ratio of saving to national income in developing countries are likely to be a function of many variables affecting the ability and willingness to save. The main determinants of the **capacity** or **ability to save** are the average level of per capita income, the rate of growth of income, the distribution of income between rich and poor, and the age composition of the population (or dependency ratio). In turn, the **willingness to save** depends mainly on monetary factors, such as the rate of interest, the range and availability of financial institutions and assets (financial deepening), and the rate of inflation. Differences in cultural attitudes towards saving may also be important, but are not easily measured.

The capacity to save

Income is the major determinant of the capacity or the ability to save. It was Keynes who first introduced into economics the idea of the consumption function (and therefore savings function), making consumption and saving primarily a function of income rather than a function of the rate of interest, as in classical theory. Saving as a function of income is known as the Keynesian **absolute income hypothesis**. We can derive the savings ratio as a function of the level of per capita income (PCY) in the following way. If we write the Keynesian savings function as $S = -a_0 + b_0(Y)$, where b_0 is the marginal propensity to save and $-a_0$ represents dissaving (or positive consumption) when income is zero, and divide by the population level (P), we have:

$$S/P = -a_1 + b_1(Y/P) \tag{13.1}$$

Then, to obtain an expression for the savings ratio, multiply equation (13.1) by P and divide by Y:

$$S/Y = b_1 - a_1(Y/P)^{-1} \tag{13.2}$$

The Keynesian absolute income hypothesis therefore predicts that savings per head (S/P) is a linear (but non-proportional) function of income per head (Y/P), and that the savings ratio (S/Y) is a hyperbolic function of the level of income per head; that is, the savings ratio will rise with the level of PCY but at a decreasing rate. As $Y/P \rightarrow \infty$, $S/Y \rightarrow$ to the asymptote b_1. This is shown in Figure 13.1.

The data on the savings ratio in Table 13.1 above suggest this type of relation, as already discussed. The savings ratio is lower in poor countries than in richer countries, but the ratio does not continue rising linearly (for ever) as PCY rises. It increases at a diminishing rate and then levels off.

Figure 13.1 The Keynesian absolute income hypothesis

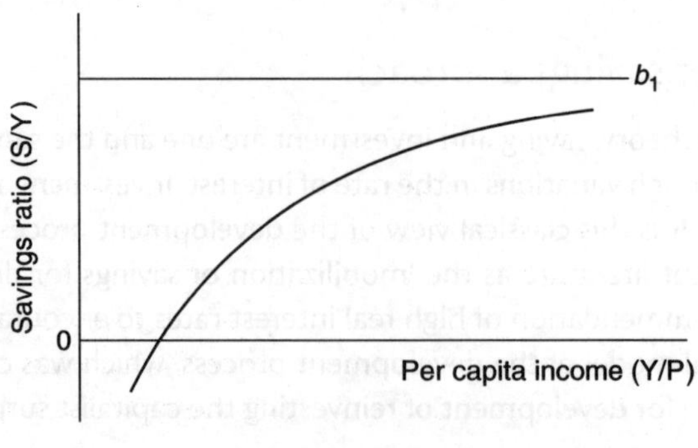

Indeed, there is even some indication that it starts falling at high levels of income, as we shall see when we come to examine the empirical evidence.

The reason why the savings ratio should rise as PCY increases and then level off is not clear-cut. It is as if saving is a luxury good in the early stages of development but then loses its appeal. Part of the reason may be purely 'statistical', arising from the way saving is normally defined in developing countries as the difference between investment and foreign capital inflows. As investment expenditure becomes more faithfully and accurately recorded as development proceeds (as per capita income rises), the savings ratio is also shown to increase. But there are also a number of economic factors that probably play a contributory role in explaining the relation. One is the growth of the money economy. As money replaces barter for transactions, the public will wish to hold a higher proportion of their income in the form of money, which they can only do by reducing consumption as a proportion of income. This hypothesis is supported by what we know about the income elasticity of demand for money in developing countries, which exceeds unity.

A second possible explanation is that population growth decreases with increases in the level of per capita income, so that population growth absorbs household saving to a lesser and lesser extent. Another plausible hypothesis is that in the early stages of development, the distribution of income, both personal and functional, grows more unequal but at a decreasing rate. If higher income groups have higher propensities to save than lower income groups, and profit earners have a higher propensity to save than wage earners, the savings ratio will be positively related to the degree of inequality in income distribution (personal income distribution) and to the share of profits in total income (functional income distribution). Some evidence of the widening distribution of income in the early stages of development was given in Chapter 3.

A second major determinant of the capacity of a country to save is the growth of income, as suggested by the **life-cycle hypothesis of saving**. The basis of the hypothesis, as originally formulated by Modigliani and Brumberg (1954), is that individuals and households attempt to spread out consumption evenly over their lifetime so that decisions to save are assumed to be a function of total lifetime earnings and the stage reached in the earnings cycle. A typical pattern of behaviour would be dissaving in youth, positive saving in middle age and dissaving in retirement. Consider now the effect of income growth within this framework. If income is rising over time, this means that the life earnings and consumption of each successive age group will be higher than the preceding one. If each successive age group is aiming for a higher level of consumption in retirement, the volume of saving of active households will exceed the dissaving of the currently retired households with a lower level of lifetime consumption. The saving ratio will then tend to rise with the rate of growth of income because the higher the growth rate, the greater the gap between the target future consumption level of the current generation of working households and the dissaving of retired people from a less prosperous generation. Thus, countries with higher growth rates might be expected to have at least higher personal savings ratios than countries with lower growth rates.

But income growth comprises two components: the growth of income per head (PCY) and the growth of population. Income growth due to population growth will affect the savings ratio according to how population growth affects the ratio of active to non-active households. Thus, a third major determinant of the savings ratio is the **dependency ratio**. If population growth rises suddenly, this will lead to a higher ratio of young dependents who consume but do not produce, and this will tend to reduce saving. Equally, however, if population growth slows for a long period, this will lead to a higher ratio of retired people, who also consume but do not produce. Thus, both high and low population growth may be associated with a high dependency ratio and a low savings ratio. To test the life-cycle hypothesis of saving, it is best to relate the savings ratio to the growth of per capita income and include the age structure of the population, or dependency ratio, as a separate variable (see Hussein and Thirlwall, 1999).

Finally, we have already mentioned the distribution of income as a determinant of the capacity to save. If the propensity to save of the rich is higher than that of the poor, the aggregate savings ratio will be positively related to the degree of inequality in personal income distribution (between individuals) and functional distribution (between wages and profits), on the assumption that the propensity to save out of profits is higher than out of wages. It will be remembered from Chapter 5 that in Lewis's model of development with unlimited supplies of labour, it is not the absolute level of per capita income that is the prime determinant of the savings ratio but the size of the capitalist surplus and the distribution of income between entrepreneurial profits and other income. According to Lewis (1955): 'if we ask why the less developed countries save so little the answer is not because they are so poor but because their capitalist sector is so small'.

Empirical studies

Let us consider four major studies of the determinants of saving across countries, which include all or some of the variables discussed above, and also other variables measuring the willingness to save that we will discuss below. These are Edwards (1996), Masson et al. (1998), Hussein and Thirlwall (1999) and Loayza et al. (2000). Edwards takes panel data for 36 countries over the period 1970–92, distinguishing between private and government savings. Masson et al. use panel data for 21 developed countries (1971–93) and 40 less developed countries (1982–93) to explain the ratio of private saving to GDP. Hussein and Thirlwall take 62 countries over the period 1967–95, taking the domestic savings ratio as the dependent variable. Finally, Loayza et al. use a dataset of 160 countries from 1964 to 1994, taking four different measures of private saving (all highly correlated). All the studies find the level and growth of per capita income highly significant as determinants of intercountry differences in the savings ratio. Masson et al. (1998) and Hussein and Thirlwall (1999) use a nonlinear specification for the level of PCY, as discussed above, and find it more significant than the linear specification, thus supporting the shape of the curve in Figure 13.1 above. Indeed, in the Masson et al. study, a quadratic term for PCY is used so that the savings ratio is first assumed to rise and then fall. For both developed and developing countries, the quadratic term turns out to be significantly negative, with the savings ratio peaking at 60% of the US level of PCY. The Loayza et al. (2000) study does separate analyses of developing countries and OECD countries and finds the impact of PCY on the savings ratio larger in developing countries than in developed countries, which is also evidence of nonlinearity. For the sample as a whole, Loayza et al. find that a 10% difference in PCY is associated with a 0.47 percentage point difference in the savings ratio. Loayza et al. (2000) conclude that 'policies that spur development are an indirect but most effective way to raise saving' and 'successful growth policies may be able to set in motion a virtuous cycle of saving, capital accumulation and growth'. The question is how to get this cumulative process started of rising income, more saving and faster growth, leading to more saving. Monetary and fiscal policy, and the sophistication of the financial system, are likely to play an important part in this process. This leads us on to the topic of the willingness to save and the role of the financial system in promoting saving and allocating resources in the most efficient manner. All the studies mentioned above include financial variables in their equations.

The willingness to save

Saving represents an intertemporal choice between consumption today and consumption tomorrow. It might be expected, therefore, that the price of present consumption, namely the real rate of interest, will affect saving positively. The higher the rate of interest, the greater the amount of saving. This assumed positive relation also reflects the classical idea of the rate of interest as the reward for waiting, and lies behind the financial liberalization programmes in developing countries, which seek to raise the real interest rate in order to encourage saving, investment and growth. Since the 1970s, there has been extensive testing of the **financial liberalization hypothesis**, and the role of the **interest rate**, in promoting saving, with mixed and largely inconclusive results. Perhaps this is not surprising since the financial liberalization argument largely refers to *financial* saving, but financial saving is only one component of total saving. If interest rates rise, financial saving may rise but at the expense of other assets, leaving total saving unchanged (see Warman and Thirlwall, 1994). It is also standard theory that any price change has both *income* and *substitution* effects. The substitution effect promotes saving, but the income effect reduces saving (because the same level of income can now be generated by less saving) and the two effects may cancel each other out.

Probably a more important determinant of the willingness to save is the **existence of financial institutions** and the **range and availability of financial assets to suit savers**. There is no *single* measure that can capture those institutional determinants of the willingness to save. The number, proximity and diversity of financial institutions serving the different needs of savers could be important. Equally, the volume and range of financial assets might matter as a measure of financial deepening. Such measures include money and quasi-money as a percentage of GDP, money and quasi-money growth, and quasi-liquid liabilities as a percentage of GDP. Domestic credit provided by the banking system as a percentage of GDP is also a measure of financial deepening, but its effect on saving is ambiguous. On the one hand, if bank credit finances investment and growth, this will have a positive effect on saving. On the other hand, an increase in bank credit will relax a liquidity constraint on consumption, resulting in a decline in saving.

Finally, the rate of inflation can be expected to affect the willingness to save, but the effect is ambiguous. On the one hand, inflation acts as a tax on money balance holdings. If individuals wish to restore the real value of their money balance holdings (the so-called **real balance effect**), saving will rise with the rate of inflation. On the other hand, it is natural to expect individuals to avoid the tax if it becomes burdensome in relation to the convenience of holding money. Even if private saving does increase, however, total saving may not increase if the government fully consumes the proceeds of the inflation tax. Inflation will also redistribute income from wages to profits within the private sector if the wage–price coefficient is less than unity. This will increase saving if the propensity to save out of profits is higher than out of wages (as discussed above), but this process can last only as long as there is money illusion and workers do not bid for wage increases to match price increases. The most likely relation between inflation and the savings ratio is an inverted U-shape (quadratic function) showing saving rising with mild inflation and then falling as inflation becomes excessive. This type of nonlinear relation is also suggested by the evidence available on the relation between inflation and growth (see later).

The evidence from the four studies cited above (and others) is that financial variables matter for the performance of saving, but financial deepening and credit availability are much more significant than interest rates. Edwards (1996) and Masson et al. (1998) find that the level of financial development is an important determinant of private saving. Hussein and Thirlwall (1999) experiment with different measures of financial deepening and find a strong positive relation between the domestic savings ratio of countries and the ratio of quasi-liquid liabilities of the banking

Table 13.2 Interest sensitivity of saving

	Initial real interest rate		
Country groupings	**3%**	**4%**	**5%**
Low-income			
Average for group	0.312	0.306	0.300
Average for 10 poorest	0.177	0.174	0.171
Lower middle-income	0.532	0.522	0.512
Upper middle-income	0.560	0.549	0.539
High-income	0.584	0.573	0.562

Note: The data refer to the change (in percentage points) in the saving rate owing to a 1 percentage point increase in the real interest rate. For example, in high-income countries with a real interest rate of 3%, a 1 percentage point rise in the real interest rate would raise the saving rate by nearly two-thirds of a percentage point (0.584 of a percentage point). At higher baseline levels of the real interest rate, the saving response diminishes slightly.

Source: Ogaki et al., 1996.

system to GDP. Loayza et al. (2000) take the ratio of M2 money to GNP as a measure of financial deepening but find it only weakly significant. More interesting, they find that higher interest rates and larger private domestic credit flows exert a *negative* effect on the private savings ratio. Loayza et al. (2000) conclude that: 'these results provide a bleaker view of the savings effects of financial liberalization than previous studies suggested'. The process and effects of financial liberalization are discussed later in this chapter.

The overall conclusion would be that while financial variables may not be as important as income variables in determining savings behaviour, economic development itself is dependent on the sophistication of the financial system, and there is evidence that saving may be more responsive to interest rates when the level of income rises above subsistence. Research on this topic by Ogaki et al. (1996) is reported in Table 13.2.

It appears that saving is very unresponsive to interest rates in the very poorest low-income countries where there is little margin of income over subsistence needs, but its responsiveness increases as consumption rises above subsistence needs and people can exercise choice about increasing their present or future consumption.

This leads us to the extensive topic of financial systems, financial policy and economic development.

Financial systems and economic development

One of the characteristic features of developing countries is that quite large sections of the economy are either non-monetized or transactions take place outside the formal financial sector. In other words, the economies of developing countries have a large sector where money is not used as the primary means of exchange, as well as having a large **informal financial sector** or **unorganized money market**. This has a number of consequences that are not conducive to development:

- If transactions take the form of barter, this is costly in time and wasteful of resources. Sellers must spend time and effort finding buyers who have things they want. Money as a means of exchange avoids the problem of the double coincidence of wants. In this sense, money is a resource and its introduction and use in an economy can be highly productive.

- Without a convenient and acceptable means of payment, the division of labour or specialization is impeded, which hinders the process of capital accumulation and reduces productivity. Remember that, for Adam Smith (see Chapter 4), it is the division of labour that is the source of increasing returns by allowing complex processes to be broken up into simpler operations that permit the use of machinery and mass production. Specialization is not worthwhile if the market is limited by the difficulty of exchanging goods.
- Saving takes the form of the acquisition of real assets as opposed to monetary assets, for example land, cattle, gold, jewellery and so on, which absorb resources and may not be used productively.
- Without the existence of financial institutions issuing monetary assets, investment will tend to take place in the sector in which the saving takes place, and this may not be the most productive sector.
- Much of the lending in the informal sector is for consumption purposes and interest rates are very high, both of which can adversely affect total investment. The informal financial sector has an important role to play in the development process, but its integration with the formal financial sector is desirable for a number of reasons.

The informal financial sector

The **informal financial sector** refers to all institutions and transactions that take place outside a country's authorized banking system. The sector plays a significant role in the financing of economic development, although exactly how significant no one really knows. Within the informal sector, there are a wide variety of institutions and multifarious arrangements between depositors, lenders and borrowers, some dating back for centuries, rooted in custom and tradition. Others are evolving constantly in response to changing economic and social conditions. The sector is characterized by a high degree of spontaneity and flexibility, with demand creating its own supply. The major participants are moneylenders, merchants, loan brokers, savings groups, and friends and relatives.

Moneylenders have a long tradition in the rural areas of developing countries. They may be landlords, merchants, shopkeepers and pawnbrokers. Loans are typically for short periods at high rates of interest, reflecting the scarcity of funds and the high demand for short-term loans to finance consumption and investment, for example the holding of stocks (inventories). Merchants often provide loans to clients based on the future sale or purchase of commodities (see Appendix to Chapter 5). Loan brokers act as intermediaries between agents who have surplus funds and those who require credit. The loans tend to be larger and the duration longer than for other sectors in the informal market.

Savings groups take different forms and have different names in various countries, and are also important sources of finance and credit in rural areas. In some cases, the savings group consists of individuals who deposit money on a regular basis with a group leader or treasurer, sometimes for special purposes such as tax payments, investment or paying for festivities. If the savings are invested, the returns may be shared by the members. Rules and regulations are shaped by local conditions and traditions. In other cases, members of the savings group take turns to borrow the collected sums of money. One particular type of savings group with a long history in Africa is the 'rotating savings and credit association', which operates like a miniature credit union based on the 'mutuality' principle, whereby members of the association make a fixed contribution to the savings fund on a periodic basis and are entitled to withdraw money on a rotational basis. Individuals can decide on the cycle of payments and withdrawals that suit their needs. The advantage is that large expenditures can be undertaken by members sooner than if they had to rely on their own personal savings.

Rural financial intermediaries (RFIs), including **microcredit institutions**, have grown in importance in recent years, operating mainly in the rural sector to provide small, unsecured, short-term loans to individuals (mainly women), households and small entrepreneurs. These intermediaries are discussed in greater detail below.

Finally, **friends and relatives** are major providers of credit. The credit is flexible and interest-free, and repayment is open-ended.

Despite the growth of the formal financial sector in the majority of developing countries, the informal financial sector continues to flourish because it fulfils needs that are not met elsewhere:

1. Many rural areas have no ready access to financial institutions, either because they are non-existent or because they are not in the immediate vicinity. The formal financial sector is predominantly urban based.
2. Where banks do exist, there are a number of institutional barriers to their use, in the form of rules of procedure for obtaining financial assistance. The conditions for obtaining loans can be stringent and hard to satisfy for a number of people. It is difficult, for instance, for the poor and illiterate to provide collateral for loans, which is usually required by the formal sector. In practice, the formal financial sector tends to be out of reach of peasant farmers, small-scale entrepreneurs and ordinary households, so the informal financial sector fills the gap in the market.
3. The informal sector sometimes acts as a complement to the formal sector. Individuals may borrow from the formal sector but find such credits inadequate and therefore resort to the informal sector to augment their borrowing. In recent years, the World Bank's structural adjustment programmes, implemented in several countries, have reduced the flow of credit from the formal sector and demand has switched to the informal sector.

A well-developed financial system serving the whole community has five main requisites, each of which can contribute to the process of **financial deepening**, as well as raising the level of saving and investment, the productivity of capital and the growth of output:

- Full monetization of the economy and the replacement of barter as a means of exchange.
- Integration of the informal and formal money markets.
- Development of a commercial banking system with central bank supervision.
- The creation of development banks and microcredit facilities for small-scale borrowing.
- Development of financial markets and financial intermediaries, issuing and dealing in financial assets.

Monetization and money market integration

Monetization of an economy provides the potential to generate a real investible surplus in several ways. As fiat (paper) money replaces barter in transactions, the demand for money relative to income rises, which releases real resources of equivalent value. The increase in real saving is equal to the increase in the real stock of money held. The issuer of money can appropriate the released resources and increase the level of investment accordingly. In a growing economy, monetary expansion is also required to allow an increased volume of transactions to take place. Monetary expansion for this purpose can also be appropriated by governments for development purposes.

The increased use of money not only releases resources, but it also saves and generates resources. It saves resources by replacing barter objects, or commodity money, which may be costly to produce, with money that is virtually costless to produce. It also saves time – which is a resource if the marginal product of labour time is positive – by avoiding the double coincidence of wants necessitated by barter. Money generates resources by facilitating exchange and thereby permitting the greater division of labour (and specialization).

Historically, the growth of the money economy has also been a powerful stimulus to the development of banking and credit mechanisms, which can themselves act as a stimulus to saving and investment. When the range of financial assets is narrow, saving tends to take the form of the acquisition of physical assets. While, in principle, this need not mean that the level of saving is reduced, in practice, it depends on how sellers of physical assets dispose of the sale proceeds. If a portion of the proceeds is consumed, the saving of one person is offset by the dissaving of another, and less resources are released for investment than if financial assets had been acquired, issued by financial institutions with an investment function.

For a number of reasons, there is also the need to promote links between the informal and formal financial sectors. The high interest rates charged in the informal sector add to costs and add to household debt, and these could be reduced if the informal sector was exposed to greater competition from the formal sector. This could be done by transforming informal institutions into more formal ones, or using the informal sector as a conduit for formal funds, taking advantage of the low transaction costs, local knowledge and greater flexibility in the informal sector. There could also be support mechanisms to guarantee loans from the informal sector.

It is also important that the capital market should be integrated, in the sense that the interest rate structure is unified. The consequence of a fragmented capital market, in which interest rates vary from one sector to another because of a lack of information and factor immobility, is that some sectors of the economy may be able to borrow funds far below the rate of interest prevailing in other sectors where the productivity of capital is higher. The allocation of capital is distorted and inefficient and the capital–output ratio is higher than it would otherwise be: the solution is to encourage funds into the organized money market, and extend the provision of financial institutions into sectors of the economy that lack them.

Paradoxically (on a classical view of the world), development of the organized money market can *lower* average interest rates in the economy at large and *raise* the level of saving because the unorganized money market tends to charge higher interest rates and lends mainly for consumption purposes, whereas in the organized money market, interest rates are lower and lending is more for investment purposes.

Developing a banking system

Developing a national banking system, comprising a central bank, a commercial banking system and special development banks, is one of the first priorities of development strategy. The functions of a **central bank** include the following:

- Issuing currency and lending to government, whereby real resources are transferred to the government in the manner described earlier (with a strong central bank, it is much easier to give priority to government and public sector needs).
- Developing a fractional reserve banking system through which it can provide liquidity and control credit (a central bank can require member banks to hold reserves in government bonds, and the growth of the bond market itself can aid development without excessive monetary expansion).
- Developing other financial institutions, especially institutions that provide long-term loan finance for development, and a market for government securities.

- Maintaining a high level of demand, through the appropriate use of monetary policy, to achieve capacity growth.
- Applying selective credit controls when necessary, in the interests of developing particular sectors of the economy.

The **commercial banking system** has two important functions: to create credit, and to encourage thrift and allocate saving in the most socially productive manner. The ability of an economic system to create credit is important for two main reasons. First, it can compensate for the failure of the economic system to generate enough investment to match planned saving. Second, it provides the means by which growth is financed. This is the real significance of the invention of paper money and credit – permitting the economic system to expand in response to the continual opportunities for growth provided by technical progress, which a barter system or a purely metallic currency do not allow.

Banks can encourage thrift and allocate savings more productively than would otherwise be the case, by offering a return on savings and enabling savings to be used outside the sector in which they originate. Banks can help to break down sectoral bottlenecks and unify interest rates. But commercial banking is still rudimentary in many developing economies. The challenge for developing countries is to promote **financial inclusion**. Approximately 2 billion people in the world lack access to bank facilities, including 500 million in Asia. The ratio of bank deposits to national income averages approximately 30% and the proportion of demand deposits to the total money supply averages 40–50%. In developed countries, in contrast, the ratio of bank deposits to national income usually exceeds 50% and the money supply consists largely of the deposits of commercial banks. The number of banks relative to population size is also small. In developing countries as a whole, the average number of banks per million of the population is about 20 compared with 200 in developed countries. Banks need to be numerous and dispersed if they are to act as catalysts for small savings. Figure 13.2 shows the financial access gap between high-income and low-income countries.

While high-income countries have 85 ATM machines per 100,000 adults and 45 branch banks, low-income countries have only 3 ATM machines and 6 branch banks. The case for **branch banking** is that it can tap small savings. If savings institutions are near at hand, people will save more than if the nearest savings institution is some distance away. Case example 13.1 describes mobile banking in Vietnam, which is an example of microcredit, discussed in the next section.

Figure 13.2 Financial access gap between high- and low-income countries, 2009

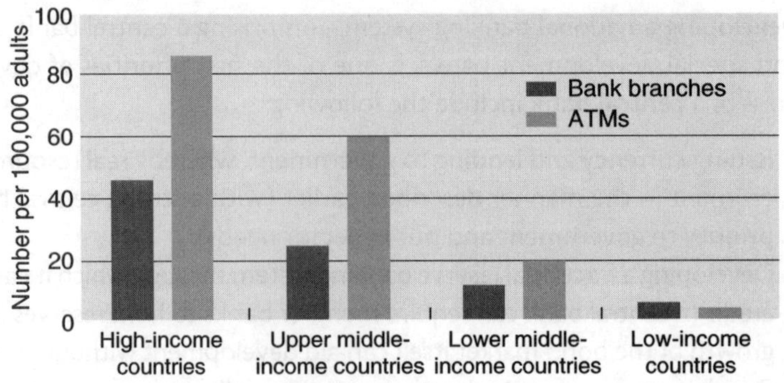

Source: Oshima and Chan, 2011.

Case example 13.1 **Vietnam's bank on wheels**

Ma Seo Sang, a Hmong widow living on less than 25 cents a day in the mountainous region of Vietnam, needed help. She had sold a pig to pay for her husband's funeral, paid a fine incurred by her son by selling one of her buffalo, and redeemed a debt with the other. She had borrowed all she could from relatives. Moneylenders, if they would even lend to her, would charge exorbitant interest (up to 10% per month). She needed money to survive.

Sang's plight raises many issues related to extreme poverty, of which lack of access to credit is one. Part of the solution is microfinance – the provision of basic financial services to the poor. Microfinance can offer a path out of poverty. But how long is the path, and can it be shortened? Vietnam's experiment with the mobile banking programme under the World Bank's Rural Finance Project provides a partial answer to those questions. It suggests that creative ways can be found not only for lenders to reach out to the poor but also for the poor to 'reach in' to lenders.

In 1998 the Vietnam Bank for Agriculture and Rural Development (Agribank) initiated a mobile banking programme modelled after similar programmes in Bangladesh and Malaysia. It procured 159 vehicles equipped to travel on dirt roads and hilly pathways, enabling loan officers to reach remote areas to process loan applications, disburse money, collect payments, and mobilize savings deposits. The visits followed a fixed calendar and were announced in advance.

Once the programme was launched, it became clear that more than just difficult access prevented the poorest from taking advantage of its services. Their isolation caused them to have feelings of helplessness and fear. In the upland ethnic group, the higher up a mountain people lived and the longer their isolation, the more they seemed to believe that they could not get credit. Suspicion was another issue. What if the lender offered a loan and then, if a payment were late, took a farmer's buffalo, as had happened to Sang?

Above all, the poorest people lacked confidence and self-esteem. For example, the illiterate poor would wonder how they could fill in applications and receipts. Others felt they could do nothing to earn extra income to repay a loan. Many were afraid to venture into activities other than cultivation and animal husbandry, even though opportunities existed.

For mobile banking to work for borrowers, the following services had to be made available: offering appropriate loan products, linking lending and saving, and combining credit and human asset building.

For lenders, it was necessary that the mobile banking experiment be financially self-sustaining. It thus required the following ingredients: group-based lending, linking formal and informal credit, and reasonable interest rates.

Barely five years in operation, the mobile banking programme has proved to be relatively cost-effective, providing financial services to 315,000 poor households. Preliminary data show that, on average, each mobile bank disbursed 1,921 loans, collected 1,387 payments, and transported cash on 75 occasions to 16 local points monthly. The excellent repayment rate suggests that the poor are good credit risks. The programme also mobilized 1,983 small savings accounts every month, showing that the poor can be good savers.

As for Ma Seo Sang, she received a loan of about $300 and used the money to buy some chickens and pigs to raise. The income she made from selling her animals helped her earn a living.

Source: Hung, 2004.

In India, 65% of Indians do not have access to financial services, only 13% have debit cards, and only 5% of Indian villages have branch banking. There is only one branch bank for every 160,000 people. Thus, India has launched a financial inclusion programme, where forty billion rupees is to be spent on the attempt to increase financial inclusion, initially focusing on villages with more than 2,000 people.

Rural financial intermediaries and microcredit[1]

Rural financial intermediaries (RFIs) and microcredit institutions play a crucial role in helping the poor and fostering the growth of small business where potential entrepreneurs are precluded from borrowing from the banking system because they are too poor and lack collateral. Within the structure of RFIs, there is a diversity of organizations and financial services. In the rural sector where most RFIs operate, and where most lending takes place, there are different niches and markets to be served. There are several case studies of successful RFIs. One such study is for Indonesia (Chaves and Gonzalez-Vega, 1996). In the 1980s and 1990s, the Indonesian government established a network of semi-independent, locally operated RFIs that have been highly successful, largely through the recruitment of local agents to gather information on borrowers, monitor their actions and enforce loan contracts. This has kept down loan defaults to less than 2% of lending. In the early 1990s, there were 13,000 such intermediaries reaching out to over 4 million people, dispensing loans of between $50 and $600. Most of the RFIs made accounting profits because fixed costs are kept low, and the effective interest rate is high, ranging from 30% to 84% per annum. Interestingly, the loans are not group-based; they are to individuals, and the pressure to repay comes from the local agents who are given appropriate incentives not to shirk, collude with the borrower, or be bribed.

This contrasts with the microcredit movement where most lending is through **joint liability lending**, which makes all members of the group jointly liable for any loan given to its members. If the group does not repay, there is no further access to loans. Thus, joint liability group lending stimulates screening, monitoring and enforcement of contracts among borrowers, reducing costs to the lenders. Because of the close proximity of borrowers within a group, information asymmetries between lenders and borrowers are reduced. Evidence shows (see Hermes and Lensik, 2007) that groups with stronger group ties have better repayment records, as do groups with written rules and a strong group leader, and which are more open geographically with no other access to credit.

There are now over 3,000 microfinance institutions across the world (some now also in developed countries), and it is estimated that at least 100 million poor people have benefited. The lobby group **Microcredit Summit Campaign** wants to see a vast expansion of such institutions, particularly to achieve the 2030 Sustainable Development Goals.

It was **Grameen** (meaning village) **Bank** in Bangladesh that pioneered the concept of microcredit in developing countries. It was formally established in 1983 (seven years after the initial idea) by Muhammad Yunus, economics professor at Chittagong University in Bangladesh, who instead of teaching the economics of poverty from an ivory tower decided to do something practical about it, based on the philosophy that everyone has the right to credit, but the poor are excluded from the conventional banking system. But the best way for people to help themselves out of poverty is to be able to borrow to set up small businesses. Thus, Grameen Bank was founded as a microcredit organization to lend sums as little as $10 to the rural poor, especially women, without collateral. A poor woman may obtain a microloan to buy an oven in order to sell hot food.

She repays the loan with interest, others can borrow, she can borrow more to buy another oven and ultimately become a prosperous trader. Another poor woman uses her microloan to buy chickens, starts selling eggs, repays the loan, borrows more and becomes a chicken farmer. These are simple, real-life stories of what is possible.

Lending and repayment take place within a group context (usually five people) where members of the group agree to monitor one another, so that there is peer pressure to use loans wisely and to repay. Each member of the group normally comes from the same village and members have a similar economic and social background. Loans are first given to two members of the group, who are closely observed for two months and must repay the loan in weekly instalments. If the repayments are made, then two others can borrow. Loan use is monitored by the staff of Grameen Bank and groups meet collectively to discuss the choice of new projects. All credit transactions are discussed openly, so there is complete transparency concerning what is going on. There can be no 'cover ups' and no corruption. The record of repayment to Grameen Bank is close to 98% of loans; far better than the record of repayment to the commercial banking system where bad debts are rife.

Muhammad Yunus

Born 1940, Chittagong, Bangladesh. Professor of Economics at Chittagong University; founder of Grameen Bank in 1983 lending small sums mainly to groups of poor women, with the philosophy that everyone has the right to credit, not just the rich with collateral. The microcredit movement has now spread throughout the developing world and lifted millions of families out of poverty. Yunus and Grameen Bank were awarded the Nobel Peace Prize in 2006.

The conventional explanation for the low default rate at Grameen Bank is the peer pressure from the group, but research shows (Pankaj, 1996) that the explanation is much deeper than this; it lies within the culture and ethos that the bank has developed among its employees, and the relationship between the bank's employees and the client borrowers. Pankaj could find no evidence of members of a group not being able to borrow if one member defaulted. The main explanation for the very high repayment rate seems to be that the bank is tightly structured, with checks on clients and borrowings at every stage. Each borrowing group has five members, and six groups make a centre, which meets weekly at a fixed time. Each centre is supervised by an employee from a Grameen branch bank who may look after 10–15 centres. Each branch bank is answerable to an area manager. The line of command is clear and there is supervision at every stage. It is this organizational structure of the bank that lies at the heart of its success. Other banks serving the poor in rural communities could learn lessons from the Grameen structure.

Grameen Bank also involves itself in social development programmes in the villages to improve the quality of life, such as encouraging members to build houses and sanitation facilities, planting trees and kitchen gardens. There is also a comprehensive training programme in maternal health, nutrition and childcare. In Bangladesh alone, there are over 1,000 branches of the bank serving 36,000 villages, which have lent more than $6 billion to 8 million people. In 2006, Muhammad Yunus and Grameen Bank were awarded the Nobel Peace Prize.

The Grameen idea has now spread to over 100 countries. Not all microcredit banks operate in the same way, but all are designed to lend to poor people denied access to credit from the commercial banking system because they have no collateral. Other well-known microcredit institutions across the world are BancoSol in Bolivia (the first microcredit bank to be set up in Latin America in 1992), Banco Compartamos in Mexico (lending mainly to women), Accion Internacional, based in the USA with affiliates in 13 Latin American countries (including Mibanco in Peru), Kenya's Rural Enterprise Programme and Bank Rakyat in Indonesia.

At the beginning of the microcredit movement, almost all the banks relied on public subsidies to operate because of the high overhead costs of administering very small loans, despite high interest rates on loans of 20–30%. In the past ten years alone, microcredit institutions (many run by NGOs) have received public subsidies of $10 billion.

The challenge for the future is to see whether microfinance can be extended more on a commercial basis without long-term subsidies, but without compromising the basic purpose of microcredit, which is to lend to the very poorest who are cut off from the normal banking system. Many profit-making microfinance institutions have sprung up in recent years, but have been criticized for high interest rates and exploitation of poor people. In Andhra Pradesh (India), more than fifty people, mainly women, committed suicide in 2010, leading state officials to intervene in the activities of commercial microlenders. Morocco, Bosnia, Nicaragua and Pakistan have all been hit by microloan payment crises in recent years.

At present, the evidence is that there seems to be a trade-off between the commercialization of microfinance and reaching out to the poor. Cull et al. (2007) attempt to examine this issue rigorously by taking a sample of 124 microcredit institutions in 49 countries to see whether there is any significant relation between the profitability of banks and their outreach to the poor. Three types of bank are distinguished: those that lend to groups (48), those that lend to individuals (56), and village lenders (20). What the evidence shows is that individual-based lenders seem to have higher profitability than group-based institutions, but the fraction of poor (and female) borrowers in the loan portfolio is lower in the latter case. Cull et al. (2007) conclude:

> we find examples of institutions that have managed to achieve profitability together with notable outreach to the poor – achieving the ultimate promise of micro-finance. *But they are so far the exceptions.* (emphasis added)

Cull et al. (2009) have also used data from the Microfinance Information Exchange covering 364 institutions with £25 billion of assets and 10 million borrowers in the period 2002–04, distinguishing between the activities of commercial microbanks and NGOs. They find that:

- Commercial microbanks account for more assets, but NGOs reach out to more people.
- More microbanks are profitable (73%) than NGOs (54%).
- Most microbanks lend to individuals, while most NGOs lend to groups.
- NGOs give much smaller loans than microbanks.
- NGOs charge higher interest rates (25% a year for the median bank) than microbanks (13%) because operating costs are higher (26 cents per $ lent for NGOs compared with 12 cents per $ for microbanks).
- Default rates don't differ between the two types of microcredit institution.

Cull et al. (2009) remark, however, that evidence on the social returns to microlending, and by how much people have been lifted out of poverty, is scant. This is the research challenge for the future. Case example 13.2 highlights a case study of a randomized control trial on the impact of microfinance in India.

Case example 13.2

A randomized control trial of microfinance in Hyderabad, India

In 2005, half of 104 slums in Hyderabad, India were randomly selected for the opening of a branch of Spandana, a microfinance institution, while the remainder were not, although other microfinance institutions were free to enter those slums. Fifteen to eighteen months after Spandana began lending to treated areas, households were 8.8 percentage points more likely to have a microcredit loan. They were no more likely to start any new business, although they were more likely to start several at once, and they invested more in their existing businesses. There was no effect on average monthly expenditure per capita. Expenditure on durable goods increased in treated areas, while expenditure on 'temptation goods' declined. Three to four years after the initial expansion, the probability of borrowing from a microfinance institution in treatment and comparison slums was the same, but, on average, households in treatment slums had been borrowing for longer and in larger amounts. There was no change in any of the development outcomes that are often believed to be affected by microfinance including health, education and women's empowerment. The results of this study are largely consistent with those of other evaluations of similar programmes in different contexts.

Source: Banerjee et al., 2013.

Another major international development organization that lends to the ultra-poor is BRAC (see Case example 13.3), which tries to tackle poverty from the bottom up in a way advocated by the World Bank (2001) in *World Development Report 2000/2001: Attacking Poverty*.

Case example 13.3

BRAC

BRAC was established in Bangladesh by Fazle Hasan Abed (now Sir) in 1972 designed to help the 'ultra-poor' (mainly women) who could not qualify even for microloans. The philosophy of the organization is to provide people with an asset base, such as a cow, goat or a few chickens, which they are taught to manage themselves. While doing so, they are given a small stipend for food. The programme is quite costly (at least $1,000 per household), but randomized control trials show that it works, and women do not fall back into poverty when the help terminates. It is estimated that the rate of return to women after going through the graduation programme is between 16 and 25%.

BRAC is the largest nongovernmental development organization in the world, now operating in eleven other countries outside Bangladesh. It employs over 100,000 people, it is 70–80% self-funded, and has helped more than 126 million ultra-poor people. In the early years, BRAC concentrated on community development through village development programmes including agriculture, fisheries, cooperatives, rural crafts, literacy, health and family planning. Since then, it has branched out into other fields including, in 1986, its rural development programme that incorporates institution building, including functional education and training, credit provision, and income and employment generation. Over the past 30 years, BRAC has given $1.5 billion in microloans – more even than Grameen Bank. BRAC also focuses on the problem of youth unemployment. To help fund its development programmes, BRAC has a number of commercial enterprises, including a retail handicraft chain called Aarong, a dairy and food project, and BRAC Salt.

Source: http://brac.net.

Development banks

Development banks play a particularly important role in the development process because it is not the explicit function of the private commercial banking system to have development priorities in mind when making loans, unless directed by the government. The function of commercial banks is to make a profit for their shareholders. This means that commercial banks are generally risk-averse and have short time horizons. It also means that they are only interested in their own cash flows and have no particular interest in the *social* profitability of the projects they lend for, or in lending to poor people. Development banks can afford to have longer time horizons, take more risks, pursue development objectives, and focus on the social profitability of lending, as well as encouraging saving.

The activities of Tonga Development Bank (where one of the authors was a consultant in 1995) provide an interesting case study. The bank was established in 1977 'to promote the expansion of Tonga for the economic advancement of the people of Tonga'. Its lending policy gives priority to projects that have the potential to increase exports or reduce imports, involve local entrepreneurship, use local inputs, contribute to increased employment opportunities, particularly for women, and increase income for the poorer sections of the community in rural areas and the outer islands. Regarding exports, if economic growth is constrained by a shortage of foreign exchange, any project financed by the bank that earns net foreign exchange will give a higher social return than private return because the growth of output will be higher than would otherwise have been the case. In Tonga, the commercial banking system would not lend to producers wishing to grow the vegetable squash, because the venture was regarded as too risky. However, Tonga Development Bank lent nearly \$10 million to squash producers, and squash now accounts for 80% of the country's export earnings. The bank reaches out to nearly 50% of households in Tonga, and it funds 70% of all loans to the private sector. It fills an important gap in the market for small loans because commercial banks will not lend for projects of less than \$5,000. There can be little doubt that Tonga Development Bank plays a pivotal role in the development of the economy of Tonga and is able to do things that the private sector would not contemplate. The positive externalities conferred fully justify interest rate subsidies.

All development banks have a role to play in stimulating the capital market. They can do this by selling their own stocks and bonds to raise finance, by helping enterprises to float or place their own securities, and by selling from their own portfolio of investments.

Financial intermediaries

The importance of having a wide variety of financial intermediaries is that they can offer a diversity of financial assets with different yields, maturities and divisibilities to suit savers and investors with different requirements and different time horizons. This can increase the level of saving and investment, and also improve the efficiency of resource allocation.

As far as the level of saving and investment is concerned, financial intermediaries offer four major advantages:

1. In general, savers wish to lend for only a short period of time (to remain liquid), while investors wish to borrow for a longer period of time. Direct lending from savers to investors, without financial intermediation, would involve savers committing themselves for longer periods than they would really like because investment does not generally generate returns immediately. Financial intermediaries, however, are able to pool risks and can borrow short and lend long, thus suiting both savers and investors.

2. The use of financial intermediaries reduces transaction costs. Direct lending, whereby savers have to find suitable borrowers or investors have to find suitable lenders, is time-consuming and costly. Reduced transaction costs encourage saving and investment.
3. Financial intermediaries can specialize in particular areas of business, which reduces information costs by accumulating knowledge of various markets. This lessens the credit risks associated with lending, and also encourages greater saving and investment.
4. Investment projects are invariably larger than the savings of any one individual or group of individuals. The existence of financial intermediaries overcomes the problem of indivisibilities.

As far as the *efficiency* of resource allocation is concerned, the great advantage of financial intermediaries is that the creation of financial assets and liabilities allows savers to hold part of their wealth in financial form. This means that investment is no longer confined to the sector where the saving takes place, thereby facilitating the allocation of resources to the most productive sectors of the economy.

Financial liberalization

The formal financial sector, consisting of a central bank, a commercial banking system and various other financial intermediaries, typically suffers from various forms of **financial repression**, which may thwart the development process. For example, the government may have a near-monopoly of the banking system and restrict the growth of financial institutions. Private sector banks may have to keep high reserve requirements and lend compulsorily to the government to finance its deficits. The central bank may impose credit rationing on the commercial banks, or insist that the banks lend to certain priority sectors. Nominal interest rates may be kept artificially low, so that with inflation the *real* rate of interest is negative, discouraging the acquisition of interest-bearing financial assets. These are all examples of financial repression.

The argument for financial liberalization is that the various forms of financial repression impede the development of financial markets. The consequences, it is argued, are a reduction of the flow of funds to the formal financial sector and distortion of the allocation of resources, leading to lower levels of saving, investment and output growth than would otherwise be the case.

The importance of the growth of the money economy and financial deepening for economic development along the lines indicated above has been stressed in the development literature for a long time (see, for example, Schumpeter, 1911, Gurley and Shaw, 1960 and Tun Wai, 1972), but it was McKinnon (1973) and Shaw (1973) who independently in 1973 first highlighted the dangers of financial repression in a rigorous way, and argued the case for maximum financial liberalization. Their views became highly influential in the thinking of the IMF and the World Bank in the design of programmes for the financial restructuring of countries as part of structural adjustment programmes. Their arguments, however, emphasize different points:

- **McKinnon's argument** is that money holdings and capital accumulation are complementary in the development process. Because of the lumpiness of investment expenditure and the reliance on self-financing, agents need to accumulate money balances before investment takes place. Positive (and high) real interest rates are necessary to encourage agents to accumulate money balances, and investment will take place as long as the real rate of return on investment exceeds the real rate of interest.
- **Shaw's argument**, on the other hand, stresses the importance of financial liberalization for financial deepening, and the beneficial effect of high interest rates on encouragement to save

Figure 13.3 The McKinnon–Shaw argument

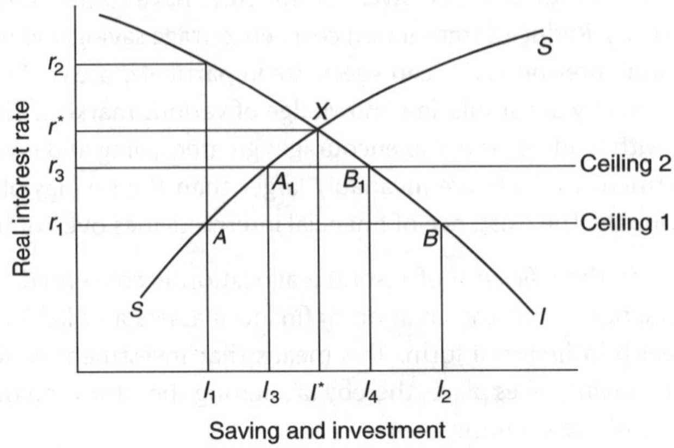

and discouragement to invest in low-yielding projects. The increased liabilities of the banking system, resulting from higher real interest rates, enable the banking system to lend more resources for productive investment in a more efficient way. Figure 13.3 can illustrate the McKinnon–Shaw argument.

Figure 13.3 is a standard classical savings and investment diagram showing saving as a positive function of the real interest rate (reflecting the idea of time preference and the interest rate as the reward for abstaining from present consumption), and investment as a negative function of the real interest rate (reflecting the diminishing marginal efficiency of investment). With no interest rate controls, the equilibrium rate of interest would be r^* and the level of saving and investment would be I^*.

Now suppose that the government imposes a ceiling on the *nominal deposit rate* for savers, giving a *real* rate of interest of r_1. This would mean that saving is I_1, and on classical assumptions that prior saving is necessary for investment, this also constrains investment to I_1. If there was no ceiling on the *loan* rate of interest, the banks could charge interest rate r_2 to investors and the gap between r_1 and r_2 would give substantial profits to banks, which they could use for various forms of non-price competition. At r_2 there is no unsatisfied demand for investment funds.

Suppose, however, that the interest rate ceiling applies to loans as well as deposits. This means that saving is still I_1, but investment demand is now I_2 and there is an excess demand for investment funds equal to *AB*. Credit will have to be rationed. There will be a tendency for banks to favour less risky projects with lower rates of return. This will lower the overall productivity of investment.

If the interest rate ceiling is raised so that real interest rates rise to r_3, this encourages saving from I_1 to I_3. This leads to more investment, credit rationing is reduced and the productivity of investment rises. From this argument, it would seem to follow that saving and investment will be optimal and credit rationing will disappear when the market is fully liberalized and the real rate of interest is left to find its market clearing level at r^*.

Critics of financial liberalization and empirical evidence

Many of the arguments for financial liberalization sound convincing on the surface, but a number of qualifications need to be made. The experience of financial liberalization across the globe has been very mixed, and we shall consider some of the empirical evidence relating to the effect of liberalization on saving, investment and growth, as we examine some of the major criticisms of the financial liberalization argument (see Gibson and Tsakolotos (1994) for a comprehensive survey of the issues involved).

First, the argument refers to *financial* saving, but financial saving is only one type of saving. Financial saving may increase as interest rates are liberalized, but there may simply be a substitution between financial assets and other assets, leaving total saving unchanged. It is also well known that any price change (in this case, the interest rate) has income as well as substitution effects. The substitution effect promotes saving by making current consumption more 'expensive', but the income effect deters saving because at higher interest rates the same income can be obtained with less saving, and the two effects may cancel each other out. This being so, it is perhaps surprising, as Dornbusch and Reynoso (1989) once remarked: 'to find so strong a belief in the ability of higher interest rates to mobilise saving'.

In fact, many of the empirical studies and surveys of the results of financial liberalization in various countries are extremely cautious in their conclusions. Research by Gupta (1987) on 22 Asian and Latin American countries over the period 1967–76 suggests that there is little support for the 'repressionist' hypothesis that the positive substitution effect of real interest rates on savings dominates the negative income effect. The most important determinant of saving is real income. Giovannini (1983) concludes from his research on eight Asian countries that his results 'cast serious doubts on the view that the interest elasticity of savings is significantly positive and easy to detect in developing countries'. Similarly, a study by Cho and Khatkhate (1990), two World Bank economists, of the financial liberalization experience of five Asian countries concluded that:

> financial reform, whether comprehensive and sweeping or measured and gradual, does not seem to have made any significant difference to the saving and investment activities in the liberalised countries. It was believed until recently that removal of the repressive policies would boost saving. The survey in this paper of the consequences of reform does not reveal any systematic trend or pattern in regard to saving ... it lends support to the conclusion that decisions to save are determined by several factors and the relationship between saving and real interest rates is at best ambiguous.

Bandiera et al. (2000) examined the liberalization experience of eight countries (Chile, Ghana, Indonesia, South Korea, Malaysia, Mexico, Turkey and Zimbabwe) over 25 years and concluded:

> our results cannot offer support for the hypothesis that financial liberalization will increase saving. On the contrary, the indications are that liberalization overall – and in particular those elements that relax liquidity constraints– may be associated with a fall in saving.

Maxwell Fry (1995), a leading authority on finance and development and an ardent advocate of financial liberalization, has conceded that:

> what is agreed ... is that if an effect [on saving] exists at all, it is relatively small [and that] positive interest effects are easier to find in Asia than in other parts of the world, but even in Asia the effects appear to have diminished over the past two decades.

If financial liberalization does not increase aggregate saving, its positive impact on development must come through a more efficient allocation of resources, which raises the productivity of investment. In other words, as stressed by Shaw (1973), financial liberalization should concentrate on the quality of investment rather than the quantity. There is not much evidence on this point, but the World Bank (1989) claimed, in its *World Development Report 1989: Financial Systems and Development*, that in countries with positive real interest rates, the average productivity of investment (as measured by the incremental output–capital ratio) is four times higher than in countries with strongly negative real interest rates. Bandiera et al. (2000) also conclude their study by saying that even if financial liberalization does not increase private saving, it does not follow that the process contracts the volume of funds applied to productive investment. For one thing, financial liberalization can increase the flow of capital from abroad, and, second, the reform process can have the effect of eliminating less productive uses of loanable funds. This is an area where more research needs to be done.

A second major criticism of the financial liberalization argument is that the model seems to treat banks simply as savings depositories, with the presumption that the supply of loans from the banking system depends on deposits held by the banks, and if deposits increase, loans will automatically increase. In short, the supply of credit is treated as exogenously determined. However, if banks have the power to create credit (which they do), backed by a central bank acting as lender of last resort, the supply of loans will depend on the demand for loans, not on the supply of deposits. The supply of loans becomes endogenous. Within this framework, what is important is not so much incentives for saving, but incentives for investment, which may require lower interest rates. This is part of the **Keynesian** and **post-Keynesian** critique of the financial liberalization school. The work of Paul Davidson (1986), the foremost post-Keynesian, is representative of this line of argument. Davidson argues that all that is needed to initiate additional real investment is finance provided by an increase in total bank loans and there is no need for prior savings, 'as long as the banks can create new finance via acceptable bank accounting practices'.

How the supply of credit responds to the interest rate, and how investment is affected by the supply of credit and the rate of interest, becomes very much an empirical matter that can only be settled by an appeal to the facts. Warman and Thirlwall (1994) found that for Mexico, over the period 1960–90, financial saving responded positively to the rate of interest, and this led to an increase in the supply of credit from the banking system to the private sector. However, while the increased supply of credit affects investment positively, there is a strong negative effect of interest rates on the level of investment, holding the supply of credit constant, and the *net* effect of higher real interest rates on investment is adverse. This is also the central conclusion of Demetriades and Devereux (1992) from research on 63 developing countries over the period 1961–90. They find that the negative effect of a high cost of capital on investment outweighs the effect of a greater supply of investible funds. Greene and Villanueva (1991), in a sample of 23 developing countries over the period 1975–87, likewise show a negative effect of real interest rates on investment.

This leads to a third worry about the financial liberalization model, which is that it ignores the adverse effect that high real interest rates can have on costs and the level of demand in an economy, which may lead to stagflation (a combination of cost inflation and rising unemployment). This is another aspect of the post-Keynesian critique of the financial liberalization model (see Dutt, 1990–91). High interest rates not only discourage investment, but may also lead to currency overvaluation by attracting capital from overseas, which leads to a fall in exports, and also increases the cost of servicing government debt, which leads to cuts in government expenditure. This has occurred in Africa (see African Development Bank, 1994). Currency overvaluation and cuts in government expenditure are both deflationary. In Latin America in the 1970s, financial liberalization went wrong because there was an explosion of government debt, economic instability and excessively high real interest rates, which led to bankruptcies, bank failures and prolonged recession. In the immortal words of Diaz-Alejandro (1985): 'Goodbye financial repression, hello financial crash.' Financial liberalization programmes were abandoned (temporarily).

A fourth critique of the financial liberalization school concerns the relationship between the formal and the informal financial sectors. Higher real interest rates are likely to attract funds away from the informal money market, or **curb market**, where there is no regulation over the use of funds. If banks are subject to reserve requirements and are forced to lend compulsorily to governments, the diversion of funds away from the informal sector may lead to the total supply of loans to the private sector being reduced. This is part of the argument of the **neostructuralist school** (see Buffie, 1984). The hypothesis is difficult to test directly without information on the supply and composition of credit from the curb market. To the extent that curb loans are mainly for consumption purposes and the government uses the reserve requirements of the banks for productive investment, the problem may not be serious. If, however, the curb loans are for investment and the government uses the banks to finance current account budget deficits, the reallocation of funds between the sectors will adversely affect the total level of saving and investment.

A final point to make is that it does not follow that credit rationing will necessarily be eliminated and resources allocated more 'efficiently' if interest rates are not controlled and are allowed to reach their market clearing level. As Stiglitz and Weiss (1981) showed in a classic paper, banks suffer from the problem of **adverse selection** because of **asymmetric information** on the part of borrowers and lenders. Borrowers know more than lenders about the risks involved in a loan transaction. A rational profit-maximizing bank may therefore be expected to practise credit rationing to reduce risk, and not simply lend to those projects that seem to offer the highest return but with more risk attached.

Where do these various criticisms leave the financial liberalization argument? Clearly, the existence of financial repression has to be taken seriously, but it does not follow that the more liberalization there is the better, when we know that financial markets have many imperfections, and that competition between banks and other financial institutions can lead to **financial distress** if there are not institutional structures in place with adequate standards of accounting and auditing to prevent bad loans. Governments will always need to intervene for prudential reasons, and also for strategic reasons either as a major borrower or to direct credit. Particular care needs to be exercised in the liberalization of interest rates because of their impact on costs, investment demand, the exchange rate and the cost of financing government deficits. This raises the intriguing question: What is the 'optimum' real rate of interest for a country? This is virtually impossible to answer (see Clarke, 1996), but even in classical terms, it is not clear that the optimum real interest rate (r^* in Figure 13.3 above) is necessarily positive. The savings and investment curves could cut below the horizontal axis if liquidity preference is very high and investment demand is very weak.

Ultimately, financial liberalization has to be judged by its impact on economic growth and development, and here the evidence is very mixed. In a major cross-section study of 80 countries over the period 1960–89, King and Levine (1993) conclude that: 'higher levels of financial development are significantly and robustly correlated with faster current and future rates of economic growth, physical capital accumulation and economic efficiency improvements'. Using cross-section analysis, however, it is difficult to test for causality. It could be that financial development is itself the product of growth and economic development. In fact, Demetriades and Hussein (1996), taking time-series data for 16 countries, find considerable evidence of bidirectional causality between levels of financial deepening and economic development, and conclude that different countries exhibit different causality patterns, reflecting differences in financial sector policies and institutional structures. Barajas et al. (2011) analyse the relationship between financial deepening, measured by private sector credit as a percentage of GDP, across over 140 developed and developing countries over the period 1975–2005 and find that the relation differs across regions depending on the concentration of bank loans, the degree of competition in the banking system, and the level of state involvement. In North Africa and in oil-producing countries, the link between financial depth and growth is weak. Arestis and Demetriades (1997) find that, in South Korea, the real interest rate and growth performance have been negatively related, and despite financial liberalization, South Korea has deliberately pursued a policy of keeping real interest rates low in order to encourage investment. This is also the message from the World Bank's (1993) report *The East Asian Miracle: Economic Growth and Public Policies*: 'a policy of moderate financial repression at positive real interest rates may have boosted aggregate investment and growth in the HPAEs [high-performing Asian economies] by transferring income from depositors, primarily households, to borrowers, primarily firms'.

De Gregorio and Guidotti (1995) suggest that the relationship between real interest rates and growth is likely to be an inverted U-shape because negative real interest rates are not conducive to financial development and growth, and very high real interest rates are also likely to reduce growth by adversely affecting investment and leading to a concentration on risky projects. Somewhere in between, growth is likely to be maximized. Fry (1997) tests this hypothesis across 85 countries for the period 1971–95 and finds broad support for the idea, with the growth rate maximized with the real interest rate at zero.

What is clear from all the evidence across countries and continents is that if financial reforms are to succeed, they must be implemented in an appropriate macroeconomic, financial and institutional framework, with proper sequencing between internal and external liberalization. Sequencing is important because if countries liberalize their external sector before or at the same time as internal liberalization, it could have severe repercussions for the exchange rate. If there is no confidence in the country, the relaxation of capital controls could lead to capital flight and downward pressure on the exchange rate. On the other hand, higher real interest rates could attract massive capital inflows, leading to excessive currency appreciation. Either way, exchange rate instability is not conducive to macroeconomic stability.

Liberalization has been more successful in Asia than in Latin America and Africa because it has taken place in an environment of greater macroeconomic stability, with a sounder institutional framework of regulation and supervision of the banking system. Macroeconomic stability means manageable fiscal and balance of payments deficits and low inflation to encourage the holding of financial assets and to allow funds to be devoted to the private sector. Confidence in the banking system is also important and requires the restructuring of bank balance sheets, the removal of bad debts, and a strengthening of the management and risk evaluation capabilities of bank managers in order to avoid bankruptcies. Governments need to strengthen banking regulation and supervision at the same time that liberalization takes place. For successful liberalization, Fry (1997) outlines the following five prerequisites:

1. Adequate prudential regulation and supervision of commercial banks, implying some minimal levels of accounting and legal infrastructure.
2. A reasonable degree of price stability.
3. Fiscal discipline.
4. Profit-maximizing, competitive behaviour by the commercial banks.
5. A tax system that does not impose discriminatory explicit or implicit taxes on financial intermediation.

The results of a meta-analysis of financial liberalization and growth are given in Case example 13.4.

Case example 13.4 **A meta-analysis of financial liberalization and economic growth**

Since the early 1970s, the relationship between financial liberalization and economic growth has been hotly debated, in policy and academic circles. On the one hand, this is because, during the past two decades, many countries have liberalized their domestic financial markets. On the other hand, views with respect to the impact of these liberalization policies differ. Whereas some have claimed that liberalization of financial markets contributes to the efficiency with which these markets can transform saving into investment, which ultimately fosters economic growth, others have pointed out that these liberalizations have contributed to various financial and economic crises in the past. Several papers have investigated the nature of the relationship between financial liberalization and economic growth. The evidence from these studies remains inconclusive.

This study aimed to provide a systematic analysis of the empirical literature by conducting a meta-analysis of the relationship between financial liberalization and economic growth based on 60 empirical studies. Two main conclusions emerge. First, the statistical results indicate that although, on average, there is a positive effect of financial liberalization on growth, the significance of this is only weak. Second, for most of the variables that may help explain the heterogeneity of results about the relationship between financial liberalization and economic growth, significant results were not found, except:

1. Data from the 1970s generate more negative coefficients, which suggests that financial liberalization policies carried out during the 1970s seem to have a stronger negative effect on growth.
2. Studies that take into account a measure of the level of development of the financial system show a weaker relationship between financial liberalization and economic growth.

Notwithstanding these qualifying remarks, the meta-analysis is highly valuable, as it provides the most comprehensive overview of the literature on the relationship between financial liberalization and economic growth available to date. Moreover, it is the first systematic analysis of this literature. The future challenge will be to improve on the meta-analytical techniques to extend the analysis of the financial liberalization growth nexus.

Source: Bumann et al., 2012.

Fiscal policy and taxation[2]

There is another arm of the prior savings approach to the financing of development from domestic resources that needs to be considered, and that is the use of fiscal policy and taxation. Fiscal policy has two major roles in the financing of development. The first is to maintain the economy at full employment so that the savings capacity of the economy is not impaired. The second is to design a tax policy to raise the marginal propensity to save of the economy as far above the average as possible without discouraging work effort and consistent with an equitable distribution of the tax burden.

Using fiscal policy to maintain full employment will involve deficit finance if unemployed or underused real resources exist in the Keynesian sense due to a deficiency of aggregate demand. While deficit finance may be inflationary in the short run until supply has had time to adjust, there is an important analytical distinction between the means by which resources are made available for investment through deficit finance at less than full employment and the means by which savings are generated by inflation. In the former case, savings are generated by an increase in real output; in the latter case, by a reduction in real consumption through a combination of factors, including a 'real balance effect on outside money' (this refers to the attempt by holders of money assets to restore the real value of their money balances, eroded by inflation, by reducing their consumption. For a fuller discussion, see below); income redistribution from low to high savers, and money illusion.

Fiscal policy to raise the marginal propensity to save above the average is concerned with the implementation of taxes to reduce consumption in the private sector. Saving brought about by taxation is **involuntary saving**. How much taxation a country raises as a proportion of national income depends on two major factors: the **taxable capacity** of the country, and the **tax effort** made by the country in relation to its taxable capacity. The taxable capacity of a country depends on factors such as the overall level of per capita income of the country, the distribution of income, the level of literacy and urbanization, the size of the industrial sector, the importance of trade, whether the country has mineral resources, and the amount of foreign investment. In turn, the tax effort depends on the extent to which a country exploits these various tax bases and on the rates of tax applied to the bases.

The overall **buoyancy** of a tax system is measured by the proportional change in total tax revenue ($\Delta T/T$) with respect to the proportional change in national income ($\Delta Y/Y$), and is composed of two parts: the elasticity of tax revenue ($\Delta T/T$) with respect to the tax base ($\Delta B/B$), and the elasticity of the base ($\Delta B/B$) with respect to income ($\Delta Y/Y$), that is:

$$(\Delta T/T)/(\Delta Y/Y) = (\Delta T/T)/(\Delta B/B) \times (\Delta B/B)/(\Delta Y/Y) \tag{13.3}$$

If the tax system is progressive (with higher tax rates applied to higher levels of income or expenditure), then the elasticity of tax revenue with respect to the base will be greater than unity, and buoyancy will be greater than unity, provided the elasticity of the base with respect to income is at least unity. If buoyancy is greater than unity, then tax revenue as a proportion of national income will rise as national income rises. The buoyancy of the tax system can be increased by increasing the rates of tax or extending the base.

Any measured change in tax revenue with respect to income is likely to consist of an automatic increase in tax revenue as income increases if the rate structure is progressive, and the effect of discretionary changes in tax rates and extension of the tax base. The **elasticity** of a tax system is measured as buoyancy minus the effect of discretionary tax changes. There are techniques for estimating the elasticity of the tax system but we will not describe them here – suffice it to say that the greater the elasticity, the more that tax revenue and saving can increase without the need for discretionary changes. This is a desirable feature of tax systems in circumstances where it may be difficult to implement discretionary changes.

Tax effort depends on the elasticity of the system and overall buoyancy, and needs to be measured in relation to capacity. One way of doing this, pioneered by the IMF (see Tait et al., 1979), is to take a cross-section of countries and relate their ratios of tax revenue to national income to the various measures of tax capacity mentioned earlier, namely per capita income, the importance of trade and industry and so on. Estimating such an international tax function gives an equation of the form:

$$T/GDP = a + b_1(PCY) + b_2(X/GDP) + b_3(I/GDP) + \text{other variables} \quad (13.4)$$

where *T/GDP* is a country's ratio of tax revenue to national income, *PCY* is per capita income, *X/GDP* is the ratio of trade to GDP, *I/GDP* is the ratio of industrial output to GDP, and the coefficients b_1, b_2, b_3 and so on measure the *average* effect of each of the variables on the tax ratio across countries. For example, if b_2 was estimated as 0.5, this would mean that a country with a trade ratio that is 1% above the average for all countries will have a tax ratio that is 0.5 percentage points above the average for all countries, other things remaining the same.

By this method, a country's tax effort can be measured by substituting its values for *PCY*, *X/GDP*, *I/GDP* and so on in equation (13.4), predicting what the tax ratio *should be* and then comparing the predicted value with the actual value of the tax ratio. If the actual value is greater than predicted, the country can be said to be making a good effort; if it is less, then the tax effort can be regarded as weak. A study of this nature has been made by Piancastelli (2001) for 75 developed and developing countries over the period 1985–95, and the results are shown in Table 13.3. Any country with a tax effort index greater than 1 has a tax ratio greater than predicted. It can be seen from Table 13.3 that there are several developing countries making a good tax effort, including some of the largest and poorest such as India, Pakistan and Ghana. Equally, however, there are other developing countries making a very poor effort, including many countries in Latin America, notably Mexico, Argentina, Venezuela, Colombia, Bolivia and Peru.

The facts on tax revenue in developing countries are that tax revenue as a percentage of national income is typically low, averaging less than 20% compared with nearly 30% in high-income countries, and taxes on income are a minor source of tax revenue compared with indirect taxes. The proportion of the population that pays income tax in developing countries is correspondingly low, averaging about 20%, compared with the vast majority of the working population in developed countries, who constitute over 40% of the total population.

On the surface, there would appear to be a great deal of scope for using tax policy to raise the level of community saving relative to income. Two important points must be borne in mind, however. The first is that the rudimentary nature of the tax system in developing countries is partly a reflection of the stage of development itself. Thus, the scope for increasing tax revenue as a proportion of income may, in practice, be severely circumscribed. There are the difficulties of defining and measuring the tax base and of assessing and collecting taxes in circumstances where the population is dispersed and primarily engaged in producing for subsistence, and where illiteracy is also rife. There is also the fact that, as far as income tax is concerned, the income of the majority of the population is so low anyway that it falls outside the scope of the tax system. Whereas 70% of national income is subject to income tax in developed countries, only about 30% is subject to income tax in developing countries.

Even if there is scope for raising considerably more revenue by means of taxation, whether the *total* level of saving will rise depends on how tax payments are financed – whether out of consumption or saving – and how income (output) is affected. It is often the case that taxes that make tax revenue highly elastic with respect to income are taxes that are met mainly out of saving or have the most discouraging effect on incentives. For example, very progressive income tax will discourage work effort if the substitution effect of the tax outweighs the income effect; and to the extent that high marginal rates of tax fall primarily on the upper income groups with a low propensity to consume, saving may fall by nearly as much as tax revenue rises.

Table 13. 3 Tax effort indices estimated over 1985–95

Countries	Actual tax ratio (a)	Predicted tax ratio (b)	Tax effort index ((c)=(a)/(b))	Countries	Actual tax ratio (a)	Predicted tax ratio (b)	Tax effort index ((c)=(a)/(b))	Countries	Actual tax ratio (a)	Predicted tax ratio (b)	Tax effort index ((c)=(a)/(b))
Fiji	20.595	9.023	2.283	Botswana	26.766	22.224	1.204	Peru	10.728	12.223	0.878
Kenya	19.991	10.497	1.908	PN Guinea	18.825	15.774	1.193	Jordan	17.733	20.938	0.847
Belgium	42.357	23.774	1.782	UK	32.752	27.542	1.189	Panama	17.881	22.197	0.806
South Africa	25.182	15.297	1.646	Luxembourg	39.923	33.653	1.186	Philippines	13.696	17.218	0.795
Netherlands	44.273	27.228	1.626	Portugal	28.667	24.307	1.179	Madagascar	9.174	11.641	0.788
Ethiopia	11.665	7.502	1.555	Sweden	34.721	29.484	1.178	Japan	15.856	20.236	0.784
Ghana	11.76	7.776	1.512	Costa Rica	20.903	17.913	1.167	Dominican Rep.	12.677	16.432	0.772
France	37.808	25.785	1.466	Cameroon	12.784	11.011	1.161	Colombia	11.895	15.431	0.771
India	10.645	7.279	1.462	Spain	28.326	24.437	1.159	El Salvador	12.265	15.979	0.768
Lesotho	23.37	16.058	1.455	Belize	21.649	18.685	1.159	Mexico	13.752	18.431	0.746
Italy	37.482	26.176	1.432	Finland	28.219	24.777	1.139	USA	18.02	24.251	0.743
Zimbabwe	21.449	15.062	1.424	Austria	32.21	28.559	1.128	Turkey	12.452	16.899	0.737

Table 13. 3 Tax effort indices estimated over 1985–95 – *continued*

Countries	Actual tax ratio (a)	Predicted tax ratio (b)	Tax effort index ((c)=(a)/(b))	Countries	Actual tax ratio (a)	Predicted tax ratio (b)	Tax effort index ((c)=(a)/(b))	Countries	Actual tax ratio (a)	Predicted tax ratio (b)	Tax effort index ((c)=(a)/(b))
Uruguay	25.515	18.089	1.411	Syria	16.334	14.576	1.121	Congo (Dem. Rep.)	6.885	9.379	0.734
Morocco	22.534	16.027	1.406	Iceland	24.347	22.018	1.106	Switzerland	19.878	28.015	0.71
Namibia	27.595	19.957	1.383	Indonesia	15.737	14.533	1.083	Nepal	7.16	10.387	0.689
Egypt	20.704	15.121	1.369	Greece	23.093	21.862	1.056	Venezuela	16.119	23.675	0.681
Romania	21.053	15.797	1.333	Brazil	17.103	16.273	1.051	Argentina	11.401	17.434	0.654
Tunisia	24.165	18.171	1.33	Malaysia	20.016	20.417	0.98	Canada	18.008	27.743	0.649
New Zealand	32.996	24.815	1.33	Chile	18.801	19.451	0.967	Bolivia	9.451	14.62	0.646
Ireland	34.487	26.496	1.302	Thailand	15.62	16.45	0.95	Sierra Leone	6.789	10.772	0.63
Norway	32.86	25.263	1.301	Mauritius	19.667	20.72	0.949	South Korea	15.619	25.678	0.608
Pakistan	12.999	10.058	1.292	Malta	25.688	27.647	0.929	Paraguay	9.139	15.754	0.58
Denmark	33.84	26.369	1.283	Germany	23.485	26.413	0.889	Guatemala	8.024	14.269	0.562
Sri Lanka	17.886	14.422	1.24	Australia	22.017	24.904	0.884	Iran	7.423	13.702	0.542
Zambia	18.286	15.133	1.208	Ecuador	14.836	16.819	0.882	Singapore	15.672	38.905	0.403

Source: Piancastelli, 2001.

To avoid such large reductions in private saving, an **expenditure tax** on upper income groups, which exempts saving from taxation, is an alternative to a progressive income tax, but the disincentive effect on work effort is not necessarily avoided. This is so because if the expenditure tax encourages saving, the tax rate must be higher to yield the same revenue as the income tax. If people work to consume and the price of consumption is raised, work effort will be curtailed if the substitution effect of the change outweighs the income effect. The more successful the expenditure tax is in stimulating saving out of a given income, the higher must be the rate of tax to keep the yields from the two taxes equal, and the greater the disincentive to work is likely to be. If the expenditure tax is in addition to the income tax, however, there is no reason to expect any substitution effect in favour of private saving, so that whether aggregate community saving increases depends on how much work effort is discouraged and the relative propensities to consume and save of those who pay the tax compared with those of the government. In general, the most effective tax policy to raise the level of saving relative to income is to impose taxes on those with a high marginal propensity to consume, namely the poor, but there are obvious considerations of equity to bear in mind in pursuing such a policy, as well as the practical consideration of political feasibility.

The prominence of agriculture in developing countries makes agricultural taxation a potentially significant source of tax revenue and a means of transferring resources into investment. There are a great variety of tax instruments for taxing agriculture, including taxes on land area, land value, net income, marketing taxes, export taxes, land transfer taxes and so on. If revenue is the aim, then marketing and export taxes are probably the most efficient and the easiest to collect. As far as exports are concerned, two main systems may be adopted; the state-controlled marketing board may pay the producer a price that is lower than the international price received, or the government may require that all foreign exchange receipts be surrendered, with compensation given in local currency at an exchange rate that overvalues the local currency.

Export taxes may, however, have disincentive effects. The substitution effect of export taxes will be to discourage production, or to switch production to the home market if the home market is not saturated. Either way, the yield from tax will fall if the tax base (the level of exports) falls more than in proportion to the rise in the export tax. Trade taxes have also been shown to be very unstable because of the volatility of primary product exports (and imports), which can lead to severe budgetary problems for countries that rely on them (see Bleaney et al., 1995).

In theory, land taxes are probably the most desirable way to transfer resources from agriculture, but, in practice, land taxes are not important as a source of tax revenue. It is also worth mentioning that no developing country has yet successfully applied a conventional income tax to agricultural income. The nearest that countries have come to this is to tax the value of land, the imputed income from land or the potential physical yield from land.

The balance between direct taxes on income and indirect taxation on expenditures and trade in the economy at large is heavily weighted in the direction of the latter, particularly in the form of import duties and sales taxes. The emphasis on indirect taxes reflects the difficulties already mentioned of levying direct taxes, and the disincentive effects that direct taxes can have. This is not to say that indirect taxes are totally devoid of disincentive effects, but they are probably less, especially if taxes such as sales taxes and import duties can be levied on necessities without too much social hardship. Indirect taxes on luxuries will raise revenue, the more so the more price inelastic the demand, but the taxes may largely be paid out of saving, to the extent that luxuries are consumed by upper income groups with a low propensity to consume. The equity grounds for such taxation, however, are still strong.

Taxes on business are relatively easy to collect and administer, but again business taxation may merely replace one form of saving with another. The marginal propensity to save out of profits is typically high. The main justification for company taxation must be to retain control of resources that might otherwise leave the country if the business is foreign-owned, or to substitute public for private investment on the grounds that public investment is more socially productive than its private counterpart.

Tax reform in developing countries[3]

Efficient utilization of the tax potential of developing countries raises problems that vary with the circumstances of each country, but there are certain fundamental changes in most of these countries that, if adopted, would make it possible to increase public revenue and reduce some of the inequities that now exist. In particular, if a tax system is to be accepted by a poor community, it must be seen to be administered honestly and efficiently, which means that every attempt must be made to minimize the scope for avoidance (legal) and evasion (illegal).

According to the classical canons of taxation, a tax system is to be judged by the standards of equity, efficiency and administrative convenience. In most developing countries, the tax system is neither equitable nor efficient and is administratively cumbersome. Avoidance and evasion are rife.

Equity requires a comprehensive definition of income and non-discrimination between income sources. A major deficiency of tax systems all over the world, and particularly in developing countries, is that there is no single comprehensive tax on all income. Typically, there is a 'cedular' system, with separate taxes on different sources of income. Wage and salary earners ('earned' incomes) tend to be discriminated against vis-à-vis the owners of property and capital and the self-employed (professional people and small traders). An equitable system should also be such that it discourages luxury consumption and makes it difficult to avoid and evade taxation.

Taxable capacity is not measured by income alone, but also by wealth. Equity therefore also requires the taxation of wealth. The ownership of wealth endows the owner with an inherent taxable capacity, irrespective of the money income the asset yields. Consider the case of a beggar with nothing and a rich man who holds all his wealth in the form of jewellery and gold, which yields no money income. Judged by income, their taxable capacity is the same: nil. No one could claim, however, that their ability to pay was the same, and that, for tax purposes, they should be treated equally.

Income tax is not only inequitable between those with property and those without, but also *between* property holders. For example, two property holders may derive the same income from property but the value of their property may differ greatly. One has a greater taxable capacity than the other. Only a combination of income and property taxes can achieve equity according to ability to pay. This is the case for a **wealth tax**.

Equity also requires that gifts between individuals be taxed, on death and *inter vivos*.

Efficiency requires that the entire tax system be self-reinforcing and self-checking so that the attempt to escape one tax increases the liability to other taxes. The system should also be based, as far as possible, on a comprehensive annual tax return.

The above considerations suggest at least four major reforms of the tax system in developing countries, which would also release resources for investment and act as an incentive to effort:

1. *All* income (including capital gains) be aggregated and taxed in the same way, at a progressive rate but not exceeding a maximum marginal rate of, say, 50%. Marginal rates above this level may not only discourage incentive but may also be counterproductive by encouraging evasion and avoidance.

2. The institution of a progressive personal expenditure tax levied on rich individuals who reach the maximum marginal rate of income tax.
3. The institution of a wealth tax.
4. The institution of a gifts tax.

Inflation, saving and growth

If voluntary and involuntary saving are inadequate, inflationary policies that 'force' saving by 'taxing' money and redistributing income between classes within the private sector are an alternative possibility. The price of financial conservatism may well be economic stagnation. The potential benefits of inflationary finance, which embrace both the Keynesian and the quantity theory approach to development finance, have been discussed by economists (including Malthus, Bentham, Thornton, Robertson and, more recently, Kaldor) at least since David Hume in the eighteenth century; and several economic historians (including Keynes) claim to have discerned a relationship in history between periods of inflation and rapid economic development. Hamilton (1952) claims that inflation was a powerful stimulant to growth in a wide number of historical contexts through the favourable effect of excess demand on profits, saving and investment, for example in England and France in the sixteenth and seventeenth centuries and in England in the latter half of the eighteenth century. Rostow (1960) also claims that inflation was important for several industrial take-offs.

Keynes, in his *Treatise on Money* (1930), similarly remarked on the apparent extraordinary correspondence in history between periods of inflation and deflation and national rise and decline, respectively. Keynes was certainly more predisposed to inflation than deflation. He described inflation as unjust and deflation as inexpedient, but of the two, inflation is to be preferred because 'it is worse in an impoverished world to provoke unemployment than to disappoint the rentier' (Keynes, 1931). While recognizing that inflation to increase capital accumulation may have regressive distributional consequences, Keynes (1930) further argued that the long-run gains to wage earners can outweigh the short-term losses:

> the working class may benefit far more in the long run from the forced abstinence which a profit inflation imposes on them than they lose in the first instance in the shape of diminished consumption so long as wealth and its fruits are not consumed by the nominal owner but are accumulated.

The Keynesian approach to the financing of development

The Keynesian approach to the financing of development by inflationary means stresses, first, that investment can generate its own saving by raising the level of income when the economy is operating below capacity, and by redistributing income from wage earners with a low propensity to save to profit earners with a higher propensity to save when the economy is working at full capacity. Second, inflation itself can encourage investment by raising the nominal rate of return on investment and reducing the real rate of interest. Only the first of these two aspects of the Keynesian approach will be considered here.

Unemployed resources provide the classic argument for Keynesian policies of inflationary finance. If resources are unemployed or underused, real output and real savings can be increased by governments running budget deficits financed either by printing money or by issuing government bonds to the banking system and the public.

In a situation of genuine 'Keynesian' unemployment, any tendency towards inflation, whatever method of deficit finance is used, should burn itself out as the supply of goods rises to meet the additional purchasing power created. Some economists have questioned, however, whether the observed unemployment of labour in developing countries is strictly of the Keynesian variety, and whether the supply of output would respond very much to increased demand. It is probably true that most unemployment in developing countries results not from a shortage of demand, but from a lack of cooperating factors of production for labour to work with (mainly capital); and the direct multiplier effects of government expenditure may be low, but some deficit-financed projects (e.g. infrastructure projects) may have considerable secondary repercussions on output if they eliminate production and marketing bottlenecks at the same time.

In the agricultural sector of developing countries, and in the production of consumer goods in the industrial sector, there are many opportunities for investment that can yield outputs several times more than the money value of capital invested in a very short space of time. In agriculture, the use of fertilizers and the provision of transport facilities are good examples. Credit expansion for these activities can soon generate sufficient output to absorb the demand-creating effects of the new money in circulation.

Thus, while it may be true that much of the unemployment in developing countries is not of the Keynesian variety, it does not follow that monetary expansion cannot generate secondary employment and output effects. The capacity-generating effects need to be considered in conjunction with the emphasis on demand in Keynesian static multiplier theory.

Let us now turn to the Keynesian full employment case. At full employment, inflation is the inevitable result of the Keynesian approach to development. In contrast to classical and neoclassical theory, Keynesian theory specifies independent saving and investment functions and allows price changes in response to excess demand in the goods market to raise saving by redistributing income. Inflation is the means by which resources are redistributed between consumption and investment. In Keynesian models, investment is not constrained by saving, but by the inflation rate willing to be tolerated by wage earners who have had their real wages cut.

If plans to invest exceed plans to save, it is reasonable to suppose that investors and consumers will both have their plans thwarted. Investment is less than firms desire, but greater than consumers plan to save. Let us assume, therefore, that the actual growth of capital is a linear combination of planned saving and planned investment:

$$\frac{dK}{K} = \alpha \frac{I}{K} + (1 - \alpha) \frac{S}{K}, \quad \alpha < 1 \tag{13.5}$$

where K is the quantity of capital, I is planned investment and S is planned saving. Now assume that the rate of inflation is proportional to the degree of excess demand, as measured by the difference between plans to invest and save:

$$\frac{dP}{P} = \lambda\left(\frac{I}{K} - \frac{S}{K}\right), \quad \lambda > 0 \tag{13.6}$$

where P is the price level. Substituting the expression for I/K into equation (13.5) gives:

$$\frac{dK}{K} = \frac{\alpha(dP/P)}{\lambda} + \frac{S}{K} \tag{13.7}$$

S/K is planned saving, and $\alpha(dP/P)/\lambda$ is forced saving, per unit of capital. Forced saving results from the inability of consumers to fulfil their planned consumption in conditions of excess demand. The underlying mechanism that thwarts the plans of consumers is inflation, which redistributes income from wage earners to profits. Other things remaining the same, if prices rise faster than wages, real consumption will fall and real saving increase as long as the propensity to save out of profits is higher than the propensity to save out of wages.

In Keynesian models, therefore, the effect of inflation on saving depends on two factors: the extent to which income is redistributed between wages and profits, and the extent of the difference in the propensity to save out of wages and profits. The relation between wages, prices and profits, and the consequent effect of income redistribution on saving, is best illustrated using simple algebra. Let Z be labour's share of national income so that:

$$Z = \frac{W}{PY} = \frac{wL}{PY} = \frac{w}{Pr} \tag{13.8}$$

where W is the wage bill, w is the wage rate, P is price per unit of output, Y is income and $r = Y/L$ is the productivity of labour. Hence, the rate of change of labour's share may be written as:

$$\frac{dZ}{Z} = \left(\frac{dw}{w} - \frac{dP}{P}\right) - \frac{dr}{r} \tag{13.9}$$

From this equation, it can be seen that given a positive rate of growth of productivity, a sufficient condition for a redistribution of income from wages to profits is that prices rise faster than wages. Note, however, that in a growing economy (with positive productivity growth), it is not a *necessary* condition. Labour's share will fall and the share of profits rise as long as $(dw/w - dP/P) \leqslant dr/r$; that is, as long as the real wage rises less than the growth of labour productivity. In a growing economy, therefore, there is no necessary clash between the real wage and profits. The real wage can rise and the share of profits in income can also rise as long as some of the gains in labour productivity are appropriated by the capitalists.

It is also obvious that on the classical savings assumption that all wages are consumed and all profits are saved, the savings ratio will rise by exactly the same amount as the wage share falls.

The basic Keynesian notion that investment determines saving forms the backbone of **neo-Keynesian growth theory**, as originally expounded by Robinson (1962) and Kaldor (1955–56). Variations in the savings ratio resulting from inflation and income redistribution are one of the many possible adjustment mechanisms for raising the warranted growth rate towards the natural rate (see Chapter 4). As Robinson (1962) used to argue, in response to the neoclassical adjustment mechanisms of variations in interest rates and the capital–output ratio, there is nothing in the laws of nature to guarantee growth at the natural rate, but if entrepreneurs wish to invest sufficient to grow at the natural rate, then saving will adapt, subject to an **inflation barrier**. (In a static economy, the 'inflation barrier' means a real wage so low that wage earners react to price increases to prevent the real wage from falling further. In a growing economy, it is the point at which labour resists any further reduction in its share of national income; that is, where labour appropriates all increases in labour productivity itself in the form of increased real wages.) When there is a steady rate of growth, the share of savings adapts to it. In effect, the actual growth rate pulls up the warranted growth rate by forcing saving. Saving adapts to investment through the dependence of saving on the share of profits in income, which rises with the level of investment relative to income in the way that has been described. Profits depend, in turn, on what happens to real wages when the system is out of equilibrium. The basic equation of Robinson's model is the distribution equation:

$$PY = wL + \pi PK \tag{13.10}$$

where π is the gross profit rate R/K, and P, Y, w, L and K are as before. Dividing by P and rearranging to obtain an expression for the profit rate, gives:

$$\pi = \frac{(Y/L) - (w/P)}{(K/L)} = \frac{R/L}{K/L} = \frac{R}{K} \tag{13.11}$$

Given the capital–labour ratio (K/L), the rate of profit depends on the relationship between output per head and the real wage. If all wages are consumed and all profits are saved, the rate of profit gives the rate of capital accumulation and the rate of growth. This follows since $S = I = \pi K$, and $\Delta K = \pi K$; therefore $\Delta K/K = \pi$. And if the capital–output ratio is fixed, $\Delta K/K = \Delta Y/Y$; hence $\pi = \Delta K/K = \Delta Y/Y$.

Variations in the rate of profit and corresponding variations in the real wage provide the mechanism that equilibrates plans to save and invest and the actual and warranted growth rates. If the actual growth rate equals the natural rate, the warranted and natural growth rates will also be equalized. If the real wage remains unchanged as investment takes place, however, saving cannot adapt and a greater volume of real investment cannot be funded. This is the inflation barrier in a static model. It appears, in fact, that in a static context, the growth rate can only be raised at the expense of the real wage, which comes close to the pessimistic development theories of Ricardo and Marx, as discussed in Chapter 4. In a growing economy, however, such pessimism would be unfounded because it can be seen from equation (13.11) that the rate of profit and capital accumulation can rise even if the real wage is rising, as long as the growth in labour productivity exceeds the increase in the real wage.

Kaldor's model also makes saving adjust to the desired level of investment through a rise in the share of profits in national income. The model consists of three basic equations:

$$Y = W + R \tag{13.12}$$

$$I = S \tag{13.13}$$

$$S = s_w W + s_r R \tag{13.14}$$

where R is profits, W is wages, s_w is the propensity to save out of wages and s_r is the propensity to save out of profits. Using the three equations we can write:

$$\begin{aligned} I &= s_w(Y - R) + s_r R \\ &= (s_r - s_w)R + s_w Y \end{aligned} \tag{13.15}$$

Making investment the independent variable in the system, and dividing by Y gives:

$$\frac{R}{Y} = \left(\frac{1}{s_r - s_w}\right)\frac{I}{Y} - \frac{s_w}{(s_r - s_w)} \tag{13.16}$$

The ratio of profits to income and the investment ratio are positively related as long as the propensity to save out of profits exceeds the propensity to save out of wages. The investment ratio must clearly be the independent variable in the system. Capitalists can decide how much they are going to consume and invest but they cannot decide how much profit they are going to make. If $s_r = 1$ and $s_w = 0$, then $I/Y = R/Y$, and, multiplying both sides of equation (13.16) by Y/K, we have Robinson's result that the rate of profit, the rate of capital accumulation and the rate of growth are all equal. A higher level of investment can raise the rate of capital accumulation by raising the profit rate and the share of saving in total income, subject, of course, to the inflation barrier. The mechanism that gives this result is rising prices relative to wages.

The Kaldor model can be used for estimating how much inflation is necessary to raise the savings ratio by a given amount (see Thirlwall, 1974 for the model). The inflation rate required depends on three main factors:

1. Labour's initial share of national income.
2. The difference in the propensity to save out of wages (s_w) and profits (s_r).
3. How fast wages chase prices (the wage–price coefficient).

If wages chase prices equiproportionately, and there is no difference in the propensity to save out of wages and profits, there can be no redistribution effects on saving by generating inflation. If there is a big difference in the savings propensities, and the wage–price coefficient is quite low, mild inflation of approximately 3% can increase the savings ratio by one percentage point. If there is only a small difference in the savings propensities, and the wage–price coefficient is very high (close to unity), over 100% inflation would be required to raise the savings ratio by one percentage point. Even Keynesians might regard such a rate as a high price to pay for extra growth (see Thirlwall, 1974 for a full range of estimates).

Reconciling the prior saving and forced saving approaches to development

There can be little doubt that the traditional development literature and the governments of most developing countries have veered towards the classical view of development when making policy prescriptions and formulating plans. But there is scope for a more eclectic approach. It is not necessary to be a classicist to recognize the importance of voluntary saving in capital-scarce economies, and it should not be necessary to be a Keynesian to admit that investors may lay claim on real resources in excess of the community's plans to save. Keynesians welcome prior saving. What they dispute is that prior saving is necessary for investment; that investment is constrained by prior saving. As Robinson (1960, vol. II) said when discussing the relation between savings and investment at full employment:

> We cannot return to the pre-Keynesian view that savings governs investment. The essential point of Keynes' teaching remains. It is decisions about how much investment is to be made that govern the rate at which wealth will accumulate, not decisions about savings.

A start at reconciliation would be for the prior savings school to admit the possibility of forced saving and to reduce their aversion to demand inflation. Equally, the Keynesians could admit that saving depends on factors other than the functional distribution of income, and that for any desired savings or investment ratio, inflation will fall as voluntary saving rises.

The quantity theory approach to the financing of development

The quantity theory approach to the financing of development stresses the effect of inflation as a tax on real money balances. Suppose a government wishes to divert more of a country's resources to investment; one of the ways it can do so is to invest on society's behalf, financing the investment by expanding the money supply. In conditions where capital is already fully employed, monetary expansion will be inflationary.

Inflation is the means by which resources are effectively transferred to government. Inflation imposes a **tax on money holdings** and consists of a reduction in the real purchasing power of money and the real resources that the holders of money must forego to restore the real value of their money holdings. The base of the tax is the level of real cash balances (M/P), and the tax rate is the rate at which the real value of money is deteriorating, which is equal to the rate of inflation (dP/P). The real yield from the tax is the product of the tax base and the tax rate; that is, $(M/P)(dP/P)$, which will be maximized (as in standard tax theory) when the elasticity of the base with respect to the rate of tax is equal to −1. If the rate of inflation is equal to the rate of monetary expansion, the real tax yield (R) will equal the real value of the new money issued; that is, $(M/P)(dM/M) = dM/P$. If $dP/P > dM/M$, some of the potential tax yield will be lost owing to a reduction in the tax base.

The inflation tax can be illustrated diagrammatically, as in Figure 13.4. *DD* is the demand for real money balances in relation to the rate of inflation. When prices are stable, the demand for real balances is *D*. At inflation rate *P*, however, which is expected to continue, the demand for real balances falls to *M*. The area 0*PXM* thus represents the amount of real income that holders of real money balances must substitute for money balances to keep real balances intact at level *M*. Since money balances must be accumulated and real income forgone at the same rate as the rate of inflation, the rate of tax is equal to the rate of inflation.

Inflation as a tax on money redistributes resources from the private sector to the government as the issuer of money – resources that are just as real as those obtained by more conventional means of taxation. Keynes was fully aware of this other aspect of inflation, as well as the tendency for demand inflation to transfer income from wages to profits. In his *Tract on Monetary Reform* (1923), Keynes describes inflation as 'a form of taxation that the public finds hard to evade and even the weakest government can enforce when it can enforce nothing else'.

The real yield from the inflation tax available for investment as a proportion of income (R_I/Y) will be the product of the money–income ratio, $(\dot{M}/P)/Y$, the rate of inflation, $dP/P = dM/M$, and the proportion of the increase in the real money supply captured for investment $(R_I)/(dM/P)$, that is:

$$\frac{R_I}{Y} = \left(\frac{M}{PY}\right)\left(\frac{dM}{M}\right)\left(\frac{R_I}{dM/P}\right) \tag{13.17}$$

Figure 13.4 Inflation tax

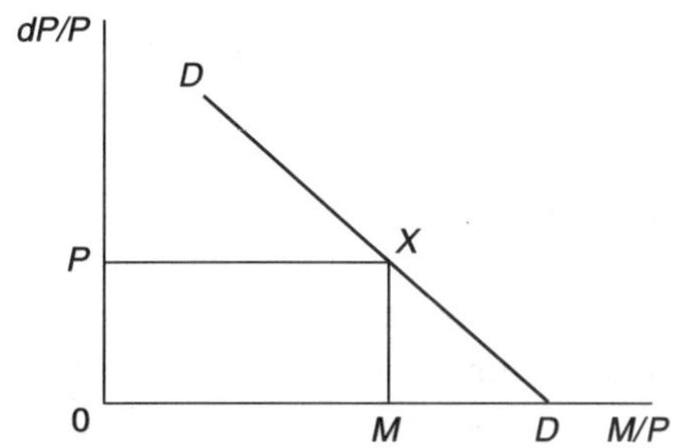

Suppose that the money–income ratio is 0.4 and 50% of new money issued is used for investment purposes, then a 10% expansion of the money supply leading to a 10% rate of inflation would yield 2% of the national income for the development programme. If all the new money is used for investment purposes, the real yield from the tax is simply the ratio of the real value of the new money issued to income (our earlier result), which in this example would be 2.5%. These calculations assume, however, that the desired ratio of money holdings to income remains unchanged regardless of the rate of inflation. In practice, the ratio is likely to be a decreasing function of the rate of inflation because the opportunity cost of holding real money balances rises. Only if the base of the tax falls more than in proportion to the inflation rate, however, will the yield from the inflation tax actually decline.

From the limited evidence available, it appears that the elasticity of the money–income ratio with respect to the rate of inflation is quite low even in high inflation countries. This suggests that inflation can operate effectively as a tax on money even in countries that have been experiencing high rates of inflation for many years. It should also be remembered that while inflation may reduce the desired ratio of money holdings to income, the ratio will have a continual tendency to rise with the gradual monetization and development of the economy. On balance, the ratio may be very little affected by monetary expansion.

The fact that the demand to hold money relative to income rises as development proceeds, and output is growing, also means that some government investment can be financed without any increase in the price level. This is easily seen taking the fundamental equation of exchange:

$$MV = PY$$

or:

$$M = K_d PY \tag{13.18}$$

where M is the nominal money supply, V is the income velocity of circulation of money, $K_d (= 1/V)$ is the demand to hold money per unit of money income, P is the average price of final goods and services, and Y is real income.

Taking rates of growth of the variables, denoted by lower-case letters, gives:

$$m = k_d + p + y \tag{13.19}$$

It can be seen that if the demand for money per unit of income is increasing ($k_d > 0$), m can be positive without the price level rising. Similarly, if the economy is growing ($y > 0$), m can also be positive without the price level rising. The government's proceeds from monetary expansion will equal $m - p$. In several developing countries, the rate of growth of the demand for money per unit of income seems to be in the order of 5% per annum. This, combined with a growth rate of output of 3% per annum, would mean that the non-inflationary growth of the money supply would be in the order of 8% per annum.

Finally, it should also be added that government investment projects financed by monetary expansion can reduce an economy's capital–output ratio (if the projects have high output–labour ratios and low capital–labour ratios), enabling a higher rate of capital accumulation for any given investment ratio, and therefore a higher rate of employment growth. Inflation is not necessarily inegalitarian if the government investment projects financed by monetary expansion help the poor in rural and urban areas by generating employment opportunities and raising productivity.

The dangers of inflation

Some of the benefits of inflation have been considered, especially the ability of inflation to release resources for development by redistributing income between classes within the private sector and from the private sector to government. Inflation is not without its dangers, however, and these must be emphasized.

First, a distinction needs to be made between the different types of inflation that may be experienced by a developing country: **demand inflation**, **cost inflation** and **structural inflation**. The argument for inflationary finance is an argument for demand inflation. Cost inflation, by reducing profits, will not be conducive to development. Structural inflation may be the inevitable price of development, but there is nothing in the process of structural inflation itself that will necessarily accelerate the development process.

There are also certain dangers and costs involved in deliberately pursuing an inflationary policy to stimulate development. The most serious threats to growth from inflation come from the effect on the balance of payments if foreign exchange is a scarce resource, and from the possibility that voluntary saving, productive investment and the use of money as a medium of exchange may be discouraged if inflation becomes excessive. If one country inflates at a faster rate than others, its balance of payments may suffer severely, leading to protection and exchange controls, and hence inefficiency in resource allocation. As far as investment is concerned, if inflation becomes excessive, investment in physical plant and equipment may become unattractive relative to speculative investment in inventories, overseas assets, property and artefacts that absorb a society's real resources. If the real rate of interest becomes negative (that is, the rate of inflation exceeds the nominal rate of interest), it may even become attractive to claim real resources and not to use them.

Inflation clearly reduces the purchasing power of money. If inflation becomes excessive, not only may voluntary saving be discouraged but the use of money as a medium of exchange may be discouraged, involving society in real resource costs and welfare losses. Since inflation reduces the purchasing power of money, holders may be expected to avoid losses by cutting down their holdings of money for transactions purposes. The cost of inflation arises from the fact that cash balances yield utility and contribute to production, and inflation causes energy, time and resources to be devoted to minimizing the use of cash balances that are costless to produce; for example the frequency of trips to the bank may increase, which absorbs labour time, and credit mechanisms may be resorted to, which absorb society's resources.

There are also the distributional consequences of inflation to consider. These are difficult to assess, but the following can be said with some confidence:

- Debtors benefit at the expense of creditors.
- Profit earners gain at the expense of wage earners in times of demand inflation and lose at the expense of wage earners in times of wage inflation.
- Real asset holders probably gain relative to money asset holders.
- The strong (in a bargaining sense) probably gain relative to the weak; and the young gain relative to the old, who tend to live on fixed contractual incomes.

In developing countries, however, the possible inegalitarian distributional consequences of demand inflation should not be allowed to constitute an argument against the use of mildly inflationary policies if one of the aims is to create additional employment. The major beneficiaries of inflationary finance should be the unemployed and the underemployed, which represents a move towards a more egalitarian structure of household incomes.

Having considered some of the potential dangers of inflation, it can be seen that there is plenty of room for disagreement over whether inflation is a help or a hindrance to development. We have seen that it can help to raise the level of real saving and encourage investment; on the other hand, it may stimulate the 'wrong' type of investment, and inflation may get out of control and retard development through its adverse effects on productive investment and the balance of payments. A lot clearly depends on the type of inflation under discussion and its rate.

Inflation targeting

Because of the perceived dangers of inflation – inflation is harmful to growth and development – many developing countries have recently copied developed countries, such as the UK and the countries of the EU under the direction of the European Central Bank, and adopted inflation targeting to control the rate of inflation. Countries such as Brazil, Chile, Colombia, Mexico, Peru, South Korea, the Philippines and Thailand all started the process in the late 1990s and early 2000s. Targeting a specific inflation rate, such as 5%, or a range between 4% and 6%, is a way of dampening inflationary expectations in an economy and lending credibility to a government's monetary and fiscal policies for controlling the economy. The question is: Does it work, without sacrificing growth and employment? To evaluate this properly, the countries adopting inflation targeting need to be compared with a control group. When this is done, the evidence for developed countries is that targeting has no significant effect on either inflation or its variability (see Lin and Ye, 2007). On the other hand, given that the credibility of central banks in developing countries is significantly less than in developed countries, it might be expected that the credibility gain from explicitly announcing an inflation target would be much more substantial in developing countries. Goncalves and Salles (2008) find this to be so in a sample of 36 emerging economies, but they do not compare their results with a control group. Lin and Ye (2009) rectify this deficiency by comparing 13 developing countries that adopted inflation targeting up to 2004, using 39 other countries as a control group. Their central conclusion is that inflation targeting has reduced the inflation rate by about 3 percentage points on average, but the experience varies between countries according to the length of time the policy has been adopted, fiscal discipline, exchange rate variability, and governments' commitment to meet the preconditions for the policy of adopting a target inflation rate. Whether any costs have been incurred, however, in terms of slower growth or higher unemployment, is not explored. But what does the empirical evidence show of the relation between inflation and growth across countries? We examine this in the next section.

Inflation and growth: the empirical evidence

The discussion so far suggests that the relation between inflation and growth is likely to be non-linear, with growth positively related to inflation up to a certain rate of inflation and then negatively related as the disadvantages of inflation outweigh the advantages. This is in line with recent empirical evidence from large datasets across developing and developed countries.

A study by Bruno (1995) at the World Bank, taking pooled annual observations for 127 countries over the years 1960–92, produced the pattern depicted in Figure 13.5. Inflation and growth are positively related up to 5% inflation, and then 'diminishing returns' to inflation set in. Inflation and growth are strongly negative once inflation rises above 30%, but for inflation rates below 20%, Bruno (1995) concludes that 'there is no obvious empirical evidence for significant long-run growth costs'.

Figure 13.5 Inflation and per capita income growth, 1960–92 (pooled annual observations, 127 countries)

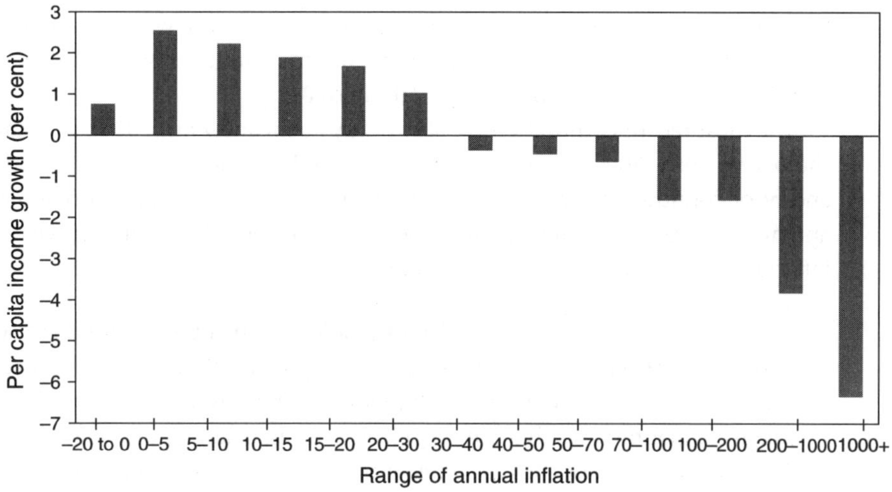

A study by Sarel (1996) at the IMF has produced a similar result. He takes 87 countries over the period 1970–90 and divides the observations into 12 inflation groupings using the inflation rate of group 6 as the standard of reference. He then estimates the effect that differential inflation has on the growth rate in the other groups. The results are shown in Figure 13.6. It can be seen that inflation has a generally positive effect on growth up to group 7, with inflation averaging 8%. Thereafter, inflation and growth are negatively related. When inflation is very high (in group 12), the difference in the effect of inflation on growth compared with group 6 is close to 4 percentage points (holding all other factors constant). (These results support the early work of Thirlwall (1974), which also showed a nonlinear relation between inflation and the savings ratio, and inflation and the investment ratio. For a survey of models of inflation and growth, and some of the early empirical evidence, see Johnson (1984). See Temple (2000) for an overview.)

Ghosh and Phillips (1998), also at the IMF, show the growth of GDP to be highest in the range of inflation 3–5% for developed countries, and in the range 5–10% for developing countries (no doubt reflecting greater structural inflation).

Figure 13.6 Effects of different inflation rates on growth

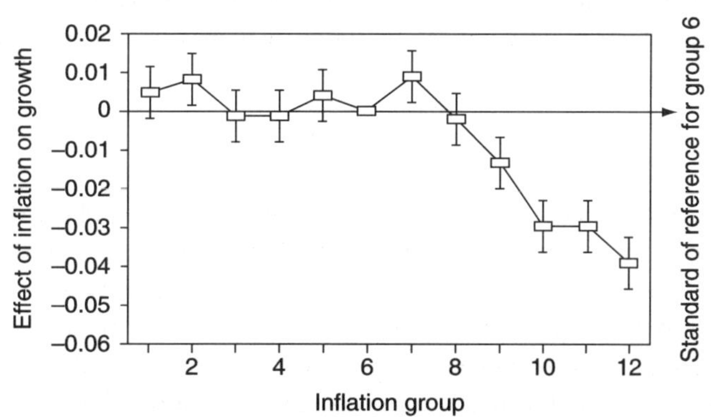

Evidence of nonlinearity between inflation and growth is also found by Stanners (1993) in a study of 9 countries over the period 1948–86 and 44 countries over the period 1980–88. First he divides the 44 countries into four groups according to the rate of inflation and shows that the highest growth occurred in the second group of countries, with an average rate of inflation of 8.2%. He then takes a scatter of 342 points for nine countries over 38 years and shows a positive correlation between inflation and growth up to 8%.

The most recent comprehensive study is by Pollin and Zhu (2006), who take 80 countries over the period 1961–2000, distinguishing between OECD (rich) countries, middle-income countries and poor countries. They find no significant relation between inflation and growth in the OECD and middle-income countries, but in the poor countries, there is a positive relation up to 15–23% inflation. Pollin and Zhu (2006) conclude:

> There is no evidence ... supportive of a policy of maintaining inflation within a low band of about 3–5 per cent, to the degree that government policy-makers are interested in promoting growth and employment, rather than low inflation as an end in itself. ... There is still a wide range of inflation rates that are very likely to be associated positively with economic growth. ... This is most especially the case when inflation is resulting from, as Bruno (1995) puts it, 'investment demand pressure in an expanding economy'.

It is not surprising from this evidence that Temple (2000) concludes his survey of inflation by saying:

> since there is not yet robust evidence that moderate inflation has an adverse impact on growth, any case for price stability which relies on a positive growth effect should continue to be regarded with considerable suspicion.

Similarly, Levine and Zervos (1993), in a review of studies of the macrodeterminants of growth, conclude that:

> given the uncharacteristically unified view among economists and policy analysts that countries with high inflation rates should adopt policies that lower inflation in order to promote economic prosperity, the inability to find simple cross-country regressions supporting this contention is both surprising and troubling.

Indeed, we can be more categorical and say that there is *no* scientific evidence to suggest that a necessary condition for faster growth is that inflation should be as low as possible. The evidence suggests that mild inflation, up to 5–8%, can be positively beneficial for growth. After that, however, the effects of inflation can be seriously damaging, certainly at rates in excess of 20%.

The inflationary experience

Having discussed the advantages of inflation and warned of the dangers of excessive inflation, the fact is that the inflationary experience of most developing countries outside Latin America, at least until the recent past, has been relatively mild. It is a myth that developing countries have been typically prone to high rates of inflation. Out of a sample of 48 developing countries over the period 1958–68, 38 recorded average rates of inflation of less than 6% per annum (see Thirlwall, 1974, p. 35 and Appendix 1). Historically, most developing countries have been very financially conservative.

From the mid-1970s, however, there was a marked acceleration of inflation worldwide, sparked by the oil price rises in 1973 and 1979, as well as other commodity price rises, and this continued into the 1980s and 1990s in many countries. Since 2000, however, the rate of inflation has subsided, at least in developed countries. The average rate of inflation country by country over the period 2000–14 is shown in Table 13.4. It can be seen that there is a wide variety of experience between countries, but, on balance, developing countries have been more prone to inflation than developed countries. In developed countries, the average rate of inflation has been about 5%, whereas in low- and middle-income countries, it has been closer to 10%. Some notable high inflation countries in the past decade have been in Africa: Ghana, 22.8%, Guinea, 16.1%, Nigeria, 15.7%, Malawi, 14.9%, and Sudan and Ethiopia, 13.7%. Some Latin American countries have also recorded some high inflation rates: Venezuela, 25.3%, Argentina, 17.3%, Brazil and Uruguay, 8%, and Paraguay, 7.5% Historically, Latin America has been the most inflation-prone continent, almost from the start of the industrialization process, and it was in Latin America that the 'structuralist–monetarist' controversy started over the causes of rapid inflation in poor countries. We conclude this chapter with an overview of the debate, which still has relevance today.

Table 13.4 Inflation

	GDP implicit deflator average annual % growth 2000–2014		GDP implicit deflator average annual % growth 2000 -2014		GDP implicit deflator average annual % growth 2000 -2014
Afghanistan	8.0	Belize	1.8	Channel Islands	3.6
Albania	2.9	Benin	2.9	Chile	5.3
Algeria	8.1	Bermuda	3.6	China	4.6
American Samoa		Bhutan	5.5	Hong Kong SAR, China	0.1
Andorra	2.4	Bolivia	7.2	Macao SAR, China	5.4
Angola		Bosnia and Herzegovina	3.3	Colombia	5.3
Antigua and Barbuda	1.9	Botswana	7.3	Comoros	3.0
Argentina	17.3	Brazil	8.0	Congo, Dem. Rep.	17.9
Armenia	4.6	Brunei Darussalam	4.9	Congo, Rep.	6.2
Aruba	4.6	Bulgaria	5.1	Costa Rica	8.7
Australia	3.7	Burkina Faso	3.0	Cote d'Ivoire	3.2
Austria	1.8	Burundi	11.9	Croatia	3.1
Azerbaijan	9.2	Cape Verde	1.9	Cuba	2.7
Bahamas, The	1.4	Cambodia	4.4	Curacao	
Bahrain	5.7	Cameroon	2.6	Cyprus	2.6
Bangladesh	6.3	Canada	2.3	Czech Republic	1.6
Barbados	1.9	Cayman Islands		Denmark	2.2
Belarus	25.6	Central African Republic	2.7	Djibouti	3.9
Belgium	1.8	Chad	5.7	Dominica	1.5

continued overleaf

Table 13.4 Inflation – *continued*

	GDP implicit deflator average annual % growth 2000–2014		GDP implicit deflator average annual % growth 2000 -2014		GDP implicit deflator average annual % growth 2000 -2014
Dominican Republic	10.6	Ireland	0.7	Mexico	5.2
Ecuador	7.4	Isle of Man	3.5	Micronesia, Fed. Sts.	2.7
Egypt, Arab Rep.	9.6	Israel	1.8	Moldova	9.6
El Salvador	3.1	Italy	2.0	Monaco	1.9
Equatorial Guinea	8.9	Jamaica	10.2	Mongolia	15.3
Eritrea	15.5	Japan	-0.9	Montenegro	5.5
Estonia	5.3	Jordan	6.2	Morocco	2.0
Ethiopia	13.7	Kazakhstan	14.2	Mozambique	6.2
Faeroe Islands		Kenya	9.1	Myanmar	6.4
Fiji	4.5	Kiribati	1.4	Namibia	6.8
Finland	1.7	Korea, Dem. Rep.		Nepal	8.2
France	1.6	Korea, Rep.	2.2	Netherlands	1.7
French Polynesia		Kosovo	2.0	New Caledonia	
Gabon	5.3	Kuwait	7.5	New Zealand	2.7
Gambia, The	5.7	Kyrgyz Republic	9.9	Nicaragua	8.5
Georgia	6.1	Lao PDR	7.1	Niger	3.7
Germany	1.2	Latvia	6.0	Nigeria	15.7
Ghana	22.8	Lebanon	2.8	Northern Mariana Islands	
Greece	2.2	Lesotho	6.9	Norway	4.4
Greenland	-2.1	Liberia	8.7	Oman	8.8
Grenada	2.4	Libya	10.4	Pakistan	11.0
Guam		Liechtenstein	0.7	Palau	2.6
Guatemala	5.4	Lithuania	3.7	Panama	3.7
Guinea	16.1	Luxembourg	3.1	Papua New Guinea	5.1
Guinea-Bissau	2.4	Macedonia, FYR	2.8	Paraguay	7.5
Guyana	11.7	Madagascar	9.7	Peru	3.4
Haiti	11.2	Malawi	14.9	Philippines	4.3
Honduras	6.1	Malaysia	4.0	Poland	2.7
Hungary	4.2	Maldives	5.5	Portugal	2.0
Iceland	5.3	Mali	3.9	Puerto Rico	4.6
India	6.1	Malta	2.9	Qatar	8.4
Indonesia	10.5	Marshall Islands	2.6	Romania	11.2
Iran, Islamic Rep.	17.9	Mauritania	8.1	Russian Federation	13.4
Iraq	11.3	Mauritius	5.0	Rwanda	9.0

Table 13.4 Inflation – *continued*

	GDP implicit deflator average annual % growth 2000–2014		GDP implicit deflator average annual % growth 2000 -2014		GDP implicit deflator average annual % growth 2000 -2014
Samoa	3.6	St. Kitts and Nevis	2.9	Turkmenistan	16.0
San Marino	2.2	St. Lucia	3.3	Turks and Caicos Islands	
Sao Tome and Principe	14.3	St. Martin (French part)		Tuvalu	2.4
Saudi Arabia	6.1	St. Vincent and the Grenadines	2.2	Uganda	8.9
Senegal	2.5	Sudan	13.7	Ukraine	15.4
Serbia	11.1	Suriname	15.5	United Arab Emirates	7.0
Seychelles	10.4	Swaziland	9.0	United Kingdom	2.5
Sierra Leone	12.2	Sweden	1.7	United States	2.1
Singapore	1.4	Switzerland	0.8	Uruguay	8.0
Sint Maarten (Dutch part)		Syrian Arab Republic	6.4	Uzbekistan	21.2
Slovak Republic	2.1	Tajikistan	17.4	Vanuatu	3.0
Slovenia	2.8	Tanzania	11.3	Venezuela, RB	25.3
Solomon Islands	6.5	Thailand	3.1	Vietnam	10.6
Somalia		Timor-Leste	4.5	Virgin Islands (U.S.)	
South Africa	7.1	Tonga	5.8	West Bank and Gaza	4.5
South Sudan		Trinidad and Tobago	5.4	Yemen, Rep.	12.0
Spain	2.2	Tunisia	3.9	Zambia	12.8
Sri Lanka	10.8	Turkey	11.1	Zimbabwe	8.4

Source: World Bank, *World Development Indicators 2015*, online (http://wdi.worldbank.org/table/4.16#).

The structuralist–monetarist debate in Latin America

The inflation rate in countries such as Argentina, Brazil, Peru, Bolivia, Chile and Uruguay has reached over 100% at times since the Second World War. In the early postwar years, a heated debate developed, which still smoulders today, over the major cause of rapid price increases. The participants in the debate polarized into two schools, frequently referred to as the **structuralists** and the **monetarists**. Although the debate is set in the Latin American context, it is nonetheless of general interest and in many ways is analogous to the Keynesian–monetarist debate that took place in developed countries in the 1970s and 1980s over the causes of inflation. It might also be said that the two debates have been equally inconclusive.

The essence of the structuralist argument is that the basic forces of inflation are structural in nature, that inflation is a supply phenomenon and can only be remedied by monetary and fiscal means at the expense of the underutilization of resources. The role of monetary expansion in propagating inflation is not denied; what is disputed is that inflation has its *origins* in monetary factors. In the structuralists' view, monetary policy can only attack the symptoms of inflation, not its root causes.

In support of the argument that inflation emanates from the supply side, the structuralists point to the characteristic features of developing countries: the rapid structural changes taking place in the economy and supply inelasticities leading to bottlenecks, and refer back to the pre-industrialization era of Latin America when inflation was much less severe than it has been in the recent past. Prior to 1930, there was relative price stability due to fairly elastic supplies of agricultural output and low population growth. But Latin America then entered the industrialization era with a capitalist class that was reluctant to invest, and with growing population pressure on food supplies, which together contributed to bottlenecks and the beginnings of inflation, subsequently exacerbated by a wage–price spiral and currency depreciation.

There is some dispute about whether this picture is accurate for the whole of Latin America, however. According to some observers, the sequence of events described by the structuralist school is more a description of a particular country, Chile. Indeed, Campos (1961) went as far as to say that any visitor to the Economic Commission for Latin America in Santiago could not help but feel that the thinking of the structuralist school had been affected by the peculiarities of Chilean inflation. But Campos was a confessed monetarist. For even in the Chilean case, he claims that the bottlenecks observed were induced by inflation itself and were not causal elements in the process. This is a more general claim of the monetarist school. They argue that supply bottlenecks are created by policies that discourage investment, for example price controls. Thus, they maintain that the act of repressing inflation, instead of tackling the monetary causes of inflation, creates bottlenecks that subsequently feed the inflation. But, in the first instance, inflation is caused by excess demand due to monetary expansion. In support of the monetarists, it does seem to be the case that in countries where prices have risen the fastest, the money supply has also grown most rapidly, but this does not answer the question of whether monetary expansion initiates inflation or simply 'finances' inflationary tendencies already present on the supply side. Moreover, if there was tighter monetary control, would it be inflation or output that would fall the most? There is no consensus, but a majority of observers seem to pinpoint supply factors as the main contributors to rising prices – particularly agricultural bottlenecks and exchange rate depreciation due to balance of payments difficulties. It is possible to argue, of course, that all balance of payments deficits are a monetary phenomenon, but the more relevant question is: What is the cause of deficits in the first place? Most balance of payments difficulties in Latin America have to do with a high income elasticity of demand for imports and low export growth because of the poor supply characteristics of domestic goods (for a 'structural' interpretation of Bolivian hyperinflation, see Pastor (1991); and see Chapter 16).

Summary

- Development requires investment, and saving is necessary to *fund* investment (although not necessarily to finance it).
- There are three main analytical approaches to the finance of development from domestic resources: the prior saving approach, the Keynesian approach and the quantity theory approach, which all focus on the ways in which saving and investment can be raised.

- The prior saving approach focuses on raising voluntary and involuntary saving through monetary and fiscal policy. The Keynesian approach emphasizes incentives to invest, which can generate its own saving. The quantity theory approach focuses on 'forcing' saving through inflationary policies.
- Voluntary saving depends on the capacity and willingness to save determined by the level of income, the growth of income, the rate of interest and the availability of financial assets.
- Most developing countries have a dual financial structure with a large informal financial sector serving the poor, rural, subsistence sector, and a formal financial sector serving those with collateral to borrow.
- Rural financial intermediaries and microcredit play an important role in the lending and borrowing activities of poor people.
- The formal financial sector often suffers various forms of financial repression impeding the growth of the financial system.
- Financial liberalization programmes have been implemented in many developing countries, often under pressure, with mixed results.
- Involuntary saving depends on tax policy. Tax effort is weak in many developing countries.
- Investment can generate its own saving through a rise in income if the economy is at less than full employment, or through a redistribution of income by inflation from wage earners with a low propensity to save to profit earners with a higher propensity to save if the economy is at full employment (this is the Keynesian argument).
- Governments can invest on society's behalf and finance the investment by monetary expansion. If this is inflationary, this will 'force' saving (the idea of inflation as a tax on money).
- Inflation poses some dangers, but the empirical evidence shows a positive relation between inflation and growth up to about 5–8% inflation.
- Many Latin American countries have experienced high inflation in the past, but the monetarist–structuralist debate, which originated there, is largely inconclusive.

Chapter 13 Discussion questions

1. What is the difference between voluntary saving, involuntary saving and 'forced' saving?
2. What are the main determinants of voluntary saving?
3. How can 'monetization' of the economy help to raise the level and productivity of capital accumulation in developing economies?
4. What are the essential features of the informal financial sector in developing countries?
5. Outline the main requisites of a well-developed financial system.
6. What forms do financial repression take in developing countries?
7. What are the dangers of financial liberalization, and on what factors does the success of liberalization depend?
8. What role do special development banks and microcredit play in financing development?

Chapter 13 **Discussion questions** – *continued*

9. Suggest reforms to the tax system in developing countries that would promote equity and more saving for investment.
10. What is meant by 'inflation as a tax on money'?
11. In what ways is demand inflation conducive to growth and development?
12. What conclusions would you draw from the recent empirical evidence on the relation between inflation and growth?

Notes

1. For a survey of microcredit, see Morduch (1999), Armendariz and Morduch (2005), and Hermes and Lensink (2007).
2. For a comprehensive discussion of the general issues in this field, see Bird (1991) and Burgess and Stern (1993).
3. For an excellent discussion of general issues, and with specific reference to Pakistan, see Ahmad and Stern (1991).

Websites on banking and finance

Microcredit

Grameen Development Bank www.grameen-info.org
BancoSol in Bolivia www.bancosol.com.bo/
Microcredit Summit Campaign www.microcreditsummit.org

Banking

Central bank list www.centralbanksguide.com/central+banks+list/

14

FOREIGN ASSISTANCE, AID, DEBT AND DEVELOPMENT

Introduction

In an open economy, domestic savings can be supplemented by many kinds of external assistance. This chapter considers the role of foreign borrowing in the development process. The emphasis is on longer term resource flows to developing countries rather than the provision of short-term balance of payments support, which is the traditional function of the International Monetary Fund (IMF), and is considered in Chapter 16.

The chapter starts by showing how the need for foreign resource inflows can be quantified, using the concept of **dual-gap analysis**, and then outlines the conditions under which foreign capital inflows will raise the growth of national income and the growth of national output.

The various magnitudes of resource inflows to developing countries are given, including official bilateral and multilateral aid flows (official development assistance, ODA), foreign direct investment (FDI) and remittances. The various donors and country recipients are identified.

We consider the debate over international assistance to developing countries, the motives for giving aid, the macroeconomic impact of aid on economies, and the critics of aid who say that it can do more harm than good.

The World Bank is a major multilateral donor, and its programmes of **structural adjustment lending** come under scrutiny.

Some resource flows, such as FDI and remittances, do not create debt, but loans from international organizations and the private banking system do, and we look at the debt burden of developing countries and the debt-servicing difficulties they face because debt has to be repaid with interest in foreign exchange, which is scarce and badly needed for imports. We ask the question: Is it possible to define an optimal level of borrowing and sustainable debt?

The 1980s witnessed a severe debt crisis for developing countries, which still lingers today, and we explore the various solutions that have been put forward for relieving the debt burden of poor, developing countries, including the World Bank's **Heavily Indebted Poor Country (HIPC) Initiative**.

The role of foreign borrowing

It is important to understand that lending and borrowing are natural features of capitalist economic activity; without them, capital accumulation would be confined to sectors of economic activity that have a surplus of income over current requirements, which, from a growth point of view, would be inefficient and suboptimal. Very often, the factors that cause the supply of capital to increase create their own demand. The most obvious example of this, at the international level, are increases in the price of oil, which create large surpluses for oil-exporting countries and the need to borrow by oil-importing countries to maintain economic growth without curtailing imports. Going back into history, sovereign lending (and the problems associated with it) has been a feature of international economic life since the Medicis of Florence started to make loans to the English and Spanish monarchs in the fourteenth century. Historically, the international lending and borrowing process has played an integral part in the development of most major industrialized countries, and continues to play a significant role in the economic transformation of today's developing countries.

Traditionally, the role of foreign borrowing has been seen by countries as a supplement to domestic saving to bridge an investment–savings gap and achieve faster growth. The concept of **dual-gap analysis**, however, pioneered by Hollis Chenery and his collaborators (e.g. Chenery and Bruno, 1962), shows that foreign borrowing may also be viewed as a supplement to foreign exchange if, to achieve a faster rate of growth and development, the gap between foreign exchange earnings from exports and necessary imports is larger than the domestic investment–savings gap, and domestic and foreign resources are not easily substitutable for one another. Foreign borrowing must fill the larger of the two gaps if the target growth rate is to be achieved. The historical sequence of experience originally suggested by Chenery was that countries in the pre-take-off stage of development would have a dominant investment–savings gap, followed by a dominant foreign exchange gap, with the possibility of a skill constraint at any stage. Most of today's developing countries, apart from China and the oil-exporting countries, have a dominant foreign exchange gap, which manifests itself in a chronic balance of payments deficit on the current account, while domestic resources lie idle. These deficits require financing not only in the interests of the countries themselves, but for the sake of the growth momentum of the whole world economy. There is an interdependence in the world economic system because countries are linked through trade. The alternative to the financing of deficits is adjustment by deflation to reduce imports, which means slower growth in the world economy as a whole.

If the historical experience of developed countries is considered, in cases where borrowing took place (mainly from Britain as the major creditor), the borrowing was ultimately converted into an export surplus, which enabled the borrowing country to repay its debt and become a net creditor. The condition for this to happen is that the marginal savings ratio should exceed the average savings ratio in order to eliminate the investment–savings gap, if that is the dominant constraint, or that the marginal propensity to export should exceed the marginal propensity to import if foreign exchange is the dominant constraint. For most developing countries today, there is little evidence that they have either the desire or the option to reduce the level of net resource inflows without a major disruption of their economies. The need for resources is as acute as ever, because of a dominant foreign exchange gap to meet development requirements and to pay interest and amortization on past borrowing. Developing countries find it difficult to convert domestic resources into foreign exchange in adequate quantities, not only cyclically when the world economy is depressed, but also secularly owing to their economic structure; that is, they produce goods whose demand tends to be both price and income inelastic in world trade.

In the first edition of this textbook (Thirlwall, 1972), I predicted that:

> unless something is done the debt-servicing problem arising from mounting resource flows may well become unmanageable in the not too distant future. It will certainly be a long time before these countries become net exporters of capital even in the absence of an investment–savings gap.

This has turned out to be true. Developing countries continue to borrow extensively; their debt now stands at over \$5,000 billion, and over \$250 billion flows out of developing countries each year to service the debts.

Dual-gap analysis and foreign borrowing

In national income accounting, an excess of investment over domestic saving is equivalent to a surplus of imports over exports. The national income equation can be written from the expenditure side as:

$$\text{Income} = \text{Consumption} + \text{Investment} + \text{Exports} - \text{Imports}$$

Since saving is equal to income minus consumption, we have:

Saving = Investment + Exports − Imports

or:

Investment − Savings = Imports − Exports

A surplus of imports over exports financed by foreign borrowing allows a country to spend more than it produces or to invest more than it saves.

Note that, in accounting terms, the amount of foreign borrowing required to supplement domestic savings is the same whether the need is just for more resources for capital formation or for imports as well. The identity between the two gaps, the investment–savings ($I - S$) gap and the import–export ($M - X$) gap, follows from the nature of the accounting procedures. It is a matter of arithmetic that if a country invests more than it saves, this will show up in the national accounts as a balance of payments deficit. Or, to put it another way, an excess of imports over exports necessarily implies an excess of the resources used by an economy over the resources supplied by it, or an excess of investment over saving. There is no reason in principle, however, why the two gaps should be equal *ex ante* (in a planned sense); that is, that *plans* to invest in excess of *planned* saving should exactly equal *plans* to import in excess of *plans* to export. This is the starting point of dual-gap analysis.

Before going into dual-gap analysis in more detail, a reminder of elementary growth theory is in order. Growth requires investment goods, which may be provided domestically or purchased from abroad. The domestic provision requires saving; the foreign provision requires foreign exchange. If it is assumed that some investment goods for growth can be provided only from abroad, a minimum amount of foreign exchange is always required to sustain the growth process. In the Harrod model of growth (see Chapter 4), the relation between growth and saving is given by the incremental capital–output ratio (c), which is the reciprocal of the productivity of capital (p), that is, $g = s/c$ or $g = sp$, where g is the growth rate and s is the saving ratio. Likewise, the growth rate can be expressed as the product of the incremental output–import ratio ($\Delta Y/M = m'$) and the ratio of investment-good imports to income ($[M/Y] = i$), that is, $g = im'$.

If there is a lack of substitutability between domestic and foreign resources, growth will be constrained by whatever factor is the most limiting – domestic saving or foreign exchange. Suppose, for example, that the growth rate permitted by domestic saving is less than the growth rate permitted by the availability of foreign exchange. In this case, **growth will be savings-limited** and if the constraint is not lifted, a proportion of foreign exchange will go unused. For example, suppose that the product of the savings ratio (s) and the productivity of capital (p) gives a permissible growth rate of 5%, and the product of the import ratio (i) and the productivity of imports (m') gives a permissible growth rate of 6%. Growth is constrained to 5%, and for a given m', a proportion of the foreign exchange available cannot be absorbed (at least for the purposes of growth). Some oil-exporting countries fall into this category; they cannot use all their foreign exchange. Conversely, suppose that the growth rate permitted by domestic savings is higher than that permitted by the availability of foreign exchange. In this case, the country will be **foreign exchange-constrained** and a proportion of domestic saving will go unused. Most developing countries fall into this category. The policy implications are clear: there will be *resource waste* as long as one resource constraint is dominant. If foreign exchange is the dominant constraint, ways must be found of using unused domestic resources to earn more foreign exchange and/or raise the productivity of imports. If domestic saving is the dominant constraint, ways must be found of using foreign exchange to augment domestic saving and/or raise the productivity of domestic resources (by relaxing a skill constraint, for example). (If there were complete substitutability between imports and domestic resources, any surplus of domestic resources could be immediately converted into foreign exchange, and any surplus of foreign exchange could be immediately converted into domestic resources, and there could only be one gap, *ex ante*, as well as *ex post*.)

Suppose now a country sets a target rate of growth, r. From our simple growth equations (identities), the required savings ratio (s^*) to achieve the target is $s^* = rc$, and the required import ratio (i^*) is $i^* = r/m'$. If domestic saving is calculated to be less than the level required to achieve the target rate of growth, an investment–savings gap is said to exist equal at time t to:

$$I_t - S_t = s^*Y_t - sY_t = (rc)Y_t - sY_t \tag{14.1}$$

Similarly, if minimum import requirements to achieve the growth target are calculated to be greater than the maximum level of export earnings available for investment purposes, there is said to exist an import–export gap, or foreign exchange gap, equal at time t to:

$$M_t - X_t = i^*Y_t - iY_t = (r/m')Y_t - iY_t, \tag{14.2}$$

where i is the ratio of imports to output that is permitted by export earnings. If the target growth rate is to be achieved, foreign capital flows must fill the larger of the two gaps. The two gaps are not additive. If the import–export gap is the larger, then foreign borrowing to fill it will also fill the investment–savings gap. If the investment–savings gap is the larger, foreign borrowing to fill it will obviously cover the smaller foreign exchange gap.

The distinctive contribution of dual-gap analysis to development theory is that if foreign exchange is the dominant constraint, it points to the dual role of foreign borrowing in supplementing not only deficient domestic saving but also foreign exchange. Dual-gap theory thus performs the valuable service of emphasizing the role of imports and foreign exchange in the development process. It synthesizes traditional and more modern views concerning aid, trade and development. On the one hand, it embraces the traditional view of foreign assistance as merely a boost to domestic saving; on the other hand, it takes the more modern view that many of the goods necessary for development cannot be produced by the developing countries themselves and must therefore be imported with the aid of foreign assistance. Indeed, if foreign exchange is truly the dominant constraint, it can be argued that dual-gap analysis also presents a more relevant theory of trade for developing countries that justifies selective protection and import substitution. If growth is constrained by a lack of foreign exchange, free trade cannot guarantee simultaneous internal and external equilibrium, and the efficiency gains from trade may be offset by the underutilization of domestic resources. We shall take up this matter in Chapter 15.

A practical example of dual-gap analysis

Now let us give a practical example of how dual-gap analysis may be applied to a country. We shall be applying equation (14.1) to estimate the investment–savings gap, and equation (14.2) to estimate the import–export gap. Suppose that the target rate of growth (r) set by the government over a five-year planning period 2015–20 is 5% per annum and the capital–output ratio is 3. The investment requirements in time t may be written as:

$$I_t = crY_t = c\Delta Y = 3\Delta Y$$

Table 14.1 Estimates of investment–savings and import–export gaps assuming a 5% growth of GDP, 2015–20 ($ million)

	Y_0	Y_1	Y_2	Y_3	Y_4	Y_5
	Base year 2015	**2016**	**2017**	**2018**	**2019**	**2020**
GDP	1,000	1,050	1,102.5	1,157.6	1,215.5	1,276.3
Savings	100	105	110.2	115.8	121.5	127.6
Investment	140	150	157.5	165.3	173.7	182.4
Investment–savings gap	**40**	**45**	**47.3**	**49.5**	**52.2**	**54.8**
Exports	210	216.3	222.8	229.4	236.3	243.4
Imports	250	262.5	275.6	289.4	303.9	319.0
Import–export gap	**40**	**46.2**	**52.8**	**60.0**	**67.6**	**75.6**

Note: The base level of investment and exports will be given by the country's national accounts and balance of payments statistics.

Now assume that 10% of income is saved, so that:

$$S_t = 0.1\ Y_t$$

Given this information and the target level of income, Y_t, for each year ($t = 1 - 5$), obtained from applying the target rate of growth to the base level of income ($Y_0 = 1{,}000$), the $I - S$ gap can be calculated for each year in the future. The results are shown in Table 14.1. All values are in dollars at constant (base year) prices.

For import requirements, let us assume that the incremental output–import ratio (m') is 0.2. Therefore:

$$M_t\,(r/m')\ Y_t = i^*\ Y_t = (0.05/0.2)\ Y_t = 0.25\ Y_t$$

Finally, assume a forecast exponential rate of growth of exports of 3% a year, namely:

$$X_t = X_0 e^{0.03t}$$

The calculated import–export gap is also shown in Table 14.1. The results show that while the two gaps are equal in the 2015 base year from the national accounts, the forecast gaps, *ex ante*, diverge through time, with the import–export gap dominant. For the target rate of growth of 5% per annum to be achieved, there would have to be foreign borrowing each year to fill the larger of the two gaps. The analysis here is brief and mechanistic, but it illustrates the principle and what can be done in a simple way as a first approach to calculating foreign resource requirements for growth and development. (See El-Shibley and Thirlwall (1981) for a case study of Sudan. Chenery's pioneer study of dual-gap analysis is in Chenery and Bruno, 1962).

Models of capital imports and growth

In the simple case where there are no repayment obligations, foreign capital inflows will raise the growth of output *and* income (g), provided the foreign inflows do not reduce the domestic savings ratio or reduce the productivity of capital. To show this, we can write:

$$g = \frac{I}{Y}(\sigma) \tag{14.3}$$

where I/Y is the ratio of investment to GDP and σ is the productivity of capital (dY/I). Now, total investment is equal to domestic saving (S) plus foreign capital inflows (F), so equation (14.3) can be written as:

$$g = \frac{(S + F)}{(Y)}\sigma = \left[s + \frac{F}{Y}\right]\sigma \tag{14.4}$$

where s is the savings ratio (S/Y). Growth is now higher than it would be with domestic saving alone, unless foreign inflows (F/Y) reduce s and σ.

If foreign inflows have to be repaid, however, the condition changes for the growth of income and output to be higher. This can be shown from the model outlined below, which incorporates the terms on which capital imports are financed. It is shown that:

- **The rate of growth of output** will be faster with capital imports, provided new inflows of foreign capital exceed the loss of domestic saving to pay interest; if, however, interest charges are met by new borrowing, capital imports must always have a favourable effect on the growth rate of output.
- **The rate of growth of income** will be faster as long as the productivity of capital imports exceeds the rate of interest.

The model is as follows. Let:

$$O = Y + rD \tag{14.5}$$

where O is output, Y is income, r is the interest rate and D is debt. The difference between domestic output and national income is net factor payments abroad (including interest, profits and dividends). From equation (14. 5), we have:

$$\Delta O = \Delta Y + r\Delta D \tag{14. 6}$$

Now:

$$\Delta O = \sigma I \tag{14. 7}$$

where σ is the productivity of capital, and:

$$I = sO + \Delta D - srD \tag{14. 8}$$

where s is the propensity to save. Substituting equation (14. 8) into equation (14. 7) and dividing by O gives an expression for output growth of:

$$\frac{\Delta O}{O} = \sigma\left(s + \frac{\Delta D - srD}{O}\right) \tag{14. 9}$$

Equation (14. 9) shows that the growth of output will be higher than the rate obtainable from domestic saving alone as long as $\Delta D > srD$, that is, as long as new inflows of capital exceed the amount of outflow on past loans that would otherwise have been saved. This is a fairly stringent condition unless it is assumed that the interest payments due are met by creating new debt. It can be seen from equation (14. 9) that if $rD = \Delta D$, the rate of growth of output with capital imports will always be higher than without capital imports as long as $s < 1$ (which is the normal case to consider). It may be concluded, then, that if interest payments on past loans can be borrowed in perpetuity, there is a permanent gain to be had from running an import surplus. In practice, however, a country that continually reschedules its debts might ultimately be classified by the international community as uncreditworthy and therefore not be able to borrow continually.

Now let us consider the rate of growth of income as the dependent variable. From equation (14. 5):

$$\Delta Y = \Delta O - r\Delta D \tag{14. 10}$$

Substituting equation (14. 8) into equation (14. 7) and the result into equation (14. 10) gives:

$$\Delta Y = \sigma(sO + \Delta D - srD) - r\Delta D \tag{14. 11}$$

Now, since $Y = O - rD$, we can also write equation (14. 11) as:

$$\Delta Y = \sigma sY + \Delta D(\sigma - r) \tag{14.12}$$

and dividing by Y, we have the following expression for the rate of growth of income:

$$\frac{\Delta Y}{Y} = \sigma s + \left(\sigma - r\right)\frac{\Delta D}{Y} \tag{14.13}$$

Equation (14.13) shows that the growth rate of income with capital imports will be higher than that obtained from domestic saving alone as long as the productivity of capital imports (σ) exceeds the rate of interest on foreign borrowing (r). This is a standard result showing that investment is profitable as long as the rate of return exceeds the rate of interest. In some circumstances, however, this condition may also be a fairly stringent one.

Capital imports, domestic saving and the capital–output ratio

From the discussion above, it would appear that import surpluses have great potential in the development process. It is sometimes argued, however, that import surpluses financed by foreign capital inflows increase the capital–output ratio (that is, reduce the productivity of capital) and discourage domestic saving; and that a large fraction of capital inflows is consumed rather than invested. The net result may be no extra growth at all or even a reduction in the growth rate. (The argument was first put forward by Griffin (1970) and has since been the subject of continual scrutiny; see the survey by White, 1992). In terms of equation (14.9) and equation (14.13), the inflow of capital ΔD may reduce s and σ and only a fraction of ΔD may be invested.

As far as the relation between capital imports and domestic saving is concerned, many studies find a negative relation. Care must be taken in interpreting the relation, however, because owing to the way saving is defined, a negative relation is bound to be found as long as a proportion of capital imports is consumed. As we said before, domestic saving is normally defined in developing countries as investment minus foreign capital inflows: $S = I - F$. If F rises and I rises by less than

F, S must fall for the equality to hold. Thus, a negative statistical relation between foreign capital inflows and domestic saving cannot necessarily be interpreted as a weakening of the development effort; it may simply reflect the fact that a proportion of foreign capital inflows is consumed. The important point is that no studies find a negative relation between capital inflows and the investment ratio. This means that capital inflows must finance some additional growth unless the productivity of capital falls drastically.

Some economists argue that foreign capital inflows do lower the productivity of capital and raise the capital–output ratio because of the tendency for international assistance to be used for prestige projects and a bias towards the use of international resource flows for infrastructure projects and social overhead capital. It should be remembered, however, that there is an important distinction to be made between the capital–output ratio of a particular project and the capital–output ratio for the economy as a whole, which is the ratio relevant to the model. It is quite possible for the overall capital–output ratio to fall even if projects financed by capital inflows are relatively capital-intensive, because the projects financed confer externalities on the rest of the economy and also relax a foreign exchange constraint on demand. There is no convincing evidence that countries with a high ratio of capital inflows to national income have a higher capital–output ratio than other countries, and no convincing evidence either that the productivity of foreign resource inflows is lower than the productivity of domestic saving.

Types of international capital flows

The main types of international capital flows to developing countries consist of:

- Official flows from **bilateral** sources and **multilateral** sources, such as the World Bank and its two affiliates, the International Development Association (IDA) and the International Finance Corporation (IFC), on concessional and non-concessional terms
- Aid provided by nongovernmental organizations (NGOs)
- Humanitarian and emergency aid
- FDI and portfolio investment
- Remittances from migrant labour.

Because of the different types of capital flow and the different terms of borrowing, there is an important distinction between the nominal value of capital flows and their worth in terms of the increased command over goods and services that they represent to the recipient. There is also a distinction between the **return** to international assistance, the **benefit** of international assistance (in a cost–benefit sense) and the **value** of international assistance:

- The **return** to international assistance is the difference between the nominal value of assistance and any repayments due, discounted by the productivity of the assistance in the recipient country. In other words, the rate of return to assistance is measured in the same way as the return to any other investment.
- The **benefit** of assistance is the difference between the nominal value of assistance and repayments discounted by the rate of interest at which the country *would have had to borrow* in the capital market. It is this calculation that we shall later refer to as the **grant element** or **aid component** of the capital flow, representing 'something for nothing' to the recipient country. Clearly, if the terms on which the country borrows from the donor are no different from those prevailing in the free market, there is no grant element or aid attached to the capital transfer and the benefit of assistance in this sense is zero.

- The **value** of the assistance may, in turn, differ from its benefit if the assistance is tied to the purchase of donor goods that differ in price from the world market price. If the prices are higher, this reduces the value of the grant element of assistance to below what it would otherwise have been (see below for calculations of the grant element).

Not all foreign resource inflows create **debt**; only those flows that involve a repayment obligation. The aid component of official flows, for example, does not create debt, nor do remittances from migrant workers or FDI, although the latter may involve an outflow of profits.

Now let us turn to a discussion of the various types of international capital flows, and the magnitudes involved. We start with a discussion of official development assistance, or international aid, and the motives behind it.

The debate over international assistance to developing countries

As indicated above, capital flows to developing countries come in many different forms: from grants or pure aid from bilateral and multilateral donors and NGOs, loans, portfolio investment and FDI by multinational companies. The magnitude of these various flows will be given later in the chapter. Donor countries and institutions provide aid, loans and investment, and developing countries accept the flows, for a mixture of reasons. But the motives of the donors and recipients, and the wider interests of developing countries as a whole, may not always coincide. The rationale and relevance of financial assistance to developing countries are very much a matter of subjective assessment, depending on the meaning and vision of the development process held by the protagonists. There is a substantial body of opinion on the right and the left of the political spectrum that argues that not only are financial resource transfers unnecessary for development, but may even be counterproductive and inimical to development by fostering dependence, weakening the domestic development effort, and leading to a distorted structure of consumption and production (as well as to debt-servicing problems and profit outflows). These criticisms are levelled at official assistance and private investment, particularly at the activities of multinational companies. We shall consider some of these concerns later, but first let us examine the motives for assistance and why developing countries accept the transfers.

The motives for official assistance

There are several motives (see Riddell, 2007 for a comprehensive text on foreign aid) that inspire financial assistance from bilateral and multilateral sources on concessionary terms, but they can be grouped under three headings:

- **Moral, humanitarian motive**: To assist poor countries, and particularly poor people in poor countries (see Opeskin, 1996). The same arguments that provide the basis for income redistribution within nations can also be applied at the global level, namely that absolute poverty is morally unacceptable and that if the marginal utility of income diminishes, total welfare will be increased by a redistribution of income from rich to poor. From a moral and welfare point of view, national boundaries are quite artificial constructions. Developing countries accept assistance with this concern in mind not only from national governments and international organizations as part of their regular aid programmes, but also from many voluntary and charitable NGOs, and from emergency and disaster relief funds.

- **Political, military and historical motives**: A large part of the US aid programme was originally designed as a bulwark against the spread of communism, and the regional and country distribution of international assistance can still be partly explained in these terms. British and French assistance tends to be concentrated on ex-colonial territories, reflecting strong historical ties and perhaps some recompense for former colonial neglect. Most developing countries are willing to accept assistance on this basis to assist their development effort, particularly when governments are threatened by hostile forces from within or without.
- **Economic motives**: Developed countries invest in developing countries not only to raise the growth rate of developing countries, but also to improve their own welfare. Hence, international assistance is seen as mutually beneficial. If the rate of interest on loans is higher than the productivity of capital in the developed donor country and lower than the productivity of capital in the developing recipient country, both parties will gain. If there are underutilized resources in the developed country that could not otherwise be activated because of balance of payments constraints, international assistance will be mutually profitable by adding to the resources in the developing country and enabling fuller utilization of the resources in the developed country. This is the strong Keynesian argument for international assistance, and forcefully recommended in the Brandt Report (discussed in Chapter 1). Developing countries accept these financial flows because most are desperately short of foreign exchange (see Chapter 16), and judge the benefits of international programmes and the projects they finance to be greater than the costs of servicing the borrowing and any unfavourable side effects.

The critics of international aid

Despite the many worthy motives for giving international assistance to developing countries, there are many critics of international aid. One extreme view is that aid has no effect on the growth performance of poor countries and can undermine development by fostering a dependency culture. This was the view of early critics, such as Bauer (1971) and Friedman (1958), and has recently been revived in polemical books such as *The White Man's Burden* (Easterly, 2006) and *Dead Aid* (Moyo, 2009). Both argue that aid to Africa has been wasted, and Moyo argues that there should be a programme of aid withdrawal from Africa and that all future capital inflows should come from the private sector, which would lead to a more responsible and efficient use of resource inflows.

It is true that international assistance may be wasted. If not directed wisely, it may help to support governments that are corrupt and profligate. It may encourage irresponsible financial policies; and if the assistance is free (pure aid), there may be no incentive to use resources productively. Critics argue that billions of dollars have been invested in Africa over the past half century, but still Africa is extremely poor.

There are several counterarguments, however, to this extreme view:

1. The amount of aid received *per head of population* in developing countries (and Africa) is very low, and poor countries have many depressive cumulative forces working against them, so that expectations relating to the impact of aid should not be exaggerated.
2. Much aid has been used for humanitarian purposes; for social investment in hospitals, public health and schools, the benefits of which are not disputed.
3. As far as corrupt governments and irresponsible economic policy-making are concerned, it is not clear that the same scenario would not prevail without aid. Indeed, the alternatives might be worse because international assistance brings a certain amount of 'leverage', which can be

used for the promotion of good governance and more enlightened policy-making. The challenge is not to stop aid, but to make it more effective.

The most valid criticism of aid is that it may lead to a weakening of the domestic development effort by supporting a culture of dependency. In particular, it may weaken a country's tax effort. In many poor developing countries, the value of aid exceeds tax revenue. To cope with this issue, Adrian Wood (2008), Oxford economist, suggests that donors collectively set an upper limit to the aid–tax ratio (say, 50%), above which aid would be phased out, but below which donors would give 50 cents more aid for every extra dollar raised in taxes. This would encourage developing countries to raise more tax, while encouraging governments to pay more attention to what their citizens want (because they are paying) rather than what donors want the aid used for.

Another less extreme view of aid is that it can have a positive effect on growth and development on average, but not in every country, and is conditional on absorptive capacity, good governance and the policies of donor countries. Some countries may not have the administrative or technical capacity to absorb much aid, in which case there will be diminishing returns to aid. There is evidence on this, which will be discussed below. There is also evidence that aid only works in good policy environments, where there is good governance and sound macroeconomic policy-making. The practices of donor countries also make a difference to the productivity of aid, whether the aid is multilateral or bilateral, whether it is tied to the purchase of donor goods or untied, and how the aid is monitored. The consensus now is that recipient countries themselves should have 'ownership' of aid programmes, and that the heavy hand of donors can be counterproductive.

There are valid criticisms of aid and how it has been administered in the past, but the fact that it can be wasted, that it doesn't help the people it is meant to, and the recipients of aid still remain poor and underdeveloped is more a challenge to the use of aid than an argument that resource flows to poor countries cannot be productive. That would defy economic logic. Case example 14.1 discusses the impact of aid on growth in Sierra Leone.

Case example 14.1 **The impact of aid on economic growth in Sierra Leone**

Sierra Leone is characterized by high levels of aid dependence and unimpressive economic performance, as well as long-term political instability and armed conflict. Development aid has historically been a high proportion of Sierra Leone's GDP and surged when the civil war, 1991–2002, ended. Annual aid dispersed to Sierra Leone in the period 1970–2007 stands at an average of 14.2% of GDP, a figure much higher than the regional average of 3.7% for Africa as a whole. Despite this level of support, Sierra Leone's economic performance has remained wanting in terms of growth and poverty reduction.

A variety of econometric approaches have been used to assess the effect of aid on economic growth in the period 1970–2007 in Sierra Leone. There are two main findings:

1. Aid had a significant positive effect on economic growth over the period as a whole, but was weak or nonexistent during the civil war.
2. Aid had a greater positive impact on growth prior to the civil war than it has in the postwar period.

These finding are largely consistent with a great portion of the macro-level aid-growth literature. Indeed, Arndt et al. (2011) find that a similar positive link between aid and

continued overleaf

Case example 14.1 **The impact of aid on economic growth in Sierra Leone** – *continued*

growth is present on a more general, cross-country level. However, case studies on Bangladesh, Cameroon, Papua New Guinea and Pakistan have not found a statistically significant link between aid and growth. There are three main reasons why this relationship may be found in Sierra Leone, but not in the other case studies:

1. The differing motivations that lead to donors granting aid may well determine how effective that aid is in promoting growth. As one of the poorest countries in the world, Sierra Leone is likely to receive aid targeted towards generating economic growth and reducing poverty.
2. Aid is likely to have a positive impact on economic growth in countries like Sierra Leone, which require capital in order to fund foreign imports essential for growing the economy. Given the high level of imports, and the likelihood that exports will be much lower, a foreign exchange gap is inevitable. Inflows of foreign aid help to fill this gap and thus promote economic growth.
3. While there is a history of corruption in Sierra Leone, it is more associated with non-official aid from countries like China and Libya than with official aid.

Source: Kargbo, 2012.

The macroeconomic impact of aid

When a country receives aid, it can do one of two things, or a combination of both. It can either spend the aid directly on imports, in which case there are no serious domestic implications (e.g. there will be no change in the exchange rate or change in foreign exchange reserves), or the government can sell the extra foreign exchange to the central bank and then use the local currency to buy domestic goods. This does have domestic implications depending on the response of governments and the Central Bank. Aiyar et al. (2005) consider four responses:

1. **Absorb and spend**: the government spends on domestic goods and the central bank sells foreign exchange, which neutralizes the increase in local currency spent by the government and finances the current account balance of payments deficit due to rising imports.
2. **Neither absorb nor spend**: the government keeps the new foreign exchange in the central bank to add to reserves. This does not assist development directly, but can act as a buffer against aid volatility in the future.
3. **Absorb but not spend**: the government reduces the money supply while the central bank sells the foreign exchange. Aid acts as a substitute for the domestic finance of government budget deficits.
4. **Spend but not absorb**: the government increases its expenditure but keeps aid in the central bank as reserves. This is equivalent to a fiscal stimulus financed by selling bonds or printing money. There is no real resource transfer to the developing country because no aid has been used to import more. This policy can be highly inflationary and lead to the currency depreciating unless the central bank sells foreign exchange to stop it.

If aid is not spent directly on imports, the first best response is to absorb and spend, but according to Aiyar et al. (2005), it is surprisingly rare, at least in the five countries they studied in detail (Ethiopia, Ghana, Mozambique, Tanzania and Uganda). In four of the countries, less than one-third of aid was absorbed.

If aid is not spent directly on imports, there is the strong possibility of exchange rate appreciation, the so-called **Dutch disease**, after what happened to the Dutch currency after the discovery of natural gas in the Netherlands in the 1970s, which can have damaging effects on the tradable goods sector of the economy, by making exports more expensive and imports cheaper. To prevent appreciation, governments can buy up foreign exchange, which adds to reserves, but then the central bank has to sell bonds if it wants to absorb the excess liquidity arising from such purchases (to prevent inflation, for example). This may lead to a rise in interest rates, which can also damage the real economy. Some studies of the impact of aid find evidence of Dutch disease (see Rajan and Subramanian, 2005), but the important point to make is that it is not inevitable, if the aid is spent on the purchase of tradable goods, which, in principle, is the best policy. There are so many goods needed for development that poor developing countries cannot produce themselves. Aid gives the chance to import them.

Two main approaches are used to assess the impact of aid on growth and development. The first is to do detailed case studies, which is the micro-approach. As representative of this approach, a study by Cassen (1994) of seven countries (Bangladesh, Colombia, India, Kenya, South Korea, Malawi and Mali) shows that most aid achieves its development objectives, although in several instances, the performance could have been improved. The provision of aid played a major part in the Green Revolution in Southeast Asia, the building of infrastructure in southern Africa, and the direct provision of basic needs and the relief of poverty in many countries. The study also found, however, that aid performance appears to be least satisfactory where it is most needed, and that, above all, improved performance requires better collaboration between aid agencies. Most microstudies find a positive impact of aid on development (Arndt et al., 2010).

The second approach to assessing the impact of aid is to conduct a detailed statistical analysis of the relation between the growth of GDP or living standards and the amount of aid (as a proportion of GDP) received by each country, controlling for other variables. This is the macro-approach. A typical estimating equation, taking a large sample of developing countries, would be:

$$y = a + b\,(\text{AID}) + c_i\,(V_i)$$

where y is the growth of per capita income, AID is the ratio of official development assistance (ODA) to GDP and V_i is a vector of control variables ($i = 1 \dots n$). Hansen and Tarp (2001) review 131 cross-section studies and conclude that most of them show a positive relation between aid and growth. Their own research shows that aid has a positive effect on growth with a coefficient (b) of approximately 0.25, although not when investment is included in the equations as one of the control variables. The implication is that aid promotes growth by encouraging investment, and this is confirmed by equations relating the ratio of investment to GDP with the ratio of aid to GDP. Dalgaard et al. (2004) also show that aid has a positive effect on the growth of living standards, with a 1 percentage point difference in the aid variable leading to (approximately) a 0.5 percentage point difference in the growth of per capita income. The impact is lower, however, in tropical countries. Dalgaard et al. (2004) conclude: 'we have confidence ... that aid has a positive impact on growth, and that the impact depends on climate-related differences'.

Addison et al. (2005) survey studies conducted between 1997 and 2005 and conclude that developing countries' growth would have been slower without aid, and that the criticism of aid that it is counterproductive is not supported by the bulk of statistical evidence.

Clements et al. (2004) distinguish different types of aid, and focus on the impact of aid specifically meant for development purposes, as opposed to aid given for political and humanitarian reasons. They take a cross-section of 67 countries over the period 1974–2001, and use a nonlinear specification of the aid–growth relationship to allow for the possibility of diminishing returns to aid. Their central estimate is that an increase in aid of 1% of GDP leads to a 0.31 percentage point increase in growth, and diminishing returns to aid seem to set in at about 8–9% of GDP (which implies 16–18% of total aid to GDP because only one-half of total aid is specifically for development purposes). These figures are three times the amount of aid actually given.

In a major study across more than 70 countries over the period 1960–2000 (and subperiods), Rajan and Subramanian (2005) conclude: 'it is difficult to discern any systematic effect of aid on growth'. This conclusion has been challenged Arndt et al. (2010), who reanalyse the Rajan and Subramanian study and estimate a long-run elasticity of growth with respect to the share of aid in GDP of 0.13, so an inflow of aid of 10% GDP would increase GDP by just over 1 percentage point in the long run.

In a meta-study of 68 countries of the aid–growth relationship, Doucouliagos and Paldam (2008) also dismiss any positive impact of aid on growth. But Mekasha and Tarp (2013) have criticized this study on methodological grounds and argue that if the meta-study is done properly, there is a statistically significant positive impact of aid on growth of about 0.1 percentage point for every 1 percentage point increase in the ratio of aid to GDP, which means that a 10 percentage point increase in the aid ratio would raise the growth of GDP by 1 percentage point. This a similar result to Arndt et al. (2010), who conclude their study by saying:

> abolishing foreign aid, or drastically cutting it back, would be a mistake and is not warranted by any reasonable interpretation of the evidence. The challenge is to improve foreign assistance effectiveness so that living standards in poor countries are substantially advanced over the next three decades.

In recent years, the World Bank has been heavily involved in attempting to assess the impact of aid, and one of its major researchers is David Dollar. The World Bank (1998) and Burnside and Dollar (2000) take a panel of 56 developing countries over the period 1970–93 and try to disentangle the circumstances in which aid 'works' and in which it does not. The major findings are that, on average, aid has had only a minor impact on the growth of GDP per head (partly because aid as a percentage of GDP is so small), but that it can be extremely effective in promoting growth and reducing poverty in the right economic and political environment where there are democratic governments pursuing sensible macroeconomic policies. In countries with good economic management, a 1 percentage point increase in aid raises the growth rate by 0.5% and reduces poverty by 1%. The World Bank (1998) calculates that an extra $10 billion of aid could lift 25 million people out of poverty if the aid is directed to countries that manage their economies well. In countries with poor management, aid is entirely wasted. There are also diminishing returns to aid. Even in good environments, the returns to aid peak when aid reaches about 10% of GDP.

The World Bank (1998) emphasizes five major points from its analysis, and indicates five policy reforms for making aid more effective:
Analysis:

- Financial aid works in a good policy environment.
- Improvements in economic institutions and policies are the key to reducing poverty.
- Effective aid and private investment are complementary.
- The value of development projects is to strengthen institutions and policies so that services can be delivered effectively.
- Aid can nurture reform even in the most distorted environments, but it requires patience and a focus on ideas, not money.

Reforms:

- Financial assistance must be targeted more effectively to low-income countries with sound economic management.
- Policy-based aid should be provided to nurture policy reform where needed.
- The mix of aid activities should be tailored to suit the needs of the country and sectoral conditions.
- Projects need to focus on creating and transmitting knowledge and capacity.
- Aid agencies need to find alternative approaches to helping highly distorted countries.

Two further reforms and improvements could make aid more effective:

1. Donors could cooperate more to pool resources for specific purposes, and to take politics out of the aid-giving process.
2. Aid should only be given if the outcomes of programmes are effective. This is referred to as 'cash on delivery', and some donors, such as Norway and Britain, are experimenting with this approach. This gives countries an incentive to achieve outcomes efficiently. Norway has promised aid for the preservation of forests, and Britain has agreed to pay Ethiopia £100 for each extra pupil sitting a school-leaving exam.

Research shows that the **unpredictability** and **volatility** of the flow of aid also affect the impact of aid on growth because they affect the composition and effectiveness of government expenditure and can deter private investment. Aid is unpredictable if recipients cannot be confident about the amount and timing of aid disbursements. Aid is volatile if it fluctuates significantly (predictably or unpredictably). Measuring the predictability of aid is not easy, but it can be done with detailed data on aid commitments and disbursements by donor agencies, such as the Development Assistance Committee (DAC) of the OECD. Celasun and Walliser (2008) found that, on average, over the period 1993–2005, disbursed budget aid differed from the amount expected by 30%, or roughly 1% of GDP. Total aid disbursements to sub-Saharan Africa deviated from aid commitments by 3.4% of GDP. Aid shortfalls cut investment, while aid windfalls encourage consumption. This aid unpredictability affects the composition of expenditure in favour of consumption. Celasun and Walliser (2008) find that an aid shortfall of 1% of GDP is associated with a cut of investment expenditure of about 0.1 to 0.2% of GDP, while a 1% aid windfall is associated with an increase in consumption of about 0.6% of GDP. In other words, more predictable aid would lead to more investment.

Aid volatility can be measured by the standard deviation of aid flows. Lensink and Morrissey (2000) take 75 countries over the period 1970–95 and find that volatility negatively affects growth performance, but when volatility is controlled for, aid itself has a positive and significant effect on growth performance.

Since the fundamental purpose of international aid is the relief of primary poverty, there is a strong case for arguing (as part of the reform of aid programmes) that assistance should be given only to countries that are committed to poverty reduction programmes and make progress towards certain targets, such as literacy, basic healthcare provision, reducing infant mortality and so on. As incentives for governments to embark on and continue the programmes, donor countries could, in turn, commit themselves to funding as long as the recipients continue to support them. This would improve the certainty of aid flows.

The World Bank (2000) is moving in these directions. In its *World Development Report 2000/2001*, it refers to the new consensus on how aid can be made more effective:

- by linking aid to policy reforms
- by improving coordination between donors

- by getting people in the recipient countries to believe that the projects or reforms will bring benefits, so that countries feel they 'own' the programmes (see below on the reform of World Bank lending).

In 1999, the World Bank launched its **Comprehensive Development Framework**, which addresses these various issues. One new approach is the sector-wide approach where donors sign on to finance a *sector* (not individual projects), and the country itself does the work. An example is given in Case example 14.2.

Case example 14.2 **Sector-wide development cooperation, mid-1990s**

To address problems of ownership, donor coordination, and fungibility, donors are experimenting with pooling their resources to support sector-wide strategies designed and implemented by the recipient government. The country, in consultation with key stakeholders, designs a sector strategy and a budget framework extending several years forward, and donors put their money into the central expenditure pool for the sector. The approach encourages country ownership of sector strategies and programmes. It also links sector expenditure with the overall macroeconomic framework. And it ensures coordination of donor and recipient activities.

Some benefits of a sector-wide programme are evident in the Zambian health sector. In 1994, the government presented its national health policy and strategy to donors and – to ensure equitable distribution of services and coherent implementation of the strategy – asked them not to fund specific provinces or projects but to fund the Ministry of Health centrally. Hesitant at first, donors began to comply. An independent evaluation in 1997 found that: 'health workers are better motivated; clinics are functioning; funds are flowing to the districts; some modicum of decentralization is in place; [and] an important part of the private sector has become formally involved'.

The approach ensures full ownership by the country and eliminates problems of donor coordination. With the country having more ownership and control over what happens, the use of resources can be much more efficient. But it also means great changes in donor–recipient relations and perhaps greater difficulties in implementation. Several sector-wide programmes have stumbled because of the recipient country's inadequate institutional capacity. Lack of consistency with the macroeconomic programme has been another problem. And donors often have too many requirements and thus too much of a problem (or too little interest) in harmonizing them. Furthermore, these arrangements greatly diminish donor control and monitoring of exactly how money is spent.

The changes required imply that gaining support for the approach will be difficult. The recipient government has to be very confident, because strict adherence to a sector-wide approach means donors that do not participate in common implementation arrangements are not allowed to act in the sector (that is, they do not have their own projects). The result may be less donor funding for a sector. Governments might therefore opt for less strict sector-wide programmes, choosing instead to allow donors to implement projects as long as they fit into the overall sector strategy.

Source: World Bank, 2000.

The total net flow of financial resources to developing countries

The total net flow of financial resources to developing countries is the total of all official and private flows to developing countries *net* of repayments of past loans (amortization). It includes flows given bilaterally by individual donor countries and multilaterally through international organizations, and includes flows both with and without concessionary terms. Most official flows are given on concessionary terms and are referred to as **official development assistance (ODA)**. To qualify as such, the concessional (or grant) element of the flow must be at least 25%. Only the concessional element of international financial flows really qualifies for the term 'aid'. The major donors of ODA are the 22 developed countries that form the **Development Assistance Committee (DAC)** of the OECD, and the various multilateral agencies. In addition, OPEC countries have lent substantial sums on concessional terms in recent years.

Other developing countries themselves, such as China and Brazil, are also starting to distribute aid, and India has set up its own agency to distribute \$11 billion over the period 2012–17. The magnitude of types of flows, including FDI and remittances, is shown in Figure 14.1, and the total net flow of resources (excluding remittances) is shown in Table 14.2. Private flows at market terms (mainly FDI and export credits) are **non-concessional flows**. The total net flows of financial resource from DAC countries to developing countries and multilateral institutions in 2014 amounted to \$577 billion, of which \$137 billion was ODA and \$402 billion consisted of non-concessional flows, mainly FDI.

The aid targets set for the developed countries of 1% of their national incomes refer to the total net flow of financial resources, while the target for ODA alone is 0.7% of donor countries' national incomes. Remember, the net flow of financial resources is not the same thing as the flow of *real resources*, since the former does not take account of interest payments and profit repatriation. If the terms of lending are steady over time, the net transfer of resources in any one year (that is, the gross capital inflow net of amortization *and* interest and profit payments) will be approximately equal to the estimated grant equivalent or aid component of assistance, the measurement of which is discussed later.

Figure 14.1 The magnitude of flows to developing countries

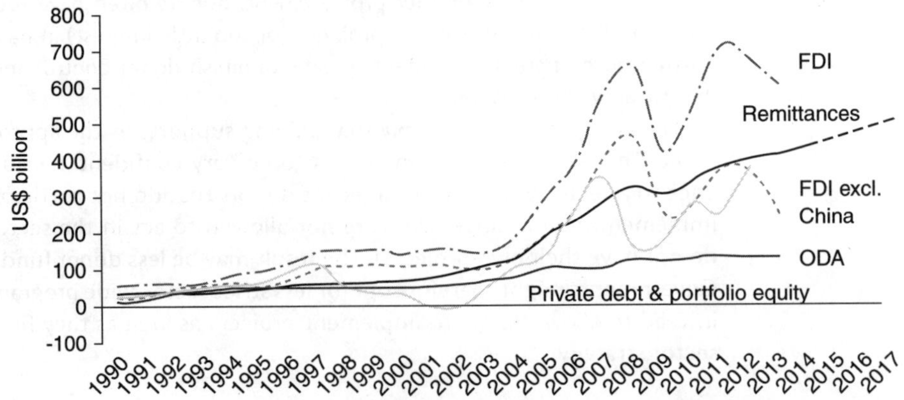

Sources: World Development Indicators and World Bank Development Prospects Group

Table 14.2 Total flow of financial resources from DAC countries to developing countries and multilateral organizations, by type of flow

	$ million	Per cent of total
	2014	2014
I. Official development assistance	137 222	23.78
1. Bilateral ODA	94 663	16.41
of which: General budget support	624	0.11
Core support to national NGOs	2 070	0.36
Investment projects	13 788	2.39
Debt relief grants	462	0.08
Administrative costs	6 347	1.10
Other in-donor expenditures	6 912	1.20
2. Contributions to multilateral institutions	42 559	7.38
of which: UN	6 803	1.18
EU	13 269	2.30
IDA	8 916	1.55
Regional development banks	4 002	0.69
II. Other official flows	4 626	0.80
1. Bilateral	4 747	0.82
2. Multilateral	- 121	-0.02
III. Private flows at market terms	402 936	69.83
1. Direct investment	189 624	32.86
2. Bilateral portfolio investment	206 979	35.87
3. Multilateral portfolio investment	3 012	0.52
4. Export credits	3 321	0.58
IV. Net grants by NGOs	32 246	5.59
TOTAL NET FLOWS	**577 030**	**100**

Source: OECD, 2015.

Official development assistance (ODA)

The total flow of ODA from the DAC countries in 2014 was $137 billion, of which approximately $94 billion consisted of grants, and $42 billion was disbursed by multilateral institutions.

The evolution of ODA in current and constant (2004) prices, and as a ratio of national income, is shown in Figures 14.2 and 14.3. The total value of ODA rose from less than $40 billion a year in 1960 to nearly $140 billion today. On the other hand, the ratio of ODA to national income fell more or less continuously from 1960 to 2004, despite the commitment in the 1970s to the 0.7% aid target, and it has only started to rise in the past decade.

The 2014 record of individual DAC countries as providers of ODA is shown in Table 14.3, together with the flow measured as a proportion of the donor's gross national income (GNI). It can be seen that only the Netherlands, Denmark, Norway, Luxembourg, Sweden and the UK

Figure 14.2 Official development assistance (ODA), 1960–2014

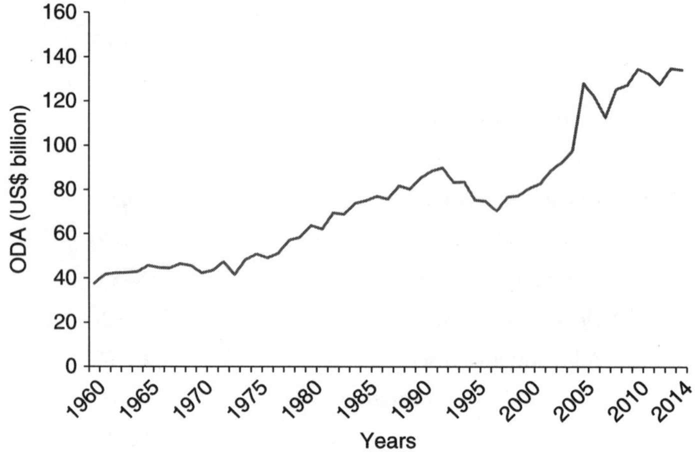

Source: Based on OECD Data-Aid Statistics.

Figure 14.3 Ratio of ODA to GNI, 1960–2014

Source: Based on OECD Data-Aid Statistics

met the aid target of 0.7% of GNI. The USA is the richest country but contributes the lowest proportion of GNI. The ratio for all DAC countries now averages only 0.3%.

Total net flow of financial resources from DAC countries

As well as providing ODA, there are other official flows on non-concessional terms from DAC countries to developing countries, and DAC countries are the major source of the various private flows. Table 14.3 also shows the total net flow of financial resources by DAC countries to developing countries and multilateral agencies, together with the total flow as a proportion of the donor's GNI. Many of the countries that failed to meet the official development assistance target managed to meet the total net financial flow target of 1% of GNI by virtue of large volumes of private lending.

Table 14.3 ODA and total net flow of financial resources from DAC countries to developing countries and multilateral agencies, 2014

	ODA		Total net flows by DAC country	
	US$ million	**% of GNI**	**US$ million**	**% of GNI**
Australia	4 382	0.31	31 975	2.29
Austria	1 235	0.28	3 284	0.76
Belgium	2 448	0.46	8 726	1.65
Canada	4 240	0.24	18 175	1.03
Czech Republic	212	0.11	106	0.06
Denmark	3 003	0.86	4 194	1.20
Finland	1 635	0.60	3 027	1.12
France	10 620	0.37	19 222	0.67
Germany	16 566	0.42	54 375	1.37
Greece	247	0.11	- 438	-0.19
Iceland	37	0.22	37	0.22
Ireland	816	0.38	1 203	0.55
Italy	4 009	0.19	8 706	0.41
Japan	9 266	0.19	40 501	0.84
Korea	1 857	0.13	10 542	0.74
Luxembourg	423	1.06	423	1.06
Netherlands	5 573	0.64	68 874	7.85
New Zealand	506	0.27	667	0.36
Norway	5 086	1.00	5 040	0.99
Poland	452	0.09	452	0.09
Portugal	430	0.19	- 331	-0.15
Slovak Republic	83	0.09	83	0.09
Slovenia	62	0.12	62	0.12
Spain	1 877	0.13	13 669	0.98
Sweden	6 233	1.09	9 325	1.64
Switzerland	3 522	0.50	4 673	0.67
United Kingdom	19 306	0.70	31 809	1.16
United States	33 096	0.19	238 648	1.34
TOTAL DAC	**137 222**	**0.30**	**577 029**	**1.24**

Source: OECD, 2015.

UK assistance to developing countries

The total flow of ODA from the UK to developing countries and multilateral agencies in 2014 was over $19 billion (see Table 14.4). Just over half the assistance is bilateral and the remainder goes to multilateral institutions. Of total bilateral aid, most goes into investment projects, including technical assistance, and for core support for NGOs working in poor countries. Recently, the UK has closed its bilateral programmes in several countries and now concentrates on just 28 of the poorest countries. Some 30% of the budget is committed to states affected by conflict.

The UK aid programme is administered by the Department for International Development (DfID) and its mission statement is given in Case example 14.3.

Case example 14.3 **DfID mission statement**

The Department for International Development (DfID) leads the UK's work to end extreme poverty. We're ending the need for aid by creating jobs, unlocking the potential of girls and women and helping to save lives when humanitarian emergencies hit.

Responsibilities

We are responsible for:

- honouring the UK's international commitments and taking action to achieve the United Nations' Global Goals (https://www.gov.uk/government/news/greening-britain-backs-the-global-goals-for-sustainabledevelopment)
- making British aid more effective by improving transparency, openness and value for money
- targeting British international development policy on economic growth and wealth creation
- improving the coherence and performance of British international development policy in fragile and conflict-affected countries
- improving the lives of girls and women through better education and a greater choice on family planning
- preventing violence against girls and women in the developing world
- helping to prevent climate change and encouraging adaptation and low-carbon growth in developing countries.

Priorities

- Strengthening global peace, security and governance.
- Strengthening resilience and response to crisis.
- Promoting global prosperity.
- Tackling extreme poverty and helping the world's most vulnerable.

Source: www.gov.uk/government/organisations/department-for-international-development.

The focus is very much on poverty reduction through social expenditure on health and education. Part of doctors' salaries in Africa are paid out of the aid budget, as well as user fees for medicines and various forms of hospital care. The aid budget is also increasingly being used to improve security in 'fragile states' (see Chapter 9).

Perhaps the most significant recent development, however, is that DfID tries not to tell the aid-receiving countries what to do; rather, it listens to what countries want to achieve and tries to help them to do so by ensuring that aid strengthens a country's system for planning, budgeting and accounting. As much aid as possible is channelled through countries' budgets so that they can assess resources and plan spending. Aid conditionality has been abandoned (see Case example 14.4).

Table 14.4 Total net flow of financial resources from the UK to developing countries and multilateral agencies, 2014

Net disbursements	**US $million**
I. Official development assistance (ODA) (A + B)	19 306
ODA as % of GNI	0.70
A. Bilateral official development assistance	11 233
of which: General budget support	87
Core support to national NGOs	394
Investment projects	916
Administrative costs	432
Other in-donor expenditures	226
of which: Refugees in donor countries	222
B. Contributions to multilateral institutions	8 073
of which: UN	855
EU	1 922
IDA	2 702
Regional development banks	464
II. Other official flows (OOF) net (C + D)	41
C. Bilateral other official flows (1 + 2)	41
1. Official export credits	–
2. Equities and other bilateral assets	41
D. Multilateral institutions	–
III. Grants by private voluntary agencies	–
IV. Private flows at market terms (long-term) (1 to 4)	12 462
1. Direct investment	–
2. Private export credits	299
3. Bilateral portfolio investment	12 761
4. Securities of multilateral agencies	–
V. Total resource flows (long-term) (I to IV)	**31 809**
Total resource flows as a % of GNI	**1.16**

Source: OECD, 2015.

Case example 14.4

Rethinking conditionality

Traditional conditionality, under which donors link aid to the implementation of particular policies by developing countries, is not compatible with the guiding principles of the country-led approach. It limits governments' freedom to design poverty reduction plans suited to the circumstances of their countries, and it compromises their accountability to their own citizens. It also undermines efforts to make aid more predictable. Conditionality has been particularly criticized when applied to privatization and trade liberalization. But even where it has been less controversial, there is little evidence that conditionality

continued overleaf

Case example 14.4 **Rethinking conditionality** – *continued*

has been effective in promoting long-term policy reform. The UK has therefore adopted a new approach, in which the key purpose is to safeguard donor resources from misuse, rather than to promote policy change in partner countries. Good policy remains vital for development, and we will continue to discuss policy options with partner countries. But we will not attempt to impose policies on them by making aid conditional on specific policy decisions. Our aid relationships will be based on three shared commitments – to poverty reduction, to human rights and other international obligations, and to sound financial management and accountability. Only if countries veer substantially away from these commitments will we consider reducing or withdrawing agreed aid.

To specify what our aid is intended to achieve, and as a basis for measuring progress, we will agree on benchmarks with partner countries, drawn from national poverty reduction plans. They will focus on outcomes and results, rather than on particular policies, and will be the basis for both partners to be accountable to their citizens for the effective use of aid. Although aid will not be conditional on the achievement of any particular benchmark, the rate and pattern of a country's progress will contribute to our assessment of its continuing commitment to poverty reduction and may be reflected in our subsequent aid allocation decisions.

Source: DfID.

The recipients of ODA

We end this statistical section by showing the distribution of ODA across the regions and continents of the world. Table 14.5 shows the total amount disbursed, the amount per head of the population, the percentage of GNI of the recipient region, and the percentage contribution that

Table 14.5 The recipients of aid, 2013

	Net official development assistance			
	$ millions	$ Per head	% of GNI	% of gross capital formation
World	150,086	21.0	0.2	0.8
Low income	43,859	72.0	11.9	44.6
Middle income	61,288	12.0	0.3	0.8
Lower middle income	45,811	16.0	0.8	3.2
Upper middle income	14,475	6.0	0.1	0.2
Low and middle income	149,928	26.0	0.6	1.8
East Asia and Pacific	11,875	6.0	0.1	0.2
Europe and Central Asia	9,026	34.0	0.5	2.1
Latin America and Caribbean	10,202	20.0	0.2	1.0
Middle East and North Africa	25,682	73.0	1.6	5.5
South Asia	14,065	8.0	0.6	2.0
Sub-Saharan Africa	46,769	49.0	2.9	13.8
High income	159	0.0	0.0	0.0

Source: World Bank, 2015.

ODA makes to total capital formation. As expected, most flows go to low-income and lower middle-income countries, but the amount per head is relatively small – $72 per head in low-income countries and only $16 per head in lower middle-income countries. On the other hand, the percentage of ODA to GNI in low-income countries exceeds 10%, and it finances 44.6% of gross capital formation. In short, the poorest countries of the world are heavily dependent on ODA for their growth and living standards. Of the continents, by far the largest recipient is Africa, where ODA per head is $49 and ODA's contribution to capital formation is 13.8%.

Aid tying

About $15 billion of DAC aid to developing countries (roughly one-fifth of total bilateral aid) is tied to the purchase of donors' goods. In this sense, capital inflows are not worth as much as they might be, as the recipients have to pay higher prices for goods and services bought with aid money than the prices prevailing in the free market. Tying tends to be of two kinds: restrictions on where the recipients can spend the aid money, and restrictions on how the aid is used. Spending restrictions take the form of tying assistance to purchases in the donor country – so-called 'procurement tying'. This reduces the real worth of aid because it prevents recipients from shopping around to find the precise goods they want in the cheapest markets. Use restrictions normally mean that the aid must be used to cover the foreign exchange costs of a defined project. Restricting the use of aid to particular projects as well as to the donor country's goods amounts to double tying. Tying can be expensive.

The price of tied goods can be 20% or more above the price of the same goods in the free market (see Jepma, 1991; Morrissey and White, 1993). Moreover, there are other costs of tying apart from the inability of the recipient to buy in the cheapest market. If there is double tying, the project for which assistance is given might not fit perfectly into the recipient's development programme, the technology might be inappropriate, the donor may raise the import content unnecessarily, the suppliers may engage in exploitation, knowing that they have a captive consumer, and servicing over the life of the investment may be expensive.

The excess cost of imported goods from the tied source represents a form of export subsidy to suppliers in the donor country, in the sense that if the aid was not tied and the suppliers had to remain competitive, the subsidy would have to be paid by the donor country itself. This subsidy to exporters in DAC countries through aid tying amounts to about $2 billion a year, or 2% of DAC assistance.

The one mitigating factor in all this is that the project for which assistance is given in tied form may have been undertaken anyway using the same source of supplies, in which case the assistance releases resources for another purpose. In other words, assistance to a certain extent is fungible because of resource switching. The fungibility of assistance also means that the balance of payments gain to the donor from tying may be quite small in practice because one form of purchase is substituted for another. This could be used as a bargaining weapon to reduce the extent of tying, the major reason for which seems to be balance of payments protection of the donors.

Remittances

Remittances from migrant workers are a growing source of resource transfer to many poor developing countries, supporting their balance of payments, and allowing the countries to grow faster than would otherwise be the case. In 2015, nearly 300 million migrant workers across the world

Table 14.6 Estimates and projections for remittance flows to developing countries

	2012	2013	2014	2015	2016	2017
	(US$ billions)					
World	**531**	**551**	**582**	**608**	**636**	**667**
Low-income countries	33	34	37	39	41	44
Middle-income	367	380	398	415	434	455
High income	131	137	148	154	161	168
Developing countries	**400**	**414**	**435**	**454**	**475**	**499**
East Asia and Pacific	108	114	122	127	134	141
Europe and Central Asia	44	48	49	50	52	54
Latin America and Caribbean	60	61	64	67	70	73
Middle-East and North Africa	49	49	51	53	55	58
South Asia	108	111	117	123	129	136
Sub-Saharan Africa	31	32	33	34	36	38

Source: World Bank calculations based on IMF balance of payments statistics.

remitted back to their homelands (developing countries) over $600 billion, more than four times higher than the volume of ODA, and more than FDI, excluding flows to China. And these are just official remittances; informal flows may be as high as formal flows. The estimated workers' remittances to developing countries by region are shown in Table 14.6. East Asia and the Pacific, and South Asia receive the most. Each migrant remits, on average, $2,000, or 20% of their earnings. For over twenty countries in the world, for example Bangladesh, Jamaica, Nicaragua and Tajikistan, remittances account for over 10% of GDP. The largest country recipient is Mexico, with flows of $30 billion. The largest remitter is Saudi Arabia (not the USA).

Remittances support the balance of payments of recipient countries and can be used either for consumption purposes or used productively to set up small businesses, to build houses, to invest in health and education. If remittances are consumed on domestic goods or imports, this increases the tax revenue of countries and enables them to spend more on socially useful purposes (see Chami and Fullenkamp, 2013). There is evidence that the children of families that receive remittances stay longer in school, and infant mortality is lower. In general, remittances help to reduce poverty.

The long-run growth effects are more controversial. The IMF (2003), using data for 100 developing countries for the period 1975–2002, finds that remittances boost growth in countries with less developed financial systems by providing an alternative way to finance investment, but remittances don't seem to impact on growth in countries with already well-functioning credit markets. Catrinescu et al. (2008) find in their study across 162 countries over 34 years that the impact of remittances on growth depends on the quality of a country's institutions; specifically: 'low level of ethnic tension; good governance; prevalence of law and order and good socioeconomic conditions are preconditions for a successful use of migrant remittances'. Their central estimate is that a 1% increase in the remittances/GDP ratio leads to a 0.04–0.05 percentage point increase in growth on average. Findings of a negative relation between remittances and growth are due to the failure to take into account the institutional structure of countries.

Multilateral assistance

The major sources of multilateral assistance to developing countries are the World Bank (the International Bank for Reconstruction and Development, IBRD) and its two affiliates, the International Development Association (IDA) and the International Finance Corporation (IFC), as well as the UN and various regional development banks.

The total disbursement in 2014 was $92 billion, of which $52 billion was on concessional terms. A detailed breakdown of the lending by the various multilateral agencies from 2010 to 2014 is given in Table 14.7. The disbursements by multilateral agencies to developing countries consist not only of the contributions of developed countries but also of funds raised on the international capital market and repayments of previous loans. As can be seen from Table 14.7, the World Bank is essentially a commercial institution lending on non-concessional terms, and it raises large sums of money on the world's capital markets.

The IDA is the 'soft' loan affiliate of the World Bank and dispenses loans at very low rates of interest with long repayment periods. It is the most important provider of concessional multilateral assistance. Since 1960, it has lent over $200 billion to over 100 countries. Only countries with less than a certain level of per capita income are eligible to receive assistance but this currently includes at least 80 countries with over 3 billion people. The EU has also become a major provider of concessional assistance through the European Development Fund (EDF). In 2014, it dispensed over £18 billion – a little more than the IDA. The major providers of non-concessional assistance in recent years (apart from the World Bank) have been the two regional development banks – the Inter-American Development Bank (IDB), lending to Latin America, and the Asian Development Bank (AsDB).

Table 14.7 Concessional and non-concessional flows by multilateral organizations, US$ million, at current prices and exchange rates

	Gross disbursements				
	2010	**2011**	**2012**	**2013**	**2014**
Concessional flows					
International financial institutions					
AfDB	2 414	2 355	2 548	2 420	2 148
AsDB	1 930	1 940	1 835	2 696	2 798
CarDB	75	72	64	92	113
EBRD	–	–	–	–	–
IDA	12 123	11 703	12 523	12 307	13 759
IDB Sp. Fund	1 994	1 703	1 619	2 169	1 938
IMF	2 973	1 455	1 506	1 212	832
Nordic Dev. Fund	65	70	56	49	50
Total IFIs	**21 575**	**19 297**	**20 151**	**20 945**	**21 638**
United Nations					
IFAD	520	621	631	612	531
UNAIDS	246	265	242	246	239

continued overleaf

Table 14.7 Concessional and non-concessional flows by multilateral organizations, US$ million, at current prices and exchange rates – *continued*

	Gross disbursements				
	2010	**2011**	**2012**	**2013**	**2014**
UNDP	613	494	487	468	463
UNFPA	316	315	349	355	340
UNHCR	393	441	424	417	480
UNICEF	1 050	1 104	1 152	1 252	1 342
UNRWA	545	608	667	539	680
UNTA	–	–	–	–	–
WFP	244	345	355	365	309
WHO	366	452	397	475	471
Other UN	151	145	148	594	153
Total UN	**4 443**	**4 792**	**4 851**	**5 325**	**5 008**
EU institutions	12 638	17 947	18 082	17 166	18 454
Adaptation Fund	22	47	24	7	13
Arab Funds	1 864	1 599	1 569	1 671	1 717
CEB	42	133	95	122	77
CIF	–	–	–	151	350
GAVI	772	819	1 068	1 544	1 415
GEF	530	474	539	574	606
GGGI	–	–	–	16	16
Global Fund	3 031	2 647	3 359	4 009	2 887
Montreal Protocol	21	10	5	37	45
OSCE	150	151	135	134	131
Total concessional	**45 085**	**47 915**	**49 878**	**51 701**	**52 356**
Non-concessional flows					
AfDB	2 042	3 051	3 510	2 304	3 045
Arab Funds	1 983	2 297	1 752	2 134	2 205
AsDB	5 272	5 626	6 900	6 163	7 600
CarDB	247	83	36	54	49
CEB	147	440	171	297	285
CIF	–	–	–	70	56
EBRD	3 399	4 022	3 501	3 961	4 823
EU institutions	8 259	982	762	1 510	868
IBRD	26 511	15 971	15 136	16 234	15 858
IDB	10 175	7 187	6 447	9 828	8 789
IFAD	44	49	63	57	92
IFC	4 184	4 733	6 414	6 743	–
Total non-concessional	**62 264**	**44 441**	**44 693**	**49 356**	**43 671**

Source: OECD, 2015.

World Bank activities

The activities of the World Bank since its creation in 1946 have broadly reflected changes in thinking about development policy and development priorities – changes that the World Bank itself has played a large part in promoting. In the early years, and throughout the 1960s, its major emphasis was on financing infrastructure projects in the field of power generation and distribution, transportation, ports, telecommunications and irrigation. There was very little support for agriculture and rural development, or industry and tourism; and programme loans (as opposed to project assistance) were largely confined to countries outside those classified as less developed.

The World Bank began to realize, however, that investment in infrastructure was not enough; that it had a role to play in lending to support directly productive activities. It also recognized the need for investment in education and managerial skills, and became increasingly aware that the development taking place in the countries it was supporting was not trickling down to the vast masses of the poor. In the late 1960s and throughout the 1970s, it began to play a more active role in agriculture and in helping both the rural and urban poor. Robert McNamara, president from 1968 to 1981, inaugurated this radical change of emphasis in his annual address to the World Bank in Nairobi in 1973. He defined absolute poverty as: 'a condition of life so degraded by disease, illiteracy, malnutrition and squalor as to deny its victims basic human necessities', and he pledged that the bank would make a concerted attack on rural poverty in order to raise the productivity of the poor and improve the incomes of small farmers. The objective was to provide most of the benefits of lending to those in the bottom 40% of the income distribution. In 1975, the World Bank announced that it would also attempt to deal with the problems of the urban poor by promoting productive employment opportunities on labour-intensive projects, and by developing basic services to serve the poor at low cost, for example water supplies, sanitation and family planning services.

Successive presidents of the World Bank have reiterated its commitment to helping the poor. It was mentioned in Chapter 2 that Lewis Preston announced in May 1992 that poverty reduction will be the 'benchmark by which our performance as a development institution will be measured', and this was reaffirmed by his successor, James Wolfensohn, president from 1995 to 2005, who wrote in the *World Development Report 2000/2001*: 'poverty amidst plenty is the world's greatest challenge. We at the Bank have made it our mission to fight poverty with passion and professionalism, putting it at the centre of all the work that we do' (World Bank, 2000). Robert Zoellich, Wolfensohn's successor, said: 'it is the vision of the World Bank Group to contribute to inclusive and sustainable globalization – to overcome poverty, enhance growth with care for the environment, and create individual opportunity and hope'. Dr Jim Yong Kim, the current president, has said: 'our mission at the World Bank is defined by two goals – to end extreme poverty by 2030, and to boost prosperity among the poorest 40% in low- and middle-income countries'.

The World Bank sees four major challenges:

1. To spur growth and overcome poverty, particularly in Africa, by provision of infrastructure, tackling corruption and raising agricultural productivity.
2. To help countries coming out of conflict, and failed states.
3. To foster regional and global public goods, for example disease control, dissemination of technology and combating global warming.
4. To advance development and opportunities in the Arab world, and to reduce social tensions particularly among young people who cannot find jobs.

It is committed to the Sustainable Development Goal of eliminating poverty by the year 2030.

Table 14.8 Distribution of World Bank lending, 2014

	% of total multilateral finance
Social and administrative infrastructure	35.0
Education	7.4
of which: Basic education	4.1
Health	3.8
of which: Basic health	2.4
Population	0.2
Water supply and sanitation	7.1
Government and civil society	10.2
Other social infrastructure/service	6.3
Economic infrastructure	43.9
Transport and communications	13.3
Energy	16.2
Other	14.5
Production	13.7
Agriculture	6.7
Industry, mining and construction	6.3
Trade and tourism	0.7
Multisector	4.4
Programme assistance	0.4
Action relating to debt	0.0
Humanitarian aid	2.4
Administrative expenses	-
Other and unspecified	0.1
TOTAL	**100.0**

Source: OECD, 2015.

The distribution of World Bank assistance for various purposes is shown in Table 14.8. The largest bulk of lending goes on economic infrastructure, which includes transport, communications and energy. Agriculture is still relatively neglected, with only 6.7% of the budget.

Structural adjustment lending

Another initiative was introduced by the World Bank in October 1979: **structural adjustment lending** to countries in order to support their balance of payments. To qualify for structural adjustment loans, a country has to adopt policies that are acceptable to the bank and designed to secure external equilibrium in the longer run without sacrificing growth. The emphasis is on improving the supply-side capacity of the economy.

The World Bank defines structural adjustment loans as 'non-project lending to support programmes of policy and institutional change to modify the structure of the economy so that it can maintain both its growth rate and viability of its balance of payments in the medium term'. The loans are geared to seven main areas:

- Supply-side reforms, for example improving the efficiency with which markets operate
- Price reforms
- Changing the price of tradable goods relative to non-tradables
- Getting the 'correct' terms of trade between agricultural goods and industrial goods
- Reducing the size of the public sector
- Financial reforms
- Tax reforms.

Governments must commit themselves to policy reform in order to qualify for a loan.

Balance of payments support has been the traditional preserve of the International Monetary Fund (IMF: see Chapter 16), but there is a difference of emphasis between the IMF and the World Bank. Whereas IMF policies focus primarily on balance of payments management, the World Bank is more concerned with promoting policies to increase efficiency and providing incentives to raise export earnings and reduce import payments. Clearly, however, the roles of the two institutions now overlap and will do so increasingly as the IMF itself insists on supply-side policies as a condition for assistance, as well as on the traditional demand-side policies of devaluation and monetary contraction. (See Taylor, 1997 for a trenchant summary and critique of IMF and World Bank policies in poor countries.) The distinct roles of the IMF and the World Bank are outlined in Case example 14.5.

Case example 14.5

The IMF and the World Bank: What's the difference?

The IMF and the World Bank were conceived at the Bretton Woods conference in July 1944 to strengthen international economic cooperation and to help create a more stable and prosperous global economy. Although these goals have remained central to both institutions, their mandates and functions differ, and their work has evolved in response to new economic developments and challenges.

The IMF promotes international monetary cooperation and provides member countries with policy advice, temporary loans and technical assistance so they can establish and maintain financial stability and external viability, and build and maintain strong economies. The IMF's loans are provided in support of policy programmes designed to solve balance of payments problems – that is, situations in which a country cannot obtain sufficient financing on affordable terms to meet international payment obligations. Some IMF loans are relatively short term and funded by the pool of quota contributions provided by its members. Others are for longer periods, including concessional loans provided to low-income members on the basis of subsidies financed by past IMF gold sales and members' contributions. In its work in low-income countries, the IMF's main focus is on how macroeconomic and financial policies can contribute to laying a basis for sustainable growth and poverty reduction. Most IMF professional staff are economists.

The World Bank promotes long-term economic development and poverty reduction by providing technical and financial support, including by helping countries

continued overleaf

Case example 14.5 **The IMF and the World Bank: What's the difference?** – *continued*

reform particular sectors or implement specific projects; for example, building schools and health centres, providing water and electricity, fighting disease, and protecting the environment. World Bank financial assistance is generally long term and is funded by member country contributions and through bond issuance. World Bank staff have qualifications that embrace a broader range of disciplines than those of IMF staff.

The IMF and the World Bank collaborate in a variety of areas, particularly in supporting governments in implementing poverty reduction strategies in low-income countries, providing debt relief for the poorest countries, and assessing the financial sectors of countries. The two institutions hold joint meetings twice a year.

Source: IMF, 2006.

Since the purpose of structural adjustment lending and the **structural adjustment programmes (SAPs)** is to improve the growth potential of countries, evaluations of these lending programmes by independent investigators and the World Bank itself have focused on the key macro variables of GDP growth, savings, investment, exports and the balance of payments. In a World Bank symposium on adjustment lending, Corbo et al. (1992) single out the following as indicators of country performance: real GDP growth, the ratio of savings to GDP, the ratio of investment to GDP, and the export ratio. Their methodology is to compare countries that have SAPs with other countries that have less intensive adjustment lending programmes and with countries that had received no adjustment loans. The performance of the three sets of countries is then compared relative to their performance in a base period before any loans were dispensed (that is, pre-1979). It appears that only the export ratio was superior in the SAP countries, and the investment ratio was much worse. This was also the conclusion of another World Bank study (1990), which found that structural adjustment lending had achieved a modest degree of success in helping countries to improve their balance of payments, but had failed to lead to an upsurge in investment or to enable countries to 'grow out of debt'. Another major study of 40 countries (Harrigan and Mosley, 1991) found that the effect on GDP growth had been negligible; export growth and the balance of payments had improved, but investment had declined. The main reason for the disappointing results appears to be the heavy requirements (or conditionality) placed on recipient governments, which have served to depress demand and confidence. There is a general consensus that the requirements should be less stringent and more selective, and more sensitive to each country's circumstances (see Mosley et al., 1991).

SAPs have particularly hit the poor in many countries. Cornia et al. (1987, 1988) called for 'adjustment with a human face', but the record is still not good. A major study by Noorbakhsh (1999), comparing the periods 1970–85 and 1986–92 in countries with SAPs and those without, found that virtually all the indicators of the standard of living – for example, infant mortality, life expectancy, adult literacy, primary school enrolment and per capita calorie supply – fared worse in countries with structural adjustment loans.

It would seem that much more care is required in the design of SAPs if they are to achieve growth with equity (see Bourguignon and Morrisson, 1992), and if the World Bank is to avoid the charge of being an anti-developmental institution, like its sister institution, the IMF (see Chapter 16). In fact, one of the most damning indictments of SAPs comes from Joseph Stiglitz

(2002), a former chief economist of the World Bank, in his powerful book *Globalization and its Discontents*, who attacks IMF policy-making at the same time. We leave the discussion until Chapter 16.

Joseph Stiglitz

Born 1943, Gary, Indiana, USA. Taught in several universities including MIT, Yale, Stanford, Princeton and Oxford. Now Professor of Economics at Columbia University. Former Chairman of the Council of Economic Advisers under President Clinton (1995–97), and Chief Economist of the World Bank (1997–2000). Most prolific economist of his generation, with major contributions to virtually every branch of economics. Highly critical of the global trade and financial architecture in such books as *Globalization and its Discontents* (2002) and *Making Globalization Work* (2006). Awarded the Nobel Prize for Economics in 2001.

The imposition of harsh conditionality, which has not worked, and the relative failure of SAPs, has led to calls for reform of World Bank lending. Gilbert et al. (1999) suggest that *ex ante* conditionality should be abandoned altogether. Instead, the World Bank should say to countries: 'If you get your own house in order you can borrow from us without conditions, and can continue to do so as long as sensible economic policies are pursued and good governance prevails.' This amounts to a form of *ex post* conditionality, but the countries would 'own' the policies rather than be dictated to by the bank. For countries without good governance and the ability to reform, it should stop lending. Instead, it should act as a knowledge bank for the dissemination of best practice techniques in economic management and policy reform. This would require more World Bank staff in the countries concerned, fulfilling a training role.

Poverty Reduction Strategy Papers (PRSPs)

World Bank policy is already moving in the direction suggested above. In a new approach announced by the World Bank and IMF in 1999, national governments are offered a role in shaping and implementing anti-poverty strategies as part of its new focus on tackling poverty directly and making debt relief conditional on countries producing **Poverty Reduction Strategy Papers (PRSPs)** (see Case example 14.6). According to the World Bank, the focus of PRSPs should be on 'identifying in a participatory manner the poverty reduction outcomes a country wishes to achieve and the key public actions – policy changes, institutional reforms, programmes and projects – that are needed to achieve the desired outcomes'. The idea is that the attack on poverty should be based on partnership between governments and all sections of society concerned with poverty reduction, with governments leading the process of setting the goals and monitoring the process.

Case example 14.6 Poverty reduction strategy in IMF-supported programmes

Poverty reduction strategies (PRS) are central to IMF-supported economic and financial programmes in low-income countries. Poverty Reduction Strategy Papers (PRSPs) assess policy challenges, describe how macroeconomic, structural and social policies and programmes can promote growth and reduce poverty, and outline external funding needs and the associated sources of financing. They are prepared by governments in low-income countries generally through a participatory process involving domestic stakeholders and external development partners.

The PRSP approach was initiated by the IMF and World Bank in 1999 in the context of the Heavily Indebted Poor Country (HIPC) Initiative (see later), and Annual Progress Reports as a basis for debt reduction. The same documents were subsequently used to anchor IMF-supported programmes for low-income countries to allow for the implementation of strategies to achieve sustained poverty reduction and growth.

The core principles of the current PRS policy in IMF-supported programmes are:

- Maintain the link between members' PRS and policies under IMF-supported programmes, with streamlined PRS documentation.
- Preserve national ownership of the PRS process.
- Provide flexibility in the scope and coverage of the PRS to reflect different country circumstances.

The authorities' PRS will be documented through an **Economic Development Document (EDD)**, and can take two forms:

1. Existing national development plans documenting countries' PRS.
2. New EDD focused on elements of the PRS that are macro-relevant under IMF-supported programmes.

These documentation requirements must be met in order for a low-income country to complete reviews under an Extended Credit Facility (ECF) arrangement.

EDDs must meet the following minimum requirements:

- A strategy or plan for poverty reduction and growth
- Specific policies, including macroeconomic and financial policies that would be pursued in the context of the strategy
- The launch date and timeframe for implementation, to ensure that the strategy underlying IMF-supported programmes is current.

In addition, they should provide a description of:

- Existing poverty situation and trends
- Factors influencing poverty, including barriers to poverty reduction
- A fiscal and debt framework, with a view to prioritizing development spending
- Spending effectiveness, that is, how well money is spent on poverty
- Safety nets and risk mitigation
- Outline of the participatory process.

Source: www.imf.org/en/About/Factsheets/Sheets/2016/08/01/16/32/Poverty-Reduction-Strategy-in-IMF-supported-Programs.

Estimating the aid component of international assistance

Because of the different nature of the various capital flows, a common procedure is required for measuring the equivalence of the different flows. Clearly, grants and loans are not equivalent since the latter have to be repaid and the former do not.

A standard procedure for making the flows equivalent is to estimate the **grant equivalent** or **aid component** of the different flows by taking the difference between the nominal flow and future repayments discounted by the free-market rate of interest, which was our earlier measure of the benefit of assistance. A capital inflow that is a pure grant (with no repayment obligations) is 'worth' its face value. A capital inflow that has to be repaid with interest is not worth its face value. How much less it is worth than its face value depends on the rate at which the repayments are discounted:

- If the rate of interest at which the country would have had to borrow in the free market is greater than the actual rate of interest it has to pay, the worth or benefit will be *positive*.
- If the rate of interest at which it would have had to borrow is less than the actual rate, the worth or benefit will be *negative* because the recipient would have had to pay back more than it need to have done (this is unlikely to happen).

The grant equivalent or aid component of assistance is measured in this differential benefit sense. The rate of return on the assistance may, of course, be much greater than the benefit if the productivity of the assistance is higher than the free-market rate of interest.

Two other factors determine the grant equivalent of a loan as well as the effective interest rate subsidy:

- The **grace period** between the disbursement of the loan and the first repayment. The longer the grace period for a loan of a given maturity, the less the present value of the future discounted repayments.
- The **maturity of the loan**. This is important because the longer the maturity, the longer the concessionary interest rate is enjoyed and the less the present value of the future discounted repayments. Through the technique of discounting, any combination of repayment terms can be brought to a common measure.

All three factors referred to – the interest rate subsidy, the grace period and the maturity of the loan – can be incorporated into a simple formula for calculating the grant equivalent of a loan. The grant equivalent or aid component of a loan (as a percentage of its face value) is called the **grant element** and is equal to:

$$\frac{G}{F} = \left[\frac{F - \left(\sum_{t=1}^{T} \frac{P_t}{(1+r)^t} \right)}{F} \right] 100$$

where F is the face value of the loan, P_t is the total repayment of principal and interest in year t, T is the maturity of the loan and r is the rate of discount. Since P_t includes interest charges, it can be seen that the lower the interest rate relative to the rate of discount (r), and the more that repayments can be delayed through time, the greater the grant element of the loan.

The grant element can be worked out for different combinations of interest rates, discount rates, grace periods and length of maturity. At the two extremes, if the financial flow is a pure grant, then $P_t = 0$ and the grant element is 100%. If the financial flow is at a rate of interest equal to the market rate of interest, and the grace period and maturity of the loan are the same as in the free market, the sum of the discounted future repayments will equal the face value of the flow and the grant element will be zero.

For combinations of conditions between the two extremes, Table 14.9 provides some illustrative calculations. For example, the grant element of a 10-year loan at 5% interest with a grace

Table 14.9 Grant element in loans at different discount rates

Rate of interest and maturity period	5%			6%			7%			10%		
	No grace period G = 0	5 years' grace G = 5	10 years' grace G = 10	G = 0	G = 5	G = 10	G = 0	G = 5	G = 10	G = 0	G = 5	G = 10
2% interest												
10 years	12.9	21.2		16.7	24.0		20.0	28.9		29.5	41.8	
20 years	22.1	27.1	31.3	27.8	34.0	39.0	32.8	40.1	45.7	39.8	48.0	53.7
30 years	28.9	34.0	37.0	35.7	40.6	45.4	41.5	47.5	52.4	54.7	62.3	67.3
40 years	34.2	38.0	41.2	41.5	46.2	49.4	47.5	52.7	56.6	60.5	61.6	73.0
3% interest												
10 years	8.6	14.1		12.5	18.0		16.0	23.2		25.8	36.6	
20 years	14.7	18.1	20.9	20.8	25.5	29.2	21.3	32.2	36.6	31.3	38.1	43.1
30 years	19.3	22.6	24.6	26.8	30.5	34.9	33.2	38.1	42.0	47.8	54.5	58.9
40 years	22.8	25.4	27.4	31.1	34.6	37.0	38.0	42.2	45.4	52.9	58.2	63.8
4% interest												
10 years	4.3	7.1		8.1	12.0		12.0	17.4		22.1	31.4	
20 years	7.4	9.0	10.4	13.9	17.0	19.4	19.8	24.2	27.5	34.1	41.1	46.0
30 years	9.6	11.3	12.3	17.8	20.3	22.8	24.9	28.6	31.5	41.0	46.7	50.5
40 years	11.4	12.7	13.7	20.7	23.0	24.6	28.6	31.7	34.1	45.3	50.0	54.6

Table 14.9 Grant element in loans at different discount rates – *continued*

Rate of interest and maturity period	5%			6%			7%			10%		
	No grace period G = 0	5 years' grace G = 5	10 years' grace G = 10	G = 0	G = 5	G = 10	G = 0	G = 5	G = 10	G = 0	G = 5	G = 10
5% interest												
10 years	0	0	0	4.2	6.0		8.0	11.5		18.4	**26.1***	
20 years	0	0	0	6.9	8.5	9.7	13.1	16.2	18.3	28.4	34.2	38.4
30 years	0	0	0	8.9	10.2	11.3	16.6	19.0	20.9	34.2	38.9	42.0
40 years	0	0	0	10.4	11.5	12.1	19.0	21.0	22.6	37.7	41.6	45.5
6% interest												
10 years	a	a	a	0	0	0	4.0	5.8		14.7	20.9	
20 years	a	a	a	0	0	0	6.6	8.1	9.2	22.7	27.4	30.7
30 years	a	a	a	0	0	0	8.4	9.6	10.6	27.4	31.1	33.6
40 years	a	a	a	0	0	0	9.6	10.6	11.4	30.1	33.3	36.4
7% interest												
10 years	a	a	a	a	a	a	0	0	0	11.1	15.7	
20 years	a	a	a	a	a	a	0	0	0	17.1	21.6	23.0
30 years	a	a	a	a	a	a	0	0	0	20.5	23.3	25.2
40 years	a	a	a	a	a	a	0	0	0	22.6	25.0	27.3

Notes: a indicates negative aid value. * Illustrative calculation referred to in the text.

Source: Ohlin, 1966, appendix.

Table 14.10 DAC members' ODA terms, 2014

	Loan share of total ODA (%)	Terms of bilateral loans			
		Average maturity (years)	Average grace period (years)	Average interest rate (%)	Grant element (%)
Australia	0.5	33.2	3.2	0.0	75.4
Belgium	0.9	29.5	10.5	0.0	82.7
Canada	4.0	5.0	5.0	2.1	31.4
France	30.5	20.5	6.6	2.2	52.8
Germany	28.7	15.0	4.5	2.3	43.5
Italy	1.9	37.4	26.5	0.0	94.2
Japan	51.1	34.7	9.2	0.6	78.1
Korea	47.4	39.9	14.5	0.1	89.6
Poland	32.2	24.2	5.0	0.2	69.0
Portugal	31.9	29.1	10.4	1.8	67.7
Total DAC	15.0	26.9	7.7	1.3	64.9

Note: Not all DAC countries report information.

Source: OECD, 2015.

period of 5 years, with the recipient discounting repayments at 10%, would be 26.1%. It can be seen that the grant element is quite sensitive to small changes in the interest rate and the discount rate but relatively insensitive to variations in the grace period and the length of maturity. Long maturities and grace periods are mainly means of providing liquidity rather than aid.

The terms of ODA from DAC members in 2014 are shown in Table 14.10. The average rate of interest charged was 1.3%, the average grace period was 7.7 years and the average maturity of loans was 27 years. The discount rate normally applied is 10%, giving a grant element of approximately 65%. In 2014, the grant element of total official development assistance was 74%. The grant element of major forms of multilateral assistance is approximately 50%.

The moral of the foregoing discussion on the grant element of loans is that identifying the real worth of assistance depends on knowledge of the alternatives. Loans that look generous on the surface because they have a lower interest rate attached may be less valuable than the alternatives if they have shorter lives and grace periods. There is also the question of the freedom of the recipient country to use the loan as it wishes, which we considered earlier in connection with aid tying.

The distribution of international assistance

The distribution of international assistance will affect the comparative rates of growth of developing countries if aid is a positive growth-inducing force. At present, the distribution of assistance in relation to the population of developing countries is extremely unequal. Whereas some countries receive less than \$5 per head per annum, others receive over \$100 per head. Assistance as a proportion of national income also differs widely between countries

Most bilateral donors refrain from making explicit the criteria on which they distribute assistance. In practice, the criteria employed often tend to be as much non-economic as economic, reflecting historical relations between countries, as well as military and political objectives. It is often said that it pays a country to be a small island of ex-colonial status in a politically sensitive part of the world. High levels of per capita assistance seem to be closely associated with these characteristics. It is difficult to discern any significant relationship between the distribution of assistance and developmental considerations such as low per capita income, slow growth, balance of payments problems or even good governance. Dictators and corrupt governments also seem to be rewarded.

One recent comprehensive study by Burnside and Dollar (2000) takes a sample of 56 countries over the period 1970–93 and tries to explain the distribution of aid as a percentage of GDP in terms of variables, such as the level of per capita income of the recipient countries (as a measure of need), population size, various strategic (political and military) interests, and whether there is good governance. There seems to be no tendency for either total aid or bilateral aid to be related to the level of poverty, or to favour countries pursuing 'good policies', although multilateral aid is more 'wisely' distributed (see also Alesina and Dollar, 2000).

Collier and Dollar (2002) derive a poverty-efficient allocation of aid and compare it with actual aid allocations across 59 countries over the period 1974–97, and conclude that the allocation of aid was radically different from the poverty-efficient allocation. With the actual allocation of aid, about 10 million people had been lifted out of poverty annually, but with an efficient allocation to reduce poverty, nearly double the number of people would have been lifted out of poverty.

Individual donor countries will continue to pursue their own objectives and set their own criteria, although there is evidence that more and more donor countries are focusing directly on the attack on poverty and favouring poor countries with sound policies, in line with World Bank thinking.

The criteria governing the distribution of multilateral assistance through international agencies, to which rich countries contribute, are of wider concern. Since loans have to be repaid in foreign exchange, one obvious criterion for distribution would be a productivity criterion measured in terms of foreign exchange, but then all sorts of questions arise concerning the measurement of productivity, the time horizon to be taken, and whether this would lead to a distribution of assistance in relation to need. Without an economically objective and value-free criterion, need is as good a criterion as any and meets the main direct objective of the World Bank, which is the 'attack on poverty' (see Chapter 2). One possibility in this connection would be to distribute assistance on a per capita basis according to some target level of per capita income, which would operate rather like an **international negative income tax**. Certain graduated rates of per capita income assistance could be applied to the gap between the actual level of per capita income and the target level. A country that fell way below the target would receive a greater amount of assistance per head of the population than a country that was closer to the target or exceeded it. Given knowledge of the total amount of resources available, rates could be fixed to ensure a wide spread of assistance across countries while not making demands on resources in excess of supply. All this would be conditional, of course, on the new guiding principle of 'good governance'.

Schemes for increasing the flow of revenue

There are two ways of increasing the net flow of financial resources to developing countries: either nominal assistance can be left unchanged and repayment obligations reduced, or nominal assistance can be increased, leaving the terms of repayment unchanged. Reducing repayment obligations means cutting interest rates, lengthening repayment periods, and generally increasing the grant element of international assistance. Other possibilities would be to allow countries to repay in local currency rather than foreign currency and to reduce the level of aid tying, as discussed earlier. We shall concentrate here, however, on measures that might be taken to increase the volume of nominal assistance.

One quick way to increase the flow would be for *all* the developed countries to meet their development assistance targets of 1% of national income for total assistance and 0.7% of national income for ODA. A significant increase in the resource flow by a deliberate budget decision in developed countries is only likely to occur, however, if there is widespread public support for the programme. In recent years, there have been signs of diminished public support for aid, based on the belief that a good deal of assistance is wasted and misused. If there is disillusion with assistance – or **aid fatigue** as it has been called – an increased flow of assistance in the future is unlikely in the absence of some recognizable improvement in the efficiency with which current assistance is used. It is difficult to convince people in developed countries, whose standard of living is not that high, to acquiesce to programmes that transfer resources from themselves if these resources are then perceived to be wasted or end up in the hands of people in recipient countries who are richer than themselves. The major reasons for the waste and misuse of resources in the past have been inefficiency and corruption on the part of recipient governments and interference from donor countries in the administration of programme assistance.

Given the political difficulties of increasing aid budgets, what the global economy needs are schemes and forms of international taxation that would raise revenue automatically, free of political debate and budgetary pressure in donor countries. The 1980 Brandt Report first raised the issue of the need for automatic revenue to support global development needs, and the UN Development Programme (UNDP) has called for more work on global taxes. There is no shortage of suggestions as to how more global finance might be raised, particularly through the taxation of global transactions. The schemes can be divided into three (overlapping) groups:

1. Taxes and charges on various international transactions and external diseconomies that damage human welfare in various ways.
2. Taxes or charges on unexploited resources over which no state has sovereignty, for example deep sea minerals.
3. International income taxes earmarked for development purposes.

A useful and interesting list of the various suggestions made has been compiled by the Overseas Development Institute in London (ODI, 1996):

Twenty recent suggestions for raising global revenue:

- A tax on all or some international financial transactions (the 'Tobin Tax'); variants include a tax on bond turnover, or on derivatives.
- A general surcharge on international trade.
- Taxes on specified traded commodities like fuel.
- A tax on the international arms trade.
- Surcharges on post and telecommunications revenues.
- An international lottery.
- A surcharge on domestic taxation (usually expressed as a progressive share of income tax).
- Dedication of some part of national or local taxes, for example on luxuries (or surcharges on them).
- Parking charges for satellites placed in geostationary orbit.
- Royalties on minerals mined in international waters.

- Charges for exploration in, or exploitation of, Antarctica.
- Charges for fishing in international waters.
- Charges for use of the electromagnetic spectrum.
- A tax or charge on international flights (or alternatively, on flights in congested sectors); a variant is a tax on aviation kerosene.
- A tax or charge on international shipping.
- Pollution charges (for example, for dumping at sea).
- A tax on traded pollution permits.
- A voluntary local tax paid to a central global agency.
- A new issue of Special Drawing Rights (SDRs), distributed to the poorer developing countries (or used for peacekeeping or other global public goods).
- Sale of part of the IMF gold stock.

These are only suggestions and possibilities. There has been no sustained discussion of any of them at the intergovernmental level, and none of them has been taken up in a serious way by any of the major aid-giving countries. A $100 billion increase in SDRs was announced in 2009 in the wake of the international financial crisis that erupted across the world in 2008 (see Chapter 16).

Apart from the idea of various taxes and charges, one of the most attractive ideas is to involve individuals in the spirit of international aid giving and to foster their interest in the challenge of development by allowing them to pay a proportion of their tax obligations in the form of donations to various development funds concerned with poverty eradication, the environment, education and so on. This already happens in a small way with tax relief on donations to charities and NGOs working in developing countries, but the principle needs to be expanded if the idea of voluntary taxation in support of development is to have a significant impact.

The proposal for new issues of SDRs and the sale of IMF gold for development purposes is discussed in Chapter 16.

Foreign direct investment (FDI) and multinational corporations

Apart from ODA, another major source of development finance is private capital flows that allow countries to import more than they export and to invest more than they save. Private capital flows are of three main types: FDI and portfolio investment, which are non-debt-creating flows, and commercial bank lending, which creates debt. In this section, we focus on FDI in developing countries. Bank lending, and the debt problems to which it gives rise, are considered in the final section.

There has been a vast increase in the amount of FDI going to developing countries in recent years, fuelled by three major factors: the rise of multinational corporations and the search for global profits, the liberalization of global capital markets, and economic liberalization within developing countries. For a comprehensive survey of the causes and effects of FDI, see de Mello (1997).

But these flows are highly concentrated in a few countries. Total flows of FDI into developing countries are now running at over $500 billion a year, compared with under $20 billion in the early 1980s, but 80% goes to only ten countries located in South America and Southeast Asia (including China), as shown in Table 14.11. Overall, FDI accounts for about 10% of total investment in developing countries and roughly 2% of GDP. In discussing the costs and benefits of FDI, the relatively small contribution of FDI to economic activity in the majority of developing countries needs to be borne in mind.

Research into the determinants of FDI shows that cost structures, differential returns, market growth, and the institutional characteristics of the host country are of prime importance. Companies wishing to invest overseas are looking for a favourable trade and investment regime, good infrastructure, property rights, political stability, macroeconomic stability, and an educated and committed workforce. Much depends on the capacity of the country to absorb the investment, which, in turn, depends on its growth prospects and ability to export.

FDI brings many advantages to recipient countries, but there are also many potential dangers and disadvantages from a development point of view. We shall first list the advantages:

1. FDI raises the investment ratio above the domestic savings ratio, which is good for growth if nothing adverse happens to the productivity of investment.
2. The investment brings with it knowledge, technology and management skills, which can have positive externalities on the rest of the economy. Foreign investment can often be a catalyst for domestic investment in the same or related fields.
3. It requires the training of labour, which is another positive externality. It is estimated that over 40 million workers are employed directly or indirectly by multinational corporations in developing countries.
4. A great deal of FDI goes into the tradable goods sector of the recipient countries, which improves the export performance of these countries and earns them valuable foreign exchange.

Recent research shows a positive relation between FDI, domestic investment and the growth of GDP. Bosworth and Collins (1999) take a sample of 58 developing countries over the period 1978–95 and find that FDI brings about a one-to-one increase in domestic investment, while capital inflows as a whole increase domestic investment by only half the amount. Coe et al. (1997) examine the empirical evidence between international research and development (R&D) spillovers and economic growth for a sample of 77 countries. They find that the variation in total factor productivity growth between countries is related to the foreign stock of R&D capital, and that East Asian countries have benefited most from foreign R&D. It has been estimated by Borensztein et al. (1995) that a 1 percentage point increase in the ratio of FDI to GDP in developing countries over the period 1971–89 was associated with a 0.4–0.7 percentage point increase in the growth of per capita GDP, with the impact varying positively with educational attainment as an indicator

Table 14.11 FDI net inflows to top ten developing countries, 2014

	Total ($ million)
China	289,097
Brazil	96,895
Singapore	67,523
India	33,871
Indonesia	26,349
Mexico	24,154
Chile	22,002
Colombia	16,151
Turkey	12,765
Malaysia	10,609

Source: World Bank, 2015.

of a country's ability to absorb technology. But there is also evidence of bidirectional causality (see de Mello, 1997). FDI affects growth positively, at least above a certain threshold, but growth also affects FDI positively; another example of a virtuous circle. Pacheco-López (2005) also finds evidence of bidirectional causality in a study of FDI in Mexico.

Now let us turn to some of the potential dangers of FDI. As we have indicated, investment by multinational corporations with headquarters in developed countries involves not only a transfer of funds (including the reinvestment of profits) but also a whole package of physical capital, techniques of production, managerial and marketing expertise, products, advertising, and business practices for the maximization of global profits. There is no doubt that such investment augments real resources directly; the question is whether such investment contributes to the broader aspects of development relating to the pattern of development and the distribution of income.

The activities of the multinationals come under attack on a variety of grounds. First, because they tend to locate in urban areas, they widen the income gap between urban and rural sectors, thus perpetuating dualism. This criticism, however, cannot be levelled exclusively against multinationals because any new industrial activity establishing in existing urban centres will have the same effect.

A second and more serious criticism is the way in which they encourage and manipulate consumption. Not only do they tend to cater for the tastes of the already well-to-do, which itself acts as a divisive force, but also they tend to encourage forms of consumption among the broad mass of people, particularly in urban areas, that are inappropriate to the stage of development and often nutritionally damaging. Prime examples are powdered baby milk and Coca-Cola. These tendencies are not only wasteful, but they encourage acquisitiveness, reduce domestic saving, and can worsen balance of payments difficulties by encouraging expensive tastes.

A third criticism, which we have already dealt with in Chapter 6, is that they may introduce inappropriate technology and retard the development of an indigenous capital goods industry. Related to this is the possibility that the multinationals may stifle indigenous entrepreneurship and destroy domestic firms, so that the net addition to capital accumulation is much less than the investment provided by the multinationals themselves.

Another aspect of the multinationals is that because of their large size and the power they wield, developing countries in which they operate lose aspects of their national sovereignty and control over economic policy. The companies may easily avoid the effects of domestic monetary policy because of easy access to foreign capital markets and their own internal resources. They can avoid tax by shifting profits abroad. Countries may wish a multinational company to do one thing, but it may not readily comply because the action may conflict with the global profit objectives of the company as a whole. Firms may exploit resources more quickly than is desirable, and exploit consumers and workers through the exercise of monopoly and monopsony power.

There is also the question of the repatriation of profits. FDI has the potential disadvantage, even compared with loan finance, that there may be an outflow of profits that lasts much longer than the outflow of debt service payments on a loan of equivalent amount. While a loan only creates repayment obligations for a definite number of years, FDI may involve an unending commitment. This has serious implications for the balance of payments and for domestic resource utilization if foreign exchange is a scarce resource. We can show with a numerical example that, in the long run, if profits are repatriated, the impact of continuous FDI on the balance of payments must be negative unless the *gross* inflow of foreign investment grows substantially from year to year. This, of course, then increases the power and influence of the foreign interests within the country concerned.

Table 14.12 Balance of payments effects of private foreign investment

Year	Gross inflow	Foreign investment at beginning of period	Foreign investment at end of period	Outflow of profits	Net inflow
1	100	100.0	110.0	10.0	90.0
2	100	210.0	231.0	21.0	79.0
3	100	331.0	364.1	33.1	66.9
4	100	464.1	510.5	46.4	53.6
5	100	610.5	671.6	61.1	38.9
6	100	771.5	848.7	77.2	22.8
7	100	948.7	1, 043.6	94.9	5.1
8	100	1, 143.6	1, 258.0	114.4	−14.4

Suppose that there is a steady gross inflow of 100 units of foreign capital per annum, that the productivity of capital is 20%, and that one-half of the profits are reinvested and the other half are repatriated. Table 14.12 shows that, on these assumptions, the balance of payments effect turns negative after the eighth year. To keep the net inflow of resources positive requires a steadily rising *gross* flow of private foreign investment, with all the implications this may have for the pattern of development in the future.

It is extremely difficult to measure the full impact and real costs of multinational investment using economic calculus alone, but this is what developing countries must do. What would be the real income gains and losses of controlling the free mobility of FDI? Other ways of taking advantage of FDI might be actively explored, including **joint ventures** and **turnkey projects**, whereby the foreign investor pays for and builds the project in collaboration with the host country, which is then run by host country nationals. There is already evidence that this is the direction in which developing countries are moving. Developing countries must lay down very clearly the conditions under which they will accept multinational investments and monitor the companies' operations so that distorted development and exploitation are avoided.

International debt and debt service problems

Developing countries not only borrow from donor countries and multilateral agencies but also commercially from the international banking system. All borrowing, whether official or private, involves repayment obligations, unless the loans are gifts or written off. First, the loan has to be repaid over a certain number of years (**amortization repayments**), and second, **interest payments** will be charged on the loan. Amortization and interest payments constitute **debt service payments.** All loans that have to be repaid with interest are **debt-creating flows.**

There has been a massive increase in debt-creating flows to developing countries since the early 1970s, caused by growing payments imbalances between countries. The total volume of debt in 2014 and the debt burden measured by various indicators – such as the debt–export ratio, the debt to national income ratio, and the ratio of debt service payments to export earnings (**the debt–service ratio**) – is shown in Table 14.13 for various groups of countries. The total debt of low- and middle-income countries is now a colossal $5,400 billion (or roughly $1,300 per head of population) and debt service payments absorb $250 billion of foreign exchange or nearly 10% of total export earnings. The debt–service ratio is particularly crucial because this measures the amount of

Table 14.13 The debt burden of developing countries, 2014

	Total external debt			Total debt service
	$ millions	% of GNI	% of exports of goods and services	% of exports of goods and services
Low income	167,105	26.6	164.0	..
Middle income	5,224,360	22.1	79.7	8.9
Lower middle income	1,527,246	27.8	104.6	14.5
Upper middle income	3,697,114	20.4	72.5	7.4
Low and middle income	5,391,465	22.2	80.9	8.9
East Asia and Pacific	1,816,587	14.6	25.7	3.8
Europe and Central Asia	1,023,990	58.0	10.5	22.8
Latin America and Caribbean	1,346,821	29.5	95.5	15.6
Middle East and North Africa	187,878	15.3	12.5	5.5
South Asia	613,379	23.5	107.0	17.5
Sub-Saharan Africa	402,811	24.5	88.8	7.3

Source: World Bank, 2015.

foreign exchange earnings that cannot be used to purchase imports and is therefore some measure of the extent to which a country might decide to default on its repayment obligations. The greater the debt service payments, the more that development is thwarted. Some of the largest debtor countries of the world, such as Brazil and Turkey, have the highest debt–service ratios.

To judge whether a country's level of debt is sustainable, the World Bank takes a debt–export ratio of 220%. This is the main criterion for relief under the HIPC Initiative (see below). By this criterion, it is mainly African countries that constitute the severely indebted low-income countries with debt–export ratios of 200% or more in some cases.

Before turning to the origins of this massive volume of debt, however, let us consider in more detail the nature of the debt-servicing problem. At the beginning of the chapter, it was shown that it is profitable for a country to borrow as long as the rate of return on the borrowing exceeds the rate of interest. In these circumstances, the rate of growth of income is higher than it would otherwise be. This gives no indication, however, of whether the borrowing can be serviced or repaid, since the loan must be repaid with interest in *foreign* currency. Thus, the profitability of borrowing and the capacity to service debt are conceptually distinct. The ability to service debt depends on whether additional foreign exchange can be earned or saved by the borrowing. This depends on the domestic economic policy pursued by the country concerned and the ability to export, which depends, to a large extent, on world economic conditions.

The debt-servicing difficulties that have arisen in recent years have had as much to do with deteriorating world economic conditions, which have depressed the foreign exchange earnings of developing countries, as with the miscalculation of rates of return on investment, the misuse of investment funds, or the use of capital inflows to increase present consumption. There was a parallel in the 1980s with the Great Depression of the 1930s when the collapse of world prices of key commodities and a general shrinkage of world trade caused major debt defaults, which subsequently dried up the flow of private capital to developing countries for the next 40 years. The trouble started in 1982 when the volume of world trade fell by 2.5%, and the terms of trade for developing countries as a whole deteriorated by over 10%.

Not even the most prudent borrower or cautious lender can foresee such events, which may occur halfway through the life of a loan commitment that was entered into under quite different economic circumstances. Lenders and borrowers can allow for risk – that is, the statistical probability that the expected outcome will not materialize – but not uncertainty, and what happened in the world economy in the 1980s was a whole shift in the probability distribution of outcomes that could not be insured against. When such unforeseen events occur, beyond the borrower's control, which make it difficult for loans to be repaid and serviced without severe economic disruption, two questions arise: What is the optimal degree of debt rescheduling? Who should bear the cost?

It is naturally in the interests of private banks that loans be repaid on schedule, but it is not necessarily in the global interest if this leads to a contraction of imports by the borrowing countries, which then reduces the exports of other (lending) countries, leading to a deflationary spiral in the whole world economy.

Optimal borrowing and sustainable debt

The benefits of borrowing to individual countries, and to the world economy at large, are clear. The question is: How far should borrowing go? Is it possible that after a certain point, even though a developing country still requires resources for development, the disadvantages of further borrowing outweigh the advantages? This raises the question of **optimal borrowing** and **the sustainability of debt**. Reasonable levels of debt are likely to enhance growth in countries short of capital if borrowing is used productively and earns foreign exchange so that debt can be serviced without deflating the economy to save imports. Debt becomes unsustainable when it accumulates at a faster rate than the borrower's capacity to service it. Expected debt service costs then discourage domestic and foreign investment, because potential investors fear the economy will be deflated or that they will be 'taxed' to service the debts.

Working out what level of debt is sustainable requires an assessment of how outstanding stocks of debt are likely to evolve over time, together with forecasts about the future interest rates, exchange rates and foreign exchange earnings. The IMF has recently developed a standardized framework for assessing debt sustainability, which takes account of a country's future growth rate, interest rate and exchange rate, and applies sensitivity analysis based on each country's history.

Several debt indicators and measures of sustainability can be used. One is the ratio of debt to GDP. There has been a progressive rise in the **ratio of debt to GDP** among developing countries, from less than 20% in the early 1970s to nearly 30% today, but it is not clear what economic significance should be attached to this ratio as a measure of the ability to service debt and therefore as a measure of debt sustainability. It is true that to service more and more debt, export earnings as a proportion of national income should rise, but this suggests more direct measures of sustainability: either the **debt–export ratio** or the **debt–service ratio**, which measures the ratio of amortization and interest payments to export earnings.

To answer the question of the sustainability of debt, Kraay and Nehru (2006) at the World Bank take 132 low- and middle-income countries over the period 1970–2002, and use probit analysis to predict debt distress defined as the inability to service debt from the Paris Club of OECD countries and from the IMF. They find that the debt–export ratio is one important factor, but that the level of debt that can be sustained depends on the quality of country institutions and policies. For a country with an average institutional/policy score, a 100% debt–export ratio would be sustainable, with a 39% probability of distress (the mean of the sample for low-income

Figure 14.4 Debt–export ratio and growth

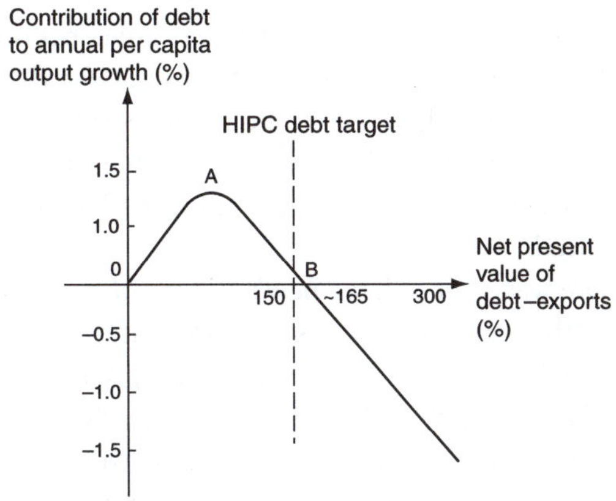

countries), while for countries with very good institutions and policies, a debt–export ratio of 400% would be sustainable.

On the relationship between the debt–export ratio and the growth of per capita income, Patillo et al. (2002) find a nonlinear relation. They take a sample of 93 developing countries over the period 1969–98 and, controlling for other variables, find that the per capita income growth of countries is maximized when the debt–export ratio is approximately 80%, and debt impacts negatively on growth when the debt–export ratio exceeds 160% – as shown in Figure 14.4. The growth differential between countries with low indebtedness (with an export–debt ratio < 100%) and those with high indebtedness (with an export-debt ratio > 367%) is, on average, more than 2 percentage points. It appears that the relationship between debt and growth is nonlinear (an inverted U-shape) and that the level of sustainable debt is, on average, close to the ratio of 150% of export earnings, which is below the ratio at which countries become eligible for debt relief under the HIPC Initiative launched by the World Bank in 1996 (see later).

These results have been corroborated by Bhattacharya and Clements (2004), who take 55 low-income countries over the period 1970–99 and find a positive relation between the debt–export ratio and per capita income growth up to a ratio of nearly 200% (and for the debt–GDP ratio up to 50%). They calculate that if the net present value of debt–GDP ratio for the most heavily indebted countries was reduced from, say, 100% to 50%, this could raise the annual growth of per capita income by 2.8 percentage points. They also calculate that a 1 percentage point reduction in the debt–service ratio could raise the investment to GDP ratio of countries by about 0.2 percentage points.

The debt crisis of the 1980s

The world debt crisis (useful texts on this subject include Cline,1984, 1995, Claudon, 1986, Lomax, 1986, Lever and Huhne, 1985 and Griffith-Jones and Sunkel, 1986) erupted in the summer of 1982, when Mexico became the first country to suspend the repayment of loans due to the private banking system and sovereign lenders. The crisis has smouldered ever since, with more and more countries, particularly in Africa, finding it difficult to service accumulated debts out of foreign exchange earnings. In 1987, Brazil became the first country to suspend interest payments to foreign creditors.

The 'crisis' aspects of debt can be looked at from different standpoints: from the point of view of the individual borrowing countries, the lenders (private and sovereign governments), or the entire world economy. As far as borrowers are concerned, when the crisis first erupted, there were essentially two types of 'problem' countries. First, there were a number of *poor commodity-dependent countries*, mainly in Africa but also elsewhere, where private banks were not heavily involved. It became a crisis for these countries when they had to cut back on essential imports in order to service their debts, but not a crisis for the banking system or the world economy, even if they had defaulted.

Second, there was a set of large *newly industrializing countries*, mainly in Latin America, which borrowed from the commercial banking system at floating rates of interest, but then their export markets became depressed. The sums of money involved were huge. In the early 1980s, 16 countries accounted for over half of the total debt of nearly $1,000 billion and for nearly 90% of the debt owed to the private banking system. In this case, the non-repayment of debt would have caused a crisis for the private banking system (which, in retrospect, had clearly overextended itself), and a crisis for individual countries if the threat of default had dried up the flow of new capital. There would also have been a crisis for the world economy if there had been a major default that led to a massive contraction of bank lending throughout the system; but this did not happen. Lending did contract sharply in the early 1980s, but then rose again as the difficulties were resolved by various forms of international cooperation and the rescheduling of debt.

The origin of the current debt difficulties of many developing countries is no mystery. Massive balance of payments surpluses arose in the early 1970s in the oil-exporting countries, with counterpart deficits elsewhere. The factors that caused the supply of capital to increase created its own demand. Private banks were anxious to lend and there was no shortage of demand. Demand was particularly strong because commodity prices were generally high, exports were buoyant and inflation had reduced the real rate of interest on loans to virtually zero. Credit looked cheap and borrowers looked like good risks from the lenders' point of view. But these circumstances suddenly changed. Depression in the developed countries, mainly self-inflicted to reduce the rate of inflation, caused world commodity prices to tumble, exports to languish and real interest rates to rise. On top of this, nominal interest rates floated upwards and the dollar appreciated. At the height of the debt crisis (in 1986) the debt–service ratio reached a peak of 30%. This has since fallen back to under 20%, partly because of lower interest rates and debt rescheduling and partly because of increased export earnings following the recovery of the world economy.

The world debt problem is a foreign exchange problem. It represents the inability of debtors to earn enough foreign exchange through exports to service foreign debts, and at the same time to sustain the growth of output (which requires foreign exchange to pay for imports). Either debt service payments have to be suspended or growth curtailed, or a combination of both. Unfortunately, for many debtor countries, it is living standards that have suffered. Many indebted developing countries have stagnated under a total burden of debt that has now reached $5,500 billion, with resource transfers to service the debt close to $250 billion per annum.

All this is part of the **transfer problem** analysed by Keynes in 1919 in the wake of the controversy over the reparation payments imposed on Germany after the First World War by the Treaty of Versailles in 1919 (Keynes, 1919). Keynes mocked the folly and futility of the whole exercise on the grounds that it was likely to be self-defeating, and so it turned out to be.

There are two aspects of the transfer problem: the **budgetary problem** for governments of acquiring domestic resources for the repayment of debt, and the problem of turning the resources into foreign exchange – or the **pure transfer problem** as Keynes called it. The **transfer burden** is the export surplus that has to be generated to acquire the necessary foreign exchange, plus the possibility of a deterioration in the terms of trade if, in order to sell more exports, prices must be reduced. Even if prices do fall, there is still no guarantee that export *earnings* will increase if the quantity sold does not rise in proportion to the fall in price. In these circumstances, the transfer becomes impossible without a contraction of domestic output to compress imports. There is substantial evidence that the indebted countries collectively are caught in this trap, since for a large part of their trade they compete with each other; and competitive price reductions leave total earnings unchanged. It is the contraction of living standards that generates the export surplus by reducing the import bill. This is not good for developing countries, or for the health of the world economy.

The debt crisis of the early 1980s has subsided, but the debt problem has not gone away. Lenders have been as irresponsible as borrowers. The developed countries must accept a large share of the responsibility for the world recession of the 1980s, as should the private banks for voluntarily overextending themselves. Shared blame requires shared solutions.

Debt relief

Debt, in many ways, is like a cancer, once it gets a grip on a country it is very hard to eradicate and may spread unless the rest of the economy can be reinforced to overcome it.

There are no easy solutions to the debt-servicing problem short of a massive programme of **debt forgiveness**, which leaves a manageable debt that the debtors can service. There has to be debt relief if there is to be any easing of the transfer burden. Without relief, further borrowing increases the size of the debt service payments and simply makes matters worse, creating what might be called a **debt trap**. Since lenders, borrowers and the whole world community have benefited from the debt creation process, there is a strong case for saying that the same three parties should share the burden of relief. It is not fair that the debtor countries (the borrowers) should bear the whole of the adjustment burden. Up to now, the world community (including the creditor countries) has done very little to ease the debtors' plight, although there are three reasons why it should:

1. The world community received an external benefit when the debt was created by the lending process in the 1970s, preventing output contraction in countries with balance of payments deficits, and thereby avoiding a world slump.
2. Much of the debt problem arose in the first place through no fault of the developing countries themselves, but as a result of events in the world economy – rising oil prices, rising interest rates, world recession, and falling commodity prices.
3. Relief could actually confer a global benefit by easing the deflationary forces associated with the huge debt overhang.

Heavily Indebted Poor Country (HIPC) Initiative

The most recent and publicized global scheme for debt relief is the **Heavily Indebted Poor Country (HIPC) Initiative** launched by the World Bank in 1996, designed to help the world's poorest indebted countries. The World Bank has always been hostile to the write-off of debt, but the share of debt service payments going to multilateral creditors has increased in recent years and now accounts for over 50% of debt service payments by some African countries. This World Bank initiative therefore marked a radical departure in thinking and attitude. At the time, James Wolfensohn, president of the bank, described the initiative as 'a breakthrough – it deals with debt in a comprehensive way to give countries the possibility of exiting from unsustainable debt. It is very good news for the poor of the world.' To qualify for debt relief, a country had to have a debt–export ratio in excess of 220% or a debt to government revenue ratio of more than 280%. Forty-one countries, mainly in Africa, originally met the criteria, with a combined debt of nearly \$200 billion. In the first three years of the initiative, however, progress was painfully slow. Only seven countries satisfied the stringent conditions laid down by the World Bank in order to receive help, and only \$10 billion of relief was dispensed.

Dissatisfaction with the original initiative led the Group of Seven (G7) rich industrialized countries to launch an **Enhanced HIPC Initiative** in Cologne in 1999, later endorsed by the World Bank and the IMF, which, according to the World Bank, was intended to be 'deeper, broader and faster'. Then, in 2005, to help accelerate progress towards the UN's Millennium Development Goals, the HIPC Initiative was supplemented by the **Multilateral Debt Relief Initiative (MDRI)**, which allows for 100% relief on eligible debts to the World Bank, the IMF and the African Development Bank.

To be considered for HIPC Initiative assistance, a country must fulfil the following four conditions:

1. Be eligible to borrow from the World Bank's International Development Agency (IDA), which provides interest-free loans and grants to the world's poorest countries, and from the IMF's Poverty Reduction and Growth Trust (formerly the Enhanced Structural Adjustment Facility) (see Chapter 16), which provides loans to low-income countries at subsidized rates.
2. Face an unsustainable debt burden that cannot be addressed through traditional debt relief mechanisms.
3. Have established a track record of reform and sound policies through IMF- and World Bank-supported programmes.
4. Have developed a Poverty Reduction Strategy Paper (PRSP) through a broad-based participatory process in the country (see Case example 14.7).

Once a country has met or made sufficient progress in meeting these four criteria, the executive boards of the World Bank and IMF formally decide on its eligibility for debt relief, and the international community commits to reducing debt to a level that is considered sustainable. This first stage under the HIPC initiative is referred to as the **decision point**. Once a country reaches this point, it may immediately begin to receive interim relief on its debt service falling due. In order to receive complete debt relief, a country must:

- Establish a further track record of good performance under programmes supported by loans from the World Bank and the IMF.
- Implement satisfactorily key reforms agreed at the decision point.
- Adopt and implement its PRSP for at least one year.

Once a country has met these criteria, it can reach its **completion point**, which allows it to receive the full debt relief committed at the decision point.

The total cost to the 39 countries currently eligible or potentially eligible for debt relief under the Enhanced HIPC Initiative is about \$75 billion at 2013 prices. Uganda was the first country to receive debt relief under the Enhanced HIPC Initiative in May 2000 based on several years of progress in implementing poverty relief programmes (see Case example 14.7).

The pre-decision point countries face common challenges, including preserving peace and stability, and improving governance and the delivery of basic services. Addressing these challenges requires continued efforts from these countries to strengthen policies and institutions, and support from the international community.

Case example 14.7

How debt relief fits into a poverty reduction strategy: Uganda's Poverty Action Fund

Improving the overall allocation of resources, including those from debt relief, through more poverty-oriented and transparent budgets, is fundamental in the fight against poverty. There are many ways of achieving this end, and in Uganda a special fund to use the savings from debt relief is proving useful.

The government created the Poverty Action Fund (PAF) as a conduit for the savings from debt relief under the HIPC Initiative (about $37 million a year; the Enhanced HIPC Initiative is expected to double this amount). The fund has been earmarked to address the poverty and social conditions highlighted in the poverty eradication action plan adopted in 1997. The plan emphasizes maintaining macroeconomic stability while increasing the incomes and the quality of life of poor people by developing rural infrastructure, promoting small businesses and microenterprises, creating jobs and improving health services and education. The PAF focuses on schools, rural feeder roads, agricultural extension, and district-level water and sanitation. Specific outcome targets have been identified, such as the construction of 1,000 additional classrooms to support the primary education programme.

Two crucial features of the PAF are its integration into the overall budget and the Ugandan government's effort to create a transparent and accountable structure of management. Reports on financial allocation are released at quarterly meetings attended by donors and NGOs. The Inspector General's office monitors the use of funds at district and national levels. This self-imposed conditionality reflects the government's strong commitment to tackling corruption. But it is also an attempt to address creditor concerns about the capacity of a debtor country to link debt relief to poverty reduction. Several measures have been proposed for improving monitoring, ranging from including district-level officials in the quarterly meetings to having local NGOs do community-based monitoring of the poverty fund's spending.

Apart from bold, imaginative, global schemes of debt relief, there have been a number of piecemeal, case-by-case initiatives in which the burden on the debtor developing countries has been ameliorated.

Debt rescheduling

The initial US response to the 1980s debt crisis was to attempt to increase **liquidity**, to give developing countries more breathing space to 'grow out' of their debt problems. This was the thinking behind the so-called **Baker Plan** of October 1988, which made provision for $20 billion of additional lending from the commercial banks and $9 billion of multilateral lending to the 15 or so most severely indebted countries, contingent on market-friendly, growth-oriented structural adjustment programmes being adopted. There was no acceptance of debt reduction by banks, and the sums of money were a drop in the ocean. In the event, most of the money was not lent because of the continued vulnerability of the banks and the deteriorating external situation.

The abortive Baker Plan was followed by the so-called **Brady Plan** of 1989, which did accept debt reduction and was more successful. The two main elements of the plan were:

1. Providing funds via the IMF and the World Bank for various forms of debt relief to those middle-income debtor countries that were willing to adopt policy reforms.

2. Encouraging countries to buy back debt from banks at a discount, thereby reducing future obligations.

One possibility was for countries to swap old loans for new long-term (30-year) bonds at a discount of some 35% and an interest rate only marginally above the market rate – the bonds were guaranteed by the IMF. Agreements of this type were reached with Mexico, the Philippines, Costa Rica, Venezuela and Uruguay. The deal with Mexico relieved it of $20 billion of debt service payments.

Other multilateral initiatives focused on the poorest debtor countries. The governments of OECD countries representing the so-called Paris Club adopted two major initiatives – the **Toronto Terms** in September 1988 and the **Trinidad Terms** in September 1990. These initiatives were related to official debt (that is, debt owed to governments) and made provision for the cancellation of a substantial proportion of the debt. For the remainder of the debt, substantial restructuring was offered.

Under the Toronto Terms, eligible countries were those receiving concessional assistance from the International Development Association, the soft loan affiliate of the World Bank, and a distinction was made between official development assistance (ODA) and non-ODA. For ODA, countries were given 25 years to pay with a grace period of 14 years, with no change in the interest rate. For non-ODA, three options were offered of different combinations of rescheduling, relief and interest rates.

Under the Trinidad Terms, heavily indebted countries with a per capita income of less than $1,195 were eligible. For ODA, countries were given 20 years to pay with a grace period of 10 years. For non-ODA, countries were given 15 years to pay with a grace period of 8 years and a market rate of interest.

In 1996 and 1999, the HIPC Initiatives were launched, as discussed above, which concentrate more on debt relief than debt rescheduling.

Apart from these official initiatives, a great deal of other debt rescheduling has been arranged privately between individual countries and the creditor banks. These ease the short-term pressure but do not reduce future repayment obligations, unless the rescheduled debt is on softer terms.

Debt service capping

Several schemes have been suggested to prevent debt service payments becoming excessive. One is for **variable maturity loans** to be issued, so that debt service payments would remain unaltered as interest rates floated upwards on private debt (rather like mortgage loans are variable in the housing market). Alternatively, maturities could be varied automatically in order to keep the debt–service ratio unchanged. This would also accommodate fluctuations in foreign exchange receipts from exports. These schemes are equivalent to capping interest payments above a certain level. In 1985, Peru unilaterally imposed a 10% ceiling on debt service payments as a proportion of export earnings.

Another possibility is to offer **zero coupon bonds**, which would delay interest payments until a loan had matured. This would reduce the present value of interest payments, but, more importantly, it would allow investment to be fully productive before there was any commitment of foreign exchange. It would not insure, however, against the bunching of repayment commitments when foreign exchange earnings might be low.

Debt buybacks and debt swaps

Another solution to the debt service problem that has gained favour in recent years is for countries to buy back their debt at a discount, or to exchange the debt in various ways that fully or partially relieve the burden of interest and principal repayments. Developing countries' debt trades in a secondary market, where some countries' debts can be bought at a discount of more than 50%. At one time, Sudanese debt could be bought in the secondary market for $2 per $100. If Sudan had been able and willing to use its foreign exchange reserves to buy its own debt, it could have wiped out, say, $1 million of debt for as little as $20,000. The secondary market, however, is generally thin, and heavy buying is likely to raise the price considerably. Even so, the use of foreign exchange reserves to buy back debt at a discount of 20–30% can make a useful contribution to debt relief. In 1995, Peru spent $600 million in the secondary market, buying $1.2 billion of its debt accumulated in the late 1970s and early 1980s at an estimated saving of $1 billion in interest payments.

Debt/equity swaps are a way of eliminating debt service payments altogether. In a debt/equity swap, the debt held by the creditor is converted into an equity stake in enterprises within the debtor country. The creditors have a claim on future profits, but the debtor countries are relieved of interest payments. Such swaps can be profitable to all parties involved. A classic example was the Nissan motor company's purchase of Mexican debt for investment in its Mexican subsidiary in 1982. Nissan bought $60 million of Mexican debt held by the Citicorp Bank at a price of $40 million – a discount of one-third. Nissan redeemed the debt certificates at the Mexican central bank for $54 million in Mexican pesos, which were then invested in its subsidiary. The bank unloaded its debt at the 'market' price, Nissan made a profit in dollars, and Mexico was relieved of interest payments in foreign currency. There have been several other debt/equity swaps since 1986, and they are increasingly linked to privatization programmes in debtor countries, but the absolute magnitude of the sums involved is still relatively small in relation to the size of the debt burden.

Debt for nature and **debt for development swaps** work in the same way as debt/equity swaps, except the debt is bought by a governmental or charitable organization and the proceeds are used for environmental or developmental purposes within the debtor country. The World Wide Fund for Nature has bought developing countries' debt at a considerable discount and exchanged it for local currency for use on environmental projects within developing countries. In 1988, UNICEF bought Sudanese debt from the Midland Bank, and this was redeemed by the Sudanese government to finance water sanitation programmes in central Sudan.

Debt for bonds is a swap scheme whereby debtor countries offer fixed interest, long-term bonds in exchange for debt held by the banks. They can be advantageous if the debt can be exchanged at a discount at a more favourable rate of interest. In 1988, Mexico launched a scheme offering $10 billion of bonds to its creditor banks, hoping to sell at a discount of 50%. The sale turned out to be disappointing, however. Only 100 out of the 500 banks bid for the bonds, and the debt was discounted by only 30%. Even so, some saving was made by the Mexican government.

Exit bonds are a particular type of bond that give a bank a lower rate of interest than on the original debt, but end the bank's liability to provide new money. One way of encouraging this type of arrangement would be for the IMF to guarantee interest payments on the exit bonds, which would encourage the banks to swap debt for this type of bond.

Long-term solutions

On a longer term basis, developed countries might set up machinery to guarantee loans from private sources (in addition to export credit guarantees) and establish a fund from which commercial interest rates could be subsidized. Such a scheme would mean that private lenders would not be deterred from lending through fear of default, developing countries would receive cheaper credit, and the donor's contribution in the form of payments to private lenders would not burden the balance of payments (if this was regarded as an obstacle to a higher level of official assistance).

Second, ODA might be given as grants rather than loans. The grant element of official assistance is already high, and this further step would not only give extra marginal help but would also eliminate the need to haggle over debt renegotiations if the need for rescheduling arose.

Finally, there is an urgent need to devise schemes to stabilize the price or terms of trade for primary commodities. A large part of the 1980s debt crisis resulted from the collapse of primary product prices, and large fluctuations in primary product prices continue to pose problems for poor countries today (see Chapter 15).

To stabilize the terms of trade, indexation may be appropriate for some commodities, for example oil. For other primary commodities, credit creation to finance merchants' stocks would assist. Special Drawing Rights (see Chapter 16) might play a useful role here for buying up surplus stocks of primary commodities that are storable, or for income compensation for commodities that are not. It seems incredible that so many years have passed since Keynes' wartime plan for an international agency for stabilizing commodity prices (see Thirlwall, 1987; and see Chapter 15 for partial schemes already in existence), yet the world still lacks the requisite international agreement and institutional structures for greater stability and a fairer deal for developing countries that live by exporting primary commodities.

Summary

- Domestic saving and investment for growth and development can be supplemented by various types of foreign resource inflows such as loans from bilateral and multilateral sources, pure aid, FDI and remittances.
- The amount of foreign resource inflows required to support a particular target rate of economic growth can be estimated using dual-gap analysis.
- Foreign borrowing will raise the growth of national income if the productivity of capital imports is greater than the rate of interest on loans, and will raise the growth of national output if new foreign borrowing exceeds the loss of domestic saving to pay interest on past borrowing.
- The total amount of foreign resource inflows into developing countries is approximately $1000 billion, including $140 billion of aid, $400 billion of FDI and $600 billion of remittances.
- The motives for aid giving are humanitarian and economic, but there are many critics of aid who argue that it weakens the domestic savings effort and fosters a 'dependency' culture.
- The macroeconomic impact of aid depends on whether it is spent directly on imports or whether the government sells the foreign exchange to the central bank and then uses the local currency to buy domestic goods.
- The World Bank is a major multilateral lender to developing countries, but its structural adjustment programmes have been criticized for being too deflationary and 'anti-developmental'.

- Foreign direct investment has benefits, particularly knowledge spillovers, but it also has costs in terms of continual profit outflows and the use of inappropriate techniques of production.
- Migrant remittances are now greater than official aid, and are non-debt-creating.
- Loans create debt that has to be repaid in foreign currency. The debt burden of developing countries is a foreign exchange problem. The volume of international debt is approximately \$5,500 billion.
- Empirically, the optimal level of country debt seems to be about 80% of the value of exports, and the impact of debt on growth becomes negative if debt grows to 160% of exports.
- The debt crisis of the 1980s, which still lingers today, was largely caused by unfavourable external circumstances, including a collapse of commodity prices and a doubling of interest rates.
- There is no solution to the debt burden of the highly indebted countries without debt forgiveness. Some poor countries qualify for the World Bank's HIPC Initiative, which allows debt to be written off if the proceeds are used for poverty reduction programmes approved by the World Bank.

Chapter 14 Discussion questions

1. What is the distinctive contribution of dual-gap analysis to the theory of development?
2. Under what circumstances will foreign borrowing raise the rate of growth of income, and raise the rate of growth of output?
3. What are the characteristics of the different types of financial flow to developing countries?
4. What factors determine the grant element of a financial flow?
5. How might the flow of resources to developing countries be augmented, and what criteria should govern their distribution between countries?
6. What is the purpose of World Bank structural adjustment lending, and how successful has it been?
7. What are the advantages and disadvantages of FDI to developing countries?
8. Discuss the view that foreign lending is merely a pernicious device for transferring resources from poor to rich countries.
9. Can countries borrow too much? What is the sustainable level of borrowing?
10. What is the nature of the debt problem in developing countries?
11. What imaginative schemes can you think of to relieve the debt-servicing burden of developing countries?
12. How successful have the World Bank's HIPC debt relief programmes been?

Websites on aid, remittances, debt and FDI

Aid

International Aid Transparency Initiative www.aidtransparency.net

International migration and remittances

International Organization for Migration www/iom/int
Global Commission on International Migration www.iom.int/global-commission-international-migration
Migration Observatory, University of Oxford www.migrationobservatory.ox.ac.uk

Debt

World Bank, Global Financial Development Report www.worldbank.org/en/publication/gfdr
OECD, Development Co-operation Directorate www.oecd.org/dac
HIPC Initiative www.worldbank.org/hipc
Make Poverty History www.makepovertyhistory.org/takeaction/

Foreign direct investment

UNCTAD www.unctad.org/en/Pages/Home.aspx
International Trade Centre, Investment Map www.investmentmap.org

Nongovernmental organizations

NGO Global Network www.ngo.org
Jubilee Debt Campaign http://jubileedebt.org.uk

V

INTERNATIONAL TRADE, THE BALANCE OF PAYMENTS AND DEVELOPMENT

15

TRADE THEORY, TRADE POLICY AND ECONOMIC DEVELOPMENT

Introduction

In Chapter 14 we discussed the important role of foreign borrowing and foreign resources inflows in the development process. Using dual-gap analysis, it was shown that foreign borrowing can be used to bridge a domestic investment–savings gap or a foreign exchange gap, whichever is the larger. We saw that the policy issue is deciding how far borrowing should go without leading to unmanageable international debt.

The empirical evidence indicates a serious conflict in many poor countries between maintaining an adequate growth rate and a sustainable balance of payments on current account. The ultimate solution must lie in improving the balance of payments through trade and faster export growth.

In this chapter, we do a number of things. First, we discuss the general relation between trade and economic growth, and establish the precise nature of the benefits from trade, including the formation of customs unions and regional trade agreements (RTAs). The static and dynamic gains from trade are distinguished, and the role of trade as a vent for surplus commodities.

We go on to outline the enthusiasm for trade liberalization in the modern era, the way the process of trade liberalization is measured, and the empirical evidence of the impact of trade liberalization on export growth, import growth, the balance of payments, and overall economic performance of developing economies. There are separate sections on trade liberalization, poverty and domestic inequality, and on trade liberalization and international inequality.

The disadvantages of free trade for development are then explored. We examine critically the underlying assumptions of the comparative advantage doctrine and free trade theory, and ask whether developing countries might fare better in a more protected environment. This leads on to the theory of protection, the debate over import substitution versus export promotion, and the use of tariffs and subsidies as protective devices.

We then turn to the issues originally raised by the well-known Latin American economist Raúl Prebisch, concerning the terms of trade between primary commodities and manufactured goods and the balance of payments consequences of free trade for developing economies. The empirical evidence of trends and cycles in terms of trade of primary commodities and the case for international commodity agreements to stabilize the price of primary commodities are documented.

We conclude that what developing countries need is 'fair trade' not free trade, and that the slogan 'trade not aid' may be misleading from an economic point of view.

Trade and growth

The growth rates of individual developing countries correlate better with their export performance than with almost any other single economic indicator, and there is a strong correlation across countries between the growth of exports and the growth of GDP, as shown in Figure 15.1, taking 124 countries over the period 2000–14. For much of the period since 1950, the export performance of developing countries lagged behind that of developed industrial countries, with their share of world trade falling, but in recent years, there has been a reversal of fortunes for some developing countries as trade barriers have come down, and with a switch in the composition of exports towards manufactured goods.

Table 15.1 shows developing countries' share of world manufacturing exports in 2013, distinguishing between resource-based (RB), low-tech (LT), medium-tech (MT) and high-tech (HT) exports. It shows how poorly low- and lower middle-income countries fare with regard to their

Figure 15.1 The relation between export growth and GDP growth across 124 countries, 2000–14

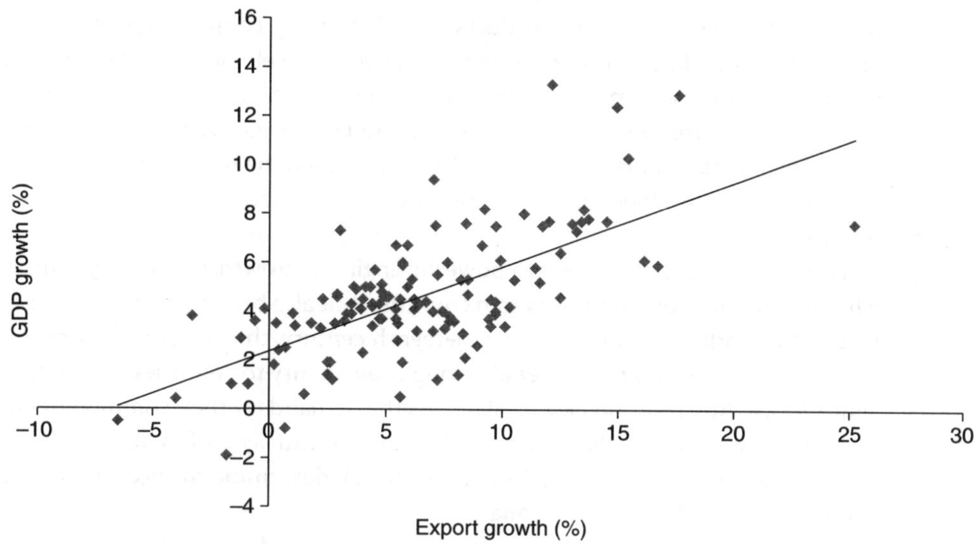

Source: Data from World Bank, 2015.

share of manufactured exports as a whole – only 6.4% of the total. The share of low-income countries in all types of manufactured exports is less than 1%. The Asian and Pacific region fares best, with 24.5% of total manufactured exports, and a 30.6% share of high-tech exports. Africa, by contrast, has a share of only 1.9% of high-tech exports. Latin America also fares relatively badly. The export trade of many poor countries, particularly in Africa, is still dominated by primary commodities.

Taking the developing countries together, however, it is not true that the world as a whole is neatly polarized into two camps: developing countries, producing and exporting *solely* primary products in exchange for manufactures from developed countries, and the developed world, producing and exporting *solely* manufactures in exchange for primary commodities from developing countries. In practice, a good deal of trade in both manufactures and primary products goes on among the developed and developing countries alike, with developed countries exporting substantial quantities of

Table 15.1 World market shares of manufactured exports by region and income level, 2013

	World market share (%)				
Region	**Total**	**RB**	**LT**	**MT**	**HT**
Asia and Pacific	24.5	15.9	38.7	18.1	30.6
Latin America	5.4	7.5	5.2	5.3	3.1
Africa	1.1	1.1	1.9	1.0	1.9
Low income	0.3	0.4	0.5	0.1	0.2
Lower middle income	6.1	8.9	8.0	3.5	6.1
Upper middle income	29.2	19.9	36.3	24.1	43.3
High income	64.4	70.8	55.2	72.3	50.4

Source: UNIDO, 2015.

primary commodities (especially temperate zone foodstuffs) and developing countries exporting a variety of manufactured goods. Developed countries, in fact, account for about 50% of the world's supply of primary products, and developing countries just over 30% of world trade in manufactures. In short, the distinction between developing and developed countries is not wholly synonymous with the distinction between primary producers and producers of manufactured goods. This needs to be borne in mind later when we discuss the terms of trade – the ratio of export to import prices. There is a distinction to be made between the terms of trade for developing and developed countries and the terms of trade for primary products and manufactured goods.

Historically, trade has acted as a powerful engine of growth, not only by contributing to a more efficient allocation of resources within countries, but also because it transmitted growth from one part of the world to another. In the nineteenth century, the demand in Europe, and in Britain in particular, for food and raw materials brought prosperity to countries such as Canada, Argentina, South Africa, Australia and New Zealand. As the demand for their commodities increased, investment in these countries also increased. Trade was mutually profitable. As Alfred Marshall (1890) wrote in the nineteenth century: '**the causes which determine the economic progress of nations belong to the study of international trade**'.

Not all countries benefited equally, however, and today the situation is somewhat different. Most world trade takes place in industrial commodities, in which many poor developing countries find it difficult to compete, and the demand for developing countries' traditional exports grows slowly relative to the demand for industrial goods. Except for spasmodic commodity booms, trade does not seem to work to the equal advantage of both sets of countries.

Three distinct factors have slowed the growth of developing countries' traditional exports:

1. The pattern of demand has shifted to types of manufactured goods with a relatively low import content of primary commodities.
2. Technological change has led to the development of synthetic substitutes for raw materials.
3. Developed countries have pursued protectionist policies that have retarded the growth of their imports of primary commodities and low value-added manufactured goods from developing countries, particularly textiles.

In view of these trading developments, and the emergence of a foreign exchange gap as a constraint on growth in developing countries, there has been a rethinking by some economists in recent years about the basis on which the gains from trade should be evaluated. The slow growth and balance of payments difficulties of developing countries has led to a shift of emphasis from viewing the effects of trade solely from the traditional classical standpoint of efficient resource allocation to viewing the impact of trade on growth and foreign exchange earnings. It is balance of payments difficulties, necessitating foreign borrowing if growth is to be sustained, that have led to the cry in recent years of **trade, not aid**. The relevance of this slogan is examined later in this chapter. The problem facing developing countries is not so much *whether* to trade but *in what commodities* to trade, and to ensure that the terms on which they trade with developed countries are favourable. There is no dispute that there are static and dynamic gains from trade. The issue is whether the overall gains would be greater, and the distribution of gains between countries fairer, if the pattern of trade were different from its present structure, and if developed countries modified their trading policies towards the developing world.

So what should developing countries do? The answer would appear to be structural change in favour of the production and export of manufactured goods, which have more favourable demand characteristics in world markets, in particular, a higher income elasticity of demand.

These dynamic considerations and the need for diversification out of primary products do not diminish the case for international specialization. What is involved is a recognition of the distinction between **natural comparative advantage** (the classical, static basis for trade) and **acquired comparative advantage**, and whether developing countries can acquire new comparative advantage on the basis of free trade. If not, what form of protection would be welfare-enhancing? Before considering these controversial and highly topical issues, let us first establish more firmly the static and dynamic gains from trade that are stressed by traditional theory.

The gains from trade

The benefits from trade in traditional trade theory are measured by the increase in the value of output and real income from domestic resources that international specialization and trade permit. This is quite distinct from the balance of payments' effects of trade. The resource gains from trade can be divided into static and dynamic gains:

- **Static gains** accrue from international specialization according to the doctrine of comparative advantage.
- **Dynamic gains** result from the impact of trade on production possibilities at large. Economies of scale, foreign investment and the transmission of technical knowledge are examples of dynamic gains.

In addition, trade can provide a **vent for surplus** commodities, which brings otherwise unemployed resources into employment. It also enables countries to purchase goods from abroad, which can be important for two reasons: first, if there are no domestic substitutes, the ability to import can relieve domestic bottlenecks in production, and, second, imports may simply be more productive than domestic resources.

The static gains from trade

Ricardo

The static gains from trade are based on the **law of comparative advantage**, first outlined by David Ricardo (1772–1823), English classical economist, in his *Principles of Political Economy and Taxation* (1817). What Ricardo showed in his remarkable theorem is that even though a country may have an absolute productivity (cost) advantage in the production of *every* good, it will still pay a country to specialize in those commodities in which it has a *comparative* advantage – that is, in those commodities in which *relative* labour productivity is the highest or for which the *opportunity cost* of production is lowest. Ricardo is not explicit about what determines relative differences in productivity and costs, but, clearly, resource endowments will be the major determinants: natural resources, labour and human capital and the level of technology.

To illustrate the gains from trade, according to the law of comparative advantage, Ricardo used the example of England and Portugal, both with the capacity to produce cloth and wine, but with England having a comparative advantage in cloth and Portugal in wine. Suppose, for example, with its given resources, England can produce 10,000 yards of cloth or 2,000 bottles of wine. The opportunity cost ratio of cloth to wine is 10:2. Portugal, on the other hand, with its resources can produce 10,000 yards of cloth and 8,000 bottles of wine. The opportunity cost ratio is 10:8. England has to sacrifice 5 yards of cloth to produce one bottle of wine, whereas Portugal only has to sacrifice 1.25 yards of cloth. Clearly, the opportunity cost of producing wine in Portugal is less than in England. However, England has to sacrifice one-fifth of a bottle of wine to produce 1 yard of cloth, whereas Portugal has to sacrifice four-fifths of a bottle of wine. The opportunity cost of producing cloth in England is lower.

What we can now show is that if there is an international rate of exchange between England and Portugal, which is between the two domestic rates of exchange of 10:2 and 10:8, both countries can benefit by specializing in what they are best at producing in an opportunity cost sense, and exchanging goods at a more favourable rate of transformation internationally than domestically. Consider Figure 15.2. The solid linear lines show the production possibility curves (or the marginal rate of transformation between the two goods) in the two countries: 10,000 yards of cloth and 2,000 bottles of wine in England, and 10,000 yards of cloth and 8,000 bottles of wine in Portugal. Before trade, each country produces combinations of cloth and wine that give the maximum utility represented by indifference curve I. The two countries produce at a and b, respectively, where the slope of the production possibility curve is tangential to the slope of the indifference curve. Now assume that with the opening of trade, there is an international price ratio of 10:5, shown by the broken line. England, if it specializes in cloth, can now exchange cloth for wine more favourably, and likewise Portugal can exchange wine for cloth more favourably. For example, in trading 5,000 yards of cloth, England can now consume 2,500 bottles of wine instead of 1,000, while Portugal, trading 4,000 bottles of wine, can now consume 8,000 yards of cloth instead of 5,000. Both countries move to higher levels of welfare at point c on indifference curve II. As a result of the international division of labour, world production increases (in this example, wine production increases from 5,000 to 8,000 bottles and cloth production stays the same) and world welfare increases.

Ricardo's theorem is a powerful one, and has been extremely influential because it lies at the heart of the free trade doctrine that countries will always benefit if they liberalize trade. There are four important caveats, however, that need to be remembered in discussing the merits of free trade:

1. There is nothing in the comparative cost doctrine that ensures equality in the distribution of the gains from trade. This depends on where the international price ratio lies between the two opportunity cost ratios. One country may lose absolutely if a decline in its terms of trade (the ratio of its export price to its import price) offsets the efficiency resource gain from specialization. This is the concept of **immiserizing growth,** first proposed by Jagdish Bhagwati (1958).
2. The gains from trade are 'once and for all'. They do not recur. Once the process of resource reallocation through trade has taken place, there are no further gains. The law of comparative advantage, therefore, has nothing to say about the growth effects of trade. **The law is static**. The growth effects of trade will depend on the types of goods countries specialize in – whether they are subject to increasing or diminishing returns, and whether they are income elastic or inelastic in demand.
3. The law of comparative advantage assumes continuous full employment, namely, that those thrown out of work in one industry (as a result of countries specializing) can find work in others. This may not be so easy for countries specializing in the production of land-based activities subject to diminishing returns where there is a limit to employment set by the point where the diminishing marginal product of labour equals the wage. If there is not continuous full employment, the real resource gains from specialization and trade may be offset by the real resource (and welfare) losses from unemployment.

Figure 15.2 Gains from trade

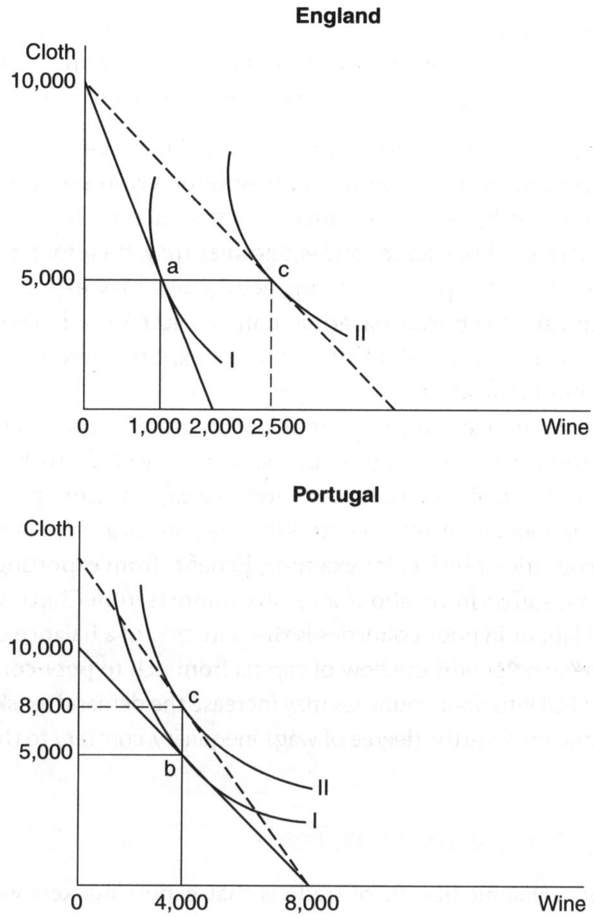

4. There is nothing in the doctrine of comparative advantage that guarantees balanced trade. Ricardo was fully aware of this, and relied on the gold standard mechanism to produce an equilibrium – with the relative price of goods rising in the surplus countries with gold inflows and falling in the deficit countries with gold outflows, with no income adjustment. But the international gold standard never worked this way, and today there is no sure mechanism that guarantees trade equilibrium. If a particular pattern of trade specialization leads to payments deficits, and the economy has to be contracted to save imports and foreign exchange, the resulting unemployment may again offset the static resource gains.

The Heckscher–Ohlin theorem

In the early twentieth century, Ricardo's doctrine of comparative advantage was developed by Eli Heckscher (1919) and Bertil Ohlin (1933), two Swedish economists who attribute differences in labour productivity and relative costs of production specifically to differences in relative factor endowments – that is, to differences in the amount of capital per unit of labour. The Heckscher–Ohlin (H–O) theorem states that poor countries with an abundance of labour and scarce capital should find it relatively cheaper to produce and export labour-intensive goods, while rich countries with more capital and a relative shortage of labour should find it cheaper to produce and export capital-intensive goods. This should not only produce welfare gains from trade, but also greater wage equality in poor countries because the demand for unskilled labour will rise relative to skilled labour. The wage gap between poor and rich countries should also narrow. As with Ricardo's theorem, however, there are a number of caveats to be made:

- Abundant labour in poor countries is not necessarily cheap labour in an economic sense, if the productivity of labour is correspondingly lower. It is the **efficiency wage** (the money wage divided by labour productivity) that determines the combination of factors used in production. Labour-abundant economies may, therefore, still export relatively capital-intensive goods and capital-abundant economies may export relatively labour-intensive goods (the so-called **Leontief paradox**, named after Wassily Leontief, 1953, who first discovered that contrary to the H–O theorem, US exports were relatively labour-intensive compared with import substitutes).
- The theorem takes only two groups of countries – poor developing countries and rich developed countries – but poor countries not only trade with rich countries but also with each other. As the demand for labour-intensive exports from poor countries rises in rich countries, wages in poor countries may rise, but may also fall as a result of competitive imports from other poor countries. Mexico, for example, benefits from exporting labour-intensive products to the USA, but suffers from labour-intensive imports from China. What happens to the wages of unskilled labour in poor countries is the outcome of a balance of forces.
- The theorem ignores the flow of capital from rich to poor countries as trade takes place. The inflow of FDI into poor countries may increase the demand for skilled labour relative to unskilled labour, and increase the degree of wage inequality, contrary to the predictions of the H–O theorem.

The dynamic gains from trade

The major dynamic benefit of trade is that export markets widen the total market for a country's producers, thereby allowing greater specialization, or division of labour. Specialization, in turn, stimulates capital accumulation and 'learning by doing'. Historically, Adam Smith recognized this benefit of trade in his famous book *An Inquiry into the Nature and Causes of The Wealth of Nations* (1776), as did John Stuart Mill in his *Principles of Political Economy* (1848), in which he wrote: 'a country which produces for a larger market than its own can introduce a more extended division of labour, can make greater use of machinery, and is more likely to make inventions and improvements in the process of production'. Mill also stressed the role of trade as a conduit for the international dissemination of ideas and technology through a number of mechanisms: first, a domestic buyer of an imported good may imitate the production technique, or adapt the new technique if it is patented, and second, there may be a direct exchange of ideas for further varieties of goods that increase welfare. 'New' growth theory (see Chapter 4), which incorporates trade, as pioneered by Grossman and Helpman (1991a, 1991b), encapsulates many of these original ideas of Mill.

Mill also recognized that the growth effects of trade depend on what a country specializes in: natural resource activities or manufacturing industries. It is the production of industrial goods, particularly research-intensive goods, that produces technical dynamism and rapid growth. Stiglitz (2006) makes the same enduring point:

> a country whose static comparative advantage lies in, say, agriculture, risks stagnation ... with limited growth prospects; ... the industrial sector is almost everywhere the source of

> innovation, [and] many of these advances spill over into the rest of the economy as do the benefits from the development of institutions, like financial markets, that accompany the growth of an industrial sector.

As alluded to above, there is a close association between the size of markets and the accumulation of capital. The larger the market, the easier capital accumulation becomes. For a small country with no trade, there is very little scope for large-scale investment in advanced capital equipment. Trade offers some escape, but a minimum size of domestic market in the first place is important to make trade viable. In this respect, larger countries such as China and India are in a more favourable position than smaller countries such as Fiji, Mauritius or the Gambia. India and China's large populations offer the basis for the establishment of capital goods industries and the production of manufactured goods, since production can take place on an economic basis before trade. The smaller country may need substantial protection for a commodity before it can be produced economically and compete in world markets. At least 60 countries classified as 'developing' have populations below 15 million. In terms of Figure 15.2 above, the dynamic benefits of trade are represented by an outward shift of the production possibility curves of both countries, leading to a higher level of community welfare.

Dynamic gains from trade are at the heart of **new trade theory** pioneered by Paul Krugman (1979, 1980, 1986), with its emphasis on increasing returns and positive externalities associated with the geographic concentration of production for trade (also providing an argument for strategic protection).

Paul Krugman

Born 1953, New York, USA. Taught at the Universities of Yale, the Massachusetts Institute of Technology, and California (Berkeley), and now Professor of Economics at Princeton University. Made many important contributions to economics; best known for his pioneering work on the role of increasing returns in explaining trade patterns (new trade theory) and the spatial concentration of industrial activities (new economic geography). Also an influential *New York Times* columnist. Awarded the Nobel Prize for Economics in 2008.

Trade as a vent for surplus

Another important potential gain from trade is the provision of an outlet for a country's surplus production, which would otherwise go unsold and represent a waste of resources. This is the so-called 'vent for surplus' gain from trade, first articulated by Adam Smith in his *An Inquiry into the Nature and Causes of Wealth of Nations* (1776). He writes:

> when the produce of any particular branch of industry exceeds what the demand of the country requires, the surplus must be sent abroad and exchanged for something for which there is a demand at home. Without such exportation a part of the productive labour of the country

> must cease, and the value of its annual produce diminish ... between whatever places foreign trade is carried on, they all of them derive two distinct benefits from it. It carries the surplus part of the product of their land and labour for which there is no demand among them, and brings back in return something else, which may satisfy part of their wants and increase their enjoyment.

In Figure 15.2 above, this vent for surplus argument is represented by a movement from a point inside the production possibility frontier to a point on the frontier, which represents a higher level of welfare. The gain implies that the 'surplus' export resources have no alternative uses and cannot be switched to domestic use. This is not an unreasonable assumption in many natural resource-rich countries. Oil wells, mines and fishing grounds, for example, have no alternative uses, and the market for their products would soon become saturated if demand was confined to domestic consumption alone. The vent for surplus theory is a much more plausible explanation for the start of trade than the comparative cost doctrine of specialization.

Theory of customs unions and free trade areas

Because of the various gains to be had from trade, **regional trade agreements (RTAs)** have become fashionable in recent years, in the form of **customs unions** and **free trade areas.** The World Trade Organization (WTO) lists over 100 that have been established or modified since 1948. The major ones are: the EU; NAFTA (the North American Free Trade Agreement); MERCOSUR (Southern Common Market), comprising Argentina, Brazil, Paraguay, Uruguay and Venezuela; APEC (Asia-Pacific Economic Cooperation); ASEAN (Association of Southeast Asian Nations); and SACU (Southern African Customs Union), comprising Botswana, Lesotho, Namibia, South Africa and Swaziland.

The essence of a customs union is that it frees trade between members and imposes a *common* external tariff (CET) on imported goods from the rest of the world. In a free trade area (FTA), by contrast, barriers to trade are brought down within the area, but there is no CET. Countries are free to impose their own specific tariffs on goods from outside the area, although often subject to agreement over the proportion of goods that must be purchased from within the area. Customs unions therefore *create* trade, but also *divert* it from lower cost suppliers outside the union. The interesting question is always whether the benefits of trade creation exceed the costs of trade diversion. FTAs also create trade, but the extent of trade diversion is likely to be much less, with the presumption that on narrow economic grounds, at least, FTAs are superior. For the same reason, customs unions are likely to be inferior to a policy of unilateral tariff reductions, and therefore need to be justified on other economic or non-economic grounds.

Before we look at the empirical evidence on these matters, however, let us consider theoretically the gains and losses of customs unions. The analysis makes the same assumptions as orthodox trade theory: perfect competition, prices reflect opportunity cost, factors of production are immobile between countries, trade is balanced (i.e. no balance of payments problems), and the full employment of resources:

- The **trade creation** effect of a union has two parts: first, a production effect, which consists of the substitution of cheaper 'foreign' goods for domestic goods from within the union, and second, a consumption effect – the gain in consumer surplus from cheaper goods.
- The **trade diversion** effect also has two parts: first, the substitution of higher priced goods from within the union for goods outside the union, and second, the loss of consumer surplus that this entails.

Figure 15.3 Gains and losses within a customs union

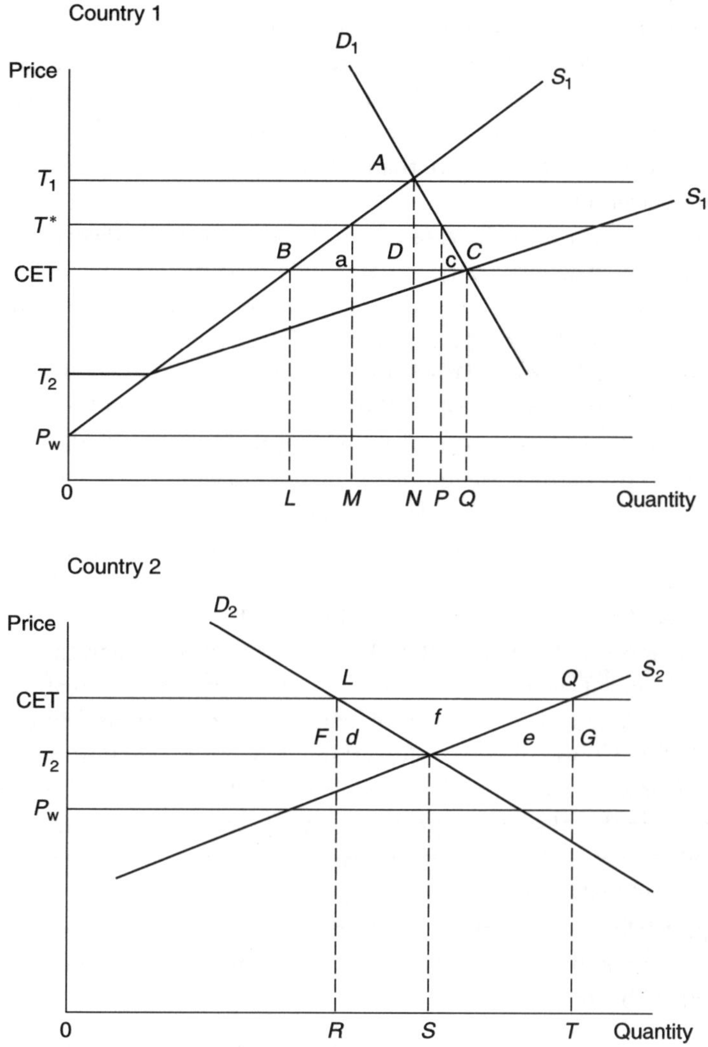

The gains and losses for two partner countries within the union are illustrated in Figure 15.3. To simplify the analysis, scale economies and terms of trade effects are ignored. The analysis that follows relies heavily on Robson (1988).

In Figure 15.3, D_1 and D_2 are the demand curves for a good in the two countries; S_1 and S_2 are the domestic supply curves; $S_1 + M_1$ is the supply curve in country 1 consisting of the domestic supply curve and the supply of the good from the partner country, which is assumed to enter duty free; and P_w is the world price. Now, suppose that before the union of the two countries, a tariff of P_wT_1 was imposed in country 1 and P_wT_2 in country 2. In this case, it can be seen that demand equals supply in both markets; there are no imports from the rest of the world, and we can focus first on the process of trade creation. A customs union is now formed with a CET that balances supply and demand of the two partners (equal to P_wCET). The CET is lower than OT_1 in country 1 and higher than OT_2 in country 2. This has consumption and production effects in the two countries.

In country 1, domestic consumption increases from *N* to *Q*, and domestic production decreases from *N* to *L*. In country 2, domestic production increases from *S* to *T*; domestic consumption decreases from *S* to *R*, and the difference between supply and demand is exported to country 1. For country 1, there has been a cost saving equal to the area *ABD*, and an increase in consumer surplus equal to the area *ADC*. The total gain of trade creation is equal to *ABD* + *ADC*. In country 2, there has been a loss of consumer surplus equal to area *d* and an increased production cost equal to area *e*, but this is more than offset by the increased export revenue of *LFGQ*, so country 2 is also better off.

Now let us consider the case where there is also trade diversion from the rest of the world. Suppose that, in country 1, the initial tariff level was lower than P_wT_1 – say, P_wT^*, so that demand exceeded supply and the excess demand was filled by imports from the rest of the world, *MP*, at price P_w. If a CET was now introduced of P_wCET, demand would increase from *P* to *Q* with an increase in consumer surplus of area *c*. Production would fall from *M* to *L* with a reduction in production cost equal to area *a*. There would be trade creation gains equal to *a* + *c*, but now there is also trade diversion. Imports, previously from outside the union, would now come from the higher cost partner. *MP* imports from abroad would be replaced at the increased cost of *MP* + P_wCET. This is the cost of trade diversion.

In evaluating the net gains from a customs union, trade creation needs to be compared with trade diversion. In general, trade creation is likely to predominate over trade diversion, the larger the union and the lower the CET. The larger the union, the greater the scope for trade creation, and the lower the CET, the less trade diversion there is likely to be. It is possible, however, even if the union as a whole is, on balance, trade-creating, that at least one country may lose. Likewise, it is possible for at least one country to gain even if the union as a whole is, on balance, trade-diverting. Everything depends on circumstances. A customs union can be devised, however, which raises the welfare of all members. This requires, first, that the union's CET is set so that the level of post-union trade with the rest of the world does not fall below its pre-union level, and, second, that lump sum compensatory taxes and transfers are imposed to offset individual country losses.

Apart from trade creation and trade diversion, customs unions may have other important effects associated with the enlargement of the market, which are neglected by the static analysis presented above:

1. The larger market may generate economies of scale. If there are economies of scale, the supply curves in Figure 15.3 above will slope downwards, and the CET can be lower than the original tariff in *both* partner countries. There will be a normal trade creation effect and a cost saving in both countries.
2. Integration is likely to promote increased competition, which is likely to favourably affect prices and costs, and the growth of output.
3. The widening of markets within a customs union is likely to attract international investment. Producers will prefer to produce within the union rather than face a CET from outside.
4. If the world supply of output is not infinitely elastic, there are terms of trade effects to consider. Specifically, if there is trade diversion, the world price of the good will fall, moving the terms of trade in favour of the customs union.

This terms of trade effect represents a welfare gain, which may partly offset the welfare loss of trade diversion. It was mentioned earlier, however, that because customs unions impose a CET, they are likely to be inferior, in terms of welfare improvement, to a policy of *unilateral* tariff reductions (continuing to make the standard assumptions, of course, of trade balance and full employment). We can now illustrate this using Figure 15.3 above. Suppose country 1 has an initial tariff level of $P_w T^*$. It enters a customs union with country 2 with a common external tariff CET, and trade creation takes place equal to $a + c$ (as before). Country 1 could also, however, reduce its tariff to $P_w T^*$ on a non-discriminatory basis. It would enjoy the same trade creation gains, but now would be able to obtain imports cheaper from the rest of the world. This means an additional gain equal to the difference between the total expenditure on imports from the union compared with the rest of the world.

At a simple level, the conclusion from this theoretical analysis is that the formation of customs unions represents a movement towards free trade, but even freer trade (i.e. no trade diversion) is better. Venables (2003) has considered theoretically which countries are likely to be winners and losers from RTAs (regional trade agreements). Outcomes depend on the comparative advantage of members relative to each other and relative to the rest of the world. In general, countries with 'extreme' comparative advantage in particular products do worse than those with comparative advantage between partners and the rest of the world. Integration between low-income countries tends to lead to divergence of per capita incomes, while agreements between high-income countries cause convergence. Venables argues that low-income countries would be better served by integration with high-income countries than other low-income countries. For poor countries, north-south agreements would be better than south-south agreements. The empirical evidence seems to bear this out.

The general experience of RTAs in developing countries has been disappointing because they have been inward-looking and protectionist, with trade diversion exceeding trade creation. Typically, the existing ratio of trade to GDP has been high in member countries, and the ratio of trade with the rest of the world has also been high, so that the scope for trade creation has been minimal and the potential for trade diversion has been great. In ECOWAS (Economic Community of West African States), founded in 1975, the amount of interregional trade is still less than 15% of total exports. Forouton (1993) concludes his study of regional integration in sub-Saharan Africa by saying:

> the structural characteristics of the SSA [sub-Saharan Africa] economies, the pursuit of import-substitution policies, and the very uneven distribution of costs and benefits of integration arising from economic differences among the partner countries, have thus far prevented any meaningful trade integration in SSA.

Of the various groupings in sub-Saharan Africa, only SACU (formed in 1910) has achieved any noticeable degree of integration in the market for goods. Otherwise, intragroup trade has remained limited. This conclusion is echoed by many of the authors' papers in Oyejide et al. (1997), which examine the experience of regional integration and trade liberalization in sub-Saharan Africa.

Research by Vamvakidis (1999) across developing countries as a whole supports this pessimistic conclusion. He takes 109 cases of participation in 18 RTAs over the period 1950–92, and regresses the growth of per capita income of countries on the growth of world income, the initial level of per capita income, education level, trade openness, plus a dummy variable if a country belongs to an RTA. The dummy variable is significantly negative. He also finds that membership of an RTA lowers the share of investment in GDP.

In related work, Vamvakidis (1998) and Arora and Vamvakidis (2005) also try to estimate the effect on a country's growth rate of the size, income and growth of neighbouring countries. They find, perhaps not surprisingly, that it pays to have neighbours that are relatively rich, open to trade and growing fast. A 1 percentage point change in the growth of a country's trading partners is associated with a 0.8 percentage point increase in its own domestic growth. In a customs union, the countries swim or sink together.

Free trade enthusiasm in the modern era

Despite the arguments for free trade laid down by classical economic theory, it was never seriously practised by countries (except by Britain post-1850) until after the Second World War (see Chang, 2002, 2005, 2007; Reinert, 2007), with the establishment of the **General Agreement on Tariffs and Trade (GATT)** in 1947 and the general commitment by developed countries to the freeing of international trade in the wake of the protectionism and 'beggar-thy-neighbour' policies practised in the interwar depression years, 1919–39. Even so, the process of liberalization took a long time to gather momentum. Many developed countries maintained quite high tariff levels, and non-tariff barriers, until the early 1970s, and many developing countries, freed from their colonial past, adopted protection, particularly in Latin America and parts of Asia. It is only since the 1970s that both developed and developing countries have made a concerted effort to liberalize trade between themselves under various pressures from GATT (and the World Trade Organization (WTO) since 1995 – the successor to GATT), the World Bank, the IMF and other international organizations, and in view of the alleged poor economic performance of countries pursuing protection.

Overall, the liberalization of trade has led to a massive growth of world trade relative to world output. Container ships have also played their part. The first container ship was launched in 1956 and the share of countries with container ports rose rapidly to 90% within 30 years. Container ships and container ports hugely facilitate the shipment of goods and reduce the cost of handling freight. While world output (or GDP) has expanded sevenfold, the volume of world trade has grown 25 times at an annual compound rate of nearly 8% per annum. In some individual countries, notably in Southeast Asia, the growth of exports has exceeded 10% per annum, and in China, 20% per annum. The evolution of world trade as a proportion of world output is shown in Figure 15.4, rising from 25% in 1960 to over 60% today.

Figure 15.4 The share of world trade in world output, 1960–2014

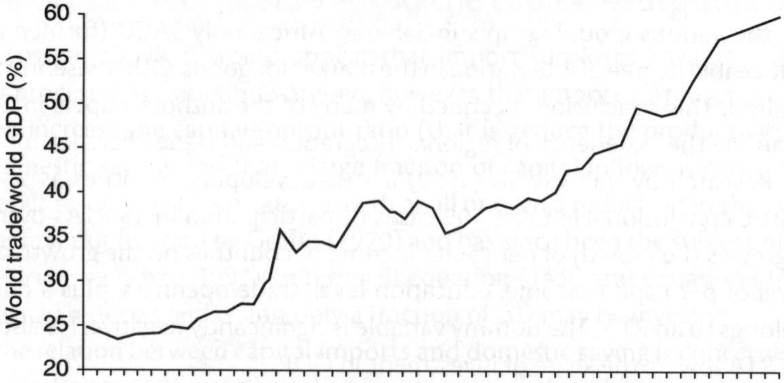

Note: Trade is measured as the sum of exports and imports of goods and services.

Source: World Bank, 2014.

Measurement and process of trade liberalization

To measure the degree and process of trade liberalization, it must be borne in mind that there are many different measures and types of protection, such as tariffs, quotas, licences, technical and environmental restrictions, and many different measures and concepts of trade liberalization and trade openness. The first thing to make clear, however, is that trade liberalization is not the same thing as trade openness. For example, a country may be very open, in the sense that it has a high ratio of trade to GDP because it has abundant natural resources that it can only export, but may operate a very illiberal trade regime, which makes trade difficult in other activities. Equally, a country with a low ratio of total trade to GDP, because it is a large country and relatively self-sufficient, may be very liberal in its trading practices.

The most common measure of trade liberalization focuses on what is happening to tariffs and non-tariff barriers (NTBs) to trade, whether trade is biased against exports in favour of import substitutes, and the general micro- and macro-environment of a country in which trade takes place, including the level of the exchange rate, whether the state has a monopoly of major exports, and monetary and fiscal conditions. Average tariff rates, export taxes, total taxes on international trade and indices of NTBs are all obvious measures of protection, but there are difficulties in using any one of these indices as a measure of trade liberalization:

1. A country may substitute one type of protection for another. For example, it may reduce NTBs, but raise tariffs to compensate, and vice versa.
2. *Nominal* tariffs on goods are not the appropriate basis for assessing the restrictive effect of a tariff structure on trade. The nominal rate does not measure how inefficient (or costly) producers can be without incurring competition and losing market share. This is measured by the protection of value-added. This is the so-called *effective rate of protection* (see below).
3. Average tariff rates are often measured in empirical work by the ratio of tariff revenues to the value of imports, but this is not a measure of the official tariff rate, but of the collected rate. In the extreme, if a very high tariff discouraged imports completely, there would be no imports, and the measured tariff rate would be zero.

It is more useful to devise measures of trade regimes that can then be ranked from illiberal to liberal, or from protectionist to liberalized, and to look at the various indices through time. One approach is to measure the extent to which the structure of protection and incentives is biased against exports. The easiest way to measure this, outlined by Krueger (1998), is by the extent to which the ratio of domestic price of import competing goods (P_{md}) to their international (world) price (P_{mw}), relative to the ratio of the domestic price of importables (P_{xd}) compared with their international price (P_{xw}), deviates from unity, that is:

$$B = \frac{p_{md}/p_{mw}}{p_{xd}/p_{xw}} \tag{15.1}$$

If we assume that $P_{mw}/P_{xw} = 1$, then if $P_{md}/P_{xd} > 1$, the trade regime is biased against exports in favour of import substitutes, and if $P_{md}/P_{xd} < 1$, the trade regime favours export promotion.

Greenaway et al. (1998), in their major study of trade liberalization and growth across 73 countries, construct a similar index to Krueger's, which also measures the relative distortion (D) of the price of exportables to importables. It is calculated as:

$$D = \frac{(1 + t)}{(1 + s)} \tag{15.2}$$

where t is the tariff on imports and s is the rate of subsidy to exports. A ratio of unity implies trade neutrality; $D > 1$ implies anti-export bias in favour of import substitution, while $D < 1$ implies an export-oriented trade strategy.

David Greenaway was very influential in the first World Bank (1987) classification of trade regimes in its *World Development Report 1987*. Four categories were identified:

1. **Strongly outward-oriented** countries, where there are very few trade or foreign exchange controls and trade and industrial policies do not discriminate between production for the home market and exports, and between purchases of domestic goods and foreign goods.
2. **Moderately outward-oriented** countries, where the overall incentive structure is moderately biased towards the production of goods for the home market rather than for export, and favours the purchase of domestic goods.
3. **Moderately inward-oriented** countries, where there is a more definite bias against exports and in favour of import substitution.
4. **Strongly inward-oriented** countries, where trade controls and incentive structures strongly favour production for the domestic market and discriminate strongly against imports.

Many investigators and international organizations devise their own measures of protection and liberalization, using multiple criteria. One is the **Sachs and Warner Openness Index**. Countries are classified as 'open' or 'closed' according to five criteria. A country is regarded as 'closed' if at least one of the following criteria is satisfied: an average tariff rate higher than 40%; non-tariff barriers covering more than 40% of imports; a socialist economic system; a state monopoly of major exports; or a black market exchange rate premium in excess of 20% (Sachs and Warner, 1995). The criteria are arbitrary, of course, but nonetheless many investigators have used this index to classify countries, and to measure the timing of liberalization (although, as we said above, openness and liberalization are not the same).

Another measure is the **Index of Economic Freedom** published since 1995 by the Heritage Foundation in Washington, which considers a broad array of institutional factors, one of which is trade policies. A trade policy score of 1–5 is given to countries based on their average tariff rate, the extent of non-tariff barriers, and the degree of corruption in the customs service. Five broad levels of protection are distinguished: very low (free), low, moderate, high, and very high (repressed). Countries can be classified according to category, and their economic performance analysed.

The process of trade liberalization can take many forms, but as Michaely et al. (1991) say in their massive volume of case studies of trade liberalization in developing countries: 'very little is known about essential attributes of a change from one [trade] regime to another; of a move away from a distorted trade policy regime towards a more neutral one'. On the other hand, we know that the issues of timing, phasing and sequencing are likely to be important in the design and implementation of a successful trade liberalization policy (see Rodrik, 1996, 2001).

Often the first stage of liberalization is the dismantling of non-tariff barriers to trade in the form of quotas and licences, not necessarily the reduction of tariffs. In fact, tariffs often rise to compensate for the removal of quantitative restrictions on imports. This makes protection more transparent and reduces rent-seeking behaviour. When protection is removed from an industry, production is likely to decline and unemployment rise. Capital is specific and will be left unutilized, and labour may not be mobile enough to be employed in other activities. This is a serious worry and can undermine the static welfare gains from trade liberalization. It is certainly an argument against liberalizing imports too rapidly. As the relative prices of factors of production and goods change, there are also likely to be considerable redistribution effects, which need taking account of in the process of liberalization (see below).

The other big worry is the effect of trade liberalization on the balance of payments. If imports rise faster than exports, balance of payments difficulties may arise, which have negative growth consequences. This has implications for the sequencing of trade liberalization. Imports should not be liberalized before the export sector has had time to adjust or respond in order for foreign exchange to be available to meet the higher import bill. In terms of policy, it means that anti-export bias needs removing, or export subsidies given, before serious import liberalization takes place (as was the case in Japan and South Korea, for example). East Asia provides an interesting case study of how countries should proceed, where the process of trade liberalization was gradual and export-oriented, in contrast to many Latin American countries, where the process of liberalization was sudden and no attention was paid to the sequencing.

Another message from the experience of liberalization is that liberalization is much more likely to be successful in an environment of internal and external stability. It is particularly important not to allow the exchange rate to appreciate, which otherwise worsens the balance between export and import growth. This means that countries need to retain control of the capital account of the balance of payments, and not to liberalize capital flows at the same time as trade. Unfortunately, many Latin American countries, such as Mexico, Argentina and Peru, when they liberalized in the 1980s and early 1990s, allowed their exchange rate to appreciate, which damaged the trade balance and impacted negatively on growth.

In short, if trade liberalization is to be successful in promoting economic development, it needs to avoid adjustment costs as a result of the poor timing and sequencing of liberalization, and it needs to avoid inegalitarian distributional consequences. See Case example 15.1 for a general assessment of trade liberalization in eight countries.

Case example 15.1

Trade liberalization in eight countries

After decades of highly interventionist trade regimes, Bangladesh, Brazil, Bulgaria, India, Jamaica, Malawi, Philippines and Zambia initiated major trade reforms in the 1980s and 1990s. There was a considerable reduction in the average tariff rates and their dispersion, and a number of quantitative restrictions on imports were eliminated or converted into their tariff equivalents. There was also the elimination of export/import licences.

What were the results? All told, it is difficult to gauge the overall legacy of the reforms. No doubt the reforms moved in the right direction, but except for India and Brazil, there was significant and painful overshooting. It would have been wiser and less costly to move gradually. Most of the countries had a shallow industrial base at the beginning of the reforms. The supply response has been extremely poor in Malawi and Zambia in particular, while neglect of the social implications in the planning of the adjustment process has had serious social welfare consequences. Government efforts to deal with economic dislocation and job losses have been at best reactive and marginal. Threatened workers and communities have had virtually no policy options other than to plea for protection after they are already in serious trouble. Even in countries that opted for a more gradual pace of liberalization, reforms have been so deep and extensive that it is no longer possible to envisage a reversal. Unemployment can no longer be addressed through a return to old-style protectionism, even if, in many cases, the economy has not yet adjusted to its full potential because of inflexible markets. In Bangladesh, Jamaica and the Philippines, emigration first provided labour markets with safety valves, and, subsequently, remittances provided financial flows for offsetting trade deficits and balance of payments disequilibria. New behind-the-border practices, be they related to competition or the labour markets, must now come into play.

Source: Tussie and Aggio, 2005.

Models of export-led growth

The impact of trade liberalization on economic performance works mainly through improving the efficiency of resource allocation, allowing greater scope for specialization, and stimulating exports, which have powerful effects on supply and demand within an economy. Before examining the empirical evidence on the relation between trade liberalization, trade performance and the economic growth of countries, it is first important to understand why exports are so crucial for economic development.

There are three main models of export-led growth:

- The neoclassical supply-side model
- The balance of payments constrained growth model
- The virtuous circle model.

The first is the orthodox model, which fits neatly into mainstream neoclassical growth theory. The latter two models are rarely articulated in the trade and growth literature, and yet may be of greater importance for understanding growth rate differences in open developing economies, especially if most developing countries are constrained in their economic performance by a shortage of foreign exchange. Moreover, orthodox growth and trade theory predicts the convergence of per capita incomes across countries (see Chapter 4), which is at variance with what we observe in the real world. What appears to happen in practice is that once a country gains an advantage through the capture of export markets, it tends to sustain that advantage through the operation of various cumulative forces, which generate 'virtuous circles' of success for favoured countries (and regions), and 'vicious circles' of slow growth and underemployment for those countries that are left behind (see Chapter 10). When studies are conducted of the relation between exports and growth, either across countries or over time, it is not always clear whether the relation found is picking up supply-side factors, demand-side influences, cumulative forces interacting with each other, or a combination of all three.

The neoclassical supply-side model

The neoclassical supply-side model of the relation between exports and growth assumes that the export sector, because of its exposure to foreign competition, confers externalities on the non-export sector, and also that the export sector has a higher level of productivity than the non-export sector. Thus, the share of exports in GDP and the growth of exports matter for overall growth performance. Feder (1983) was the first to provide a formal model of this type to explain the relation between export growth and output growth. The output of the export sector is assumed to be a function of labour and capital in the sector; the output of the non-export sector is assumed to be a function of labour, capital and the output of the export sector (to capture externalities); and the ratio of respective marginal factor productivities in the two sectors is assumed to deviate from unity by a factor δ. These assumptions produce an augmented neoclassical growth equation of the form:

$$G = a(I/Y) + b(dL/L) + [\delta/(1 + \delta) + F_x](X/Y)(dX/X) \tag{15.3}$$

where I/Y is the investment ratio; dL/L is the growth of the labour force; dX/X is the growth of exports; X/Y is the share of exports in GDP; $\delta/(1 + \delta)$ is the differential productivity effect; and F_x is the externality effect. Feder originally tested the model by taking a cross-section of 19 semi-industrialized countries and a larger sample of 31 countries over the period 1964–73. First, he tested the model without export growth, and then with the growth of exports included. The inclusion of dX/X considerably improves the explanatory power of the equation, and the effect of export growth is always statistically significant. The coefficient on export growth, however, is an amalgam of an externality effect and a productivity differential effect. To decompose the two, equation (15.3) can be fitted excluding the export share term (X/Y), which then isolates the externality effect. The difference between the total effect of export growth and the externality effect is the productivity differential effect. When this is done, Feder (1983) found substantial differences in productivity between the export and non-export sectors and also evidence of externalities. The results should not surprise. The export sector is likely to be more 'modern' and capital-intensive than the non-export sector, which, to a large extent, consists of low productivity agriculture and petty service activities. The externalities conferred are part of the dynamic gains from trade discussed at the beginning of the chapter, associated with the transmission and diffusion of new ideas from abroad relating to production techniques and efficient management practices.

The Feder (1983) model is a pure supply-side argument, which has plausibility, but there are other (non-neoclassical) supply-side arguments, and also demand-side considerations, which would also be consistent with finding export growth and GDP growth positively correlated over the long term. From the supply side, export growth may raise output growth through externalities, but also faster export growth permits faster import growth. If countries are short of foreign exchange, and domestic and foreign resources are not fully substitutable, more imports permit a fuller use of domestic resources. In particular, more foreign exchange allows the greater import of capital goods, which may not be produced domestically.

The balance of payments constrained growth model

The major weakness of the orthodox supply-side model of the role of exports is that it doesn't go far enough; it neglects the importance of demand for the growth of output. All components of domestic demand – consumption, investment, government expenditure and exports themselves – have an import content that must be paid for. Exports are unique in this respect, because exports are the only component of demand that provide the foreign exchange to pay for the other components of demand, which otherwise would be constrained. It is important to stress this, because this insight lies at the heart of demand-oriented theories of growth and development in an open economy.

Most factors of production in the growth and development process are *endogenous* to demand and not exogenously determined as neoclassical growth theory assumes. Capital is a produced means of production and is as much a consequence of the growth of output as its cause. The demand for labour is a derived demand from output. Labour input responds to demand in a variety of ways through reductions in unemployment; increases in labour force participation; increases in hours worked; shifts of labour from low productivity to high productivity sectors; and, in the last resort, through international migration. In labour surplus economies, such as most developing countries, it stretches credulity to assume an exogenously given supply of labour that determines output in a *causal* sense. Productivity growth is also largely endogenous to output growth, working through induced capital accumulation, embodied technical progress, and static and dynamic returns to scale. To understand growth rate differences between countries, it is necessary to understand why demand growth differs between countries, and the constraints on demand that exist within countries.

In most developing countries, the major constraint on the growth of demand is the current account of the balance of payments and the shortage of foreign exchange. Export growth relaxes a balance of payments constraint on demand and allows all other components of demand (consumption, investment and government expenditure) to grow faster without running into balance of payments difficulties. This is the simplest of all explanations of the relationship between export growth and output growth. The fact is that, in the long run, no country can grow faster than that rate consistent with balance of payments equilibrium on current account, unless it can finance ever-growing deficits, which, in general, it cannot. Ratios of payments deficit to GDP of more than 2–3% start to make the international financial markets nervous (witness the experience of Mexico, Brazil and the countries of East Asia in recent years), and *all* borrowing *eventually* has to be repaid. We will show in Chapter 16 that if relative price (or exchange rate) changes do not act as an efficient balance of payments adjustment mechanism, the rate of growth of output of a country (g) can be approximated by the simple formula:

$$g = x/\pi \qquad (15.4)$$

where x is the growth of export volume (determined by the growth of 'world' income and the income elasticity of demand for exports) and π is the income elasticity of demand for imports. The correlation between g and x is immediately apparent.

The virtuous circle model of export-led growth

Finally, it needs to be recognized that exports and growth may be interrelated in a cumulative process. This raises the question of causality but, more important, such models provide an explanation of why growth and development through trade tends to be concentrated in particular areas of the world, while other regions and countries have been left behind. These models provide a challenge to orthodox growth theory and trade theory, which predict the long-run convergence of living standards across the world. In neoclassical growth theory, capital is assumed to be subject to diminishing returns so that rich countries should grow slower than poor countries for the same amount of investment undertaken (see Chapter 4). Neoclassical trade theory predicts convergence through the assumption of factor price equalization. The empirical evidence is at odds with the theory: there is no evidence that living standards across the world are converging. A simple cumulative model, driven by exports as the major component of autonomous demand, was outlined in Chapter 10. Output growth is a function of export growth; export growth is a function of price competitiveness and foreign income growth; price competitiveness is a function of wage growth and productivity growth; and productivity growth is a function of output growth – the so-called Verdoorn law working through static and dynamic returns to scale, including learning by doing. It is this induced productivity growth that makes the model 'circular and cumulative', since if fast output growth (caused by export growth) induces faster productivity growth, this makes goods more competitive and therefore induces faster export growth. The Verdoorn relation not only makes the model 'circular and cumulative', but also gives rise to the possibility that once an economy obtains a growth advantage, it will tend to keep it. Suppose, for example, that an economy obtains an advantage in the production of goods with a high income elasticity of demand in world markets, such as high-tech goods, which raises its growth rate above other countries. Through the Verdoorn effect, productivity growth will be higher and the economy will retain its competitive advantage in these goods, making it difficult, without protection or exceptional industrial enterprise, to establish the same commodities. In such a cumulative model, it is the difference between the income elasticity characteristics of exports (and imports, if balance of payments equilibrium is a requirement, as argued earlier) that is the essence of divergence between industrial and agricultural economies, or between 'centre' and 'periphery'. This simple model can go a long way in explaining differences in the level of development between countries and the forces that perpetuate divergences in the world economy. The forces are *structural*, relating to the production and demand characteristics of the goods produced and traded.

What you export matters

The argument that what a country exports matters for its growth performance can be formally tested using a procedure developed by Hausmann et al. (2007). First, they measure what is called the 'productivity' (PRODY) of each commodity (i) exported to see what country income level the good is associated with. Second, they calculate an EXPY for each country, which is the weighted sum of all the PRODYs that the country exports. If a country is specializing in high-income goods, it will have a high EXPY, and if it is specializing in low-income goods the EXPY will be low. Cross-country analysis shows a high correlation between a country's EXPY and its growth and export performance.

The calculation of PRODY is:

$$\text{PRODY}_i = \sum_j \left(\frac{(x_{ij}/X_j)}{\sum_j (x_{ij}/X_j)} \right) Y_j$$

where x_{ij} is the export of commodity i from country j, X_j is the country's total exports, x_{ij}/X_j represents a country's specialization in commodity *i*, $\sum_j (x_{ij}/X_j)$ is the share of commodity *i* in total world exports, and Y_j is the income per capita of each country exporting the good *i*. PRODY_i will be low if low-income countries specialize in that good, and high if high-income countries specialize in that good.

The calculation of EXPY is:

$$\text{EXPY}_j = \sum_i \text{PRODY}_i (x_{ij}/X_j)$$

This is simply the weighted average of the PRODYs for that country where the weights are the value shares in the country's total exports. As would be expected, the relationship between the level of per capita income of countries and EXPY is strong, but, more significantly, there is a strong relation between EXPY, output growth and export growth across countries (controlling for the other determinants of GDP growth). Some developing countries such as China have an EXPY higher than would be expected on the basis of their level of per capita income, indicating that they are producing and exporting sophisticated goods more associated with high-income countries. This is one reason why China is so successful (see also Felipe, 2009). A 10% higher level of EXPY gives a country extra growth of about 0.4 percentage points. The calculations are picking up the higher income elasticity of demand for more sophisticated goods, and this is why the structure of exports matters for economic performance.

Trade liberalization and export growth

What is the empirical evidence on the relation between trade liberalization and export growth? Because various forms of trade restrictions, including export duties, cause anti-export bias, the presumption must be that trade liberalization will raise the growth of exports, but by how much?

There are two broad types of empirical work on the relationship between trade liberalization and export performance. First, there are large multicountry studies that examine in detail the process of trade policy reforms within individual countries and its consequences. Pioneer studies of this type include Little et al. (1970), Balassa (1971) and Michaely et al. (1991). Second, there are econometric studies using time-series, cross-section or panel data analysis (pooling time-series and cross-section data). The evidence gives mixed and conflicting results, which suggests that the context in which trade liberalization takes place is of primary importance, particularly world economic conditions and domestic economic policies being pursued at the same time, especially with regard to the exchange rate.

Individual country (or industry) case studies that show a positive effect of liberalization on export performance include Joshi and Little's (1996) analysis of India's trade reforms in 1991, Ahmed's (2000) study of Bangladesh, Jenkins' (1996) study of manufactured exports from Bolivia, and Pacheco-López's (2005) study of Mexico after the trade reforms of 1985–86. Multicountry case studies that show a positive impact of liberalization on export growth include the cross-section analysis by Thomas et al. (1991), Helleiner's (1994) collection of theoretical and empirical studies, and Bleaney's (1999) panel data study of manufactured exports for ten countries of Latin America.

One of the most comprehensive studies is that by Santos-Paulino and Thirlwall (2004) (see also Santos-Paulino, 2002a), who take a panel of 22 countries that have adopted trade liberalization policies since the mid-1970s. A dummy variable for the year(s) of liberalization is included in an export growth equation using between 350 and 500 observations (depending on the method of estimation), and the central conclusion is that, controlling for other variables, liberalization has raised export growth by nearly 2 percentage points compared with the pre-liberalization period. The impact appears to have been the greatest in Africa (3.6 percentage points, p.p.) and the least in Latin America (1.6 p.p.). There is also evidence that liberalization has increased the sensitivity of export growth to world income growth; that is, liberalization has increased the income elasticity of demand for exports by inducing structural change.

The high-performance Asian countries are perhaps the most spectacular examples of economic success linked to export performance, but, interestingly, this has not always been based on free trade. The economies of Japan, South Korea, Taiwan, Singapore, Hong Kong, Malaysia, Indonesia and Thailand have recorded some of the highest GDP growth rates in the world since 1965 (averaging as a group nearly 6% per annum) and also some of the highest rates of growth of exports (averaging more than 10% per annum). While some of the countries have been very laissez-faire, however, others have been very interventionist, for example Japan and South Korea, pursuing relentless export promotion but import substitution at the same time.

Another interesting case study is China, which still restricts trade, but is now the world's second-largest exporter after Germany. Since China launched its 'open door' policy in 1978, after three decades of inward-oriented trade, its exports have been growing at over 10% per annum and its average GDP growth rate has been 8%. This is another classic example of export-led growth deliberately promoted by the government through the establishment of special economic zones and 'open cities' (originally in the provinces of Guangdong and Fujian), which act as magnets for investment and provide incentives for exporters. Typical incentives for exporters in all export-orientated economies consist of:

- Exemption from duties and tariffs on inputs that go into exports
- Investment grants
- Tax holidays
- Favourable retention rights over foreign exchange if exports are in certain sectors
- Favourable treatment of foreign investment.

In China, a 25% investment share was enough to give joint venture status to foreign investors, who then qualified for tax incentives, and no limit was placed on foreign equity investment in Chinese companies.

For a country's overall economic performance to improve, however, it is not enough for export growth to accelerate. Export growth must be shown to outpace import growth, otherwise balance of payments difficulties will arise.

Trade liberalization, import growth and the balance of payments

The main function of tariffs and non-tariff barriers, such as quantitative import controls, quality standards and government procurement policies, is to control the level and growth of imports in order to protect and promote domestic industry. If tariffs are reduced, and quantitative restrictions are lifted, imports can be expected to increase. There will be an 'autonomous' increase, and also imports are likely to become more sensitive to income and relative price changes domestically. If the income elasticity of demand for imports increases, this tightens the balance of payments constraint on growth (see equation (15.4); and Chapter 16). Country studies by Melo and Vogt (1984) for Venezuela, Mah (1999) for Thailand, and Bertola and Faini (1991) for Morocco all show a significant impact of trade liberalization on import growth and the sensitivity of imports to domestic income growth.

The most comprehensive study to date is by Santos-Paulino and Thirlwall (2004) (see also Santos-Paulino, 2002b), who take the same 22 countries as for export growth, discussed previously, and find that trade liberalization, by itself, controlling for other factors, has increased the growth of imports by 5–6 p.p. (more in countries initially highly protected and less in others), and also increased the income elasticity of demand for imports by 0.2–0.5 p.p. Pacheco-López and Thirlwall (2006) have also examined the direct effect of liberalization on the income elasticity of demand for imports in 17 Latin American countries over the period 1977–2002 and find a rise from 2.08 p.p. in the pre-liberalization period to 2.63 p.p. in the post-liberalization period.

If trade liberalization raises the growth of imports by more than exports, or raises the income elasticity of demand for imports by more than in proportion to the growth of exports, the balance of trade (or payments) will worsen for a given growth of output, unless the currency can be manipulated to raise the value of exports relative to imports. The consequence is that the growth of output may have to be constrained to avoid balance of payments crises.

The first major studies of this topic were by Parikh for UNCTAD (1999) and for WIDER (Parikh, 2002). The first study examined 16 countries over the period 1970–95, with the main conclusion that trade liberalization seems to have worsened the trade balance by 2.7% of

GDP, which is substantial. The second study extends the analysis to 64 countries with the general conclusion:

> the exports of most of the liberalizing countries have not grown fast enough after trade liberalization to compensate for the rapid growth of imports during the years immediately following trade liberalization. The evidence suggests that trade liberalization in developing countries has tended to lead to a deterioration in the trade account.

Santos-Paulino and Thirlwall (2004) take the same sample of 22 developing countries as for the impact of liberalization on export and import growth previously discussed and find that the switch to a more liberal trading regime worsened, on average, the trade balance by 2% of GDP (which is similar to the Parikh estimate), and the current account by 1% of GDP. For a separate group of 17 least developed countries, Santos-Paulino (2007) finds a deterioration in the trade balance ratio of 4% of GDP. For a sample of 17 Latin American countries over the period 1997–2002, Pacheco-López and Thirlwall (2007) find a deterioration in the trade balance of 1.3–2.3% of GDP (depending on the method of estimation used).

Ju et al. (2009) at the IMF take a sample of 39 countries over the period 1970–2004 to estimate the effect of trade liberalization on the trade balance. They find that liberalization raised the export/GDP ratio, but raised the import/GDP ratio by more, and using the Wacziarg and Welch (2008) dates of liberalization, calculate a negative effect on the trade balance/GDP ratio of −1.3%.

All these results show that trade liberalization has impacted unfavourably on the trade balance and current account balance of liberalizing countries. Such a deterioration, if it cannot be financed by sustainable capital inflows, may either trigger a currency crisis or necessitate a severe deflation of domestic demand (and therefore growth) to control imports. As UNCTAD (2004) argues in its *Least Developed Countries Report 2004* on the theme of linking international trade with poverty reduction: 'this critical [balance of payments] constraint on development and sustained poverty reduction is conspicuously absent in the current debate on trade and poverty'.

Indeed, the ultimate test of successful trade liberalization, at least at the macro-level, ignoring distributional effects, is whether it lifts a country on to a higher growth path consistent with a sustainable balance of payment; in other words, whether it improves the trade-off between growth and the balance of payments, as illustrated in Figure 15.5.

Figure 15.5 The trade-off between growth and the balance of payments

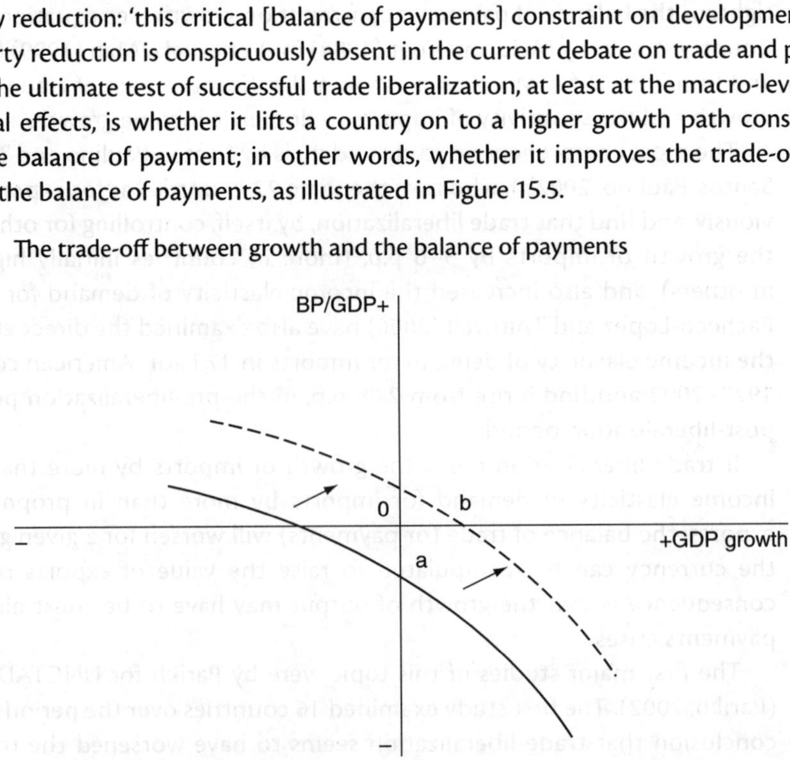

The ratio of the current balance (or trade balance) to GDP (BP/GDP) is measured on the vertical axis, and the growth of GDP on the horizontal axis. The solid line curve gives the negative trade-off curve, showing how the balance of payments deteriorates as growth accelerates. The curve is deliberately drawn here to represent a serious situation where the balance of payments is in deficit (point a) even at zero growth. The objective of trade policy should be to shift the curve upwards to, say, point b on the horizontal axis so that some positive growth is possible without running into payments difficulties. It is possible to estimate such a trade-off curve and see whether liberalization has shifted it favourably. Pacheco-López and Thirlwall (2007) do this for 17 Latin American countries using pooled time-series/cross-section data over the period 1977–2002 and find that trade liberalization *worsened* the trade-off by 3.6 percentage points. Before liberalization, the curve cut the vertical axis at a deficit of 1.39%; after liberalization, it cuts the curve at a −4.99 deficit/GDP ratio. This may be one of the reasons why it is difficult to find robust results showing that trade liberalization has improved the growth performance of countries.

Trade liberalization and economic performance

It is fairly clear that trade liberalization has improved export performance, but liberalization and export growth are not the same and should not be confused in the discussion of trade liberalization and economic growth. As Stiglitz (2006) notes:

> Advocates of liberalization cite statistical studies claiming that liberalization enhances growth. But a careful look at the evidence shows something quite different … It is exports – not the removal of trade barriers – that is the driving force of growth. Studies that focus directly on the removal of trade barriers show little relationship between liberalization and growth. The advocates of quick liberalization tried an intellectual sleight of hand, hoping that the broad-brush discussion of the benefits of globalization would suffice to make their case.

The early work of Edwards (1992, 1993, 1998) and Dollar (1992) showed a positive relation between the outward orientation of countries, the removal of trade distortions and the growth of countries. This work, however, has been heavily criticized by Rodriguez and Rodrik (2000) on methodological grounds and for lack of robustness. They themselves find no significant relationship between either import duties or the percentage of imports covered by non-tariff barriers and the growth of per capita income (controlling for other variables).

The work of Dollar and Kraay (2004) has been highly influential, especially with the World Bank. They take a sample of 73 developing countries from the 1970s to the 1990s and rank them according to their share of trade (exports plus imports) in GDP. The top one-third of countries are called 'the post-1980s globalizers', and these countries (24 in all) are compared with the rest of the sample. Per capita income in the 'globalizer' countries is shown to have grown much more rapidly decade by decade compared with the 'non-globalizers'. The influence of Dollar and Kraay on the views of the World Bank can be vividly seen in its report, *Globalization, Growth and Poverty* (2002), in which it claims:

> Some 24 developing countries – with 3 million people – have doubled their ratio of trade to income over the past two decades. The rest of the developing world trades less than 20 years ago. The more globalizing developing countries have increased their per capita growth rate from 1 percent in the 1960s to 3 percent in the 1970s, 4 percent in the 1980s and 5 percent in the 1990s; … much of the rest of the developing world – with about 2 billion people – is becoming marginalized.

Dollar and Kraay's results need to be treated with some care, however. Dowrick and Golley (2004) show that the faster growth of the 'globalizing' countries is entirely due to the fast growth of China and India. If these two countries are excluded from the sample, the remaining 22 'globalized' countries grew slower over the period 1980–2000 than the 'non-globalized' ones. They also show that the 'globalizing' countries were not the most open or liberal. Their share of trade in GDP rose the most, but the countries started from a low base and were still less open economies than the 'non-globalizers', at least until the 1990s.

Another major influential study of trade orientation and growth is that by Sachs and Warner (1995), which takes 79 countries over the period 1979–89. They find that open economies (see before for the definitions of 'open' and 'closed') grew on average 2.44 percentage points faster than closed economies. Rodriguez and Rodrik (2000) argue, however, that it is not tariffs and non-tariff barriers that distinguish the two sets of countries but a combination of the black market exchange rate premium and the state monopoly of exports. The black market exchange rate is highly correlated with turbulent macroeconomic conditions – debt, terms of trade deterioration and wars – and this was the major cause of their slower economic growth. Wacziarg and Welch (2008) extend the Sachs and Warner study into the 1990s when 78 countries are classified as open and 27 closed (compared with 31 open and 74 closed during the period studied by Sachs and Warner), and find that there appears to be no significant effect of openness on economic growth.

Greenaway et al. (1998, 2002) examine the relationship between trade liberalization and growth within a 'new' growth theory framework (see Chapter 4) using panel data analysis for up to 73 countries over the period 1975–93. Different measures of liberalization are used, and they also look for lagged effects. What they find is that in the first year of liberalization, the impact is negative (although not significantly so); in the second year, it is positive but not significant; but in the third year, it is positive and significant. This suggests a J-curve effect of liberalization on growth, with the effects taking time to come through. On the other hand, there is no indication of whether the positive impact lasts.

In conclusion, there is some evidence that trade liberalization promotes growth and a higher growth of living standards; on the other hand, the results are not always robust, and depend on the measure of liberalization used, the time period taken and the estimation method. Rodriguez and Rodrik (2000) conclude their evaluation of trade orientation and economic growth by saying that the indicators of openness and liberalization used are either poor measures of trade barriers or are highly correlated with other determinants of domestic performance. They are particularly concerned that the priority given to trade policy reforms has generated expectations that are unlikely to be met, and may preclude other institutional reforms, which would have a greater impact on economic performance. In other words, trade liberalization cannot be regarded as a substitute for a comprehensive trade and development strategy. To quote Rodrik (2001): 'deep trade liberalization cannot be relied upon to deliver high rates of economic growth and therefore does not deserve the high priority it typically receives in the development strategies pushed by leading organizations'.

Trade liberalization, poverty and domestic inequality

Poverty

There may be static efficiency gains from trade liberalization and a greater volume of trade, but there will also be welfare losses if domestic firms cannot compete as trade barriers fall and those thrown out of work cannot find alternative employment. In other words, the gains from trade to a country may not be equally distributed between people within a country, and some may lose absolutely. George (2010) cites production losses of more than 20% in some poor countries as a result of liberalization.

If more trade leads to faster economic growth, this should lift more people out of poverty and reduce the poverty rate, depending on the elasticity of the poverty rate with respect to growth (see Chapter 2), but as we saw earlier, trade liberalization does not guarantee faster economic growth, and even if the poverty rate declines, the income distribution may still become more unequal if the richest in the country gain relative to the poorest.

The impact of trade liberalization on poverty depends mainly on its effects on employment and prices. Two main groups in society need distinguishing: workers (or wage earners) and producers (or profit earners). Profit earners include not only firms and enterprises, but also the self-employed who are consumers as well as producers, such as peasant farmers in rural areas, and those working in the petty service sector in urban areas.

Wage earners will be affected by trade liberalization in three main ways: by what happens to the wage rate, to employment and to the prices of goods they consume. There are many possibilities. If liberalization increases productivity, and real wages rise, workers will benefit. Increased competition in import-competing activities, however, may destroy jobs and lower wages. In Kenya, cotton farming and textile production have been badly hit by liberalization. Cotton production fell by 70% between the mid-1980s and the mid-1990s and textile employment fell from 120,000 to 85,000 in ten years (Christian Aid, 2005). Two million Mexican maize farmers have lost their jobs since the NAFTA was signed in 1994 because they cannot compete with subsidized maize from the USA. Case example 15.2 discusses the impact of trade liberalization on employment and poverty in Africa.

Case example 15.2

Impact of trade liberalization in Africa

Trade liberalization has cost sub-Saharan Africa US$272 billion over the past 20 years. Had they not been forced to liberalize as the price of aid, loans and debt relief, sub-Saharan African countries would have had enough income to wipe out their debts and have sufficient left over to pay for every child to be vaccinated and go to school. Two decades of liberalization have cost sub-Saharan Africa roughly what it has received in aid. Effectively, this aid did no more than compensate African countries for the losses they sustained meeting the conditions attached to the aid they received.

When trade is liberalized, imports climb steeply as new products flood in. Local producers are priced out of their markets by new, cheaper, better marketed goods. Exports also tend to grow, but not by as much. Demand for the kind of things sub-Saharan African countries export, such as raw materials, doesn't change much, so there isn't a lot of scope for increasing exports. This means that, overall, local producers are selling less than they were before trade was liberalized.

It is often poor farmers who suffer most when trade is liberalized. The fall in domestic demand that results from increased imports hits them particularly hard. Poor farmers have little access to capital or technology to increase their productivity or improve the quality of what they sell in response to more competition. They are also competing in an extremely unequal market, where imports from developed countries are often heavily subsidized. Manufacturing industries have not grown up to employ people who are no longer able to make a living from farming. Instead, manufacturing has also been hard hit by trade liberalization.

continued overleaf

Case example 15.2 **Impact of trade liberalization in Africa** – *continued*

Trade liberalization, therefore, means a 'double whammy' for poor people, stifling the development of industry that would replace lost jobs in agriculture. Export trends bear this out. Although exports did increase in most cases following trade liberalization, most countries simply exported more of the same – they did not start to export more manufactured goods, or more higher value-added agricultural goods

It is clear that trade liberalization is not driving the development of a more dynamic diversified or pro-poor pattern of development. On the contrary, it is locking Africa into greater dependence on a few agricultural products whose prices have been declining for 50 years. Liberalization is hitting manufacturing hard, and it is the development of manufacturing that Africa needs if it is ever to trade its way out of poverty.

Source: Christian Aid, 2005.

Real income also depends on the price of consumption goods. Price changes will have distributional effects depending on the weight of each good in each worker's basket. If the price of food falls, the poor will gain more than the rich because they spend a higher proportion of their income on food. If liberalization raises the price of food, however, because of the removal of subsidies for example, the poor are likely to suffer severely.

Producers will also be affected in a variety of ways, in particular by what happens to output prices, to input prices, and to the prices of the basket of goods bought for consumption in the case of self-employed producers. Producer prices are likely to fall with trade liberalization. In Senegal, after liberalization, the price farmers received for their tomatoes fell by 50%, and tomato production fell by 70%, leaving many farmers without a cash crop (Christian Aid, 2005). But the price of inputs is also likely to fall, so whether producers gain or lose depends on the prevailing protective structure of their output and inputs.

If any generalization can be made from case studies, it seems that when all price and wage effects are taken into account, rural families tend to lose and urban households tend to gain, at least in circumstances where workers retain their jobs. Ravallion (2006) concludes, on the basis of his micro-case studies of trade liberalization in Morocco and China, that: 'the most vulnerable households tend to be rural dependent on agriculture, with relatively few workers, and with weak links to the outside economy through migration'. He also looks at the relationship between trade liberalization and the poverty rate across 75 countries in which there have been at least two household surveys on poverty (giving 178 cases in all), and finds no significant relation, positive or negative. Ravallion (2006) concludes: 'it remains clear that there is considerable variation in the rates of poverty reduction at a given rate of expansion of trade volume'. Equally, however, he says: 'based on the data available from cross-country comparison, it is hard to maintain the view that expanding trade, in general, is a powerful force for poverty reduction in developing countries'.

Likewise, Winters et al. (2004) conclude their major survey on trade liberalization and poverty by saying:

> there can be no simple relationship between trade liberalization and poverty. Theory provides strong presumption that trade liberalization [should] be poverty-alleviating in the long run and on average … equally, however, it does not assert that the static and microeconomic effects of liberalization will always be beneficial to the poor. Trade liberalization

necessarily implies distributional changes; it may well reduce the well-being of some people (at least in the short term) and some of these may be poor.

See also Thorbecke and Nissanke (2006) on the transmission mechanisms through which trade liberalization can affect poverty.

To protect the poor as trade liberalization takes place, countries need to consider a number of policy issues:

- **Sequencing of liberalization**: To ameliorate the costs of adjustment, great care needs to be taken with the sequencing of liberalization, so that vulnerable sectors are given time to adjust.
- **Provision of social safety nets**: For those already poor and adversely affected by liberalization, governments need to put in place social safety nets in the form of, for example, unemployment and income insurance. These could be supported by World Bank programmes.
- **Labour mobility and training**: Improved worker mobility and worker training can help those who lose jobs to find new ones.
- **Development of markets**: To take advantage of new market opportunities, the poor and other disadvantaged groups require training and technical assistance in traditional and non-traditional activities. Access to credit is particularly important for the start of new businesses.
- **Infrastructure development**: In agriculture, improved and cheaper transport is important to allow poor farmers to take advantage of new market opportunities. They should be a core component of 'aid for trade' programmes.
- **Poverty Reduction Strategy Papers**: A conscious effort needs to be made to integrate pro-poor trade strategies into Poverty Reduction Strategy Papers (see Chapter 14) that have to be prepared by countries for international organizations, such as the World Bank, to qualify for debt relief (see UNCTAD, 2004).

Income inequality

Let us now turn specifically to the issue of the impact of trade liberalization on wage and income inequality within countries, which is not necessarily the same as the impact on poverty or the poverty rate. Poverty can fall, but wage and income inequality can rise because the share of income going to the top income recipients rises by more than the share going to the bottom. In general, what will happen to the income distribution as trade liberalization takes place will depend on how the wage distribution is affected, how the distribution of assets changes, and what happens to the rate of return on assets. Goldberg and Pavcnik (2007), in their survey of the distributional effects of globalization in developing countries, say: 'while inequality has many different dimensions, all existing measures of inequality for developing countries seem to point to an increase in inequality which in some cases is severe'. Table 15.2 gives the Gini ratios (as a measure of distribution – see Chapter 2) for a selection of developing countries in the 2000/2010s. Gini ratios are generally higher in Latin America than in Asia or Africa, and in most countries in the past decade, inequality has increased.

The major cause of income inequality is wage inequality between skilled and unskilled workers. Orthodox trade theory (e.g. the Heckscher–Ohlin theory) predicts a narrowing of wage inequality in poor countries because their comparative advantage lies in the production and export of goods using abundant unskilled labour, which should raise wages of unskilled workers relative to skilled. But this narrowing has not happened. Robbins (1996), Freeman and Oostendrop (2001), Zhu and Trefler (2005) and Anderson (2005) all give extensive evidence of a worldwide trend

Table 15.2 Income inequality in selected developing countries measured by the Gini ratio

Country	Latest date in the 2000/2010s	Gini ratio
Bangladesh	2010	32.0
Bolivia	2013	48.1
Brazil	2013	52.9
Chile	2013	55.5
China	2011	30.7
Colombia	2013	53.5
Dominican Republic	2013	47.1
Egypt	2008	30.8
Ghana	2006	42.8
Honduras	2013	53.7
India	2012	33.6
Indonesia	2010	35.6
Jamaica	2004	45.5
Mexico	2012	48.1
Nigeria	2009	43.0
Pakistan	2010	29.6
Peru	2013	44.7
Philippines	2012	43.0
Sri Lanka	2012	38.6
Thailand	2012	39.3
Venezuela	2006	46.9

Source: World Bank, 2015.

towards greater wage inequality between skilled and unskilled labour in poor countries. There are four major reasons for this:

1. The competition between poor countries themselves. Orthodox theory takes a two-country world – rich and poor. But poor countries trade with each other, for example Mexico and China. Mexico's trade with the USA may raise the wages of unskilled relative to skilled labour in Mexico, but trading with China may reduce the wages of unskilled labour in Mexico.
2. The flows of FDI to poor countries, and rich developed countries shifting the production of intermediate inputs to poor countries, or outsourcing (see the model of Feenstra and Hanson, 1997). This increases the demand for skilled labour in poor countries. Foreign-owned plants in Mexico that export pay wages 60% higher than plants that do not export.
3. The trade-related, skill-biased technical change in poor countries, either as a result of increased competition and trying to 'catch up', or the increased import of machinery from rich countries, which increases the demand for skilled labour (see Wood, 1993, 1995, 1997).
4. If trade liberalization causes balance of payments problems and the economy has contracted, this depresses the demand for unskilled labour and reduces relative wages (see Arbache et al., 2004 for a case study of Brazil).

Wage differences between skilled and unskilled workers are not the only source of income inequality, although according to Goldberg and Pavcnik (2007), income inequality tends to move in the same direction as wage inequality. Greater trade openness may alter the gap in earnings between men and women, between regions within a country and between rural and urban areas, and also change the rate of return on assets – all of which affect a measure of income inequality such as the Gini ratio. What is the evidence?

The most highly publicized and 'rose-tinted' view that trade openness has not worsened the income distribution and that 'growth is good for the poor', is found in the studies by Dollar and Kraay (2002, 2004). First, they plot changes in the Gini ratio against changes in trade shares for more than 100 developed and developing countries, and find no relation. Second, they take 80 countries over 40 years and regress the growth of per capita income of the poorest 20% of the population on the growth of average income per head, and find the relation is 1:1, that is, an elasticity of unity, and that the level of openness makes no difference to the coefficient. Dollar and Kraay express some surprise that they do not find a negative effect of openness on the poor, given all the assertions and adverse publicity of the anti-globalization movement. They do various tests of robustness and stick with their original conclusion, which is that: 'openness to trade increases the income of the poor to the same extent that it increases the income of the other households in society'.

This is not the general consensus, however, of most other studies in this field. One directly contrary study is by Edward (2006), who uses world consumption data and finds that for roughly 1 billion people between the 50th and 70th percentile of the consumption distribution, consumption hardly changed between 1993 and 2001, and among the $2 a day poor, the ratio of their consumption growth to average growth was not 1:1 but 1:2. He concluded that: 'growth is good for the poor but much better for the rich'.

The most detailed study of the impact of trade liberalization on the distribution of income is by Milanovic (2005). In his introductory survey of the existing literature, Milanovic remarks:

> The conclusions run nearly the full gamut, from openness reducing the real income of the poor to openness raising the income of the poor proportionately less than the income of the rich to raising both the same in relative terms. Note, however, that there are *no* results that show openness reducing inequality; that is, raising the income of the poor more than the income of the rich – let alone raising the absolute income of the poor by more.

Milanovic's (2005) own research takes 321 household income surveys from 95 countries in 1988, and 113 countries in 1993 and 1998 covering 90% of the world's population. The income is divided up into deciles, and inequality is measured by the income of the ith decile (i = 1–10) of the population relative to the mean level of income of the whole population. For each decile, income inequality is then related to trade openness measured by the ratio of total trade to GDP, and also to openness interacted with the level of income, to test whether the effect of openness on inequality varies with the level of income. Two striking results emerge. First, increased openness *reduces* the income share of the bottom six deciles. Second, the adverse effect of openness on inequality is greater the lower a country's per capita income. The poor only start to benefit relative to the rich at an income per capita of about $7,500 at 1990 prices. Barro (2000) and Spilimbergo et al. (1999) also find that openness worsens income inequality up to a certain point, and then the effect diminishes. Milanovic (2005) concludes: 'openness would therefore seem to have a particularly negative impact on poor and middle income groups in poor countries – directly opposite to what would be expected from the standard Heckscher–Ohlin framework'.

Trade liberalization and international inequality

In Chapter 2, we documented the historical widening of the international and global distribution of income, and the recent slight fall. Bourguignon (2015), in his book *The Globalization of Inequality*, argues that falling inequality between nations and rising inequality within nations (where it exists) can both be explained by globalization, because the process of freeing trade has allowed some populous poor countries to grow fast and catch up with richer countries, while free trade and flows of foreign direct investment have widened the gap between skilled and unskilled wages within rich and poor countries.

How much of the persistent inequality across the world is due to trade liberalization? Is freer trade equilibrating or disequilibrating? These are not easy questions to answer, but attempts can be made. One methodological approach is to interact a measure of trade openness with the level of per capita income (PCY) to test whether the impact of openness varies with the level of development. This is what Dowrick and Golley (2004) do, taking over 100 countries for two separate time periods, 1960–80 and 1980–2000. For the first period, a higher trade share of one percentage point (p.p.) is associated with 0.11% faster growth, and the poorer the country, the slightly greater the benefit from openness, meaning that trade liberalization was a force for convergence. But for the second period, this result is reversed. The impact of the trade share on the growth of PCY is now negative, and poor countries suffered more than rich countries, leading to divergence. Dividing the 1980–2000 sample of countries into 30 poorest countries and the rest shows no significant effect of the trade share on growth in the poorest countries, but the richer countries gained about 0.012% growth for a 1 p.p. increase in the trade share. Specialization in primary products had a strong negative effect on growth in the 1980–2000 period, reducing it on average by nearly 1% and the impact was even stronger in the poor country group, a difference of 1.7%. Dowrick and Golley's conclusion is that 'trade has promoted strong divergence in productivity [between countries] since 1980'. A new study of the period since 2000 is badly needed.

Ghose (2004) has also examined this issue, and reaches a more neutral conclusion. He takes 96 countries over the period 1981–97, and examines the relationship between the rate of change of the trade/GDP ratio (as a measure of trade liberalization) and both the level of PCY in 1981 and the size of population. Overall, he finds that the effect of trade liberalization on growth performance has been much the same for poor and rich countries, and that, therefore, trade liberalization has had no discernible effect on international inequality. On the other hand, there seems to be a positive relationship between trade performance and population size, and this may have contributed to the decline in the population-weighted Gini ratio mentioned above. The result is heavily influenced by China and India, the two most populous countries in the world, both of which started with a very low trade base in 1981. In both cases, however, export growth has been the driving force, not trade liberalization per se.

All we can say with some confidence is that there is little evidence that free trade has contributed to a narrowing of the income gap between countries, as predicted by orthodox trade and growth theory. Despite growing trade between countries, income disparities continue to persist.

Disadvantages of free trade for development

Even if trade-liberalized countries did perform (on average) better than non-liberalized countries, this does not mean that all developing countries should liberalize as quickly as possible, and that there is no role for protection and government intervention to improve trade and growth performance. Indeed, we have seen that this is exactly what many successful East Asian countries have done. It is also worth remembering that historically no country developed on the basis of free trade. The countries of Europe, North America and Scandinavia all developed their industrial sectors with the aid of tariff and non-tariff protection (see Chang, 2002, 2005, 2007; Reinert, 2007). Trade liberalization is not a substitute for a trade and development strategy.

Let us consider, therefore, the potential disadvantages of free trade and the weaknesses of the comparative cost doctrine that underlies it. Like most micro-welfare theories, the comparative advantage/free trade argument is a *static* one based on restrictive and often unrealistic assumptions. The doctrine assumes, for example, the existence of full employment in each country (otherwise there would be no opportunity cost involved in expanding the production of commodities), that the prices of resources and goods reflect their opportunity cost (that is, that perfect competition exists), and that factor endowments are given and unalterable. Moreover, the doctrine ignores the effect of free trade on the terms of trade (movements in which affect real income) and the balance of payments consequences of free trade. As a result, it can be argued that the principle of comparative advantage is not very useful in the context of developing countries, which are in need of rapid structural change and are as much concerned with long-term development as short-term efficiency. As many economists have commented, the doctrine of comparative advantage is more useful in explaining the *past* pattern of trade than in providing a guide as to what the future pattern of trade should be as a stimulus to development.

The question is not whether there should be trade but whether there should be *free trade*, as the doctrine of comparative advantage implies. Perhaps the long-run needs of developing countries would be better served, at least initially, by various forms of protection.

The development considerations that the doctrine of free trade overlooks are numerous. First, it ignores the balance of payments' effects of free trade, and the effect of free trade on the terms of trade. If the demands for different commodities grow at different rates owing to differences in their price and income elasticity of demand, free trade will work to the benefit of some countries and to the relative detriment of others. In classical theory, Torrens, J.S. Mill, Marshall, Edgeworth and Taussig all conceded that unilateral substitution by a country of free trade for protection would move the terms of trade against the country. But most 'free traders' ignored the issue. In general, the implicit assumption was that moving from protection to free trade would not alter the commodity terms of trade, or if it did, the gains from trade would more than offset any unfavourable terms of trade effect. If the terms of trade effect does offset the gains from trade, this is a valid argument for protection (see below).

A second factor that the free trade doctrine tends to overlook is that some activities are subject to increasing returns while others are subject to diminishing returns. The commodities most susceptible to diminishing returns are primary products, where the scope for technical progress may also be less than in the case of manufactured goods. This being so, one might expect a rise in the ratio of primary to manufactured goods prices, and diminishing returns would not matter so much if the goods were price inelastic. In practice, however, there has been a substitution of synthetic alternatives for primary products, and the terms of trade have deteriorated (see below), partly because of substitution and partly because the demand for primary commodities in general, in relation to supply, has expanded much less than for manufactured commodities. But whatever the movement in the terms of trade, it would surely be perverse to base a trade and development strategy on activities subject to diminishing returns, particularly in light of the theory of cumulative causation (see Chapter 10).

A third disadvantage of adherence to the comparative advantage doctrine is that it could lead to excessive specialization in a narrow range of products, putting the economy at the mercy of outside influences. The possibility exists of severe balance of payments instability arising from specialization, which could be damaging to development.

Fourth, static comparative cost analysis ignores the fact that comparative advantage can be altered by deliberate policies to promote certain activities. There is no reason why countries should be condemned to the production and export of the same commodities forever. No country was endowed with the *natural* ability to produce industrial goods. Now that technology and capital accumulation, rather than natural resources, are the basis for trade, comparative advantage is no longer predetermined or predictable. Hausmann and Rodrik (2003) document how countries somehow stumble on lucrative niche markets almost by accident: hats in Bangladesh, cut flowers in Colombia, footballs and bed sheets in Pakistan and software in India, to give just a few examples. If there is any explanation at all, it is entrepreneurial trial and error. If comparative advantage is not given by nature but can be altered, the case for initial protection is strengthened (the classic infant industry argument).

It should also be remembered that the concept of comparative advantage is based on calculations of private cost. But we observed in Chapter 9 that social costs in developing countries may diverge markedly from private costs, and that social benefits may exceed private benefits because of externalities. If private costs exceed social costs in industry (because wage rates are artificially high, for example), and social benefits from industrial projects exceed private benefits, there is a strong argument for protecting industry in order to encourage the transfer of labour from other activities into industry to equate private and social cost and private and social benefit.

Finally, the export growth of some activities has relatively little secondary impact on other activities. Primary commodities fall into this category. There is abundant evidence that the export growth of primary commodities has not had the development impact that might have been expected from the expansion of industrial exports. The reasons for this are not hard to understand. Primary production has very few backward or forward linkages, and historically it has tended to be undertaken by foreign enterprises, with a consequent outflow of profits. The secondary repercussions of the pattern of trade are overlooked by the free trade doctrine.

Theory of protection: tariffs versus subsidies

We have seen that trade can bring substantial benefits, but it does not follow that the freer the trade the better. There are many disadvantages that the doctrine of free trade overlooks when trade is considered in a long-run development context, as opposed to the static short-run context of the doctrine of comparative advantage. Furthermore, free trade does not guarantee an equal distribution of the gains from trade, and this is an important consideration for countries that naturally look to their relative position compared with others, and not only at their absolute performance.

We can summarize the **arguments for protection** as follows (see Johnson, 1964). First, there are purely **economic arguments** that comprise all arguments in favour of protection as a means of increasing real output or income above what it would otherwise be. These include the following:

- The infant industry argument – allowing industries to reach their optimum size in terms of minimum average costs of production.
- The existence of external economies in production, where the social cost of production is less than the private cost.

- Distortions in the labour market that make the social cost of using labour less than the private cost.
- International distortions that cause the domestic rate of transformation between goods to diverge from the foreign rate of transformation, due, for example, to monopoly power in international trade. This argument for protection is often referred to as the **optimum tariff argument**.

This category of economic arguments might also include two factors previously stressed: terms of trade deterioration and balance of payments difficulties arising from the pattern of trade. Johnson (1964) and others of neoclassical persuasion have argued that these are non-arguments because in the case of the terms of trade, the restriction of imports will not reduce import prices for a small country; and in the case of the balance of payments, equilibrium can be achieved automatically by letting the exchange rate float freely.

The terms of trade argument may be correct, but the balance of payments argument suffers from confusion between a balance of payments equilibrium on the current account, which affects the real economy, and balance in the foreign exchange market. The two are not the same. A floating exchange rate, by definition, will equilibrate the foreign exchange market, but will not necessarily equilibrate the balance of payments on current account. If terms of trade deterioration and balance of payments difficulties constrain growth and lead to unemployment, the social cost of labour will be less than the private cost, which is a domestic distortion and an economic argument for protection.

Second, **non-economic arguments** for protection tend to be arguments in favour of protection for its own sake rather than to increase output or income above what it would otherwise be. Industrialization at any price and self-sufficiency for strategic reasons are examples of this type of argument.

Having summarized the arguments in favour of protection, the question then is: What is the best means of protection? It can be shown that tariffs are appropriate only under special circumstances: when the distortions are international (the optimum tariff argument) and when self-sufficiency is the objective. All other arguments for protection are arguments for subsidies, the reason being that when distortions are domestic, a tariff will introduce further distortions, and according to the **theory of the second best**, there is no way of knowing *a priori* whether the situation will be made better or worse.

The argument can be illustrated with a diagram. Consider Figure 15.6, where a good that is producible domestically is subject to a domestic distortion such that the private cost of production S´S´ is *d* per cent above the social cost (*SS*). The demand curve is *DD* and the good is also

Figure 15.6 Welfare gains and losses from protection

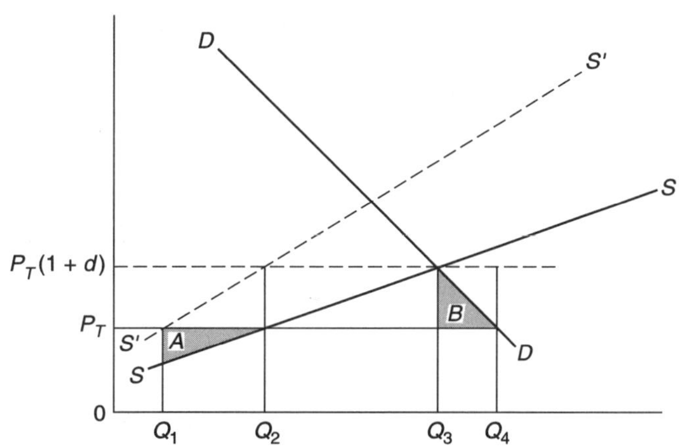

importable at the international price, P_t. Under free trade, domestic producers will produce up to Q_1 and Q_1 to Q_4 will be imported. Q_1 to Q_2 imports could be replaced, however, by additional domestic production, with real savings equal to the shaded area *A*, if domestic producers were given a subsidy of *d* per cent. The same real income gain could be achieved by a tariff of the same percentage, but because the domestic price rises to $P_T(1 + d)$, there will be a loss of consumer surplus equal to the shaded area *B* owing to the restriction of consumption by Q_3Q_4. The loss of consumer surplus may be greater than the real income gain, reducing total welfare. The balance of advantage depends on the relative slopes of the supply and demand curves. In these circumstances, a subsidy to labour is unequivocally first best.

Now let us consider the relative merits of tariffs and subsidies where the arguments in favour of protection are non-economic. Suppose, for example, the objective of protection is simply to increase domestic output. Here, subsidies are also superior to tariffs because tariffs impose a consumption cost and add nothing more to the achievement of increased production. Consider Figure 15.7. We assume that there is no domestic distortion, so the *SS* curve represents both the private and the social cost of production. Now suppose that the object is to raise domestic production from Q_1 to Q_2. This can be done with a tariff or subsidy of *d* per cent that uses extra resources equal to the shaded area *A*. The tariff, however, imposes an extra consumption cost equal to area *B* as a result of a rise in the price from P_T to $P_T(1 + d)$.

On the other hand, if the objective is self-sufficiency and to cut back imports, we can show that tariffs are the least costly. The reason for this is that it is more efficient to reduce imports by jointly restricting consumption and increasing domestic production, than by doing either of these on their own. Consider Figure 15.7 again. A tariff of *d* per cent reduces imports to Q_2Q_3 at a cost of $A + B$. To get the same reduction with a subsidy requires a subsidy in excess of *d* per cent in order to induce extra domestic production Q_2Q_5 (equal to the cutback in consumption through the tariff of Q_3Q_4). This involves an extra cost equal to the area $C + D$. Since $C > B$, the cost of the subsidy policy is obviously greater than the cost of the tariff.

If subsidies are first best, they may be effectively granted by exemption from taxation. If this exemption is from existing taxes, it will have revenue implications for the government budget. In the long run, however, subsidies can be 'self-financing' by the increased output they stimulate.

A further argument against tariffs and in favour of subsidies is that tariffs are very inward-looking, whereas protection through subsidies is much more outward-looking. Tariffs adjust the

Figure 15.7 Tariffs and subsidies

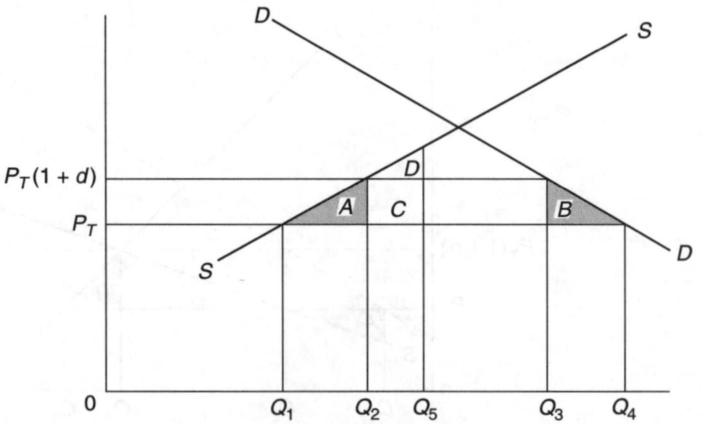

internal price structure to the (high) internal cost structure. This may lead to inefficiencies and make it difficult for exports to compete when the effects of import substitution policies cease. Subsidies, in contrast, adjust the internal cost structure to the (low) external price structure and make it possible for exports to compete more easily in world markets.

Effective protection

In assessing the restrictive effect that a tariff structure has on trade, however, it is not enough just to look at the nominal tariff on finished goods. For one of the original theoretical expositions, see Corden (1966); see also the pioneering work of Balassa (1971). The nominal rate does not measure how inefficient (or costly) producers can be without incurring competition and losing their market. This is measured by the protection of **value-added**, which is the difference between the value of output and the value of inputs. The protection of value-added is the so-called **effective rate of protection**. Since value-added is the difference between the value of output and inputs, not only is the tariff on output important when measuring the degree of protection, but also the tariff on inputs.

Formally, the effective rate of protection is measured as the excess of domestic value-added over value-added at world prices, expressed as a percentage of the latter. Thus, the effective rate of protection of industry X may be defined as:

$$EP_x = \frac{V_x' - V_x}{V_x} = \frac{V_x'}{V_x} - 1$$

where V_x' is domestic value-added under protection and V_x is value-added under free market conditions (at world prices). Domestic value-added is equal to the sale of the industry's product minus the sum of intermediate inputs, all valued at domestic market prices; that is, including the effect of tariffs on the finished good and on the inputs into the finished good. The free market value-added can be defined identically, but with the final product and input prices measured exclusive of tariffs on them. It is clear that the height of the effective tariff rate depends on three variables:

- The level of nominal tariffs on output
- The proportion of value-added to total output
- The level of nominal tariffs on the industry's inputs.

The higher the nominal tariff, the lower the tariff on imported inputs, and the higher the proportion of value-added to total output, the higher the effective rate of protection. If the tariff on finished goods is very high and the tariff on inputs is low, domestic value-added can be very high; in turn, world value-added may be very low, giving enormous rates of effective protection, sometimes in excess of 1,000%.

Let us now give a practical example. Suppose Indian textiles have a world price of \$5, of which \$3 represents raw material costs and \$2 represents value-added. Suppose that imports of Indian textiles into a developed country are subject to a tariff of 20%, while domestic producers must pay a tariff of 10% on textile raw materials. To remain competitive, the domestic producer must produce the commodity for not more than \$6. The value-added can be \$6 minus the cost of raw materials plus the tariff on raw materials, that is, \$6 – (\$3 + \$0.30) = \$2.70. The effective rate of protection is the difference between domestic value-added and Indian value-added (that is, value-added at world prices), expressed as a percentage of Indian value-added, that is, (2.70 – 2)/2 = 35%. This is the effective rate of protection, equal to the difference between the gross subsidy on value-added provided by the tariff on the final product (\$(1/2) = 50%) and the implicit tax on value-added as a result of the tariff on raw materials (\$(0.30/2) = 15%). This is the extent (35%) to which production can be more costly in the developed country without losing competitive advantage; in other words, it is the degree to which Indian textile producers would have to be more productive to compete in the developed country market.

Effective rates of protection almost always exceed nominal rates. At one extreme, if a country obtains raw material inputs that are duty free (at world prices) but puts a tariff on the final good, the effective rate must be higher than the nominal rate. At the other extreme, if a country puts a tariff on inputs but no tariff on the finished good, the effective rate of protection is negative. Students might like to prove these propositions for themselves, using the formula for the effective rate of protection.

Calculation of the effective rate of protection also depends on the exchange rate. If the exchange rate of a country in the protected situation is overvalued, the price of imported inputs measured in domestic currency will be undervalued, and this will affect the calculation of the domestic value-added and the value-added at world market prices. Without adjustment for this factor, effective rates of protection are described as 'gross'; with adjustment, they are referred to as 'net'.

Our example of the effective rate of protection also assumes that all inputs are traded. Some inputs will be non-traded, however, and their price enters into the value of total output and total inputs. If the effect of protection on the price of non-traded goods is ignored, the rates of effective protection will be overestimated. In practice, it is not easy to estimate the effect of protection on the price of non-traded goods.

The theory of effective protection suggests that the same *nominal* tariff cuts mean different degrees of change in effective rates of protection, and thus it may be unwise for developing countries to press for across-the-board tariff cuts on all commodities. **Reductions in tariffs against their primary products will increase the effective rate of protection against their manufactures,** which, we have argued, are the more important exports as far as long-run development prospects are concerned. The average nominal level of protection in developed countries is about 4%, but effective protection against the goods of developing countries may well be in the region of 30% or more. Developing countries themselves may give their own producers very high rates of effective protection.

Import substitution versus export promotion

In the early stages of production, the protectionist strategy of import substitution using tariffs is undoubtedly the easiest and many countries have pursued it, particularly in Latin America in the 1950s to the 1970s. However, there are different stages of import substitution, and some are easier than others. The first easy stage involves the replacement by domestic production of imports of non-durable consumption goods such as clothing, footwear, leather and wood products. Countries in the early stages of industrialization are naturally suited to these products and relatively little protection is required. Once this stage is over, the maintenance of high growth rates then requires the import substitution of other goods if the strategy is to be continued.

The problem with this second stage of import substitution is that relatively high rates of protection are required, because intermediate goods such as steel and producer durables are subject to substantial economies of scale, internal and external, so that unit costs are very high if output is low. The problem with high rates of protection is that they breed inefficiency and, more importantly, act as a tax on exports by keeping costs and the exchange rate high. The catalogue of costs and distortions introduced by protective import substitution policies is formidable. Import substitution tends to shift the distribution of income in favour of the urban sector and higher income groups with a higher propensity to import, thereby worsening the balance of payments. Protection taxes agriculture since it raises the price of industrial goods relative to agricultural goods. Furthermore, since protection maintains an artificially high exchange rate, it reduces receipts in terms of domestic currency from a given quantity of agricultural exports, which may discourage agricultural production. Import substitution may also worsen unemployment by encouraging capital-intensive activities.

Despite the dangers of the second stage of import substitution, this is the strategy that many Latin American, Southeast Asian and Eastern European countries adopted in the immediate postwar years. The consequence was that the export of manufactures was discouraged and the terms of trade turned against agriculture within the countries, discouraging agricultural output and reducing the growth of demand for industrial products internally. In the 1960s, reforms were undertaken in several countries, but there was a distinct difference in emphasis and approach between Latin America and Southeast Asia. In Latin America, policies became more outward-looking but still favoured production for the domestic market. Although subsidies were given to exports, exporters were still required to use domestic inputs produced under protection, and the subsidies were generally insufficient to provide an incentive to export that was comparable to the protection of domestic markets; thus, there was a continued bias in favour of import substitution. In East and Southeast Asia, in contrast, the policy has always been one of relentless export expansion – in Japan, South Korea, Singapore, Taiwan and other countries, as outlined earlier. Now, most developing countries are attempting to follow this route with varying degrees of success.

The Prebisch doctrine: an alternative approach to trade in developing countries

Raúl Prebisch (1901–86) was one of the first development economists to question the mutual profitability of the international division of labour for developing countries on existing lines. Prebisch was executive secretary of the Economic Commission for Latin America, 1950–63, and secretary-general of UNCTAD, 1963–69 (for a biography of Prebisch, see Dosman, 2008). He looked at the relation between trade and development from the standpoint of the balance of payments rather than the augmentation of real resources. His major claim was that the unfavourable impact of unrestricted trade on the terms of trade and balance of payments of developing countries can far outweigh any advantages with respect to a more efficient allocation of resources. His concern was with two distinct, but not unrelated, phenomena. One is the transference of the benefits of technical progress from developing to developed countries through terms of trade deterioration. The second is the balance of payments' effects of differences in the income elasticity of demand for different types of products. He divided the world into industrial 'centres' and 'peripheral' countries, and then conducted his analysis within the framework of the traditional two-country, two-commodity case of international trade theory – equating developing countries with primary producers (the 'periphery') and developed countries with industrial producers (the 'centre').

Technical progress and the terms of trade

As stated earlier, in theory, the barter terms of trade might be expected to move in favour of developing countries. For one thing, primary product production tends to be subject to diminishing returns, and for another, technical progress tends to be more rapid in manufacturing industry than in agriculture. If prices are related to costs, one would expect that, in theory, the ratio of primary product prices to industrial good prices would rise. According to Prebisch (1950), however, the ratio had shown a long-run historical tendency to fall. He advanced two explanations of this and hence why the benefits of technical progress tend to flow from developing to developed countries and not the other way round. His first explanation concerns the relation between incomes and productivity. He suggested that whereas factor incomes tend to rise with productivity increases in developed countries, they rise more slowly than productivity in developing countries owing to surplus labour. Thus, there is a greater upward pressure on final goods' prices in developed than in developing countries, causing the ratio of prices to move in the opposite direction to that suggested by the pace of technical progress. All this is on the supply side.

On the demand side is the fact that the demand for primary products grows more slowly than that for industrial products as world income grows, for two major reasons:

1. Many primary commodities have an intrinsically low income elasticity of demand because they are necessities.
2. Many primary commodities have been substituted by synthetics, for example natural rubber.

Putting these demand and supply factors together gives the picture in Figure 15.8, which shows what is likely to happen to the terms of trade of primary commodities through time.

In the centre, the supply and demand curves for industrial goods are relatively elastic, and in the periphery, the supply and demand curves for primary products are relatively inelastic. Assume initially that the supply and demand curves intersect at the same point in both sectors, so that the prices of industrial and primary products are 'equal' (that is, the terms of trade = 1). In the centre, technical progress will first shift the supply curve (*SS*) outwards, but let us assume that increases in wage costs push it back inwards to S_1S_1. In the periphery, in contrast, technical progress shifts the supply curve outwards to S_1S_1, but there is no inward shift due to rising wage costs. In the centre, the demand for industrial goods grows strongly from *DD* to D_1D_1, while in the periphery, the demand for primary products grows only slowly. The price of industrial goods rises to P_{I2}, while the price of primary products in this example has actually fallen to P_{p2}. The terms of trade of primary products has deteriorated by the amount *ab* for fundamental economic reasons associated with the characteristics of products and the institutional structures of the countries that produce them.

Figure 15.8 Movements in the terms of trade

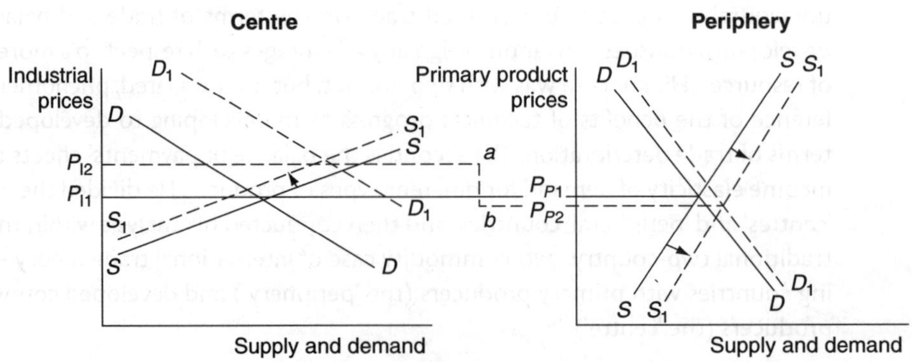

The income elasticity of demand for products and the balance of payments

According to Prebisch, the second factor working to the disadvantage of developing countries is the balance of payments' effects of differences in the income elasticity of demand for different types of product. As mentioned, it is generally recognized and agreed that the income elasticity of demand for most primary commodities is lower than that for manufactured products. On average, the elasticity is probably less than unity, resulting in a decreasing proportion of income spent on those commodities (commonly known as **Engel's law**). In the two-country, two-commodity case, the lower income elasticity of demand for primary commodities means that for a given growth of world income, the balance of payments of primary producing, developing countries will *automatically* deteriorate vis-à-vis the balance of payments of developed countries producing and exporting industrial goods. A simple example will illustrate the point (see also Chapter 10).

Suppose that the income elasticity of demand for the exports of developing countries is 0.8 and that the growth of world income is 3.0%: exports will then grow at 2.4%. Now suppose that the income elasticity of demand for the exports of developed countries is 1.3 and the growth of world income is 3.0%; exports of developed countries will then grow at 3.9%. Since there are only two sets of countries, developing countries' exports are the imports of developed countries and developed countries' exports are the imports of developing countries. Thus, developing countries' exports grow at 2.4% but imports grow at 3.9%; developed countries' exports grow at 3.9% and imports at 2.4%. Starting from equilibrium, the balance of payments of developing countries automatically worsens, while that of developed countries shows a surplus. This has further repercussions on the terms of trade. With imports growing faster than exports in developing countries, and the balance of payments deteriorating, the terms of trade will also deteriorate through depreciation of the currency, which may cause the balance of payments to deteriorate even more if imports and exports are price inelastic.

It is easily seen that the price of balance of payments equilibrium is slower growth for developing countries. If their exports are growing at 2.4%, import growth must be constrained to 2.4%, which means that with an income elasticity of demand for imports of 1.3, income growth in developing countries must be restrained to $2.4/1.3 = 1.85\%$ for balance of payments equilibrium. In the absence of foreign borrowing to bridge the foreign exchange gap, or a change in the structure of exports, the result of different income elasticities of demand for primary and manufactured products is slower growth in the primary producing countries – perpetuating the development 'gap'.

For terms of trade and balance of payments reasons (which are connected), Prebisch therefore argued for import substitution and the protection of certain domestically produced goods. Prebisch's balance of payments argument reinforces the classical infant industry and optimum tariff (terms of trade improvement) argument for protection.

There are several benefits that Prebisch expected from protection:

- Protection would enable scarce foreign exchange to be rationed between different categories of imports, and could help to correct balance of payments disequilibrium resulting from a high-income elasticity of demand for certain types of imports.
- It could help to arrest the deterioration in the terms of trade by damping down the demand for imports.
- It could provide the opportunity to diversify products and to start producing and exporting goods with a much higher income elasticity of demand in world markets.
- Following our earlier analysis, however, protection by tariffs is only appropriate if the arguments for protection do not arise from domestic distortions.

Recent trends in the terms of trade

Primary commodities

Whether the terms of trade have moved unfavourably against primary commodities and developing countries is an empirical question. Prebisch originally suggested an average deterioration of the terms of trade of primary commodities between 1876 and 1938 of 0.9% per annum. Work by Hans Singer at the UN in 1949 also suggested a trend deterioration of 0.64% per annum over the same period, and thus the **Prebisch–Singer thesis** of the declining terms of trade for primary commodities was born (see Singer, 1950). In a detailed reappraisal of Prebisch's work, Spraos (1980) confirmed the historical trend deterioration, but at the lower rate of approximately 0.5%, having corrected the statistics for the changing quality of goods, shipping costs and other factors. Extending the data to 1970, however, Spraos concluded that there had been no significant trend deterioration. Sapsford (1985, 1988), however, shows that it is the wartime structural improvement (1940–51) that makes the whole series look trendless. If the series is divided into two subperiods – prewar and postwar – there is a trend deterioration in both subperiods and the estimated trend deterioration over the whole period 1900–82 is 1.2% per annum, allowing for the wartime structural break.

Hans Singer

Born 1910, Elberfield, Germany. Died 2006. In 1933, came to England as a refugee to work on his PhD with Keynes at Cambridge. Joined the UN in 1947; was instrumental in the establishment of bodies such as the International Development Association of the World Bank, the United Nations Development Programme, and the World Food Programme; and taught at the New School for Social Research in New York. Joined the Institute for Development Studies at the University of Sussex in 1969, and travelled and lectured widely, advising several countries and development institutions. Championed the world's poor in his prolific writing, and was a passionate advocate of international aid. Linked with the name of Prebisch and the thesis of a declining terms of trade of primary commodities.

Since the original Spraos and Sapsford evaluations of the Prebisch–Singer thesis, there has been an outpouring of further studies using different time periods and different statistical estimating techniques. Grilli and Yang (1988) at the World Bank constructed their own series of the terms of trade and also looked at individual commodities, but reached similar conclusions to Sapsford. Over the period 1900–83, they put the percentage terms of trade deterioration of all primary commodities at 0.5% per annum, and 0.6% per annum for non-fuel commodities (allowing for a wartime structural break). For individual commodities, the trend deterioration is estimated as follows: food, –0.3% per annum; cereals, –0.6% per annum; non-food agricultural commodities, –0.8% per annum; and metals, –0.8% per annum. Only tropical beverages registered an improvement of 0.6% per annum. Bleaney and Greenaway (1993) updated the Grilli–Yang series to 1991 and estimated a trend deterioration of 0.8% per annum, with a big structural break in the early

1980s associated with world recession and the supply response of developing countries attempting to export themselves out of debt difficulties. Ocampo and Parra (2003) take the same 24 commodities as Grilli and Yang and estimate the decline in the real terms of trade over the whole of the twentieth century. They estimate a cumulative decline of 0.8% per annum, the same as Bleaney and Greenaway. The estimates of decline for each commodity by subperiods is shown in Table 15.3. Only six commodities experienced an improvement over the whole period.

Another study is by Cashin and McDermott (2002) at the IMF, who look at trends and cycles in both the nominal and real price (i.e. the terms of trade) of non-food commodities over the period 1862–1999. The graphs of both indices are shown in Figure 15.9.

Nominal prices were relatively stable from 1862 to 1932 (except during the First World War), but since then have been very volatile around a rising trend. The real price index, however, or the terms of trade of primary commodities, has always been very volatile around a generally declining trend. The average trend decline over the whole period 1862–1999 is 1.3% per annum. From an index of 120 in 1862 to an index of 20 in 1999, real commodity prices lost 85% of their value. Or,

Table 15.3 Changes in the real terms of trade for commodities (annual average percentage growth rates)

	1920–30	1980–90	1900–2000	1900/04–1996/2000
Aluminium	1.8	2.8	−1.1	−1.3
Bananas	5.8	0.1	0.0	−0.1
Beef	−0.2	−6.6	1.0	0.9
Cocoa	−0.7	−9.5	−1.3	−1.0
Coffee	0.4	−8.3	−0.1	0.4
Copper	1.4	−1.1	−0.7	−0.6
Cotton	−3.0	−6.1	−1.0	−1.1
Jute	−0.9	0.6	−0.4	−0.7
Lamb	−0.1	−3.9	1.6	1.7
Lead	0.7	4.2	−0.8	−0.3
Leather	4.7	1.3	−0.8	−1.1
Maize	−1.2	−5.3	−0.8	1.2
Palm oil	−2.3	−2.8	−0.3	0.0
Rice	3.7	−6.9	−1.3	−1.2
Rubber	−9.5	−7.6	−2.8	−2.8
Silver	−5.3	−16.2	−0.3	−1.0
Sugar	−16.8	−10.5	−1.3	−1.1
Tea	7.6	−4.0	−0.7	0.7
Timber	−2.2	−1.5	1.1	−1.5
Tin	0.1	−10.2	0.1	0.2
Tobacco	−2.7	−0.4	0.8	−0.7
Wheat	4.5	−3.1	−0.6	−0.9
Wool	−3.1	−5.5	−1.2	−0.4
Zinc	−0.9	4.7	0.3	0.1

Source: Ocampo and Parra, 2003.

Figure 15.9 Nominal and real price indices of non-food primary commodities, 1862–1999

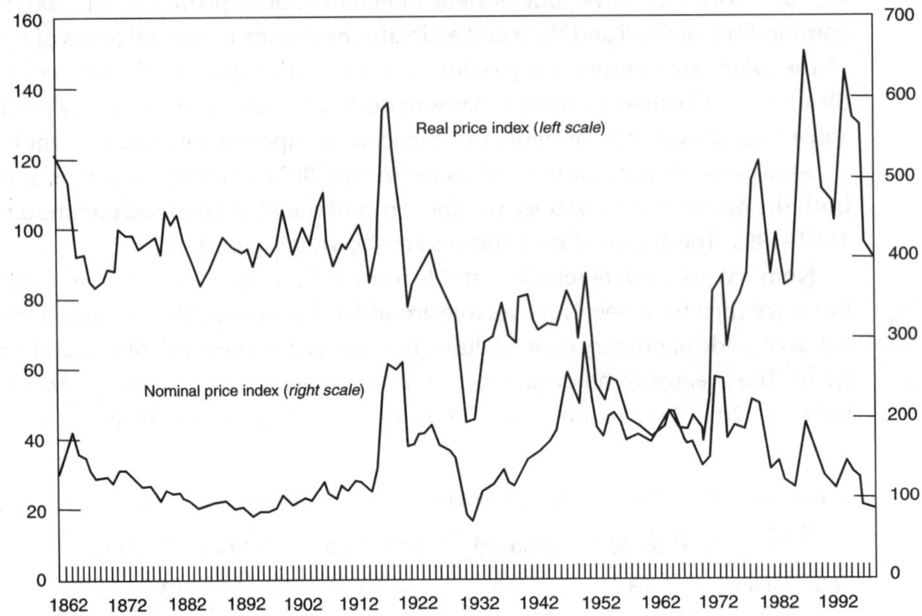

to put it another way, in 1999, primary commodities could only buy 20% of the industrial goods that they could buy in 1862. This represents a substantial real income loss. The estimated trend decline is even more serious if the commodity boom years of 1951 or 1973 are taken as the starting point for analysis.

Cashin and McDermott (2002) also focus on the magnitude and length of the cycles in real commodity prices, which they believe to be more serious than the trend decline. They find 13 occasions since 1913 when the annual price change was more than 20% in one year. This is serious volatility. They also find that average price slumps last longer than price booms (4.2 years compared with 3.6 years).

Cashin and McDermott (2002) conclude their study by saying:

> Although there is a downward trend in real commodity prices, this is of little policy relevance, because it is small compared with the variability of prices. In contrast, rapid, unexpected and often large movements in commodity prices are an important feature of their behaviour. Such movements can have serious consequences for the terms of trade, real incomes, and fiscal positions of commodity-dependent countries, and have profound implications for the achievement of macroeconomic stabilisation.

Erten and Ocampo (2013) have identified four supercycles of real commodity prices over the period 1865–2010 ranging between 30 and 40 years, with an amplitude 20–40% higher or lower than the long-run trend. The mean of each supercycle of non-oil commodities is generally lower than that for the previous cycle, supporting the Prebisch–Singer hypothesis. The cycles are 1894–1932, peaking in 1917; 1932–71, peaking in 1951; 1971–99, peaking in 1973, and post-2000, when real commodity prices rose to 2012 and then started to dip.

Blattman et al. (2007) have looked historically at the relationship between terms of trade volatility and growth, taking 35 countries over the period 1870–1939 and find a negative relationship, and this is one of the major reasons why the income gap between the 'periphery' primary producing countries and the industrial countries widened during this period. One major adverse effect of volatility was the deterrent to foreign direct investment.

The most comprehensive historical study to date of the commodity terms of trade is by Harvey et al. (2010), who look at 25 commodities over the past four centuries from 1650 and find that in the 'very long run, a secular deteriorating trend is a relevant phenomenon for a significant proportion of primary commodities', particularly for aluminium, coffee, hides, jute, silver, sugar, tea, tobacco, wheat, wool and zinc. For other commodities, no significant trend can be detected – either up or down – and Harvey et al. (2010) conclude: 'there is simply no statistical evidence that relative commodity prices have ever trended upwards'.

Developing countries

As already indicated, the terms of trade of primary commodities relative to manufactures is not necessarily the same as the terms of trade of developing countries relative to developed countries, because both sets of countries export and import both types of goods (albeit in different ratios), but, in practice, there is likely to be a close overlap and parallel movement between the two. Sarkar (1986) has looked at the export prices of developing countries relative to those of developed countries, and also at the prices of exports from developing to developed countries relative to the prices of imports from developed countries into developing countries (both excluding fuel). In the first case, the trend deterioration was 0.51% per annum; in the second, the relative deterioration was 0.93% per annum.

Bleaney and Greenaway (1993) find that over the period 1955–89, a 1% deterioration in the terms of trade of primary products translated into a 0.3% deterioration in the terms of trade for developing countries as a whole, although this would have been substantially greater for Africa and Latin America, which are more commodity-dependent than Asia.

Sarkar and Singer (1991) have also looked at the terms of trade of *manufactures* exported by developing countries relative to those of developed countries over the period 1970–87, and find a deterioration of approximately 1% per annum. If this is the case (this result has been challenged by Bleaney, 1993, and particularly by Athukorala, 1993, who show that the result apparently depends on the inclusion of non-ferrous metals in the manufacturing export price series), it would appear that developing countries suffer double jeopardy. Not only do the prices of their primary products decline relative to those of manufactured goods, but also the prices of their manufactured exports decline relative to those of developed countries; reflecting, no doubt, the commodity composition of these exports – their lower value-added and lower income elasticity of demand in world markets. This is confirmed by Erten (2011), who has carefully examined the terms of trade for different groups of developing countries using UNCTAD data (e.g. countries exporting mainly primary commodities, countries exporting mainly manufactures, the least developed countries and the highly indebted countries), and finds in all cases a decline in their terms of trade from 1960 to 2006 of between 1 and 3% per annum, with a severe structural break in the mid-1970s.

Finally, there is a distinction between the **barter (or commodity) terms of trade**, which measures the ratio of export to import prices, and the **income terms of trade**, which is the ratio of export to import prices times the quantity of exports, that is, $(Px/Pm) \times Qx$. The income terms of trade is thus a measure of the total purchasing power of exports over imports. From the point of view of development, measured by per capita income, the income terms of trade is perhaps the more relevant concept to consider than the barter terms of trade. It may well be, for instance, that the prices of exports fall relative to those of imports owing to increased efficiency in the exporting country, and this releases resources for further exports, which subsequently expand more than proportionately to the fall in price. The barter terms of trade will have worsened, but the country will be better off. It is also worth remembering that when a country devalues its currency, it deliberately worsens its barter terms of trade in the hope that the balance of payments will improve, providing scope for a faster growth of real income through a rapid improvement in the income terms of trade. On the other hand, if the demand for a country's exports is price inelastic, then a decline in the barter terms of trade will also mean a deterioration in the income terms of trade.

In the long run, if world trade is buoyant, all countries can experience an improvement in their income terms of trade. The question is not who are the gainers and who are the losers, as in the case of the barter terms of trade, but what are the *relative* rates of improvement in the income terms of trade?

Fair trade not free trade: trade policies towards developing countries

Developed countries, supported by multilateral institutions such as the IMF, the World Bank and the WTO, preach the virtues of trade liberalization and free trade for developing countries, but fail to practise it themselves. In particular, rich countries still protect their agricultural sectors with subsidies and tariffs, which make it difficult, and sometimes impossible, for poor developing countries to compete in world markets. The case of cotton is highlighted in Case example 15.3. Agricultural subsidies in the EU and the USA amount to over $100 billion per annum. Developed countries also impose tariffs on agricultural imports from developing countries, and subsidize exports. The average tariff against agricultural imports into developed countries is 23%. US rice farmers receive a 72% subsidy. The dumping of artificially cheap crops from rich country agribusiness has destroyed thousands of small farmers in developing countries.

Case example 15.3 **Unfair trade in cotton**

The USA spends $3.3 billion a year on subsidies to 25,000 cotton farmers, which profoundly affects the livelihoods of 10 million cotton farmers in the west and central African countries of Burkina Faso, Benin, Chad and Mali. This subsidy to US cotton producers is three times the US aid budget to the whole of Africa. The tragedy is that the World Bank has encouraged these African countries to produce more cotton on the pretext of comparative advantage, but they find it impossible to compete against such subsidies. The US trade representative at the Doha Round of WTO trade negotiations in 2002 had the audacity to tell the cotton farmers of Africa that 'they should do something else'.

The protection afforded to agriculture is also given to many low value-added manufactured goods in which developing countries have a static comparative advantage – particularly for a wide range of textile goods. Trade barriers against the exports of developing countries cost these countries approximately $100 billion a year, which is almost equal to the amount they receive in official development assistance.

When it comes to the reality of free trade, as opposed to the rhetoric, there appears to be one law for rich developed nations and another for the poor. As long as the terms of trade of primary products continue to decline, and developing countries' agricultural products are discriminated against in world markets, trade between the developed and developing countries cannot be fair. The playing field between rich and poor countries is not level, and the rich countries seem to want to keep it that way. What developing countries want is fair trade not free trade. See Oxfam's (2002) compelling indictment of the world's unfair trading system.

The **World Trade Organization (WTO)**, established in 1995 (formerly the General Agreement on Tariffs and Trade, GATT, founded in 1947) is the major international body that negotiates multilateral tariff reductions between countries. Up to now, however, it has been singularly unsuccessful in freeing trade in agricultural commodities. The **Kennedy Round** (1964–67), the **Tokyo Round** (1973–79) and the **Uruguay Round** (1986–94) of world trade negotiations all focused mainly on reducing tariffs on trade in manufactures (with some preferential treatment for developing countries). It was in Seattle in 1999 that developing countries began to raise their voice concerning agricultural protection, but the talks ended in failure. The rich countries refused to make any concessions over agriculture, and the trade round collapsed amid recriminations and violent street protests. In November 2001, the **Doha Round** was launched. This was supposed to be a 'development' round (to help poor countries), but in 2009, the talks ended with no agreement being reached because of the insistence by rich countries that they will only cut farm subsidies and trade barriers if developing countries allow them access to their markets for manufactured goods and the financial services sector, and enforce stricter competition rules and transparency in government procurement. The US reaction to the breakdown of the Doha Round has been to start bilateral trade deals with countries that it favours politically.

The main multilateral pressure group for a fairer trading deal between developed and developing countries is the **United Nations Conference on Trade and Development (UNCTAD)**, which was first convened in Geneva in 1964, with Raúl Prebisch as secretary-general. The organization exists as a continuous pressure group with the aim of assisting developing countries through fairer trade, and also aid. Among its stated objectives are:

- Greater access to the markets of developed countries through the reduction in trade barriers
- More stable commodity prices
- Raising the level of aid from developed countries to the UN target of 0.7% of donors' GNI
- Compensation to developing countries for fluctuations in export earnings and terms of trade deterioration.

It has had some limited success in persuading developed countries to grant preferential access to the exports of developing countries, but mainly in the field of manufactured goods, benefiting the larger and more advanced developing countries.

Perhaps the most significant trade agreement negotiated to date to help poorer developing nations is the **Lomé Convention**, which was signed in 1975 by the European Economic Community (EEC, now the European Union, EU) and 46 (now 77) developing countries in Africa, the Caribbean and the Pacific (the so-called ACP countries). The Lomé Convention provides for free access to the European market for all developing countries' manufactured goods and 90% of their agricultural exports. In addition, agreement was reached to stabilize the foreign exchange earnings of 12 key commodities (the so-called **Stabex scheme**). The Lomé Convention also dispenses aid to the ACP countries through the **European Development Fund (EDF)**. Since 1975, the Lomé Convention has been renegotiated five times. The latest agreement reached in Cotonou (Benin) in 2000 is designed to last for 20 years, with revisions possible every 5 years. In 2000, the Stabex scheme was discontinued. Instead, support for fluctuations in export earnings will come from the EDF as part of a **Country Support Strategy** drawn up for each ACP state.

In the voluntary sector, the **fair trade movement** is gathering widespread support, and is making a difference to the lives of poor farmers in many developing countries. The movement was founded in 1979 with the main objective of guaranteeing a price to producers above the world price with a sufficient premium above the cost of production to allow producer cooperatives to invest in community projects such as housing, healthcare and public utilities. More than 7 million farmers and their families in over 60 countries participate and benefit. Importers of fair trade products such as coffee, tea, chocolate, sugar, bananas, fruit juices and so on must buy directly from Fairtrade-certified producers, and agree to establish long-term, stable relationships with them. This cuts out the middleman, or monopsonist – often a large multinational corporation in the case of many primary commodities. The fair trade movement has encouraged farmers to join cooperatives, which have much greater bargaining power in dealing with buyers. Many supermarkets and other retail outlets now stock a range of Fairtrade products.

The value of retail sales is still a drop in the ocean – £1.8 billion in the UK in 2015 and £4.4 billion globally. Unfortunately, however, the fair trade movement cannot alter fundamental economic forces, which drive down the price of commodities relative to the prices of manufactured goods and services. The only long-run solution to this dilemma is structural change, which requires the protection of new industries, and this is what rich, developed countries do not like. They want access to poor developing countries' markets, while continuing to protect their own. The fair trade movement can, however, make a major contribution to raising public awareness of the inequities in the global trading system, which, in turn, can exert pressure on rich developed countries' governments for fundamental reform of the terms on which developed and developing countries trade with each other.

Trade strategy for development

So what trade strategy should poor developing countries pursue? The overriding objective must be to acquire dynamic comparative advantage. For this, the private sector of an economy needs government support in the form of incentives and various types of 'protection' to mitigate investment risks. It is one thing to argue against anti-export bias; it is another to argue that poor developing countries should abandon all forms of protection of domestic industry. Improved market access to developed countries for poor developing country exports merely perpetuates static comparative advantage. As Rodrik (2001) argued in the lead-up to the Doha Round of trade negotiations: 'the exchange of reduced policy autonomy in the South for improved market access in the North is a bad bargain where development is concerned'. Poor developing countries need time and policy space to nurture new (infant) industrial activities as developed countries did historically, and as many newly industrializing economies still do today. As Hausmann and Rodrik (2003) say in their important work on the concept of 'self-discovery':

> the fact that the world's most successful economies during the last few decades prospered doing things that are most commonly associated with failure (e.g. protection) is something that cannot easily be dismissed.

Dani Rodrik

Born 1957, Istanbul, Turkey. Professor of Political Economy, Harvard University; one of the foremost development economists of his generation, working on the importance of institutions for economic development and the relation between trade and development. Strong critic of free trade orthodoxy and the WTO in his book, *The Global Governance of Trade: As if Development Really Mattered* (2001). Also pioneered, with Ricardo Hausmann and others, new thinking in development economics relating to 'self-discovery' and 'growth diagnostics', and important work on the analysis of 'growth accelerations'. His latest books include *The Globalization Paradox* (2012) and *Towards a Better Global Economy* (2014).

Hausmann and Rodrik's (2003) argument is that there is much randomness in the process of a country discovering what it is best at producing, and a lack of protection reduces the incentive to invest in discovering which goods and services they are. Poor, labour-abundant economies have thousands of things they could produce and trade, but, in practice, their exports are highly concentrated. Sometimes, over 50% of exports are accounted for by less than ten products. Bangladesh and Pakistan are countries at similar levels of development, but Bangladesh specializes in hats and Pakistan in bed sheets. This specialization is not the result of resource endowment; it is the result of chance choice by enterprising entrepreneurs who 'discovered' (*ex post*) where relative costs were lowest. Other 'chance' investments include cut flowers in Colombia for export to North America, camel cheese in Mauritania for export to the EU, high-yield maize in Malawi, and squash in Tonga. The policy implications of the Haussmann and Rodrik observation and model are that governments need to encourage entrepreneurship and invest in new activities *ex ante*, but push out unproductive firms and sectors *ex post*. Intervention needs to discriminate as far as possible between innovators and imitators. Normal forms of trade protection turn out not to be the ideal policy instruments, because they do not discriminate, and earn profits only for those selling in the domestic market. Export subsidies avoid anti-export bias, but still do not discriminate between the innovators and the copycats and are, in any case, illegal under WTO rules. The first best policy is public sector credit or guarantees, which can discriminate in favour of the innovator and be used as a 'stick' if firms do not perform well.

There is much that the international community can also do to promote trade for development, as opposed to pursuing trade liberalization for its own sake. The whole world trade system works against the majority of poor developing countries, because:

1. They depend on primary commodities (the 'curse' of natural resources) and low value-added manufactures.
2. The 'rules of the game' governing trade between rich and poor countries are biased in favour of the rich.
3. The agenda for trade reform is largely set by the rich developed countries.

The only permanent solution to primary commodity dependence is structural change, which requires the establishment of new, non-traditional industries; but the rich developed nations are hostile to this move. They want free access to poor developing countries' markets while continuing to protect their own. The most recent example of this is the ongoing debate between the EU and the African, Caribbean and Pacific (ACP) countries over **Economic Partnership Agreements (EPAs)** to replace the trade preferences that the ACP countries used to enjoy under the Lomé Convention. The EU is insisting that poor developing countries reduce restrictions on imports of manufactured goods and service activities in return for continued access to the EU market for their agricultural products. The EU is refusing to look at alternatives to free trade EPAs, but concedes that EPAs could lead to the collapse of the manufacturing sector in many poor countries. As Stiglitz (2006) remarks in his powerful book *Making Globalization Work*: 'the US and Europe have perfected the art of arguing for free trade while simultaneously working for trade agreements that protect themselves against imports from developing countries'. If developed countries really wanted to help poor developing countries, they could reduce and eliminate tariffs and barriers against all their goods. In addition, developing countries might be allowed 'infant *country* protection', which would be equivalent to a currency devaluation, but has the advantage of raising revenue for spending on public goods. One of the severe drawbacks of tariff reductions in poor countries is a loss of tax revenue.

If trade is to promote development, the WTO, which now governs world trade, needs radical reform and rethinking (Wade, 2003). *The Agreement Establishing the WTO* (WTO, 1995) lists as one of its purposes:

> Raising standards of living, ensuring full employment and a large and steady growing volume of real income and effective demand, and expanding the production of, and trade in, goods and services, while allowing for the objective of sustainable development, seeking both to protect and preserve the environment and to enhance the means of doing so in a manner consistent with their respective needs and concerns at different levels of development.

The aim is laudable, but unfortunately there is a divorce between rhetoric and reality because the WTO treats trade liberalization and economic development as synonymous. As we have seen, however, the historical and contemporary evidence is that domestic economic policy, institution-building and the promotion of investment opportunities are far more important than trade liberalization and trade openness in determining economic success in the early stages of economic development. Rodrik (2001) reminds us (see also Chang, 2002, 2005, 2007; Reinert, 2007) that:

> No country has [ever] developed simply by opening itself up to foreign trade and investment. The trick has been to combine the opportunities offered by world markets with a domestic investment and institution-building strategy to stimulate the animal spirits of domestic entrepreneurs.

But now, under WTO rules, all the things that, for example, South Korea, Taiwan and other East Asian countries did to promote economic development in the 1960s, 1970s and 1980s are severely restricted. Some countries that break the rules are succeeding spectacularly. China is one obvious example, but another would be Vietnam, which, while promoting FDI and exports, also protects its domestic market, maintains import monopolies and engages in state trading. The WTO should shift away from trying to maximize the flow of trade to understanding and evaluating what trade regime will maximize the possibility of development for individual poor developing countries.

A new world trade order is required that acts on behalf of poor developing countries, and poor developing countries need a louder voice in any reformed structure.

International commodity agreements[1]

Developing countries in particular, and the world economy in general, suffer several problems from the uncontrolled movement of primary commodity prices. First, there is the gradual trend deterioration in the prices of primary commodities relative to industrial goods, which directly reduces the real income and welfare of developing countries. Second, the prices of primary products are much more cyclically volatile than those of industrial goods.

This volatility has a number of detrimental consequences. First, it leads to a great deal of instability in the foreign exchange earnings and balance of payments position of developing countries, which makes investment planning and economic management much more difficult than would otherwise be the case.

Second, because of asymmetries in the economic system, volatility imparts inflationary bias combined with tendencies to depression in the world economy at large. When the prices of primary products fall, the demand for industrial goods falls but their prices are sticky downwards. When the prices of primary products rise, prices of industrial goods are quick to follow suit and governments depress demand to control inflation. The result is stagflation.

Third, the price volatility of primary products leads to volatility in the terms of trade, which may not reflect movements in the equilibrium terms of trade between primary products and industrial goods in the sense that supply and demand are equated in both markets. In these circumstances, world economic growth becomes either supply constrained if the prices of primary products are 'too high', or demand constrained if they are 'too low' (see Chapter 5). On all these macroeconomic grounds, there is a *prima facie* case for attempting to introduce a greater degree of stability into markets for primary commodities (including oil).

Price falls can, however, be dramatic and persistent. Cashin et al. (2000) look at shocks to the prices of 60 commodities over the period 1957–98 and find them typically long-lasting and not just temporary blips: 17 of the commodities experienced price shocks that persisted for longer than five years. This means depressed prices for a long time, and makes price stabilization and income compensation schemes more difficult and costly to manage (see below).

The issue of primary product price instability is not something new. It preoccupied Keynes before and during the Second World War. In 'The International Regulation of Primary Commodities', Keynes (1942) remarked: 'one of the greatest evils in international trade before the war was the wide and rapid fluctuations in the world price of primary commodities … It must be the primary purpose of control to prevent these wide fluctuations'. Keynes (1942) followed up his observations and proposals with a more detailed plan for what he called **commod control** – an international body representing leading producers and consumers that would stand ready to buy 'commods' (Keynes' name for typical commodities), and store them, at a price (say) 10% below the fixed basic price and sell them at 10% above. Figure 15.10 illustrates how the scheme would operate.

In Figure 15.10, P_n is the fixed basic price. When the price rises outside the 10% upper range, the commod control scheme would sell, pushing the price downwards towards the 'normal' price. Similarly, when the price falls outside the 10% lower range, the commod control scheme would buy, pushing price upwards within the range. The basic price would have to be adjusted according to whether there was a gradual run-down or build-up of stocks, indicating that the price was

Figure 15.10 Keynes' commod control scheme

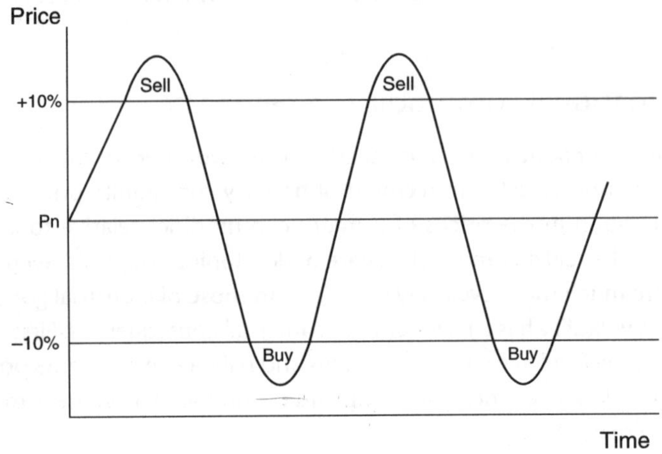

either 'too low' or 'too high'. If production did not adjust (at least downwards), Keynes recognized that production quotas might have to be implemented. Commodities should be stored as widely as possible across producing and consuming centres.

This proposal is of some contemporary relevance as a means of responding quickly to conditions of famine. For example, there could be a system of granaries strategically placed across the world under international supervision to store surpluses and release them in times of need. The finance for the storage and holding of 'commods' in Keynes' scheme would have been provided through his proposal for an international clearing union, acting like a world central bank, with which 'commod controls' would keep accounts.

The finance for storage and holding could now be provided through the issue of Special Drawing Rights (SDRs) by the IMF (see Chapter 16). A commod control scheme could make a major contribution to curing the international trade cycle, with all its attendant implications. Over 70 years have passed since Keynes' wartime proposal, but primary product price fluctuations still plague the world economy. The world still lacks the requisite international mechanisms to rectify what is a major source of instability for the world economy.

In the recent past, there have been five main international commodity agreements in operation – for sugar, tin, rubber, coffee and cocoa, and accounting for some 35% of non-oil exports of the developing countries – but all have had their difficulties and broken down. Maizels (1992) and Gilbert (1996) both provide a comprehensive discussion of international commodity agreements and commodity problems in general. The basic problem with all agreements is getting suppliers to abide by quotas to restrict output in the face of declining prices. Participants must share a common purpose. The most successful 'commodity agreement' of all is the EU's Common Agricultural Policy, but this does not help developing countries.

Small fluctuations in the export earnings of developing countries, arising from falling prices, are capable of offsetting the entire value of foreign assistance to developing countries in any one year. A 10% fall in export earnings is approximately equivalent to the annual flow of official development assistance. Stable export earnings, it would appear, are at least as important as foreign assistance. For a summary of the measures of instability and the empirical evidence of the effects of instability on developing countries' economies, see Lim (1991) and Love (1987).

In general, unstable export proceeds are the product of variations in both price and quantity. Large fluctuations in earnings may be causally related to four factors:

1. Excessive variability of supply and demand
2. Low price elasticity of supply and demand
3. Excessive specialization in one or two commodities
4. A concentration of exports in particular markets.

If the source of instability does come from the supply side, stabilizing prices will not, of course, stabilize earnings. It will reduce them in times of scarcity and boost them in periods of glut. If there is a tendency towards perpetual oversupply and demand is price inelastic, price stabilization will maintain earnings, but price stabilization will further encourage supply, which may then necessitate production quotas and lead to inefficiency in production, if producing countries are allocated quotas to satisfy equity rather than efficiency.

This is not to argue that there is not a case for compensation, but that methods should be avoided that encourage overproduction or inefficiency. It may be better to let prices find their own market level and for producing countries to be compensated by the beneficiaries under long-term agreements, the compensation being used to encourage some producers into other activities. Alternatively, income compensation schemes could be worked out, especially in cases where export instability results from variations in domestic supply. Several alternative methods of price stabilization have been tried or recommended, including buffer stock schemes, export restriction schemes and price compensation schemes. These are examined briefly below.

Buffer stock schemes involve buying up the stock of a commodity when its price is abnormally low and selling the commodity when its price is unusually high. The success of such schemes rests on the foresight of those who manage them. Purchases must be made when prices are low relative to future prices and sold when prices are high relative to future prices. Clearly, buffer stock schemes are only suitable for evening out price fluctuations. They cannot cope with persistent downward trends in price without accumulating large stocks of the commodity, which must be paid for – and presumably sold in the future at still lower prices. Storage schemes are only appropriate for goods that can easily be stored, and for which the cost of storage is not excessive. Apart from internationally managed buffer stock schemes, governments of individual countries often take an active role in stabilizing prices via commodity boards. Again the problem arises, however, that if there is excess supply, the government will acquire large stocks of the commodity and the budgetary burden of maintaining the price becomes prohibitive.

Restriction schemes are concerned with maintaining prices by restricting supply to the market. The essence of a restriction scheme is that major producers or nations (on behalf of producers) get together and agree to restrict the production and export of a good whose price is falling, thus maintaining or increasing (if demand is inelastic) revenue from a smaller volume of output. In practice, it is difficult to maintain and supervise schemes of this nature, because it becomes extremely attractive for any one producer or nation to break away from, or refuse to join, the scheme.

The disadvantages of restriction schemes are, first, that demand may not be inelastic in the long run, so that raising the price by restricting supply may reduce export earnings in the long run. Restriction schemes may ultimately lead to substitution for the product and falling sales. Second, restriction schemes can lead to serious resource allocation inefficiencies stemming from the arbitrary allocation of export quotas between countries and production quotas between producers within countries, unless the quotas are revised regularly to take account of changes in the efficiency of production between producers and between regions of the world. Restriction schemes are often operated by producer cartels, the classic example being the oil-producing countries belonging to OPEC (Organization of the Petroleum Exporting Countries), which managed to raise the price of crude oil by 800% between 1973 and 1980 (although it has not been so successful since then at stabilizing prices at a consistently high level).

Developing countries are not only producers of raw materials, however; they are also consumers, and what some countries gain with respect to the production and exportation of one commodity they may lose with respect to the importation and consumption of another. Developing countries that are poor in all raw materials may not benefit at all. It is not clear, except in the case of a few special commodities such as oil, that cartelization and monopoly pricing of the product will necessarily redistribute income from developed to developing countries taken as a whole. If this is so, bilateral commodity agreements between developing country producers and developed country users are probably preferable as a means of ensuring that all developing countries benefit.

Price compensation agreements lend themselves to the above form of bilateral arrangement. For example, if the price of a commodity falls, two countries could agree on a sliding scale of compensation such that the importing country pays an increasing sum of money to the exporter as the price falls below a 'normal' price specified in advance. The sliding scale of compensation could be applied to deviations of the actual price from the 'normal' price. Since restrictions on output and quotas are not part of the scheme, arrangements of this kind have the beauty of divorcing the efficiency aspects of pricing and commodity arrangements from the distributional aspects. The commodity would be traded at world prices, and the lack of full compensation would ensure that, if world prices were falling, some countries would decide to shift resources, so maintaining some degree of allocative efficiency.

There is no reason why price compensation schemes should not run concurrently with other types of international commodity agreement. Indeed, if the price of a commodity continually declines, it may be necessary to couple a restriction scheme with a price compensation scheme, otherwise importing countries will be *persistently* subsidizing the exporting countries. There is also the danger in this case, and also in the case of price support schemes, that one form of assistance will replace another. If developed countries continually have to pay more than the market prices for their primary products, and argue at the same time that the major constraint on financial assistance to developing countries is their balance of payments, they might use price compensation agreements as an excuse for cutting other forms of assistance. If so, what primary producers gain in the form of higher prices or higher export earnings than if the market were free, they lose in other ways.

If fluctuations in price emanate from the supply side and not from changes in demand, price compensation will operate perversely on the stabilization of *export earnings*. This is illustrated in Figure 15.11. Price in the market is determined by the intersection of the supply and demand curves, D_1D_1 and S_1S_1, giving equilibrium price, P_1. Now suppose that there is a decrease in demand to D_2D_2, causing price to fall to P_2. Earnings before the price fall were $0P_1XS_1$; after the price fall, they are $0P_2X_1S_1$. Assume that P_1 is the 'normal' price agreed under the price compensation scheme, and that P_2C represents the appropriate amount of price compensation in relation to the deviation from the 'normal' price following the decrease in demand. Total revenue under the price compensation scheme will be $0CC_1S_1$, which is not far short of total revenue before the fall in price. Consider, however, an equivalent fall in price from P_1 to P_2 as a result of an increase in supply from S_1S_1 to S_2S_2. Under the same price compensation scheme, total revenue is now $0CC_2S_2$, which is greatly in excess of the original total revenue (before the price fall) of $0P_1XS_1$. Conversely, if the supply falls and the price rises above the 'normal' price, revenue will be less than before the

Figure 15.11 Price compensation and export earnings

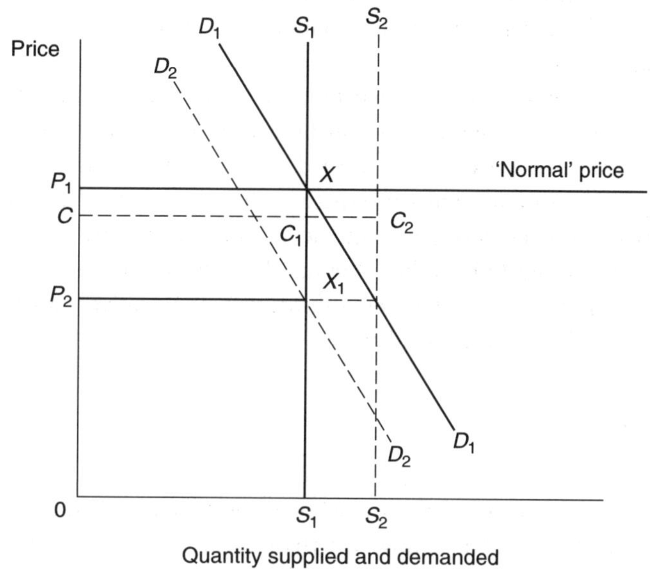

price rise, since the exporting country will presumably be compensating the importing country – unless the scheme works only one way.

The only way to overcome the induced instability of price compensation schemes is to formulate an **income compensation scheme** that takes account of both price and quantity changes. The practical difficulty is reaching agreement on a 'normal' level of income. If the trend rate of growth of output is positive for most commodities, to settle for a fixed level of 'normal' income would be unjust.

The way most income compensation schemes work is that each year's compensation is based on deviations of actual export earnings from the moving average of a series of previous years. The IMF's Compensatory and Contingency Financing Facility used to operate along these lines. The Stabex scheme – once operated by the EU under the Lomé Convention – was another example of an income compensation scheme. But there must be sufficient funds available. Furthermore, the compensation is paid to governments, so producers do not necessarily reap the benefits.

For stability and a greater degree of certainty over export earnings, producers and governments are increasingly looking to **futures markets** for risk management. To be able to sell forward in futures markets guarantees the producer a price and therefore earnings, depending on supply. Futures markets are not well developed, however, and very often cover is not available for more than one year in advance. Where private risk management is not available, there is a case for publicly subsidized agencies to increase the access of commodity producers in developing countries to insurance against price volatility – perhaps offering price floor guarantees to producers. This may be cheaper in the long run than compensating countries for commodity price fluctuations.

Trade versus aid

'Trade not aid' has become a popular slogan in developing countries in recent years. Let us now consider whether a unit of foreign exchange from exports is really worth more than a unit of foreign exchange from international assistance, or whether the slogan is more an understandable reaction to the debt-servicing problems arising from *past* borrowing (the benefits of which may have been forgotten) and to the political interference and leverage that may accompany international assistance.

If the meaning of aid is taken literally (that is, a free transfer of resources), Johnson (1967) showed a long time ago that a unit of foreign exchange from exports can never be as valuable as a unit of foreign exchange from aid. The reason for this is that exports do not provide additional resources for investment directly, only indirectly by the opportunity provided to transform domestic resources into goods and services more cheaply than if the transformation had to be done domestically. Aid, on the other hand, not only provides resources directly, but also indirectly by *saving the excess cost of import substitution*. The relative worth of exports compared with pure aid can therefore be expressed as:

$$\frac{cX}{(1 + c)A} \tag{15.5}$$

where X is the value of exports, A is the value of pure aid and c is the proportional excess cost of import substitution. The relative worth of exports will rise with the excess cost of import substitution, but it is clear that the worth of exports can never match the worth of an *equal* amount of pure aid ($X = A$), since $c < (1 + c)$. The fact that aid may be tied to higher priced goods makes some difference to the argument, but it can be shown that the excess cost of import substitution and the excess cost of tied goods would have to be relatively high for the worth of aid not to exceed the worth of trade. Let r be the ratio of the price of tied goods to the price of the same goods in the free market. The relative worth of exports may then be written as:

$$\frac{cX}{(1 + c)A} \times r \tag{15.6}$$

Now exports will be worth more than aid if $cr > (1 + c)$. Different combinations of c and r could be thought of to satisfy this condition, but both c and r would have to be quite high, for example $c = 2.0$ and $r = 1.5$.

The more important consideration, however, is that the term 'aid' in the slogan 'trade not aid' should probably not be interpreted literally. The comparison that developing countries are making is not between trade and pure aid, but either between trade and the aid component of an equal amount of foreign assistance, or simply between trade and an equal amount of foreign assistance. If these are the comparisons being made in practice, two interesting questions arise: Under what circumstances will trade be more valuable? Which is the most appropriate comparison to make?

Consider first the comparison between exports and the aid component of an equal amount of foreign assistance. If this is the comparison that is being made by developing countries, the Johnson formula can be modified by letting $A = Fg$, where A is the aid component of assistance (see Chapter 14), F is the nominal amount of foreign assistance and g is the aid component as a proportion of nominal assistance (that is, the grant element). Substituting Fg for A in equation (15.5) gives the relative worth of exports compared with the aid component of an equal amount of foreign assistance:

$$\frac{cX}{(1 + c)Fg} \tag{15.7}$$

or, if the aid is tied:

$$\frac{cX}{(1 + c)Fg} \times r \tag{15.8}$$

From equation (15.7) the value of exports will exceed the value of the aid component of an *equal* amount of foreign assistance ($X = F$) if $c > g(1 + c)$, and, from (15.8), if $cr > g(1 + c)$. The relative worth of exports is the greater, the higher the excess cost of import substitution, the higher the excess cost of tied aid and the lower the grant element of assistance. It is still the case, however, that c and r would have to be quite high and g relatively low for the worth of exports to exceed the worth of the aid component of an equal amount of foreign assistance.

But even if a comparison of exports with the aid component of an equal amount of foreign assistance showed exports to be worth more, it is not clear that this is the correct comparison to make when justifying the slogan 'trade not aid'. Equations (15.7) and (15.8) assume that only the aid component of assistance saves the excess cost of import substitution. In fact, foreign borrowing *on any terms* saves the excess cost of import substitution. This being so, there are strong grounds for arguing that the comparison that should underlie the slogan 'trade not aid' is a comparison of the worth of exports with the worth of an equal amount of foreign assistance, which provides resources directly equal to Fg and indirectly equal to Fc. The relative worth of exports compared with foreign assistance can thus be expressed as:

$$\frac{cX}{Fg + Fc} = \frac{cX}{(g + c)F} \tag{15.9}$$

or, with tied assistance:

$$\frac{cX}{(g + c)F} \times r \tag{15.10}$$

The conditions for the worth of exports to exceed that of foreign assistance are clearly more stringent than for the worth of exports to exceed the worth of the aid component of an equal amount of foreign assistance. Now, ignoring the potential excess cost of tying, foreign assistance is always worth more than an equal value of exports as long as some grant element is attached to the assistance (that is, as long as $g > 0$).

The values of g, c and r give a practical guide to any country of the relevance of the slogan 'trade not aid', ignoring the secondary repercussions and the side effects of the two resource flows. For some illustrative calculations, see Thirlwall (1976). Morrissey and White (1993) argue that only the face value of assistance should be deflated by the excess cost of tying and not the repayments, but this makes little practical difference. The values of g, c and r for most developing countries are probably not such as to justify the slogan 'trade not aid' on narrow economic grounds. As far as secondary repercussions are concerned, however, there is the question of the productivity of resources from abroad compared with those released by exports, and of the additional saving generated by the two means of resource augmentation. There is little evidence on the first point, but on the second, it is sometimes claimed, as we saw in Chapter 14, that foreign assistance discourages saving, while export earnings contribute positively to saving. There is no disputing that some foreign assistance may be 'consumed', but this is not the important consideration. The question is: Which resource flow leads to the most investment? If 50% of the foreign assistance is 'saved' and the propensity to save of the export sector is 50%, the contribution of the two sources of foreign exchange to growth is exactly the same.

There is no evidence to suggest that the propensity to 'save' out of foreign assistance is less than the propensity to 'save' out of exports. Given that export income may be highly concentrated in the hands of the government or multinational firms, the propensity to save out of export income could be high. If the propensity was, say, 0.6, then 40% of foreign assistance would have to be 'consumed' for foreign assistance not to contribute as much to saving as exports. This is unlikely. If anything, therefore, the secondary economic repercussions of exports and assistance favour assistance.

Summary

- Trade (or more accurately export growth) has been the 'engine' of growth for many countries, both historically and in the contemporary world economy since the Second World War.
- There is nothing in the theory of free trade, however, to guarantee an equitable distribution of the gains from trade between rich and poor countries. This depends on the terms of trade and the balance of payments consequences of different patterns of specialization.
- There are static gains from trade based on the law of comparative advantage, dynamic gains from trade from wider markets and the flow of knowledge, and gains by allowing surplus production over domestic consumption to be exported (e.g. many natural resource products).
- There has been extensive trade liberalization and growth in trade since 1945, under the auspices of GATT since 1947 and the WTO since 1995.
- Trade liberalization in developing countries has boosted export growth, but raised import growth by more and worsened the balance of payments.
- The overall effect of trade liberalization on developing countries' performance has been disappointing. Positive growth effects are hard to discern, the impact on reducing poverty has been minimal, and the income distribution within countries has worsened.
- There are many disadvantages of free trade for development. The law of comparative advantage is static and does not consider the supply and demand characteristics of goods produced and traded, which affect the future growth performance of countries. There are several respectable economic arguments for protection, including the infant industry argument.
- Structural change is important for developing countries to acquire new comparative advantage in non-traditional goods. *What* you export matters.
- Ideally, import substitution and export promotion should be pursued together, as happened in most successful Southeast Asian countries, and now in China.
- The long-run deterioration in the terms of trade of primary commodities (first outlined by Prebisch and Singer in 1950), and the cyclicality of primary product prices, damages the economies of many developing countries. There is a case for international commodity price stabilization schemes.
- What developing countries need is fair trade, not free trade.
- Trade is not necessarily more beneficial than 'aid' in providing resources for development. It depends on the terms of capital inflows, and the excess cost of import substitution.

Chapter 15 Discussion questions

1. What is the essence of the distinction between static and dynamic gains from trade?
2. What fundamental assumptions of free trade theory may be violated in the context of developing countries?
3. Why might there be a tendency for the terms of trade to move against primary products and primary producing countries, and what does the empirical evidence show?
4. Outline the various arguments for protection.
5. Under what conditions are tariffs a first best policy of protection?
6. Discuss the relative merits of import substitution versus export promotion.
7. Why are regional trade agreements (RTAs) inferior to the generalized freeing of trade?
8. What has been the impact of trade liberalization on exports and economic growth in developing countries?
9. To what extent do you think that the 'East Asian miracle' has been based on export-led growth?
10. Why do some economists argue that the gains from trade should be looked at more from the point of view of the effect of trade on the balance of payments than from the traditional viewpoint of real resource augmentation?
11. In what ways is trade not 'fair' between developed and developing countries?
12. What do you understand by the concept of 'effective protection', and how is it measured?
13. What problems do unstable commodity prices pose for a country and for the world economy?
14. What are the theoretical and practical difficulties of stabilizing the price and export earnings of primary products?

Note

1. For a discussion of the issues involved in this section, see Maizels (1987) and Gilbert (1996).

Websites on trade

Trade negotiations

WTO www.wto.org
International Trade Centre www.intracen.org

Fair trade

Oxfam www.oxfam.org.uk
Fairtrade Foundation www.fairtrade.org.uk
New Economics Foundation www.neweconomics.org

Trade agreements

MERCOSUR www.mercosur.int/msweb/portal%20intermediario/es/index/htm
NAFTA www.naftanow.org
Regional Trade Agreements Information System http://rtais.wto.org/UI/PublicMaintainRTAHome.aspx

16

THE BALANCE OF PAYMENTS, INTERNATIONAL MONETARY ASSISTANCE AND DEVELOPMENT

Introduction

We have seen how the composition of trade of developing countries can lead to severe balance of payments difficulties, which can act as a constraint on growth, and how vulnerable many developing countries are to exogenous shocks that adversely affect their export earnings and import payments.

In this chapter we develop a simple model of balance of payments constrained growth, first of all without capital flows and then allowing current account deficits to be financed by capital inflows. It is shown that growth consistent with current account equilibrium depends on four major factors:

1. What is happening to the real terms of trade (or real exchange rate) and the price elasticities of demand for exports and imports.
2. The growth of world income.
3. The income elasticity of demand for a country's exports.
4. The income elasticity of demand for imports.

We show that if the real terms of trade are constant, a country's growth rate can be approximated by the ratio of export growth to the income elasticity of demand for imports.

The model has several policy implications relating to exchange rate policy, industrial policy to improve the income elasticity of demand for exports, and trade policy to reduce the income elasticity of demand for imports. Different types of exchange rate regimes are considered, from fixed pegs to free floating, and a cautionary tale is told from the East Asian financial crisis of 1997.

The model with capital flows shows how capital inflows can relax the constraint of current account equilibrium, but the extra growth is minimal because there are limits to the current account deficit to GDP ratio (and the international debt to GDP ratio).

The original purpose of the International Monetary Fund (IMF) was to provide short-term balance of payments support to countries and it does this through various facilities, such as Stand-By Arrangements, Extended Fund Facility, Extended Credit Facility, Standby Credit Facility, Poverty Reduction and Growth Facility and other special facilities. But the IMF imposes conditions on lending, and the more lending, the harsher the conditions. We examine the results of the IMF's programmes in developing countries and the criticisms of the policies imposed.

The chapter ends with a discussion of the potential of Special Drawing Rights (SDRs) to aid developing countries without them having to adjust to balance of payments difficulties by deflating their economies.

Balance of payments constrained growth

Poor countries are in balance of payments deficit most of the time, but the deficits fluctuate according to internal and external economic circumstances. In the 1970s, for example, owing to the oil shocks in 1973 and 1979 and the slowdown of world growth, the deficits grew considerably, despite a slowdown of internal growth that reduced the demand for non-oil imports. In the early 1980s, the deficits contracted because most developing countries were forced to adjust (that is, deflate their economies) in order to repay debt out of diminished export earnings. In the late 1980s, the deficits increased again, with some internal recovery and a greater willingness of the international capital markets to resume lending. By 1996, the deficits totalled $98 billion, over half of which was accounted for by Thailand, Indonesia, the Philippines, Malaysia and South Korea, which all experienced serious financial crises in 1997. These countries had to readjust, and since 2002, East Asia and the Pacific have been in big surplus. Today, China has a huge surplus, but many African countries have deficits in excess of 10% of GDP. The world as a whole is plagued with serious payments imbalances. For any country or continent, the observed deficit (*ex post*) measures the extent to which it has been able and willing to finance the difference between the value of import payments and the value of export receipts.

All countries have a growth rate that is consistent with balance of payments equilibrium on the current account, and with its overall balance on the current and capital account. What determines the growth rate that is consistent with current account balance on the one hand, and overall balance on the other? If we specify the equilibrium equations and the determinants of import and export demand, we can immediately see the major factors of importance, and we can, in turn, understand the various policy measures taken by individual countries and the international community to raise the growth rate of less developed countries consistent with balance of payments equilibrium. For the original development of this model, see Thirlwall (1979). For an overview of the literature, see McCombie and Thirlwall (1997, 2004), Thirlwall (2011) and Soukiazis and Cerqueira (2012).

The current account balance of payments of a country, measured in its own *domestic* currency, may be written as:

$$P_d X = P_f M E \tag{16.1}$$

where X measures the quantity of exports and P_d is the average price of exports, so $P_d X$ is the value of exports in domestic currency. M is the quantity of imports, P_f is the average (foreign) price of imports and E is the nominal exchange rate measured as the domestic price of foreign currency, which thus converts the value of imports measured in foreign currency ($P_f M$) into a domestic currency equivalent.

The condition for the balance of payments to remain in equilibrium in a *growing* economy through time is that the *rate of growth* of export earnings should equal the *rate of growth* of import payments, that is:

$$(p_d + x) = (p_f + m + e) \tag{16.2}$$

where the lower-case letters represent rates of change of the variables.

Now let us consider what the growth of export and import volume depends on. Export demand may be expected to depend primarily on the price of a country's exports relative to the foreign price of similar goods (expressed in a common currency) and on the level of 'world' income, which determines the purchasing power over a country's goods. Similarly, import demand may be expected to depend on the price of imports relative to domestic substitutes and on the level of domestic income. If the price and income elasticities of demand for exports and imports are assumed to be constant, we may write the export and import functions in the following (multiplicative) way:

$$X = A\left(\frac{P_d}{P_f E}\right)^{\eta} Z^{\epsilon} \tag{16.3}$$

and:

$$M = B\left(\frac{P_f E}{P_d}\right)^{\psi} Y^{\pi} \tag{16.4}$$

where Z measures 'world' income; Y measures domestic income; η is the price elasticity of demand for exports (< 0); ϵ is the income elasticity of demand for exports (> 0); ψ is the price elasticity of demand for imports (< 0); π is the income elasticity of demand for imports (> 0); and A and B are constants.

Taking small rates of change of the variables in equations (16.3) and (16.4), we can see what the growth of exports and imports depends on:

$$x = \eta(p_d - p_f - e) + \epsilon(z) \tag{16.5}$$

and:

$$m = \psi(p_f + e - p_d) + \pi(y) \tag{16.6}$$

In other words, **export growth** depends on:

1. How fast domestic prices are changing relative to foreign prices, taking into account variations in the exchange rate (*e*), multiplied by the price elasticity of demand for exports.
2. How fast world income is changing, together with the value of the income elasticity of demand for exports.

We rule out here the possibility that developing countries can sell any amount of their goods on world markets at the going price, which would mean that the income elasticity of demand, and what is happening to world purchasing power, does not matter, and that export growth is simply supply determined. This may be true in the case of *some* commodities from some *small* countries, but the proposition that demand conditions do not matter for export performance does not stand up to empirical scrutiny as a general rule. There are very few countries that are pure price-takers in international trade.

Likewise, **import growth** depends on:

1. How fast import prices are changing relative to domestic substitutes (taking account of exchange rate changes), multiplied by the price elasticity of demand for imports.
2. How fast domestic income (as a proxy for expenditure) is changing, together with the income elasticity of demand for imports.

Since the growth of imports depends on the growth of domestic income, if we substitute equations (16.5) and (16.6) into equation (16.2) (which gives the condition for a moving balance of payments equilibrium through time), we can derive an expression for a country's growth of income that is consistent with current account equilibrium, which depends on certain key variables and parameters. Substitution of (16.5) and (16.6) into (16.2) gives:

$$p_d + \eta(p_d - p_f - e) + \epsilon(z) = p_f + \psi(p_f + e - p_d) + \pi(y) + e \tag{16.7}$$

so that:

$$y = \frac{(1 + \eta + \psi)(p_d - p_f - e) + \epsilon(z)}{\pi} \tag{16.8}$$

Before embarking on discussion, let us identify in words what this growth rate depends on, which must be binding if current account deficits cannot be financed:

1. It depends on the rate at which the real terms of trade are changing ($p_d - p_f - e$). The real terms of trade are the ratio of export to import prices measured in a common currency ($P_d/P_f E$). A rise in this ratio, that is ($p_d - p_f - e$) > 0, raises real income growth consistent with current account equilibrium (other things being constant), and a fall in this ratio lowers the balance of payments equilibrium growth rate. This is the **pure terms of trade** effect on income growth.
2. If the real terms of trade are changing, the growth rate depends on the **price elasticities of demand** for exports (η) and imports (ψ), which determine the magnitude of the volume response of exports and imports to relative price changes. For surveys of estimating export and import demand functions, see Senhadji and Montenegro (1999) and Senhadji (1998).
3. One country's growth depends on the growth rates of other countries (z) – which neatly illustrates the **interdependence of the world economy** – but the rate at which one country grows relative to others depends crucially on the income elasticity of demand for its exports (ϵ), which depends on the tastes of foreign consumers, the characteristics of goods, and a whole host of **non-price factors** that determine the demand for goods in international trade. One of the main reasons why some countries have a healthier balance of payments and a higher growth rate than others is related to the characteristics of the goods they produce and export in world trade. What you export matters (Hausmann et al., 2007).
4. The growth rate depends on a country's **appetite for imports**, as measured by π, the income elasticity of demand for imports. The higher is π, the lower the growth rate that is consistent with balance of payments equilibrium on the current account.

These factors show the rationale for agreements to prevent the terms of trade deteriorating for developing countries, for exchange rate policy, for international Keynesianism to maintain the growth of world income, and for policies to induce structural change – through export promotion or import substitution – in order to raise the income elasticity of demand for exports and to reduce the income elasticity of demand for imports. Let us take up some of these issues in turn.

The terms of trade

The effect of terms of trade deterioration (import prices rising faster than export prices, other things remaining the same) is to worsen the balance of payments at a given rate of growth or, what amounts to the same thing, to reduce the rate of growth of income consistent with current account equilibrium. For example, if in equation (16.8), import prices were rising at 10% per annum while the price of exports was rising at only 5% per annum, this would mean a lower y than if the terms of trade were constant. In theory, this 'terms of trade effect' could be offset by a continual **appreciation** of the currency; that is, by a continual percentage fall in E($e < 0$), but very few developing countries, if any, are in a position to appreciate their currencies even if they wanted to. Terms of trade stability in real terms must depend, or rely, on international commodity agreements to stabilize the prices of the exports of developing countries relative to the prices of the goods they import. Within this framework of analysis, the rationale for terms of trade agreements is apparent.

It is not clear, however, that terms of trade deterioration is always a bad thing, because what happens to export earnings and import payments, and hence to the balance of payments equilibrium growth rate, depends not only on changes in relative prices but also on the volume response of exports and imports to price changes. Since the price elasticities, η and ψ, are defined as negative, it can be seen from equation (16.8) that if their sum exceeds −1, $p_d < p_f$ will mean that y is higher than would be the case if $p_d > p_f$. In other words, the export and import volume response to domestic export prices rising more slowly than import prices is sufficient to offset the fact that more has to be paid for a given volume of imports relative to exports. If, however, the price elasticity of demand for the exports of a developing country is low because of the nature of the product in question (for example, a primary product), and the price elasticity of demand for imports is also low because the imports are necessities, the balance of payments will *worsen* if the terms of trade deteriorate, and growth will have to be constrained for the preservation of balance of payments equilibrium. In these circumstances, commodity agreements assume great importance and it would be beneficial if the ratio of export prices to import prices were to rise. In Chapter 15, we considered various commodity schemes aimed at stabilizing export prices, or changing the relative price of exports and imports. We also noted that this will not necessarily stabilize export earnings if there are fluctuations in export supply. The international response to this has been to devise schemes to compensate for loss of export earnings. In the past, the IMF operated a Compensatory and Contingency Financing Facility to cover shortfalls of export earnings, but now countries must use other emergency financing facilities (see below).

Another argument for stabilizing the export prices of developing countries and maintaining their incomes is that price and income instability tend to depress the world economy as a whole and the developing countries with it, given the interdependence between countries in the world economy. Falling prices and incomes in developing countries reduce the purchasing power over industrial goods, inducing recession, while rising commodity prices may also induce recession by raising the price of manufactured goods and inducing deflation in developed countries. For the smooth growth of the world economy, there is a lot to be said for attempting to stabilize the prices of primary products so that the purchasing power of the producers and exporters of these commodities grows in line with supply. One suggestion is that Special Drawing Rights (SDRs) (see below) might be used to purchase primary products in order to stabilize their price in times of glut, on the lines of Keynes' 'commod control' scheme (see Chapter 15).

The exchange rate and devaluation

Now suppose that export prices do rise more quickly than import prices, improving the terms of trade, but that the sum of the price elasticities of demand for exports and imports exceeds unity, what then? This will worsen the balance of payments and reduce the balance of payments equilibrium growth rate. It is in these circumstances that **exchange rate depreciation** may become relevant, and is often resorted to. It can be seen from equation (16.8) that if a country's rate of price increase is above that of other countries ($p_d > p_f$), this can, in principle, be compensated for by allowing the exchange rate to depreciate continually ($e > 0$) by the difference between p_d and p_f in order to hold 'competitiveness' steady. The conventional approach to balance of payments adjustment, and the policy pursued relentlessly by the IMF in countries experiencing balance of payments difficulties, is downward adjustment of the exchange rate. Note, however, that the rationale of such a policy presupposes a number of things:

- That the source of the difficulties is price uncompetitiveness.
- That the price elasticities are 'right' (that is, they sum to greater than unity) for a depreciation to reduce the imbalance.
- That the *real* terms of trade (or the *real* exchange rate) can be changed by devaluation.

A fall in the nominal exchange rate, however, that is, $e > 0$, may lead either to a fall in P_f ($p_f < 0$) or a rise in P_d($p_d > 0$), both of which would nullify the effect of the devaluation (see equation (16.8)). A fall in P_f might come about if foreign suppliers desired to maintain their competitiveness as the devaluing country became more competitive. This is known as **pricing to market**; that is, foreign exporters reduce their markups in response to nominal exchange rate changes in order to remain competitive in world markets. A rise in P_d may come about as the domestic price of imports rises as a result of devaluation, which is then followed by a domestic wage–price spiral. Either way, within a short space of time, relative prices measured in a common currency may revert to their former level and devaluation will have been ineffective in this respect. Edwards (1989) has looked at the effectiveness of devaluation in reducing a country's *real* exchange rate. He studied 39 cases of devaluation in 25 developing countries in the period 1962–82, and found that, in most cases, devaluation had been eroded by domestic inflation within three years. Devaluation must be backed by restrictive monetary and fiscal policies if it is to be effective, but this can lead to unemployment. A detailed case study of Mexico by Kamin and Rogers (2000) shows that devaluation has nearly always been associated with high inflation and economic contraction.

Note also that a *one-shot* devaluation or depreciation of the currency cannot put a country on a *permanently higher growth path* that is consistent with balance of payments equilibrium. Currency depreciation would have to be continuous (that is, $e > 0$ permanently) for this to happen, unless devaluation can somehow induce favourable structural changes at the same time. Countries must look very carefully at the prevailing conditions before embracing currency devaluation as a panacea for the relief of balance of payments constrained growth. There are three major worries.

First, raising the domestic price of imported goods can be a highly inflationary policy for an open economy that is heavily dependent on imports, as many developing countries have discovered to their cost, particularly in Latin America, and some countries have had the courage to resist IMF support, which has been conditional on devaluation. In the eyes of some, the acronym IMF stands for (I)nflation, (M)isery and (F)amine.

Second, depreciation can be dangerous because it prematurely shifts resources into the tradable goods sector, where productivity may be lower than in the non-tradable goods sector. This is argued forcefully by Yotopoulos (1996), who believes that there is a tendency for the real exchange rate to be *undervalued* because of weakness on the capital account of the balance of payments, depressing the nominal exchange rate. In the early stages of development, developing countries should therefore protect the nominal exchange rate from depreciation through the use of controls and intervention in the foreign exchange market, and only start to liberalize once the foreign exchange market has become more fully developed and currencies are not regarded as 'soft' by the outside world. In the 33 countries studied by Yotopoulos (1996), there was a *negative* relation between changes in the real exchange rate and the growth of per capita income for most of the 1970s and 1980s (holding other factors constant).

Third, the effect of currency devaluation is to make countries more competitive in the range of goods that were the source of their balance of payments difficulties in the first place. A devalued currency might encourage export sales of new (manufactured) goods with a high price elasticity in world trade, but it might be inappropriate for the traditional range of goods produced and exported with a low price elasticity of demand. For example, if a country is a large supplier and a price-maker in world markets, currency devaluation coupled with low price elasticity will *reduce* export earnings. If the country is a price-taker, devaluation will raise the domestic price of the commodity and cause inflation. It is true that production for export will become more profitable and might encourage a greater supply response, but there are other less inflationary ways to encourage supply than devaluation. The different types of exchange rate systems available in developing countries are discussed below.

The IMF supply-side approach to devaluation

Devaluation, as well as permitting a reduction in the foreign currency price of exports, may also increase the profitability of exporting, by raising the price of tradable goods relative to the price of non-tradables, and by providing exporters with more domestic currency per unit of foreign exchange earned. The IMF, having conceded that the price elasticity of demand for many of the goods exported and imported by developing countries (particularly as a group) is low, now increasingly uses this supply-side argument as a justification for devaluation. If output is stimulated, this will, to a certain extent, also mitigate the contraction of aggregate monetary demand that results from devaluation and any accompanying expenditure-reducing policies.

The IMF supply-side approach to devaluation was first articulated in print by Nashashibi (1980) with reference to the Sudan. The approach first requires the calculation of foreign exchange earnings per unit of domestic resources employed for a range of tradable goods. Export (and import substitute) activities can then be arranged on a profitability scale and, according to the supply-side argument, the appropriate devaluation is the one that goes down the scale far enough to ensure the profitability of traditional exports, as well as (perhaps) to encourage new activities. Thus, if the current exchange rate for the Sudan was, say, US\$2 to S£1 and foreign exchange earnings per unit of domestic resources were calculated to be less than this for most commodities, it would clearly be unprofitable to produce for export, and the exchange rate should be devalued to bring the production of tradables within the margin of profitability. Foreign exchange earnings per unit of domestic resources are measured as:

$$C = \frac{(P_x X - P_m M)r}{P_d D} \tag{16.9}$$

where X refers to exports, P_x is the world price of exports in domestic currency, M is the quantity of imported inputs, P_m is the price of imported inputs in domestic currency, D is the amount of domestic resources used in production, P_d is the price of domestic inputs and r is the exchange rate measured as the foreign price of domestic currency. If $C > r$, production is not profitable at the existing exchange rate.

It is clear from equation (16.9) that if devaluation is to improve profitability, the rise in $(P_x X - P_m M)/P_d D$ must be more than the reduction in r. Unfortunately, this cannot be taken for granted. It depends on the response of $P_x X$, $P_m M$, P_d and D to the change in r. The implicit assumptions underlying the approach are that developing countries are price-takers, so that P_x will rise in proportion to the devaluation, that X will increase, that M will decrease, and that these favourable effects will not be offset by rises in P_m and $P_d D$. In practice, there may not be a complete 'pass through' of devaluation to export prices (P_x), the elasticity of export supply may be very low because of structural rigidities and factor immobility, and the elasticity of import prices and domestic prices may be very high. The end result may be that the profitability of exporting remains largely unchanged. This was the conclusion of a detailed study of devaluations in the Sudan by Nureldin-Hussain and Thirlwall (1984), which looked at the profitability of cotton, groundnuts, sesame and gum arabic.

The Sudan and many other developing countries fall into the 'rigid country' classification distinguished by Branson (1983) in his useful taxonomic discussion of trade structures and devaluation. 'Rigid' countries are those that produce agricultural-based raw materials with low supply elasticities and whose demand for imports is very inelastic in the short run, particularly for imports used as intermediate inputs. In addition, the price elasticity of demand for exports may be high but not infinite, and real wages may be sticky. In these circumstances, devaluation may be a second best policy compared with 'structural' intervention to raise foreign exchange earnings per unit of domestic inputs.

The growth of world income and structural change

Now let us turn to the growth of world income: z in equation (16.8). There is nothing that individual poor countries can do about the growth of world income, but since all countries are linked through trade, the interdependence of countries and the importance of global prosperity is only too apparent. This should be the overriding function of supranational institutions and mechanisms: to keep world income and trade buoyant in the face of exogenous shocks and to avoid the beggar-thy-neighbour policies that characterized the 1930s, when the whole world economy slumped. The purpose of the IMF was to avoid a repetition of the 1930s – to help countries in balance of payments difficulties and to avoid recourse to widespread protectionism, which can export unemployment from one country to another in a downward spiral. This is the same purpose that underlies various schemes for the recycling of export surpluses and for managed trade; that is, to relieve the balance of payments constraint on growth in countries that tend to have a chronic deficit while other countries are in perpetual surplus. This was a major theme of the 1980 Brandt Report discussed in Chapter 1, and the major concern of countries during the financial and economic crisis that hit the world economy in 2008.

While individual countries have no control over the growth of world income, they do have some control over the income elasticity of demand for their exports, which determines how fast exports grow as a result of world income growth. Likewise, countries have some control over the income elasticity of demand for imports, because both these parameters are a function of the type and characteristics of the goods being produced for sale in international trade. Thus, they are a function of the industrial and trade strategy being pursued.

In Chapter 15, we discussed export promotion versus import substitution strategies. Import substitution is designed to lower the import elasticity, but there is a limit to import substitution, and the policy itself may lower the export elasticity at the same time by creating a rigid and inefficient industrial structure. A much more fruitful strategy, which has been pursued relentlessly and successfully by several Southeast Asian countries, is to concentrate on raising the export elasticity, which may, at the same time, reduce the import elasticity if the goods produced for export also compete with imports.

Application of the balance of payments constrained growth model

How well does the balance of payments constrained growth model outlined in equations (16.1)–(16.8) fit the growth experience of developing countries? Or, to put it another way, how well does equation (16.8) predict the growth performance of developing countries? To answer this question, it is convenient to simplify the model by assuming either that the sum of the price elasticities of demand ($\eta + \psi$) does not differ significantly from unity, in which case equation (16.8) reduces to $y = \epsilon z/\pi$, and/or that relative prices in international trade do not change in the long run (or the real exchange rate remains constant), in which case equation (16.8) reduces to $y = \epsilon z/\pi = x/\pi$. This latter result is often referred to as the **dynamic Harrod trade multiplier result**, because it is the dynamic analogue of the static Harrod trade multiplier result $Y = X/m$, where Y is the *level* of income, X is the *level* of exports, m is the marginal propensity to import, and $1/m$ is the foreign trade multiplier (Harrod, 1933). *Prima facie* evidence that a country is balance of payments constrained in its growth performance would be to find that its actual growth is close to or just above its balance of payments equilibrium growth rate (financed by sustainable long-run capital inflows – see below), combined with unemployed domestic resources.

A number of studies have applied this simple model to individual or groups of developing countries, and most are supportive that GDP growth can be predicted from the ratio of export growth to the income elasticity of demand for imports. McCombie and Thirlwall (1994, 1997) give a survey of studies up to 1996, McCombie and Thirlwall (2004) reprint 18 studies with an introductory survey up to 2003, and Thirlwall (2011) lists over 40 studies in a history and overview of the balance of payments-constrained growth model. Recent country studies include Nell (2003) for South Africa, Razmi (2005) for India, Britto and McCombie (2009) for Brazil, and Felipe et al. (2010) for Pakistan. Recent studies for groups of countries include Perraton (2003) for 51 developing countries, Pacheco-López and Thirlwall (2006) for 17 Latin American countries, Gouvea and Lima (2010) for 4 Asian and 4 Latin American countries, and Gouvea and Lima (2013) for a panel of 90 countries. Case example 16.1 applies the model to Latin American countries.

Studies are supportive of the model for two main reasons:

1. It is shown overwhelmingly that real exchange rate changes are not an efficient balance of payments adjustment weapon; it is income that adjusts to preserve balance of payments equilibrium.
2. Capital flows make no substantial difference to the prediction of the current balance model because there is a limit to the current account deficit to GDP ratio that countries can sustain.

The results of these studies add weight to the idea and importance of export-led growth, discussed in Chapter 15.

Case example 16.1 **Application of the balance of payments constrained growth model to 17 Latin American countries, 1977–2002**

Countries	Actual GDP growth (y) (%)	Export growth (x) (%)	Income elasticity of demand for imports (π)	Predicted balance of payments constrained growth rate (x/π) (%)
Argentina	1.33	6.07	3.66	1.66
Bolivia	1.89	3.46	1.82	1.90
Brazil	2.70	8.07	1.59	5.08
Chile	5.50	8.62	2.03	4.24
Costa Rica	3.94	7.38	2.27	3.25
Dominican Rep	.4.23	7.84	0.92	8.52
Ecuador	2.57	5.38	1.83	2.94
El Salvador	1.66	5.03	2.47	2.04

Case example 16.1 **Application of the balance of payments constrained growth model to 17 Latin American countries, 1977–2002 – (*continued*)**

Countries	Actual GDP growth (y) (%)	Export growth (x) (%)	Income elasticity of demand for imports (π)	Predicted balance of payments constrained growth rate (x/π) (%)
Guatemala	2.93	2.14	3.78	0.57
Honduras	3.41	2.44	1.41	1.73
Mexico	3.30	11.38	3.17	3.59
Nicaragua	0.45	1.40	0.97	1.44
Paraguay	3.73	7.01	2.48	2.83
Peru	1.93	5.25	1.56	3.37
Uruguay	1.43	4.05	2.13	1.90
Venezuela	1.13	1.74	3.76	0.46

Source: Pacheco-López and Thirlwall, 2006.

Capital flows

So far we have assumed growth to be constrained by the necessity to preserve current account equilibrium on the balance of payments. In practice, of course, countries are allowed to run deficits, sometimes for substantial periods of time, financed by capital inflows from abroad from a variety of sources. The extent to which the value of imports can exceed the value of exports to finance a correspondingly higher level of income is determined by the *net* level of capital inflows. Thus, we may write the equation for the overall balance of payments as:

$$P_dX + C = P_fME \tag{16.10}$$

where C measures net capital inflows (including reductions in foreign exchange reserves) in domestic currency. Taking the rates of change of this identity gives:

$$\frac{E}{R}(p_d + x) + \frac{C}{R}(c) = p_f + m + e \tag{16.11}$$

where E/R and C/R represent the proportion of total receipts to finance the import bill that come from export earnings (E) and capital inflows (C), respectively. If we now substitute our expressions for x and m (equations (16.5) and (16.6)) into equation (16.11), we can solve for the growth rate associated with overall balance of payments equilibrium. This rate will depend on all the factors already mentioned, and on the rate of growth of *real* capital inflows ($c - p_d$). On substitution, we obtain:

$$y = \frac{(1 + \frac{E}{R}\eta + \psi)(p_d - p_f - e) + \frac{E}{R}(\epsilon[z]) + \frac{C}{R}(c - p_d)}{\pi} \tag{16.12}$$

This model is known as the **extended version of the dynamic Harrod trade multiplier result** (that is, extended to allow for capital flows). Apart from the weight, E/R, attached to the two export elasticities, η and ϵ, the only difference between equation (16.12) and our earlier result in equation (16.8) is the addition of the last term $(c - p_d)$, which measures the growth of *real* capital inflows (the growth of the nominal flows, c, minus the rate of domestic inflation, p_d). A positive growth of capital inflows will allow a country to grow faster than would be the case if it was constrained to maintain balance of payments equilibrium on the current account. On the other hand, it must be said that a continually positive rate of growth of capital inflows implies an *ever-growing* burden of debt, which is not sustainable in the long run. Thus, running current account deficits to finance growth is not a feasible option in the long run, and other long-run strategies must be pursued that relate to the determinants of the growth rate consistent with current account equilibrium. For the original development of this model, see Thirlwall and Nureldin-Hussain (1982).

This model has been applied by Nureldin-Hussain (1999) to a sample of African and Asian countries over the period 1970–90, with interesting results (Table 16.1). Each country's growth rate (column 1) is disaggregated into three components according to equation (16.12). The first is the terms of trade effect, the second is the export volume effect, and the third is the effect on growth of real capital inflows. It can be seen that the model fits remarkably well for most countries, but the contribution of the different effects differs between countries, and between the two continents of Africa and Asia. Africa has grown much more slowly than Asia, on average, and over one-half of Africa's growth (excluding that arising from oil exports) has been financed by capital inflows. Movements in the terms of trade have also had an adverse effect on growth in Africa. In Asia, by contrast, a much higher proportion of growth has been permitted by the rapid growth of exports, and terms of trade movements have had a favourable effect on growth.

Table 16.1 Estimates of extended version of dynamic Harrod foreign trade multiplier, 1970–90 (annual percentage average)

	Actual growth rate	Terms of trade effect (A)	Export volume effect (B)	Real capital inflow effect (C)	Predicted growth rate = (A) + (B) + (C)
African countries					
Egypt	6.90	−2.37	4.36	7.31	9.30
Congo, Dem. Rep.	6.59	0.42	3.88	2.38	6.67
Kenya	6.24	−0.50	1.62	5.59	6.71
Mauritius	5.80	0.92	5.13	0.19	6.23
Tunisia	5.69	0.87	5.24	1.48	7.59
Burundi	5.60	1.69	3.21	−1.26	3.65
Cameroon	5.50	−1.12	7.08	0.00	5.97
Gabon	5.10	0.49	6.81	−0.04	7.33
Algeria	4.90	10.15	4.21	−8.72	5.64
Morocco	4.62	−1.34	2.83	3.47	4.96
Côte d'Ivoire	4.50	0.39	4.23	0.81	5.43
Lesotho	4.40	−3.43	6.62	1.55	4.74

Table 16.1 Estimates of extended version of dynamic Harrod foreign trade multiplier, 1970–90 (annual percentage average) – (*continued*)

	Actual growth rate	Terms of trade effect (A)	Export volume effect (B)	Real capital inflow effect (C)	Predicted growth rate = (A) + (B) + (C)
Burkina Faso	4.20	−5.17	3.03	5.63	3.50
Somalia	3.40	−1.10	0.18	5.00	4.07
Zimbabwe	3.23	−2.40	2.23	−1.24	−1.41
Sudan	3.10	0.14	1.13	1.92	3.20
Benin	2.90	1.44	0.96	1.35	3.75
Tanzania	2.90	0.33	−0.55	5.01	4.79
Togo	2.90	0.08	2.31	0.61	3.00
Senegal	2.67	0.23	1.56	1.05	2.83
Nigeria	2.50	2.37	1.28	−1.17	2.48
South Africa	2.42	−1.03	1.32	7.74	8.03
Mauritania	2.30	0.68	1.58	0.42	2.69
Ethiopia	2.20	−0.09	0.74	2.53	3.17
Sierra Leone	1.58	−0.23	−0.67	2.65	1.75
Zambia	1.40	−0.31	−1.29	0.58	−1.02
Ghana	1.40	−3.81	0.15	2.88	−0.79
Niger	0.81	−5.07	1.79	3.47	0.20
Madagascar	0.48	−0.10	0.06	0.95	0.91
Average	3.66	−0.27	2.45	1.80	3.98
Average excluding oil exporters	3.40	−0.84	1.99	2.49	3.64
Asian countries					
Korea, Rep. of	9.11	−0.81	13.47	−2.49	10.17
Hong Kong	9.07	−0.07	8.34	1.01	9.28
Indonesia	10.76	1.82	3.18	5.76	7.58
China	8.20	−0.02	6.43	0.26	6.67
Malaysia	7.08	−0.69	6.60	2.21	8.12
Thailand	6.80	0.96	5.45	2.61	9.02
Pakistan	5.04	−0.44	4.28	4.40	8.24
India	4.31	−0.85	3.16	1.96	4.27
Sri Lanka	4.30	−0.65	2.33	3.00	4.68
Japan	4.20	−1.42	9.73	−4.63	3.68
Philippines	3.70	0.22	2.00	0.26	2.48
Average	6.60	−0.18	5.91	1.31	6.74
Average excluding Japan and Korea	6.58	0.03	4.46	2.39	6.70

Source: Based on Nureldin-Hussain, 1999.

Exchange rate systems for developing countries

All countries have a wide choice of exchange rate systems, ranging from completely fixed to freely floating, with a number of options in between. Which system a developing country chooses must depend on its circumstances at the time, what exchange rate arrangements other countries are using, and the long-run goals of economic policy. For example, a country may wish to pursue exchange rate stability because of the instability and perceived disadvantages of floating rates, in which case it will wish to choose some form of fixed exchange rate regime. Alternatively, a country may wish to use its exchange rate to achieve various real objectives in the domestic economy, such as a faster rate of growth and full employment, and therefore sets a target for the *real* exchange rate. With changing domestic and foreign prices, a real exchange rate target will require frequent variations in the nominal exchange rate, in which case the country will wish to choose some form of flexible exchange rate regime. On the other hand, if inflation is the most serious problem within a country, currency depreciation to maintain a given real exchange rate may simply exacerbate inflation, and a country may wish to anchor its currency to that of another country or even adopt the currency of another country in order to gain monetary credibility. This would be an extreme form of exchange rate pegging.

There is also the question of capital flows. If a country has liberalized its capital markets and the capital account of the balance of payments, and capital is free to move in and out, it will be difficult, if not impossible, for a country to pursue an exchange rate target and operate an independent monetary policy at the same time. This is called the **impossible trinity**. Capital outflows, for example, will cause a currency to depreciate in value. The only effective way to stop this is to raise domestic interest rates, which depress the internal economy. The reverse dilemma occurs with capital inflows. The only way to reconcile internal and external equilibrium is either to control capital movements, or to allow the exchange rate to float. Theoretically, free floating allows a country to pursue a completely independent monetary policy geared to the goals of the domestic economy, but, in practice, no country is completely indifferent to the value of its exchange rate, particularly as it is a characteristic of the foreign exchange market that exchange rates may considerably overshoot their true 'equilibrium' value. These are just a few examples of the considerations and conditions that countries need to bear in mind in choosing an exchange rate regime. For useful surveys of exchange rate policy in developing countries, see Argy (1990), Frenkel (1999), Fischer (2001), Ghosh et al. (2002) and Ghosh and Ostey (2009). The spectrum of alternatives, from hard pegs to floating, is given in Table 16.2.

Each country must find its own solution, in the light of its own circumstances. The IMF generally respects a country's choice of exchange rate regime, and gives advice to support that choice. The different options are discussed below, but the historical experience of the past 30 years or so points to three broad policy conclusions (Fischer, 2001):

1. Intermediate positions between hard pegs and floating (what might be called 'soft' pegs) are not sustainable without capital controls.

Table 16.2 Types of exchange rate regime

Hard pegs	Intermediate regimes	Floating
Currency boards	Pegged exchange rates	Free float
Currency unions	Crawling peg	Managed float
Dollarization, or adopting the currency of another country	Exchange rate band Crawling band	

2. While countries have shifted from intermediate regimes to either end of the spectrum (more towards floating than hard pegs), a wide range of flexible rate arrangements still remains possible.
3. Countries are not indifferent to exchange rate movements, so independent floating is not an option and can be dangerous.

Let us now briefly consider the different types of exchange rate regime listed in Table 16.2, and their advantages and disadvantages.

A **currency board** is an extreme form of hard peg that requires each unit of a country's currency to be backed by an equal amount of a reserve currency, such as the US dollar. The currency board system was widely practised in Africa under British rule before independence. More recently, Argentina decided to anchor its currency to the US dollar in this way but went into serious recession with the appreciation of the US dollar in 2000–01, and the currency peg was eventually abandoned. Linking a weak currency to a stronger currency can be a useful anti-inflation device to gain monetary credibility. Indeed, the system is reminiscent of the old gold standard system, where the currency had to be backed up by gold, with the money supply expanding and contracting according to the balance of payments and changes in international reserves. The two major disadvantages of currency board systems are:

1. The credit for entrepreneurs to invest is not elastic to the needs of trade (because it depends on the availability of foreign exchange reserves),
2. If the reserve currency appreciates in value, so too does the currency that is linked to it. This can cause serious problems of competitiveness with other trading partners, and damage exports and the balance of payments.

Another extreme form of hard peg is a **currency union**, where countries decide to adopt a common currency, so that, by definition, exchange rates between member countries of the union disappear. Countries may decide to enter a currency union if they feel that multiple currencies, exchange rate volatility and uncertainty are seriously damaging trade, and that the overall benefits of surrendering monetary independence exceed the costs. The conditions for an **optimal currency area**, in which the benefits to the members exceed the costs, are that:

1. Economic cycles should be synchronized and economic shocks symmetrical so that a single monetary policy is suitable for all members.
2. Labour and capital are freely mobile.
3. Fiscal transfer mechanisms exist to help disadvantaged regions.
4. Multiple currencies are seriously damaging trade.

It is never easy for a country to know whether the benefits will exceed the costs, and decisions are often taken on political, as well as economic, grounds. It is important to stress, however, that the fact that a country has no exchange rate to defend vis-à-vis its partners does not mean that the country avoids balance of payments problems; they just show up in a different form (Thirlwall, 2007). If plans to import exceed plans to export, balance of payments difficulties will manifest themselves in falling output and rising unemployment, unless there are compensating capital transfers between the members of the currency union. The francophone countries of West Africa are part of a currency union that now uses the euro as the common currency, and the eurozone, the largest currency union in the world, comprises 19 (of the 28) countries of the EU with the euro as its common currency.

Another form of hard peg is to simply adopt the currency of another country, referred to as **dollarization** in the case of adopting the US dollar. As far as monetary and exchange rate policy is concerned, the country becomes an adjunct to the country issuing the currency. This is a last resort for countries unable to manage their own affairs. In recent years, Ecuador and El Salvador have dollarized.

Pegged exchange rates are fixed exchange rates, but adjustable. This was the system set up at Bretton Woods in 1944, by which each country's currency was pegged to the US dollar, so that all bilateral rates of exchange between countries were also pegged. The system was called the 'adjustable peg system', however, because if countries found themselves in fundamental balance of payments disequilibrium, with unsustainable deficits, they were allowed to adjust the rate of exchange with the dollar and therefore other currencies too. The system gave exchange rate stability, and avoided competitive devaluation by countries that characterized the beggar-thy-neighbour policies of the 1930s, but proved difficult to sustain in a world of increasing capital mobility. This is the problem for any country wishing to peg its exchange rate. If a currency is under pressure, the existence of a peg gives a one-way option for speculators. The currency markets anticipate that the peg can be adjusted only downwards, which then makes the currency vulnerable to speculative attacks. With large amounts of capital freely mobile, it is very difficult to maintain a pegged rate while attempting to pursue an independent monetary policy, because the interest rate has to be used to defend the currency. It was largely speculative capital flows, and the inability of the USA to meet the promise of exchanging dollars for gold, that caused the international monetary system established at Bretton Woods to break down in 1972. Since then, other countries that have tried to peg rates have met with a similar fate. To quote Fischer (2001): 'in recent years, fixed or pegged exchange rates have been a major factor in every major emerging market financial crisis – Mexico at the end of 1994; Thailand, Indonesia and Korea in 1997; Russia and Brazil in 1998; Argentina and Turkey in 2000 … and 2001'.

If countries do decide to peg their exchange rate, there are three broad choices of peg:

1. Pegging to a single currency such as the dollar, pound or euro.
2. Pegging to an individually tailored basket of currencies reflecting the trade of the country concerned.
3. Pegging to a common basket of currencies such as the SDR (special drawing rights), which, since 2016, has been a weighted basket of the world's five major currencies – the dollar, the yen, the euro, the pound and the Chinese yuan (renminbi).

The question is: Which peg to choose? This will depend on what the country is trying to achieve. If it is macroeconomic stability, pegging against just one currency is unlikely to be optimal since movements in a country's exchange rate may bear no relation to its own balance of payments, but instead will move according to the balance of payments of the country that the currency is pegged to. Ideally, the pegged rate needs to balance out the effect of individual *bilateral* exchange rate changes over the economy as a whole. This requires pegging to a basket of currencies, where the weights should reflect the direction and elasticity of total trade (exports and imports) between the country and its trading partners. Pegging to a common basket of currencies, such as the SDR, is likely to be superior to pegging to just one currency, but inferior to an individually tailored basket of currencies.

To preserve the advantages of a fixed exchange rate, but to minimize the speculative pressures that can build up with the prospect of currency depreciation, there are various, more flexible, intermediate exchange rate regimes.

One possibility is a **crawling peg**. Under a crawling peg, a country maintains its pegged exchange rate within agreed margins at a level equal to the moving average of the market exchange rate over a previously agreed time period. This allows a country's currency to drift gradually lower if circumstances warrant, but avoids the upheaval of devaluation under an adjustable peg system and the possibility of excessive depreciation under free floating. To avoid speculation against the currency, the interest rate can be raised by a margin equal to the permitted rate of depreciation.

A variant of the crawling peg is an **exchange rate band**, whereby the country allows the exchange rate to vary within a specified range. A **crawling band** allows the exchange rate band itself to move over time.

The furthest extreme of flexibility is to allow a currency to float completely independently without any intervention at all. This implies that the country is completely indifferent to its exchange rate. In practice, no country can be indifferent if it is concerned with macroeconomic stability. Exchange rates can overshoot wildly, which can be very disruptive, and a rapidly depreciating currency can be a serious source of inflation by raising the domestic price of imports. It also needs to be stressed that although free floating, by definition, guarantees equilibrium in the foreign exchange market (because the exchange rate is the price that equilibrates the supply and demand for foreign exchange), it does *not* guarantee equilibrium on the current account of the balance of payments because the demand elasticities for imports and exports may not be of the right order of magnitude. This may then involve the unsustainable build-up of debt if deficits are financed by foreign borrowing.

Although many countries claim to have moved towards greater exchange rate flexibility in recent years, in practice, they intervene. This is called **managed floating**. Countries have no target rate of exchange, no peg, no official band, but they intervene on a daily basis according to circumstances. Managing the exchange rate is easier when there are controls on capital flows. Capital controls insulated China from the exchange rate turmoil that hit many countries in Southeast Asia in 1997 (see Case example 16.2). In 1998, Malaysia imposed capital controls in order to manage its exchange rate more effectively (see Athukorala, 2001). For a short time, Chile imposed a tax on capital inflows so that it could operate a policy of monetary contraction to control inflation without leading to destabilizing capital inflows.

Case example 16.2

The 1997 East Asian financial crisis: a cautionary tale

The financial crisis in East Asia erupted in July 1997 when pressure on the Thai baht became so severe that the government was compelled to cease defending the fixed exchange rate and to allow the currency to float, in order to avoid defaulting on its international obligations. There was rapid contagion throughout the region, leading to a collapse of the currencies of Thailand, Indonesia, Malaysia, the Philippines and Korea (the Asia-5) within a matter of weeks. Accompanying the currency collapse were steep falls in these countries' stock markets, which spread to other economies such as Singapore and Hong Kong, whose currencies remained relatively stable. The turmoil rapidly turned into a major world financial crisis and not only had dramatic effects on the region's growth performance, but also substantially reduced world economic growth. What happened in East Asia in 1997 provides an illuminating case study, and cautionary tale, of the danger to countries of attempting to run large balance of payments deficits financed by short-term capital inflows, while trying to maintain a fixed exchange rate.

continued overleaf

Case example 16.2 **The 1997 East Asian financial crisis: a cautionary tale** – *continued*

The question is: Why did this region, previously described by economists and commentators as representing a 'growth miracle', plunge into one of the world's most serious postwar recessions? The answer is that, for some time, there had been a major imbalance in the external accounts of the Asia-5 countries, but no one warned of the danger, not even the IMF, who did not see the crisis coming. The deficits of 5% and more of GDP were being financed by shorter term volatile capital inflows. Volatile flows constituted over 60% of external financing in the years prior to 1997. The massive capital inflows led to imprudent lending by the domestic banks, and a rapid expansion of credit, leading to asset and property bubbles. The latter encouraged even further capital inflows. It became clear to investors that the exchange rate could not be maintained, and once market sentiment changed, a self-fulfilling prophecy developed, leading to a vicious circle of capital flight, falling exchange rates and a collapse in the regional stock exchanges. Once capital begins to move out of a region and the exchange rate begins to fall, no one wants to be caught holding assets valued in domestic currency. The capital loss caused by a depreciating currency can far outweigh any possible gains in higher returns or in higher interest rates that are imposed to try to restore confidence.

The East Asian financial crisis exposed some fundamental weaknesses in the Asian growth process, although not the underlying factors that gave rise to rapid growth rates in the first place. Particularly, it showed the danger (and this is a warning to other countries) of the rapid liberalization of international capital flows before the domestic banking system has developed sufficient regulatory control, and of financing ever-growing balance of payments deficits relative to GDP by increasingly short-term capital flows. The balance of payments becomes the ultimate constraint on the growth performance of nations.

Source: Based on McCombie and Thirlwall, 1999.

Finally, it needs to be said that an optimal exchange rate strategy for a developing country ought to recognize the **dual structure** of most countries and that a single exchange rate for all commodities may not be appropriate. Either a **dual exchange rate** is required, or some system of taxes and subsidies to achieve the same effect. A classic early reference arguing the case for dual exchange rates is Kaldor (1964). Under a dual exchange rate system, a fixed (official) rate could apply to primary commodity exports (and to essential imports to keep their domestic price low) and a free (devalued) rate could apply to manufactured exports with a high price elasticity of demand (and to inessential imports). With a foreign exchange shortage, the free rate would produce a domestic price of foreign exchange well above the official rate. The higher the free rate, or the greater the degree of devaluation, the greater the stimulation of manufactured exports and the greater the discouragement of inessential imports.

The main administrative problem with dual exchange rates is to separate the two markets, to ensure that export proceeds from primary commodity exports are surrendered at the official rate and that foreign exchange bought at the official rate is used for essential imports. The former can be achieved through state marketing boards, the latter through strict licensing. Currency auctions – selling foreign exchange for non-essential purposes to the highest bidder – is another form of dual (or multiple) exchange rate policy. In the early days of the IMF, dual and multiple exchange rates were discouraged and frowned upon as interfering with free trade and exchange, but in more recent years, greater tolerance has been shown.

Recent research on the relation between the exchange rate regime adopted by countries and the functioning of the real economy shows the following:

- Under pegged regimes, inflation is lower, the growth of output is not affected, but output volatility is higher than under flexible exchange rate regimes (Ghosh et al. 2002).
- Pegged regimes are more prone to currency crises than floating exchange rate regimes, particularly in countries more integrated with international financial markets, but intermediate regimes are even more prone to crisis than the bipolar extremes of hard pegs or free floating (Bubula and Otker-Robe, 2004).
- Countries with flexible exchange rate regimes absorb terms of trade shocks more easily than countries with fixed exchange rate regimes, so that output is less volatile (Broda, 2004).

So, trade-offs are involved. Pegged exchange rates are best for controlling inflation, but they constrain the use of other macroeconomic policies such as scope for countercyclical fiscal policy because agents fear that countries will intervene to control expected currency depreciation. Pegs also impede timely external adjustment so payments imbalances build up. Intermediate regimes deliver faster growth of output of about 0.5% per annum, but inflation is higher (Ghosh and Ostry, 2009). The countries currently pursuing different types of exchange rate regime are shown in Table 16.3. It can be seen that there is quite a variety of exchange rate systems in operation. Forty three countries still peg their currency to the US dollar in one form or another and 26 countries peg to the euro. At the other end of the spectrum, 36 countries operate a managed float and 29 countries have free floating. Neither free floating nor managed floating mean that countries are indifferent to the exchange rate; merely that there is no formal peg to which the currencies are anchored.

Table 16.3 Countries classified by exchange rate regime, 2014

Exchange rate arrangement	Exchange rate anchor					
	US dollar (43)		Euro (26)		Composite (12)	Other (9)
No separate legal tender	Ecuador El Salvador Marshall Islands Micronesia	Palau Panama Timor-Leste Zimbabwe	Kosovo Montenegro	San Marino		Kiribati Tuvalu
Currency board	Djibouti Hong Kong SAR **ECCU** Antigua and Barbuda Dominica Grenada	St. Kitts and Nevis St. Lucia St. Vincent and the Grenadines	Bosnia and Herzegovina Bulgaria	Lithuania		Brunei Darussalam

continued

Table 16.3 Countries classified by exchange rate regime, 2014 *– continued*

Exchange rate arrangement	Exchange rate anchor			
	US dollar (43)	**Euro (26)**	**Composite (12)**	**Other (9)**
Conventional peg	Aruba The Bahamas Bahrain Barbados Belize Curaçao and Sint Maarten Eritrea Jordan Oman Qatar Saudi Arabia South Sudan Turkmenistan United Arab Emirates Venezuela	Cabo Verde Comoros Denmark Sao Tome: and Principe **WAEMU** Benin Burkina Faso Cote d'Ivoire Guinea-Bissau Mali Niger Senegal Togo **CEMAC** Cameroon Central African Rep. Chad Rep. of Congo Equatorial Guinea Gabon	Fiji Kuwait Libya Morocco Samoa	Bhutan Lesotho Namibia Nepal Swaziland
Stabilized arrangement	Guyana Iraq Kazakhstan Lebanon Maldives Suriname Trinidad and Tobago	FYR Macedonia	Singapore Vietnam	
Crawling peg	Nicaragua		Botswana	
Crawl-like arrangement	Honduras Jamaica	Croatia		
Pegged exchange rate within horizontal bands			Tonga	
Other managed arrangement	Cambodia Liberia		Algeria Iran Syria	
Managed Floating	Afghanistan Kenya Madagascar Malawi Mozambique Albania Brazil Colombia Georgia Ghana Hungary Papua New Guinea Seychelles Siena Leone Tanzania Ukraine Uruguay Iceland Indonesia Israel Korea Moldova New Zealand Paraguay Peru Philippines Romania Serbia South Africa	India Mauritius Mongolia Zambia		

Table 16.3 Countries classified by exchange rate regime, 2014 – *continued*

Exchange rate arrangement	**Exchange rate anchor**			
	US dollar (43)	**Euro (26)**	**Composite (12)**	**Other (9)**
	Thailand Turkey Uganda			
Free floating	Australia Canada Chile Japan Mexico Norway Poland Sweden United Kingdom	Somalia United States **EMU** Austria Belgium Cyprus Estonia Finland France Germany Greece Ireland Italy Latvia Luxembourg Malta Netherlands Portugal Slovak Rep. Slovenia Spain		

Source: IMF, 2014.

The international monetary system and developing countries

The world's international monetary system is governed largely by the **International Monetary Fund (IMF)**, which was established at Bretton Woods in 1944 in the aftermath of the Great Depression of the 1920s and 1930s and in preparation for the postwar peace. There was a fear that the protectionism and beggar-thy-neighbour policies that characterized the interwar period would rear their ugly heads again, to the detriment of the world economy at large, if not all the individual countries within it. Thus, the IMF was originally conceived as an institution for stabilizing the world economy, rather than as an agency for development, providing short-term loans to member countries in temporary balance of payments difficulties. Responsibility for development was given to the IMF's sister institution, the **World Bank**, established at the same time. Because the IMF was not allowed to create money, John Maynard Keynes (one of the architects of the IMF) used to complain (and joke) that his proposal for a bank had become a fund, and what was, in fact, a fund had been called a bank.

Over the years, however, and particularly in recent years, the role of the IMF has changed. It has increasingly become the bank manager of poor countries, and much more of a development agency, advancing longer term loans to cover what are now perceived as longer term structural balance of payments difficulties. The role of the World Bank has also been changing, and now it too provides loans as a means of balance of payments support (the traditional preserve of the IMF), for programmes of structural adjustment (see Chapter 14). In turn, the IMF instituted a Structural

Adjustment Facility in 1986, and an Enhanced Structural Adjustment Facility in 1987 (see below). The roles of the IMF and the World Bank have almost merged, reflecting the fact that the balance of payments is the principal long-run constraint on the growth of output in developing countries.

The IMF and the World Bank also roughly agree on the same policies and reforms that should be applied in developing countries – often referred to as the **Washington Consensus**. The term 'Washington Consensus' was originally coined by John Williamson of the Institute for International Economics in 1989 to refer to an agenda for reform in Latin America, which he believed the IMF and the World Bank would endorse (see Williamson 1990, 1993). The reforms quickly came to be seen as a model for the wider developing world. The package of reforms suggested by Williamson comprised the following:

- Fiscal discipline
- Redirection of public expenditure towards education, health and infrastructure investment
- Tax reform – broadening the tax base and cutting marginal tax rates
- Interest rates that are market determined and positive (but moderate) in real terms
- Competitive exchange rates
- Trade liberalization – replacement of quantitative restrictions with low and uniform tariffs
- Openness to foreign direct investment
- Privatization of state enterprises
- Deregulation – abolition of regulations that impede entry or restrict competition, except for those justified on safety, environmental and consumer protection grounds, and prudential oversight of financial institutions
- Legal security for property rights.

The Washington Consensus extols the virtues of the free market and free trade for the achievement of more rapid economic progress (see Taylor, 1997), but Williamson objects to the interpretation of it as 'neoliberal', because neoliberalism also embraces a political ideology relating to minimal state interference in economic and social affairs, low tax rates, individualism, and a general indifference to the income distribution produced by market forces.

The wisdom of the Washington Consensus was always a matter of dispute among economists, but its initial appeal did not last long because, in the 1990s, several developing countries that adopted the package of reforms, under pressure from the IMF and the World Bank, suffered severe financial and economic crises, which toppled governments, reduced living standards, and left millions of people worse off. Free-market forces turned out to be as disruptive and destructive as government regulations and controls. Economists now question the pace and sequencing of the deregulation and liberalization of markets, and call for stronger domestic institutions and policies to be put in place before countries open up to floods of imports and capital inflows. The need to mix institution-building with the freeing of markets is sometimes called the **post-Washington Consensus**. However, the ideology and practical policy-making of the IMF and the World Bank have hardly changed.

One country that has resisted the pressure of the Washington Consensus is China. It has forged its own development strategy, the **Beijing Consensus**, which does not allow the economy to be buffeted by the unfettered forces of free-market capitalism, either domestic or international. It is becoming increasingly attractive to other (large) developing countries (e.g. Brazil) looking for an alternative approach to economic policy-making, which puts the needs of people first, not the interests of bankers and international speculators. China's declared goal is to achieve fast, sustainable growth, combined with equity and poverty reduction. China recognizes that to achieve this requires a degree of economic independence to insulate it from turbulence in the world economy. This makes it cautious about free trade and the free movement of international capital, although not about attracting long-term foreign direct investment. China is fortunate to be large enough (and stable enough) to go its own way. Many developing countries are either too small, too vulnerable or too unstable to resist the orthodoxy because they are dependent on loan support from the IMF and the World Bank.

How the IMF works

The IMF has three main roles:

1. It oversees the international monetary system and monitors the economic and financial policies of its 189 member countries. As part of this surveillance process, which takes place at the global level and in individual countries, the IMF highlights possible risks to stability and advises on needed policy adjustments.
2. It helps its member countries design economic policies and manage their financial affairs more effectively by strengthening their human and institutional capacity through expert advice and training, which it calls 'capacity development'.
3. It provides loans to member countries experiencing actual or potential balance of payments problems to help them rebuild their international reserves, stabilize their currencies, continue paying for imports, and restore conditions for strong economic growth, while correcting underlying problems.

The IMF is a source of four main forms of financial assistance, or liquidity, to developing countries:

- Drawings from the ordinary facilities provided by the IMF
- Drawings made under special facilities
- Facilities for low-income countries
- The periodic issue of Special Drawing Rights (SDRs).

Members' drawing rights, their share of SDR allocations, and indeed their subscription to the IMF and voting power are all based on **quotas**. Every member must subscribe to the IMF an amount equal to its quota – 25% in the form of reserve assets and the remainder in local currency. Initial quotas are based on a formula relating to the economic circumstances of individual countries, such as living standards, importance in world trade and so on, which are then modified in various ways in the light of the conditions and quotas of other countries. The USA has the largest quota, amounting at present to 83 billion SDRs out of the total value of quota subscriptions of 471 billion SDRs. When countries draw on the IMF, they buy the currency they need with their own currency, and when they repay, they repurchase their own currency with foreign currency acceptable to the IMF. The size of the quotas comes under continual review. The 14th General Review of Quotas took place in 2015.

The IMF may supplement its quota resources by borrowing any country's currency. This was institutionalized by the **General Arrangements to Borrow (GAB)** in January 1962, which was a four-year arrangement concluded with ten industrialized countries. Since then, the GAB has been extended several times. The IMF also borrows from the private capital market and makes bilateral deals with countries.

The IMF also borrows to finance special facilities as a means of recycling the balance of payments surpluses of some member countries. The IMF argues that while it has no desire to supplant ordinary commercial banks in the recycling process, its ability to advocate adjustment policies effectively and convincingly in deficit countries is enhanced by the capacity to make substantial financial resources available to member countries. Thus, while the IMF continues to place reliance on quota subscriptions as the main source of its finance, it is also in the market to borrow. Now that the IMF sees its role as providing larger amounts of finance over longer and longer periods for countries with chronically weak balance of payments in relation to their growth objectives, it has an ever-growing need for resources.

A country making use of the IMF's resources is generally required to carry out a programme of balance of payments adjustment as a condition of support. This requirement is known as **conditionality** and reflects the IMF principle that financing and adjustment must go hand in hand. What constitutes balance of payments equilibrium is not rigidly defined. It need not mean current account equilibrium, but the measure must be defined free of restrictions on trade and payments, in keeping with the underlying liberal free trade philosophy of the IMF. The enforced programmes of balance of payments adjustment typically consist of currency devaluation and restrictions on government expenditure and the money supply, coupled with the liberalization of trade and capital movements.

These conditionality practices, which were developed during the 1950s and 1960s under pressure from the USA, have been severely criticized (see below) and have undergone continual review. They are harsh, but perhaps less harsh than they were. Countries are encouraged to approach the IMF early before payments problems become acute, and it recognizes the need for a longer adjustment period. When helping countries to design adjustment programmes, the IMF is supposed to have due regard to the socioeconomic and political characteristics of the country concerned (although there is still not much evidence of this). The IMF now recognizes that balance of payments difficulties associated with an acceptable growth of output may have as much to do with the structural characteristics of a country as with relative price distortions and excessive government expenditure. The emphasis has also shifted from demand contraction to supply-side policies to increase the efficiency of resource allocation and supply potential. For a comprehensive review of the evolution of the conditionality practices of the IMF, see Guitian (1982) and Dell (1981).

IMF lending

Table 16.4 shows the IMF's major non-concessional lending facilities, and Table 16.5 shows the IMF's concessional lending facilities for low-income countries. Currently, there are five major non-concessional facilities. First, there is the **Stand-By Arrangement (SBA)**, created in 1952 to provide short- to medium-term assistance to countries with short-term balance of payments difficulties. Normally, certain performance criteria relating to money supply targets and government expenditure must be met before resources are released. A strong programme is required to rectify balance of payments disequilibria, which almost always consists of deflation and depreciation of the exchange rate. Typically, an SBA covers a 12- to 18-month period, and repayments must be made within 3–5 years of each drawing. Countries may draw up to 200% of quota annually and 600% cumulatively.

Second, there is the **Extended Fund Facility (EFF)**, created in 1974 to provide longer term assistance to support countries' structural reforms to address long-term balance of payments difficulties. The repayment schedule is longer, 4–10 years, but the conditions are stringent. The country must provide a detailed statement of policies and measures every 12 months. The resources are provided in instalments, with performance criteria attached. Nonetheless, the introduction of the EFF represented an important and significant shift in emphasis from viewing the balance of payments as a stabilization problem, to recognizing the balance of payments as a fundamental long-term constraint on growth that cannot be rectified in a short period of time by conventional means. Structural change is required.

In the wake of the 2007–09 global financial crisis, the IMF strengthened its lending policies through the creation of three new facilities: the **Flexible Credit Line (FCL)**, the **Precautionary and Liquidity Line (PLL)** and the **Rapid Financing Instrument (RFI)** (see Table 16.4 for details).

Table 16.4 IMF's non-concessional lending facilities

Credit facility (year adopted)	Purpose	Conditions	Access limits	Repayment schedule (years)
CREDIT TRANCHES AND EXTEND FUND FACICITY				
Stand-By Arrangement (SBA) (1952)	Short- to medium-term assistance for countries with short-term balance of payments difficulties	Adopt policies that provide confidence that the member's balance of payments difficulties will be resolved within a reasonable period	Annual: 200% of quota; cumulative: 600% of quota	3¼–5
Extended Fund Facility (EFF) (1974) (Extended Arrangements)	Longer term assistance to support members' structural reforms to address long-term balance of payments difficulties	Adopt up to 4-year program, with structural agenda and annual detailed statement of policies for the next 12 months	Annual: 200% of quota; cumulative: 600% of quota	4½–10
Flexible Credit Line (FCL) (2009)	Flexible instrument in the credit tranches to address all balance of payments needs, potential or actual	Very strong ex ante macroeconomic fundamentals, economic policy framework, and policy track record	No preset limit	3¼–5
Precautionary and Liquidity Line (PLL) (2011)	Instrument for countries with sound economic fundamentals and policies	Sound policy frameworks, external position, and market access, including financial sector soundness	250% of quota for 6 months; 500% of quota available upon approval of 1- to 2-year arrangements; total of 1,000% of quota after 12 months of satisfactory progress	3¼–5
SPECIAL FACILITES				
Rapid Financing Instrument (RFI) (2011)	Rapid financial assistance to all member countries facing an urgent balance of payments need	Efforts to solve balance of payments difficulties (may include prior actions)	Annual: 50% of quota cumulative: 100% of quota	3¼–5

Source: IMF, 2014.

In addition to the IMF's ordinary lending facilities, there are three special lending facilities for low-income countries: the **Extended Credit Facility (ECF)**, the **Standby Credit Facility (SCF)**, and the **Rapid Credit Facility (RCF)**, all related to protracted balance of payments difficulties (see Table 16.5 for details). Note that the ECF supersedes the Poverty Reduction and Growth Facility, which was set up in 1999 to assist poor countries facing persistent balance of payments problems, and was designed to work alongside the IMF and World Bank's Heavily Indebted Poor Country Initiative (see Chapter 14) for debt relief for poor countries, and requires the preparation of a Poverty Reduction Strategy Paper. This is still a requirement under the EFF.

Total IMF credit outstanding for all 189 IMF members in March 2016 was nearly 55 billion SDRs, having fallen from a peak of 96 billion SDRs in December 2012 in the wake of the world financial crisis.

Table 16.5 IMF concessional lending facilities to low-income countries

	Extended Credit Facility (ECF)	Standby Credit Facility (SCF)	Rapid Credit Facility (RCF)
Objective	Help low-income countries achieve and maintain a stable and sustainable macroeconomic position consistent with strong and durable poverty reduction and growth	Very strong ex ante macroeconomic fundamentals, economic policy framework, and policy track record	Approved access available up front throughout the arrangement period, subject to a midterm review after 1 year
Purpose	Address protracted balance of payments problems	Resolve short-term balance of payments needs	Low-access financing to meet urgent balance of payments needs
Eligibility	Countries eligible under the Poverty Reduction and Growth Trust (PRG1)	Efforts to solve balance of payments difficulties (may include prior actions)	Outright purchases without the need for full-fledged program or reviews
Qualification	Protracted balance of payments problem; actual financing need over the course of the arrangement, though not necessarily when lending is approved or disbursed	Potential (precautionary use) or actual short-term balance of payments need at the time of approval; actual need required for each disbursement	Urgent balance of payments need when upper- credit-tranche (UC1) program is either not feasible or not needed
Poverty Reduction and Growth Strategy	IMF-supported program should be aligned with country-owned poverty-reduction and growth objectives and should aim to support policies that safeguard social and other priority spending		
	Submission of Poverty Reduction Strategy (PRS) document by second review	Submission of PRS document not required; If financing need persists, SCF user would request an ECF with associated PRS documentation requirements	Submission of PRS document not required; move to ECF facilitated in cases of repeated use by preparation of a Poverty Reduction Strategy Paper (PRSP)
Conditionality	UCT; flexibility on adjustment path and timing	UCT; aim to resolve balance of payments need in the short term	No UCT and no conditionality based on ex post review; track record used to qualify for repeat use (except under shocks window)
Access policies	Annual limit of 100% of quota; cumulative limit (net of scheduled repayments) of 300% of quota. Exceptional access: annual limit of 150% of quota; cumulative limit (net of scheduled repayments) of 450% of quota		
	Norms: access declines with total outstanding credit; 120% of quota if outstanding credit is less than 100% of quota; 75%	Sublimits (given lack of UCT conditionality): annual 25% of quota, 100% of quota cumulative (net of	

Table 16.5 IMF concessional lending facilities to low-income countries – *continued*

	Extended Credit Facility (ECF)	Standby Credit Facility (SCF)	Rapid Credit Facility (RCF)
Objective	of quota if outstanding credit is greater than or equal to 100% of quota; SCFs treated as precautionary annual access limit 75% of quota, average annual access limit 50% of quota	scheduled repayments); under the shocks window: 50% annual and 125% cumulative (net of scheduled repayments)	
Financing terms	Interest rate: Zero Repayment terms: 5½–10 years	Interest rate: 0.25% Repayment terms: 4-8 years Availability fee: 0.15% on available but undrawn amounts under precautionary arrangement	Interest rate: Zero Repayment terms: 5½–10 years

Source: IMF, 2014.

Other IMF activities

As well as providing finance and loans to member countries, the IMF has a number of other responsibilities connected with the smooth functioning of the world economy, including the surveillance of exchange rates and promoting the health of the world financial system. One of the mandates of the IMF is to monitor the exchange rate policies of countries. Article IV, Section I of the original (1947) IMF Charter states that member countries should 'avoid manipulating exchange rates ... to prevent effective balance of payments adjustment or to gain an unfair advantage over other members'. By manipulating the exchange rate, the IMF means countries indulging in practices that keep an exchange rate undervalued in order to maintain large balance of payments surpluses. The assessment of exchange rate levels, however, is not easy because an 'equilibrium' rate depends on how the internal balance of a country is defined, and what is regarded as the optimal level of international reserves. There are different 'equilibrium' exchange rates for different levels of employment and unemployment, different growth rates, and reserves to import ratios. But, the IMF lacks any power to influence the exchange rate policy of countries, except persuasion. The sanction of fining countries in persistent surpluses, which Keynes proposed at Bretton Woods, was never adopted.

Criticisms of the IMF

The policy prescriptions of the IMF in developing countries have been, and still are, based on a blend of finance and adjustment. Few would dispute the need for international institutions to provide finance to ease the burden of balance of payments adjustment. In its adjustment policies, however, the IMF has come in for severe criticism; so much so that it has been described as **anti-developmental**. In its approach to adjustment, the IMF is conditioned by the beliefs and philosophy of the organization itself and the prevailing orthodoxy of neoclassical economic theory. The IMF denies that it has a rigid doctrinaire approach to economic policy, but it clearly has a particular philosophy based on the Washington Consensus. It is a major bastion of support of an international economic system that prefers capitalism to socialism, favours private investment over public investment, extols the virtues of free trade and the operation of the price mechanism, and encourages the free flow of private capital to and from developing countries. Gore (2000) argues that this consensus that emerged within the IMF (and World Bank) was more than just a paradigm shift from the idea of state-led development to market-oriented policies. There was a deeper shift in the way development problems were perceived in an increasingly globalized world, and the IMF's policies have been a response to these changes in the world economy. The fact remains, however, that a particular orthodoxy has been applied to the vast majority of developing countries as if they were one homogeneous mass and can be properly treated in exactly the same way.

Joseph Stiglitz (2002), formerly a chief economist of the World Bank, has severely criticized the IMF for serving the needs of global finance, rather than the needs of global stability, by encouraging premature internal and external financial liberalization. He has satirized the methods of the IMF by describing what he calls a four-step programme for every country, regardless of circumstances and already 'pre-drafted' by IMF officials before they reach the country, for 'voluntary' signature by the country concerned. No signature, no help. The four core elements of each programme are privatization of state industries, capital market liberalization, market-based pricing, and free trade.

Capital market liberalization has been disastrous for many countries not ready and able to cope with volatile capital inflows and outflows. The IMF has, in fact, admitted that opening economies prematurely to free flows of capital constituted 'an accident waiting to happen', and now concedes that capital controls are justified in some circumstances. The IMF was undoubtedly shaken by the 1997 East Asian crisis, which it did not foresee even though there was a massive build-up of current account deficits and capital had started to flow out of Southeast Asia long before the crisis hit.

Market-based pricing has also been disastrous in many instances, leading to civil unrest. When food and fuel subsidies for the poor were lifted in Indonesia in 1998, the country exploded into riots.

Free trade, we saw in Chapter 15, is not optimal from a development point of view. If imports grow faster than exports, the balance of payments worsens.

The neoliberal, neoclassical approach to economic thinking and policy-making colours, to a large extent, the IMF's diagnosis of balance of payments problems and their appropriate solution. Deficits are invariably seen as related to, or caused by, price uncompetitiveness and excess monetary demand, to be 'cured' by devaluation and demand contraction. But, the IMF still lacks a comprehensive theoretical apparatus to deal with two basic questions regarding devaluation: How is the degree of *overvaluation* of a currency determined? How is the optimal pace of adjustment from the overvalued to the equilibrium rate of exchange decided? In keeping with the IMF's philosophy, devaluation and retrenchment are coupled with other measures that, from a balance of payments point of view, work in the opposite direction – namely the relaxation of foreign exchange controls, the removal of import restrictions, and the dismantling of subsidies and price controls.

Critics of the IMF argue with some justification that there is one law for the poor and another for the rich. While poor countries must remove controls over foreign exchange and imports as a condition of assistance, rich countries continue to impose restrictions on imports from developing countries. To support the liberalization programme, the country then has to depress aggregate demand sufficiently to accommodate devaluation in the attempt to achieve balance of payments equilibrium, which leads to slow growth and unemployment. The symptoms of balance of payments disequilibrium are tackled, but not the root causes of the perpetual tendency towards disequilibrium. As we argued in Chapter 15, the balance of payments problems of most developing countries must be regarded as primarily *structural* in nature, relating to the characteristics of the goods produced and traded. This implies a very different approach to balance of payments adjustment than one of continual devaluation, demand contraction and dismantling of the public sector. At the very least, it calls for policies – using a judicious mix of subsidies and controls – to alter the *structure* of production.

Another criticism of the IMF is that it ignores 'structural' *surpluses* on the balance of payments – the counterpart of 'structural' deficits – and critics argue that the burden of adjustment ought to be shared more equitably between deficit and surplus countries, instead of the major part of the burden being shouldered by debtor developing countries, as at present. If surplus countries do not attempt to adjust by expanding their own economies, or by appreciating their currencies, they should be penalized, and deficit countries ought to be allowed to discriminate against the goods of these countries. This would be a revival of the idea of 'scarce currencies', and of the right of countries to control imports from 'scarce currency' countries, that is, from those with surpluses.

Critics would also argue that if the IMF is genuinely concerned with development as well as providing balance of payments support, it could distribute all new issues of SDRs to developing countries to spend in developed countries. After all, if the developed countries were not able to earn their reserves by selling goods to developing countries in exchange for SDRs, they would have to earn them in some other way. We shall return to this matter below.

The IMF has become sensitive to some of these criticisms in recent years, particularly to the charge that it is 'anti-developmental'. Along with the World Bank, the IMF now declares itself committed to poverty reduction and allowing countries to 'own' their own policies through the formulation of Poverty Reduction Strategy Papers. Instead of countries having to fulfil a mass of individual conditions for loan support, governments can now specify just a few broad outcomes relating to poverty reduction, health and education. To what extent it will change its attitude to balance of payments difficulties and the need for devaluation and deflation, however, is still an open question.

The IMF also now has an **Independent Evaluation Office (IEO)**, established in 2001, to monitor its lending activities and research the effects of its lending policies. The IEO chose three subjects for its first studies:

- fiscal adjustment in IMF-supported programmes
- the role of the IMF in three capital account crises (Indonesia and Korea, 1997–98 and Brazil, 1998–99)
- prolonged use of IMF resources.

Kenen (2004) surveys the results of the studies so far. On fiscal policy, the IEO criticizes IMF programmes for not paying enough attention to raising income and property taxes, and combating tax evasion, and for focusing too heavily on cutting public employment or capping wages in periods of fiscal crisis. In general, fiscal policy has not been 'too tight', although the fiscal outcome has normally been tighter than forecast. In Korea and Indonesia, however, in 1997–98, there was too much fiscal stringency because the IMF did not foresee the collapse of investment and output, so that IMF policies made the situation worse. The prolonged use of IMF resources has increased in recent years because, as Keynes once said: 'if you owe a bank a little, the bank owns you, but if you owe the bank a lot *you* own the bank'. The IMF has been reluctant to pull out of countries in case it doesn't get repaid at all. The evaluation reaches some interesting findings, which have general lessons:

- Excessively detailed conditionality does not appear to be effective.
- Conditionality that is focused on policy rules or procedures, rather than on discretionary one-time actions, seems to be most effective.

The International Financial Institution Advisory Commission, known as the **Meltzer Commission**, appointed by the US Congress, which reported in 2000, recommended that the IMF should withdraw from the development field entirely and concentrate on the role of 'lender of last resort' to emerging economies facing financial crisis. This would be a return to its original function of lending to countries in short-term balance of payments difficulties. Likewise, the World Bank should pare down its activities, lending only to really poor countries, and not to countries able to attract private capital. In line with the focus on poverty reduction, lending should be confined to countries with an income of less than $4,000 per head with low credit ratings. For the poorest countries, there should be grants not loans. Lending to Asia and Latin America could largely be left to the regional development banks in those regions. In general, there should be a much clearer distinction between the activities of the IMF and the World Bank. This would be a return to the original conception at Bretton Woods that the World Bank would act as the development agency and the IMF would be like a bank to be used in emergencies only, but not get involved in detailed policy-making itself in the countries concerned. A move in this direction would disarm many of the IMF's critics.

The results of IMF programmes

The effects of the IMF's programmes on countries' economic performance have been very mixed. In an early study, Reichmann and Stillson (1978) examined the effects of IMF programmes in developed and developing countries in the period 1963–72, comparing the two years after the implementation of the programme with the two years before. Taking the balance of payments as a whole (current plus capital account), of the 75 cases examined, only 18 showed a statistically significant improvement and 4 showed an actual worsening. In the 29 cases where the inflation rate had exceeded 5% before the programme, it had worsened in 6 cases and in 16 cases there was no significant change. As far as GDP growth is concerned, of the 70 cases examined, the performance had improved in 33 but deteriorated in 28. A study by Donavan (1982) of the non-oil-developing countries for the period 1971–80 revealed a similar pattern: some improvement in the balance of payments, mixed effects on growth and some tendency towards inflation.

Following a major analysis of over 30 IMF stabilization programmes supported by upper-tranche credits between 1964 and 1979, Killick (1984a, 1984b) advocated what he called a 'real economy approach to balance of payments' or 'adjustment with growth', which would be a more flexible supply-oriented approach with demand management subservient.

One of the purposes of the Extended Fund Facility and the (now defunct) Structural Adjustment Facility was to permit the IMF to deal with structural disequilibrium, but as far as the EFF is concerned, the programmes were no different from conventional demand management programmes built around monetary and fiscal contraction coupled with trade liberalization and some production incentives.

In a follow-up study of IMF programmes in developing countries, Killick (1995) criticized the IMF's overreliance on conditionality and performance criteria, which invariably leads to the breakdown of IMF programmes. To avoid breakdowns and pressure on IMF resources, he calls for the relaxation of standardized reform packages and a greater emphasis on locally initiated programmes of stabilization and reform. Above all, the programmes should set a growth target of at least 1% above population growth, and sufficient financing for this should be mobilized. Killick finds that the main victim of IMF programmes is investment, and that there is no evidence that IMF financing acts as a catalyst for private investment.

Taylor (1988) reports the results of studies of 18 countries, conducted under the auspices of the World Institute for Development Economics Research (WIDER) in Helsinki. The principal finding of the authors of the country studies is that 'past policies could have been designed to better effect, and that programmes of the Fund/Bank type are optimal for neither stabilization nor growth and income redistribution in the Third World'. This is a serious indictment of policy from some of the world's leading development economists. There are alternative programmes to those implemented by the IMF, but they would be more interventionist and more directly concerned with the targets than with the precise instruments. There is a role for selective import controls, export subsidies, multiple exchange rates, low interest rates and so on, but these are all frowned on by the IMF. The IMF conducts its own in-house studies of programmes and is naturally more sanguine, but is conscious that the design of programmes can be improved. In a study of 45 IMF lending arrangements approved between mid-1988 and mid-1991, Schadler (1996) reports striking gains on the external accounts, but virtually no improvement in inflation, investment and growth. Four explanations are given:

- Countries coming to the IMF too late
- Too much emphasis on the external objective of balance of payments equilibrium rather than domestic objectives
- The breaking of monetary targets
- Not enough emphasis on raising domestic saving.

Research on the effect of IMF programmes on the growth of per capita income by Przeworksi and Vreeland (2000) and Dreher (2006) shows a negative effect. Dreher's (2006) study examines data for 98 countries over the period 1970–2000 and, overall, finds a negative effect of 1.7 percentage points per annum (on average), although the compliance with conditionality mitigated the negative effect. Dreher's conjecture is that 'the short-term effect of demand compression takes place very quickly, while the compliance measures pick up later adherence to the more structural aspects of policy conditions'.

Special Drawing Rights (SDRs) and developing countries

One possibility for increasing the flow of resources to developing countries is to distribute to them most, if not all, of the saving accruing to developed countries from the issue of costless SDRs as a means of international payment. The IMF established SDRs in July 1969. To date, there have been only four allocations of SDRs: 9.3 billion between 1970 and 1972; 12.1 billion between 1979 and 1981; 161.2 billion in 2009, and a one-off injection of 21.5 billion in the wake of the financial crisis and world economic recession in 2008–09, allocated mainly to low-income countries.

The normal basis of allocation of SDRs between countries is the member countries' quota subscriptions to the IMF. This means that approximately 70% of the new international money created has been distributed to the world's richest countries, while the poorest countries have received only 30%. If the SDRs had been distributed on a per capita basis, the distribution would have been almost exactly the reverse.

There can be no doubt about the potential benefits of international money, such as SDRs, for the world as a whole, but there are several objections to the present distribution, and reasons to believe that a redistribution of SDRs in favour of developing countries could increase world welfare. First, the balance of payments adjustment costs of developing countries are generally higher than those of developed countries, and this in itself constitutes an economic argument for revising the present allocation rules. But second, SDRs represent a social saving because they are costless to produce (unlike gold), and do not have to be earned by exporting (unlike dollars). The view that the social saving to SDRs should be distributed to the developing countries has spawned several proposals for a so-called **link between development assistance and SDRs**, which would have several advantages:

1. If there was a regular expansion of SDRs a link would provide a useful mechanism by which total development aid could be guaranteed to rise with the long-term growth of world trade and production. At present, there is no guarantee that aid will rise in proportion to world income. Aid programmes are chopped and changed according to the balance of payments situation of donor countries.
2. A link scheme would increase the proportion of total international aid that is untied, and this would not impose any reserve losses on the donor, as when a country unties its aid unilaterally. All donor countries would gain reserves in exchange for the exports they provide to the developing countries.
3. If the link scheme operated through such international financial institutions as the World Bank or one of its affiliates, these multilateral institutions would be provided with a regular flow of resources without the necessity of entering into time-consuming negotiations with national governments.

The historical origin of the link idea can be traced back to Keynes' plan, proposed at Bretton Woods in 1944, for an International Clearing Union (ICU) with the power to issue international money for collectively agreed purposes. The function of the ICU was not only to be a world central bank but also to lend to international organizations pursuing internationally agreed objectives, in particular, at that time, for postwar relief work and the management of international commodities.

The variety of link proposals that have been put forward can be classified into three types: a direct link, an organic link and an inorganic (or indirect, voluntary) link.

As far as a **direct link** is concerned, the simplest method would be to allocate more SDRs directly to developing countries, as was done in 2009. Alternatively, the IMF quotas to developing countries could be increased.

An **organic link** refers to the possibility of channelling SDRs to developing countries via developed countries, development agencies, or both. The direct allocation of SDRs to development agencies probably has the most advantages and the least drawbacks among the organic link proposals. Development agencies would have accounts with the IMF to which SDRs would be credited. The development agencies would then lend in the normal way. When goods were purchased from exporters by developing countries, the IMF would then transfer the SDRs from the account of the development agencies to the account of the exporting country. The country would then pay its exporters in its domestic currency. The scheme has the advantage of being simple and could be introduced with minimal amendments to the IMF Articles of Agreement.

A tied version of the organic link was Scitovsky's (1966) original plan for a new international currency to be issued to deficit countries with unemployed resources, which would relinquish domestic currency in exchange. This could then be lent to developing countries, but could only be spent in the issuing country. This would serve several purposes. It would provide developing countries with unrequited imports at no opportunity cost to developed countries and remedy developed countries' deficits at the same time. This is also a way of eliminating deflationary bias in the world economy.

An **inorganic link** would involve developed countries agreeing to make voluntary contributions to the multilateral aid-giving agencies whenever new SDRs were allocated. The contributions would be in national currencies but would represent a uniform proportion of each contributor's SDR allocation. The drawback of the proposal is its voluntary nature – one or two major countries might not contribute or might make their contribution dependent on their balance of payments. This would introduce a great deal of uncertainty into the scheme. Also, national governments would have to agree appropriations and this would create the same difficulties as regular foreign aid appropriations. There do not seem to be many advantages in an inorganic link.

Several objections have been raised against the link proposals but none is very convincing. Some have argued against the link on the grounds that the creation of reserves should be kept separate from the transfer of real resources. But this has never been the case historically. Resource transfers have always been involved in the acquisition of gold and dollars. Since SDRs save real resources, it is entirely appropriate that, in the process of reserve creation, the saving should be distributed to developing countries.

A second objection to the link is that it would mean the loss of control over the granting and distribution of assistance by national governments. Under the link scheme, the distribution of the burden of assistance would depend on where the SDRs were spent, which, it is argued, could not be accurately forecast. This is a weak argument for two reasons. The same objection may be levelled against *all* forms of untied bilateral aid. There is never an automatic correspondence between the financial burden of aid and the real resource burden of aid. It all depends on whether the national governments that grant aid allow the resources to be transferred, which depends primarily on their policy towards the balance of payments.

A further objection is that the link is likely to be inflationary. It is true that developing countries will tend to spend new international money rather than add to their reserves, but whether or not the resulting claims on developed countries are inflationary will depend on whether developed countries are willing to release resources to the extent of the claims on them. In practice, SDRs could be less inflationary than the dollar standard by instituting multilateral control over international liquidity rather than unilateral control by the USA, which, because of the need for dollars, has not been subject to the anti-inflationary discipline that is normally present in other countries.

A final objection is that development assistance is not likely to increase under the link because governments will cut down on their normal budgetary aid appropriations. Critics argue that it is highly unlikely that developed countries would be willing to give extra aid through the link but not in other forms. This objection can also be challenged. First, the reserve effects of the two forms of assistance are not the same. Conventional aid worsens the donor's balance of payments, whereas the link scheme would improve the balance of payments of countries where SDRs were spent and thus improve the reserve position. Second, governments often wish to provide aid for specific purposes and this desire would not be undermined by a link. Moreover, since it is difficult for a country to know how much aid it is providing through the link, it would be difficult for a country to offset it. The link deserves much more consideration in international monetary circles than it has received to date. To paraphrase Pirandello, if ever there were an instrument in search of a policy, it is SDRs.

Summary

- A major constraint on the growth of output in many developing countries is a deficit on the current account of the balance of payments, or, in other words, a shortage of foreign exchange to pay for imports.
- The International Monetary Fund (IMF) was established at the Bretton Woods conference in 1944 to give financial support to countries in temporary balance of payments difficulties, but the deficits of developing countries are structural and long term, relating to the nature of the goods they export and import.
- A country's growth rate consistent with balance of payments equilibrium on current account depends on changes in the real exchange rate, the price elasticities of demand for exports and imports, the growth of world income, and the income elasticity of demand for exports and imports.
- If the real exchange rate is constant over time, the long-run growth of GDP can be approximated by the ratio of the growth of export volume and the income elasticity of demand for imports.
- Capital inflows can lift a balance of payments constraint on growth, but only by a small amount for realistic values of the sustainable ratio of deficits (or international debt) to GDP.
- Currency depreciation needs to be continuous to raise a country's growth rate permanently consistent with balance of payments equilibrium, but currency depreciation can be very inflationary.
- No single exchange rate regime can be prescribed for all developing countries. Each country needs to choose its own regime consistent with other economic objectives.
- The IMF has many lending facilities, but access is mainly related to the size of a country's quota with the IMF, not to the scale of difficulties confronting the country.
- IMF conditionality has been severely criticized as deflationary, and insensitive to the circumstances and needs of countries. The results of IMF policies have been disappointing.
- Special Drawing Rights (SDRs) could be distributed to developing countries as a means of financial support, to be spent in developed countries. This would increase developed countries' reserves and transfer resources to developing countries.

Chapter 16 Discussion questions

1. What factors determine the demand for a country's exports and imports?
2. Can the devaluation of a country's currency guarantee balance of payments equilibrium on the current account?
3. What factors determine the income elasticity of demand for a country's exports?
4. Why are developing countries more prone to balance of payments disequilibrium than developed countries?

Chapter 16 **Discussion questions** – *continued*

5. What do you understand by the IMF's 'supply-side approach to devaluation' in developing countries?
6. What factors need to be taken into account in choosing a country's exchange rate regime?
7. What are the lessons of the financial crisis in Southeast Asia in 1997?
8. How do the ordinary and special facilities of the IMF work? What do you understand by 'conditionality'?
9. What criticisms have been levelled against the IMF in its policies of support to developing countries?
10. What have been the effects of IMF policies in developing countries?
11. How could SDRs be used simultaneously as an instrument of aid to developing countries and as a means of employment creation in developed countries?

Websites on balance of payments and IMF

International Monetary Fund www.imf.org
UNCTAD Handbook of Statistics http://unctad.org/en/Pages/Publications/Handbook-of-Statistics.aspx
UN Comtrade comtrade.un.org

REFERENCES AND FURTHER READING

Chapter 1 The study of economic development

Banerjee, A.J. and Duflo, E. (2011) *Poor Economics: A Radical Rethinking of the Way to Fight Global Poverty* (New York: Public Affairs).

Bardhan, P. (1993) 'Economics of Development and the Development of Economics', *Journal of Economic Perspectives*, 7(2): 129–42.

Black, R and White, H. (2006) *Targeting Development: Critical Perspectives on the Millennium Development Goals* (London: Routledge).

Brandt Commission (1983) *Common Crisis: North–South Co-operation for World Recovery* (London: Pan).

Brandt Report (1980) *North–South: A Programme for Survival* (London: Pan).

Chang, H.-J. (2002) *Kicking Away the Ladder: Development Strategy in Historical Perspective* (London: Anthem Press).

Domar, E. (1947) 'Expansion and Employment', *American Economic Review*, 7(2): 129–42.

Fischer, S. (2003) 'Globalization and its Challenges', *American Economic Review*, 93(2): 1–30.

Furtado, C. (1964) *Development and Underdevelopment* (Berkeley, CA: University of California Press).

Galbraith, J.K. (1980) *The Nature of Mass Poverty* (Harmondsworth: Penguin).

Goulet, D. (1971) *The Cruel Choice: A New Concept in the Theory of Development* (New York: Atheneum Books).

Goulet, D. (2006) *Development Ethics at Work* (London: Routledge).

Griffin, J.P. (1986) *Well-Being: Its Meaning, Measurement and Moral Importance* (Oxford: Clarendon Press).

Harrod, R. (1939) 'An Essay in Dynamic Theory', *Economic Journal*, 49(1): 14–33.

Hirschman, A. (1981) 'The Rise and Decline of Development Economics', in *Essays in Trespassing: Economics to Politics and Beyond* (Cambridge: Cambridge University Press).

Kanbur, R. (2005) 'New Directions in Development Economics: Theory or Empirics?', *Economic and Political Weekly*, 15(40): 1515–26.

Krugman, P. (1992) 'Towards a Counter-Revolution in Development Theory', *World Bank Economic Review (Supplement): Proceedings of the World Bank Annual Conference on Development Economics* (Washington, DC: World Bank).

Lal, D. (1983) *The Poverty of Development Economics* (London: Hobart).

Lewis, W.A. (1984) 'The State of Development Theory', *American Economic Review*, 74(1): 1–10.

Lipton, M. (1977) *Why Poor People Stay Poor* (London: Temple Smith).

Little, I.M.D. (1982) *Economic Development: Theory, Policies and International Relations* (New York: Basic Books).

Myrdal, G. (1957) *Economic Theory and Underdeveloped Regions* (London: Duckworth).

Naqvi, S.N.H. (1995) 'The Nature of Economic Development', *World Development*, 23(4): 543–56.

Naqvi, S.N.H. (1996) 'The Significance of Development Economics', *World Development*, 24(6): 975–87.

Pearson Report (1969) *Partners in Development*. Report of the Commission on International Development (London: Pall Mall Press).

Qizilbash, M. (1996) 'Ethical Development', *World Development*, 24(7): 1209–21.
Ravallion, M. (2013) 'The Idea of Antipoverty Policy', NBER Working Paper 19210 (Cambridge, MA: NBER).
Rawls, J. (1972) *A Theory of Justice* (Oxford: Oxford University Press).
Reinert, E. (2007) *How Rich Countries Got Rich and Why Poor Countries Stay Poor* (London: Constable & Robinson).
Sen, A.K. (1981) *Poverty and Famines, An Essay on Entitlement and Deprivation* (Oxford: Clarendon Press).
Sen, A.K. (1983) 'Development: Which Way Now?', *Economic Journal*, 93(372): 745–62.
Sen, A.K. (1999) *Development as Freedom* (Oxford: Oxford University Press).
Thirlwall, A.P. (1995) 'In Praise of Development Economics', *METU Studies in Development*, 1 and 2 (1984), repr. in A.P. Thirlwall, *The Economics of Growth and Development: Selected Essays*, vol. 1 (Aldershot: Edward Elgar).
Todaro, M. and Smith, S.C. (2015) *Economic Development in the Third World* (London: Longman).
UN (United Nations) (2015) *Global Sustainable Development Report* (New York: UN).
UNDP (UN Development Programme) (1999) *Human Development Report* (New York: Oxford University Press).
UNDP (2002) *Human Development Report* (New York: Oxford University Press).
World Bank (2000) *World Development Report 2000/2001: Attacking Poverty* (New York: Oxford University Press).

Chapter 2 The development gap and the measurement of poverty

Alkire, S. and Santos, M.E. (2010) 'Acute Multidimensional Poverty: A New Index for Developing Countries', *OPHI Working Paper* 38 (Oxford Poverty and Human Development Initiative, University of Oxford).
Atkinson, A.B. and Brandolini, A. (2010) 'On Analysing the World Distribution of Income', *World Bank Economic Review*, 24(1): 1–37.
Banerjee, A.J. and Duflo, E. (2007) 'The Economic Lives of the Poor', *Journal of Economic Perspectives*, 21(1):141–67.
Banerjee, A.J. and Duflo, E. (2011) *Poor Economics: A Radical Rethinking of the Way to Fight Global Poverty* (New York: Public Affairs).
Basu, K. (2006) 'Globalization, Poverty and Inequality: What is the Relationship? What Can be Done?', *World Development*, 34(8): 1361–73.
Baumol, W. (1986) 'Productivity Growth, Convergence and Welfare: What the Long-run Data Show', *American Economic Review*, 76(5): 1072–85.
Besley, T. and Burgess, R. (2003) 'Halving Global Poverty', *Journal of Economic Perspectives*, 17(3): 3–22.
Bourguignon, F. (2015) *The Globalisation of Inequality* (Princeton, NJ: Princeton University Press).
Bourguignon, F. and Morrisson, C. (2002) 'Inequality among World Citizens: 1820–1992', *American Economic Review*, 92(4): 727–44.
Chen, S. and Ravallion, M. (2008) 'The Developing World is Poorer than we Thought, but no Less Successful in the Fight Against Poverty', Policy Research Paper 4703 (Washington, DC: World Bank).
Collier, P. (2007) *The Bottom Billion* (Oxford: Oxford University Press).
Deaton, A. (2013) *The Great Scape: Health, Wealth and the Origins of Inequality* (Princeton, NJ: Princeton University Press).
Dollar, D. and Kraay, A. (2000) *Growth is Good for the Poor* (Washington, DC: World Bank).
Dowrick, S. (1992) 'Technological Catch-up and Diverging Incomes: Patterns of Economic Growth 1960–1988', *Economic Journal*, 102: 600–10.
Easterlin, R. (2000) 'The Worldwide Standard of Living since 1800', *Journal of Economic Perspectives*, 14(1): 7–26.
Edward, P. (2006) 'Examining Inequality: Who Really Benefits from Global Growth?', *World Development*, 34(10): 1667–95.
Eichengreen, B., Park, D. and Shin, K. (2011) 'When Fast Growing Economies Slow Down: International Evidence and Implications for China', NBER Working Paper 16919 (Cambridge, MA: NBER).
Ghose, A.K. (2004) 'Global Inequality and International Trade', *Cambridge Journal of Economics*, 28(2): 229–52.

Jones, C. (1997) 'On the Evolution of the World Income Distribution', *Journal of Economic Perspectives*, 11(3): 19–36.

Maddison, A. (2001) *The World Economy: A Millennial Perspective* (Paris: OECD).

Maddison, A. (2003) *The World Economy: Historical Statistics*, Development Studies Centre (Paris: OECD).

Milanovic, B. (2005) *Worlds Apart: Measuring International and Global Inequality* (Princeton, NJ: Princeton University Press).

Milanovic, B. (2011) *The Haves and the Have-Nots* (New York: Basic Books).

Milanovic, B. (2016) *Global Inequality: A New Approach for the Age of Globalization* (Cambridge, MA: The Belknap Press of Harvard University Press).

Norwegian Institute of International Affairs (2000) *Globalisation and Inequality: World Income Distribution and Livings Standards, 1960–1998* (Report to the Norwegian Ministry of Foreign Affairs).

Pritchett, L. (1997) 'Divergence: Big Time', *Journal of Economic Perspectives*, 11(3): 3–17.

Ravallion, M. (1997) 'Good and Bad Growth: Human Development Reports', *World Development*, 25(5): 631–8.

Ravallion, M. (2001) 'Growth, Inequality and Poverty: Looking Beyond Averages', *World Development*, 29(11): 1803–11.

Ravallion, M. (2013) 'How Long Will It Take to Lift One Billion of People Out of Poverty?', *The World Bank Research Observer*, 28(2): 139–58.

Sala-i-Martin, X. (2002) 'The Disturbing Rise of Global Income Inequality', NBER Working Paper 8904 (Cambridge, MA: NBER).

Sutcliffe, R. (2004) 'World Inequality and Globalization', *Oxford Review of Economic Policy*, 20(1): 15–37.

Svedberg, P. (2004) 'World Income Distribution: Which Way?', *Journal of Development Studies*, 40(5): 1–32.

Thirlwall, A.P. (2012) 'Poor Economics: A Radical Rethinking of the Way to Fight Global Poverty: A Review Article', *Journal of Development Studies*, 48(10): 1554–7.

Thorbecke, E. and Nissanke, M. (2006) 'Introduction: The Impact of Globalization on the World's Poor', *World Development*, 34(8): 1333–7.

UNDP (UN Development Programme) (1992) *Human Development Report 1992* (New York: Oxford University Press).

UNDP (1997) *Human Development Report* (New York: Oxford University Press).

UNDP (2014) *Human Development Report 2014* (New York: UNDP).

Wade, R. (2001) 'The Rising Inequality of World Income Distribution', *Finance & Development*, 38(4): 37–9.

Wade, R. (2004) 'Is Globalization Reducing Poverty and Inequality?', *World Development*, 35(11): 1836–57.

World Bank (2000a) *World Development Report 2000/2001: Attacking Poverty* (New York: Oxford University Press).

World Bank (2000b) *The Voices of the Poor* (Washington, DC: World Bank).

World Bank (2008) *The Growth Report: Strategies for Sustained Growth and Inclusive Development* (Washington, DC: Commission on Growth and Development, World Bank).

World Bank (2015) *World Development Indicators, 2015* (Washington, DC: World Bank), http://data.worldbank.org/products/wdi.

World Bank (n.d.) World Bank Country and Lending Groups, https://datahelpdesk.worldbank.org/knowledgebase/articles/906519-world-bank-country-and-lending-groups.

Zind, R.G. (1991) 'Income Convergence and Divergence within and between LDC Groups', *World Development*, 19(6): 719–27.

Chapter 3 The characteristics of underdevelopment and structural change

Acemoglu, D. (2003) 'Root Causes: A Historical Approach to Assessing the Role of Institutions in Economic Development', *Finance & Development*, 40(2): 27–30.

Acemoglu, D., Johnson, S. and Robinson, J. (2001) 'The Colonial Origins of Comparative Development: An Empirical Investigation', *American Economic Review*, 91(5): 1369–1401.

Adelman, I. and Morris, C.T. (1971) 'An Anatomy of Income Distribution Patterns in Developing Countries', *AID Development Digest*, October.

Ahluwalia, M.S., Carter, N. and Chenery, H. (1979) 'Growth and Poverty in Developing Countries', *Journal of Development Economics*, 6(3): 299–341.

Baldacci, E., Clements, B., Cui, Q. and Gupta, S. (2005) 'What Does it Take to Help the Poor?', *Finance & Development*, June.

Chang, H.-J. (2002) *Kicking Away the Ladder: Development Strategy in Historical Perspective* (London: Anthem Press).

Chang, H.-J. (ed.) (2003) *Rethinking Development Economics* (London: Anthem Press).

Chatterji, M., Gilmore, B., Strunk, K. and Vanasin, J. (1993) 'Political Economy, Growth and Convergence in Less Developed Countries, *World Development*, 21(12): 2029–38.

Chenery, H. and Syrquin, M. (1975) *Patterns of Development 1950–1970* (Oxford: Oxford University Press).

Chenery, H., Robinson, S. and Syrquin, M. (1986) *Industrialisation and Growth: A Comparative Study* (New York: Oxford University Press).

Chenery, H., Ahluwalia, M., Bell, C., Duloy, J. and Jolly, R. (eds) (1974) *Redistribution with Growth* (Oxford: Oxford University Press).

Clark, C. (1940) *The Conditions of Economic Progress* (London: Macmillan).

Collier, P. (2007) *The Bottom Billion* (Oxford: Oxford University Press).

Deininger, K. and Squire, L. (1996) 'A New Data Set Measuring Income Inequalities', *World Bank Economic Review*, 10(3): 565–91.

Di Meglio, G., Gallego, J., Maroto, A. and Savona, M. (2015) 'Services in Developing Countries: A New Chance for Catching Up', SPRU Working Paper Series, WWPS 2015–32.

Dollar, D. and Kraay, A. (2000) *Growth is Good for the Poor* (Washington, DC: World Bank).

Easterly, W. and Levine, R. (2002) 'Tropics, Germs and Crops: How Endowments Influence Economic Development', NBER Working Paper 9106 (Cambridge, MA: NBER).

Felipe, J. (2009) *Inclusive Growth, Full Employment and Structural Change* (London: Anthem Press).

Felipe, J. and Hasan, R. (eds) (2006) *Labour Markets in Asia: Issues and Perspectives* (Basingstoke: Palgrave Macmillan).

Finance & Development (2005) 'Cultivating Minds: How Investing in Education Boosts Development' (Washington, DC: IMF).

Fisher, A.G.B. (1939) 'Production: Primary, Secondary and Tertiary', *Economic Record*, 15(1): 24–38.

Forbes, K.J. (2000) 'A Reassessment of the Relationship between Inequality and Growth', *American Economic Review*, 90(4): 869–87.

Godfrey, M. (1986) *Global Unemployment: The New Challenge to Economic Theory* (Brighton: Wheatsheaf).

Guo, D., Dall'erba, S. and Le Gallo, J. (2012) 'The Leading Role of Manufacturing in China's Regional Economic Growth: A Spatial Econometric Approach of Kaldor's Laws', *International Regional Science Review*, 36(2): 139–66.

Gylfason, J. (2001) 'Nature, Power and Growth', *Scottish Journal of Political Economy*, 48(5): 558–88.

Hansen, J.D. and Zhang, J. (1996) 'A Kaldorian Approach to Regional Economic Growth in China', *Applied Economics*, 28: 679–85.

ILO (International Labour Organization) (2009) *Labour Force Statistics* (Geneva: ILO).

ILO (2015) *Labour Force Statistics* (Geneva: ILO).

Imbs, J. and Wacziarg, R. (2003) 'Stages of Diversification', *American Economic Review*, 93(1): 63–86.

Kaldor, N. (1966) *Causes of the Slow Rate of Economic Growth of the United Kingdom* (Cambridge: Cambridge University Press).

Kaldor, N. (1967) *Strategic Factors in Economic Development* (Ithaca: Cornell University Press).

Kuznets, S. (1955) 'Economic Growth and Income Inequality', *American Economic Review*, 45(1): 1–28.

Kuznets, S. (1963) 'Quantitative Aspects of the Economic Growth of Nations: Distribution of Income by Size', *Economic Development and Cultural Change*, 11(1): 1–80.

Libanio, G. (2006) 'Manufacturing Industry and Economic Growth in Latin America; A Kaldorian Approach', www.policyinnovations.org/ideas/policy_library/data/01384/_res/id=sa_File1/Libanio_manufacturing.pdf.

Maddison, A. (1991) *Dynamic Forces in Capitalist Development* (Oxford: Oxford University Press).

Marconi, N., de Borja Reis, C.F. and de Araújo, E. (2016) 'Manufacturing and Economic Development: the Actuality of Kaldor's First and Second Laws', *Structural Change and Economic Dynamics*, 37: 75–89.

Milanovic, B. (2011) *The Haves and the Have-Nots* (New York: Basic Books).

Myrdal, G. ([1957]1963) *Economic Theory and Underdeveloped Regions* (London: Methuen).

Naqvi, S.N.H. (1995) 'The Nature of Economic Development', *World Development*, 23(4): 543–56.

Necmi, S. (1999) 'Kaldor's Growth Analysis Revisited', *Applied Economics*, 31(5): 653–60.

Oxfam (2007) *Africa's Missing Billions*, Briefing Paper 107, October (IANSA, Oxfam and A Safer World).

Pacheco-López, P. and Thirlwall, A.P. (2014) 'A New Interpretation of Kaldor's First Law of Growth for an Open Developing Economy', *Review of Keynesian Economics*, 3: 384–98.

Paukert, E. (1973) 'Income Distribution at Different Levels of Development: A Survey of Evidence', *International Labour Review*, 108: 97–125.

Pieper, U. (2003) 'Sectoral Regularities of Productivity Growth in Developing Countries: A Kaldorian Interpretation', *Cambridge Journal of Economics*, 27(6): 831–50.

Reinert, E. (2007) *How Rich Countries Got Rich and Why Poor Countries Stay Poor* (London: Constable & Robinson).

Rodrik, D., Subramanian, A. and Trebbi, E. (2004) 'Institutions Rule: The Primacy of Institutions over Geography and Integration in Economic Development', *Journal of Economic Growth*, 9(2): 131–65.

Rodrik, D. (2007) *One Economics, Many Recipes* (Princeton, NJ: Princeton University Press).

Rodrik, D. (2016) 'Premature Deindustrialization', *Journal of Economic Growth*, 21(1): 1–33.

Rostow, W.W. (1960) *The Stages of Economic Growth: A Non-Communist Manifesto* (Cambridge: Cambridge University Press).

Rowthorn, R. and Ramswamy, R. (1999) 'Growth, Trade and Deindustrialisation', *IMF Staff Papers*, 46(1): 18–41.

Sachs, J. (2008) 'Institutions Matter but not for Everything: The Role of Geography and Resource Endowments in Development Shouldn't be Underestimated', in G. Secondi (ed.) The Development Economics Reader (London: Routledge).

Sachs, J. and Warner, A. (2001) 'The Curse of Natural Resources', *European Economic Review*, 40(2): 38–41.

Schmidt-Hebbel, K., Serven, L. and Solimano, A. (1994) *Saving, Investment, and Growth in Developing Countries: An Overview*. Policy Research Working Paper no. 1382 (Washington, DC: World Bank).

Stewart, F. (2001) *Horizontal Inequalities: A Neglected Dimension of Development* (WIDER: Helsinki).

Streeten, P. et al. (1981) *First Things First: Meeting Basic Human Needs in the Developing Countries* (Oxford: Oxford University Press for the World Bank).

Szirmai, A. (2012) 'Industrialization as an Engine of Growth in Developing Countries, 1950–2005', *Journal of Structural Change and Economic Dynamics*, 23(4): 325–46.

Szirmai, A. and Verspagen, B. (2015) 'Manufacturing and Economic Growth in Developing Countries, 1950–2005', *Journal of Structural Change and Economic Dynamics*, 36: 45–59.

Szirmai, A., Naude, W. and Alcorta, L. (eds) (2013) *Pathways to Industrialisation in the 21st Century* (Oxford: Oxford University Press).

Thirlwall, A.P. (ed.) (1983) 'Symposium on Kaldor's Growth Laws', *Journal of Post Keynesian Economics*, 5(3): 341–79.

Thorbecke, E. (1973) 'The Employment Problem: A Critical Evaluation of Four ILO Comprehensive Country Reports', *International Labour Review*, 107(5): 393–423.

Tregenna, F. (2009) 'Characterising Deindustrialisation: An Analysis of Changes in Manufacturing Employment and Output Internationally', *Cambridge Journal of Economics*, 33(3): 433–66.

UN DESA (UN Department of Economic and Social Affairs) (2015) World Population Prospects: The 2015 Revision (New York: UN).

UNDP (2004) *Cultural liberty in today's diverse world*, (UNDP: New York).

UNIDO (UN Industrial Development Organization) (2012) 'Climbing the Stairways of Development: Structural Change as the Driver of Economic Growth', Policy Brief, May.

Wade, R. (1990) *Governing the Market: Economic Theory and the Role of Government in East Asian Industrialisation* (Princeton, NJ: Princeton University Press).

Wells, H. and Thirlwall, A.P. (2003) 'Testing Kaldor's Growth Laws across the Countries of Africa', *African Development Review*, 15(2/3): 89–105.

White, A. and Anderson, E. (1991) 'Growth versus Distribution: Does the Pattern of Growth Matter?', *Development Policy Review*, 19(3).

World Bank (1995) *World Development Report 1995: Workers in an Integrating World* (Oxford: Oxford University Press).

World Bank (2009) *World Development Indicators, 2009* (Washington DC: World Bank).

World Bank (2012) *World Development Report 2013: Jobs* (Washington DC: World Bank).

World Bank (2015) *World Development Indicators 2015* (Washington DC: World Bank).

Chapter 4 Theories of economic growth: old and new

Abramovitz, M. (1956) 'Resource and Output Trends in the United States since 1870', *American Economic Review, Papers and Proceedings*, 46(2): 5–23.

Abramovitz, M. (1986) 'Catching-up, Forging Ahead and Falling Behind', *Journal of Economic History*, 46(2): 385–406.

Amable, B. (1993) 'Catch-up and Convergence: A Model of Cumulative Growth', *International Review of Applied Economics*, 7(1): 1–25.

Arrow, K. (1962) 'The Economic Implications of Learning by Doing', *Review of Economic Studies*, 29(3): 155–73.

Barro, R. (1991) 'Economic Growth in a Cross-Section of Countries', *Quarterly Journal of Economics*, 106(2): 407–33.

Barro, R. (1998) *Determinants of Economic Growth*. Lionel Robbins Lectures (Cambridge, MA: MIT Press).

Barro, R. and Lee, J.-W. (1993) 'Losers and Winners in Economic Growth', *Proceedings of the World Bank Conference on Development Economics* (Washington, DC: World Bank).

Barro, R. and Sala-í-Martin, X. (2003) *Economic Growth*, 2nd edn (New York: McGraw Hill).

Baumol, W. (1986) 'Productivity Growth, Convergence and Welfare: What the Long-Run Data Show', *American Economic Review*, 76(5): 1072–85.

Benhabib, J. and Spiegel, M.M. (1994) 'The Role of Human Capital in Economic Development: Evidence from Average Cross Section Data', *Journal of Monetary Economics*, 34(2): 143–73.

Blaug, M. (1996) *Economic Theory in Retrospect*, 5th edn (Cambridge: Cambridge University Press).

Bosworth, B. and Collins, S. (2007) 'Accounting for Growth: Comparing China and India', NBER Working Paper 12943 (Cambridge, MA: NBER).

Chaudhuri, P. (1989) *Economic Theory of Growth* (Iowa: Iowa State University Press).

Cobb, C. and Douglas, P. (1928) 'A Theory of Production', *American Economic Review*, 18(1): 139–65.

Collier, P. and Gunning, J.W. (1999) 'Explaining African Economic Performance', *Journal of Economic Literature*, 37(1): 64–111.

Cornwall, J. and Cornwall, W. (1994) 'Structural Change and Productivity in the OECD', in P. Davidson and J. Kregel (eds) *Employment Growth and Finance: Economic Reality and Economic Theory* (Aldershot: Edward Elgar).

De Gregorio, J. (1992) 'Economic Growth in Latin America', *Journal of Development Economics*, 39(1): 59–84.

De Mello, L. (1996) *Foreign Direct Investment, International Knowledge Transfers and Endogenous Growth: Times Series Evidence* (Department of Economics, University of Kent).

Denison, E. (1962) *The Sources of Economic Growth in the US and the Alternatives before Us* (New York: Committee for Economic Development, Library of Congress).

Domar, E. (1947) 'Expansion and Employment', *American Economic Review*, 37(1): 34–55.

Douglas, P. (1948) 'Are There Laws of Production?', *American Economic Review*, 38(1): 1–41.

Dowrick, S. and Gemmell, N. (1991) 'Industrialisation, Catching-up and Economic Growth: A Comparative Study across the World's Capitalist Economies', *Economic Journal*, 101: 363–75.

Dowrick, S. and Nguyen, D.T. (1989) 'OECD Comparative Economic Growth 1950–85: Catch-Up and Convergence', *American Economic Review*, 79(5): 1010–30.

Dray, M. and Thirlwall, A.P. (2011) 'The Endogeneity of the Natural Rate of Growth for a Selection of Asian Countries', *Journal of Post Keynesian Economics*, 33(3): 451–68.

Durlauf, S. (1996) 'Controversy: On the Convergence and Divergence of Growth Rates: An Introduction', *Economic Journal*, 106: 1016–18.

Easterly, W. and Pritchett, L. (1993) 'The Determinants of Economic Success: Luck and Policy', *Finance & Development*, 30(4): 38–41.

Easterly, W. and Levine, R. (2001) 'It's not Factor Accumulation: Stylised Facts and Growth Models', *World Bank Economic Review*, 15(2): 177–219.

Eltis, W. (1984) *The Classical Theory of Economic Growth* (London: Macmillan).

Felipe, J. (1999) 'Total Factor Productivity Growth in East Asia: A Critical Survey', *Journal of Development Studies*, 35(4): 1–41.

Gomulka, S. (1971) *Inventive Activity, Diffusion and the Stages of Economic Growth* (Aarhus: Aarhus University Press).

Gomulka, S. (1990) *The Theory of Technological Change and Economic Growth* (London: Routledge).

Grossman, G. and Helpman, E. (1990) 'Trade, Innovation and Growth', *American Economic Review Papers and Proceedings*, 80(2): 86–91.

Grossman, G. and Helpman, E. (1991) *Innovation and Growth in the Global Economy* (Cambridge, MA: MIT Press).

Harrod, R. (1939) 'An Essay in Dynamic Theory', *Economic Journal*, 49(1): 14–33.

Hausmann, R., Pritchett, L. and Rodrik, D. (2005) 'Growth Accelerations', *Journal of Economic Growth*, 10(4): 303–29.

Hausmann, R., Rodrik, D. and Velasco, A. (2008) 'Growth Diagnostics', in J. Stiglitz and N. Serra (eds) *The Washington Consensus Reconsidered: Towards a New Global Governance* (New York: Oxford University Press).

Hirschman, A. (1958) *Strategy of Economic Development* (New Haven, CT: Yale University Press).

Hu, Z.F. and Khan, M.S. (1997) 'Why is China Growing So Fast?', *IMF Staff Papers*, 44(1): 103–31.

Hulten, C. and Isaksson, A. (2007) 'Why do Development Levels Differ: The Sources of Differential Growth in a Panel of High and Low Income Countries', NBER Working Paper 13469 (Cambridge, MA: NBER).

Islam, N. (2003) 'What Have we Learnt from the Convergence Debate?', *Journal of Economic Surveys*, 17(3): 309–62.

Kaldor, N. (1957) 'A Model of Economic Growth', *Economic Journal*, 67(268): 591–624.

Kaldor, N. (1961) 'Capital Accumulation and Economic Growth', in F. Lutz (ed.) *The Theory of Capital* (London: Macmillan).

Kaldor, N. (1967) *Strategic Factors in Economic Development* (Ithaca: Cornell University Press).

Kaldor, N. (1972) 'Advanced Technology in a Strategy for Development: Some Lessons from Britain's Experience', in *Automation and Developing Countries* (Geneva: ILO).

Kaldor, N. (1985) *Economics without Equilibrium* (Cardiff: University College Cardiff Press).

Kennedy, C. and Thirlwall, A.P. (1972) 'Surveys in Applied Economics: Technical Progress', *Economic Journal*, 82(325): 11–72.

Kenny, C. and Williams, D. (2001) 'What Do We Know About Economic Growth? Or, Why Don't We Know Very Much?', *World Development*, 29(1): 1–22.

Keynes, J.M. (1936) *The General Theory of Employment, Interest and Money* (London: Macmillan).

Kim, K. (2015) 'Demand and Structural Change in Adam Smith's View of Economic Progress', *Cambridge Journal of Economics*, 39(1): 245–64.

Knight, M., Loayza, N. and Villanueva, D. (1993) 'Testing the Neoclassical Theory of Economic Growth', *IMF Staff Papers*, 40(3): 512–41.

Krugman, P. (1994) 'The Myth of Asia's Miracle', *Foreign Affairs*, 73(6): 62–78.

Leon-Ledesma, M. and Thirlwall, A.P. (2002) 'The Endogeneity of the Natural Rate of Growth', *Cambridge Journal of Economics*, 26(4): 441–59.

Levine, R. and Renelt, D. (1992) 'A Sensitivity Analysis of Cross-Country Growth Regressions', *American Economic Review*, 82(4): 942–63.

Levine, R. and Zervos, S. (1993) 'What We Have Learned About Policy and Growth From Cross-Country Regressions', *American Economic Review, Papers and Proceedings*, 83(2): 426–30.

Libanio, G. (2009) 'Aggregate Demand and the Endogeneity of the Natural Rate of Growth: Evidence from Latin American Countries', *Cambridge Journal of Economics*, 33(5): 967–84.

Lucas, R. (1988) 'On the Mechanics of Economic Development', *Journal of Monetary Economics*, 22(1): 3–42.

Maddison, A. (1970) *Economic Progress and Policy in Developing Countries* (London: Allen & Unwin).

Malthus, T. ([1798]1983) *An Essay on the Principle of Population* (London: Penguin).

Mankiw, N.G., Romer, D. and Weil, D.N. (1992) 'A Contribution to the Empirics of Economic Growth', *Quarterly Journal of Economics*, 107(2): 407–37.

Marshall, A. (1890) *Principles of Economics* (London: Macmillan).

Marx, K. ([1867]1967) *Capital: A Critique of Political Economy*, vol. 1 (New York: International Publishers).

Myrdal, G. (1957) *Economic Theory and Underdeveloped Regions* (London: Duckworth).

Nadiri, M. (1972) 'International Studies of Factor Inputs and Total Factor Productivity: A Brief Survey', *Review of Income and Wealth*, 18(2): 129–54.

Nell, K. and Thirlwall, A.P. (2016) 'Explaining Differences in the Marginal Product of Capital across Countries in the Context of New Growth Theory', manuscript.

Pack, H. (1994) 'Endogenous Growth: Intellectual Appeal and Empirical Shortcomings', *Journal of Economic Perspectives*, 8(1): 55–72.

Pritchett, L. (2000) 'Understanding Patterns of Growth: Searching for Hills among Plateaus, Mountains and Plains', *World Bank Economic Review*, 14(2): 221–50.

Pugno, M. (1995) 'On Competing Theories of Economic Growth: Cross-Country Evidence', *International Review of Applied Economics*, 9(3): 249–73.

Putterman, L. (2000) 'Can an Evolutionary Approach to Development Predict Post-War Economic Growth?', *Journal of Development Studies*, 36(3): 1–30.

Ricardo, D. ([1817]1992) *Principles of Political Economy and Taxation* (London: Everyman).

Robinson, S. (1971) 'The Sources of Growth in Less Developed Countries: A Cross-Section Study', *Quarterly Journal of Economics*, 85(3): 391–408.

Rodrik, D. (2010) 'Diagnostics before Prescription', *Journal of Economic Perspectives*, 24(3): 33–44.

Rodrik, D. (2013) 'Unconditional Convergence in Manufacturing', *Quarterly Journal of Economics*, 128(8): 165–204.

Romer, P.M. (1986) 'Increasing Returns and Long-Run Growth', *Journal of Political Economy*, 94(5): 1002–37.

Romer, P.M. (1990) 'Endogenous Technical Change', *Journal of Political Economy*, 98(5): 71–102.

Romer, P.M. (1994) 'The Origins of Endogenous Growth', *Journal of Economic Perspectives*, 8(1): 3–22.

Ruttan, V. (1998) 'New Growth Theory and Development Economics: A Survey', *Journal of Development Studies*, 35(2): 1–26.

Sala-í-Martin, X. (1997) 'I Just Ran Two Million Regressions', *American Economic Review*, 87(2): 178–83.

Senhadji, A. (2000) 'Sources of Economic Growth: An Extensive Growth Accounting Exercise', *IMF Staff Papers*, 47(1): 129–57.

Smith, A. (1759) *The Theory of Moral Sentiments* (London: Millar and Kincaid).

Smith, A. (1776) *An Inquiry into the Nature and Causes of the Wealth of Nations* (London: Strahan and Cadell).

Solow, R. (1956) 'A Contribution to the Theory of Economic Growth', *Quarterly Journal of Economics*, 70(1): 65–94.

Solow, R. (1957) 'Technical Change and the Aggregate Production Function', *Review of Economics and Statistics*, 39(3): 312–20.

Solow, R. (1962) 'Technical Progress, Capital Formation and Growth', *American Economic Review, Papers and Proceedings*, 52(2): 76–86.

Summers, R. and Heston, A. (1991) 'The Penn World Table (Mark 5): An Expanded Set of International Comparisons, 1950–1988', *Quarterly Journal of Economics*, 106(2): 327–68.

Swan, T. (1956) 'Economic Growth and Capital Accumulation', *Economic Record*, 32(2): 334–61.

Temple, J. (1999) 'The New Growth Evidence', *Journal of Economic Literature*, 37(1): 112–56.

Thirlwall, A.P. and Sanna, G. (1996) '"New" Growth Theory and the Macro Determinants of Growth: An Evaluation and Further Evidence', in P. Arestis (ed.) *Employment, Economic Growth and the Tyranny of the Market* (Aldershot: Edward Elgar).

Vogel, L. (2009) 'The Endogeneity of the Natural Rate of Growth: An Empirical Study for Latin American Economies', *International Review of Applied Economics*, 23(1): 45–53.

World Bank (1991) *World Development Report 1991* (Washington, DC: World Bank).

World Bank (2008) *The Growth Report: Strategies for Sustained Growth and Inclusive Development* (Washington, DC: World Bank).

Young, A. (1995) 'The Tyranny of Numbers: Confronting the Statistical Realities of the East Asian Growth Experience', *Quarterly Journal of Economics*, 110(3): 641–80.

Young, A.A. (1928) 'Increasing Returns and Economic Progress', *Economic Journal*, 38(152): 527–42.

Chapter 5 The role of agriculture and surplus labour for industrialization

Abrar, S., Morrissey, O. and Rayner, A. (2004) 'Crop-Level Supply Response by Agro-Climate Regions in Ethiopia', *Journal of Agricultural Economics*, 55(2): 289–311.

Adelman, I. (1984) 'Beyond Export-led Growth', *World Development*, 12(9): 937–49.

Africa Progress Panel (2010) *Raising Agricultural Productivity in Africa: Options for Action, and the Role of Subsidies*, Policy Brief, September (Geneva: Africa Progress Panel).

Askari, H. and Cummings, J. (1976) *Agricultural Supply Response: A Survey of the Econometric Evidence* (New York: Praeger).

Bardhan, P. (1980) 'Interlocking Factor Markets and Agrarian Development: A Review of the Issues', *Oxford Economic Papers*, 32(1): 82–98.

Bardhan, P. (1984) *Land, Labour and Rural Poverty: Essays in Development Economics* (Oxford: Oxford University Press).

Bardhan, P. and Udry, C. (1999) *Development Microeconomics* (New York: Oxford University Press).

Barnum, A.N. and Sabot, R.H. (1977) 'Education, Employment Probabilities and Rural–Urban Migration in Tanzania', *Oxford Bulletin of Economics and Statistics*, 39(2): 109–26.

Besley, T. and Burgess, R. (2000) 'Land Reform, Poverty and Growth: Evidence from India', *Quarterly Journal of Economics*, 115(2): 389–430.

Binswanger, H. and Deininger, K. (1997) 'Explaining Agricultural and Agrarian Policies in Developing Countries', *Journal of Economic Literature*, 35(4): 1958–2005.

Chang, H.-J. (2009) 'Rethinking Public Policy in Agriculture: Lessons from History, Distant and Recent', *Journal of Peasant Studies*, 36(3): 477–515.

Chhibber, A. (1988) 'Raising Agricultural Output: Price and Non-Price Factors', *Finance & Development*, June: 44–7.

Dorner, P. (1972) *Land Reform and Economic Development* (Harmondsworth: Penguin).

Dorner, P. (1992) *Latin American Land Reform in Theory and in Practice: A Retrospective Analysis* (Madison: University of Wisconsin Press).

Duranton, G. (1998) 'Agricultural Productivity, Trade and Industrialisation', *Oxford Economic Papers*, 50(2): 220–36.

Floro, M. and Ray, D. (1997) 'Vertical Links between Formal and Informal Financial Institutions', *Review of Development Economics*, 1(1): 34–56.

Floro, M. and Yotopoulos, P. (1991) *Informal Credit Markets and the New Institutional Economics: The Case of Philippine Agriculture* (Boulder, CO: Westview Press).

Foster, A. and Rosenzweig, M. (2010) 'Is There Surplus Labour in Rural India?', Working Paper 85, Yale University, Department of Economics.

Ghatak, S. and Ingersent, K. (1984) *Agriculture and Economic Development* (Brighton: Wheatsheaf).

Gollin, D. (2014) 'The Lewis Model: A 60-Year Retrospective', *Journal of Economic Perspectives*, 28(3): 71–88.

Gollin, D., Parente, S. and Rogerson, R. (1997) 'The Role of Agriculture in Development', *American Economic Review, Papers and Proceedings*, 92(2): 160–4.

Islam, N. and Yokota, K. (2008) 'Lewis Growth Model and China's Industrialisation', *Asian Economic Journal*, 22(4): 359–96.

Johnston, B.F. and Mellor, J. (1961) 'The Role of Agriculture in Economic Development', *American Economic Review*, 51(4): 566–93.

Johnston, B.F. (1970) 'Agriculture and Structural Transformation in Developing Countries: A Survey of Research', *Journal of Economic Literature*, 8(2): 369–404.

Jorgenson, D. (1966) 'Testing Alternative Theories of the Development of a Dual Economy', in I. Adelman and E. Thorbecke (eds) *The Theory and Design of Economic Development* (Baltimore, MD: Johns Hopkins University Press).

Kaldor, N. (1979) 'Equilibrium Theory and Growth Theory', in M. Baskia (ed.) *Economics and Human Welfare: Essays in Honor of Tibor Scitovsky* (New York: Academic Press).

Kim, K. (2015) 'Demand and Structural Change in Adam Smith's View of Economic Progress', *Cambridge Journal of Economics*, 39(1): 245–64.

Kirkpatrick, C. and Barrientos, A. (2004) *The Lewis Model After Fifty Years*, Development Economics and Public Policy, Working Paper Series Paper No. 9 (University of Manchester).

Knight, J.B. (1972) 'Rural–Urban Income Comparisons and Migration in Ghana', *Oxford Bulletin of Economics and Statistics*, 34(2): 199–228.

Lehmann, D. (ed.) (1974) *Agrarian Reform and Agrarian Reformism: Studies of Peru, Chile, China and India* (London: Faber & Faber).

Lewis, W.A. (1954) 'Economic Development with Unlimited Supplies of Labour', *Manchester School*, 22: 139–91.

Lewis, W.A. (1955) *The Theory of Economic Growth* (Homewood, IL: Irwin).

Lewis, W.A. (1958) 'Unlimited Supplies of Labour: Further Notes', *Manchester School*, 26(1): 1–32.

Lin, J.Y. (1992) 'Rural Reforms and Agricultural Growth in China', *American Economic Review*, 82(1): 34–51.

Lipton, M. (2011) *Land Reform in Developing Countries: Property Rights and Property Wrongs* (London: Routledge).
Lipton, M. and Longhurst, R. (1989) *New Seeds and Poor People* (London: Routledge).
Lockwood, W.W. (1954) *The Economic Development of Japan: Growth and Structural Change 1868–1938* (Princeton, NJ: Princeton University Press).
Mehra, S. (1966) 'Surplus Labour in Indian Agriculture', *Indian Economic Review*, 1(1): 111–29.
Otsuka, K., Chuma, H. and Hayami, Y. (1992) 'Land and Labour Contracts in Agrarian Economies', *Journal of Economic Literature*, 30(4): 1965–2018.
Powelson, J.P. and Stock, R. (1987) *The Peasant Betrayed: Agriculture and Land Reform in the Third World* (Boston, MA: Oelgeschlager, Gunn & Hain).
Ranis, G. (2004) 'Arthur Lewis's Contribution to Development Thinking and Policy', *Manchester School*, 72(6): 712–23.
Ranis, G. and Fei, J. (1961) 'A Theory of Economic Development', *American Economic Review*, 51(4): 533–65.
Ray, D. (1998) *Development Economics* (Princeton, NJ: Princeton University Press).
Schiff, M. and Montenegro, C.E. (1997) 'Aggregate Agricultural Supply Response in Developing Countries: A Survey of Selected Issues', *Economic Development and Cultural Change*, 45(2): 393–410.
Schultz, T.W. (1964) *Transforming Traditional Agriculture* (New Haven, CT: Yale University Press).
Schultz, T.W. (1980) 'Nobel Lecture: The Economics of Being Poor', *Journal of Political Economy*, 88(4): 639–51.
Sen, A.K. (1964) 'Size of Holdings and Productivity', *Economic and Political Weekly*, 16(5/6/7): 323–6.
Sen, A.K. (1966) 'Peasants and Dualism With and Without Surplus Labour', *Journal of Political Economy*, 74(5): 425–50.
Smith, A. (1776) *An Inquiry into the Nature and Causes of the Wealth of Nations* (London: Strahan and Cadell).
Southworth, H. and Johnston, B.F. (eds) (1967) *Agricultural Development and Economic Growth* (Ithaca: Cornell University Press).
Stark, O. (1991) *The Migration of Labour* (Oxford: Blackwell).
Stiglitz, J. (1974) 'Incentives and Risk Sharing in Sharecropping', *Review of Economic Studies*, 41(2): 219–55.
Thirlwall, A.P. (1986) 'A General Model of Growth and Development on Kaldorian Lines', *Oxford Economic Papers*, 38(2): 199–219.
Todaro, M. (1969) 'A Model of Labour Migration and Urban Unemployment in Less Developed Countries', *American Economic Review*, 59(1): 138–48.
Todaro, M. (1971) 'Income Expectations, Rural–Urban Migration and Employment in Africa', *International Labour Review*, 104(5): 387–413.
Todaro, M. (1976) *Internal Migration in Developing Countries* (Geneva: ILO).
Udry, C. (1994) 'Risk and Insurance in a Rural Credit Market: An Empirical Investigation in Northern Nigeria, *Review of Economic Studies*, 61(3): 495–526.
Vogel, S. (1994) 'Structural Changes in Agriculture: Production Linkages and Agricultural Demand-led Industrialization', *Oxford Economic Papers*, 46(1): 136–56.
Weisdorf, J. (2006) 'From Domestic Manufacture to Industrial Revolution: Long-Run Growth and Agricultural Development', *Oxford Economic Papers*, 58(2): 264–87.
World Bank (1979) *World Development Report 1979* (Washington, DC: World Bank).
World Bank (1982) *World Development Report 1982* (Washington, DC: World Bank).
World Bank (2007) *World Development Report 2008: Agriculture for Development* (Oxford: Oxford University Press for the World Bank).
World Bank (2013) 'Raising Agricultural Productivity' in *World Bank Group Agricultural Action Plan 2013–2015* (Washington: World Bank).
World Bank (2015) *World Development Indicators 2015* (Washington, DC: World Bank).
Yap, L.Y.L. (1977) 'The Attraction of Cities: A Review of the Migration Literature', *Journal of Development Economics*, 4(3): 239–64.

Chapter 6 Capital accumulation, technical progress and techniques of production

Ahiakpor, J. (1989) 'Do Firms Choose Inappropriate Technology in LDCs?', *Economic Development and Cultural Change*, 37(3): 557–71.
Arrow, K. (1962) 'The Economic Implications of Learning by Doing', *Review of Economic Studies*, 29(3): 155–73.

Arslanalp, S., Bornhorst, F. and Gupta, S. (2011) 'Investing in Growth', *Finance & Development*, 48(1): 34–7.

Bell, M. and Pavitt, K. (1992) 'Accumulating Technological Capability in Developing Countries', *World Bank Economic Review, Supplement* 6: 257–81.

Bruton, H. (1987) 'Technology Choice and Factor Proportions Problems in LDCs', in N. Gemmell (ed.) *Surveys in Development Economics* (Oxford: Blackwell).

Burns, A. (2008) 'Bridging the Technology Divide', *Finance & Development*, 45(2): 44–5.

Calderón, C., Moral-Benito, E. and Servén, L. (2015) 'Is Infrastructure Capital Productive? A Dynamic Heterogeneous Approach', *Journal of Applied Econometrics*, 30(2): 177–98.

Dasgupta, P. (1993) *An Inquiry Into Well-Being and Destitution* (Oxford: Clarendon Press).

Dobb, M. (1955) 'A Note on the so-called Degree of Capital Intensity of Investment in Underdeveloped Countries', in *On Economic Theory and Socialism* (London: Routledge & Kegan Paul).

Fagerberg, J., Scholec, M. and Knell, M. (2007) 'The Competitiveness of Nations: Why Some Countries Prosper While Others Fall Behind', *World Development*, 35(10): 1595–620.

Forsyth, D. and Solomon, R. (1977) 'Choice of Technology and Nationality of Ownership in a Developing Country', *Oxford Economic Papers*, 29(2): 258–82.

Grossman, G. and Helpman, E. (1991) *Innovation and Growth in the Global Economy* (Cambridge, MA: MIT Press).

Harrod, R. (1948) *Towards a Dynamic Economics* (London: Macmillan).

Helleiner, G.K. (1975) 'The Role of Multinational Corporations in the Less Developed Countries: Trade in Technology', *World Development*, 3(4): 161–89.

Hicks, J. (1932) *The Theory of Wages* (London: Macmillan).

Hulten, C. and Isaksson, A. (2007) 'Why Development Levels Differ: The Sources of Differential Income Growth in a Panel of High and Low Income Countries', NBER Working Paper 13469 (Cambridge, MA: NBER).

Jenkins, R. (1990) 'Comparing Foreign Subsidiaries and Local Firms in LDCs', *Journal of Development Studies*, January.

Keller, W. (2004) 'International Technological Diffusion', *Journal of Economic Literature*, 42(3): 752–82.

Lall, S. (1978) 'Transnationals, Domestic Enterprises and Industrial Structures in Host LDCs: A Survey', *Oxford Economic Papers*, 30(2): 217–48.

Lall, S. (1992) 'Technological Capabilities and Industrialisation', *World Development*, 20(2): 165–86.

Lewis, A. (1955) *The Theory of Economic Growth* (London: Allen & Unwin).

Navaretti, G.B. and Tarr, D.G. (2000) 'International Knowledge Flows and Economic Performance: A Review of the Evidence', *World Bank Economic Review*, 14(1): 1–15.

Pack, H. (1974) 'The Employment-Output Trade-Off in LDCs: A Microeconomic Approach', *Oxford Economic Papers*, 26(3): 388–404.

Pack, H. (1976) 'The Substitution of Labour for Capital in Kenyan Manufacturing', *Economic Journal*, 86(431): 45–58.

Rostow, W.W. (1960) *The Stages of Economic Growth* (Cambridge: Cambridge University Press).

Schumpeter, J. (1934) *The Theory of Economic Development* (Cambridge, MA: Harvard University Press).

Schumpeter, J. (1943) *Capitalism, Socialism and Democracy* (London: Allen & Unwin).

Sen, A.K. (1968) *Choice of Techniques*, 3rd edn (Oxford: Basil Blackwell).

Sen, A.K. (1969) 'Choice of Technology: A Critical Survey of a Class of Debates', in UNIDO, *Planning for Advanced Skills and Technology* (New York: UNIDO).

Sen, A.K. (1975) *Employment, Technology and Development* (Oxford: Clarendon Press).

Stewart, F. (1977) *Technology and Underdevelopment* (London: Macmillan).

Straub, S. (2008) 'Infrastructure and Growth in Developing Countries: Recent Advances and Research Challenges', Policy Research Working Paper 4460 (Washington, DC: World Bank).

Thirlwall, A.P. (1977) 'The Shadow Wage when Consumption is Productive', *Bangladesh Development Studies*, 5(4): 439–42.

Thirlwall, A.P. (1978) 'Reconciling the Conflict between Employment and Saving and Employment and Output in the Choice of Techniques in Developing Countries', *Rivista Internazionale di Scienze Economiche e Commerciali*, February.

White, L. (1978) 'The Evidence on Appropriate Factor Proportions for Manufacturing in LDCs: A Survey', *Economic Development and Cultural Change*, 27(1): 27–59.

World Bank (1994) *World Development Report 1994: Infrastructure or Development* (Oxford: Oxford University Press).

World Bank (2004) *World Development Report 2005: A Better Investment Climate for Everyone* (Washington, DC: World Bank).

World Bank (2005) *World Development Report 2006: Equity and Development* (Washington, DC: World Bank).

Chapter 7 Human capital: education, the role of women, nutrition and health

Baldacci, E., Clements, B., Cui, Q. and Gupta, S. (2005) 'What does it Take to Help the Poor?', *Finance & Development*, 42(2): 20–31.

Barro, R. (1991) 'Economic Growth in a Cross-Section of Countries', *Quarterly Journal of Economics*, 106(2): 407–43.

Behrman, J.R. (1993) 'The Economic Rationale for Investing in Nutrition in Developing Countries', *World Development*, 21(11): 1749–71.

Bliss, C. and Stern, N. (1978) 'Productivity, Wages and Nutrition, Part II: Some Observations', *Journal of Development Economics*, 5(4): 363–98.

Burde, D. and Linden, L.L. (2012) 'The Effect of Village-Based Schools: Evidence from a Randomized Controlled Trial in Afghanistan', National Bureau of Economic Research, Working Paper 18039.

Cole, M. and Neumayer, E. (2006) 'The Impact of Poor Health on Total Factor Productivity', *Journal of Development Studies*, 42(6): 918–38.

Dasgupta, P. (1993) *An Enquiry into Well-Being and Destitution* (Oxford: Clarendon Press).

Deaton, A. (2013) *The Great Escape: Health, Wealth, and the Origins of Inequality* (Princeton, NJ: Princeton University Press).

Denison, E. (1962) *The Sources of Economic Growth in the US and the Alternatives before Us* (New York: Committee for Economic Development, Library of Congress).

Drèze, J. (ed.) (1999) *The Economics of Famine* (Cheltenham: Edward Elgar).

Drèze, J. and Sen, A.K. (1989) *Hunger and Public Action* (Oxford: Clarendon Press).

Drèze, J. and Sen, A.K. (2013) *An Uncertain Glory: India and its Contradictions* (London: Allen Lane).

Finance & Development (2005) 'Cultivating Minds: How Investing in Education Boosts Development' (Washington, DC: IMF).

Gallup, J.L. and Sachs, J.D. (2001) 'The Economic Burden of Malaria', *American Journal of Tropical Medicine and Hygiene*, 64(1): 85–96.

IFPRI (International Food Policy Research Institute) (2015) *Global Nutrition Report 2015: Actions and Accountability to Advance Nutrition and Sustainable Development* (Washington, DC: IFPRI).

IMF (International Monetary Fund) (2015) *IMF Annual Report 2015, Tackling Challenges Together* (Washington, DC: IMF).

Klugman, J., Hanmer, L., Twigg, S. et al. (2014) *Voice and Agency: Empowering Women and Girls for Shared Prosperity* (Washington, DC: World Bank).

Lagarde, C. (2014) 'The Economic Power of Women's Empowerment', keynote speech, 12 September, Tokyo.

McCarthy, F.D., Wolf, H. and Wu, Y. (2000), 'The Growth Costs of Malaria', Working Paper 7541, National Bureau of Economic Research.

Mincer, J. (1974) *Schooling, Experience and Earnings* (New York: National Bureau of Economic Research).

Montenegro, C. and Patrinos, H. (2014) 'Comparable Estimates of Schooling Around the World', Policy Research Working Paper 7020 (Washington DC: World Bank).

Murray, C.J. and Lopez, A.D. (eds) (1996) *The Global Burden of Disease*, vol. 1 (Geneva: WHO).

O'Grada, C. (2007) 'Making Famine History', *Journal of Economic Literature*, 45(1): 5–38.

Psacharopoulos, G. (1985) 'Returns to Education: A Further International Update and Implications', *Journal of Human Resources*, 20(4): 583–604.

Psacharopoulos, G. (1991) *Education for Development* (Washington, DC: World Bank).

Pascharopoulos, G. (1994) 'Returns to Investment in Education: A Global Update', *World Development*, 22(9): 1325–43.

Ram, R. (1996) 'Level of Development and Rates of Return to Schooling: Some Estimates from Multi-Country Studies', *Economic Development and Cultural Change*, 44(4): 839–57.

Ravallion, M. (1997) 'Famines and Economics', *Journal of Economic Literature*, 35(3): 1205–42.

RBM (Roll Back Malaria) and UNDP (UN Development Programme) (2013) *Multisectoral Action Framework for Malaria* (New York/Geneva: RBM and UNDP).

Save the Children (2015) *The Urban Disadvantage: State of World's Mothers* (Fairfield, CT: Save the Children).

Schultz, T.W. (1961) 'Investment in Human Capital', *American Economic Review*, 51(1): 1–17.

Sen, A.K. (1999) *Development as Freedom* (Oxford: Oxford University Press).

Sen, A.K. (1981a) *Poverty and Famines: An Essay on Entitlement and Deprivation* (Oxford: Clarendon Press).

Sen, A.K. (1981b) 'Ingredients of Famine Analysis: Availability and Entitlements', *Quarterly Journal of Economics*, 96(3): 433–64.

Steinberg, C. and Nakane, M. (2012) 'Can Women Save Japan?', Working Paper WP/12/248 (Washington, DC: IMF).

Te Lintelo, D. and Lakshman, R. (2015) 'The Hunger and Nutrition Commitment Index (HANCI 2014): Measuring the Political Commitment to Reduce Hunger and Undernutrition in Developing Countries', IDS Evidence Report No 150.

Te Lintelo, D. and Nisbett, N. (2015) 'Global Goals Must Fight the Poor Nutrition that Kills 3 Million Children Every Year', *The Guardian*, 30 September.

UNAIDS (Joint UN Programme on HIV/AIDS) (2015) *How AIDS Changed Everything, MDG: 15 Years, 15 Lessons of Hope from AIDS Response* (Geneva: UNAIDS).

UNDP (UN Development Programme) (2014) *Human Development Report 2014: Sustaining Human Progress* (New York: Oxford University Press).

UNESCO (UN Educational, Scientific and Cultural Organization) (2015) *Education For All 2000–2015: Achievements and Challenges, Global Monitoring Report 2015* (Paris: UNESCO).

UN Women (2015) *Progress of the World's Women 2015–2016: Transforming Economies, Realizing Rights* (New York: UN Woman).

Utzinger J. and Tanner, M. (2013) 'Socioeconomic Development to Fight Malaria, and Beyond', *Lancet*, 382(9896): 920–2.

WHO (World Health Organization) (2008) *The Global Burden of Disease, 2004 update.* (Geneva: WHO).

WHO (2012) *Health Statistics and Information Systems: Estimates for 2000–2012*, Global Summary estimates, www.who.int/healthinfo/global_burden_disease/estimates /en/index2.html and http://www.who.int/gho/mortality_burden_disease/daly_rates/text/en/, accessed 10 February 2016.

WHO (2014a) *Global Nutrition Targets 2025: Stunting Policy Brief* (Geneva: WHO), http://apps.who.int/iris/bitstream/10665/137094/1/9789241564809_eng.pdf accessed 10 February 2016.

WHO (2014b) *Global Tuberculosis Report 2014* (Geneva: WHO), http://apps.who.int/iris/bitstream/10665/137094/1/9789241564809_eng.pdf accessed 10 February 2016.

World Bank (1980) *Education Sector Policy* (Washington, DC: World Bank).

World Bank (1990) *World Development Report 1990* (Washington, DC: World Bank).

World Bank (2010) *World Development Indicators 2010* (Washington, DC: World Bank).

World Bank (2012) *World Development Report 2012: Gender Equality and Development*, (Washington, DC: World Bank).

World Bank (2013) *World Development Indicators 2013* (Washington, DC: World Bank).

World Bank (2015) *World Development Indicators 2015* (Washington, DC: World Bank).

Chapter 8 The role of institutions in economic development

Acemoglu, D. (2008) 'Root Causes: An Historical Approach to Assessing the Role of Institutions in Economic Development', in G. Secondi (ed.) *The Development Economics Reader* (London: Routledge).

Acemoglu, D. and Robinson, J.A. (2012) *Why Nations Fail: The Origins of Power, Prosperity and Poverty* (New York: Crown Publishers).

Acemoglu, D., Johnson, S. and Robinson, J.A. (2001) 'The Colonial Origins of Comparative Development: An Empirical Investigation', *American Economic Review*, 91(5): 1369–1401.

Acemoglu, D., Johnson, S. and Robinson, J.A. (2002) 'Reversal of Fortune: Geography and Institutions in the Making of the Modern World Income Distribution', *Quarterly Journal of Economics*, 117(4): 1231–94.

Alesina, A. and Perotti, R. (1994) 'The Political Economy of Growth: A Critical Survey of the Recent Literature', *World Bank Economic Review*, 8(3): 351–71.

Alesina, A. and Rodrik, D. (1994) 'Distributive Politics and Economic Growth', *Quarterly Journal of Economics*, 109(2): 465–90.

Aron, J. (2000) 'Growth and Institutions: A Review of the Evidence', *The World Bank Research Observer*, 15(1): 99–135.

Bardhan, P. (1993) 'Symposium on Democracy and Development', *Journal of Economic Perspectives*, 7(3): 45–9.

Bardhan, P. (2005a) *Conflicts and Cooperation: Essays in the Political and Institutional Economics of Development* (Cambridge, MA: MIT Press).

Bardhan, P. (2005b) 'Institutions Matter, But Which Ones?', *Economics of Transition*, 13(3): 499–532.

Bardhan, P. and Udry, C. (1999) *Development Microeconomics* (New York: Oxford University Press).

Barro, R. (1991) 'Economic Growth in a Cross Section of Countries', *Quarterly Journal of Economics*, 106(2): 407–33.

Barro, R. (1996a) 'Democracy and Growth', *Journal of Economic Growth*, 1(1): 1–27.

Barro, R. (1996b) 'Institutions and Growth: An Introductory Essay', *Journal of Economic Growth*, 1(2): 213–41.

Barro, R. (2008) 'Democracy and Growth', in G. Secondi (ed.) *The Development Economics Reader* (London: Routledge).

Chang, H.-J. (ed.) (2003) *Rethinking Development Economics* (London: Anthem Press).

Fosu, A.K. (2013) 'Institutions and African Economies: An Overview', *Journal of African Economies*, 22(4): 491–8.

Gastil, R.D. (1983) *Freedom in the World: Political Rights and Civil Liberties, 1983–1984* (Westport, CT: Greenwood).

Gastil, R.D. (1986) *Freedom in the World: Political Rights and Civil Liberties, 1986–1987* (Westport, CT: Greenwood).

Harris, J., Hunter, J. and Lewis, C.M. (eds) (1996) *The New Institutional Economics and Third World Development* (London: Routledge).

Hausmann, R., Pritchett, L. and Rodrik, D. (2005) 'Growth Accelerations', *Journal of Economic Growth*, 10(4): 303–29.

Hoff, K. (2003) 'Paths of Institutional Development: A View from Economic History', *The World Bank Research Observer*, 18(2): 205–26.

Kaufman, D., Kraay, A. and Zoido-Lobaton, P. (1999) Governance Matters, Policy Research Working Papers 2196, World Bank.

Keefer, P. and Knack, S. (1995) 'Institutions and Economic Performance: Cross-Country Tests Using Alternative Institutional Measures', *Economic and Politics*, 7(3): 207–27.

Lin, J.V. and Nugent, J. (1995) 'Institutions and Economic Development', in J. Behrman and T. Srinivasan (eds) *Handbook of Development Economics* (Amsterdam: North-Holland).

Mauro, P. (1995) 'Corruption and Growth', *Quarterly Journal of Economics*, 110(3): 681–712.

North, D. (1994) 'Economic Performance Through Time', *American Economic Review*, 84(3): 359–68.

North, D. (1990) *Institutions, Institutional Change and Economic Performance* (New York: Cambridge University Press).

Olson, M. (1982) *The Rise and Decline of Nations* (New Haven, CT: Yale University Press).

Rodrik, D. (2000) 'Institutions for High-Quality Growth and How to Acquire Them', *Studies in Comparative International Development*, 25(3): 3–31.

Rodrik, D. (2008) *One Economics: Many Recipes* (Princeton, NJ: Princeton University Press).

Rodrik, D. and Subramanian, A. (2008) 'The Primacy of Institutions and What This Does and Does Not Mean', in G. Secondi (ed.) *The Development Economics Reader* (London: Routledge).

Rodrik, D., Subramanian, A. and Trebbi, E. (2004) 'Institutions Rule: The Primacy of Institutions over Geography and Integration in Economic Development', *Journal of Economic Growth*, 9(2): 131–65.

Sachs, J. (2008) 'Institutions Matter but not for Everything: The Role of Geography and Resource Endowments in Development Shouldn't be Underestimated', in G. Secondi (ed.) *The Development Economics Reader* (London: Routledge).

Secondi, G. (ed.) (2008) *The Development Economics Reader* (London: Routledge).

Shirley, M. (2008) *Institutions and Development* (Cheltenham: Edward Elgar).

Trebilcock, M.J. and Prado, M.M. (2011) *What Makes Poor Countries Poor?* (London: Edward Elgar).

World Bank (2002) *World Development Report 2002: Building Institutions for Markets* (Washington, DC: World Bank).

Chapter 9 The role of the state in economic development

Abed, G. and Gupta, S. (eds) (2002) *Governance, Corruption and Economic Performance* (Washington, DC: IMF).

Arndt, H.W. (1988) '"Market Failure" and Underdevelopment', *World Development*, 16(2): 219–29.

Bardhan, P. (1997) 'Corruption and Development: A Review of Issues', *Journal of Economic Literature*, 35(3): 1320–46.

Chang, H.-J. and Rowthorn, R. (eds) (1995) *The Role of the State in Economic Change* (New York: Oxford University Press).

Collier. P. (2007) *The Bottom Billion* (Oxford: Oxford University Press).

Collier, P. (2009) *Wars, Guns and Votes* (London: The Bodley Head).

Crabtree, D. and Thirlwall, A.P. (eds) (1993) *Keynes and the Role of the State* (London: Macmillan).

Elliott, K.A. (ed.) (1997) *Corruption and the Global Economy* (Washington, DC: Institute for International Economics).

Ghani, A. and Lockhart, C. (2008) *Fixing Failed States: A Framework for Rebuilding a Fractured World* (Oxford: Oxford University Press).

Ghosh, P.K. (ed.) (1984) *Development Policy and Planning: A Third World Perspective* (Westport, CT: Greenwood Press).

Griffin, K. and Enos, J. (1970) *Planning Development* (Reading, MA: Addison-Wesley).

Gupta, S., Clements, B., Bhattacharya, R. and Chakravarti, S. (2002) 'The Elusive Peace Dividend: How Armed Conflict and Terrorism Undermine Economic Performance', *Finance & Development*, 39(4): 49–51.

Hagen, E. (1963) *Planning Economic Development* (Homewood, IL: Irwin).

Hirschman, A.O. (1958) *Strategy of Economic Development* (New Haven, CT: Yale University Press).

Hirschman, A.O. (1963) *Journeys Towards Progress: Studies in Economic Policy-Making in Latin America* (New York: Twentieth Century Fund).

Hirschman, A.O. (1971) *A Basis for Hope: Essays on Development and Latin America* (New Haven, CT: Yale University Press).

Kaldor, N. (1972) 'The Irrelevance of Equilibrium Economics', *Economic Journal*, 82(328): 1237–55.

Kaufmann, D. (2005) 'Back to Basics: Ten Myths about Governance and Corruption', *Finance & Development*, 42(3): 41–3.

Killick, T. (1977) 'The Possibilities of Development Planning', *Oxford Economic Papers*, 28(2): 161–84.

Killick, T. (1989) *A Reaction Too Far: Economic Theory and the Role of the State in Developing Countries* (London: Overseas Development Institute).

Lewis, A. (1955) *The Theory of Economic Growth* (London: Allen & Unwin).

Lewis, A. (1966) *Development Planning* (London: Allen & Unwin).

Meier, R. (1965) *Developmental Planning* (New York: McGraw-Hill).

Nurkse, R. (1953) *Problems of Capital Formation in Underdeveloped Countries* (Oxford: Oxford University Press).

Rosenstein-Rodan, P. (1943) 'Problems of Industrialisation of East and South-East Europe', *Economic Journal*, 53(209): 202–11.

Scitovsky, T. (1954) 'Two Concepts of External Economies', *Journal of Political Economy*, 62(2): 143–51.

Sen, A.K. (1957) 'Some Notes on the Choice of Capital Intensity in Development Planning', *Quarterly Journal of Economics*, 71(4): 561–84.

Sen, A.K. (1968) *Choice of Techniques*, 3rd edn (Oxford: Basil Blackwell).

Stern, N. (1989) 'The Economics of Development: A Survey', *Economic Journal*, 99(397): 597–685.

Stewart, F. (2001) *Horizontal Inequality: A Neglected Dimension of Development* (WIDER: Helsinki).

Stewart, F. and Ghani, E. (1991) 'How Significant are Externalities for Development?', *World Development*, 19(6): 569–94.

Stiglitz, J. (1990) *Economic Role of the State* (London: Allen & Unwin).

Streeten, P. (1993) 'Markets and States: Against Minimalism', *World Development*, 21(8): 1281–98.

Tanzi, V. (1998) 'Corruption around the World', *IMF Staff Papers*, 45(4): 559–94.

Transparency International (2015) *Corruption Perceptions Index*, at www.transparency.org/cpi2015#results-table.

Wade, R. (1990) *Governing the Market: Economic Theory and the Role of Government in East Asian Industrialisation* (Princeton, NJ: Princeton University Press).

Waterson, A. (1966) *Development Planning: Lessons of Experience* (Oxford: Oxford University Press).
World Bank (1997) *World Development Report 1997: The State in a Changing World* (New York: Oxford University Press).
World Bank (2004) *Doing Business in 2004: Understanding Regulation* (New York: Oxford University Press).
World Bank (2011) *World Development Report 2011: Conflict, Security and Development* (Washington DC: World Bank).

Chapter 10 Dualism, centre–periphery models and the process of cumulative causation

Amin, S. (1974) *Accumulation on a World Scale: A Critique of the Theory of Underdevelopment* (New York: Monthly Review Press).
Baran, P. (1957) *The Political Economy of Growth* (New York: Monthly Review Press).
Barro, R. and Sala-í-Martin, X. (1992) 'Convergence', *Journal of Political Economy*, 100(2): 223–51.
Berger, S. (ed.) (2009) *The Foundations of Non-Equilibrium Economics: The Principle of Circular and Cumulative Causation* (Abingdon: Routledge).
Cherodian, R. and Thirlwall, A.P. (2015) 'Regional Disparities in Per Capita Income in India: Convergence or Divergence?', *Journal of Post Keynesian Economics*, 37(3): 384–407.
Dixon, R. and Thirlwall, A.P. (1975) 'A Model of Regional Growth Rate Differences on Kaldorian Lines', *Oxford Economic Papers*, 27(2): 201–14.
Dos Santos, T. (1970) 'The Structure of Dependence', *American Economic Review, Papers and Proceedings*, 60(2): 231–6.
Dos Santos, T. (1973) 'The Crisis of Development Theory and the Problem of Dependence in Latin America', in H. Bernstein (ed.) *Underdevelopment and Development* (Harmondsworth: Penguin).
Emmanuel, A. (1972) *Unequal Exchange: A Study of the Imperialism of Trade* (New York: Monthly Review Press, translated from the French).
Fagerberg, J. and Verspagen, B. (1996) 'Heading for Divergence? Regional Growth in Europe Reconsidered', *Journal of Common Market Studies*, 34(3): 431–48.
Fagerberg, J., Verspagen, B. and Caniels, M. (1996) *Technology, Growth, and Unemployment Across European Regions*, Working Paper, 565 (Norwegian Institute of International Affairs).
Frank, G. (1967) *Capitalism and Underdevelopment in Latin America* (New York: Monthly Review Press).
Gallup, J., Sachs, J. and Mellinger, A. (1998) 'Geography and Economic Development', in B. Pleskovic and J. Stiglitz (eds) *Annual World Bank Conference on Development Economics1998* (Washington, DC: World Bank).
Higgins, B. (1956) 'The "Dualistic Theory" of Underdeveloped Areas', *Economic Development and Cultural Change*, 4(2): 99–115.
Hirschman, A. (1958) *Strategy of Economic Development* (New Haven, CT: Yale University Press).
Kaldor, N. (1970) 'The Case for Regional Policies', *Scottish Journal of Political Economy*, 17(3): 337–48.
Krugman, P. (1989) 'Differences in Income Elasticities and Trends in Real Exchange Rates', *European Economic Review*, 33(5): 1031–54.
Krugman, P. (1991) *Geography and Trade* (Cambridge, MA: MIT Press).
Krugman, P. (1995) *Development, Geography and Economic Theory* (Cambridge, MA: MIT Press).
Krugman, P. (1998) 'The Role of Geography in Development', in B. Pleskovic and J. Stiglitz (eds) *Annual World Bank Conference on Development Economics 1998* (Washington, DC: World Bank).
Krugman, P. and Venables, A. (1995) 'Globalization and the Inequality of Nations', *Quarterly Journal of Economics*, 110(4): 857–80.
Lipton, M. (1977) *Why Poor People Stay Poor* (London: Temple Smith).
Lucas, R. (1990) 'Why Doesn't Capital Flow from Rich to Poor Countries?', *American Economic Review, Papers and Proceedings*, 80(2): 92–6.
McCombie, J. and Thirlwall, A.P. (1994) *Economic Growth and the Balance of Payments Constraint* (London: Macmillan).
McCombie, J. and Thirlwall, A.P. (2004) *Essays on Balance of Payments Constrained Growth* (London: Routledge).
Myrdal, G. (1944) *An American Dilemma: The Negro Problem and Modern Democracy* (New York: Harper Brothers).

Myrdal, G. ([1957] 1963) *Economic Theory and Underdeveloped Regions* (London: Methuen).
Myrdal, G. (1968) *Asian Drama: An Inquiry into the Poverty of Nations* (London: Pantheon).
Prebisch, R. (1950) *The Economic Development of Latin America and its Principal Problems* (New York: ECLA, UN Dept. of Economic Affairs).
Prebisch, R. (1959) 'Commercial Policy in the Underdeveloped Countries', *American Economic Review, Papers and Proceedings*, 44(2): 251–73.
Rodriguez-Pose, A. and Gill, N. (2006) 'How Does Trade Affect Regional Disparities?', *World Development*, 34(7): 1201–22.
Shankar, R. and Shah, A. (2003) 'Bridging the Economic Divide within Countries: A Scorecard on the Performance of Regional Policies in Reducing Income Disparities', *World Development*, 31(8): 1421–41.
Soukiakis, E. and Cerquiera, P. (eds) (2012) *Models of Balance of Payments Constrained Growth: History, Theory and Empirics* (Basingstoke: Palgrave Macmillan).
Thirlwall, A.P. (1983) 'Foreign Trade Elasticities in Centre–Periphery Models of Growth and Development', *BNL Quarterly Review*, September.
Thirlwall, A.P. (2014) 'Kaldor's 1970 Regional Growth Model Revisited', *Scottish Journal of Political Economy*, 61(4): 341–7.
Toner, P. (1999) *Main Currents in Cumulative Causation* (London: Macmillan).
Williamson, J.G. (2013) *Trade and Poverty: When the Third World Fell Behind* (Cambridge, MA: MIT Press).
World Bank (2009) *World Development Report 2009: Reshaping Economic Geography* (Washington, DC: World Bank).

Chapter 11 Population and development

Bloom, D.E. (2016) 'Demographic Upheaval' *Finance & Development*, March.
Cassen, R. (1976) 'Population and Development: A Survey', *World Development*, 4(10/11): 785–830.
Cassen, R. (ed.) (1994) *Population and Development: Old Debates, New Conclusions* (Washington, DC: Overseas Development Council).
Dasgupta, P. (1995) 'The Population Problem: Theory and Evidence', *Journal of Economic Literature*, 33(4): 1879–1902.
Ehrlich, P. (1968) *Population Bomb* (New York: Ballantine Books).
Enke, S. (1971) 'Economic Consequences of Rapid Population Growth', *Economic Journal*, 81(324): 800–11.
Findlay, A. and Findlay, A. (1995) *Population and Development in the Third World* (London: Routledge).
Hoover, E. and Coale, A. (1958) *Population Growth and Economic Development in Low Income Countries* (Princeton, NJ: Princeton University Press).
Kelley, A.C. (1988) 'Economic Consequences of Population Change in the Third World', *Journal of Economic Literature*, 26(4): 1685–1728.
Kremer, M. (1993) 'Population Growth and Technology Change: One Million BC to 1990', *Quarterly Journal of Economics*, 108(3): 681–716.
Leibenstein, H. (1957) *Economic Backwardness and Economic Growth* (New York: Wiley).
Malthus, T. ([1798]1983) *An Essay on the Principle of Population* (London: Penguin).
Meade, J. (1967) 'Population Explosion, Standard of Living and Social Conflict', *Economic Journal*, 77(306): 233–55.
Modigliani, F. (1970) 'The Life Cycle Hypothesis of Saving and Inter-Country Differences in the Savings Ratio', in W. Eltis et al. (eds) *Induction, Growth and Trade: Essays in Honour of Sir Roy Harrod* (Oxford: Oxford University Press).
Neher, P.A. (1971) 'Peasants, Procreation and Pensions', *American Economic Review*, 61(3): 380–9.
Petty, W. (1682) *Essay Concerning the Multiplication of Mankind* (London: Mark Pardoe).
Rawls, J. (1972) *A Theory of Justice* (Oxford: Oxford University Press).
Reader, J. (2005) *Cities* (London: Heinemann).
Sidgwick, H. (1874) *Methods of Ethics* (London: Macmillan).
Simon, J. (ed.) (1992) *Population and Development in Poor Countries* (Princeton, NJ: Princeton University Press).
Simon, J. (1996) *The Ultimate Resource 2* (Princeton, NJ: Princeton University Press).
Simon, J. (1997) *The Economics of Population: Key Modern Writings*, vols 1 and 2 (Aldershot: Edward Elgar).

Smith, A. (1776) *An Inquiry into the Nature and Causes of the Wealth of Nations* (London: Strahan and Cadell).
Thirlwall, A.P. (1972) 'A Cross Section Study of Population Growth and the Growth of Output and Per Capita Income in a Production Function Framework', *Manchester School*, 40(4): 339–56.
Thirlwall, A.P. (1988) 'Population Growth and Development', in D. Ironmonger, J.O. Perkins and T.V. Hoa (eds) *National Income and Economic Progress: Essays in Honour of Colin Clark* (London: Macmillan).
UN DESA (UN Department of Economics and Social Affairs), Population Division (2003) *World Population Policies* (New York: UN).
UN DESA (UN Department of Economic and Social Affairs) (2015) *World Population Prospects: The 2015 Revision* (New York: UN).
World Bank (1984) *World Development Report 1984: Population Change and Development* (New York: Oxford University Press for the World Bank).
World Bank (2015) *World Development Indicators 2015* (Washington, DC: World Bank).

Chapter 12 Development and the environment

Barbier, E.R. (1989) *Economics, Natural Resource Scarcity and Development* (London: Earthscan).
Barnett, H.J. and Morse, C. (1963) *Scarcity and Growth: The Economics of Natural Resource Availability* (Baltimore, MD: Johns Hopkins University Press).
Baumol, W. and Oates, W. (1988) *The Theory of Environmental Policy*, 2nd edn (Cambridge: Cambridge University Press).
Blackman, A., Mathis, M. and Nelson, P. (2001) *The Greening of Development Economics* (Washington, DC: Resources for the Future).
Blowers, A. and Glasbergen, P. (1996) *Environmental Policy in an International Context* (Chichester: John Wiley).
Bond, R., Curran, J., Kirkpatrick, C., Lee, N. and Francis, P. (2001) 'Integrated Impact Assessment for Sustainable Development: A Case Study Approach', *World Development*, 29(6): 1011–24.
Booth, D.E. (1994) 'Ethics and the Limits of Environmental Economics', *Ecological Economics*, 9(3): 241–52.
Boulding, K.E. (1966) 'The Economics of the Coming Spaceship Earth', in H. Jarrett (ed.) *Environmental Quality in a Growing Economy* (Baltimore, MD: Johns Hopkins University Press).
Bowers, J. (1997) *Sustainability and Environmental Economics: An Alternative Text* (Harlow: Longman).
Bushby, J.W. (2009) 'The Climate Security Connection: What it Means for the Poor', in L. Brainard, A. Jones and M. Purvis (eds) *Climate Change and Global Poverty: A Billion of Lives in the Balance* (Washington, DC: Brooking Institution Press).
Brainard, L., Jones, A. and Purvis, M. (eds) (2009) *Climate Change and Global Poverty: A Billion Lives in the Balance* (Washington, DC: Brookings Institution Press).
Carson, R. (1962) *Silent Spring* (Boston, MA: Houghton Mifflin).
Cole, M.A. (2003) 'Development, Trade and the Environment: How Robust is the Environmental Kuznets Curve?', *Environment and Development Economics*, 8(4): 557–80.
Common, M. (1996) *Environmental and Resource Economics: An Introduction*, 2nd edn (London: Longman).
Common, M. and Stagl, S. (2005) *Ecological Economics: An Introduction* (Cambridge: Cambridge University Press).
Commoner, B. (1972) *The Closing Circle* (London: Cape).
Conable, B. (1989) 'Development and the Environment: A Global Balance', *Finance & Development*, December.
Dasgupta, P. (1982) *The Control of Resources* (Oxford: Blackwell).
Dasgupta, P. (2007) 'Comments on the Stern Review's Economics of Climate Change', *National Institute Economic Review*, 199(1): 4–7.
Dasgupta, P. (2008) 'Creative Accounting', *Nature*, October.
Dasgupta, P. and Heal, G.M. (1979) *Economic Theory and Exhaustible Resources* (Cambridge: Cambridge University Press).
Dawkins, R. (1976) *The Selfish Gene* (Oxford: Oxford University Press).
De Bruyn, S. (2001) *Economic Growth and the Environment* (Dordrecht: Kluwer).
Ehrlich, P.R. and Ehrlich, A.H. (1970) *Population, Resources, Environment: Issues in Human Ecology* (San Francisco, CA: Freeman).
Ellerman, D., Marcantonini, C. and Zaklan, A. (2016) 'The EU ETS: Ten Years and Counting', *Review of Environmental Economics and Policy*, 10(1): 89–107.

Fankhauser, S. (1995) *Valuing Climate Change: The Economics of the Greenhouse* (London: Earthscan).

Forrester, J. (1971) *World Dynamics* (Cambridge: Wright-Allen Press).

Garrod, G.D. and Willis, K. (1999) *Economic Valuation of the Environment* (Cheltenham: Edward Elgar).

Goldsmith, E., Allen, R., Allaby, M., Davoli, J. and Lawrence, S. (1972) *Blueprint for Survival* (London: Penguin).

Greenstone, M. and Jack, B.K. (2015) 'Envirodevonomics: A Research Agenda for an Emerging Field', *Journal of Economic Literature*, 53(1): 5–42.

Grossman, G. and Krueger, A. (1995) 'Economic Growth and the Environment', *Quarterly Journal of Economics*, 110(2): 353–77.

Hanley, N. and Atkinson, G. (2003) 'Economics and Sustainable Development: What Have we Learnt, and What do we Still Need to Learn?', in F. Berkhout, M. Leach and I. Scoones (eds) *Negotiating Environmental Change* (Cheltenham: Earthscan).

Hanley, N., Shogren, J. and White, B. (2013) *Introduction to Environmental Economics*, 2nd edn (Oxford: Oxford University Press).

Hanley, N. and Spash, C. (1993) *Cost Benefit Analysis and the Environment* (Aldershot: Edward Elgar).

Hardin. G. (1968) 'The Tragedy of the Commons', *Science*, 162(3859): 1243–8.

Hensher, D.A., Rose, J.M. and Greene, W.H. (2015) *Applied Choice Analysis*, 2nd edn (Cambridge: Cambridge University Press).

Hicks, J. (1946) *Value and Capital*, 2nd edn (Oxford: Oxford University Press).

Horta, K. (1996) 'The World Bank and International Monetary Fund', in J. Werksman (ed.) *Greening International Institutions* (London: Earthscan).

Hotelling, H. (1931) 'The Economics of Exhaustible Resources', *Journal of Political Economy*, 39(2): 137–75.

IMF (International Monetary Fund) (2008) *Climate Change, the Environment and the Work of the IMF* (Washington, DC: IMF).

IPCC (Intergovernmental Panel on Climate Change) (1990) *First Assessment Report* (Cambridge: Cambridge University Press).

IPCC (2007) *Fourth Annual Report* (Cambridge: Cambridge University Press).

IPCC (2014a) *Summary for Policymakers*, in *Climate Change 2014: Impacts, Adaptation, and Vulnerability* (Cambridge: Cambridge University Press).

IPCC (2014b) *Climate Change 2014: Mitigation of Climate Change, Fifth Assessment Report* (Cambridge: Cambridge University Press).

IUCN (International Union for the Conservation of Nature and Natural Resources) with UNEP and WWF (1980) *World Conservation Strategy* (Gland, Switzerland: IUCN).

Kay, J. and Mirrlees, J. (1975) 'The Desirability of Natural Resource Depletion', in D.W. Pearce (ed.) *The Economics of Natural Resource Depletion* (London: Macmillan).

Kneese, A.V., Ayres, R.V. and D'Arge, R.C. (1970) *Economics and the Environment: A Materials Balance Approach* (Baltimore, MD: Johns Hopkins University Press).

Lancaster, K. (1966) 'A New Approach to Consumer Theory', *Journal of Political Economy*, 74(2): 132–57.

Lawrence, D.P. (2003) *Environmental Impact Assessment: Practical Solutions to Recurrent Problems* (Oxford: Wiley).

Lele, S. (1991) 'Sustainable Development: A Critical Review', *World Development*, 19(6): 607–21.

Lomberg, B. (2001) *The Skeptical Environmentalist: Measuring the Real State of the World* (Cambridge: Cambridge University Press).

Malthus, T. ([1798]1983) *Essay on the Principle of Population* (London: Penguin).

Marshall, A. (1890) *Principles of Economics* (London: Macmillan).

Meadows, D.H., Meadows, D.L., Randers, R. and Behrens, W.W. (1972) *The Limits to Growth* (New York: Universe Books).

Mill, J.S. ([1856]1986) *The Principles of Political Economy* (London: Penguin).

Nature (1998) 'When Self-interest is Key to a Better Environment', *Nature*, 395(6701): 428–9.

Nordhaus, W.D. (2007) 'A Review of the Stern Review of Economics of Climate Change', *Journal of Economic Literature*, 45(3): 703–24.

Nordhaus, W.D. and Tobin, J. (1972) 'Is Growth Obsolete?', in National Bureau of Economic Research, *Economic Growth* (Columbia: Columbia University Press).

Norton, B.G. (1987) *Why Preserve Natural Variety?* (Princeton, NJ: Princeton University Press).

Nyong, A. (2009) 'Climate Change Impacts in Developing Countries: Implications for Sustainable Development', in L. Brainard, A. Jones and M. Purvis (eds) *Climate Change and Global Poverty: A Billion Lives in the Balance* (Washington, DC: Brookings Institution Press).

Ostrom, E. (1990) *Governing the Commons: The Evolution of Institutions for Collective Action* (Cambridge: Cambridge University Press).

Ostrom, E. (2000) 'Collective Action and the Evolution of Social Norms', *Journal of Economic Perspectives*, 14(3): 137–58.

Pagiola, S., Arcenas, A. and Platais, G. (2005) 'Can Payments for Environmental Services Help to Reduce Poverty? An Exploration of the Issues and the Evidence to Date from Latin America', *World Development*, 33(2): 237–53.

Pearce, D. and Turner, R.K. (1990) *Economics of Natural Resources and the Environment* (Hemel Hempstead: Harvester Wheatsheaf).

Pearce, D., Atkinson, G. and Mourato, S. (2006) *Cost-Benefit Analysis and the Environment* (Paris: OECD).

Perman, R., Ma, Y., Common, M., Maddison, D. and McGilvray, J. (2011) *Natural Resources and Environmental Economics*, 4th edn (Boston, MA: Addison Wesley).

Pigou, A.C. (1920) *The Economics of Welfare* (London: Macmillan).

Pindyck, R.S. (2007) 'Uncertainty in Environmental Economics', *Review of Environmental Economics and Policy*, 1(1): 45–65.

Ricardo, D. ([1817]1992) *Principles of Political Economy and Taxation* (London: Everyman).

Sagoff, M. (1988) *The Economy of the Earth* (Cambridge: Cambridge University Press).

Sandmo, A. (2015) 'The Early History of Environmental Economics', *Review of Environmental Economics and Policy*, 9(1): 1–21.

Schumacher, E. (1973) *Small is Beautiful: Economics as if People Mattered* (London: Blond & Briggs).

Sen, A.K. (1967) 'Isolation, Assurance and the Social Rate of Discount', *Quarterly Journal of Economics*, 81(1): 112–24.

Stern, N. (2006) *The Stern Review: The Economics of Climate Change* (Cambridge: Cambridge University Press).

Stern, N. (2008) 'The Cost of Tackling Global Climate Change Has Doubled Warns Stern', *The Guardian*, 26 June.

Stern, N, (2013) 'The Structure of Economic Modeling of the Potential Impacts of Climate Change: Grafting Gross Underestimation of Risk onto Already Narrow Science Models', *Journal of Economic Literature*, 15(3): 838–59.

Sterner, T. (2003) *Policy Instruments for Environmental and Natural Resource Management* (Washington, DC: World Bank).

Stokke, O.S. and Thommessen, O.B. (2003) *Yearbook of International Co-operation on Environment and Development 2003/2004* (London: Earthscan).

Tarbuck, E.J., Lutgens, F. and Tusa, D. (2008) *Earth Science*, 12th edn (London: Pearson Education).

Tietenberg, T. and Johnstone, N. (2004) 'Ex Post Evaluation of Tradable Permits: Methodological Issues and Literature Review', in T. Tietenberg and N. Johnstone (eds) *Tradable Permits: Policy Evaluation, Design and Reform* (Paris: OECD).

Tietenberg, T. and Lewis, L. (2008) *Environmental and Natural Resource Economics*, 8th edn (London: Pearson Education).

UN (United Nations) (1993) *Earth Summit: Agenda 21: United Nations Programme of Action from Rio* (New York: UN).

UN (2005) *World Summit Outcome 2005* (New York: UN).

UNCTAD (UN Conference on Trade and Development) (2009) *Trade and Development Report 2009* (Geneva: UNCTAD).

UNEP (UN Environment Programme) (2012) *UNEP Year Book: Emerging Issues in our Global Environment* (Nairobi: UNEP).

UN WCED (UN World Commission on Environment and Development) (1987) *Our Common Future* (Brundtland Report) (Oxford: Oxford University Press).

Varian, H. (2005) *Intermediate Microeconomics: A Modern Approach*, 7th edn (New York: Norton).

Warren, R.N., Arnell, W., Nicholls, R., Levy, P.E. and Price, J. (2006) 'Understanding the Regional Impacts of Climate Change: Research Report Prepared for the Stern Review on the Economics of Climate Change', Tyndall Working Papers 90 (Norwich).

Wilson, E.O. (2002) *The Future of Life* (New York: Vintage).

World Bank (1992) *World Development Report 1992* (New York: Oxford University Press).

World Bank (2001) *Making Sustainable Commitments: An Environment Strategy for the World Bank* (Washington, DC: World Bank).

World Bank (2002) *World Development Report: Sustainable Development in a Dynamic World* (Washington, DC: World Bank).

World Bank (2003) *Poverty and Climate Change: Reducing the Vulnerability of the Poor through Adaptation* (Washington, DC: World Bank).

World Bank (2010) *World Development Report 2010: Development and Climate Change* (Washington, DC: World Bank).

World Bank (2011) *The Changing Wealth of Nations: Measuring Sustainable Development in the New Millennium* (Washington, DC: World Bank).

Wright, B.D. (2014) 'Data at our Fingertips, Myths in our Minds: Recent Grain Price Jumps as the "Perfect Storm"', *Australian Journal of Agricultural and Resource Economics*, 58: 538–53.

Chapter 13 Financing development from domestic resources

African Development Bank (1994) *African Development Report 1994: Financial Structures, Reforms and Economic Development in Africa* (Abidjan: African Development Bank).

Ahmad, E. and Stern, N. (1991) *The Theory and Practice of Tax Reform in Developing Countries* (Cambridge: Cambridge University Press).

Arestis, P. and Demetriades, P. (1997) 'Financial Development and Economic Growth: Assessing the Evidence', *Economic Journal*, 107(442): 783–99.

Arestis, P. and Demetriades, P. (1999) 'Financial Liberalisation: The Experience of Developing Countries', *Eastern Economic Journal*, 25(4): 441–57.

Armendariz, B. and Morduch, J. (2005) *The Economics of Microfinance* (Cambridge MA: MIT Press).

Athukorala, P. (1998) 'Interest Rates, Savings and Investment: Evidence from India', *Oxford Development Studies*, 26(2): 153–69.

Balkenhol, B. (ed.) (2007) *Microfinance and Public Policy* (Geneva: International Labour Office).

Bandiera, O., Caprio, G., Honohan, P. and Schiantarelli, F. (2000) 'Does Financial Reform Raise or Reduce Saving?', *Review of Economics and Statistics*, 82(2): 239–63.

Banerjee, A., Duflo, E., Glennerster, R. and Kinnan, C. (2013) 'The Miracle of Microfinance? Evidence from a Randomized Evaluation', National Bureau of Economic Research, No. w18950.

Barajas, A., Chami, R. and Yousefi, R. (2011) 'Differing Benefits', *Finance & Development*, 48(3).

Beck, T. and Demirguc-Kunt, A. (2009) 'Access to Finance: An Unfinished Agenda', *Journal of Economic Perspectives*, 22(3): 383–96.

Bird, R.M. (1991) *Tax Policy and Economic Development* (Baltimore, MD: Johns Hopkins University Press).

Bleaney, M., Gemmell, N. and Greenaway, D. (1995) 'Tax Revenue Instability with Particular Reference to sub-Saharan Africa', *Journal of Development Studies*, 31(6): 883–902.

Braverman, A. and Guasch, J. (1986) 'Rural Credit Markets and Institutions in Developing Countries: Lessons for Policy Analysis from Practice and Modern Theory', *World Development*, 14(10–11): 1253–67.

Bruno, M. (1995) 'Does Inflation Really Lower Growth?', *Finance & Development*, 32(3): 35–8.

Bruno, M. and W. Easterly (1998) 'Inflation Crises and Long Run Growth', *Journal of Monetary Economics*, 41(1): 3–26.

Buffie, E.F. (1984) 'Financial Repression, the New Structuralists and Stabilisation Policy in Semi-industrialised Economies', *Journal of Development Economics*, 14(3): 305–22.

Bumann, S., Hermes, N. and Lensink, R. (2012) *Financial Liberalisation and Economic Growth: A Meta-Analysis, Technical Report* (London: EPPI-Centre, University of London). Taken verbatim from conclusion at http://eppi.ioe.ac.uk/cms/Portals/0/PDF%20reviews%20and%20summaries/Financial%20liberalisation%202012Bumann.pdf?ver=2013-03-07-140718-677.

Burgess, R. and Stern, N. (1993) 'Taxation and Development', *Journal of Economic Literature*, 31(2): 762–826.

Campos, R. (1961) 'Two Views on Inflation in Latin America' in A. Hirschman (ed.), *Latin American Issues* (New Haven, Conn: Yale University Press).

Chaves, R. and Gonzales-Vega, C. (1996) 'The Design of Successful Rural Intermediaries: Evidence from Indonesia', *World Development*, 24(1): 65–78.

Chelliah, R.J., Bass, H.J. and Kelly, M.R. (1975) 'Tax Ratios and Tax Effort in Developing Countries 1969–71', *IMF Staff Papers*, 22(1): 187–205.

Cho, Y.C. and Khatkhate, D. (1990) 'Financial Liberalisation: Issues and Evidence', *Economic and Political Weekly*, May.

Clarke, R. (1996) 'Equilibrium Interest Rates and Financial Liberalisation in Developing Countries', *Journal of Development Studies*, 32(3): 391–413.

Cull, R., Demirguc-Kunt, A. and Morduch, J. (2007) 'Financial Performance and Outreach: A Global Analysis of Leading Microbanks', *Economic Journal*, 117(517): 107–33.

Cull, R., Demirguc-Kunt, A. and Morduch, J. (2009) 'Microfinance Meets the Market', *Journal of Economic Perspectives*, 23(1): 167–92.

Davidson, P. (1986) 'Finance, Funding, Saving, and Investment', *Journal of Post Keynesian Economics*, 9(1): 101–10.

De Gregorio, J. and Guidotti, P. (1995) 'Financial Development and Economic Growth', *World Development*, 23(3): 433–48.

Demetriades, P.O. (1997) 'The Direct Costs of Financial Repression: Evidence from India', *Review of Economics and Statistics*, 79(2): 311–20.

Demetriades, P.O. and Hussein, K.A. (1996) 'Does Financial Development Cause Economic Growth? Time Series Evidence from 16 Countries', *Journal of Development Economics*, 51(2): 387–411.

Demetriades, P.O. and Devereux, P. (1992) 'Investment and "Financial Repression": Theory and Evidence from 63 LDCs', Working Paper in Economics, 92/16, Keele University.

Diaz-Alejandro, C. (1985) 'Good-bye Financial Repression, Hello Financial Crash', *Journal of Development Economics*, 19(1/2): 1–24.

Dornbusch, R. and Reynoso, A. (1989) 'Financial Factors in Economic Development', *American Economic Review, Papers and Proceedings*, 79: 204–9.

Dutt, A. (1990–91) 'Interest Rate Policy in LDCs: A Post Keynesian View', *Journal of Post Keynesian Economics*, 13(2): 210–32.

Edwards, S. (1996) 'Why are Latin America's Savings Rates so Low? An International Comparative Analysis', *Journal of Development Economics*, 51(1): 5–44.

Fitzgerald, E.V.K. (1993) *The Macroeconomics of Development Finance: A Kaleckian Approach* (London: Macmillan).

Fry, M. (1989) 'Financial Development: Theories and Recent Experience', *Oxford Review of Economic Policy*, 5(4): 13-28.

Fry, M. (1995) *Money, Interest and Banking in Economic Development* (Baltimore, MD: Johns Hopkins University Press).

Fry, M. (1997) 'In Favour of Financial Liberalisation', *Economic Journal*, 107(442): 754–70.

Ghatak, S. and Sanchez-Fung, J. (2006) *Monetary Economics in Developing Countries* (Basingstoke: Palgrave Macmillan).

Ghosh, A. and Phillips, S. (1998) 'Warning: Inflation may be Harmful to Your Growth', *IMF Staff Papers*, 45(4): 672–710.

Gibson, H. and Tsakolotos, E. (1994) 'The Scope and Limits of Financial Liberalisation in Developing Countries: A Critical Survey', *Journal of Development Studies*, 30(3): 578–628.

Gillis, M. (ed.) (1989) *Tax Reform in Developing Countries* (Durham, NC: Duke University Press).

Giovannini, A. (1983) 'The Interest Rate Elasticity of Savings in Developing Countries', *World Development*, 11(7): 601–7.

Giovannini, A. (1985) 'Saving and the Real Interest Rate in LDCs', *Journal of Development Economics*, 18(2/3): 197–217.

Goncalves, C. and Salles, J. (2008) 'Inflation Targeting in Emerging Economies: What Do the Data Say?', *Journal of Development Economics*, 85(1/2): 312–18.

Goode, R. (1993) 'Tax Advice to Developing Countries: An Historical Survey', *World Development*, 21(1): 37–53.

Greene, J. and Villanueva, D. (1991) 'Private Investment in Developing Countries: An Empirical Analysis', *IMF Staff Papers*, 38(1): 33–58.

Gupta, K.L. (1987) 'Aggregate Savings, Financial Intermediation and Interest Rates', *Review of Economics and Statistics*, 69(2): 303–11.

Gurley, G.J. and Shaw, E. (1960) *Money in a Theory of Finance* (Washington, DC: Brookings Institution).

Hamilton, E. (1952) 'Prices as a Factor in Business Growth: Prices and Progress', *Journal of Economic History*, 12(4): 325–49.

Hermes, N. and Lensink, R. (2007) 'The Empirics of Microfinance: What Do We Know?', *Economic Journal*, 117(517): 1–10.

Hermes, N. and Lensink, R. (eds) (2011) 'Special Issue: Microfinance: Its Impact, Outreach and Sustainability', *World Development*, 36(1): 938–48.

Hossain, A. and Chowdhury, A. (1996) 'Monetary and Financial Policies', in *Developing Countries: Growth and Stabilisation* (London: Routledge).

Hulme, D. and Thankom, A. (eds) (2008) *Microfinance: A Reader* (London: Routledge).

Hung, G.N.T. (2004) 'Bank on Wheels', *Finance & Development*, 41(2): 41–3.

Hussein, K. and Thirlwall, A.P. (1999) 'Explaining Differences in the Domestic Savings Ratio across Countries: A Panel Data Study', *Journal of Development Studies*, 36(1): 31–52.

Johnson, O.E.G. (1984) 'On Growth and Inflation in Developing Countries', *IMF Staff Papers*, 31(4): 636–60.

Kaldor, N. (1955–56) 'Alternative Theories of Distribution', *Review of Economic Studies*, 23(2): 83–100.

Kaldor, N. (1980) *Reports on Taxation II, Collected Economic Essays*, vol. 8 (London: Duckworth).

Keynes, J.M. (1923) *Tract on Monetary Reform* (London: Macmillan).

Keynes, J.M. (1930) *Treatise on Money*, vol. 2 (London: Macmillan).

Keynes, J.M. (1931) *Essays in Persuasion* (London: Macmillan).

King, R.G. and Levine, R. (1993) 'Finance and Growth: Schumpeter Might be Right', *Quarterly Journal of Economics*, 108(3): 717–38.

Levine, R. (1997) 'Financial Development and Economic Growth: Views and Agenda', *Journal of Economic Literature*, 35(2): 688–726.

Levine, R. and Zervos, S. (1993) 'What we have Learned About Policy and Growth From Cross-Country Regressions', *American Economic Review, Papers and Proceedings*, 83: 426–30.

Lewis, A. (1955) *The Theory of Economic Growth* (London: Allen & Unwin).

Lin, S. and Ye, H. (2007) 'Does Inflation Targeting Really Make a Difference? Evaluating the Treatment Effect of Inflation Targeting in Seven Industrial Countries', *Journal of Monetary Economics*, 54(8): 2521–33.

Lin, S. and Ye, H. (2009) 'Does Inflation Targeting Make a Difference in Developing Countries?', *Journal of Development Economics*, 89(1): 118–23.

Loayza, N., Schmidt-Hebbel, K. and Serven, L. (2000) 'What Drives Private Saving Across the World?', *Review of Economics and Statistics*, 82(2): 165–81.

McKinnon, R. (1973) *Money and Capital in Economic Development* (Washington, DC: Brookings Institution).

Mahmud, W. and Osmani, S. (2011) *The Theory and Practice of Microcredit* (Abingdon: Routledge).

Masson, P., Bayoumi, J. and Samiei, H. (1998) 'International Evidence on the Determinants of Private Saving', *World Bank Economic Review*, 12(3): 483–501.

Mikesell, R. and Zinser, J. (1973) 'The Nature of the Savings Function in Developing Countries: A Survey of the Theoretical and Empirical Literature', *Journal of Economic Literature*, 11(1): 1–26.

Modigliani, F. and Brumberg, R. (1954) 'Utility Analysis and the Consumption Function: An Integration of Cross Section Data', in K.K. Kurihara (ed.) *Post-Keynesian Economics* (New Brunswick, NJ: Rutgers University Press).

Molho, L.E. (1986) 'Interest Rates, Saving and Investment in Developing Countries: A Re-examination of the McKinnon–Shaw Hypothesis', *IMF Staff Papers*, 33(1): 90–116.

Morduch, J. (1999) 'The Microfinance Promise', *Journal of Economic Literature*, 37(4): 1569–614.

Newbery, D. and Stern, N. (1987) *The Theory of Taxation for Developing Countries* (Oxford: Oxford University Press for the World Bank).

Ogaki, M., Ostry, J.D. and Reinhart, C.M. (1996) 'Saving Behaviour in Low- and Middle-Income Developing Countries: A Comparison', *IMF Staff Papers*, 43(1): 38–71.

Oshima, A. and Chan, J.A. (2011) 'Branching Out', *Finance & Development*, 48(1): 57.

Ostry, J.D. and Reinhart, C.M. (1995) 'Savings and the Real Interest Rate in Developing Countries', *Finance & Development*, December.

Pankaj, J. (1996) 'Managing Credit for Rural Poor: Lessons from the Grameen Bank', *World Development*, 24(1): 79–89.
Pastor, M. (1991) 'Bolivia: Hyperinflation, Stabilisation and Beyond', *Journal of Development Studies*, 27(2): 211–37.
Piancastelli, M. (2001) 'Measuring the Tax Effort of Developed and Developing Countries: Cross Country Panel Data Analysis 1985–95', mimeo, University of Kent at Canterbury.
Pollin, R. and Zhu, A. (2006) 'Inflation and Economic Growth: A Cross-Country Non-Linear Analysis', *Journal of Post Keynesian Economics*, 28(4): 593–614.
Robinson, J. (1960) 'Notes on the Theory of Economic Development', in *Collected Economic Papers* (Oxford: Blackwell).
Robinson, J. (1962) 'A Model of Accumulation', in *Essays in the Theory of Economic Growth* (London: Macmillan).
Rostow, W.W. (1960) *The Stages of Economic Growth* (Cambridge: Cambridge University Press).
Sarel, M. (1996) 'Nonlinear Effects of Inflation on Economic Growth', *IMF Staff Papers*, 43(1): 199–215.
Schumpeter, J. (1911) *The Theory of Economic Development* (Cambridge, MA: Harvard University Press).
Shaw, E. (1973) *Financial Deepening in Economic Development* (London: Oxford University Press).
Stanners, W. (1993) 'Is Low Inflation an Important Condition for High Growth?', *Cambridge Journal of Economics*, 17(1): 79–107.
Stiglitz, J. and Weiss, A. (1981) 'Credit Rationing in Markets with Imperfect Information', *American Economic Review*, 71(3): 393–410.
Tait, A.A., Gratz, W. and Eichengreen, B. (1979) 'International Comparisons of Taxation for Selected Developing Countries, 1972–1976', *IMF Staff Papers*, 26(1): 123–56.
Tanzi, V. (1987) 'Quantitative Characteristics of the Tax System of Developing Countries', in D. Newbery and N. Stern (eds) *The Theory of Taxation for Developing Countries* (Oxford: Oxford University Press for the World Bank).
Tanzi, V. (1991) *Public Finance in Developing Countries* (Aldershot: Edward Elgar).
Temple, J. (2000) 'Inflation and Growth: Stories Short and Tall', *Journal of Economic Surveys*, 14(4): 395–432.
Thirlwall, A.P. (1974) *Inflation, Saving and Growth in Developing Economies* (London: Macmillan).
Thirlwall, A.P. (1976) *Financing Economic Development* (London: Macmillan).
Thirlwall, A.P. (1987) *Nicholas Kaldor* (Brighton: Wheatsheaf).
Tun Wai, U. (1972) *Financial Intermediaries and National Savings in Developing Countries* (New York: Praeger).
Warman, F. and Thirlwall, A.P. (1994) 'Interest Rates, Savings, Investment and Growth in Mexico 1960–90: Tests of the Financial Liberalisation Hypothesis', *Journal of Development Studies*, 30(3): 629–49.
Williamson, J. and Mohar, M. (1999) *A Survey of Financial Liberalisation, Essays in International Finance*, 211 (Princeton University).
Woo Jung, S. (1986) 'Financial Development and Economic Growth: International Evidence', *Economic Development and Cultural Change*, 34(2): 333–46.
World Bank (1989) *World Development Report 1989: Financial Systems and Development* (Washington, DC: World Bank).
World Bank (1993) *The East Asian Miracle: Economic Growth and Public Policies* (Oxford: Oxford University Press).
World Bank (2001) *World Development Report 2000/2001: Attacking Poverty* (New York: Oxford University Press).
World Bank (2015) *World Development Indicators 2015* (Oxford: Oxford University Press).

Chapter 14 Foreign assistance, aid, debt and development

Adams, R. and Page, J. (2005) 'Do International Migration and Remittances Reduce Poverty in Developing Countries', *World Development*, 33(10): 1645–69.
Addison, T., Mavrotas, G. and McGillivray, M. (2005) 'Development Assistance and Development Finance: Evidence and Global Policy Agendas', WIDER Research Paper 23 (Helsinki: WIDER).
Aiyar, S., Berg, A. and Hussain, M. (2005) 'The Macroeconomic Challenge of Aid', *Finance & Development*, 42(3): 28–31.
Alesina, A. and Dollar, D. (2000) 'Who Gives Foreign Aid to Whom and Why?', *Journal of Economic Growth*, 5(1): 33–63.

Allsopp, C. and Joshi, V. (1991) 'The Assessment: The International Debt Crisis', *Oxford Review of Economic Policy*, 2(1): i–xxxiii.

Arndt, C., Jones, S. and Tarp, F. (2010) 'Aid, Growth and Development: Have We Come Full Circle?', *Journal of Globalisation and Development*, 1(2): 1–29.

Arndt, C., Jones, S. and Tarp, F. (2011) *Aid Effectiveness: Opening the Black Box* (Helsinki: UNU-WIDER).

Bauer, P. (1971) *Dissent on Development* (London: Weidenfeld & Nicolson).

Bhattacharya, R. and Clements, B. (2004) 'Calculating the Benefits of Debt Relief', *Finance & Development*, 51(4): 48–50.

Borensztein, E., de Gregorio, J. and Lee, J.W. (1995) 'How Does Foreign Investment Affect Growth?', NBER Working Paper 5057 (Cambridge, MA: NBER).

Bosworth, S. and Collins, S. (1999) 'Capital Flows to Developing Economies: Implications for Savings and Investment', *Brookings Papers on Economic Activity*, 30(1): 143–80.

Bourguignon, F. and Morrisson, C. (1992) *Adjustment and Equality in Developing Countries: A New Approach* (Paris: OECD).

Bourguignon, F. and Platteau, J.P. (2017) 'Does Aid Availability Affect Effectiveness in Reducing Poverty? A Review Article', *World Development*, 90(2): 6–16.

Burnside, C. and Dollar, D. (2000) 'Aid, Policies and Growth', *American Economic Review*, 90(4): 847–68.

Cassen, R. (1994) *Does Aid Work?*, 2nd edn (Oxford: Clarendon Press).

Catrinescu, N., León-Ledesma, M., Piracha, M. and Quillin, B. (2008) 'Remittances, Institutions and Economic Growth', *World Development*, 37(1): 81–92.

Celasun, O and Walliser, J. (2008) 'Managing Aid Surprises', *Finance & Development*, 45(3): 34–7.

Chami, R. and Fullenkamp, C. (2013) 'Beyond the Household', *Finance & Development*, 50(3): 48–51.

Chenery, H. and Bruno, M. (1962) 'Development Alternatives in an Open Economy: The Case of Israel', *Economic Journal*, 72(285): 79–103.

Claudon, M.P. (ed.) (1986) *World Debt Crisis* (Cambridge, MA: Ballinger).

Clements, M., Radelet, S. and Bhavnani, R. (2004) 'Counting Chickens When they Hatch: The Short-Term Effect of Aid on Growth', Working Paper 44 (Centre for Global Development, Washington, DC).

Cline, W.R. (1984) *International Debt: Systematic Risk and Policy Response* (Washington, DC: MIT Press for the Institute for International Economics).

Cline, W.R. (1995) *International Debt* (Harlow: Longman).

Coe, D., Helpman, E. and Hoffmaister, A. (1997) 'North–South R&D Spillovers', *Economic Journal*, 107(440): 139–49.

Collier, P. and Dollar, D. (2000) *Aid Allocation and Poverty Reduction* (Washington, DC: World Bank).

Collier, P. and Dollar, D. (2002) 'Aid Allocation and Poverty Reduction', *European Economic Review*, 46(8): 1475–1500.

Collier, P. and Dollar, D. (2004) 'Development Effectiveness: What Have We Learnt?', *Economic Journal*, 114(496): F244–71.

Corbo, V., Fischerand, S. and Webb, S.B. (1992) in *Adjustment Lending Revisited: Policies to Restore Growth* (Washington, DC: World Bank).

Cornia, G., Jolly, R. and Stewart, F. (1987, 1988) *Adjustment with a Human Face*, vols I and II (Oxford: Oxford University Press).

Dalgaard, C.J., Hansen, H. and Tarp, F. (2004) 'On the Empirics of Foreign Aid and Growth', *Economic Journal*, 114(496): 191–216.

Daseking, C. (2002) 'Debt: How Much is too Much?', *Finance & Development*, December.

De Mello, L. (1997) 'Foreign Investment in Developing Countries and Growth: A Selective Survey', *Journal of Development Studies*, 34(1): 1–34.

Doucouliagos, H. and Paldam M. (2008) 'Aid Effectiveness and Growth: A Meta Study', *European Journal of Political Economy*, 24(1): 1–24.

Doucouliagos, H. and Paldam, M. (2013) 'The Robust Result of Meta-Analysis of Aid Effectiveness: A Response to Mekasha and Tarp', *Journal of Development Studies*, 49(4): 584–7.

Easterly, W. (2002) 'How Did Heavily Indebted Poor Countries Become Heavily Indebted? Reviewing Two Decades of Debt Relief', *World Development*, 30(10): 1677–96.

Easterly, W. (2006) *The White Man's Burden* (Oxford: Oxford University Press).
El Shibley, M. and Thirlwall, A.P. (1981) 'Dual-Gap Analysis for the Sudan', *World Development*, 9(2): 193–200.
Fajnzylber, P. and Humberto Lopez, J. (eds) (2008) *Remittances and Economic Development: Lessons from Latin America* (Washington, DC: World Bank).
Frank, A.G. (1981) *Crisis in the Third World* (London: Heinemann).
Friedman, M. (1958) 'Economic Aid: Means and Objectives', *Yale Review*, 47(4): 500–16.
Gibson, H.D. and Thirlwall, A.P. (1989) 'An International Comparison of the Causes of Changes in the Debt Service Ratio 1980–85', *BNL Quarterly Review*, March.
Gilbert, C. and Vines, D. (eds) (2000) *The World Bank: Structure and Policies* (Cambridge: Cambridge University Press).
Gilbert, C., Powell, A. and Vines, D. (1999) 'Positioning the World Bank', *Economic Journal*, 109: 598–633.
Greenaway, D. and Morrissey, O. (1993) 'Structural Adjustment and Liberalisation in Developing Countries: What Lessons Have We Learnt?' *Kyklos*, 46(2).
Griffin, K. (1970) 'Foreign Capital, Domestic Savings and Economic Development', *Bulletin of the Oxford Institute of Economics and Statistics*, 32(2): 99–112.
Griffith-Jones, S. and Sunkel, O. (1986) *Debt and Development Crisis in Latin America* (Oxford: Clarendon Press).
Hansen, H. and Tarp, F. (2001) 'Aid and Growth Regressions', *Journal of Development Economics*, 64(2): 547–70.
Harrigan, J. and Mosley, P. (1991) 'Evaluating the Impact of World Bank Structural Adjustment Lending 1980–87', *Journal of Development Studies*, 27(3): 63–94.
Hermes, N. and Lensink, R. (eds) (2001) 'Changing the Conditions for Development Aid', *Journal of Development Studies*, 37(6): 1–16.
IMF (International Monetary Fund) (2003) *World Economic Outlook: Growth and Institutions* (Washington, DC: IMF)
IMF (2006) *IMF in Focus: A Supplement of the IMF Survey* (Washington, DC: IMF).
Jepma, C. (1991) *The Tying of Aid* (Paris: OECD).
Kargbo, M. (2012) 'Impact of Foreign Aid on Economic Growth in Sierra Leone: Empirical Analysis', *WIDERAngle*, May.
Kennedy, C. and Thirlwall, A.P. (1971) 'Foreign Capital, Domestic Savings and Economic Development: Some Comments', *Bulletin of the Oxford Institute of Economics and Statistics*, 33(2): 135–8.
Keynes, J.M. (1919) *Economic Consequences of the Peace* (London: Macmillan).
Kraay, A. and Nehru, V. (2006) 'When is External Debt Sustainable?', *World Bank Economic Review*, 20(3): 341–65.
Lensink, R. and Morrissey, O. (2000) 'Aid Instability as a Measure of Uncertainty and the Positive Impact of Aid on Growth', *Journal of Development Studies*, 31(6): 883–902.
Lever, H. and Huhne, C. (1985) *Debt and Danger: The World Financial Crisis* (Harmondsworth: Penguin).
Lomax, D.F. (1986) *The Developing Country Debt Crisis* (London: Macmillan).
Mekasha, T. and Tarp, F. (2013) 'Aid and Growth: What Meta-Analysis Shows', *Journal of Development Studies*, 49(4): 564–83.
Morrissey, O. and White, H. (1993) 'How Concessional is Tied Aid?', *CREDIT Research Paper*, 93/13 (University of Nottingham).
Mosley, P. (1987) *Overseas Aid: Its Defence and Reform* (Brighton: Wheatsheaf).
Mosley, P., Harrigan, J. and Toye, J. (1991) *Aid and Power: The World Bank and Policy Lending*, vol. 1, *Analysis and Policy Proposals*, vol. 2, *Case Studies* (London: Routledge).
Mosley, P., Hudson, J. and Verschoos, A. (2004) 'Aid, Poverty and the "New Conditionality"', *Economic Journal*, 114(496): F217–43.
Moyo, D. (2009) *Dead Aid* (London: Allen Lane).
Noorbakhsh, F. (1999) 'Standards of Living, Human Development Indices and Structural Adjustment in Developing Countries: An Empirical Investigation', *Journal of International Development*, 11(1): 151–75.
ODI (Overseas Development Institute) (1996) *New Sources of Finance for Development*, Briefing Paper (London: ODI).
OECD (Organisation for Economic Co-operation and Development) (2015) *Statistics on Resource Flows to Developing Countries* (Paris: OECD).

Ohlin, E. (1966) *Foreign Aid Policies Reconsidered* (Paris: OECD).
Opeskin, B.R. (1996) 'The Moral Foundations of Foreign Aid', *World Development*, 24(1): 21–44.
Pacheco-López, P. (2005) 'Foreign Direct Investment, Exports and Imports in Mexico', *World Economy*, 28(8): 1157–72.
Pattillo, C., Poirson, C.H. and Ricci, L. (2002) 'External Debt and Growth', *Finance & Development*, 39(2): 101–2.
Pearson Report (1969) *Partners in Development, Report of the Commission on International Development* (London: Pall Mall Press).
Pesmazoglu, J. (1972) 'Growth, Investment and Savings Ratios: Some Long and Medium Term Associations by Groups of Countries', *Bulletin of the Oxford Institute of Economics and Statistics*, 34(4): 309–28.
Raffer, K. and Singer, H. (1994) *The Foreign Aid Business* (Aldershot: Edward Elgar).
Rajan, R.G. and Subramanian, A. (2005) 'Aid and Growth: What Does the Cross-Country Evidence Show', IMF Working Paper 05/127 (Washington, DC: IMF).
Rajan, R.G. and Subramanian, A. (2008) 'Aid and Growth: What Does the Cross Country Evidence Really Show?', *Review of Economics and Statistics*, 90(4): 643–65.
Riddell, R. (2007) *Does Foreign Aid Really Work?* (Oxford: Oxford University Press).
Sachs, J.D. (1990) 'A Strategy for Efficient Debt Reduction', *Journal of Economic Perspectives*, 4(1): 9–29.
Sahn, D.E., Dorosh, P.A. and Younger, S.D. (2000) *Structural Adjustment Reconsidered* (Cambridge: Cambridge University Press).
Stiglitz, J. (1999) 'The World Bank at the Millennium', *Economic Journal*, 109(459): 577–97.
Stiglitz, J. (2002) *Globalization and its Discontents* (London: Allen Lane).
Stiglitz, J. (2006) *Making Globalization Work* (New York: W.W. Norton).
Taylor, L. (1997) 'The Revival of the Liberal Creed: the IMF and the World Bank in a Global Economy', *World Development*, 25(2): 145–52.
Thirlwall, A.P. (1972), *Growth and Development, with Special Reference to Developing Economies* (London: Macmillan).
Thirlwall, A.P. (1986) 'Foreign Debt and Economic Development', *Studies in Banking and Finance* (Supplement to the *Journal of Banking and Finance*), 4.
Thirlwall, A.P. (ed.) (1987) *Keynes and Economic Development* (London: Macmillan).
Trumbull, W. and Wall, H. (1994) 'Estimating Aid-Allocation Criteria with Panel Data', *Economic Journal*, 104(425): 876–82.
White, H. (1992) 'The Macroeconomic Impact of Development Aid: A Critical Survey', *Journal of Development Studies*, 28(2): 163–240.
Wood, A. (2008) 'How Donors Should Cap Aid to Africa', *Financial Times*, 4 September.
World Bank (1990) *Adjustment Lending: Ten Years of Experience* (Washington, DC: World Bank).
World Bank (1998) *Assessing Aid: What Works, What Doesn't, and Why* (New York: Oxford University Press).
World Bank (2000) *World Development Report 2000/2001: Attacking Poverty* (New York: Oxford University Press).
World Bank (2014) *Migration and Development Brief* 23 (Washington: Migration and Remittances Team, Development Prospects Group).
World Bank (2015) *World Development Indicators 2015* (Oxford: Oxford University Press).

Chapter 15 Trade theory, trade policy and economic development

Ahmed, N. (2000) 'Export Responses to Trade Liberalisation in Bangladesh: A Cointegration Analysis', *Applied Economics*, 32(8): 1077–84.
Allen, F., Behrman, J.R., Birdsall, N. et al. (2014) *Towards a Better Global Economy: Policy Implications for Citizens Worldwide in the 21st Century* (Oxford: Oxford University Press).
Anderson, E. (2005) 'Openness and Inequality in Developing Countries: A Review of Theory and Recent Evidence', *World Development*, 33(7): 1045–63.
Arbache, J., Dickerson, A. and Green, F. (2004) 'Trade Liberalisation and Wages in Developing Countries', *Economic Journal*, 114(493): 73–96.

Arora, V. and Vamvakidis, A. (2005) 'How Much do Trading Partners Matter for Economic Growth?', *IMF Staff Papers*, 52(1): 24–40.

Athukorala, P. (1993) 'Manufactured Exports from Developing Countries and Their Terms of Trade: A Reexamination of the Sarkar–Singer Results', *World Development*, 21(10): 1607–13.

Athukorala, P. (2000) 'Manufactured Exports and Terms of Trade of Developing Countries: Evidence from Sri Lanka', *Journal of Development Studies*, 36(5): 89–104.

Balassa, B. (1971) *The Structure of Protection in Developing Countries* (Baltimore, MD: World Bank).

Barro, R. (2000) 'Inequality and Growth in a Panel of Countries', *Journal of Economic Growth*, 5(1): 5–32.

Bertola, G. and Faini, R. (1991) 'Import Demand and Non-Tariff Barriers: The Impact of Trade Liberalisation', *Journal of Development Economics*, 34(1/2): 269–86.

Bhagwati, J. (1958) 'Immiserizing Growth: A Geometrical Note', *Review of Economic Studies*, 25(3): 201–5.

Blattman, C., Hwang, J. and Williamson, J.G. (2007) 'Winners and Losers in the Commodity Lottery: The Impact of Terms of Trade Growth and Volatility in the Periphery 1870–1939', *Journal of Development Economics*, 82(1): 156–79.

Bleaney, M. (1993) 'Manufactured Exports of Developing Countries and their Terms of Trade since 1965: A Comment', *World Development*, 21(10): 1615–16.

Bleaney, M. (1999) 'Trade Reform, Macroeconomic Performance and Export Growth in Ten Latin American Countries 1979–95', *Journal of International Trade and Economic Development*, 8(1): 89–105.

Bleaney, M. and Greenaway, D. (1993) 'Long Run Trends in the Relative Prices of Primary Commodities and in the Terms of Trade of Developing Countries', *Oxford Economic Papers*, 43(3): 349–63.

Bourguignon, F. (2015) *The Globalisation of Inequality* (Princeton, NJ: Princeton University Press).

Cashin, P. and McDermott, C.J. (2002) 'The Long-Run Behavior of Commodity Prices: Small Trends and Big Variability', *IMF Staff Papers*, 49(2): 175–99.

Cashin, P., Liang, H. and McDermott, C.J. (2000) 'How Persistent are Shocks to World Commodity Prices?', *IMF Staff Papers*, 47(2): 177–217.

Cashin, P., McDermott, C.J. and Scott, A. (2002) 'Booms and Slumps in World Commodity Prices', *Journal of Development Economics*, 69(1): 277–96.

Chang, H.-J. (2002) *Kicking Away the Ladder: Development Strategy in Historical Perspective* (London: Anthem Press).

Chang, H.-J. (2005) *Why Developing Countries Need Tariffs* (Geneva: South Centre).

Chang, H.-J. (2007) *Bad Samaritans: Rich Nations, Poor Policies and the Threat to the Developing World* (New York: Random House).

Christian Aid (2005) 'The Economics of Failure: The Real Cost of Free Trade for Poor Countries', Briefing Paper, June.

Cline, W. (1997) *Trade and Income Distribution* (Washington, DC: Institute for International Economics).

Corden, W.M. (1966) 'The Structure of a Tariff System and the Effective Rate of Protection', *Journal of Political Economy*, 74(3): 221–37.

Darity, W. and Davis, L. (2005) 'Growth, Trade and Uneven Development', *Cambridge Journal of Economics*, 29(1): 141–70.

De Mello, J. and Panagariya, A. (eds) (1993) *New Dimensions in Regional Integration* (Cambridge: Cambridge University Press).

Diakosavvas, D. and Scandizzo, P.L. (1991) 'Trends in the Terms of Trade of Primary Commodities, 1900–1982: The Controversy and Its Origin', *Economic Development and Cultural Change*, 39(2): 231–64.

Dollar, D. (1992) 'Outward-Oriented Developing Countries Really Do Grow More Rapidly: Evidence from 95 LDCs 1976–1985', *Economic Development and Cultural Change*, 40(3): 523–44.

Dollar, D. and Kraay, A. (2002) 'Growth is Good for the Poor', *Journal of Economic Growth*, 7(3): 195–225.

Dollar, D. and Kraay, A. (2004) 'Trade, Growth and Poverty', *Economic Journal*, 114(493): 22–49.

Dosman, E. (2008) *The Life and Times of Raúl Prebisch 1901–1986* (Montreal: McGill-Queens Press).

Dowrick, S. and Golley, J. (2004) 'Trade Openness and Growth: Who Benefits?', *Oxford Review of Economic Policy*, 20(1): 38–56.

Edward, P. (2006) 'Examining Inequality: Who Really Benefits from Global Growth?', *World Development*, 34: 1667–95.

Edwards, S. (1992) 'Trade Orientation, Distortions and Growth in Developing Countries', *Journal of Development Economics*, 39(1): 31–57.

Edwards, S. (1993) 'Openness, Trade Liberalization and Growth in Developing Countries', *Journal of Economic Literature*, 31(3): 1358–93.

Edwards, S. (1998) 'Openness, Productivity and Growth: What do we Really Know?', *Economic Journal*, 108: 383–98.

Erten, B. (2011) 'North-South Terms of Trade from 1960 to 2006', *International Review of Applied Economics*, 25(2): 171–84.

Erten, B. and Ocampo, J.A. (2013) 'Super Cycles of Commodity Prices since the Mid-Nineteenth Century', *World Development*, 44: 14–30.

Feder, G. (1983) 'On Exports and Economic Growth', *Journal of Development Economics*, 12(1/2): 59–74.

Feenstra, R. and Hanson, R. (1997) 'Foreign Direct Investment and Relative Wages: Evidence from Mexico's Maquiladoras', *Journal of International Economics*, 42(3/4): 371–93.

Felipe, J. (2009) *Inclusive Growth, Full Employment and Structural Change* (London: Anthem Press).

Forouton, F. (1993) 'Regional Integration in Sub-Saharan Africa: Past Experience and Future Prospects', in J. de Melo and A. Panagariya (eds) *New Dimensions in Regional Integration* (Cambridge: Cambridge University Press).

Freeman, R. and Oostendrop, R. (2001) 'The Occupational Wages Around the World Data', *International Labour Review*, 140(4): 380–401.

George, C. (2010) *The Truth About Trade: The Real Impact of Liberalization* (London: Zed Books).

Ghose, A. (2004) 'Global Inequality and International Trade', *Cambridge Journal of Economics*, 28(2): 229–52.

Gilbert, C. (1987) 'International Commodity Agreements: Design and Performance', *World Development*, 15(5): 591–616.

Gilbert, C. (1996) 'International Commodity Agreements: An Obituary Notice', *World Development*, 24(1): 1–19.

Goldberg, P. and Pavcnik, N. (2007) 'Distributional Effects of Globalisation in Developing Countries', *Journal of Economic Literature*, 45(1): 39–82.

Greenaway, D. and Milner, C. (1993) *Trade and Industrial Policy in Developing Countries* (London: Macmillan).

Greenaway, D. and Sapsford, D. (1994) 'What Does Liberalisation do for Exports and Growth?', *Weltwirtschaftliches Archives*, 1.

Greenaway, D., Morgan, W. and Wright, P. (1998) 'Trade Reform, Adjustment and Growth: What Does the Evidence Tell Us?', *Economic Journal*, 108(450): 1547–61.

Greenaway, D., Morgan, W. and Wright, P. (2002) 'Trade Liberalisation and Growth in Developing Countries', *Journal of Development Economics*, 67(1): 229–44.

Grilli, E.R. and Yang, M.C. (1988) 'Primary Product Prices, Manufactured Goods Prices, and Terms of Trade of Developing Countries: What the Long Run Evidence Shows', *World Bank Economic Review*, 2(1): 1–47.

Grossman, G. and Helpman, E. (1991a) *Innovation and Growth in the Global Economy* (Cambridge, MA: MIT Press).

Grossman, G. and Helpman, E. (1991b) 'Trade, Knowledge Spillovers and Growth', *European Economic Review*, 35(2/3): 517–26.

Hanson, G.H. and Harrison, A. (1999) 'Trade Liberalisation and Wage Inequality in Mexico', *Industrial and Labour Relations Review*, 52(2): 271–88.

Harvey, D., Kellard, N., Madsen, J. and Wohar, M. (2010) 'The Prebisch-Singer Hypothesis: Four Centuries of Evidence', *Review of Economics and Statistics*, 92(2): 367–77.

Hausmann, R. and Rodrik, D. (2003) 'Economic Development as Self-Discovery', *Journal of Development Economics*, 72(2): 603–33.

Hausmann, R., Hwang, J. and Rodrik, D. (2007) 'What You Export Matters', *Journal of Economic Growth*, 12(1): 1–25.

Heckscher, E. (1919) 'The Effect of Foreign Trade on the Distribution of Income', *Ekonomisk Tidskrift*, 21: 497–512.

Helleiner, G. (ed.) (1994) *Trade Policy and Industrialisation in Turbulent Times* (London: Routledge).

Jenkins, R. (1996) 'Trade Liberalization and Export Performance in Bolivia', *Development and Change*, 27(4): 693–716.

Johnson, H.G. (1964) 'Tariffs and Economic Development: Some Theoretical Issues', *Journal of Development Studies*, 1(1): 3–30.

Johnson, H.G. (1967) *Economic Policies Towards Less Developed Countries* (London: Allen & Unwin).

Joshi, V. and Little, I.M.D. (1996) *India's Economic Reforms 1991–2001* (Oxford: Oxford University Press).

Ju, J., Wu, Y. and Zeng, L. (2009) 'The Impact of Trade Liberalisation on the Trade Balance of Developing Countries', *IMF Staff Papers*, 57(2): 427–49.

Keynes, J.M. (1942) 'The International Regulation of Primary Commodities', in D. Moggridge, (ed.) (1980) *The Collected Writings of J.M. Keynes*, vol. 27: *Activities 1940–1946: Shaping the Post-War World: Employment and Commodities* (London: Macmillan).

Kim, K. (2015) 'Demand and Structural Change in Adam Smith's View of Economic Progress', *Cambridge Journal of Economics*, 39(1): 245–64.

Krueger, A. (1997) 'Trade Policy and Economic Development: How We Learn', *American Economic Review*, 87(1): 1–22.

Krueger, A. (1998) 'Why Trade Liberalisation is Good for Growth', *Economic Journal*, 108(450): 1513–22.

Krugman, P. (1979) 'Increasing Returns, Monopolistic Competition and International Trade', *Journal of International Economics*, 9(4): 469–80.

Krugman, P. (1980) 'Scale Economies, Product Differentiation and the Pattern of Trade', *American Economic Review*, 70(5): 950–9.

Krugman, P. (1986) *Strategic Trade Policy and the New International Economics* (Cambridge, MA: MIT Press).

Leamer, E. (1988) 'Measures of Openness', in R. Baldwin (ed.) *Trade Policy and Empirical Analysis* (Chicago: Chicago University Press).

Leontief, W. (1953) 'Domestic Production and Foreign Trade: The American Position Re-examined', *Proceedings of the American Philosophic Society*, 97(4): 332–49.

Lim, D. (1991) *Export Instability and Compensatory Finance* (London: Routledge).

Little, I., Scitovsky, T. and Scott, M. (1970) *Industry and Trade in Some Developing Countries* (Oxford: Oxford University Press).

Love, J. (1987) 'Export Instability in Less Developed Countries', *Journal of Economic Studies*, 14(2): 3–80.

McCulloch, N., Winters, A. and Cirera, X. (2001) *Trade Liberalisation and Poverty: A Handbook* (London: Centre for Economic Policy Research).

Mah, J.S. (1999) 'Import Demand, Liberalisation and Economic Development', *Journal of Policy Modeling*, 21(4): 497–503.

Maizels, A. (ed.) (1987) 'Primary Commodities in the World Economy: Problems and Policies', *World Development*, 15(5): 537–49.

Maizels, A. (1992) *Commodities in Crisis* (Oxford: Oxford University Press).

Marshall, A. (1890) *Principles of Economics* (London: Macmillan).

Melo, O. and Vogt, M. (1984) 'Determinants of Demand for Imports in Venezuela', *Journal of Development Economics*, 14(3): 351–8.

Michaely, M., Papageorgiou, D. and Choksi, A. (eds) (1991) *Liberalising Foreign Trade*, vol. 7: *Lessons from Experience in the Developing World* (Oxford: Basil Blackwell).

Milanovic, B. (2005) 'Can we Discern the Effects of Globalization on Income Distribution?', *World Bank Economic Review*, 19(1): 21–44.

Mill, J.S. (1848) *Principles of Political Economy* (London: Longmans, Green and Co.).

Morrissey, O. and White, H. (1993) 'How Concessional is Tied Aid?', *CREDIT Research Paper*, 93/13 (University of Nottingham).

Ocampo, J.A. and Parra, M. (2003) 'The Terms of Trade for Commodities in the Twentieth Century', *CEPAL Review*, 79: 7–35.

Ohlin, B. (1933) *Interregional and International Trade* (Cambridge, MA: Harvard University Press).

Oxfam (2002) *Rigged Rules and Double Standards: Trade, Globalization and the Fight Against Poverty* (Oxford: Oxfam).

Oyejide, A., Elbadawi, I. and Collier, P. (eds) (1997) *Regional Integration and Trade Liberalisation in Sub-Saharan Africa*, vol. 1: *Framework Issues and Methodological Perspectives* (London: Macmillan).

Pacheco-López, P. (2005) 'The Impact of Trade Liberalisation on Exports, Imports, the Balance of Payments and Growth: The Case of Mexico', *Journal of Post Keynesian Economics*, 13(3): 343–75.

Pacheco-López, P. and Thirlwall, A.P. (2006) 'Trade Liberalization, the Income Elasticity of Demand for Imports and Growth in Latin America', *Journal of Post Keynesian Economics*, 21(4): 460–90.

Pacheco-López, P. and Thirlwall, A.P. (2007) 'Trade Liberalisation and the Trade-off between Growth and the Balance of Payments in Latin America', *International Review of Applied Economics*, 21: 469–97.

Parikh, A. (2002) 'Impact of Liberalisation, Economic Growth and Trade Policies on Current Accounts of Developing Countries: An Econometric Study', WDP 2002/63 (Helsinki: WIDER).

Prebisch, R. (1950) *The Economic Development of Latin America and its Principal Problems* (New York: ECLA, UN Dept. of Economic Affairs).

Prebisch, R. (1959) 'Commercial Policy in the Underdeveloped Countries', *American Economic Review, Papers and Proceedings*, 44(2): 251–73.

Ram, R. (1987) 'Exports and Economic Growth in Developing Countries: Evidence from Time Series and Cross Section Data', *Economic Development and Cultural Change*, 36(1): 51–72.

Ravallion, M. (2001) 'Growth, Inequality and Poverty: Looking Beyond Averages', *World Development*, 29(11): 1083–15.

Ravallion, M. (2006) 'Looking Beyond Averages in the Trade and Poverty Debate', *World Development*, 34(8): 1374–92.

Reinert, E. (2007) *How Rich Countries Got Rich and Why Poor Countries Stay Poor* (London: Constable & Robinson).

Ricardo, D. (1817) *On the Principles of Political Economy and Taxation* (P. Sraffa, ed.) (Cambridge: Cambridge University Press).

Robbins, D.J. (1996) 'Evidence on Trade and Wages in the Developing World', OECD Development Centre Technical Paper 119, December.

Robbins, D.J. and Gindling, T.H. (1999) 'Trade Liberalisation and the Relative Wages for More-Skilled Workers in Costa Rica', *Review of Development Economics*, 3(2): 140–54.

Robson, P. (1998) *The Economics of International Integration*, 4th edn (London: Routledge).

Robson, P. (1988) *Integration, Development and Equity: Economic Integration in West Africa* (London: Allen & Unwin).

Rodriguez, F. and Rodrik, D. (2000) 'Trade Policy and Economic Growth: A Skeptic's Guide to the Cross-National Evidence', in B. Bernanke and K. Rogoff (eds) *Macroeconomics Annual 2000* (Cambridge, MA: MIT Press).

Rodrik, D. (1996) 'Understanding Economic Policy Reform', *Journal of Economic Literature*, 34(1): 9–41.

Rodrik, D. (2001) *The Global Governance of Trade: As if Development Really Mattered* (New York: UNDP).

Rodrik, D. (2012) *The Globalization Paradox: Why Global Markets, States, and Democracy Can't Coexist* (Oxford: Oxford University Press).

Sachs, J.D. and Warner, A. (1995) 'Economic Reform and the Process of Global Integration', *Brookings Papers on Economic Activity*, 26(1): 1–118.

Salvatore, D. and Hatcher, T. (1991) 'Inward Oriented and Outward Oriented Trade Strategies', *Journal of Development Studies*, 27(3): 7–25.

Santos-Paulino, A. (2002a) 'Trade Liberalisation and Export Performance in Selected Developing Countries', *Journal of Development Studies*, 39(1): 140–64.

Santos-Paulino, A. (2002b) 'The Effects of Trade Liberalisation on Imports in Selected Developing Countries', *World Development*, 30(6): 959–74.

Santos-Paulino, A. (2007) 'Aid and Trade Sustainability under Liberalisation in Least Developed Countries', *World Economy*, 30(6): 972–98.

Santos-Paulino, A. and Thirlwall, A.P. (2004) 'The Impact of Trade Liberalisation on Export Growth, Import Growth, and the Balance of Payments of Developing Countries', *Economic Journal*, 114(493): 50–72.

Sapsford, D. (1985) 'The Statistical Debate on the Net Barter Terms of Trade between Primary Commodities and Manufactures', *Economic Journal*, 95(379): 781–8.

Sapsford, D. (1988) 'The Debate over Trends in the Terms of Trade', in D. Greenaway (ed.) *Economic Development and International Trade* (London: Macmillan).

Sapsford, D. and Balasubramanyam, V.N. (1994) 'The Long-Run Behaviour of the Relative Price of Primary Commodities: Statistical Evidence and Policy Implications', *World Development*, 22(11): 1737–45.

Sarkar, P. (1986) 'The Singer–Prebisch Hypothesis: A Statistical Evaluation', *Cambridge Journal of Economics*, 10(4): 355–71.

Sarkar, P. and Singer, H. (1991) 'Manufactured Exports of Developing Countries and their Terms of Trade since 1965', *World Development*, 19(4): 333–40.

Singer, H. (1950) 'The Distribution of Gains between Investing and Borrowing Countries', *American Economic Review*, 40(2): 473–85.

Skarstein, R. (2007) 'Free Trade: A Dead End for Underdeveloped Countries', *Review of Political Economy*, 19(3): 347–67.

Smith, A. (1776) *An Inquiry into the Nature and Causes of the Wealth of Nations* (London: Strahan and Cadell).

Spilimbergo, A., Londono, J. and Szekely, M. (1999) 'Income Distribution, Factor Endowments and Trade Openness', *Journal of Development Economics*, 59(1): 77–101.

Spraos, J. (1980) 'The Statistical Debate on the Net Barter Terms of Trade between Primary Commodities and Manufactures', *Economic Journal*, 90(357): 107–28.

Stiglitz, J. (2006) *Making Globalization Work* (New York: W.W. Norton).

Thirlwall, A.P. (1976) 'When is Trade More Valuable than Aid?', *Journal of Development Studies*, 13(1): 35–41.

Thirlwall, A.P. (1986) 'A General Model of Growth and Development on Kaldorian Lines', *Oxford Economic Papers*, 38(2): 199–219.

Thirlwall, A.P. (2000) 'Trade Agreements, Trade Liberalisation and Economic Growth: A Selective Survey', *African Development Review*, 12(2): 129–60.

Thirlwall, A.P. and Bergevin, J. (1985) 'Trends, Cycles and Asymmetries in the Terms of Trade of Primary Commodities from Developed and Less Developed Countries', *World Development*, 13(7): 805–17.

Thirlwall, A.P. and Pacheco-López, P. (2008) *Trade Liberalisation and The Poverty of Nations* (Cheltenham: Edward Elgar).

Thomas, V., Nash, J. and Edwards, S. (1991) *Best Practices in Trade Policy Reform* (Oxford: Oxford University Press for the World Bank).

Thorbecke, E. and Nissanke, M. (eds) (2006) 'Introduction: The Impact of Globalization on the World's Poor', *World Development*, 34(8): 1333–7.

Tussie, D. and Aggio, C. (2005) 'Economic and Social Impacts of Trade Liberalisation', in UNCTAD, *Coping with Trade Reforms: Perspective on the WTO Industrial Tariff Negotiations* (Geneva: UNCTAD).

UNCTAD (UN Conference on Trade and Development) (1999) *Trade and Development Report* (Geneva: UN).

UNCTAD (2004) *The Least Developed Countries Report 2004* (Geneva: UN).

UNIDO (UN Industrial Development Organization) (2015) *Industrial Development Report 2016* (Vienna: UNIDO).

Vamvakidis, A. (1998) 'Regional Integration and Economic Growth', *World Bank Economic Review*, 12(2): 251–70.

Vamvakidis, A. (1999) 'Regional Trade Agreements or Broad Liberalisation: Which Path Leads to Faster Growth?', *IMF Staff Papers*, 46(1): 42–68.

Venables, A. (2003) 'Winners and Losers from Regional Integration Agreements', *Economic Journal*, 113(490): 747–61.

Wacziarg, R. (2001) 'Measuring the Dynamic Gains from Trade', *World Bank Economic Review*, 15(3): 393–429.

Wacziarg, R. and Welch, K. (2008) 'Trade Liberalisation and Growth: New Evidence', *World Bank Economic Review*, 22(2): 187–231.

Wade, R. (2003) 'What Strategies are Viable for Developing Countries Today? The World Trade Organisation and the Shrinking of "Development Space"', *Review of International Political Economy*, 10(4): 621–44.

Winters, A., McCulloch, N. and McKay, A. (2004) 'Trade Liberalisation and Poverty: The Evidence So Far', *Journal of Economic Literature*, 42(1): 72–115.

Wolf, M. (2005) *Why Globalization Works* (New Haven, CT: Yale University Press).

Wood, A. (1993) *North–South Trade: Employment and Inequality* (Oxford: Clarendon Press).

Wood, A. (1995) 'How Trade Hurt Unskilled Workers', *Journal of Economic Perspectives*, 9(3): 57–80.

Wood, A. (1997) 'Openness and Wage Inequality in Developing Countries: The Latin American Challenge to East Asian Conventional Wisdom', *World Bank Economic Review*, 11(1): 33–57.

World Bank (1987) *World Development Report* (Washington, DC: World Bank).

World Bank (2002) *Globalization, Growth and Poverty* (Washington, DC: Oxford University Press).

World Bank (2014) *World Development Indicators 2014* (Washington, DC: World Bank).

World Bank (2015) *World Development Indicators 2015* (Washington, DC: World Bank).
WTO (World Trade Organization) (1995) *The Agreement Establishing the WTO* (Geneva: WTO).
Zhu, S. and Trefler, D. (2005) 'Trade and Inequality in Developing Countries: A General Equilibrium Analysis', *Journal of International Economics*, 65(1): 21–48.

Chapter 16 The balance of payments, international monetary assistance and development

Ansari, M., Hashemzadeh, N. and Xi, L. (2000) 'The Chronicle of Economic Growth in Southeast Asian Countries: Does Thirlwall's Law Provide an Adequate Explanation?', *Journal of Post Keynesian Economics*, 22(4): 573–88.
Argy, V. (ed.) (1990) *Choosing an Exchange Rate Regime: The Challenge for Smaller Industrial Countries* (Washington, DC: IMF).
Athukorala, P. (2001) *Crisis and Recovery in Malaysia: The Role of Capital Controls* (Cheltenham: Edward Elgar).
Bairam, E. (1993) 'Income Elasticities of Exports and Imports: A Reexamination of the Empirical Evidence', *Applied Economics*, 25(1): 71–4.
Bird, G. (1987) *International Financial Policy and Economic Development* (London: Macmillan).
Bird, G. (1995) *IMF Lending to Developing Countries: Issues and Evidence* (London: Routledge).
Bird, G. (2001) 'IMF Programs: Do They Work? Can They be Made to Work Better?', *World Development*, 29(11): 1849–65.
Bird, G. (2003) *The IMF and the Future: Issues and Options Facing the Fund* (London: Routledge).
Branson, W. (1983) 'Economic Structure and Policy for External Balance', *IMF Staff Papers*, 30(1): 39–66.
Britto, G. and McCombie, J. (2009) 'Thirlwall's Law and the Long-Run Equilibrium Growth Rate: An Application to Brazil', *Journal of Post Keynesian Economics*, 32(1): 115–36.
Broda, C. (2004) 'Terms of Trade and Exchange Rate Regimes in Developing Countries', *Journal of International Economics*, 63(1): 31–58.
Bubula, A. and Otker-Robe, I. (2004) 'The Continuing Bipolar Conundrum', *Finance & Development*, 41(1): 31–5.
Collier, P. and Gunning, J. (1999) 'The IMF's Role in Structural Adjustment', *Economic Journal*, 109(459): 634–51.
Corden, W.M. (1993) 'Exchange Rate Policies for Developing Countries', *Economic Journal*, 103(416): 198–207.
Crockett, A. (1977) 'Exchange Rate Policies for Developing Countries', *Journal of Development Studies*, 13(2): 125–43.
Dell, S. (1981) *On Being Grandmotherly: The Evolution of IMF Conditionality, Essays in International Finance*, 144 (Princeton University).
Donavan, D.J. (1982) 'Macroeconomic Performance and Adjustment under Fund-Supported Programs: The Experience of the Seventies', *IMF Staff Papers*, 29(2): 171–203.
Dreher, A. (2006) 'IMF and Economic Growth: The Effects of Programs, Loans and Compliance with Conditionality', *World Development*, 34(5): 769–88.
Edwards, S. (1989) *Real Exchange Rates, Devaluation and Adjustment: Exchange Rate Policy in Developing Countries* (Cambridge, MA: MIT Press).
Felipe, J., McCombie, J. and Naqvi, K. (2010) 'Is Pakistan's Growth Rate Balance of Payments Constrained?', *Oxford Development Studies*, 38(4): 477–96.
Fischer, S. (2001) 'Exchange Rate Regimes: Is the Bipolar View Correct?', *Journal of Economic Perspectives*, 15(2): 3–24.
Frenkel, J. (1999) *No Single Currency Regime is Right for all Countries at all Times, Essays in International Finance*, 215 (Princeton University).
Ghosh, A. and Ostry, J. (2009) 'Choosing an Exchange Rate Regime', *Finance & Development*, 46(4): 38–40.
Ghosh, A., Gulde, A. and Wolf, H. (2002) *Exchange Rate Regimes: Choices and Consequences* (Cambridge, MA: MIT Press).
Gore, C. (2000) 'The Rise and Fall of the Washington Consensus as a Paradigm for Developing Countries', *World Development*, 28(5): 789–804.
Gouvea, R. and Lima, G. (2010) 'Structural Change, Balance-of-Payments Constraint and Economic Growth: Evidence from the Multi-sectoral Thirlwall's Law', *Journal of Post Keynesian Economic*, 33(1): 169–204.

Gouvea, R. and Lima, G. (2013) 'Balance of Payments Constrained Growth in a Multisectoral Framework: A Panel Data Investigation', *Journal of Economic Studies*, 40(2): 240–54.

Guitian, M. (1982) *Fund Conditionality: Evolution of Principles and Practices* (Washington, DC: IMF).

Harrod, R. (1933) *International Economics* (Cambridge: Cambridge University Press).

Hausmann, R., Hwang, J. and Rodrik, D. (2007) 'What You Export Matters', *Journal of Economic Growth*, 21(1): 1–25.

Helleiner, G.K. (1983) *The IMF and Africa in the 1960s, Essays in International Finance*, 152 (Princeton University).

IMF (International Monetary Fund) (2014) *Annual Report on Exchange Arrangements and Exchange Restrictions* (Washington, DC: IMF).

Johnson, O.E.G. (1976) 'The Exchange Rate as an Instrument of Policy in a Developing Country', *IMF Staff Papers*, 23(2): 334–48.

Kaldor, N. (1964) 'Dual Exchange Rates and Economic Development', *Economic Bulletin for Latin America*, September (reprinted in *Collected Economic Essays*, II; London: Duckworth, 1981).

Kamin, S. and Rogers, J.H. (2000) 'Output and the Real Exchange Rate in Developing Countries: An Application to Mexico', *Journal of Development Economics*, 61(1): 85–109.

Kenen, P. (2004) 'Appraising the IMF's Performance', *Finance & Development*, 41(1): 41–5.

Khan, M. (1990) 'The Macroeconomic Effects of Fund-supported Adjustment Programs', *IMF Staff Papers*, 37(2): 195–231.

Killick, T. (ed.) (1982) *Adjustment and Financing in the Developing World* (Washington, DC: IMF).

Killick, T. (ed.) (1984a) *The Quest for Economic Stabilisation: The IMF and the Third World* (London: Heinemann for the ODI).

Killick, T. (ed.) (1984b) *The IMF and Stabilisation: Developing Country Experiences* (London: Heinemann for the ODI).

Killick, T. (1995) *IMF Programmes in Developing Countries: Design and Impact* (London: Routledge).

Lim, D. (1991) *Export Instability and Compensatory Financing* (London: Routledge).

Love, J. (1987) 'Export Instability in Less Developed Countries: Consequences and Causes', *Journal of Economic Studies*, 14(2): 3–80.

McCombie, J. and Thirlwall, A.P. (1994) *Economic Growth and the Balance of Payments Constraint* (London: Macmillan).

McCombie, J. and Thirlwall, A.P. (1997) 'The Dynamic Harrod Foreign Trade Multiplier and the Demand-Oriented Approach to Economic Growth: An Evaluation', *International Review of Applied Economics*, 11(1): 5–26.

McCombie, J. and Thirlwall, A.P. (1999) 'The East Asian Crisis: Retrospect and Prospect', *Asia and Australasia: Regional Overview, 3rd Quarter*, Economic Intelligence Unit.

McCombie, J. and Thirlwall, A.P. (2004) *Essays on Balance of Payments Constrained Growth: Theory and Evidence* (London: Routledge).

Moreno-Brid, J.C. (1998) 'Balance of Payments Constrained Economic Growth: The Case of Mexico', *BNL Quarterly Review*, 51(207): 413–33.

Moreno-Brid, J.C. and Perez, E. (1999) 'Balance of Payments Constrained Growth in Central America', *Journal of Post Keynesian Economics*, 22(1): 131–47.

Nashashibi, K. (1980) 'A Supply Framework for the Exchange Reform in Developing Countries: The Experience of Sudan', *IMF Staff Papers*, 27(1): 24–79.

Nell, K. (2003) 'A "Generalised" Version of the Balance of Payments Constrained Growth Model: An Application to Neighbouring Regions', *International Review of Applied Economics*, 17(1): 1–22.

Nowzad, B. (1981) *The IMF and its Critics, Essays in International Finance*, 146 (Princeton University).

Nureldin-Hussain, M. (1999) 'The Balance of Payments Constraint and Growth Rate Differences among African and East Asian Economies', *African Development Review*, 11(1): 103–37.

Nureldin-Hussain, M. and Thirlwall, A.P. (1984) 'The IMF Supply-Side Approach to Devaluation: An Assessment with Reference to the Sudan', *Oxford Bulletin of Economics and Statistics*, 46(2): 145–67.

Pacheco-López, P. (2005) 'The Effect of Trade Liberalisation on Exports, Imports, the Balance of Payments and Growth: The Case of Mexico', *Journal of Post Keynesian Economics*, 27(4): 595–617.

Pacheco-López, P. and Thirlwall, A.P. (2006) 'Trade Liberalisation, the Income Elasticity of Demand for Imports and Economic Growth in Latin America', *Journal of Post Keynesian Economics*, 29(1): 41–61.

Pastor, M. (1987) 'The Effects of IMF Programs in the Third World: Debate and Evidence from Latin America', *World Development*, 15(2): 249–62.

Payer, C. (1974) *The Debt Trap* (Harmondsworth: Penguin).

Perraton, J. (2003) 'Balance of Payments Constrained Growth and Developing Countries: An Examination of Thirlwall's Hypothesis', *International Review of Applied Economics*, 17(1): 1–22.

Przeworski, A. and Vreeland, J. (2000) 'The Effect of IMF Programs on Economic Growth', *Journal of Development Economics*, 62(2): 285–556.

Razmi, A. (2005) 'Balance of Payments Constrained Growth Model: The Case of India', *Journal of Post Keynesian Economics*, 15(4): 507–14.

Reichmann, T.M. and Stillson, R. (1978) 'Experience with Programs of Balance of Payments Adjustment: Stand-by Arrangements in the Higher Tranches, 1963–72', *IMF Staff Papers*, 25: 292–310.

Schadler, S. (1996) 'How Successful are IMF Supported Adjustment Programs?', *Finance & Development*, 33(2): 14–17.

Scitovsky, T. (1966) 'A New Approach to International Liquidity', *American Economic Review*, 56(5): 1212–20.

Senhadji, A. (1998) 'Time-Series Estimation of Structural Import Demand Equations: A Cross-Country Analysis', *IMF Staff Papers*, 46(3): 236–68.

Senhadji, A. and Montenegro, C. (1999) 'Time Series Analysis of Export Demand Equations: A Cross-Country Analysis', *IMF Staff Papers*, 46(3): 259–73.

Soukiazis, E. and Cerqueira, P. (2012) *Models of Balance of Payments Constrained Growth* (Basingstoke: Palgrave Macmillan).

Spraos, J. (1986) *IMF Conditionality: Ineffectual, Inefficient, Mistargeted, Essays in International Finance*, 166 (Princeton University).

Stiglitz, J. (2002) *Globalization and its Discontents* (London: Allen Lane).

Taylor, L. (1988) *Varieties of Stabilisation Experience* (Oxford: Clarendon Press).

Taylor, L. (1997) 'The Revival of the Liberal Creed: the IMF and the World Bank in a Global Economy', *World Development*, 25(2): 145–52.

Thirlwall, A.P. (1979) 'The Balance of Payments Constraint as an Explanation of International Growth Rate Differences', *BNL Quarterly Review*, 32(128): 45–63.

Thirlwall, A.P. (2003) *Trade, the Balance of Payments and Exchange Rate Policy in Developing Countries* (Cheltenham: Edward Elgar).

Thirlwall, A.P. (2007) 'Regional Problems are Balance of Payments Problems', *Regional Studies*, 14(5): 419–25.

Thirlwall, A.P. (2011) 'Balance of Payments Constrained Growth Models: History and Overview', *PSL Quarterly Review*, 64(259): 307–51.

Thirlwall, A.P. and Nureldin-Hussain, M. (1982) 'The Balance of Payments Constraint, Capital Flows and Growth Rate Differences between Developing Countries', *Oxford Economic Papers*, 34(3): 498–510.

Triffin, R. (1971) 'The Use of SDR Finance for Collectively Agreed Purposes', *BNL Quarterly Review*, March.

Vreeland, J.R. (2003) *The IMF and Economic Development* (Cambridge: Cambridge University Press).

Williamson, J. (ed.) (1983) *IMF Conditionality* (Washington, DC: Institute for International Economics).

Williamson, J. (1990) 'What Washington Means by Policy Reform', in J. Williamson (ed.) *Latin American Adjustment: How Much Has Happened?* (Washington, DC: Institute for International Economics).

Williamson, J. (1993) 'Democracy and the "Washington Consensus"', *World Development*, 21(8): 1329–36.

Williamson, J. (2000) *Exchange Rate Regimes for Emerging Markets: Reviving the Intermediate Option* (Washington, DC: Institute for International Economics).

Yotopoulos, P. (1996) *Exchange Rate Parity for Trade and Development: Theory, Tests and Measurement* (Cambridge: Cambridge University Press).

Other introductory texts

Chenery, H. and Srinivasan, T.N. (eds) (1988) *Handbook of Development Economics*, vols 1 and 2 (Amsterdam: North-Holland).

Clunies-Ross, A., Forsyth, D. and Huq, M. (2009) *Development Economics* (London: McGraw-Hill).

Cypher, J.M and Dietz, J.L. (2014) *The Process of Economic Development*, 4th edn (London: Routledge).

Herrick, B. and Kindleberger, C. (1983) *Economic Development*, 4th edn (New York: McGraw-Hill).

Meier, G. and Rauch, J.E. (2005) *Leading Issues in Economic Development*, 8th edn (Oxford: Oxford University Press).

Nafziger, E.W. (2012) *The Economics of Developing Countries*, 4th edn (Englewood Cliffs, NJ: Prentice Hall).

Perkins, D., Radelet, S., Lindauer, D. and Block, S. (2013) *Economics of Development*, 7th edn (New York: W.W. Norton).

Ray, D. (1998) *Development Economics* (Princeton, NJ: Princeton University Press).

Secondi, G. (ed.) (2008) *The Development Economics Reader* (London: Routledge).

Thirlwall, A.P. (2013) *Economic Growth in an Open Developing Economy: the Role of Structure and Demand* (Cheltenham: Edward Elgar).

Todaro, M.P. and Smith, S.C. (2015) *Economic Development in the Third World*, 12th edn (London: Longman).

Van Den Berg, H. (2016) *Economic Growth and Development*, 3rd edn (New York: McGraw-Hill).

NAME INDEX

In this index c denotes case example, f figure, n note and t table. Page references in **bold** indicate extended discussion.

SUBJECT INDEX

In this index c denotes case example, f figure, n note and t table. Page references in **bold** indicate extended discussion.